50

Jackie Newlin
P.O. 72
Lebo, KS
66856

Group Counseling
Second Edition

Group Counseling
THEORY AND PROCESS
Second Edition

James C. Hansen
State University of New York at Buffalo

Richard W. Warner
Auburn University

Elsie J. Smith
State University of New York at Buffalo

Rand McNally College Publishing Company / Chicago

Rand McNally Education Series
B. Othanel Smith, Advisory Editor

Credits for copyrighted
material appear on p. 577

Sponsoring editor: Louise Waller
Project editor: Erek Smith
Designer: Iris Rothstein

80 81 82 10 9 8 7 6 5 4 3 2 1

Contents

Preface

In recent years there has been a growing appreciation of the value of group counseling, which has become a preferred mode of treatment in resolving interpersonal conflicts. Group experience also has a significant role in assisting personal development of individuals who are not experiencing specific problems. The rapid growth of the group movement has created some problems, among them the use of the group process by untrained leaders and the assumption that a "good" individual counselor is automatically a "good" group counselor. The purpose of this book is to provide a basic knowledge from which a group leader can build his or her own approach to conducting groups. The authors believe that a leader developing a personal approach with groups needs to examine the prominent theoretical strategies and the general concepts and procedures through which strategies are implemented into the counseling process.

It is essential for individuals working in groups to have an understanding of the concepts and processes of group functioning. Therefore Part I of the book presents various theoretical approaches to group counseling and assists the reader in comparing the concepts and techniques. Part II examines the practical aspects of group counseling that have been taken from the literature. The process section of the book integrates the literature from various group approaches instead of focusing on any one approach.

Chapter 1 discusses some general concepts regarding the phenomena of a group, a definition and rationale for group counseling, and a brief description of the process. It also deals with the importance of theory for a group counselor, looks at the relationship of theory to understanding the members and the process in the group, and offers ideas for selecting and evaluating a theoretical approach.

Chapters 2 through 9 are overviews of various theoretical contributions to group counseling. These chapters are not an exhaustive coverage of each approach, but they provide the general background and techniques so that readers can build their own theoretical concepts. The chapters deal with personality development, maladaptive behaviors, counselor and member roles, and techniques and methods of conducting the group. The personality development and maladaptive behavior sections are included because they are the foundation for the theorists' concepts of the goals of the group, member and leader behaviors, and the process of the group.

Theory chapters begin with the psychoanalytic approach, which was the first to be applied to groups. Many of its principles have been adopted in modified form by other approaches. Alderian concepts about group counseling, including Dreiker's work, are covered in the third chapter. Although T-groups and sensitivity groups are not specific to group counseling, many of their concepts and techniques have become a part of this field. The encounter group movement, too, has had a marked effect on the conduct of groups. The self-theory approach to groups has evolved over the years from nondirective leadership to the encounter group concept. Gestalt encounter groups are covered to illustrate yet another concept with some variation in technique. Two rational approaches to groups, Reality Therapy and Rational-Emotive Therapy, are presented in one chapter. Transactional analysis and behavioral counseling approaches in groups are offered as two developing positions that have considerable applicability.

Chapter 10 is an assessment of the similarities and differences in the theoretical concepts and techniques of these approaches. The chapter shows some generally accepted therapeutic aspects in group counseling and highlights some of the unique ideas that exist. It presents conceptual models to help readers understand group counseling theories and techniques.

Part II focuses on the practical aspects of group counseling. It examines the techniques of leadership, the behavior of group members, techniques with various ages and problems, and the general process of group development. These chapters are eclectic in nature, pulling together concepts and research from all types of groups and applying them to group counseling. The authors believe that the counselor is a specialist in his or her setting and can apply the general concepts to clients of all kinds.

Chapter 11 discusses techniques that are appropriate with clients of a variety of ages and with different types of problems. Chapter 12 is concerned with counselors as persons, as well as with their roles and techniques in leading a group. Chapter 13 covers group members and the contribution of their personalities to role behavior. In addition, this chapter presents two models of communication that will be useful in understanding group members' behavior. Chapters 14 and 15 involve a five-stage sequential conception of group process and functioning. These chapters begin with the task of the counselor in preparing for a group, and then follow the development through the five stages of initiation, conflict and confrontation, cohesiveness, productiveness, and termination.

Throughout the book, problems, issues, and concerns confronting the group counselor are examined. Chapter 16 focuses specifically on two areas: ethics and training. Functional guidelines for ethical conduct of groups are provided, and the didactic training and supervised practice necessary before attaining full leadership status are explored.

The authors have received help from a number of commentators. We wish especially to acknowledge with thanks Professor Nicholas Colangelo of The University of Iowa, Professor James O. Mathis of Sam Houston State University, and Professor David P. Meyer of Oakland University.

J.C.H.
R.W.W.
E.J.S.

PART ONE

GROUP COUNSELING: THEORY

1
Group Counseling and Theory

Much of what individuals believe about themselves comes from feedback garnered from interactions with other people. Normal everyday interactions do not allow individuals to check the reactions of others as they can do in a group experience. By analyzing their behavior in a group, individuals can see how they act in the everyday world. The group is a microcosm of society, and while people try hard to mask certain behaviors, the same self that one displays in the real world will emerge. The group can help people to examine and understand themselves and to interpret their behaviors.

Group experience has existed in various forms throughout history but has only recently come into focus and been recognized as a relevant and respected form of counseling. The value of group approaches lies in helping individuals achieve a sense of identity: who they are, where they are, what it is they are doing, and where they are going (self-discovery, self-realization, self-direction). These values have been generally accepted, and counselors have implemented them to a degree irrespective of the underlying theory.

THE GROUP

In terms of counseling, a group is more than a collection of people. Group members share some common attitudes and values, accept each other, and relate to each other in many ways. They accept membership in the group to deal with the problems they have in common as well as to satisfy some individual needs.

They desire this membership enough to conform at least minimally to the group standards. Cartwright and Zander (1968) offer the following statements as characteristic of individuals in groups:

They engage in frequent interactions.

They define themselves as group members.

They are defined by others as belonging to the group.

They share norms concerning matters of common interest.

They participate in a system of interlocking roles.

They identify with one another as a result of having set up the same *model—objective—or ideals* in their superego.

They find the group to be rewarding.

They pursue *promotively interdependent* goals.

They have a collective perception of their unity.

They tend to act in a unitary manner toward the environment (p. 48).

Most groups start as a collection of people: the members do not begin with the above-mentioned characteristics. The more of these characteristics the group members develop, the stronger the group will be. A group passes through several stages of development in this process.

Loeser (1957) describes the essential properties of a group as: (1) dynamic interaction, (2) a common goal, (3) an appropriate number of members for the proposed function, (4) their volition and consent, and (5) the development of a capacity for self-direction. If the members are going to learn from each other, it is necessary for some type of relationship—and subsequent interaction based on this relationship—to develop. The kind of feedback members want, and their willingness to give to each other, will depend upon having a general common goal. For those wanting to examine themselves and secure feedback for developing a self-concept or behavior change, a rather small number of members are necessary. The concept of volition and consent for counseling is particularly important. Involuntary members would not explore themselves in a group and would not be open to feedback regarding themselves. Finally, if the group is voluntary and becomes meaningful, the willingness to govern and control will evolve and the group will move in terms of self-direction.

GROUP COUNSELING

Group counseling is an interpersonal process involving a counselor and several members who explore themselves and their situations in an attempt to modify their attitudes and behaviors. From a survey of prominent contributors to the field of group counseling, Gazda, Duncan, and Meadows (1967) generated a composite definition.

> Group counseling is a dynamic interpersonal process focusing on conscious thought and behavior and involving the therapy functions of permissiveness, orientation to reality, catharsis, and mutual trust, caring, understanding, acceptance, and support.

The therapy functions are created and nurtured in a small group through the sharing of personal concerns with one's peers and the counselor(s). The group counselees are basically normal individuals with various concerns which are not debilitating to the extent requiring extensive personality change. The group counselees may utilize the group interaction to increase understanding and acceptance of values and goals and to learn and/or unlearn certain attitudes and behaviors (p. 306).

Group counseling may be preventative and/or remedial for the person. Preventative counseling permits an individual to resolve concerns before serious problems develop. For those individuals who have developed more serious problems, group counseling can be a process of intervention to change behavior. The group is more powerful than a counselor in individual counseling, and this power can be exercised in two directions. Because the group is made up of peer members, the feedback is more potent and more important to the member than is that of a single counselor. However, the group also can exert power against the counselor in an attempt to protect the individual. That is, the individual will feel more secure in a group of peers than he or she would in meeting the counselor in a one-to-one relationship. In this way, the group can provide an element of security.

Some confusion exists between the terms *group counseling* and *group psychotherapy*. Group counseling generally has been described as a therapeutic experience for normal people without serious emotional problems. Psychotherapy has been defined as a longer experience for emotionally disturbed persons. Gazda (1969) places group counseling and psychotherapy on "a continuum with overlapping goals and professional competencies, but the subtle distinctions are evident in expressions such as 'basically normal' counselees 'focusing on conscious thought and behavior,' and 'concerns which are not debilitating to the extent requiring extensive personality change,' found in references to group counseling." Accordingly, Ohlsen (1977) believes counseling and psychotherapy differ primarily in terms of the people involved rather than the process. Various theoretical positions presented in this book—and their procedural differences—are compared in Chapter 10. Some of the positions did not develop as group counseling approaches but have made significant contributions to the process.

Rationale for Group Counseling

The rationale for group counseling seems deeply rooted in the nature of human beings and their societal relationships. Personality is largely the product of interaction with other significant human beings. The need of men and women to be closely related to others thus seems as basic as any biological need and essential to their survival. If one's self-concept is dependent upon the appraisal or perceptions of significant others, then one must become aware of this transaction. Also, an individual must be able to understand, accept, and cope with problems that arise when there is a discrepancy between how others perceive him or her and how the individual perceives himself or herself. One of the values of the group process is that it provides a situation where individuals are able to discuss their perceptions of themselves and receive immediate feedback on how the members of the group perceive them.

With the recognition that people are indivisible, social, decision-making beings whose actions have a social purpose, the rationale for group counseling takes on an added dimension. Verbal and nonverbal interactions and transactions then become vital to an awareness of what transpires when people interact. One's self-concept and philosophy of life thus are transparent and consistent in the way one approaches life and life's processes. The group becomes a microcosm of society where the members and the leader can observe patterns of behavior and then work through problems that need to be resolved. These problems usually are based to some extent on a social interaction and thus are best solved or resolved in a social setting—a group.

One of the values or goals of group counseling is the creation of an atmosphere in which the members achieve a sense of belonging. This need to belong seems to be a constant entreaty of people today. Listen to the words of popular songs, read contemporary literature and poetry, or attend the latest movies; over and over again the endless search of people for others is reiterated.

Ruitenbeek (1970) maintains that the desire for intimacy, relatedness, care, and affection are not unusual. Previously, people came together naturally to talk and share themselves in a spontaneous and unstructured manner. Some examples of this are revival meetings and discussion groups formulated between friends and particularly within families. The necessity now for formulating groups to come together in a somewhat structured manner is an indication that society has changed and often is unable to meet the needs of its people. The reasons for this inability are many. Sociologists have a number of suppositions for the breakdown in communication: technological advancement; the mobility prevalent among people today; urbanization and increasing density of populations; decline in community life; and changes in family relationships. Accompanying the material advancement people have gained has come a loss of closeness, intimacy, and communication among the members of society. Ruitenbeek (1970) cites this loss of sense of community and the absence of meaningful social activities as the reason for the increased interest in participation in groups. He contends that the group experience affords the participants an opportunity to discuss matters of concern to themselves and also to establish genuine and meaningful relationships.

Given that the above perceptions hold a sense of truth, the concept of the group process is an attempt to meet these needs of men and women. As society changes, so must the techniques and methods of serving humanity change. The group process is a natural outgrowth of our times, one that bears study, consideration, and implementation.

Contributions of the Group to Personal Development The group offers a great range of momentary and continuing experiences that enable its members to grow and develop. It is composed of persons, often from diverse racial, social, and cultural backgrounds, who come together for the attainment of common and individual goals: forming a better self-concept, achieving better relationships with others, and leading more productive lives. Just being a part of the group often facilitates the growth and development of those who participate.

Personal Exploration and Feedback   Group counseling enables an individual to move toward meeting certain psychological needs: to belong, to be accepted, to release negative feelings, and to participate in a supportive atmosphere where self-exploration is encouraged. Within the group setting, individuals are able to give to each other. Each responds to the other members, providing immediate feedback and giving each the opportunity to come to the realization of how he or she is perceived by others. The opportunity to discuss perceptions and possible alternatives is available, and one can thus adopt the behavior one chooses.

Given a conducive environment, the individual can risk dropping defenses and can begin to explore areas that normally are threatening. The individual often feels that he or she is unique, with certain problems that no one else has ever experienced. In bringing these problems to the group, the person often finds that others have faced the same or similar problems. In the sharing of common problems and feelings, alternatives can be discussed and methods formulated to so change the situation that the individual can cope with it more effectively. This is not to say that unique problems do not exist—they do. However, they still can be discussed and worked through within the group when the atmosphere conveys a sense of understanding, sensitivity, and assistance. Self-worth is enhanced because no matter who one is or what one says or does, he or she can be accepted and cared for. Of significance is the fact that the individual is free to identify unique concerns and to make his or her own decisions about whether or not to focus upon them. This element fosters the development of a sense of responsibility to self.

Reality Testing   Many of the areas with which an individual is concerned are social in nature. Perhaps one of the greatest contributions to personal development that a group affords an individual is an opportunity not only to talk about the problems but to engage in reality testing.

In the group, a member can evaluate performance and ideas by the acceptance they receive from the group. The acting out and trying of new behaviors, followed by examination and appraisals from others, give the member an idea of how such behaviors will be accepted in the outside world. The individual thus develops the confidence to extend these behaviors outside the group setting. In essence, one of the values of group counseling is the opportunity made available to the individual member for greater awareness of the social purposes of behaviors and the consequences that result.

Responsibilities to Others   Through reality testing, not only is each member able to generalize behaviors from the group setting to other situations outside the group, but through this experience he or she can develop a sense of responsibility to self and also to others. The development of one's sense of responsibility to self has been mentioned above. It is significant here to note the development of a sense of responsibility to others. In order for a group to function properly or to its maximum potential, a sense of trust must develop between the members. A member then assumes the responsibility of contributing to the group's development by responding to each individual member and by working to achieve the overall goals or purposes predetermined by the group. This acceptance of responsibility can be generalized to outside situations where a commitment of self has been given.

The Group Counseling Process

Kelman (1963) suggested three types of behavior that are required within the counseling situation for behavior change to occur: engaging in the counseling process; commitment to the purposes of the group; and internalization of behavior-modifying experiences. Through this process the individual can experience a progression of self-exploration, leading to self-understanding, leading to behavior change.

(1) **Engagement in the Process**   For the group to move forward effectively and for a participant to achieve self-understanding and eventually change behaviors, he or she must become involved in the process. Most individuals approach a group with ambivalent feelings. They would like to improve their behavior but they are frightened about the experience and in most cases really do not want to change. The counselor will help the individual deal with these ambivalent feelings by communicating that they are common and appropriate, and that they can be discussed. The counselor will probably direct the tone of the meeting by following some topics and ignoring others. An active counselor may interpret statements and on occasion may confront an individual. A less active counselor will show the direction he or she wishes to go by responding to some statements and not to others. The members respond to such cues and learn to act appropriately.

Of course, an individual could learn the right phrases without any emotional involvement. An individual who is committed just at a superficial level will not have the meaningful insight that would lead to behavior change. Although the counselor is important in the process of counseling, members also will sanction behaviors and put pressure on each other to deal with group standards. One of the strongest pressures is the individual's desire to become accepted by the other group members. During the engagement stage, the counselor and the group members cooperate to create a situation in which each individual becomes engaged in the process of counseling. Once this has occurred, the individual has to decide how much of a commitment to counseling he or she is willing to make.

(2) **Commitment to the Process**   The individual must be personally committed to the counseling process for real behavior change to occur. He or she must be motivated to stay with the group in order to benefit from it. If the group situation is not perceived as a safe one, the individual will not feel free to engage in self-expression or self-exploration. Without self-exploration, the individual will not receive from the other members of the group the feedback which would assist in self-understanding.

Identification with the group is important in building meaningful relationships between the group members. Participants learn that they can be accepted for what they are, even with obvious deficiencies. This acceptance may be more important to the individual than being accepted by the counselor. Commitment to the process of counseling is also fostered by membership in the group. The group member will discover that he or she is not isolated and that there are other people with similar difficulties. This awareness of similar difficulties and a common fate increases identification with the group and personal commitment to it. An individual may become so attached to the group and its members' acceptance, however, that feedback does not lead to behavior change. It is important then for individuals to be accepted, but they must move beyond the point of dependence on the group.

New Behavior Patterns   In the first stage of the group, the individual learns how to get involved and work in a group. In the second stage, changes are fostered by the relationship of the group members. Beyond that, however, behavior changes are dependent on the member's internalization of a new, more realistic behavior pattern. This is achieved by an objective self-evaluation of past behavior through self-exploration and with feedback from the group members. As a result of new understanding, the member can develop a more realistic attitude and behavior pattern. Reality testing within the group continues to give the individual behavior-modifying experiences. When the individual exhibits old behavior patterns, he or she can be confronted not only with their self-defeating nature but also with the reaction that these behavior patterns elicit in other people.

These three types of behavior are an integral part of the life stages of a group. Chapters 14 and 15 focus on the group process through the stages of initiation, conflict and confrontation, cohesiveness, production, and termination.

THE PLACE OF THEORY IN GROUP COUNSELING

Counseling theories should be guidelines for producing desirable changes. Although there are disagreements regarding how these changes take place, each theory proposes a process whereby the counselor and group can participate in the process of changing the member's behavior.

As the counselor is confronted with an array of information from the member, he or she needs some structure to organize that information and also a plan to resolve the problem. A theory, as a plan of attack, is a framework upon which the information central to the solution of the problem can be arranged. It enables the counselor to organize data properly and to develop the relationship between each of the bits of data.

A theory should help the counselor understand what he or she is doing. It gives the counselor a structural basis for judging how much progress is being made toward a desired outcome. Implicit in this statement is the assumption that a theory will influence what is being done, since it is a guideline for the counselor's conception and behavior.

Theories regarding the purpose and process of counseling stem from conceptions of the nature of human beings, what they should do, and how they change. In philosophical terms, counseling theories rely on concepts of the human organism, motivation, and learning theory. As Stefflre and Matheny (1968) point out, the relative importance of each of these bases will be different for each theorist, although all would seem to be present in each person's theory.

Theory

A theory must be considered as a conceptual model used to make sense out of the events we observe. Group counseling theories are systematic ways of understanding the participants' behavior, as well as systematic ways of viewing the counseling process and providing a guideline for the counselor's behavior. Hall and Lindzey (1957) view theory as a cluster of related assumptions, systematically related to each other and to a set of empirical definitions. The elements of data, postulates, and relevant assumptions are all parts of a theory. Stefflre and Matheny (1968) conclude that definitions regarding theory contain elements of both reality and belief. Reality is the data of behavior, that which a counselor would see and try to explain, while belief is the way the counselor would try to make sense out of the data by relating it to conceivable explanations. A theory, then, is a map—a few points are known but the road between them is inferred.

Shertzer and Stone (1974) have delineated four major functions of theory:

1. A theory serves to summarize and generalize a particular body of knowledge. It brings together a body of related knowledge and, in shorthand fashion, attempts to put the separate findings into a meaningful and useful package.

2. A theory serves to increase the understanding of a particular body of knowledge. It attempts to order data and to demonstrate those pieces of the puzzle that are the most important.

3. A theory provides the tools by which predictions may be made. It is like a diagram that depicts the various points and what may be expected to occur at these points. For the practitioner, it acts as a guide to the particular pathways that are possible and what may result if certain routes are followed. It points out the relationship between means and ends.

4. A theory serves to encourage further research into the area. It makes no difference whether the theory is proved correct or incorrect; the importance of the theory is that it stimulates further investigations into the particular phenomena with which it is concerned. This is the point to which we refer when we state that a theory is always in the process of becoming. As new research evidence is accumulated, the theory is substantiated, revised, or simply rejected.

Any theory can be measured against certain formal attributes. Stefflre and Matheny (1968) offer several criteria by which a theory may be judged. The first requirement is clarity. It should be easily understood, and the assumptions of hypotheses contained in the theory should be stated in such a way as not to contradict one another. Second, a theory should be comprehensive, explaining as many events as possible in various situations. A third requirement is explicitness; the theory should be stated in precise, definable statements. A theory that is stated clearly, explicitly, and comprehensively can be used to stimulate research, which in turn can validate the theory and contribute to its modification. Whether it is a formal research or an ongoing action research, it will provide a check on the theory to determine if it is appropriate and useful.

Theory and the Counselor

How does a theory develop? If a theory is a structure, the structure is based on smaller pieces of information drawn from experience. One may think of theory building in terms of a pyramid. The base of the pyramid is simple observation of a series of events or behaviors. After careful observations over a period of time, inferences are made about what has been observed. The counselor begins to relate some of these events or behaviors with one another. If the counselor observes these events over a period of time, the inferences may become a hypothesis. A series of separate but related hypotheses may be formed from many observations and inferences. These related hypotheses are the bases upon which the structure of a theory about a client's behavior can be established. Thus, in all theory development, an individual starts with observable events; inferences about the relationship between these events are made, and over a period of time become hypotheses; assumptions about the relation of these hypotheses are then made, and the framework for a theory is formed. Once formed, however, the theory is not static. There is a tendency to think of a theory as a law, which it is not. The theory is always in process. As new observations of events are made, new inferences and hypotheses are developed, and they will change the structure of the theory.

Most counselors do not go through this process of developing a complete theory for each client. They are more likely to rely on a theory that has already been developed. Even so, they will place each client into the structure of an overall theory and develop a minitheory for each client.

Stefflre and Matheny (1968) conclude that a theory is derived from personal, historical, sociological, and philosophical bases. Shoben (1962) suggests that it is the counselor's own psychological need structure—not what research tells him or her—that indicates which theory the counselor will adopt. It would seem that both the theory builder and the person who is adopting a theory should look closely at their own needs to determine the real reason for choosing one theory over another. The development of a theory is tied to the period in time in which it is formulated. Its history and the point in time, as much as anything else, dictates the kind of resolution to problems that will be considered at least plausible. Closely related to the time variable are the sociological and cultural elements that surround a theorist. In addition, the development or adoption of a particular theory is influenced by the philosophical realm. The prevailing mind set of the time or place in which the theorist works dictates to some degree the kind of theory to be used or developed. In part, it is philosophy that defines the goals for which one should strive. Hence, the theory that is developed and used will reflect the dominant philosophy of the time, the culture, and the personal needs of the counselor.

Particularly in counseling, it is important that a theory be useful. For a scientist, the theory may be subjected to experimental testing; for a counselor, however, a theory must provide adequate guidelines for understanding clients and for proposing specific techniques. The theory adopted by a counselor will be related to the desired outcomes he or she seeks. It will be consistent with the counselor's techniques and have some relationship with the desired end product of counseling. Furthermore, the techniques that the counselor uses will also have some relationship to the outcome expected.

Relationship of Theory to Process

Ford and Urban (1963) have conceptualized the relationship between theory and practice in a type of pyramid. At the base of the pyramid are the general theories of human development and personality. These theories are established in the fields of psychology, sociology, and anthropology and consist of abstract ideas, concepts, and assumptions. This level provides the knowledge and understanding of appropriate and inappropriate behaviors. At the second level on the pyramid, a counselor depends on more specific theories of behavior change. These theories are broader applications than counseling theories, which make up the third level on the pyramid. It is apparent, however, that a counseling theory is based on other theories of behavior change, such as learning theory. At the top of the pyramid is the counseling practice or the specific techniques that a counselor would use. So the specific technique that a counselor uses is based on a theory of counseling, which is built upon a theory of behavior change, which is really evolved from broader theories of human development and personality.

Evolving theory into practice is a whole process. The following model may be helpful to the counselor in examining established theories to use for developing a personal theory of counseling. A counselor begins with some general assumptions about personality, moves to more specific assumptions about behavior changes, and then to a counseling theory that indicates techniques which he or she can implement. A beginning counselor may profit from learning established theories in the field and examining the research regarding those theories. The counselor may then wish to utilize the theory that feels most comfortable and through action research modify, reformulate, or discard part of it based upon personal experiences. Without such procedures, a counselor cannot hope to know where she or he is going with clients.

Theory, then, is important in counseling for two primary reasons: as a method of helping the counselor understand clients, and as a set of guidelines for counseling behavior.

Understanding Clients The counselor uses a theory to help distinguish between what is normal or rational behavior and what is abnormal or irrational. It helps in understanding the possible causes of behavior that is damaging to the client. Each client will have somewhat different experiences; a theory enables the counselor to make some assumptions about the general causes of such behaviors.

Counseling theory needs to be derived from a theory of personality development. The counselor must have knowledge of general personality development from childhood through adulthood and of the normal development of personality, as well as an understanding of how maladaptive behavior is derived and maintained. Only when he or she understands the development of both adaptive and maladaptive behaviors can the counselor find ways of helping clients. This, of course, requires the counselor to deal with his or her conception of the nature of human beings.

A set of logically interdependent hypotheses, propositions, or principles about human behavior is crucial for the counselor. He or she cannot preselect problems and measure the phenomena through an interest in a particular aspect of the behavior. Participants in a group will confront the counselor with complicated and varying sets of behavior patterns that are of concern to them, but with which the counselor may have little experience or about which little may be known. The most desirable basis other than verified knowledge to use as a guide in dealing with the problem is a logically interrelated set of hypotheses about behavior; that is, a theory that can be used as if it were verified knowledge.

The concept of a counselor as a hypothesis maker or model builder has been supported by many. Pepinsky and Pepinsky (1954) suggest that the counselor be a model builder by forming a "micro-theory" of the client's behavior. They believe that the counselor must distinguish between observation and inference, state testable hypotheses, test them, and reconstruct the micro-theory in light of the new information. The counselor's responses in the interview would follow from his or her conception or understanding of the client. Meehl (1954) also considers the counselor a model builder. He describes the process thus: the counselor brings events and circumstances together at the moment into a "conception of this person." Through this process, the counselor maintains a continuing understanding by formulating a personal theory for the client. That theory is generally based on some larger theory of personality development, maladjustment, and counseling theory.

A theory helps the counselor to be systematic in his or her observation. The particular advantages of a systematic approach are the elaboration, evaluation, and verification of new ideas and their relation to one another. Systematic conceptualizing behavior helps the counselor to focus attention on concrete behavioral events. Without a theory, the counselor would be likely to observe a client's concern over one area for a while, then jump to observation of another area, and later change to a third concern simply because it seemed interesting and important at the moment. But if the counselor had specific assumptions about the relationship between the three different aspects that occurred in the group and why they were occurring, he or she would have a better understanding and more appropriate techniques for helping the group members express themselves. A systematic approach also facilitates a comparison of different observations, which is essential for accurate generalizations about one member's behavior or the behavior of the group members in general.

Guide to Counselor Behavior   Most counseling theories contend that counseling is a learning process. The differences in theories involve *how* this process of learning takes place. The counseling theory will include ideas about the appropriate role for the counselor. The counselor's behavior in the counseling process will be determined by the theoretical frame of reference from which he or she works. It will determine how personally involved the counselor will become in the process and how active he or she is in the session.

In addition to providing systematic procedures both for observation and under-standing of the client, a theory also affords procedures for modifying behaviors. Beyond influencing the choice of events to be observed, the theory can influence which observations are chosen to be analyzed and evaluated, and what responses the counselor will eventually make. With the multitude of events occurring simul-taneously and continuously in a group, counseling theory can help the counselor generate ideas for potentially effective courses of action. Consistent procedures can be formulated explicitly and then replicated successfully from one group to another. Specification and explicit description make the method reliable and com-municable, and the observations that follow can be checked.

Hence, a counseling theory is not remote and impractical or merely idealistic. It is part of counseling practice. As a problem is confronted, the theory can be used to enlarge the number of events that need attention in order to derive an adequate solution. It is practical because it helps the counselor make systematic observa-tions, encourages bringing together various conceptions of counseling, and helps the counselor approach a prediction, evaluation, and improvement of outcomes.

Group Counseling Theory

There is no exclusive theory of group counseling. Various theories of counseling have viewed the group situation as an extension of individual counseling. This thinking has been based on concepts that pertain to a dyadic approach, with some elaborations to accommodate certain features of the group situation. A number of the theoretical positions reviewed in this book will indicate technical considerations for groups, but not a complete formulation of appropriate concepts. Another dif-ficulty involves nearly complete reliance on group dynamic concepts without the use of personality theory to help understand the clients. In some instances, this has led to "techniques in running groups" that have lost sight of the individual. The leader uses techniques, phrases, and gimmicks without sufficient knowledge of the effect on the individuals. Although meaningful attempts have been made to devel-op a theory of group counseling, we still lack a comprehensive theory that ac-counts for the phenomena of interest to a group counselor (Lieberman, Lakin, and Whitaker, 1969).

A general theory is needed, based on the specifics of individual change within a group. Seven critical issues for developing such a theory of group treatment are presented by Lieberman, Lakin, and Whitaker (1969). Although their original intent was to integrate psychoanalytic and group dynamic theories, they call for a gen-eral theory based on the specifics of therapeutic change, rather than integration based on an amalgam of concepts. Other writers can be used to elaborate on these propositions.

First, there is the need for a theory that explicates the psychology of group membership from the perspective of the client. In order to accomplish this task, we must articulate categories that describe how the client experiences the group. A theory of the phenomenology of group experiences must then in-dicate how subjective experiences of group members influence the therapeutic process.

Second, there is a need for more knowledge about the significance and function of the counselor's role. How influential is the leader, how does the leader derive his or her influence, and how much is useful or detrimental? Kernberg (1975) posits that we need an understanding of how the ego system of the individual leader functions as the modal point in activating a particular target system or subsystem in the group to a temporary position of ascendance. In essence, we need to comprehend the leader's function as a decision maker who is influenced by his or her own internal needs and values as he or she responds to and stimulates the social, cultural, and personal conflicts impinging on the group at any moment.

Third, a general theory should consider the major regulatory forces encroaching upon group members. It must account for the development and relationship of norms and implicit and explicit values that affect the process and outcome of the group experience. Haskell (1975) concurs that values have exerted a major influence on the group movement and posits that the major obstacle to date in the construction of a theoretical framework on which to formulate group principles has been our failure to explicate and to question five basic presumptions and ideologies that permeate group work. These include the belief that phenomena such as group stages, revolt against the leader, or resistances are lawful and indigenous to the group process; the presumption that group wisdom is to be trusted above that of any leader or a minority of individuals; the emphasis on the here and now and the superiority of feeling and emotion over rationality; the presumption that democratically run groups are superior and that the conditions necessary for a democratic model to work exist in the group situation; and finally, the presumption of functionalism, that is, the assumption that because a certain power structure exists, it functions to facilitate social exchanges that benefit all members of the group. To provoke further research, he asks: To what extent are group phenomena that we regard as lawful really the result of specific group techniques? To what extent does the belief in democracy and functionalism really serve to foster the status quo? And finally, to what extent is group wisdom really the wisdom of the group leader?

The fourth issue concerns how a group develops into a therapeutic instead of a nontherapeutic organization. Although all theories discuss the qualities of the relationship and levels of communication that are important in producing an effective group, a general theory would require specification of how these are developed. Is the existence of a therapeutic relationship sufficient to produce positive behavior change? Grunebaum (1975), Carpenter (1977), and Parloff and Dies (1977) argue that ultimately we must specify what interventions and techniques work with a particular client type if we are to explain the development of a therapeutic group.

Fifth, what changes can occur as a result of participation in group counseling? Are the changes different from those in individual counseling? Some theories emphasize intrapsychic changes, such as decreased anxiety or increased self-esteem, while other theories emphasize overt behavior change. A general theory should account for the usefulness of both.

A sixth requirement for a general theory is an adequate concept to account for the generalization of learning from the group to other life situations. What factors account for the perpetuation of newly acquired behaviors or attitudes or for the regression to prior levels of functioning?

Finally, a general theory should explain how group counseling compares with other forms of treatment, particularly individual counseling. This requires the specification of help-giving and help-getting. "Without a help-giving model that will enable us to characterize similarities and differences among treatments, precision about the group therapeutic process will elude us (Lieberman, Laken, and Whitaker, 1969, p. 138)."

These seven issues embrace what the group counselor needs to know. Some of the issues are covered in several of the theories, but taken together they cannot be answered by any one position. An attempt to combine theories may illustrate contradictions. The seven requirements may be used to evaluate the various theoretical positions and to assist the counselor in selecting and developing a personal position.

The Research to Date Bachrach (1972) has described two fundamental methods of research. The predominant methodology in science is the formal theoretical approach involving observation, hypothesis formulation, experimentation, empirical testing of experimental hypotheses, and modification of the theory. In this approach, theory is a reasonable stage between experimentation and the formulation of laws. Critics of the formal theoretical approach argue that theories are not necessary to research. They fear that theories may begin to determine research rather than to integrate research data. These advocates of the informal theoretical method contend that a researcher need only proceed from observation to experimentation resulting in an understanding of the relationships among variables. They believe such understanding will ultimately lead to the formulation of laws. Basic to their approach is a reliance on hunches as opposed to formal hypotheses and careful investigation of the single case or the individual in the group rather than large groups of subjects or group comparisons.

Both methodologies offer relevant approaches to our understanding of group phenomena. The burgeoning of the group movement has fostered a spate of research, much of it sporadic, ill-designed, and inconclusive. A major issue is the failure of researchers to confirm the claims of clinicians that group counseling is effective. Parloff and Dies (1977) contend the major reason for this inconsistency is clinical conceptual rather than research technical. If we are to advance the field of group counseling, we must replace the global conceptualizations guiding present research with specific questions and specific definitions. It will not suffice merely to ask "Is group counseling effective?" Rather, we must ask "Effective for what? What kinds of changes occur, with what kinds of individuals, and under what kinds of conditions?" (Parloff, 1970, p. 182)

Not only must we learn to ask the right questions, but we must also be systematic and specific in our methodology. Highest priority must be placed upon the development of specific definitions of terms and treatment modalities (Parloff and Dies, 1977; Carpenter, 1977). Researchers must then propose specific hypotheses matching specific treatments with particular client needs (Parloff and Dies,

1977; Grunebaum, 1975). Frank (1975) proposes that if we are to comprehend the process of group therapy, we must understand the meaning of a particular behavior for the leader, the client exhibiting the behavior, and the others in the situation. He proposes that researchers undertake situational analyses of happenings in groups, always in relation to the total context in which they occur.

In summary, the clinician and the researcher must fuse their efforts in furthering research. Writers have reached the stage of posing pertinent questions, formulating specific hypotheses, and designing appropriate strategies. It may be that they will generate a general theory of group counseling. Until that time, counselors must select a theory that will best help them understand clients and provide a guide for their behavior. Although there are weaknesses in any stated theory, a counselor can use one to guide informal observation and research in an effort to develop a personal theoretical approach.

Selection of a Theory

A counselor is faced with a multiplicity of behavior changes desired by the members and with a variety of theories and techniques from which to choose. On what basis can he or she decide which set of theories and techniques will produce the desired changes for the specific individuals in the group? Ford and Urban (1963) review several procedures that counselors use in selecting a basic approach to counseling. One criterion is based on personal experience—what seems satisfactory to the counselor. This is an idiosyncratic criterion. As a counselor works with several individuals, certain procedures are found to be useful in achieving whatever goals he or she is aiming toward. Since they worked with one client or one group, perhaps they will work with another. This type of approach has many hazards. At best, a counselor's observations are distorted by a limited number and restricted variety of clients and groups. At worst, this approach leads to counseling solely on the basis of what "feels good." A second criterion used in choosing a theory is based on a consensus of experts. It does provide a wider variety of experiences from which to make judgments, and the effects of systematic personal biases may be somewhat reduced. A major difficulty with this criterion can be that it exerts a strong pressure for conformity and restricts experimentation with new procedures. A closely related criterion is prestige. Many young counselors will adopt a form of theory that is presently in vogue or will adopt the theoretical position of their supervisor. A fourth criterion for selecting a theory is the amount and quality of the verified body of knowledge supporting it. (The chapters that follow in Part One will present such information for each position discussed.)

"It seems essential to recognize that a theory is a tool of discovery, chosen partially because of the utility it has had and our discovery of ourselves in the ordering of events and experiences of which our own lives are made (Shoben, 1962, p. 617)." Theory makes articulate a set of ideas that the counselor can discover or provides a structure out of the confusion of the counseling process. It is important for the counselor to have a thorough knowledge of self and his or her theoretical frame of reference. Shoben believes that the counselor's adaptation to any particular theory is a reflection of personality traits.

Williamson (1962) describes the counselor as a "technique," indicating that the counselor's philosophy of human development should show through his or her behavior and that efforts at relating effectively with the client must come from the counselor's own self-acceptance. The counselor is a technique not only in what he or she does or says but also in the manner of nonverbal communication. Even the counselor's life-style can be an important effective technique in counseling.

Lister (1964) maintains that a beginning counselor has already spent a number of years formulating, testing, and modifying hypotheses about self and others. He believes that, as a consequence, the counselor has a personal theory and that this personal theory refers to the hypotheses the counselor has come to view as a reliable guide to personally effective and satisfying human relations. "Although many such hypotheses are largely implicit and inarticulate, they nevertheless constitute patterns for counseling behavior even before the students are introduced to formal courses in counseling or personality theory (p. 310)."

The formal theory chosen by a counselor is probably related to personal theory. To the extent that a choice of a theory depends on something other than the internal consistency of a system of ideas, its comprehensiveness, or the degree to which it is clearly buttressed by evidence that meets the criteria of scientific validity, it seems at least possible that mere personal and temperamental factors may be determinative. The choice of a theory may be "partially a function of the extent to which such ideas validate one's inarticulate and implicit impressions of how behavioral events can be ordered and understood (Shoben, 1962, p. 81)."

SUMMARY

An individual's behavior is largely the product of interactions with other significant human beings. It seems appropriate to resolve problems or enhance productive behaviors through human interactions in a group. Group counseling is not spontaneous; it involves planning and direction. Theories can provide guidelines for the conduct of group counseling by assisting a counselor in understanding the group members and his or her role in the group. The union of personal and textbook theories can provide an explication for those who feel comfortable using the client-centered approach, learning theory, or any other systematic counseling approach. The ease with which one adopts a formal theory depends upon one's access to a formal theory that articulates one's personal theory and upon the freedom to adopt and implement that theory. A counselor may begin by leaning more heavily on a formal theory to understand and explain the group member's behavior as well as his or her own counseling behavior, but with more experience the counselor may rely less on the formal theory and more on personal theory, using the theoretical terms only to explain feelings and to communicate with others. The following chapters provide several theoretical conceptions that are used in group counseling. Each chapter presents a concept of behavior development, maladaptive behaviors, theory, and group process to be used in group counseling.

References

Bachrach, A. *Psychological research.* New York: Random House, 1972.

Brown, T. You're OK, we're OK. *Group Practice,* 1976, *25,* 24–26.

Buirski, P. Some contributions of ethology to group therapy: Dominance and hierarchies. *International Journal of Group Psychotherapy,* 1975, *25,* 227–35.

Carpenter, J. Further considerations on "A theoretical framework for group psychotherapy": A summary and critique. *Journal of Contemporary Psychotherapy,* 1977, *9,* 83–88.

Cartwright, O., and A. Zander. *Group dynamics.* New York: Harper and Row, 1968.

Cox, M. Group psychotherapy as a redefining process. *International Journal of Group Psychotherapy,* 1973, *23,* 465–73.

Ford, D., and H. Urban. *Systems of psychotherapy: A comparative study.* New York: Wiley, 1963.

Frank, J. Some problems of research in group psychotherapy. *International Journal of Group Psychotherapy,* 1975, *25,* 141–44.

Galinsky, M., and J. Schopler. Warning: Groups may be dangerous. *Social Work,* 1977, *22,* 89–94.

Gazda, G. *Theories and methods of group counseling.* Springfield, IL.: Charles C Thomas, 1969.

Gazda, G., J. Duncan, and M. Meadows. Counseling and group procedures: Report of a survey. *Counselor Education and Supervision,* 1967, *6,* 305–10.

Gazda, G., J. Duncan, and P. Sisson. Professional issues in group work. *Personnel and Guidance Journal,* 1971 *49,* 637–43.

Glasser, P., R. Sarri, and R. Vinter. *Individual change through small groups.* New York: The Free Press, 1974.

Gootnick, I. Transference in psychotherapy with schizophrenic patients. *International Journal of Group Psychotherapy,* 1975, *25,* 379–88.

Grunebaum, H. A soft-hearted review of hard-nosed research on groups. *International Journal of Group Psychotherapy,* 1975, *25,* 185–97.

Hall, C., and G. Lindzey. *Theories of personality.* New York: Wiley, 1957.

Haskell, R. Presumptions of group work: A value analysis. *Small Group Behavior,* 1965, *6,* 469–85.

Hawkins, D., B. Norton, C. Eisdorfer, and D. Gianturco. Group process research: A factor analytical study. *American Journal of Psychiatry,* 1973, *130,* 916–19.

Jones, R., and P. Jones. The behavior of individuals in small groups. In *Sociology in medicine.* New York: Wiley, 1975, 135–45.

Kaplan, A. *The conduct of inquiry.* New York: Chandler Publishing Company, 1964.

Kelman, H. The role of the group in the induction of therapeutic change. *International Journal of Group Psychotherapy,* 1963, *13,* 251–75.

Kernberg, O. A systems approach to priority setting of intervention in groups. *International Journal of Group Psychotherapy,* 1975, *25,* 251–75.

Kubie, L. Unsolved problems in the use of group processes in psychotherapy. *The Journal of Nervous and Mental Disease,* 1973, *157,* 434–41.

Lieberman, M., M. Laken, and D. Whitaker. Problems and potential of psychoanalytic and group-dynamics theories for group psychotherapy. *International Journal of Group Psychotherapy, 1969, 19, 131–41.*

Lister, J. The counselor's personal theory. *Counselor Education and Supervision,* 1964, *3,* 207–13.

Loeser, L. Some aspects of group dynamics. *International Journal of Group Psychotherapy,* 1957, *7,* 5–19.

Lubin, D., W. Reddy, C. Stransberry, and A. Lubin. The group psychotherapy literature: 1976. *International Journal of Group Psychotherapy,* 1977, *27,* 521–52.

Meehl, P. *Clinical and statistical prediction.* Minneapolis: University of Minnesota Press, 1954.

Milman, O., and G. Goldman. *Group process today.* Springfield, IL: Charles C Thomas, 1974.

Naar, R. A theoretical framework for group psychotherapy. *Journal of Contemporary Psychotherapy,* 1975, *7,* 50–55.

Ohlsen, M. *Group counseling.* New York: Holt, 1970.

Parloff, M. Group therapy and the small group field: An encounter. *International Journal of Group Psychotherapy,* 1970, *20,* 267–304.

Parloff, M., and R. Dies. Group psychotherapy outcome research 1966–1975. *International Journal of Group Psychotherapy,* 1977, *27,* 281–319.

Pepinsky, M., and P. Pepinsky. *Counseling: Theory and practice.* New York: Ronald Press, 1954.

Piper, W., E. Debbane, and J. Garant. Group psychotherapy outcome research: Problems and prospects of a first-year project. *International Journal of Group Psychotherapy,* 1977, *27,* 321–41.

Ruitenbeek, H. *The new group therapies.* New York: Avon Books, 1970.

Schutz, W. Not encounter and certainly not facts. *Journal of Humanistic Psychology,* 1975, *15,* 7–18.

Shertzer, B., and S. Stone. *Fundamentals of counseling.* Boston: Houghton Mifflin, 1974.

Shoben, E. The counselor's theory as a personal trait. *Personnel and Guidance Journal,* 1962, *40,* 617–21.

Siegel, M. Individual and group psychotherapy: Fads and foolishness. *Psychotherapy: Theory, Research and Practice,* 1973, *10,* 261–64.

Stefflre, B., and K. Matheny (Eds.). *The function of counseling theory,* Guidance Monograph Series. Boston: Houghton Mifflin, 1968.

Williamson, E. The counselor as technique. *Personnel and Guidance Journal,* 1962, *41,* 108–11.

2
Psychoanalytic Approaches to Groups

Psychoanalysis is first and foremost a method of individual treatment for people with emotional problems who seek assistance. What has become known as analytic group therapy or counseling is basically an extension of psychoanalytic techniques formulated primarily for individual therapy and modified later to encompass treatment of individuals within groups. Yet, whether one talks of individual or group analysis, psychoanalytic theory constitutes the foundation for both of these approaches. It is the focal point around which all else that could be called psychoanalytic revolves.

For the most part, counselors view individual and group psychoanalysis as incompatible with educational settings (Aubrey, 1971; Fullmer, 1971). This stance is taken primarily because counselors tend to distinguish between what constitutes counseling and what comprises psychotherapy. Traditionally, the psychoanalytic approach to group treatment has been placed in the province of psychotherapy rather than in the domain of counseling. That is, psychoanalysis is generally seen as a method of treatment for individuals suffering from deeply imbedded personality problems rather than a method of treatment for individuals experiencing difficulties in coping with the everyday problems of life.

GROUP PSYCHOTHERAPY OR GROUP COUNSELING?

As noted in Chapter 1, whether or not one can definitively separate group counseling from group psychotherapy remains open to discussion. If groups are in any way similar to other situations in life, it would seem that there might be an area of overlap between group counseling and group psychotherapy. This idea is supported by some of the developments that have occurred in groups during the past decade. In recent group counseling literature, for example, the phrase "group psychotherapy for normal individuals" has become increasingly popular. Theorists are saying that one must pay attention to the pathology of everyday living. Different types of behavior disorders such as anxiety neurosis, obsessive-compulsive neurosis, or schizophrenia are simply subclassifications of that broad area labeled conflicts in living. What differs in each case is the manifestation of symptoms. In each case, however, the common denominator is that the individual is having difficulty with life.

Szasz (1961) has done more, perhaps, than anyone else to question counselors' and psychotherapists' use of the term mental illness. He has raised the questions: What is mental illness, and who is mentally ill? In Szasz's opinion, mental illness is a myth and tends to be whatever psychiatrists say it is. He states, "Although mental illness might have been a useful concept in the nineteenth century, today it is scientifically worthless and socially harmful (p. ix)." Szasz also argues that it is impossible to answer the question: What is psychotherapy? The term encompasses almost everything a helping professional might attempt to do for a person in need of his or her services. The primary benefit of psychotherapy, according to Szasz, sounds a great deal like what other theorists have said about the parameters and goals of counseling. That is, "psychotherapy is an effective method of helping people—not to recover from an 'illness,'—but rather to learn about themselves, others, and life (p.xi)."

Given this point of view, the debate about whether group psychoanalysis is counseling or psychotherapy seems to lose some of its importance. The problem is human suffering, and who is to say that the pathology of the normal hurts any less or has any fewer negative ramifications than the pathology of those who are labeled sick, mentally ill, or disturbed? As Dreikurs (1960) has pointed out, "We may well have to think in terms of organizing therapy groups not only for our emotionally sick but for the normal population which is emotionally unbalanced in a world of unrest and suspicion, hardly anywhere permitting sincere cooperation (p. 19)." It is partly upon this rationale that the psychoanalytic approach is included here. Other reasons for presenting this approach are: (1) the psychoanalytic school was one of the first to apply its theory of human behavior systematically to group treatment; (2) some of the basic principles underlying psychoanalytic theory are used in modified form by the other group approaches described in the book; and (3) the psychoanalytic approach to groups is still used in a variety of settings other than the school—child and adult clinics, family and marriage counseling centers, and private practice, to name a few.

FREUD AND PSYCHOANALYTIC THEORY

Freud is the acknowledged father of psychoanalytic theory and, perhaps, of modern human psychology itself. He not only provided the major and original structure of psychoanalytic theory, but he also introduced the concept of psychic determinism—the idea that every behavioral action and emotional reaction has a cause that is usually related to both the interpersonal and the intrapsychic (Locke, 1961). Moreover, Freud's topographical structure of personality (the trilogy of the id, ego, and superego), his emphasis upon early childhood experiences, his delineation of psychosexual stages of development, and his stress on the importance of the unconscious and dreams were all revolutionary landmarks in explicating the science of human behavior. With Freud's many contributions to psychoanalytic theory, it is little wonder, then, that psychoanalytic theory has become almost synonymous with Freudian theory—despite the fact that modifications have been made in his original formulations.

Although Freud's contributions are primarily in the area of personality theory, *Group Psychology and the Analysis of the Ego* (1922) was a pioneering work in the area of group psychology. Possibly because of his interest in individual psychology and possibly for other reasons, Freud's work in group psychology stopped short. It has been left to some of his followers to translate and to enlarge upon his formulations concerning group psychology and translate them to the field of group psychotherapy.

The practice of psychoanalysis in groups is not commonly used in group therapy. In fact, during the early days of group psychotherapy, many analysts rejected the idea that psychoanalysis was possible in a group context. Today, this position has changed and is reflected by the works of such renowned group psychoanalysts as Wolf, Slavson, and Foulkes.

PSYCHOANALYTIC APPROACH TO GROUPS

The psychoanalytic approach to groups symbolizes the conventional method of group treatment, although the proponents contend that this orientation produces a more lasting effect on the behavioral change of individuals than do the more recent group approaches. Analytic groups are considered conventional because of the goals of treatment, the roles of the therapist and the group members, and the methodological arrangements of the group. Typically, such groups meet once a week for one hour and a half with eight or nine members who interact with each other by exchanging their problems and their interpretations of each other's actions and words. The group therapist customarily assumes a relatively passive role, at times offering some direction and interpretation of what is taking place.

As the newer group methods have become more popular, individuals have begun to challenge the conventional approach of analytic group treatment. They have questioned the relevancy of this type of treatment for the problems facing modern women and men—namely those of an overwhelming sense of alienation and dehumanization. Is it necessary, such individuals ask, to reconstruct the family and to deal with the unconscious motivators of behavior? What good does the interpretation of one's behavior do? To a certain extent, the neo-Freudians have made the analytic approach to groups more palatable to modern men and women, but despite their efforts the psychoanalytic tradition in groups has not captured the imagination of the general public.

One of the goals of this chapter is to examine the salient principles of psychoanalytic theory. What are some of its basic assumptions about individuals? What is its theory of personality development, and does this conceptualization of a person's psychic development relate to analytic group therapy? In what types of settings is the psychoanalytic method appropriate? To what extent are the methods and the techniques of analytic group therapy similar to or different from those used in individual therapy? What are some of the modern derivatives of the psychoanalytic tradition? In addition to an examination of these questions, this chapter contains a summary of analytic personality theory, makes some historical observations on the development of analytic group therapy, discusses the theory and techniques of this method, and provides examples of analytically oriented groups from the research literature. Emphasis is placed upon classical psychoanalytic group counseling—that is, on a decidedly Freudian orientation. This stance is taken primarily for the sake of parsimony. In keeping with the position previously presented, no attempt is made to differentiate between group counseling and group psychotherapy; the terms are used interchangeably. Similarly, the terms counselor and therapist also are used interchangeably. (Early literature on psychoanalysis in groups used "therapist" almost exclusively, but recent trends reflect a growing shift to "counselor.")

PSYCHOANALYTIC PERSONALITY THEORY AS A FOUNDATION FOR GROUP THERAPY

Begun some eighty years ago by Freud, the psychoanalytic theory of personality development provides a frame of reference for evaluating both the normal and the abnormal behavior of individuals (Brenner, 1957). There has been, however, an overriding concern with psychoanalytic hypotheses regarding abnormal development. It is this morbid obsession with or lure of the negative which has caused some individuals to confuse or associate the psychoanalytic theory of personality development with pathology. The roots of analytic group counseling are found in classical psychoanalytic personality theory. Analytic group counselors tend to borrow heavily from Freud's notion of the levels of human awareness and his outline of the structural components of an individual's personality.

Human Nature

One of the trademarks of psychoanalytic theory is its adherence to Freud's basic assumptions concerning human nature. From the classical psychoanalytic view, human beings are not seen as the masters of their own destinies. Instead, their behavior is motivated by a need to gratify fundamental biological urges and instincts. Moreover, an individual's behavior is not a random chance event but is determined largely by his or her life history of experiences. Thus, according to classical psychoanalytic theory, men and women are captives of fundamentally evil instincts and drives, which must be bridled via the process of socialization lest they career out of control and wreak havoc on the orderly functionings of society. Since classical analysts believe that an individual's personality is substantially formed by the age of five, it is important in group counseling to focus upon unresolved conflicts originating from early childhood experiences. Thus, the early years are like the coming attractions of a movie, in the sense that they define and guide later behavior. It seems only a natural sequel that psychoanalytic group therapy is founded upon the concept that the present behavior of a member of a group is most understandable when one looks at his or her life history of experiences.

Levels of Awareness

Levels of awareness assume a prominent role in classical psychoanalytic theory. Freud (1935) posited that an individual has three different levels of awareness that are significant in personality development and analytic counseling. From least to most significance, these levels are the conscious, the preconscious, and the unconscious. As the term implies, the conscious level consists of those acts, feelings, or behaviors of which a person is aware. The preconscious contains those thoughts or feelings which, although not a part of the conscious, can be summoned into consciousness. Freud described the unconscious as the most important level of awareness—mainly because of the role it has in shaping a person's behavior. The unconscious contains those thoughts or feelings to which an individual does not have access. Since a person cannot bring them into consciousness by individual effort, counseling or therapy is needed. They are normally repressed because they are considered unacceptable, both to oneself and to society in general. One potential result of this kind of repression of unconscious and unpleasant thoughts may be that the person experiences internal conflict represented in the form of symptoms—symptoms that disguise and distort the original cause of the problem.

Part of the counselor's job is to deal with the client's levels of awareness—not only to bring into awareness those unconscious repressed thoughts that manifest themselves in the form of maladaptive behavior but also to assist the person in working through these unresolved conflicts. In dealing with a participant's unconscious motivators of behavior, the primary techniques of the group therapist are ones of uncovering, exploring and interpreting the client's conflict. This approach is often hindered by what psychoanalysts view as the two basic characteristics of emotional problems: (1) a resistance to changing one's way of living, and (2) a proclivity to relive, repeat, and redo in the present those behaviors that belong more appropriately to yesteryear's way of life (Slavson, 1964).

In addition to describing an individual's levels of awareness and the effect they may have upon personality development, Freud (1935) delineated three structural divisions of personality. The interaction of these three structural divisions results in a system of both reciprocally urging and checking forces.

The Id Freud's first structural division of personality is the id (meaning "it"), chosen as a deliberately neutral term. It is inherited at birth—unconscious, irrational, unorganized, and pleasure-oriented. The id is also the source of the libido—that fixed reservoir of sexual energy available to a person. Since the id's primary aim is immediate gratification of pleasure, it has no sense of morality or unity of purpose. Freud believed that the id contains all that is inherited, i.e., that is present at birth.

The Ego The ego constitutes the second structural part of an individual's personality. Unlike the id, the ego is not present at birth but develops gradually.

As the ego matures, its functions may be classified into the following two groups: (1) physical growth, or the genetically determined development of the central nervous system, as manifested by greater muscular or sensory control; and (2) experience or experiential factors (Hartmann & Kris, 1945). Throughout this process, the ego becomes an individual's library of memories (Rapaport, 1951).

Ego identification with persons or objects within one's environment is an important function of this structure of an individual's personality. Identification is the process that individuals experience as they attempt to become like someone or something in one or several aspects of thought or behavior (Brenner, 1957). For example, an infant learns to imitate the smile of an adult and to speak by imitation. Identification plays a significant part in diverting psychic energy from the id to the ego. The "becoming like" quality of identification produces a change in the ego. One possible result of this change is that either all or part of the psychic energy directed toward the mental representation of an object becomes attached to the copy of that object in the ego.

Another function of the ego is to deal with anxiety-arousing events precipitated by conflicts of interest between the id and the superego, the third topographical structure of an individual's personality. The ego has two primary devices to deal with anxiety-provoking situations: (1) it may employ its attributes of problem-solving behavior—its reality-based reasoning powers; or (2) it may use methods to deny, falsify, or distort reality. These methods are called ego defense mechanisms.

Ego Defense Mechanisms   Ego defense mechanisms are an individual's source of psychological protection from anxiety and from becoming unglued in the face of pressure from two competing personality subsystems. They may be used beneficially or detrimentally. Freud (1949) delineated a number of ego defense mechanisms, pointing out that each individual tends to develop a characteristic pattern for using such defenses. The sheer number of ego defense mechanisms which are potentially at a person's disposal explains, in part, the variety of personality types that may develop among individuals.

One major ego defense mechanism is repression. Repression operates to prevent the entry of unconscious thoughts that are anxiety-arousing into consciousness (Fenichel, 1945). It is an attempt by the individual to protect himself or herself. Although repression is, to some degree, necessary for normal personality development, it can be overused. Other illustrative examples of ego defense mechanisms are projection, regression, and sublimation.

The Superego   The third component of an individual's personality structure is the superego, which, in large part, resembles the conscience. Freud conceived of the superego as the core of parental moral attitudes and social behavior learned during childhood (Freud, 1949). Thus, the superego acts toward the ego in the same way as the child's parents once acted toward the child. By internalizing parental criticism and approaches toward solving problems, individuals, in some measure, carry their parents around within themselves.

Thoughts connected with the superego lead to an evaluation of some behaviors as either good or bad. A harmonious matching of the superego and the ego moves people toward realizing their ego-ideal—what people would like to be like. Since many individuals rarely completely attain their ego-ideal, compromise must take place. Failure to compromise, or the inharmonious relationship between the superego and the ego or the ego and the ego-ideal, may lead the individual to adopt maladjustive behaviors. Thus, the two major aspects of the superego are its moral restrictions and the ego-ideal.

Psychosexual Stages of Development

There is more to an individual's personality development than the structural and functional distinctions between the id, ego, and superego. According to classical psychoanalytic theory, an individual's personality develops as she or he passes through a series of stages. These stages are defined by their areas of pleasure-seeking activities. The term *psychosexual stages of development* implies, therefore, that a relationship exists between an individual's pleasure-seeking activities and psychological maturation. Although few individuals proceed smoothly from one stage to another, Freud assumed that for the vast majority of individuals, normal personality development entailed passing through the stages he outlined.

In accordance with his belief that an individual's personality is largely formulated by the fifth year of life, Freud emphasized the psychosexual stages of development during these years. The first three stages occur in what he called the pregenital periods. These are the oral, anal, and phallic stages, and their primary erotogenic or pleasure-seeking zones are respectively the mouth (as exemplified by the child's sucking behavior); the anal area (characterized by toilet training); and the genitals (exemplified by early childhood sexual exploration and identification). While the oral and anal stages occur in infancy, the phallic period takes place in early childhood. The two remaining stages are latency (the learning and socialization period which occurs about the fifth year of life) and the genital stage, which comes with the onset of puberty and the development of relationships with members of the opposite sex.

The importance of the psychosexual stages of maturation is that at each juncture the individual develops certain patterns of personality development, particularly in relationship with the ego. As noted, not all persons proceed smoothly from one stage to another. Fixation is likely to occur if the individual does not receive appropriate socialization. That is, although the person is able to pass on to other stages, he or she does so at the expense of having left unfulfilled some basic libidinal or pleasure-seeking strivings. The residual effects of these unmet pleasures are like skeletons hanging in one's closet. They may haunt an individual or crop up at the most unexpected and inopportune time. Unconsciously, a person may expend a lifelong effort trying to regain what has been lost in terms of satisfaction of early childhood pleasure zones. As Shakespeare once said, what is done cannot be undone. In psychotherapy, the counselor seeks to assist the client in understanding what was done and how he or she can most satisfactorily move through an understanding of past events to more fruitful and personally satisfying adaptive behavior.

In summary, the psychoanalytic theory of personality posits that an individual's behavior is determined by heredity and environmental interaction. His or her basic motivating tendency is to reduce psychological and biological tensions. Early childhood experiences have a direct bearing on adult behavior, since individuals tend to repeat earlier behaviors in order to gain control of the current stimulants surrounding them. Optimum gratification of pleasure-arousing zones during each psychosexual stage allows the young person's ego to mature. The maturation of the ego, in turn, helps the individual to relate better to the world. With a healthy maturation of the ego, there is a greater chance that the libidinal drives of the id and the demands of the superego will be better integrated. Good mental health occurs, therefore, as a result of judicious balancing of the forces of the id, ego, and superego. Much of this mental juggling is done unconsciously. The concepts of levels of awareness and structural components of personality pervade all facets of classical psychoanalytic group therapy. Freud was convinced that personality development is almost completely formed by the end of a child's fifth year and that continued development was mainly a process of elaboration on this basic structure.

Inappropriate Behavioral Development

Classical psychoanalytic theory postulates that the two major factors which lead to inappropriate behavioral development are: (1) ineffectual functioning of a person's psychic apparatus, and (2) early learnings. One can examine maladjustment by exploring the various ways in which the id, ego, and superego—the psychic apparatus—function. The ego acts as the executor of an individual's conduct. When the ego fails to integrate the other two subsystems of a person's personality, inappropriate behavior is likely to take place. For example, if the id is controlled too harshly by the ego and its defense mechanisms, adequate outlets for the expressions of the id may be blocked. This phenomenon is noticeable in people who seem to lack the capacity for finding pleasure from their environment. In terms of the id and the ego relationship, there are two possible dangers to normal development: (1) the id may override the ego "in which no trace will be left of the previous character of the individual and the entrance into adult life will be marked by a riot of uninhibited gratification of instincts" (Freud, A., 1948, p. 163); and (2) the ego may reign over the id and restrict it to a limited area, constantly guarded by the person's defense mechanisms.

Failure to integrate the demands of the superego may also lead to maladjustment. The superego may be overly harsh and demand impossible perfection; it may be unduly lenient; or it may even be an inconsistent mixture of the two. More important, it may not allow people to distinguish adequately between their wishes and those of their parents or parental equivalents. Hence people may be continually torn between what they should do and what they would like to do. Just as in the case of the improperly regulated id, people who operate mainly on the basis of "shoulds" find out that they are not master of their own ship.

In addition to ineffectual functioning of the psychic apparatus, learned behavioral disorders assume a prominent role in the development of maladaptive behavior. One of Freud's basic propositions is that the learning associated with behavioral disorder occurs in infancy and early childhood and that, consequently, all later learnings are effectuations of that learned disorder (Fenichel, 1945). Freud maintained that behavior is learned for two purposes: (1) to reduce psychological energies or drives so that they conform to social mores, and (2) to control drives that might lead to immediate gratification but that also have severe penalties or consequences attached to their fulfillment. He grouped practically all learned responses under his concept of the ego (Ford and Urban, 1963).

The common element of most behavior pathologies is the approach-avoidance conflict. As psychological energy and tensions mount, they stimulate behavior aimed at reducing the conflict. Thus, the symptoms of learned behavior disorder usually result from compromises between fulfilling the unconscious wish of the psychological energy and the negative evaluation of doing so. The types of responses contained in the conflict and the person's efforts to resolve it may vary. Different types of behavior disorders such as anxiety neurosis, obsessive-compulsive neurosis, or schizophrenia are simply subclassifications of the kinds of responses contained in the conflict and in the particular individual's attempts to resolve it. Hence the maladaptive process is essentially the same. What differs is the manifestation of various symptoms.

In analytic group counseling, the counselor seeks to understand the conflict behind the symptom. Counseling is directed toward assisting the individual to develop a better integrative function of the ego over the impulses which have been repressed. The goal of group psychoanalysis is not to try to relieve the individual of the basic conflicts of living, but rather to help the person develop greater awareness of his or her psychological desires, self-evaluative thoughts and feelings, and the dictates of the reality situation.

PSYCHOANALYSIS AND GROUPS: HISTORICAL OBSERVATIONS

The historical involvement of psychoanalysis in groups is significant for two fundamental reasons: (1) as a background for understanding the events and thoughts that led to what can be called loosely the psychoanalytic group model; and (2) as a means by which the present controversies concerning the applicability of psychoanalysis to groups can be examined.

Group Psychology and Freud

The year 1922 is a significant one in psychoanalytic history, for during that year Freud's work *Group Psychology and the Analysis of the Ego* was first published. Already a seminal figure in individual psychology, Freud, using the works of Le Bon (1895) and McDougall (1921), applied his psychoanalytic theory to the study of groups. He addressed himself to answering three basic questions: (1) What is a group? (2) How does the group come to exert an influence over an individual's mental functioning? (3) What changes does the group produce in the mental life of a person? Freud was concerned with outlining principles of group psychology; he did not deal with the subject of group treatment or group psychotherapy.

In switching his focus of interest from the study of individuals to the study of groups, Freud noted that this was not a sign of inconsistency on his part. Pointing out that the contrasts made between individual and group psychology were superficial distinctions and that one could profit most from a study of both these areas, he stated:

> The contrast between individual psychology and social or group psychology which at first glance may seem to be full of significance, loses a great deal of its sharpness when it is examined more closely. It is true that individual psychology is concerned with the individual man and explores the paths by which he seeks to find satisfaction for his instinctual impulses, but only rarely and under certain exceptional conditions is individual psychology in a position to disregard the reactions of this individual to others. In the individual's mental life someone else is invariably involved, as a model, as an object, as a helper, as an opponent (Freud, 1959, pp. 1–2).

Freud's ideas on group psychology emphasized the following: (1) the importance of ego development and ego identifications in groups; (2) the significance of the leader in the group; and (3) the reconstruction of the family unit among group members. Three possible types of identification are suggested in *Group Psychology and the Analysis of the Ego:* "First . . . the original form of emotional tie with an object; secondly, . . . introjection of the object into the ego; and thirdly, . . . perception of a common quality shared with some other person (p. 65)."

Freud was one of the first theoreticians to stress the importance of the leader in group formation and functioning (Slavson, 1964). In his view, the leader is the central figure in every group, since it is the leader who becomes the common ego-ideal of members of the group. This centrality occurs because the leader is the common object of libidinal cathexis that ties group members together. That is to say, the link among group members is their common investment of emotional energy onto the group leader.

Group leaders function as parental figures for the members of the group. That is, group members unconsciously project onto the leader their attitudes toward parental figures, particularly their feelings toward their fathers. (Freud did not take into account what would happen if the group leader were a female.) Therefore, in some respects, the original family constellation is reestablished in groups (Slavson, 1964). As the group begins to take on the characteristics of the family, there is a tendency on the part of its members to regress to earlier childhood dependency stages. Presently, the psychoanalytic approach to group counseling is based mainly on these ideas.

One of Freud's greatest limitations was that he looked at the group as a form of mob psychology—more specifically, his basic propositions on groups arose from the primal horde concept. His parallels between the group leader and the leader of a primal horde leave much to be desired. As Slavson (1964) points out, "Freud's conclusion that the 'group' is similar to the 'primal horde' has to be questioned. It would be more correct if the word 'mass' were to be substituted for 'groups' (p. 25)."

Beyond explaining the significance of the leader and the tendency of members to regress to earlier childhood dependency stages, Freud stopped short—possibly because he had chosen inappropriate organizations (the Catholic Church and the army) from which to formulate general principles of group dynamics. Considering the time period as well as the country in which he lived, Freud's choice of organizations to study group psychology is understandable. Freud came from an authoritarian society, and members of the army and the Catholic Church were dependent upon their leaders.

Since Freud's provisional statement about groups, certain reformulations have been made. Notable among these is the repudiation of the group as a horde or mob. The basic tenets of his theory of personality, however, are still integrally connected with group analysis.

Group Analysis

Trigant Burrow first applied the term *group analysis* to the therapeutic treatment of individuals in groups. Burrow's motivation for developing group analysis was simple: he had become increasingly disenchanted with Freud's lack of emphasis on the social forces affecting behavior. In *The Social Basis of Consciousness* (1927), Burrow explained that in group analysis no one individual would hold an authoritative position except to the extent that an individual's thoughtfulness or intelligence qualified him or her to act in a responsible capacity. His concern was that each group member would endeavor to discover the nature of their motivation and expression and would begin to test these discoveries against the spontaneous reactions from other participants. After 1932, Burrow's contributions to group psychotherapy were minimal, possibly because he had turned his attention to psychoanalysis, which stressed the biological principles of behavior.

Since Trigant Burrow, a number of psychoanalysts have completed therapeutic work with groups using the psychoanalytic model. One of the pioneers in this area was Alexander Wolf, who stumbled onto the use of groups for therapy almost by accident. In 1938 Wolf suggested to a number of his adult clients who were experiencing the financial strains of the 1930s that they continue their analytic treatment in a group context. Since all expressed interest, Wolf conducted his first meeting. As a result of both the clients' and Wolf's enthusiasm, the word spread to other individuals. By 1940, Wolf was conducting five groups, one of which was composed of married couples.

Wolf cites a number of reasons for the attraction of people to analytic groups during this time. First, the economic depression of the 1930s had created a society in which people were collectively trying to cope with the problems of poverty and emotional stress. Second, most people as a result of the depression could not afford individual analysis. Third, individuals could not only receive treatment in depth but could also obtain the support of others who were having similar struggles in life. Wolf is noted for initiating the meeting of group members at alternate sessions without the presence of the therapist.

Samuel Slavson, although an engineer by training, is another analytically oriented group therapist noted for his early efforts. He is perhaps best known for his development of activity therapy for children and play therapy.

Representing the British school, Foulkes and Anthony have combined Lewin's field theory with analytic group psychotherapy. They stress the group process, whereas Slavson places primary emphasis on the individual in group treatment.

Criticisms

One of the common criticisms made against group psychoanalysis is that true free association is not possible in group counseling. That is, the chain of free association for any particular person in a group may be broken by interruptions from other group members. Locke (1961), however, dismissing the necessity of having a chain of uninterrupted free associations, points out that another person's interruption or attempt to pick up on the train of thought of the first speaker may be viewed as a very significant second free association that the therapist must also interpret. Commenting on the position of those who adhere to the traditional concept of free association, Locke (1961) observes, "Their thinking generally circles around the syllogism of the couch: if there is no couch, there is no free association; if there is no free association, there is no psychoanalysis (p. 7)."

Another criticism of analytic group counseling is that it focuses too much on overt behavior—the presenting problem—rather than upon the unconscious underlying cause of a person's problem. This situation is, in part, due to the presence of others in the therapy setting. Group members are predisposed toward picking up on the here and now of another participant's behavior. Consequently, unconscious material may not be brought out in the group.

In addition, individuals may also be unduly influenced by the behavior of other participants. Although recognizing the importance of the group in assisting an individual to make new identifications that may improve ego and superego functioning, Slavson (1964) likewise acknowledges that discussions and reactions that occur in a group may exceed a person's ego tolerance. To mitigate against the possibility of ego destruction, he proposes that the counselor carefully select individuals for any particular group.

The examination of differences between individual and group analysis leads back to the original question: Is psychoanalysis possible in group psychotherapy? Locke (1961) argues that the controversy attendant upon group analysis may be seen as: (1) just a difference of opinion on the group approach, or (2) a flat rejection of analytic group counseling. He affirms that the objections raised against the possibility of using the psychoanalytic method in groups are based on easily surmountable technical difficulties.

Acknowledging the differences between individual and group analysis, Foulkes and Anthony (1965) also take the stance that psychoanalysis is still possible in groups. The authors declare, however, that although group dynamics do exist, they have no effect on the ongoing psychoanalysis. Wolf and Schwartz (1962) maintain a similar position. A significant feature of their approach is that they first prepare their clients with individual psychotherapy before admitting them to group therapy.

Slavson (1964) maintains that analytic group counseling cannot stand alone as a separate therapeutic tool or theory. Since it is a direct descendant of individual therapy, it must base its methods, techniques, and understandings on the former. Hence, in his opinion, analytic group counseling is only a modification of individual counseling and not, at least as yet, a completely different method or school.

Representing psychoanalysts of another persuasion, the Tavistock Clinic in London postulates that the psychoanalyst uses exactly the same principles in the group as he would in the individual situation. Their point of departure from other group analysts is that they see the whole group as one client. Thus, the most important point of departure among analytic group therapists seems to be the degree of emphasis attached to the group situation itself. Is it group analysis or analysis of an individual within the group context? From a survey of the research, it seems that the majority of psychoanalysts agree that what has become known as group psychoanalysis is, in reality, group psychotherapy that has an analytic orientation.

Group Dynamics in Psychotherapy

Durkin (1964) has attempted to reconcile the cleavage between analytic group therapists and that group of social scientists known as group dynamicists. Group dynamicists use general systems theory to analyze the group process. Broadly speaking, general systems theory conceptualizes the individual as a process or system. Given this approach, a person's behavior can be best understood as an integral part of the social matrix or the larger dynamic system.

Group dynamicists conduct group therapy on the premise that potent group currents have profound influences on individual members. The task of group leaders is to identify the underlying group themes which elicit such reactions and to analyze the effects of these topics on the members. Thus, the therapeutically oriented group dynamicist seeks to modify group-generated determinants of maladaptive behavior. This goal is accomplished by the leader's clarification of the ongoing group process as well as the responses it evokes in group members (Sager and Kaplan, 1972). The assumption is that the insight the participant obtains from the therapy group will help the participant function more effectively with family, work, and community groups.

Bion (1959) is one of the leading proponents of the group dynamicist approach to analytic group therapy. Bion operates on the assumption that both constructive and destructive or pathological group forces exist. Either of these forces may greatly influence the individual group member. The problem is that usually the group member is not consciously aware of these forces or their impact upon his or her behavior. The role of the therapist is to explain whatever irrational group assumptions may be functioning in the group (for instance, pairing, fight-flight, and dependency) and to facilitate the development of a healthy "work group."

From her thorough investigation of the two schools, Durkin concluded that for all practical purposes there was no group therapy presently conducted solely on the basis of group dynamics principles by group dynamicists. Instead, social psychologists, like the British psychoanalysts who purportedly engaged in group dynamic therapy, tended to combine group dynamics with psychoanalysis. The important distinction between those of the dynamics orientation and other group analysts is that the former see the group forces rather than the individual as the primary source of group therapy. Given this position, group dynamics is the new ingredient that distinguishes dynamic therapy. According to Durkin, the common ground of these two groups is that both adhere to analyzing transference and resistance in the group to obtain basic personality change in individual members.

Clearly, psychoanalytic group psychotherapy has many subdivisions beyond those differences in orientation that can be observed in individual psychoanalysis (Durkin, 1964). Some of the old differences among analytic therapists have had a carry-over effect into groups. While some analytic schools continue to ignore libido theory, others emphasize interpersonal factors. Sullivanians, for instance, have characterized the group "as an effective laboratory to explore and vividly verify one's patterns of interpersonal reaction as a prelude to learning their historical perspective and eventually changing one's behavior (Goldman, 1957, p. 391)." Disciples of Horney contend that "the group can help appreciably to modify the member's exaggerated self-idealization and distorted concepts of the world which come from childhood. In its striving toward a cooperative mutuality it can, under the therapist's guidance, develop a healthy feeling of belongingness in the members based on the essential humanness of each (Rose, 1957, p. 380)."

Revision of Freudian Group Concepts

Much of what has been presented is a long way from the old Freudian point of view. Durkin (1964) enumerates five ways in which analytic psychotherapy groups have deviated from Freud's position. First, most present-day group analysts do not subscribe completely to the idea that the individual automatically and irrevocably substitutes the leader for his or her own ego-ideal; an intricate set of transference situations is established through which this process occurs.

Second, group members do not seem to be as inactive as Freud suggested. They may respond ambivalently toward the group, acting passively at times and taking a more active part on other occasions. Neither are members as dependent as Freud implied, for in the group they employ defenses that have evolved out of childhood to resist strongly the leader's therapeutic efforts.

Third, the interaction between the group leader and members and the resultant group standards that develop are not derived entirely from accepting the leader's standards. Group standards also emerge from the struggle among the members concerning their individual values. The standards of the group, and not necessarily those of the leader, are used to modify a person's own ego-ideal.

Fourth, the group member's reaction to the leader and to the group is not, as Freud proposed, always the same because of identification with the same loved object (the counselor). For example, group members may gravitate from perceiving the therapist as the all-giving omnipotent parent who has final answers and a magical cure for them to perceiving the therapist more realistically. During this process of modification of their identifications with the counselor, they may become angry and disappointed. Thus, the analysis of the individual's conflicts allows one to desist from idealizing the counselor (Durkin, 1964).

Fifth, Durkin asserts that represssion of aggression factors is not as complete as Freud imagined. Using the model of the family to analyze groups, Freud posited, for example, that competition for parents' (leaders') love is normally repressed when these feelings threaten the child's (member's) relationship to the parent. Durkin (1964) maintains that current experience in therapy groups indicates that such repressions are not only superficial but also are easily detectable—despite camouflage attempts. She states, "Hostility rises quickly and disproportionately to the surface whenever a member detects or imagines preferences on the part of the therapist, with the result that equality and justice come into question frequently (p. 87)."

Although there are fundamental differences in theoretical orientations among group analysts, there is also a great deal of overlapping (Monroe, 1955). Yet, despite the differences among analytic group therapists, it is possible to distinguish them sufficiently from their nonanalytic counterparts. For instance, regardless of their orientation, most group analysts agree upon the basic principles of intervention that earmark the psychoanalytic experience. These principles are concerned with the unconscious and the interpretation of resistance, defense reactions, and transference.

DIFFERENCES BETWEEN INDIVIDUAL AND ANALYTIC GROUP COUNSELING

Distinguishing between individual and group analysis has assumed much importance in the psychoanalytic school. In fact, considerable debate has developed around the differences between these two treatment modalities. While some analysts maintain that it is not possible to use the psychoanalytic method in groups, others have stated just the opposite. Debate has also centered on the properties of the group and whether the individual client or the group itself should be the primary focus of concern.

Theorists who adhere to a strict application of Freudian concepts of personality development and treatment techniques have tended to differentiate individual and group counseling by concentrating on differences that occur within the client and within the group leader. Those who have taken a more psychodynamic view have tended to stress the properties of the group. Each of these perspectives is important for understanding the varied approaches used in analytic group counseling.

Wolf (1975) is one of the most prominent analytic group therapists who has stressed that psychoanalysis is possible in groups. According to him, analytic group counseling must entail the systematic application of analytic concepts, especially transference, resistance, and interpretations. The differences which Wolf and Schwartz (1971) emphasize may be categorized in terms of client changes, variations in therapists' behavior, and dynamics of the treatment setting.

Client Differences

According to Wolf and Schwartz (1971), analytic group counseling produces behavioral differences in the client that are both quantitatively and qualitatively different from those produced in the individual relationship.

Client Affirmation of Self   Wolf and Schwartz (1971) maintain that one of the benefits of analytic group counseling is that clients get a chance to affirm themselves more than in the individual treatment setting. The presence of peers in the group context tends to give the individual the support needed to challenge the authority of the leader. For example, group participants may support one another in expressing anger toward the therapist. In the individual situation, such clients may have been hesitant to assert themselves when they were alone with the therapist. The support of one's peers helps the individual to gain the ego strength needed in order to stand up to the therapist. Hence, the therapist is inclined to exert less control over the client.

Client Privacy and Exposure   Individual group treatment affords clients a sense of privacy and reduces the chances of their exposing their problems to others. As Wolf (1949) has pointed out, initially clients have feelings of dread and insecurity when they are told that others will be with them in the therapeutic setting. They fear that their confidences will be betrayed by group participants. Another concern is that they will be rejected by group members because of their shortcomings and will, therefore, no longer be able to wear the masks to which they have become accustomed. Conversely, other individuals may prefer group treatment because they believe that the therapist has a professional responsibility to understand their shortcomings. Such individuals may seek and/or need a group to test the reality of human compassion and understanding with others.

Relatedness   Wolf and Schwartz (1971) assert that significant differences exist in the relatedness clients feel in individual and group counseling. In individual treatment, the client-therapist relationship is closer and more related than in the group context. This situation is inclined to occur because the client and therapist are more deeply involved in the nature of their relationship and in greater exploration of the client's intrapsychic life. Relatedness in the individual context may constitute more of a fantasy relationship. The individual is less likely to experience the counselor as a person, since the counselor strives to maintain anonymity in individual counseling.

Whereas the dyadic relationship only gives the client one person to relate to, the group provides opportunities for multiple contacts. Hence, the individual tends to feel less isolated. While the client's relationship with the therapist is symbolic in both counseling modalities, the group offers the individual a chance for more realistic relationships with others. Moreover, group participants usually feel closer to one another than to the therapist. As Wolf and Schwartz (1971) have indicated, the relatedness of the client and the counselor in the individual setting may be pseudoclose, especially when the client is experiencing a deep transference neurosis. The client feels close to the counselor because of the transference of symbiotic ties from the mother or father to the counselor. The counselor becomes imbued with characteristics which he or she does not have. In individual therapy, then, the client experiences more of a pseudocloseness to the therapist than in group therapy. Client relatedness to the therapist is, therefore, limited but intense in individual treatment.

Client Accountability   The individual is forced to be more accountable for her or his behavior in the group setting than in the individual context. In individual analysis, clients are generally not held accountable for their fantasies of love, hate, incest, or sexuality. The therapist allows the client to speak freely and regress without fear of retaliation in order to have the client explore underlying psychic material. That is, the therapist allows the client the illusion of nonaccountability by letting the client talk about irresponsible fantasies. Wolf and Schwartz (1971) assert that it is dangerously irresponsible for the therapist to allow the client the illusion of nonaccountability for too long without limiting it and without indicating to the client the consequences of his or her thoughts, feelings, and actions, if planned.

Group members not only hold each other responsible, but they also demand a kind of accountability from each other. For example, group members may respond with fear, anger, and hostility to another participant's wild fantasies, dreams, thoughts, or feelings. Such reactions from the group make the individual aware that he or she is held accountable for what he or she says and does.

The group demand for member accountability may have other benefits. For instance, it may cultivate a sense of social responsibility among participants and may have a therapeutic humanizing value. The whining, dependent individual may be encouraged by group members to change such behavior in order to be accepted as an adult by other group members. Group members can more easily and rightfully demand from other participants certain kinds of responsible behavior than can the therapist conducting individual analysis. This situation exists partly because the therapist conducting individual analysis must retain the posture of the "blank screen" on which the client can project early parental conflict.

Forced Interaction   Individuals in the one-to-one counseling situation may more easily limit their active involvement in counseling than they do in the group situation. Group members tend to demand a kind of give-and-take relationship from each other. Forced interaction within the group also means that the counselor must assume a multiplicity of roles. Group members may offer suggestions for dealing with problems to each other. Whereas the counselor in the dyadic modality may have to be less spontaneous and less aggressive to prevent misunderstanding of the plan of treatment, the analytic group leader is often asked and required to assume a more dynamic role.

Multiple Transferences   The analytic group provides the individual with multiple opportunities for transference more readily than does the analyst alone in individual counseling. Each group member may project upon other participants a variety of roles. For instance, group members may project or respond to other participants as if they were siblings. Participants may also respond to their peers as if their peers were parental figures. The client's initial investment of parental qualities to a peer may make it easier to work through parental distortions placed upon the therapist, since the resolution of a parental transference to the therapist is not only more difficult but also more threatening. The fact that the group, through sheer numbers and differences in behavior, provides the client with opportunities for multiple transferences usually means that the client can re-create or reconstruct the family circle more easily.

In individual analysis, parental transference is normally the most frequent distortion. Transferences involving sibling conflicts may not take place. Moreover, transference tends to be more inflexible in individual counseling, most probably because the therapist is limited by his or her own being and personality in the types of transference stimuli he or she can evoke. In individual counseling, the therapist must often rely on the client's verbal accounts of interpersonal exchanges to other persons. Such reports may be inaccurate and are less clear than those that occur in the group with other participants.

Differences in Analyst's Role

Wolf and Schwartz (1971) maintain that group counseling also produces both quantitative and qualitative changes in the therapist. The analytic group counselor still uses the basic methods and concepts of psychoanalytic treatment employed in individual counseling, but basic differences exist in how the analyst proceeds and what forces she or he takes into account.

As noted previously, in individual analysis the therapist concentrates on the intensity of parental transferences directed toward him or her. In contrast, the analytic group leader also focuses on the interactions that take place among group participants. The counselor adheres to the necessity of working through sibling as well as parental transferences invested in peers. As the therapist's concept of transference is broadened, the therapist's efforts change to resolve such conflicts.

In one-to-one counseling, the therapist is likely to assume the role of the leader in a most unequivocal fashion. The pressure of the group, however, may lead a therapist to deny his or her leader status. The give-and-take of the group situation may even make the analytic group counselor question the appropriateness of such authority status.

The issue of the status of the analytic therapist in either setting may provide the motivating forces for an analyst's preference of either the group or the individual setting. Group therapy tends to attract analysts at both ends of the authoritarian pole—those who are very authoritarian as well as those who are self-devaluating. Authoritarian-oriented therapists may prefer individual analysis, since they have more control over the client, while less authoritarian-oriented leaders may prefer the group method; they may view group participants as capable group co-therapists.

In the group situation, the counselor may unmask and reveal himself or herself more to the clients. This situation occurs because of the sheer number of clients and the therapist's obligation to face them all in a circle. The therapist cannot hide behind the couch; thus the therapist's verbal and nonverbal responses to individual clients are more open to scrutiny in the group than in the individual setting. The group may also encourage the therapist to let down his or her guard and expose his or her reactions to clients.

The structural setting of the group makes it difficult for the therapist to elude clients' scrutiny. For example, Wolf and Schwartz (1971) cite the case of how a therapist attempted to convince a client in individual therapy that the client's suspicions regarding his unresponsiveness to her were unfounded, childlike, and perhaps a manifestation of transference neurosis. When the client suddenly sat up on the couch and swirled to face the therapist, she discovered that the therapist was opening his mail. In actuality, the client was aware of reality, but the analyst was telling her that her perceptions were distorted. Wolf and Schwartz (1971) concluded that no group therapist could have succeeded in deluding an individual for so long with such a misrepresentation of reality. The required face-to-face contact in groups would have long exposed the therapist's unresponsive behavior.

Moreover, the counselor has the potentiality of doing more harm in the individual than in the group situation, since there are no other clients present to exert control via their critical remarks. The analyst is less able to dominate the membership of the group. In the group context, the clients move more to a feeling of parity with the counselor. Such is not the case in individual treatment. The dyadic relationship fosters within a client a sense of inferiority with respect to the counselor; the counselor is viewed as all-knowing.

Differences in Treatment Process

The group setting also provides for differences in the treatment process. The psychoanalytic method is still used, but the presence of others may either dilute or intensify the treatment that an individual receives. The group modality differs from individual treatment in that the principle of shifting attention takes place (Wolf and Schwartz, 1971). This principle basically means that the focus of attention moves from one client to another. No one individual in the therapy group has the exclusive attention of the counselor. The more clients there are in the group, the greater is the diffusion of attention from both the counselor and the individual client.

For some individuals, the shifting of attention that occurs gives them time to digest and work through the insights they have gained from other group participants or the counselor. It also allows the client some freedom from the type of continuous scrutiny given in individual treatment. Some clients may even use the shifting of attention in the group to avoid dealing with the self in any depth. Shifting of attention also gives group participants the opportunity to assume different roles. For instance, as the group changes its focus from one client to another, the first client may now serve in the role of co-counselor—as offerer as well as receiver of help. The dyadic interview does not provide an opportunity for these changes in clients' roles to take place.

The group process likewise raises some issues concerning the timing that occurs with respect to interpretations. On some occasions, group participants may offer interpretations or insights that a client is not prepared or able to accept. Instances of poor timing may be more controlled in the individual setting, primarily because it is the therapist who makes the majority of interpretations regarding the client's behavior.

The group setting may make it more difficult for the counselor to have clients complete the "working through" process of their intrapsychic problems. The group counselor may be inundated with material from participants; hence, clients may not have a chance to undergo an in-depth experiencing of their problems as they normally would in individual counseling. On the other hand, the forces inherent within the group often mitigate against the clients' incomplete working through of their problems. The interactions among group members make it more probable to discover the repetitive core of the individual's intrapsychic difficulties, even the transference neurosis. Likewise, the presence of others supplies the client with multiple transference possibilities to help work out conflicts.

The extent to which unconscious material can be exposed and worked through is used as a measure of the depth of therapy. Individual treatment is usually regarded as a more in-depth therapeutic experience than group analysis because the client can experience a deeper regression to the symbiotic attachment to the mother.

The group can also help protect the client from the therapist's overprotection. Wolf and Schwartz (1971) point out, for example, how group treatment can temper the therapist's preoccupation with the fragility of new members. The therapist in question had experienced considerable anxiety over his decision to admit a seriously ill schizophrenic. He prepared group members for the entrance of the new applicant by telling them how fragile she was. Upon entering the group, the client exhibited all kinds of bizarre behavior and verbally attacked members. Not being able to withstand her verbal abuse any longer, one group participant called her crazy and told the client how the group leader had prepared the other participants for her entry. The abused participant then turned to the therapist and blamed him for forcing him to submit to such treatment; other group members also joined in with their criticism of the therapist.

As these exchanges took place between the other participants and the group leader, the new female participant burst into tears and became equally critical of the therapist. The net effect was that everyone was relieved. The woman had wanted someone to care enough about her to no longer put up with her bizarre behavior. Personal and social realities had emerged within the group regarding individuals' responsibility for their behavior. The therapist was rightfully held responsible for his overprotective concern and for letting things get out of hand. In the ensuing sessions, the client in question interacted freely with increasing responsiveness to group members and leader.

The Unit of Conceptual Analysis   Generally speaking, Wolf and Schwartz's (1971) delineation of differences between individual and analytic group counseling is based on the belief that the unit of conceptual analysis is that of the individual personality. This conceptualization accounts for the fact that few of the differences Wolf and Schwartz make between individual and group treatment have to do with the group as an organized, dynamic organism in its own right. Group interaction is analyzed in terms of what it reveals about the pathology or characteristic behaviors of each individual client. The therapist does not attend to group process variables; the group is not seen to have a life of its own. Insightful interpretations directed toward an individual's psychodynamics displayed within the group are seen to concentrate part of the core of analytic group counseling.

The differences that Foulkes and Anthony (1965) cite between individual and group counseling are both similar to and different from those that Wolf and Schwartz cite. Part of this variation can be attributed to Foulkes and Anthony's concept of the group in analytic counseling. Their approach to analytic group counseling, and hence the differences they note between the two treatment approaches, is more closely akin to the group-dynamic approach. Foulkes and Anthony (1965) conceptualize the group as a genuine, organized, and dynamic organism in its own right. The group can be compared in many respects to the strict psychoanalytic conceptualization of the individual personality. According to these theorists, the group process must be carefully nurtured and guided by the therapist. The curative factors which emerge from the group are seen to be the most significant factors in analytic group counseling. Hence, the therapist's task in analytic group counseling is quite different from that in individual analytic counseling. Foulkes and Anthony (1965) maintain that the group counselor must attend to group process variables as much as to the content of individual members' intrapsychic conflicts. By focusing attention equally on group process concerns, the therapist is able to make interventions which keep group tensions and group avoidances at a level which encourages participants to express themselves and their conflicts.

The psychoanalytic leader of Foulkes and Anthony's leaning makes process interventions which treat the group as a whole. The group is seen to have a personality, much in the same way that an individual does. For example, one may speak of the group's ego. One of the fundamental differences, then, that Foulkes and Anthony note between individual and group counseling is that there are two units of concern in group counseling but only one in individual counseling. The unit for concern in individual counseling is the personality of the individual. In the group setting, the units of concern are: (1) the individual's personality; and (2) the group itself.

Foulkes and Anthony (1965) delineate other differences in individual and in group analysis, many of which are similar to those provided by Wolf and Schwartz. First, whereas in individual psychoanalysis only the client free associates (a technique requiring an individual to initiate thoughts but to avoid any controlling of content or sequence in reporting these thoughts to the therapist), in group analysis the spontaneous contributions of members encourage a type of free group association or multiple primary and secondary associations, as members build upon the experiences or comments of others. Second, in group analysis the interpretation is done by the members as well as the group analyst, thereby resulting in a "group as a whole background of interpretation."

Third, Foulkes and Anthony (1965) posit that whereas individual analysis promotes unitary transference and encourages regressive behavior, in the group setting multiple transference relationships occur; regression is not encouraged. Multiple transference refers to a transference relationship not only in terms of the leader but also in relationship to other group members. Since the group approach limits regression and transference, the member becomes less dependent upon the counelor. Finally, the counselor is inclined to assume a more active role in the group situation than in individual therapy.

Locke (1961) likewise specifies certain differences between individual and group analysis. His emphasis, however, is upon the advantages of the group situation over the individual one. According to him, one of the important advantages of the group is that it rebuilds the original setting in which members experience their first conflicts. This provides a setting in which individuals can reenact their styles of adjustment and reveal repetitive, ineffective patterns of behavior in relationship to others.

Difficulties of Definition   Distinguishing between individual and group analysis has been a major concern of the psychoanalytic school. Most analytic group therapists have maintained that in order for analytic group counseling to exist, it must be distinguished sufficiently from individual counseling; otherwise what one has is most likely individual analysis in a group setting. To conduct analytic group counseling, one must understand how it differs from individual treatment—what its distinguishing features are. Part of the emphasis on the differences between individual and analytic group counseling was to separate these two forms of treatment.

It seems clear that analytic group theorists have differed over what constitutes analytic group counseling. Therapists who believe that analytic group counseling is possible seem to be divided in their opinions on: (1) the concept of the group; and (2) the application of psychoanalytic concepts. According to one school of thought, analytic group counseling can only exist if there is a systematic application of psychoanalytic concepts. The personality of the individual must be the major conceptual unit of concern. Group processes are only taken into consideration to the extent they help clarify or resolve an individual's intrapsychic conflicts. The group itself is not viewed as having a life of its own.

A second school emphasizes the importance of the group process. Theorists of this persuasion tend to view the group as having an ego of its own—both the group personality as well as that of the individual are the units of concern. The therapist makes group-centered as well as individual-centered interventions.

The cleavage which has developed within the psychoanalytic school concerning analytic group counseling has resulted in criticisms from both sides. Many of these criticisms have implications for group counseling.

For example, if people's past behavior pattern is to withdraw because they are reliving previous experiences in the family situation that caused them to retreat from others, then they will display such behavior in the group. The interaction with other group members, however, may serve to hasten the therapeutic process primarily because of the instant feedback from both the group analyst and other participants. In short, the group supplies a more real-life setting than does individual therapy.

Besides the usefulness of reconstructing the original family, Slavson (1964) asserts, one of the real advantages of group psychotherapy is that it reemphasizes the importance of interpersonal factors in the development and correction of personality disturbances. For example, he asserts individuals in analytic group counseling develop a type of "social hunger." Participants' desire for acceptance by the group and the therapist becomes the motive for emotional growth.

Slavson also notes that one of the major values of group counseling is the influence it has in lessening superego restraints and ego defenses. The fact that other members of the group may have similar problems and that one is not unique in one's pecularities helps to weaken one's self-protectiveness. Slavson points out that many adolescent clients will at first attempt to conceal the true state of affairs in their homes. Adolescents may describe their parents as loving and devoted when in reality they are not. The need to describe parents in ways other than what they are arises from the clients' desire to make a good impression and thereby protect their own ego. Slavson maintains that group counseling affords a member greater opportunities for new identifications that offer additional possibilities for improving that individual's ego and superego structure.

CONCEPTUALIZATION OF PSYCHOANALYTIC GROUP PROCESS

Key Concepts in Psychoanalysis

The unique features of the psychoanalytic approach to both individual and group counseling are founded upon the underlying theoretical constructs of the psychoanalytic model of personality, structural assumptions concerning the human psyche, and the genesis and dynamics of various forms of maladjustment (Sager and Kaplan, 1972). Locke (1961) suggests further that if a therapist's work meets three criteria: (1) method, (2) material, and (3) interpretation, it may be described as psychoanalytic.

The psychoanalytic method concentrates on exploring and uncovering. An individual has a problem; the therapist seeks to assist the client by uncovering the problem's root cause. However, the method of exploring and uncovering is often hindered by the client's desperate fight not to have the problem exposed. The task of psychoanalysis is exposure of the problem.

The material of analytic counseling is the unconscious. Slips of the tongue, dreams, and fantasies are considered manifestations of the client's unconscious motivations. The stress on unconscious material is one of the trademarks that distinguishes psychoanalytic theory from the newer theories that give prominence to the here-and-now of a client's behavior.

Interpretation is the final and, perhaps, the key element in the analytic approach to both individual and group counseling. The therapist uses interpretations to get at the real meaning of the client's communications—to help the individual understand what she or he is experiencing beneath the level of consciousness and how he or she may be distorting the present.

Although these three elements are present in both individual and group counseling, they are not exactly equivalent. In the group situation, they may be changed or transformed to take into account the dynamics that occur when other individuals are present in therapy.

Goals of Treatment

Generally speaking, goals may be said to be an expression of a desired therapeutic outcome. They indicate how group leaders will attempt to influence group members through their behavior. Moreover, goals also reveal what is sought by having a person in a group, what is anticipated, and what is thought important to achieve as a result of group treatment. Goals not only give potential group members some idea of the benefits they are to achieve from group counseling but also indicate how a person will be treated in the group by the therapist and other participants.

It is instructive to realize that goals in almost every school of group counseling can be categorized into two groups: attainable and ideal. The ideal goals point to the type of client change for which the therapist strives. Underlying these goals will be a basic concept of personality change, a fundamental view of people, and a concept of what constitutes group counseling. Conversely, attainable goals are those the client and counselor will most likely achieve. Such goals constitute the middle ground in life and are mediated by the counselor's level of skill as well as the client's readiness, ability, and current psychological state. Attainable goals represent a readjustment of what theoretically constitutes the ideal objective of group counseling—namely, personality reorganization and maturation. Psychoanalytic group counseling goals provide a point of comparison with other group approaches discussed in this book.

The overall goal of analytic group counseling is to help the individual to resolve neurotic conflicts which prevent him or her from constructive growth and development. Another objective is to help the individual to accept reality, to face up to life instead of running away from it. Analytic group treatment is designed to integrate and to bring into harmony the intrapsychic and interpersonal aspects of an individual. It emphasizes the exploration and working through of unconscious, intrapsychic processes.

What distinguishes psychoanalytic group counseling goals from those of other theoretical schools are: (1) the analytic conceptualization of human nature and personality development; and (2) the methods of treatment. For instance, analytic group counseling is founded on the Freudian concept of human beings. There is an emphasis on psychic determinism or the belief that every behavioral action and emotional reaction has a cause that is tied to an individual's intrapsychic and interpersonal history. One objective of analytic group counseling is to help the individual become aware of these underlying determinants of behavior.

The analytic group counseling goal of helping the individual to resolve neurotic conflicts is based on the Freudian concept of what constitutes healthy personality development. That is, individuals have neurotic conflicts because they have not passed adequately through certain psychosexual stages. Problems in current living have their origins in early childhood relationships with one's parents and family. It is no small wonder, then, that many psychoanalysts believe that the re-creation of the family within the group setting is basic to the therapeutic process. Psychoanalysts base many of their interventions on the belief that an individual's relationship patterns with his or her family members and others are reproduced within the group. The manner in which family members are reproduced is a fundamental concern of analytic group counseling. This one feature of analytic group counseling provides the rationale for the group therapist's emphasis on transference relations that are believed to take place within the group.

As with other group approaches, the psychoanalytic model of group counseling has both attainable and ideal goals. Since little is said about the attainable goals of analytic group counseling, emphasis is placed on examining the ideal goals of this particular group approach.

The ideal goal of the psychoanalytic group method is client personality maturation. This goal is based upon the belief that the key to a happier and more fully functioning life is helping one outgrow emotional immaturities in order to realize one's potential in life. A measure of the success of this objective is the degree to which the individual has the ability to feel, think, and respond appropriately in normal situations and to deal with potentially new, traumatic experiences in an adequate manner. The goal is to relieve the individual from being bogged down in the feelings of a child.

Group counseling is oriented to facilitate the goal of personality maturation by: (1) helping the client deal with the forces that prevent the client from meeting his or her maturational needs; and (2) assisting the individual to relinquish maladaptive behavior. In the group setting, therapists help group members to gain personality maturation by arousing, analyzing, interpreting, and resolving transference investments. The therapist extends supports for analyzing an individual's transference investments onto group members and onto himself or herself. The therapist helps the client to relinquish maladaptive behavior which thwarts the individual's personality maturation by helping the client to understand and work through transference investments displayed in the here-and-now of the group.

In classical, psychoanalytic group counseling, the focus is placed on the personality maturational changes which need to take place within each individual group member. The bases for the therapist's actions or interventions are founded on Freudian concepts of individual personality development. The counseling group provides the backdrop or stimulus for understanding and overcoming an individual's personality immaturity. Change is sought within the individual rather than in some kind of collectivity called the group. Analytic group counseling is geared toward the achievement of long-range, ideal counseling goals. The stages or levels of group treatment outlined in this chapter reflect the counselor's scheme to attain the ideal goal of personality maturation for each individual.

Stages of Analytic Group Treatment

Classic analytic group therapists do not subscribe to stages of group development. Instead, they emphasize stages of analytic group treatment. Some of the rationale for this position has been alluded to previously.

Basically, classic psychoanalytic group leaders believe that the group itself does not have a life of its own. Such theoretical concepts as "group emotion," "group symptom," and "group formation" are, therefore, not used by analytic group therapists in describing what takes place within the group (Wolf and Schwartz, 1971; Slavson, 1964). Instead, group leaders stress that each client must remain a detached entity in whom intrapsychic changes must take place. The client works on individual problems within the group rather than on group problems, as is the case with some of the other group therapies.

Moreover, the therapist focuses on the latent content of what is being said by each individual rather than on the "group process." This does not mean that the therapist excludes awareness of the emotional effect group participants have on each other. On the contrary, the therapist uses the interactions between participants to get at transference relations and intrapsychic material for each person. Clients talk about their problems and those of others as individuals. Seldom is there a group problem or a group aim. The prevailing conceptual unit is the intrapsychic functioning of the individual.

The classic psychoanalytic group therapist's emphasis on the individual as the proper unit of study has ramifications for the stages of treatment. According to Wolf (1963), all clients do not pass through the same stage of treatment at the same time. An individual participant may be at one stage while the rest of the members of the group are at another. An individual tends to pass through consecutive stages at his or her own pace. Given the types of problems individuals have and the success they have had in dealing with their problem, a majority of group participants may be at a certain stage. The use of open or continuous groups tends to ensure that all group members will not be at the same treatment stage. Except for the first stage, then, all stages of treatment can be said to coexist in analytic group counseling.

Stage 1: *Preliminary Individual Analysis*   During the first stage of psychoanalytic group treatment, the therapist seeks to prepare the individual for group therapy. The individual is given an interview alone with the therapist, during which time the therapist explores the individual's present difficulties. For instance, the therapist might ask for biographical material, present and recurrent dreams, and, in general, the client's complaints. The therapist talks with the client to find out whether the father or the mother is the central figure in the emotional constellation and to what degree siblings, grandparents, and others have contributed to the development of the client's difficulties. The therapist also explores each individual's goals, ideals and identifications, and beliefs about personal strengths and weaknesses.

The goal of this procedure is to obtain an initial impression of the client's character structure and to make a diagnosis of the problem. Moreover, from the material gained, the therapist makes tentative plans for the course of treatment she or he will follow with the client. Decisions are made concerning the depth of treatment necessary. The therapist establishes a treatment plan, which may be later modified for each member of the group.

There is no set time for the preliminary individual analysis stage. Individuals are told that they are being prepared for therapy. In some instances, the person may be referred to individual therapy. During the preliminary stage, individuals are told that if they become too anxious or unsettled by the group, they may leave and return to individual treatment. Wolf (1975) indicates that clients who leave the group because they are too anxious usually return to the group situation after one or two individual analytic sessions. Wolf (1975) also maintains that an individual's entry into a group is determined by the person's diminishing resistance and anxiety about joining a group.

The first few meetings of the group are also included in the first treatment stage. The purpose of these meetings is to have participants get to know each other and to discuss the guidelines along which the group will be conducted. The therapist explains the procedures he or she will use, sets limits on client behavior (for example, the rule of no sexual intimacy among participants), and discusses the issue of confidentiality.

Stage 2:   Establishment of Rapport through Dreams and Fantasies During the first session in which there is active client participation, the therapist asks the clients within the group to describe a recent or recurrent dream. The major purpose of having clients report dreams is to engage them in participating in the group and to establish interpersonal interaction or discussion among the members of the group. Group members are asked to interpret or free associate as a group concerning the material reported in another person's dream. If individuals report that they have had no recent or recurrent dreams, they are asked by the therapist to present their fantasies or daydreams.

The therapist may use a number of other techniques to engage group participants. For example, the counselor might ask each person to state briefly what his or her problem is. Another therapist may establish rapport by asking group members to describe their feelings about joining the group.

The technique of going around may also be used to involve members in an analytic group, particularly those who have been silent. In using the going around technique, the therapist asks each individual to say whatever enters his or her mind about each member in turn without too much deliberation. This technique also fosters a kind of free association about one's fellow members in a group.

As people have become more used to and oriented toward involvement in groups, many of the techniques described here are not necessary to bring about interpersonal interaction among group members. Such interaction normally occurs spontaneously, and the establishment of rapport is not a major issue.

Stage 3:   The Analysis of Resistance   As clients continue to free associate about each other, their resistances emerge before the group. Stage three is essentially the stage in which resistances are analyzed. During this period, group members' defenses are discovered, examined, and delineated. According to Wolf (1963), there are a number of ways in which group members manifest their resistance. For example, an individual may assume the role of a voyeur—that is, assume the role of one who looks at what is taking place in the group but does not become involved in group interaction. At some point, group members are likely to demand that the onlooker become involved in the interaction and expose himself or herself as others have done.

Hiding behind the analysis of others is another common form of resistance. Individuals who evidence this form of resistance tend to concentrate on the neurotic behavior of others while evading any analysis of themselves. They may also be adept at redirecting the group's attention to any person who dares to analyze them by pointing out that the tone of the person who offered the interpretive remark was hostile or interesting. In an effort to deflect attention, a person might also offer a self-analysis in place of the one that was given by the other participant.

Providing the group with historical data is another common method of resistance used by some individuals. Talk of what happened in childhood amounts to rehearsing the past. As Wolf (1949, p. 29) says: "Long irrelevant biographies, usually distorted by the narrator, can be a continual evasion. Even a recital of yesterday's events can assume this character. . . . History has the greatest significance when evoked and recalled by the discovery and analysis of resistance and transference in the moment of their occurrence—that is, when history has a bearing on the present which is meaningful to both the patient and the therapist." By talking about a problem in the past, the individual attempts to avoid its resolution.

Resistance by individual group members may also take other forms, such as frequent or uninterrupted silences and assuming the role of assistant to the therapist. The individual who assumes the position of assistant to the therapist initially astounds group members with astute observations and interpretations regarding other members of the group. It usually takes group members a while to discover that the therapist's unasked-for assistant is not getting anything out of the group and is avoiding dealing with personal conflicts.

There are perhaps as many ingenious ways to demonstrate resistance as there are people in a group. While some individuals try to resist by hiding in a group, others resist by coming late to meetings and by "using" their tears to evoke sympathy from the group. The task of the therapist is to penetrate the many forms of resistance displayed by group participants.

Stage 4: The Analysis of Transference According to Wolf (1975), the discovery, analysis, and resolution of transference is the most important work of analytic group counseling. Transference experiences are important because they repeatedly interfere with an individual's true estimate of reality. Moreover, transference prevents an individual from responding to a person on the basis of that individual's qualities, primarily because the person who is transfering responds to the transference object in ways that originally blocked a full relationship to a family member. That is, transference relations are feelings and defenses that are carryovers from the past; they are not responses to the actual characteristics of other people and situations. The goal of this stage is to help individual clients understand the extent to which they project parental and sibling qualities onto members of the group, the therapist, and significant others in their lives.

The therapist begins this stage of treatment by explaining the features and importance of transference. The therapist indicates that people inherit from their childhood conditioned reflexes which make them endow "the present with old forms" and that investing others with attributes which they do not possess indicates a distorted character structure in the person who invests. Therapeutic progress is measured by the extent to which individuals can correct their transferences.

From this point on, the group leader describes the other qualities of transference. Transferences are irrelevant, repetitious, and irrational ways of viewing others. Feelings of anxiety, mild tension, and helplessness usually occur when an individual transfers to another. These qualities of transference produce an immobilizing effect on an individual.

The therapist may begin to demonstrate transference relations by analyzing something that has just occurred in the group or by asking every group member to examine what investments he or she makes onto others and the therapist. Group members are likewise asked to assist each other in their interpretations of transference relations. The group leader stresses that the presentation and analysis of a transference relation should take place as close as possible to the moment of its occurrence. This discourages group members from looking backward into history to understand their behavior and to furnish transference material.

As the group progresses, individual members become adept at analyzing both their own transference behavior and that of others. Toward the end of this stage, group members should evidence a better understanding of how they project their past familial relationships onto others in the present. To pass successfully through this stage of treatment, individual clients must have gained insight into transference behavior.

Stage 5: Working Through The process of working through is one of the most difficult stages the client undergoes. This is a stage wherein insight without appropriate accompanying client change is not tolerated. As Wolf (1950) has stated: "This is a period of intense struggle with one's own transference reactions, when they cannot be justified and conciliated; when insight without action cannot be tolerated; when character change must replace explaining and when group discipline demands personal reformation (p. 544)."

One test of an individual's readiness for termination is the extent to which he or she can analyze and resolve or dispose of transference investments. Another yardstick is the degree to which the client does not permit other group members to project or invest on the client qualities that he or she does not have.

Generally speaking, it is the therapist who decides when an individual should be terminated from group therapy. The client's ability to resolve transference investments is usually a good indication that he or she is ready for termination.

Stage 6: Reorientation and Social Integration This is the final stage of analytic group treatment. The goals of this level of treatment can perhaps be best understood by examining the skills the client now possesses. Basically, the individual develops and displays a surer, more positive, and more constructive approach to life. The individual can be with others without having a compulsive need to please and be accepted. The individual is able to cope with reality and withstand the pressures of everyday living. He or she has adopted new ways of living and is relatively free from using previous neurotic solutions to conflicts in life.

In psychoanalytic group counseling, none of these stages of treatment is as distinct as presented here. Most of the stages outlined in this section have been based on the works of Wolf and on general principles drawn from psychoanalytic group literature. Hence, it might be more appropriate to label the stages outlined as levels of development which indicate the psychoanalytic approach for bringing about constructive personality change. As noted previously, the stages of treatment are based heavily on the classical psychoanalytic school of group therapy.

Role of the Leader

Slavson (1964) outlines four generic functions of the analyst: directional, stimulative, extensional, and interpretive. The directional function is used by the leader when the group seems to be bogged down by feedback overload that has no objective or conclusion in sight. The counselor identifies the underlying theme the group is struggling with and helps the group to focus on and follow the theme which preoccupies them.

The leader assumes the stimulative role when "because of repression, resistance, emotional fatigue, or lagging interest," the group becomes impassive or begins to discuss inconsequential minutiae (Slavson, 1964, p. 425). To revitalize the group, the leader takes on a more active role. He or she questions members, recalls ideas previously discussed, and generally retraces the group process.

The extensional service is the third function of the leader. Herein, she or he extends the group's communications beyond their areas of fixation. Slavson conceives of the extensional function as the foundation of ego treatment. The counselor makes connections between the conscious and unconscious ego in group participants.

The interpretive function has been previously described. Interpretation is essentially the leader's effort to bring to the surface submerged meanings of a person's communications. It should only occur when the individual has sufficiently unraveled repressions and resistances or exhibits a certain readiness for insight.

The psychoanalytic group leader is typically not quite a member of the group, but is more aloof than the other participants. Locke (1961) asserts that the counselor must not take the position of leader when the group is a peer group. If he or she does, participants may not perceive the necessary family relationships.

Wolf (1969) also suggests a number of qualities the psychoanalytic group leader should possess. The group leader must be able to deal with the variety of transferences with which he or she is invested by group members. That is, the leader must be able to withstand the hostility and praise of group members as they might variously see her or him—for example, parent figure, authority figure. The leader must be strong enough to admit errors and secure enough in the leadership position to relinquish it to the group or to individual members as the situation of the moment demands. Moreover, the leader should be skilled in resolving intragroup conflict; be able to interpret problems; and avoid assuming dogmatic attitudes. The most significant function of the group leader, according to Wolf, is to emphasize in the terminal stages of treatment the relationship between the individual's freedom to do as he or she pleases and the needs of the group.

In summary, the analytic group leader is the symbol of hope, growth, and the potential constructive forces of the group. While his or her leadership is desired by some, it is also resented and resisted by others. Group members may fear the leader as an authority figure and project upon the leader their own hatred, distrust, and contempt for themselves. As progress is made in the analytic group process, members tend to see the leader as being more human and less authoritative. There is a feeling of equality with the leader, even though members may still respect his or her therapeutic skills. Thus the reduction of alienation between the group members and the leader is one of the more significant therapeutic goals.

Methodological Concerns

Part of the controversy in analytic group counseling centers around methodology. For example, what should the group composition be? What is the benefit of a leaderless group? Should individuals be allowed to have combined treatment?

Client Selection   In analytic group counseling, each prospective participant is thoroughly screened. Moreover, the counselor takes a history of the client's family background, life experiences, and medical background. A major concern is to determine if the individual has a reasonably strong and flexible ego. The purpose of screening individuals before admitting them to group counseling is twofold. First, it is important to understand the client, the client's defense structure, and the extent to which the client projects onto others. Second, screening provides the counselor with information which will indicate if the individual can benefit from group treatment.

Psychoanalytic group leaders vary in the criteria they use for client selection. For example, Slavson (1954) maintains that clients with intense sexual disturbances, pronounced narcissism, and regressive and infantile characters should be excluded from group counseling. Wolf and Schwartz (1971) assert that current alcoholics and drug addicts, the mentally retarded, seriously handicapped stutterers, suicidal and homicidal individuals, the psychopathics, the very depressed, and the manic should be excluded from group treatment.

Group Composition   Generally, psychoanalysts concur that heterogeneous groups are preferable to homogeneous therapy groups. Wolf and Schwartz (1962) delineate three reasons for their preference for heterogeneous therapy groups. First, they view the heterogeneous group as more representative of the real world. Since one of the goals of psychoanalysis is to assist the individual in achieving a healthier and more normal life in the real world, the heterogeneous group is a natural choice.

Second, a heterogeneous group is less likely to foster conformity to a uniform group standard. Once a group is organized along homogeneous lines, restrictions will be placed on the degree to which analytic exploration can be done. Participants, too, tend to demand a heterogeneous group. For instance, analytic groups containing exclusively women usually request at some point that men be introduced to the group. In short, heterogeneity in group composition brings out the kind of diversity that facilitates the progress of analytic groups.

Third, Wolf and Schwartz (1962) maintain that a heterogeneous therapy group provides a much greater opportunity for multiple transferences to take place. Group members' sex, age, and conflict problems promote a greater multiplicity of transferences.

The Alternate Session   The alternate session concept [see p. 32] refers to the situation in which the regular therapy group meeting is held with the counselor and the next, or alternate one, is held without the counselor. Wolf and Schwartz (1962) are the main proponents of the alternate session. The alternate session technique is based upon the belief that some counselees may feel safer in the peer session because they do not have to risk the counselor's disfavor. During this time, they may be better able to express negative feelings toward the group leader. Once the group members give those individuals support in expressing negative feelings toward the leader, those persons may be able to confront the leader more directly in the regular session. On the other hand, some participants may view the counselor as the protector and prefer the regular session. In addition, the peer group session offers an opportunity for the group members to become more adultlike and autonomous, since they are compelled to assume responsibility for the session in the absence of the leader.

Combined Treatment   Combined treatment is the term used to denote the situation in which a group member is simultaneously seen in individual therapy with either the group counselor or another therapist. Locke (1961) argues that individual and group work are not compatible. One will tend to rob the other. In combined treatment, the client may be inclined to play off one session against the other, while resisting in each. Reserving the individual session for the real therapeutic material, the person may use the group for social reasons. Individual sessions may also prolong the client's dependency upon the therapist.

Likewise, Wolf and Schwartz (1962) do not recommend the combined treatment approach on the grounds that the client is predisposed to view the group as supplementary to individual therapy. Individual treatment, they suggest, should be used only as preparatory work for group membership.

UNIQUE FEATURES AND CONTRIBUTIONS OF PSYCHOANALYTIC GROUP COUNSELING

The psychoanalytic group method can be credited with providing the first systematic application of a well-developed body of human development to group treatment. Freud's book on *Group Psychology and the Analysis of the Ego* was seminal in that it provided the foundation for later conceptualizations of human beings' psychological behavior in groups. His belief that each individual reconstructs his or her family group in group treatment has remained a dominant idea not only in analytic group counseling but also in other group therapies. Likewise, the analytic emphasis on group members' efforts to deal with authority issues, especially as personified by the group leader, is central to many theorists' views on group troatment and development. For example, a large part of T-group theory is based on authority issues with which members preoccupy themselves. In some T-groups, members become concerned about the nature of their relationship with the leader and what they should do if the group leader does not direct them or assume a typical leadership role. Some of the theoretical groundwork for the T-group was provided by Freud and his followers.

Moreover, many of the terms which have become commonplace today have their origins in psychoanalytic theory—for example, transference, countertransference, and resistance. These terms and concepts have become an integral part of many group approaches. Furthermore, analytic group counselors have worked perhaps the hardest, or at the very least have fought the longest battles, over how individual treatment differs from group treatment. The effort to distinguish between these two treatment modalities is a contribution in and of itself.

The role of the psychoanalytic group leader as a blank screen is another unique feature and contribution of analytic counseling. T-group theorists later used this concept of the detached leader in their laboratory experiments.

Analytic group counselors are noted for their emphasis on the importance of client selection criteria and client readiness for group counseling. Analytic group counselors screen their prospective group members more thoroughly than most other theoretical schools. Such screening helps to reduce the instances in which client casualties occur in group treatment. The lack of careful screening of clients to see what their ego-strength is constitutes a major failure of some of the newer approaches to groups—notably encounter and T-groups. Few other schools make a systematic effort to prepare their clients for group treatment. The person who selects analytic group counseling is usually given, at the minimum, one consultation during which an extensive client history is taken, or else preliminary individual analysis if his or her ego-strength is considered too fragile for group work.

The extensive and long-term training required of analytic group counselors is another distinctive feature of this school. The individual who selects analytic treatment can usually be reasonably assured that the therapist has undergone extensive training. This situation does not exist with some of the newer group approaches, such as encounter groups and T-groups.

The analytic school may be distinguished from some of the other group approaches in terms of its goal—personality maturation. Group counseling under the analytic framework is long-term and eschews any promises of magical or quick cures found in some group models. Classical group psychoanalysis evidences little preoccupation with group dynamics or what the group is feeling, group themes, and group climate. These topics are seen to divert clients' emphasis from their own intrapsychic concerns. The classical psychoanalytic group therapist stresses that each person is different from the other in history, development, and psychological dynamics. In essence the classical analyst is more concerned with the emerging wholesome development of the individual ego than with the collective effort of the group. The classical analyst affirms that the more emphasis that is placed upon client similarities, the more the group counselor is limited to the manifest behavior of the client.

Moreover, by analyzing transference behavior the counselor helps the client to understand the extent to which she or he distorts relationships with others in the group. Psychoanalysts maintain that some of the newer group therapies encourage acting out and do not analyze transference relations when they occur in the group setting. Classical psychoanalytic group therapists believe that the newer group therapies' pursuit of "limitlessness" is an irrational goal.

References

Aubrey, R. F. Misapplication of therapy models to school counseling. In C. E. Becr (Ed.), *Philosophical guidelines for counseling.* Dubuque, IA: Wm. C. Brown, 1971, 202–7.

Becker, B. J. The psychodynamics of analytic group psychotherapy. *American Journal of Psychoanalysis,* 1972, *32,* 177–85.

Berzon, B., C. Pious, and R. Parson. The therapeutic event in group psychotherapy: A study of subjective reports by group members. *Journal of Individual Psychology,* 1963, *19,* 204–12.

Bessell, H. The content is the medium: The confidence is the message. *Psychology Today,* 1968, *1,* 32–35 and 61.

Bion, W. *Experiences in groups.* New York: Basic Books, 1959.

Bordin, E. S., B. Nachmann, and S. T. Segal. An articulated framework for vocational development. *Journal of Counseling Psychology,* 1963, *10,* 107–16.

Brammer, L. M., and E. L. Shostrom. *Therapuetic psychology: Fundamentals of actualization counseling and psychotherapy.* Englewood Cliffs, NJ: Prentice-Hall, 1968. (2nd ed.)

Brenner, C. *An elementary textbook of psychoanalysis.* Garden City, NY: Doubleday, 1957.

Brill, A. A. *Basic principles of psychoanalysis.* Garden City, NY: Doubleday, 1949.

Burrow, T. *The social basis of consciousness.* New York: Harcourt, Brace and World, 1927

Dreikurs, R. *Group psychotherapy and group approaches: The collected papers of Rudolf Dreikurs.* The Alfred Adler Institute of Chicago, 1960.

Durkin, H. E. *The group in depth.* New York: International Universities Press, 1964.

Feifel, H., and J. Eells. Patients and therapists assess the same psychotherapy. *Journal of Consulting Psychology,* 1963, *27,* 310–18.

Fenichel, O. *The psychoanalytic theory of neurosis.* New York: W. W. Norton, 1945.

Ford, D. H., and H. B. Urban. *Systems of psychotherapy: A comparative study.* New York: John Wiley, 1963.

Foulkes, S. H., and E. J. Anthony. *Group psychotherapy: The psychoanalytic approach.* Baltimore, MD: Penguin Books, 1965. (2nd ed.)

Freud, A. *The ego and the mechanism of defense.* New York: International Universities Press, 1948.

Freud, S. *A general introduction to psychoanalysis.* New York: Liveright, 1935. (First published in 1920)

Freud, S. *An outline of psychoanalysis.* New York: Norton, 1949.

Freud, S. *Group psychology and the analysis of the ego.* New York: Liveright, 1959. (Volume 18 of *The Standard Edition of the Complete Psychological Works of Sigmund Freud.*) London: Hogarth Press, 1964.

Fullmer, D. W. *Counseling: Group theory and system.* Scranton, PA: International Textbook Co., 1971.

Goldman, G. D. Some applications of Harry Stack Sullivan's theories to group psychotherapy. *International Journal of Group Psychotherapy,* 1957, *7,* 385–91.

Hartmann, H. *Essays on ego psychology.* New York: International Universities Press, 1964.

Hartmann, H., and E. Kris. The genetic approach in psychoanalysis. In *The psychoanalytic study of the child.* New York: International Universities Press, 1945, vol. 1, 11–29.

Hinkley, R. G., and L. Herman. *Group treatment in psychotherapy.* Minneapolis: University of Minnesota Press, 1951.

King, P. T., and K. F. Bennington. Psychoanalysis in counseling. In B. Stefflre and W. H. Grant (Eds.), *Theories of counseling.* New York: McGraw-Hill, 1972, 177–242.

Le Bon, G. *The crowd: A study of the popular mind.* New York: Viking Press, 1960. (First published in 1895)

Locke, N. *Group psychoanalysis: Theory and technique.* New York: New York University Press, 1961.

McDougall, W. *The group mind.* New York: Arno, 1921.

Menninger, K. *Theory of psychoanalytic technique.* New York: Basic Books, 1958.

Monroe, R. L. *Schools of psychoanalytic thought: An exposition, critique, and attempt at integration.* New York: Dryden Press, 1955.

Osipow, S. H. *Theories of career development.* New York: Appleton-Century-Crofts, 1973. (2nd ed.)

Rapaport, D. The autonomy of the ego. *Bulletin of the Menninger Clinic,* 1951, *15,* 113–23.

Redl, F. Group emotion and group leadership. *Psychiatry,* 1942, *5,* 573–96.

Rose, H. Horney concepts in group psychotherapy. *International Journal of Group Psychotherapy,* 1957, *7,* 376–83.

Ruitenbeek, H. M. *The new group therapies.* New York: Avon Books, 1970.

Sager, C. J., and H. S. Kaplan (Eds.). *Progress in group and family therapy.* New York: Brunner-Mazel, 1972.

Slavson, S. R. *A textbook in analytic group psychotherapy.* New York: International Universities Press, 1964.

Stern, M. The ego aspect of transference. *International Journal of Psychoanalysis,* 1957, *38,* 146–57.

Szasz, T. S. *The myth of mental illness.* New York: Dell, 1961.

Talland, G., and D. Clark. Evaluations of topics in therapy group discussions. *Journal of Clinical Psychology,* 1954, *10,* 131–37.

Watson, R. I. *Psychology of the child.* New York: John Wiley, 1965. (2nd ed.)

Wepman, J. M., and R. W. Heine. *Concepts of personality.* Chicago: Aldine, 1967.

Wolf, A. The psychoanalysis of groups. *American Journal of Psychotherapy,* October 1949, 16–60; and January 1950, 525–58.

Wolf, A. Psychoanalysis of groups. In M. Berger and M. Rosenbaum (Eds.), *Group psychotherapy and group function.* New York: Basic Books, (2nd ed.),1975, 273–327.

Wolf, A., and E. K. Schwartz. *Psychoanalysis in groups.* New York: Grune & Stratton, 1962.

Wolf A., and E. K. Schwartz. Psychoanalysis in groups. In H. I. Kaplan and B. Sadock (Eds.), *Comprehensive group psychotherapy.* Baltimore, MD: Williams and Wilkins, 1971, 241–91.

Yalom, I. D. *The theory of group psychotherapy.* New York: Basic Books, 1970.

3

Adlerian Approach to Groups

The term neo-Freudian generally refers to a collective group of psychoanalysts who, for varying reasons, disagreed with Freud on certain theoretical issues. Some of their contributions to psychoanalytic theories of personality and of groups will be reviewed briefly here. Admittedly, there is no attempt to balance completely the theoretical formulations of classical psychoanalysts and neo-analysts. This is for reasons of parsimony and because the neo-analytic contributions to the psychoanalytic school are seen as extensions of Freudian theory rather than as entirely new and separate systems (Ford and Urban, 1963). In recent years Adler's concepts have been applied to counseling and teaching in educational settings, subsequently receiving nationwide attention.

Some of the modifications that neo-Freudians have made in classical psychoanalytic theory are: (1) greater stress on the cultural determinants of an individual's behavior; (2) more focus on the quality of the therapeutic relationship and the individual's perception of it; (3) less stress on sexual needs and greater attention to needs and feelings of inferiority, love, mastery, and ambivalence; and (4) more emphasis on the rational functions of the ego in solving life difficulties (Brammer and Shostrom, 1977).

Adler was one of the early disciples who later abandoned some of Freud's basic contentions. Instead of viewing clients as helpless victims of their impulses, Adler (1930, 1939) stressed the goal directedness or purposiveness of human beings. In contrast to Freud, Adler believed that power and status motives were more important for behavior development than sexual drives. Likewise, Adler accentuated the unity and integration of behavior rather than the conflict of different elements. He proposed a holistic view of people.

Adler posited that human beings are motivated primarily by social urges. Because men and women are social beings involved in social activities, they acquire a life-style that is predominantly social in orientation. In Adler's opinion, social activities are determined by the society in which people are born. He underscored the consciousness of personality, while recognizing at the same time that some individual goals may also be beneath the conscious level. Emphasizing the conscious aspects of personality, Adler saw an individual as capable of planning and guiding his or her actions with a real awareness of their meaning (Adler, 1930).

One of the first proponents of a subjectivistic psychology, Adler believed that an individual's behavior could only be explained by analyzing that person's "inner nature." The crucial determinants of an individual's behavior are internal. They consist of values, interests, attitudes, and ideas. Subjective reality, or a person's thoughts and interpretations of reality, are the primary determinants of the way in which a person behaves (Ansbacher and Ansbacher, 1956). According to Adler, the basic drive of people is a "striving for superiority" or a "striving to overcome." According to him, individuals make self-evaluations of their own inferiority, leading to actual feelings of inferiority and a striving for superiority. Adler reduced the importance of the id and the unconscious almost to the vanishing point.

Another of Adler's points of emphasis is the social interest or life-style. A favorite technique of Adlerian therapists is to ask clients for their first remembrances. Replies to this kind of question give the therapist clues as to the experiences upon which the client's life-style is based. Assisting clients to become more aware of their own unique life-style, self-images, and ego-ideal is also a major goal of the Adlerian therapist.

Many of Adler's basic tenets are carried over into analytic group psychotherapy. For instance, Adlerian group counselors tend to stress the establishment of counseling conditions that they believe will help members to gain self-esteem, to become more social, and to restructure their "subjective apperceptive schemes" and find more realistic life-styles (Durkin, 1964).

ADLERIAN INDIVIDUAL PSYCHOLOGY AS A FOUNDATION FOR GROUP COUNSELING

The basis for Adler's concept of personality development is found in his Theory of Individual Psychology. It is within this theory that he discusses the human condition, the fundamental strivings of people, and the causes of maladaptive behavior. As with other theories discussed in this book, Adlerian concepts of personality development can not be dealt with at length. At best, one can only present the most prominent tenets of Adlerian psychology which have a bearing on the theory and process of group counseling that has evolved from it.

Basically, Adler espoused a subjectivistic psychology of human behavior. He stressed the importance of studying the way people feel, think, and see themselves (Adler, 1927, 1930). According to him, the personalities of individuals are largely reflections of how they have conceived reality over a period of time. Objective events were given much less weight than how an individual perceived these events, regardless of how accurate or distorted such perceptions were in reality. This philosophical position provided, in large measure, Adler's rationale for naming his theory Individual Psychology. He wanted to underscore the fact that he was studying behavior from the perspective of the individual.

Adler's subjectivistic psychology of human development is noteworthy in that it is perhaps the first major theory which espoused a phenomenological view of people and of therapy. Later theorists, such as Carl Rogers and Albert Ellis, have not merely expanded upon Adler's notion of subjective reality as a major determinant of behavior. They have also made this concept a major underpinning of their theoretical formulations.

Despite his emphasis on the subjective reality of people, Adler also noted that there is need for taking into account objective reality factors (Ansbacher and Ansbacher, 1956). Distorted perceptions of reality were labeled "fictions." People developed fictions, or distorted views of reality, to support their own private inner logic or their subjective views of life. Objective reality, then, was significant only insofar as it was an indirect determinant of behavior and provided insight to fictions people developed.

Another aspect of Adlerian personality development is that it is primarily cognitive in nature. Behavior is maintained, sustained, or abolished by what people tell themselves about life and the people around them. The thought processes of individuals provide clues to the inner logic of individuals. The idea that people control their own behavior through their thoughts rather than by anything others do to them is one of Adler's important contributions to counseling. Later on, Albert Ellis picks up on this feature of Adler's theory and makes it a central part of his theory of rational emotive therapy.

In short, Adler's theory of personality development is subjectivistic in that it maintains the importance of studying behavior from the perspective of the individual. It is phenomenological in that it stresses dealing with individuals' total perceptual life field. And it is cognitively oriented in that it asserts that thought processes control individuals' actions.

ADLERIAN PRINCIPLES OF PERSONALITY DEVELOPMENT

The Adlerian concept of personality development is based on several guiding principles. These principles are: (1) people are social beings, primarily and exclusively; (2) all behavior is goal-directed and purposeful; (3) there exists within all humans a unity of behavior; and (4) behavior is lawfully organized. Other concepts that were pivotal in Adler's theory of personality development include: organ inferiority; feelings of inferiority; striving for superiority; family constellation and birth order; social interest; and life-style.

Social Nature

According to Adler, people are social beings, primarily and exclusively (Dreikurs, 1957). Human behavior is developed within a social context and, therefore, should be studied within that context. Moreover, all human conflicts are essentially social or manifestations of difficulties in social interaction. The transactions and interactions that take place between people provide the clues to understanding their behavior (Dinkmeyer and Muro, 1971). Since the basic desire of people is to belong, people can only fulfill themselves and become significant within a group context. The group provides the vehicle for individuals' personal development.

Adler's view of the nature of people is basically positive. People are not only essentially good but as infants they enter the world with an innate response pattern of love and affection. According to Adler, individuals have an innate human potentiality for social interest. In this instance, social interest is described as both the ability to participate and the willingness to contribute to society (Dreikurs, 1957). To function adequately socially, people must develop sufficient social interest; otherwise, deficiency and maladjustment take place.

The development of feelings of inferiority on the part of people is considered part of the human condition and inevitable. All individuals at some juncture of their lives (usually early childhood) experience evaluations of inferiority, which in turn lead to actual feelings of inferiority. The nature of human beings is to try to overcome feelings of inferiority developed in childhood by striving to become superior in self-selected designated areas. In Adler's opinion, feelings of inferiority were not necessarily negative; they provided the motivations for later adolescent and adult achievement in life.

Adlerian philosophy likewise proffers that people have a basic desire to belong. The desire to belong is a lifelong pursuit and is characterized by individuals' efforts to find their "place in life."

Adler's concept of the nature of people differed markedly from Freud's. Freud portrayed people as driven primarily by instincts which had to be controlled or transformed into socially acceptable behavior. Adler (1927, 1930, 1939), on the other hand, asserted that human behavior was primarily learned rather than instinctual. Behavior was acquired in relation to other people and oneself. He also affirmed that people are in control of their behavior and the situations they encounter. The fundamental nature of people is primarily social.

Adler's views on the nature of human beings are well suited for group counseling. The group provides the social context in which people can develop a sense of belonging and demonstrate their social interest. Given that a safe environment is provided, individuals may bring to the group their feelings of inferiority as well as their strivings for superiority.

Goal-Directed, Purposeful Behavior

Human behavior is purposeful and goal-directed. It is based upon the fact that the individual is a self-determining organism. Every action of an individual is directed toward a goal he or she is struggling to attain. To understand individuals, one must first find out what their goals are. Goals form the basis of each individual's personality.

Children's personalities are formed on the basis of the goals they set in life. Basically, children set two types of goals: immediate and long-range. Immediate goals are decidedly the easier ones with which counselors can work. They are observable in the day-to-day functioning of children (Dreikurs, 1957). Long-range goals indicate children's private, inner logic and constitute their basic outlook on life. Both immediate and long-range goals have important influences on a child's personality development.

Significant differences exist in the relative influence of immediate and long-range goals. Children establish long-range goals early in life—usually by the age of three or four. Children's perceptions of their interactions with significant others in the family constellation influence the types of goals they set for themselves, and subsequently their personality development. The private logic and goals of children can be understood by analyzing their experiences within the family constellation and by listening to their recollections and perceptions of their interactions between themselves, parents, siblings, and other relatives. Children's early recollections of interactions that occurred within the family constellation form the foundation for the concept of life they have developed and maintained since childhood.

This situation exists, in part, because people tend to remember from their early childhood only those incidents which fit into the concept of life they have developed and maintained since childhood (Dreikurs, 1957). For example, one individual disclosed that the earliest thing he could remember about his mother was that she always told him that "he did not belong to himself." He recalled the resentment that he felt during the times she made those statements as if they had occurred just yesterday. He further explained that he never quite understood what his mother meant by this saying; however, for reasons unclear to himself, he never confronted his mother about his feelings or asked her for a clarification of what she meant.

The earliest remembrance of another client involved her mother's toilet training of her. The client recalled backing herself into a corner as her mother yelled and screamed at her for soiling her pants. Although she was rescued by a sympathetic family caretaker, the client vividly remembered her mother's anger. It was only when the client had reached middle age that she could admit that she felt dominated by her mother and was tired of trying to appease her whims. By this time, the client's practice of avoiding conflicts and of seeking approval from others had become firmly entrenched as a basic modus operandi.

Individuals' perceptions of interactions in the family not only are pivotal in their establishment of long-range goals; such perceptions also become guiding principles for their concept of life. If children perceive that they are rejected or unloved by one or both of their parents, their basic goal in life may be to obtain love from others, regardless of the cost. Such children adopt a basic goal of being liked by others. An alternate reaction might be that such children establish a long-range goal of punishing their parents for their lack of love. This type of behavior is quite noticeable in the angry child, the delinquent adolescent, and others who may seek to harm their parents by harming themselves. Maladjusted long-range goals can only be changed through an intensive form of therapy. Oftentimes it matters little if individuals' early recollections are accurate or inaccurate. What really counts are the thoughts which people tell themselves as a result of their perceptions.

Immediate goals differ from long-range ones in that they are not only easier to discern but also easier to change. An individual may pursue several immediate goals simultaneously. Such goals tend to be suitable for an individual's current situation, and they are generally in harmony with his or her actions.

Immediate goals can be changed through counseling. They do not require intensive exploration of the individual. The primary differences, then, between immediate and long-range goals may be summarized as follows: Long-range goals are established early in life; they are more rigid and less susceptible to change; they require in-depth therapy; and they provide the guiding principles for an individual's behavior.

Both immediate and long-range goals may be based on distorted perceptions of reality. Children establish "fictitious" goals when they do not feel they have found their place in life. Fictitious goals are substitute goals. They represent individuals' attempts to obtain their desired or "real" goals through mistaken and misguided ways. For instance, children may assume the fictitious goal of acting out because their real goal is to obtain attention. Fictitious goals are selected through the process of trial and error. That is, children and adults develop certain behaviors associated with fictitious goals because they find that others are responsive to such behavior—for example, shouting or pouting to gain attention, withdrawing love to gain love, or acting helpless to obtain what one wants. The possibilities are endless and are limited only to the extent that those whom they want to respond to their goals actually respond. Mistaken or inaccurate conclusions that people develop in their early formative years provide the motivating factors of their behavior and the foundation for personality development.

According to Adler, individuals' awareness or consciousness of their goals is self-determined. In contrast to immediate goals, most people are not aware of their long-range goals. Adler posited, however, that people choose to be aware or unaware of their goals or intentions. In choosing, individuals are inclined to do what they intend to do and to deny, when confronted, their awareness of their intentions. Statements such as "I didn't intend to hurt you" or "I didn't mean any harm" may be the individual's way of disguising true intentions to inflict pain or cause harm. Along such lines, guilt feelings may be conceptualized as pretenses of good intentions which people do not have (Dreikurs, 1957). That is, people feel guilty primarily when they are not willing to do what they think they should do socially.

Adlerian principles of the goal directedness and purposefulness of behavior may be summarized in the following manner. All human actions have a purpose and that purpose is fundamentally of a social nature. All human qualities express movement, especially in relation to others. Individuals set both immediate and long-range goals. People operate according to the long-range and short-range goals they set for themselves. Individuals may or may not be consciously aware of the goals they set. Goals are individuals' attempts to find their place in life. The movement toward a goal is always in relation to others and oneself.

Unity of Behavior

The Adlerian theory of personality development posits a holistic concept of people. Individuals are greater than the sum of their acts. Clients should not be analyzed from the perspective of urges and drives but rather from the perspective of the total field in which they operate. The individual is an indivisible whole. The Adlerian concept of the unity of behavior is similar to Gestalt psychologists' view of behavior.

Behavior is Lawfully Organized: Life-Style

One of the basic principles of Adlerian personality development is that behavior is lawfully organized. Each person develops a generalized pattern of responses to most situations. Adler called the generalized pattern of responses a person's life-style. All behavior is organized around an individual's life-style. Life-style, then, is a habitual pattern of behavior which is unique to each individual.

Life-style is the internal organizer of an individual's behavior. Life-style is all-inclusive. It encompasses individuals' goals, their opinions of themselves and the world, and the habitual behaviors they use for achieving desired outcomes. Life-style is a product of learning that is created by each child by the age of five. After this point, it becomes firm and generally impervious to change. Life-style helps an individual to achieve what one might designate as internal consistency of thoughts, behavior, feelings, and actions.

Once an individual's life-style is developed, it assumes the role of a sovereign. That is, it becomes the "whole" that commands the "parts."

Feelings of Inferiority

According to Adler, all human beings begin their psychological life with feelings of inferiority. Such feelings may be attributed to children's early recognition of their inherently subordinate position to adults and to nature. Feelings of inferiority are initiated with individuals' perception and self-evaluation of situational events in which they have felt inadequate. Feelings of inferiority are displeasurable and constitute a minus state that people seek to overcome. Adler characterized such feelings as inevitable, universal, and normal (Ansbacher and Ansbacher, 1956).

Striving for Superiority

People attempt to overcome or compensate for their feelings of inferiority by striving for superiority. Striving for superiority is an all-inclusive term in that it is used to explain individuals' drive to master external obstacles, to gain power and status, and to arrive at a plus or positive state. It may be compared to later theories of drive reduction. Since people cannot ever completely rid themselves of feelings of inferiority, striving for superiority becomes a dominant motif of their lives. In women, the drive for mastery takes the form of a "masculine protest." Similar to Freud's idea of penis envy, Adler believed that women envied the status and power of men. Group counseling provides the context in which people can deal openly with their feelings of inferiority and their strivings for superiority.

Birth Order

Adler was one of the first theorists to emphasize the importance of an individual's birth order in the family. He posited that individuals' birth order in the family increased the probability that certain behavior patterns would develop. These behavior patterns were seen to influence a person's life-style and interpersonal relationships with others. For example, the only child was characterized as one who had a high probability of being overindulged by his or her parents and of developing limited interpersonal response skills. The older child was conceptualized as one who had been dethroned and who had had great demands placed upon her or him. As a consequence, such a child had a greater than normal chance of developing behavior patterns which reflected a fear of competition, concern about the attitudes of authority figures, and assumption of leadership positions. The second child was seen to develop deep convictions of inadequacy and less concern over obedience to authority. The youngest child was apt to evidence a high degree of egocentrism and feelings of being a baby all of his or her life.

Maladjustment

Adler's principles of normal personality development formed the basis for his views on maladjustment. The maladjusted individual is essentially a caricature of a normally healthy person. Life is distorted for the maladjusted person. This distortion may be based on real, precipitating situational events that occurred in childhood or inaccurate perceptions of events.

People develop maladjusted or disordered behavior primarily because: (1) they have greater feelings of inferiority than what might be normally expected as a result of the human condition; and (2) they acquire an accompanying set of inappropriate compensatory responses to offset their deep-seated feelings of inferiority. The difference, then, between normal and abnormal adjustment is one of degree and exaggeration of behavior. The normally healthy individual manifests feelings of inferiority and striving for superiority. These feelings and strivings are, however, exaggerated in the maladjusted individual.

Adler attributed a number of child-rearing practices and parental mistakes to individuals' development of disordered or inappropriate behavior. Three concepts which seemed to assume the most importance were: (1) organ inferiority; (2) pampering; and (3) neglect. Children developed organ inferiority because of their negative perceptions of physical handicaps or infirmities they were either born with or developed shortly upon entering the world. For example, the sickly child or the child who suffers from underdeveloped muscular capability are two cases in point. Parents' undue concern over their children's physical handicaps tend to confirm their children's negative perceptions of their infirmity.

Although both the pampered and the neglected child received different kinds of parental treatment, the end results of that treatment were basically the same. Parental overprotection and inattentiveness led to children's feelings of inadequacy.

Adler used a number of characteristics to describe the maladjusted or neurotic individual. The neurotic individual was inclined to be rigid in thought, to see life in dichotomous or black-and-white terms, to have excessive fears, to vacillate, and to be dependent rather than independent. These characteristics seemed to be general character traits most neurotics or maladjusted persons shared. What distinguished one maladapted individual from another was the "safeguarding tendencies" each individual acquired to protect himself or herself from feelings of inferiority. The type of safeguarding response chosen differentiated the type of disorder the individual developed. Adler considered an individual's selection of a safeguarding response a "creative act."

In short, Adlerian psychology conceptualized maladjustment as the individual's development of exaggerated feelings of inferiority and exaggerated striving for superiority.

ADLERIAN APPROACHES TO GROUPS

The Adlerian approach to groups is based on the principles Adler described in his theory of Individual Psychology (Adler, 1930). Similar to other theorists, however, Adler did not develop a formal theory of group counseling. His involvement with groups, and the subsequent Adlerian group method, came about as a result of his personal philosophy of the social nature of people and his early work with groups at the child guidance clinic in Vienna in 1921.

Adler's early involvement with groups laid the foundation for later teleoanalytic approaches to groups. His initial rationale was to teach parents how they could have a more positive impact on the lives of their children. To achieve this overall goal, Adler took his practice directly to the schools. There he interviewed and counseled parents and their children before other groups of parents and professionals in the schools (Sonstegard and Dreikurs, 1973). It soon became clear that there were other benefits of using the demonstrational approach within the educational and clinic settings. He could teach the principles of individual psychology to a wide audience of people. He could demonstrate to professionals in the schools how to work with children and their parents toward a common goal.

Many of the strands of Adler's work with groups remain today. Adlerian group counseling is still primarily an educational process. It focuses on the family and children. The technique of involving both parents and their children in a public setting with an audience of other potential participants is still prominent today. Adlerian group counseling is usually conducted in educational and clinic settings.

Although Adler used the group method as early as 1921 in his child guidance clinics in Vienna, most Americans have become acquainted with the Adlerian approach to groups through the efforts of Rudolf Dreikurs, a Viennese psychiatrist trained by Adler. Shortly after 1934, Dreikurs emigrated to Chicago. There he established child guidance centers similar to the ones Adler had set up in Vienna (Sonstegard and Dreikurs, 1973).

Up until his death in 1972, Dreikurs applied Adlerian principles to the group treatment of individuals of all age levels. Of particular interest, however, are his formulations concerning group counseling with children and families. Much of Dreikurs' work with young people has been done in collaboration with Manford Sonstegard. Other students of Dreikurs, such as Corsini (1957), Dinkmeyer (1969), and Grunewald (1955), have made significant applications of the group approach in schools and other settings. The major contribution of Dreikurs and his students is that they refined many of Adler's concepts. They are also responsible for developing a step-by-step approach to the phases of group counseling.

Attention is placed in this chapter upon the goals of group counseling, the group process, key concepts and techniques of counseling, the role of the group leader, and the roles of group members. The group procedures described are mainly those developed by Dreikurs and his associates. A later section focuses on the two primary populations upon whom the Adlerian or teleoanalytical method of group counseling has been applied: (1) families; and (2) children. The commonalities that exist between family group counseling and group counseling of children are explored. Teleoanalytic or Adlerian contributions to group counseling are also analyzed.

General Goals of Adlerian Group Counseling

There exist within the Adlerian method overall goals which apply to both group counseling of children and of families. Generally speaking, the most therapeutic goal in Adlerian group counseling is to help individuals deal with their feelings of inferiority. This goal is important because feelings of inferiority are considered the main source of individual maladjustment. Moreover, such feelings tend to decrease individuals' self-confidence, lower their self-esteem, and restrict their sphere of social interest (Dreikurs, 1957). Without self-confidence and restored faith in one's own worth and ability, a person cannot grow and improve. The group process in the teleoanalytic method is designed to help individuals regain their self-respect. This process is usually accomplished by having group participants face up to their actual feelings of inferiority and by actively encouraging them to recognize that they are worthwhile human beings.

Another objective of teleoanalytic group counseling is to help participants gain a sense of belonging. A feeling of belonging is necessary for an individual's social and emotional well-being. As Dreikurs (1957, p. 173) has stated: "Not belonging is the worst contingency man can experience; it is worse than death. This explains the supreme significance of status." The degree of an individual's social interest can be measured by the areas in which he or she feels a sense of belonging. Although individuals may develop devious means to find their places in life, they never lose their desire to do so. In group counseling of individuals, it is significant to discover the techniques that people use to maintain a sense of belonging. These techniques must not only be revealed to the individual in question; the counselor must also help the participant discover more personally rewarding techniques of belonging. A sense of belongingness must be, however, transferable outside the group counseling situation. The teleoanalytic group leader strives to help participants learn how to leave the security of the group and deal effectively with real life situations in which others do not necessarily understand their emotional difficulties.

The development of social interest is another objective of group counseling. As noted previously, Adlerians consider the development of social interest vital to an individual's mental health. Social interest is important because it helps the individual to reach beyond his or her immediate concerns. It tends to reduce the morbid preoccupation with oneself. The greater social interest an individual has, the less vulnerable he or she will feel in the presence of others. This situation can be best exemplified by the good feeling and sense of accomplishment one obtains from helping others. When individuals are actively concerned with others' well-being, they are oftentimes better able to put their own problems in a more realistic perspective.

The task of the counselor is to build upon the social interest of group participants through role modeling of desirable behaviors. Social interest is vital to the development of group cohesiveness. The greater the degree to which the counselor can generate social interest in the group, the more cohesive the group will be. For example, a counselor might state: "I'm concerned about Jim's feelings of isolation and hopelessness. Is there any way that we can reach out to him to let him know that we understand his feelings?" Such open-ended questions encourage group participants to reach out to others and to become less preoccupied with their own difficulties.

Group Process

Group process in the teleoanalytic method is a dynamic one. Emphasis is placed on how group members affect each other and the types of transactions that occur between them. The group is viewed as a value-forming agent; it influences the beliefs and attitudes of its members more so than does the counselor. For example, Dreikurs (1957) cites his experience in working with a group comprised almost entirely of depressed clients. As group members took turns explaining why they were correct in their own individual pessimism and hopelessness about life, the others tried to convince the person in question that all was not hopeless. When group members recognized what they were saying to each other, a dramatic improvement occurred in the attitudes of all participants. They came to realize that all was not hopeless, either for themselves or for others.

A similar situation existed for a group of adolescents. For example, Sonstegard and Dreikurs (1973) report how the influence of a group affected a young female adolescent's views on dating and staying out late. The teenager had complained about her parents' lack of understanding concerning her dating behavior. When other participants began to express how they would not consider going out with anyone their parents had not met, the teenager was forced to reevaluate her thinking and actions. Again, the group had served as a value-forming agent.

Essentially, the Adlerian group process posits that people learn from each other and that counseling is an educational process. Participants can see the validity of the counselor's interpretation when they recognize themselves in others. What helps them to overcome their resistance is their observation of a similar resistance in other participants. Most psychological interpretations in the group are not made for the benefit of the person to whom they are directed, but rather for the benefit of the others who learn from them (Dreikurs, 1957). Group counseling is a vehicle for social reorientation of individuals. It is not only a means to help a person find a sounder approach to social living but also a way to help the person learn how to cooperate.

Hence, the group process focuses on examining the here-and-now of behavior (Dinkmeyer and Muro, 1971). Group members are encouraged to explore how their present transactions affect their immediate goals. Interactions that take place in the group situation among participants are used to clarify the goals and consequences of individuals' behavior.

Despite Adlerians affirmation of democratic principles, the group process is basically leader-centered. The counselor takes an active role in directing and encouraging participants to understand the purpose of their actions. The group process in teleoanalytic counseling is action-oriented, leader-centered, and here-and-now focused.

Phases of Adlerian Group Counseling

As mentioned earlier, the Adlerian group process is divided into four phases: (1) the establishment and maintenance of an appropriate counseling relationship; (2) psychological investigation or analysis; (3) interpretation or the revelation of goals; and (4) reorientation of goals. It is not necessary for groups to move in linear fashion from phase one to phase four. In teleoanalytic group counseling, more emphasis is placed on the progress of individuals within the group than on the stages of group development. None of the stages of the group process are considered mutually exclusive. On the contrary, some overlap exists within the dynamics of each of the phases of group counseling.

The Counseling Relationship Similar to most other group counseling theorists, Adlerians maintain that the establishment of a good counseling relationship is basic to the therapeutic process. The counselor helps to create a good counseling relationship by developing an atmosphere of mutual respect and trust. According to Sonstegard and Dreikurs (1973), counselor sincerity is of the utmost importance in establishing participant trust. Counselors must be willing to be as they are and not pretend they are something they are not. This means that the counselor must take risks in expressing what he or she sees taking place in the group, even though such statements may be viewed negatively by the participants.

Central to the establishment of a good group counseling relationship is the agreement between the counselor and the individual on the goals of the latter's participation in the group. Agreement upon the goals of counseling promotes a constructive relationship because it suggests that the counselor and client are working toward common objectives. If there is disagreement on the goals and interests of the individual and the counselor, a satisfactory relationship cannot be established. Lack of client-counselor alignment of goals tends to engender client resistance as to the purposes of group counseling. Hence, what might seem to be resistance on the part of the individual is little more than a discrepancy between the goals of the counselor and the individual. Because of its emphasis on the alignment of client and counselor goals of counseling, the teleoanalytic school can be viewed as the forerunner of the contractual method established by transactional analysts.

To establish a good counseling relationship, the counselor must convey to group participants an anticipation of success. The counselor must communicate to participants a feeling that they can be helped and, perhaps more importantly, that they can learn how to help themselves. More recently, Yalom (1975) has relabeled the Adlerian concept of anticipation as the "installation of hope." According to him, the installation of hope is a basic curative factor in all of the group counseling approaches. Hope is required to keep the client in counseling, while faith in the treatment mode or process is in itself therapeutically effective. Yalom also concurs with the Adlerian conviction that counselors must convey to group participants the feeling that they believe in themselves and in the efficacy of group counseling. As Yalom (1975, p. 7) has stated: "No less important is that the therapist believe in himself and in the efficacy of his group. It is my conviction that I am able to help every patient who commits himself to therapy and remains with the group for at least six months. In my first meetings with each patient, I share this conviction with him and attempt to imbue him with my optimism."

Many of the Adlerian tenets regarding the necessary characteristics of the counseling relationship have been adopted by other theoretical schools. For example, Rogers (1961) used the term counselor congruency to indicate that counselors must be willing to be themselves within the group situation. Berne (1966) renamed the Adlerian concept of alignment of client-counselor goals the contractual agreement in transactional analysis. Yalom made the Adlerian notion of anticipation of success one of his basic curative factors in group counseling. These brief examples underscore the influence of the teleoanalytic school on other group approaches.

In summary, several elements comprise the Adlerian concept of the counseling relationship. These characteristics are: mutual respect and trust, counselor sincerity and honesty, agreement upon goals, and anticipated success.

Psychological Investigation   The second phase of the teleoanalytic group counseling method involves psychological investigation. In other group models, it is usually labeled diagnosis. During the psychological investigation period, the counselor analyzes the psychodynamic forces operating within the individual. This phase has two major objectives: (1) to explore the premises of the person's goal; and (2) to understand the dynamics which support the person's present state of conflict. Psychological investigation is essentially a data-gathering phase in which the group leader attempts to put together "the missing parts" and to formulate hypotheses concerning the nature of the person's conflicts. The underlying assumption of this phase is that an analysis of past and present relationships will provide clues to the person's present character and personality.

Adlerian group counselors used specific methods and procedures to determine the psychodynamic forces of each group participant. Generally, before an individual is accepted into a group, a complete history is taken on the individual. Such background information may be obtained from the participant, family members, teachers, or, in general, the referring person. A large part of the counselor's data gathering also takes place within the group. Hence, the counselor basically uses two settings to gather information related to the client's problem: (1) an interview, and (2) the group itself.

Regardless of the setting in which data are collected, the counselor usually explores certain fundamental areas. The counselor first examines the individual's subjective condition. Questions are designed to find out what the individual's complaints are, how the individual feels, and how the individual views his or her problem. Next, the counselor focuses on the objective nature of the client's situation. The counselor investigates how the individual functions in the social environment. For children, the social environment may constitute the school, their relationships with peers, and their interactions within the family. The counselor analyzes the objective situation of adults by inquiring about their work situation, their involvement with people outside of the work setting, and the family.

Having arrived at both a subjective and an objective understanding of the client's present conflicts, the counselor makes a tentative analysis of the underlying causes of the client's complaints. If the client is an older child (adolescent) or adult, his or her life-style is examined. Life-style is determined by: (1) exploring each client's family constellation; and (2) examining the client's earliest recollections to ascertain the types of conclusions the client reached from interactions in the family group (Sonstegard and Dreikurs, 1973). For example, the counselor might say to the client: "Tell me something that happened to you when you were little." The underlying assumption of this procedure is that the individual will only remember those experiences which reflect his or her scheme for living. Much of what people remember is based upon their ordinal position—oldest child, middle child, youngest child, only child—within the family. The ordinal position influences how people perceive all family events and how siblings have played a significant part in the growth of their character.

Adlerians maintain that certain life-styles are more prominent than others. Some examples of characteristic types of life-style that are frequent in our culture include, according to Dinkmeyer and Dreikurs (1963), the following:

1. I belong or have a place in life if I obtain the approval I want.

2. I belong or feel I have a place in life if I am in complete control.

3. I belong or feel I have a place in life if I am intellectually superior and right.

4. I belong or feel I have a place in life if I am taken care of by others.

The counselor also conducts a psychological investigation of clients within the group counseling situation. According to Dreikurs (1957), a person's goals and movements are much more obvious in group interaction than in an individual interview with the counselor. In the group situation the client's facade may become more visible. During group counseling, the investigation begins with the client's here-and-now problems. The counselor analyzes the individual's problems from the perspective of determining the purpose of the individual's actions. Whenever the counselor observes a particular person's action within the group, the counselor asks himself: "For what purpose is he or she behaving this way? What is his or her goal in behaving in this manner?"

Adler placed a great deal of emphasis on using hunches to correctly guess the psychological movement of an individual (Dinkmeyer, 1963). Following Adler's steps, Dreikurs developed the "hidden reason" technique. Basically, the "hidden reason" technique was designed to understand what takes place in an individual's private logic. It is used when an individual does something out of the ordinary which she or he does not understand. For example, an individual might say: "I don't know why I behaved that way; it's really not like me." The counselor would then try to guess or use hunch to help the individual determine under what circumstances certain behaviors make sense. The counselor next asks what the individual was thinking about when he or she behaved in the puzzling manner. If the counselor can help the individual to find the exact words that were on his or her mind at the time of the incident, the client is helped to find the hidden reason for the puzzling behavior.

Psychological investigation is used to understand the source and systems of beliefs of an individual. Rehabilitation of a client is based upon the counselor's having a complete analysis of all of the previous familial and social relationships which have helped to form an individual's character and personality.

Interpretation or Revelation of Goals   During this phase of group counseling, the counselor tries to make the individual aware of the goals or purposes of his or her behavior. Little significance is attached to the whys or the causes of an individual's behavior. The individual is encouraged to understand actions, not feelings. As Dinkmeyer (1971, p. 237) has noted: "Little time is spent in description of feelings or straight reflection of feelings. The emphasis is focused on the purpose of feelings."

This strategy is based on the Adlerian belief that the functions of emotions are more important than the emotions themselves. According to Dreikurs (1957), people create their emotions in order to support their own self-determined goals. The anxious feelings that a person has serve a purpose, as do feelings of depression. For example, an individual may use feelings of depression to support an inner private logic which says, "I am helpless," "I am hopeless," or "Life is unfair." To help a client, a counselor must understand what purpose feelings of depression serve.

Client insight is an important occurrence during this phase of counseling. Adlerians maintain, however, that "insight is not the basis for cure, improvement, or adjustment; it is merely a step toward it, and not even a necessary prerequisite" (Dreikurs, 1957).

The group tends to promote the process of insight. As individuals listen to and interact with others, they may come to see themselves more clearly. Group members may not only learn from the disclosures of others but may also become adept in deciphering each other's goals. Young children are usually more receptive to feedback from their peers than from adults.

Dinkmeyer (1971) proposes that in counseling children the proper sequence in the insight interpretation stage entails asking the child the following questions: Do you know why you are acting this way? Would you like to know why you are acting this way? Could it be that you are . . .? or I'm getting the impression that. . . . This procedure is called the "mirror technique." In other words, clients are confronted with the goals and intentions of their behavior.

Reorientation or Reeducation   Reorientation is the most important phase of group counseling. A basic objective of this stage is to help the client redirect his or her goals. The counselor helps the individual to see alternate ways of behaving and thinking.

To achieve this end, the counselor challenges and encourages the individual to give up the faulty premises on which he or she has been living. This suggests that the client must make a fundamental change in his or her attitudes toward life or, in the case of adults, life-style. The counselor demonstrates that the client has willpower, that the client can decide either to relinquish or maintain the incorrect premises on which life has heretofore been based. One way of testing to see if clients have reoriented themselves is to ask them their earliest recollections. If there is a change in their earliest recollections, they have adjusted their basic outlook on life. If there is no change, they are still clinging to the past and to the faulty premises upon which they have consistently based their lives.

During the reorientation phase, the individual is encouraged to adopt a sounder approach to living—to develop more social interest in others. Both the counselor and group members attempt to help the client deal with feelings of inferiority by encouraging him or her to demonstrate evidence of self-respect. Adlerians posit that inferiority feelings must be dealt with before a person can begin to reorient behavior. The group provides the type of support which helps a person deal with inferiority feelings.

The reorientation phase relates insight to behavior change. In this respect, Adlerian group counseling can be said to be the forerunner of many group approaches which emphasized that insight is not enough. Adlerians help their clients to relinquish the faulty premises upon which they have nurtured their guilt feelings, their isolation, and their desire for prestige. They attempt to teach individuals to understand the consequences of their behavior and goals and to cooperate with others. They also try to teach individuals to find healthier sources of satisfaction and to take life in stride.

The Adlerian Group Leader

Adlerians describe the role of the group leader in terms of two primary functions: (1) attributes as a person and (2) skill and effectiveness as a professional technician. In order to be an effective group leader, the Adlerian counselor must sincerely desire to help others. Teleoanalysts believe that clients can discern when a counselor is insincere. Sincerity is the cornerstone of establishing a positive counseling relationship.

Moreover, Adlerian counselors must be willing to be as they are and not pretend to be something they are not. They express openly what they see and interpret it, even when working with children. Adlerian counselors present themselves as equals and emphasize the democratic principles of being in a group. Despite this emphasis, teleoanalytic counselors do not abdicate their role as leader on the group. In fact, teleoanalytic group leaders assume that they are superior in knowledge and experience. Such a position does not mean that counselors consider themselves or feel superior to group members. It is simply a matter of the counselor's having more skills in working with groups.

According to Sonstegard and Dreikurs (1973), Adlerian counselors may be more honest in their approach than some other therapists. Teleoanalytic counselors do not refrain from directing and asking clients questions; this behavior, however, does not make them autocratic. The autocratic counselor is often one who wants to give the appearance of letting clients find their own answers. Such a position closely resembles that of the autocratic chief "who decides what to divulge and what to hold back, regardless of the desires or needs of the group (Sonstegard and Dreikurs, 1973, p. 74)." Moreover, the counselor who refuses to participate and withholds knowledge that the group realizes the counselor possesses demonstrates a basic lack of respect for the group and a failure to consider them as equals.

To be truly teleoanalytic, the counselor must be open and frank with clients. Such behavior on the part of the counselor demonstrates a fundamental respect for individuals who are in need of his or her help. There are no magical cures in teleoanalytic group counseling. The counselor proceeds on the basis of agreed upon goals on which both counselor and client will work.

Initial behaviors of the group counselor are those which entail observing the individual, conducting a psychological investigation, agreeing on the goals to be worked on in the group, and establishing the basis for a counseling relationship built upon mutual respect and leader sincerity. It is the counselor's task to develop within group members an anticipation of success from their counseling experience. Adlerians believe that counselor influence depends upon an ability to win the active support of group members.

Adlerian group counseling is both action-oriented and leader-centered. The group leader focuses on the here-and-now of an individual's behavior. Whether working with children or families, the Adlerian group counselor views counseling as an educational process in which the members' emotional experiences reinforce their intellectual learning.

The techniques of the Adlerian group leader may vary. The group leader encourages individuals to improve, recognize, and correct value systems that work against their desirable social functioning. During group sessions, the counselor helps participants to understand their goals and the ways in which they seek to achieve their goals. Initially, the leader may confront individuals with their purposes and, in this respect, serves as a model so that group participants may later assist in the exploration of individuals' purposeful behavior. The counselor confronts the client in a caring manner; and teleoanalytic interpretations are made tentatively and in terms of the individual's unique goal. In working with children, the teleoanalytic group counselor uses primarily the techniques of encouragement and the law of natural consequences. Adult group counseling may entail multiple group therapy, that is, more than one therapist may work with a family.

Adlerian group counselors consider it important to work with teachers, parents, and school administrators. They have adapted many of their group counseling techniques for the classroom setting; and many of them have trained parents and teachers how to work with children.

It is important for the teleoanalytic group counselor to possess certain skills.

Sonstegard and Dreikurs (1973) assert that the counselor must have the ability to conduct an effective psychological investigation. Likewise, the counselor must be able to engage in pattern fitting in order to discern how the data gathered on the individual clarifies that individual's goals or purposes in life.

Moreover, a counselor should be able to apply his or her skills toward redirecting an individual's mistaken goals. To achieve this end, the counselor must obtain specific training in the application of the last three phases of Adlerian counseling. It is suggested that counselors receive training at one of the Alfred Adler Institutes.

SPECIAL APPLICATIONS OF THE ADLERIAN APPROACH

Group Counseling with Children

Dreikurs and Sonstegard (1968) focused a major portion of their professional lives on working with children. Long before parent effectiveness training became popular, Dreikurs outlined many of the principles one needs to understand in working with children. Dreikurs' work with children was on several levels. First, he worked directly with the child in group counseling. Second, he went into the schools to work with counselors, teachers, and administrators to help them to relate better to children. Third, he worked with parents themselves. This section focuses on Dreikurs' and his associates' working with children in the schools and in the Family Education Centers which he helped to establish. A separate section will deal with Adlerian family group counseling.

A great deal of Dreikurs' writings reflect an orientation toward both group counseling and group guidance. His writings may be considered group guidance oriented because he describes approaches that a classroom teacher can use in his or her relationship with students. The primary differences between group guidance and group counseling are: (1) the number of individuals involved—in counseling usually small groups of six to ten persons; (2) the person who conducts the sessions—in the case of group guidance, the teacher, and the counselor for group counseling; and (3) the fact that the counselor deals more directly with the mistaken goals of the child.

Much of Dreikurs' underlying philosophy of working with children is common to both group guidance and counseling. Counselors and teachers also share a common base of techniques. The settings in which the techniques are employed modifies or influences the degree to which the individual will pass through certain phases previously described.

It is important to realize that Dreikurs was one of the first to take counseling to the schools. The model or approach that Dreikurs describes applies to both group counseling of children and counselor consultation within the classrooms. Dreikurs' rationale for working with teachers was clear from the start. From his perspective, children of all groups required help and guidance beyond what many counselors could provide in their attempt to service an entire school. He reacted strongly to what he called the new discipline of child psychiatry, which he saw operating on the assumption that children are "emotionally sick." According to Dreikurs and Sonstegard (1968), the disturbed child was not necessarily sick, and the teacher as well as the counselor, parent, social worker, or psychiatrist could be effective in working with the child. As Dreikurs and Sonstegard (1968, p. ix) have stated: "The disturbed child has wrong ideas about himself and life and uses socially unacceptable means to find his place. Anyone who can win his confidence, who understands him, who can show him alternatives can redirect the child."

It is within this frame of reference that Dreikurs' premises about working with children is presented. It matters little who does the counseling of the child, or whether one labels the process of helping children as group guidance or group counseling. What does matter are positive answers to the questions: Is the child helped? Does the person better understand the child? Has the disturbed or misbehaving child redirected his or her goals in a much more positive fashion?

According to proponents of the teleoanalytic method, researchers on children have exhibited little understanding in the motivation of children who are deficient or experiencing difficulties. Researchers have generally tended to use labels which attempt to explain the child's behavior. Thus, children are labeled as immature, lazy, passive-aggressive, or inclined to daydream. Adlerians maintain that most of these labels are attempts to explain the child's behavior but in reality they merely describe it. To understand a child's behavior one must comprehend the goals of that behavior.

The Misbehaving Child   Dreikurs' assumptions concerning the goals of the misbehaving child have particular significance for the counselor. From an understanding of the child's goals, the counselor may be able to enter more effectively into the child's frame of reference. As noted previously, the fundamental desire of each child is not only to find a place in the group but also to feel that she or he belongs. A well-behaved and well-adjusted child has been able to find social acceptance by conforming to the requirements of a particular group and by making meaningful contributions to it. The underlying assumption of the misbehaving child is that his or her actions will provide a sense of importance or social status within a group.

The misbehaving child is essentially a discouraged child. The discouraged child manifests an entire set of psychodynamics. The discouraged child does not see the possibility of ever solving his or her problems or of even moving toward potential solutions.

Dinkmeyer and Dreikurs (1963) maintain that discouraged children have little or no confidence in their own ability or in life; they have negative expectations about life. They fear being failures, being proven inadequate or humiliated in some way. The key to helping discouraged people is to change their expectations about life and themselves. This situation exists because expectations are the strongest human motivations. People act according to what they anticipate will happen and not necessarily on the basis of past experiences and hereditary predispositions. Moreover, the past is not subject to change, but an individual can alter his or her expectations. To help a discouraged person, one has to first encourage that person. As Dinkmeyer and Dreikurs (1963, p. 37) have stated:

An examination of all the influences which shape a person's belief or doubt in his own strength and ability can clearly indicate the encouraging and discouraging stimulations to which he is exposed. In our time, the scale balances heavily on the negative side. We all discourage one another more than we encourage; we all are much better prepared to discourage.

The Family: The Crucible of Competition   The process of discouragement usually begins within the family. Oftentimes family members discourage each other more than would normally be permitted or acceptable in other settings, particularly that of work. The tendency of people to look down on each other has to be kept to a minimum at work and at other social settings; otherwise such behavior would tend to disrupt the work team or social affair (Dinkmeyer and Dreikurs, 1963). Individuals are inclined to control what they say and do at work and at social gatherings so that a certain level of cooperation and surface harmony can take place. Such control does not always exist in the family. Family members may say and do things to each other which they would never do to outsiders.

The teleoanalytic school emphasizes that competition among siblings may foster an individual's feelings of discouragement. Dinkmeyer and Dreikurs (1963) differentiate between sibling competition and sibling rivalry. Rivalry may be defined as an "open contest for immediate gratification and advantages (p. 40)." Competition is more subtle; it means that each child attempts to establish his or her superiority over the other child. Since equality does not usually exist within families, each child will be viewed as inferior or superior to the others. In an effort to avoid feeling inferior, the child looks for the primary competitor's weak spots. As Dinkmeyer and Dreikurs (1963, p. 40) have stated: "Competitors within the family are thus characterized by the development of opposite character traits, abilities, interests, and temperaments. Each child seeks success where another fails, and, in turn, intensifies the other's sense of failure and inadequacy by his own success." Since the main competition is between the first and second child, they reflect the greatest difference in personality traits in the family.

Adlerians assert that although parents may be unaware of the reasons for the differences in their children, they, nevertheless, reinforce their children's differences by stresssing the weaknesses and strengths of each child. Parents abdicate their influence on a child to that child's siblings when they reinforce differences between children. That is, children establish their siblings' inferiority or superiority, while parents confirm such beliefs by the manner in which they treat each child. If a child is convinced that he or she can never match a sibling in certain areas, then that child may not even try to apply himself or herself in that area.

Adlerians maintain that teachers and community people may also reinforce a child's basic sense of discouragement by stressing differences between siblings in their academic achievements or social skills. When this occurs, the child may develop academic deficiencies. Deviancy, delinquency, and failures are other side effects of discouragement.

To counsel children effectively, the counselor must be aware of the psychodynamics, process, and effects of discouragement. During the psychological investigation phase of counseling, the group leader attempts to find out: To what extent is the child discouraged? What factors in the child's family life—for example, birth order and sibling competition—led to the child's feelings of discouragement? What are the effects of discouragement on the child's behavior?

Goals of the Misbehaving Child   As noted previously, there are four goals of the misbehaving child. The function of the group counselor is to help the child become aware of and redirect or change ineffectual goals into more positive ones.

The first goal of the child is labeled the attention-getting mechanism goal. The child misbehaves in order to gain special attention and service. The attention-getting mechanism is found among children who feel that they are not able to become a part of the group through any useful contributions of their own. Finding that socially acceptable means of gaining attention are ineffective, they will try any method that will confirm their existence or make people take notice of them.

Children who use the attention-getting mechanism may be either active or passive and may use constructive or destructive methods. If children feel accepted, they will use constructive attention-getting methods. The extent to which children respond actively or passively is dependent on their self-confidence and courage. The more self-confidence children have, the more likely they are to use both constructive and active attention-getting mechanisms.

For example, children who evidence active-constructive behavior have the overpowering ambition to be the first in the class. Conversely, the active destructive child usually becomes the class clown, the bully, the impertinent, and the rebel. Passive-constructive children manage to receive special attention and favor by their charm and not necessarily by doing anything themselves. On the other hand, the passive-destructive child exemplifies laziness and stubbornness. Attention-getting is the only goal which is achieved by the two associate pairs of behavior patterns. Children who have found little success in using the active-constructive attention-getting behavior pattern may turn to active-destructive behavior.

Frequently, the eldest child in a family may try all four behavior patterns of the attention-getting goal. First children in a family may feel that they have to be first to have any place in a group because they were dethroned by a younger child and, subsequently, had to fight to maintain their superiority in the family (Dreikurs, 1968). Usually, the oldest child strives to reestablish superiority through active-constructive means. If these efforts fail, the child may turn to active-destructive behavior—for example, being silly, clowning, or acting tough. The child decides that if she or he cannot be first in being good, she or he will be first in being bad.

The child who exhibits passive-constructive behavior may be a only, a youngest, or a sickly child (Dreikurs, 1968). Such a child receives attention by being cute or a clinging vine. If constructive efforts fail, the child may force others to become preoccupied with him or her by feigning sickness or helplessness.

Obtaining power and defeating others is another goal of the misbehaving child. The struggle for power is usually to show that the child can control others and do what he or she wants to do. Adult efforts to control children may convince them of the value of power, thereby giving them added determination to strike back with stronger methods. Children who have power as their major goal may attempt to provoke teachers and parents into a struggle for power. For example, children may respond to their parents that they are not going to bed at the time specified. In turn, the parents attempt to show that they have more power than the children and will, therefore, make the children go to bed. What ensues, then, is a fight between parent and child. The child has succeeded in his or her goal by getting the parents involved in a power struggle.

Third, children may misbehave to gain revenge, to hurt others because they themselves feel hurt and abused. Here children secure a place for themselves in the group by making others hate them. Having exhausted other means, their victory comes from being considered vicious by others.

Fourth, children may feign deficiency in order to avoid situations that demand that they perform tasks or function as a member of society. Children who hide behind a display of real or imagined inferiority are usually so discouraged that they anticipate only defeat and failure. Their behavior is guided by the belief that further participation will only result in more humiliating and embarrassing experiences.

Techniques and Principles of Counseling Children

Counselors who use the teleoanalytic approach believe that the child has become a dysfunctioning person as a result of mistaken approaches to finding his or her place in the group. As a result, one of the goals of counseling children in groups is to give them an opportunity to experience new social interaction patterns and experiences. By being presented with alternative social interaction patterns, children become aware of the way they approach life tasks.

Group counseling with children follows essentially the same four phases described earlier. In the case of working with children, however, counselors must be able to recognize certain principles which foster healthy development of the child. Two of these principles are: encouragement, and the law of natural consequences.

Moreover, teleoanalytic group counseling addresses itself to the "immediate goals, the changes in the child's immediate behavior, and the motivation that brings about the changes (Sonstegard and Dreikurs, 1973, p. 54)." Even though a child's actions are congruent with immediate goals, she or he is not aware of these goals.

Observation of the Child   Observation of the child is extremely important in teleoanalytic group counseling. Generally speaking, observation is designed for prescriptive rather than diagnostic purposes (Dinkmeyer and Dreikurs, 1963). During the observation period, the counselor must:

1. Understand the subjective field in which the child's behavior occurs. To achieve this end, the counselor must see the situation through the eyes of the child.

2. Look for the child's purposes and the goals of the child's actions.

3. Record and observe all related behavior, since every movement of the child is believed to have meaning.

4. Recognize that the child's behavior is a creative act designed to help the child find a place in life.

5. Look for recurring patterns of behavior under different situations.

6. Be aware of the child's stage of development.

Counselor observation of children in either a classroom or in a group counseling situation may reveal that some children only participate when they feel they are the leaders in a group situation (active-constructive attention-getting mechanism). Other children will obtain the leader's attention by being silent within the group—passive-constructive attention-getting mechanism. Conversely, the group monopolizer may use the technique of talking to gain group members' attention. Group monopolizers may become anxious when attention shifts to another member. In essence, the monopolizer is a recognition-seeker who tries to maintain a place in the center of the group. According to Dinkmeyer and Muro (1971), monopolists are often not aware of their behavior and may actually feel that they are behaving correctly.

Hostile group members may be those whose goal is to engage the counselor in a contest of power or to seek revenge for their feelings of being hurt, let down, or abandoned by a person whose love and acceptance they wanted. Hostile group members tend to be sullen and defiant. They often seek open confrontation with the group leader. To work effectively with such children, the counselor must be aware that their goal is to engage the counselor in a power conflict or to vent their hurt feelings.

The child who feigns or displays inadequacy may evidence similar patterns in the classroom and in the group counseling situation. In the classroom situation, discouraged children who are having difficulty in reading, for example, may believe that they cannot compete successfully with other children; therefore, they give up entirely. Their goal is to have the teachers eventually give up on them also. In the group counseling situation, such children may withdraw, display great dependency on other group members, or absent themselves from the group.

The child who withdraws from the group presents an obvious challenge to both the group and the counselor for them to demonstrate their care and concern by trying to bring him or her into the group. For instance, such children may place their chairs apart from the group or sit in a manner which creates physical barriers between themselves and the group members. In many instances, such children are waiting for the group counselor and members to ask them to become a part of and to contribute to the group.

Another method children may use to get special attention is to absent themselves from the group. Children may use absence as a means of testing the limits of acceptance in the group and to determine their status within it. The absent members may expect and want other group members to inquire about their whereabouts.

Special attention or service may also be attained by children acting dependently in the counseling group. In both the classroom and the counseling group, dependent children operate from a position of either feigned or perceived weakness. Dependent children look for someone to show them what they want, how they desire it, and, in general, the why of everything in order to solve their problem. In the group context, such individuals tend to treat others as experts and view others as the only means of assistance available. According to Ohlsen (1970), dependent children have had their dependent behaviors reinforced by significant others who needed to have someone dependent upon them; hence, during the process of growing up, they did not learn how to behave independently. In group counseling, dependent children attempt to get others to take control and hence do not have to face the anxiety which may accompany being independent. These children become the clinging vines of both their teachers and their counselors. To help overly dependent children, the counselor must encourage and reinforce their independent actions within the group and place them in meaningful choice-making situations.

It is important that the group counselor learn how to observe his or her own emotional response to children's disturbing behavior (Dreikurs, 1968). Such an observation will not only provide clues to children's goals but also give the counselor some measure of self-understanding. Dreikurs (1968, p. 47) maintains that "it is good policy not to do what the child expects; this means not to follow one's first impulse, but to do the opposite." This statement is based on the belief that the counselor's first impulse would most likely satisfy the child's achievement of a mistaken goal. Instead, the counselor must up-end the client's expectations.

Observation of the child using the teleoanalytic method occurs within and outside of the counseling group. The counselor looks for mistaken goals and recurring patterns within the child's behavior. The counselor is sometimes encouraged to check his or her views with parents and teachers. Likewise, the counselor observes his or her own behavior in response to the child's action or the four goals of the misbehaving child. The counselor is sensitive to the child's expectations of an encounter. Up-ending of the client's expectations takes place as the counselor is careful not to respond in the characteristic manner the child expects.

Encouragement: Principle and Technique   Encouragement is both a principle and a technique which pervades all of teleoanalytic group counseling; however, it is especially important when working with children in groups. It is viewed as a basic requirement for corrective group counseling of children.

Adlerians maintain that encouragement is necessary for children's healthy development. Children become what they are encouraged to become (Dinkmeyer and Dreikurs, 1963). The counselor uses encouragement in group counseling when he or she expresses faith and belief in the child and translates such feelings to the child. Throughout the process of child counseling, the counselor should encourage the child and convey a feeling of anticipated success rather than failure. Dinkmeyer and Dreikurs (1963) suggest that the encouraging counselor:

1. Values the child as is.

2. Demonstrates faith in the child.

3. Tries to build the child's self-concept.

4. Gives the child recognition for his or her efforts.

5. Uses the group to promote the child's development.

6. Concentrates on the strengths and assets of the child.

Because group counseling with children should emphasize encouragement, teleoanalytic group counselors are less concerned with why a child misbehaves than with the purpose of the child's misbehavior. Moreover, teleoanalysts assert that references to the past may be pointless to the child. Likewise, references to a child's jealousy, insecurity, lack of self-confidence, feelings of being dominated or neglected, and feelings of self-pity may only discourage a child further. Conversely, children respond much more positively when they are made aware of what they want in the present: that is, to obtain attention, to show power, to obtain revenge, or to get special service or consideration. Interpretation with children is usually concerned solely with the child's present attitudes and immediate purposes.

Moreover, the counselor's telling children that they could perform so much better, that they could be so nice "if only . . ." frequently conveys clearly to children that they are not nice, that it is their fault that they are not doing better. Adlerians do not consider such statements as examples of encouragement but rather as instances of possible discouragement to the child (Dreikurs, 1968).

The process of encouragement may perhaps be better understood by examining the Adlerian concept of security and courage. From the Adlerian perspective, security is something a child obtains from somewhere or something—or fails to secure. Conversely, courage is something the child has inside; the child cannot get it from outside forces, even though the environment may foster or hinder its development. Counselors must recognize, then, that children must be helped to develop their own courage to cope with life.

Law and Technique of Natural Consequences   The concept of natural consequences is a basic principle of teleoanalytic group counseling (Dreikurs, 1968). Briefly, natural consequences are used to denote a logical and immediate result of a child's transgression that is not imposed on him or her by any authority other than the situation itself. In other words, the counselor does not attempt to delineate or outline to a child the consequences of his or her actions. Instead, the counselor works to help the child understand the effect of his or her behavior on others by a stance of noninterference. The situation itself and reality factors will convey to the child the impact of his or her actions. In such instances, the counselor assumes the role of the friendly bystander, that is, one who is willing to help the child understand the impact of behavior, but, nevertheless, one who does not preach or moralize to the child. Natural consequences reflect the power of the existing social order rather than that of an individual person in the role of the group leader. It suggests that a child learns and corrects maladaptive behavior not by punishment but rather by allowing the situation to take care of itself.

A counselor who uses natural consequences does not try to force the child to do anything. Rather, the counselor allows the child to find out the effects of his or her actions on others. For example, a child may have been referred to the counselor because of repeated lateness to school. Instead of preaching the virtues of punctuality in the group counseling situation, the counselor gives the child the opportunity to find out how other group members respond to lateness. The group member who is late to group counseling sessions soon finds out that he or she is at a disadvantage. The group member who attempts to monopolize the group counseling situation soon finds out that fellow group participants respond negatively.

Adlerian Family Counseling

In recent years, the Adlerian approach to family counseling has received much attention. As with the Adlerian method of counseling children, a great deal of the work in this area has been done by Dreikurs and his associates. Central to Dreikurs' approach to family counseling is the use of group techniques to teach and to counsel parents on how to get along with their children and spouses.

Underlying Philosophy   The foundation for the Adlerian approach to family counseling is found in Adler's basic philosophical assumptions: people are fundamentally social beings; as such, they try to find their places in society by becoming members of groups, and all people are motivated by social interests. It is their social nature that distinguishes them from other animals. All human problems are, therefore, of a social nature. An individual who has not developed sufficient social interest—meaning the ability to participate in and willingness to contribute to groups—is likely to experience social maladjustment. The individual who believes in his or her own inadequacy or inferiority is inclined to seek compensations for such feelings within the family.

Adlerian philosophy emphasizes the equality of individuals in terms of basic human rights. Children, as well as adults, have rights that should not be denied them. For instance, each person within a family has the right to be respected. The family, then, is a network of cooperative social relationships. Within this network or enterprise, each individual must assume responsibility in helping the family to accomplish its group goals. Finally, the behavior of each member of a family is goal-directed. To understand why one family member behaves the way he or she does toward another family member, one must know the former's goals.

Conflict Within the Family   According to Dreikurs (1967), the basic cause of conflict within a family is a disturbed human relationship. It is not in laws, financial difficulty, sexual incompatibility, or a difference in interests or temperament. These are the convenient reasons to which people cling to explain their problems in adjusting to family life. They provide a kind of smokescreen to conceal the real source of conflict, which is a faulty equilibrium in the social relationships between the members of a family. In Dreikurs' (1967) opinion, the commonly given reasons for family strife are only test situations. That is, in-laws, financial hardships, and misbehaviors of children merely "test the solidity of the existing relationship between husband and wife, between parents and children (p. 248)."

To a certain extent, all families tend to have their own set of problems. What makes a problem destructive depends upon the individual family member's perception of its gravity. It is the attitude of an individual toward a family problem, and not the actual nature of the problem, that makes it seem destructive. For example, while some family members may see financial difficulties as a rallying point, other families may perceive the same problem as the cause of family disintegration. The attitudes of family members toward their problems are determined by the kinds of relationships members have established with each other. In families with poor social relationships, small problems mushroom into major ones.

Family relationships based on mutual respect, confidence, and cooperation tend to reduce conflict. Families that operate on democratic principles are inclined to have fewer problems. For example, Dreikurs (1967) postulates that the traditional unequal relationships of husband and wife and of parents and children are doomed to create strife in a society that espouses democratic rights for all individuals. Partial support for this position is seen in the current women's movement and the rebellion of youth. Today, women seem less willing to accept the role of the inferior sex. Men who attempt to live their lives according to the masculine pattern of the past are finding it ever more difficult to get along with wives who protest the continuation of the pattern of masculine superiority.

Relationships built upon the inferiority of any family member tend to produce disharmony, since feelings of inferiority are often accompanied by destructive competition. When there is a feeling of competition instead of cooperation, agreement among family members on even small issues becomes almost impossible. Each decision becomes a contest for power, a test to see who will be the winner and who will be the loser. This situation exists for husbands and wives as well as for children and their parents.

In keeping with the Adlerian notions of equality and democracy, Dreikurs (1960) maintains that "all mistakes in child-rearing constitute either a violation for the respect of the child or a violation by the parent of his own dignity and self-respect (p. 23)." To correct this situation, Dreikurs and his associates have proposed nonspecific principles for improving family relationships. Some of these principles deal with encouragement, the law of natural consequences, and the comprehension of goals. Briefly, Dreikurs asserts that all individuals within a family need encouragement. A child misbehaves when discouraged and does not believe that she or he can succeed with useful behavior. The law of natural consequences refers to the child's learning the logical and immediate effect of transgression, not by any punishment imposed by an authority but by the situation itself. Parents often may overprotect their children by not letting them learn the natural consequences of their actions. In order for children to function well in society, they must learn to respect reality and order. Finally, parents must try to understand the goal of a child's behavior, for it is the child's goal that guides his or her actions.

Adlerians have also taken a position on the issue of communication within the family as a basis for conflict. According to Dreikurs (1967), "Communication in the contemporary American family has not broken down; it exists, but not always for beneficial purposes (p. 189)." For example, frequently family members use communication to defeat one another. In essence, destructive family relationships may thrive on a communication system that is all too clear and all too open. It is not the breakdown in family communication that is so important to Adlerians, but rather the relationships family members have established with each other that facilitate the process of communication. This is true whether the communication is positive or negative. Real misunderstandings in communication (sometimes labeled as a breakdown in communication) can be easily rectified if the relationship established among family members is a healthy one.

To clarify how communication works in a family, Dreikurs gives the example of a young girl who continued to play with her toys despite the fact that she had heard her mother call her to dinner twice. When a stranger who was observing this interchange asked the young girl why she continued to play, the girl responded, "Oh, Mother hasn't called the third time yet. It's when she screams that I usually go to dinner." Obviously a pattern of communication had been established between them, one that was perhaps more implicit than explicit.

The family "communication problem" is usually a relationship problem. Talk or communications may serve to intensify conflict as well as to reduce it. When this situation occurs, Dreikurs (1967) suggests that "to reestablish language as a means of communication within the family would require the avoidance of talk whenever conflicts arise." This is essential "if words are to be instruments of positive and constructive communication in the service of harmony and peaceful living (pp. 203–4)."

Goal of Counseling   The basic goal of Adlerian family counseling is social adjustment. Social adjustment implies a reorientation in one's family relationship. Such a reorientation does not involve complete personality change. Philosophically, Adlerians tend to maintain that any change in an individual can, in its broadest sense, be viewed as a complete change, since the person who has made even the smallest change is no longer exactly the same person he or she was previously. The fundamental thrust of Adlerian family counseling is to help each involved person to become aware of the disturbed relationship and the concomitant faulty and negative attitudes toward oneself and other family members which tend to support that relationship.

Procedures and Methods of Family Group Counseling   Much of the Adlerian family counseling is conducted in Child Guidance or Family Counseling Centers. Chicago is generally viewed as the headquarters for Adlerian counseling centers, for it was there that Dreikurs (until his death in 1972) worked to train individuals in this approach. The counseling centers are based in part upon Adler's early child guidance centers in Vienna. They are customarily operated on the basis of voluntary financial support from interested citizens, school districts, or universities.

The typical clients of the centers are parents who are having difficulties with their children, although group counseling is also available for couples without children. For the sake of parsimony, however, the focus here will be on family counseling for parents experiencing conflicts with their children. The source of much of what follows is taken from *Adlerian Family Counseling* (1959), a manual for counseling centers edited by Dreikurs, Corsini, Lowe, and Sonstegard.

The procedures for arranging family counseling are relatively free of red tape.

Typically, prospective participants sign an attendance sheet and indicate their interest in family counseling. Individuals are then asked to observe a group counseling session involving two other families. One of the purposes of this procedure is to make individuals aware that other people are also having problems. Thus, from the very beginning, efforts are made to show prospective counselees that their family difficulties are not a reflection of any personal inadequacies on their part. Other objectives for having individuals observe families in group counseling sessions are: (1) They become familiar with Adlerian family group counseling procedures; and (2) They may gain insight into their own problems from listening to cases similar to and different from their own.

After observing a group counseling session involving two other families, one or both parents may ask to enroll in counseling. A preliminary interview is then arranged with a social worker. From this meeting, the social worker prepares a first interview summary. At the conclusion of this session, parents are asked to bring their children to the center for additional interviews.

On the next visit to the center, four things usually occur: (1) Parents and children are interviewed separately by a counselor; (2) The children are taken to a playroom where their behavior is observed and recorded by a worker; (3) The children are interviewed by the counselor; and (4) The counselor meets with parents and playroom observers, and gives recommendations and impressions. It should be noted that the counselor interviews the parents and the children within the context of a group setting including two other families. The purpose of this procedure is to teach parents by having them discuss a problem before a group of their peers who are likewise experiencing difficulties.

The basic position of the Adlerian counselor is that parents come to the center for counseling, not psychotherapy. This means that the counselor deals with the parents' behavior in terms of immediate and specific situations. It is felt that changes in the attitudes of the parents will lead to modifications in their children's behavior. Group counseling of parents involves the four basic steps that were described earlier: (1) establishing a relationship; (2) interpretation; (3) insight; and (4) reorientation of behavior and goals. Although the counselor assumes an active role in all four stages, he or she tends to focus upon interpreting the dynamics of the family situation to the parents and helping them to acquire new methods of resolving conflicts and establishing better family relationships. Also, the child's goals are revealed to the child by the counselor.

The methods for family group counseling are relatively direct. What follows is a brief description of a typical beginning counseling session. Group counseling tends to be an ongoing experience at the centers. New members are usually introduced to the group and then asked to inform group members of their family problems. At this time efforts are made to make the parents feel welcome and to lessen their anxiety. Following the parents' initial statement of their overall family problem, each spouse may be asked to describe an average day in his or her life. For example, a parent might be asked, "What are some of the things that bother you when you get up in the morning?" or "How do the children get along with you?"

In other words, the interview is structured to elicit information regarding the types of relationships parents have with each other and their children. Exploring the family routine not only lessens parents' uneasiness in front of the group but also provides valuable insights as to the goals of family members.

During this part of the counseling session, the counselor usually takes the leading role. The primary technique used here is one of asking questions to uncover the source of the conflict. Group members generally remain silent, observing the interchange between the counselor and the parents. The purpose of this procedure is to have the entire group participate in the learning process.

Near the end of the first part of the group counseling session, the counselor may reveal a tentative hypothesis concerning the new participants' family problems. For the second part of the group session, parents leave the room and the playroom director brings their children into the room. Upon the arrival of the children to the group, the counselor's first task is to try to put them at ease. Children may be asked: "What is your name?" "How are things going in the family?" "Do you know why your mommie and daddy brought you here?" The primary purpose of the interview with the children is to learn what are their goals and their perspective of the problems.

After the children's departure, the parents are called back in. The playroom director also enters the group and gives a report on his or her observation of the children of the couples in question. The major thrust of the report deals with the behavior of the children in the playroom—how they played and interacted with other children. Parents tend to listen to these reports with great interest. The counselor may ask them how the playroom report coincides with their knowledge of their children.

Following the playroom director's report, the counselor begins to try to pull things together by offering tentative hypotheses concerning the reasons for the family's problems. The focus here is upon each family member's goals. Other group members are asked to participate in the discussion and to offer their own ideas concerning how the new family may cope with its problem. At times group members may disagree with the counselor's tentative hypotheses. Such disagreement is usually welcomed, since Adlerians believe that no one individual is the expert in the group—regardless of his or her leadership position.

Group discussion is more than a cathartic experience for members. It is designed to be primarily a learning experience that focuses upon a reorientation in the parents' behavior. In keeping with this goal, group members may offer specific suggestions to each other. They may also reveal how they have met success or failure in dealing with their own particular family problems. Thus, a significant outcome of the group discussion is that members learn that they are not alone in having family problems. From their interaction in the group, participants learn about their own goals and their pattern of social relationships.

If the parents agree, arrangements for follow-up group sessions are made. The procedures for succeeding group counseling sessions are similar to those just described.

UNIQUE FEATURES AND CONTRIBUTIONS
OF THE ADLERIAN METHOD

The Adlerian method of group counseling is characterized by its own unique features and contributions to group counseling. For example, Adlerians were among the first to see and use the benefit of the public forum for group counseling. They demonstrated in both their parent and children groups that group counseling not only could be conducted while others watched (the public forum setting) but also could be beneficial for those who were involved in the group situation. Parents who came to observe group counseling sessions were given the opportunity to observe the process of counseling and to decide for themselves if the Adlerian approach was what they wanted. Moreover, they could learn from observing the behavior of other parents involved in the group. Parents who were involved in counseling groups learned how not to be so conscious of the difficulties they experienced in bringing up their children. Moreover, Adlerians developed a complete system of parent education in child rearing. In this respect, the teleoanalytic school can be said to be one of the forerunners of the current parent effectiveness training schools.

Other contributions also exist. The teleoanalytic method was one of the first major theoretical departures from classical psychoanalysis. Adler stressed the social nature of individual behavior and the importance of social interest and individual goals. People were not conceptualized as prisoners of biological needs and urgings, as Freud has stressed. Instead, within each individual, one could see psychological movement toward certain goals in life.

Adler was one of the first to emphasize the importance of assuming the subjective role of the individual and the importance of a person's perceptions. It was not until the major publications of the writings of Carl Rogers that the individual's phenomenological or perceptual field was elevated to any height of significance. Carl Rogers' emphasis that individuals are self-determining organisms is an affirmation of the position Adler maintained more than twenty years earlier.

In many respects, Adlerians changed significantly the role of both the counselor and the client. Adlerian emphasis on the importance of alignment of client-counselor goals represented a major departure from classical psychoanalysis. Not only was the client seen as capable of defining his or her own goals in entering the therapeutic process but also the alignment of client-counselor goals was seen as pivotal in establishing a positive counseling relationship. Behaviorists and transactionalists have picked up on the Adlerian emphasis on goal alignment or contractual arrangements and made this a major feature of their process of helping people in groups. Adlerian emphasis on redirection of client goals has become a focal point of behavioral group counseling.

Adlerians significantly changed the role of the therapist. The role of the counselor as a "blank screen" for transference purposes received considerably less attention. In the teleoanalytic method, both the individual and the group counselor assume an active role in the therapeutic process. Adlerians stressed counselor sincerity and the importance of counselors being themselves—what Carl Rogers later renamed as counselor congruency.

The Adlerian group counselor was not only active but also directive. The counselor constantly challenged the "faulty premises" or mistaken goals upon which the client based his or her life. More recently, Albert Ellis has assumed a similar posture in his group counseling of individuals. Ellis (1962) combines the best of Adler in that he posits that individuals are guided by certain irrational ideas or motives—for example, the desire to be liked by everyone. The irrational ideas or motives which Ellis describes are remarkably similar to the mistaken goals or "faulty premises" that Adler delineated both in people in general and the disturbed or misbehaving child in particular. Similar to Adlerians, Ellis maintains that the process of counseling must deal with uncovering, interpreting, and changing an individual's irrational thoughts and faulty premises regarding life. In both the teleoanalytic and the rational-emotive approach to group counseling the leader has no peer; through the help of others, the counselor moves relentlessly to help the client give up faulty premises and change his or her behavior.

The teleoanalytic stress on client responsibility and working with teachers and counselors has been picked up by Glasser (1965) and his reality theory of group counseling. Similar to teleoanalytic group counseling, reality therapy group counseling is geared toward client assumption of responsibility. Moreover, Glasser stresses the Adlerian belief that group counseling is a process of helping an individual to accept the responsibility that he or she should have learned in the "growing-up process" of life. Glasser underscores the teleoanalytic principles that individuals need to feel worthwhile in their own eyes and that their basic motivation is to love and be loved.

Adlerians have made significant contributions in: (1) the concept of personality formation and individual motivation; (2) the roles of the group counselor and client, especially multiple group therapy; (3) the procedures of helping individuals—Family Education Centers and community mental health; and (4) the process by which group counseling is to be conducted.

In short, Adler made a number of contributions in personality development as well as in group counseling, as carried out by Dreikurs and his associates. By stressing an individual's efforts to overcome uncomfortable feelings, he focused needed attention on ego defenses and the adaptive functions of the ego. He was one of the first therapists to take into account character structure and the whole person as the proper province of dynamic group therapy. As with many modern therapists, he emphasized the purposive or intentional aspects of human behavior and existence.

Today, the Adlerian approach to both individual and group counseling has lost much of its uniqueness and appeal. It has been co-opted and subsumed by other group approaches, especially that of client-centered therapy, rational-emotive counseling, and reality therapy. For example, striving for superiority, feelings of inferiority (and the ensuing concept of inferiority complex), encouragement, irrational thoughts, and parent effectiveness training have become an integral part of public psychological knowledge. Despite his contributions to psychology and the group method, Adler has had scant followers outside a narrow band of disciples. Currently, there are few Adlerian training institutes, and the likelihood of there being an Adlerian renaissance does not appear very probable. The contributions of Adler and his disciples have been primarily absorbed or subsumed into the mainstream of the other theoretical schools of personality development and group counseling.

SUMMARY

Neo-Freudians represent a diverse approach to group counseling. Although many neo-Freudians departed in significant ways from Freud, they still retained some of the distinctive features of psychoanalytic group counseling. Emphasis is placed in group counseling on the cultural and social aspects of client maladaptive behavior. Adler was keenly interested in the degree to which the counseling group provided a means to get at the interpersonal and social nature of an individual's difficulties. The Adlerian school of group counseling provided the foundation for the new group approaches to counseling.

References

Adler, A. *Understanding human behavior.* New York: Greenberg, 1927.

Adler, A. *Guiding the child.* New York: Greenberg, 1930.

Adler, A. Individual psychology. In D. Murchison (Ed.), *Psychologies of 1930.* Worcester, MA: Clark University Press, 1930.

Adler, A. *Social interest.* New York: Putnam, 1939.

Ansbacher, H., and R. Ansbacher. *The individual psychology of Alfred Adler.* New York: Basic Books, 1956.

Berne, E. *Principles of group treatment.,* New York: Oxford University Press, 1966.

Brammer, L. M., and E. L. Shostrom. *Therapeutic psychology: Fundamentals of counseling and psychothcrapy* (3rd ed.). Englewood Cliffs, NJ: Prentice-Hall, 1977.

Corsini, R. *Methods of group psychotherapy.* New York: McGraw-Hill, 1957.

Dinkmeyer, D. Group counseling: Theory and techniques. *School Counselor,* 1969, *17,* 150–67.

Dinkmeyer, D. Contributions of teleoanalytic theory and techniques to school counseling. In C. E. Beck (Ed.), *Philosophical guidelines for counseling.* Dubuque, IA: Wm. C. Brown, 1971, 233–37.

Dinkmeyer, D., and R. Dreikurs. *Encouraging children to learn.* Englewood Cliffs, NJ: Prentice-Hall, 1963.

Dinkmeyer, D., and J. Muro. *Group counseling: Theory and practice.* Itasca, IL: Peacock, 1971.

Dreikurs, R. Group psychotherapy from the point of view of Adlerian psychology. *International Journal of Group Psychotherapy,* 1957, *7,* 363–75.

Dreikurs, R. *Group psychotherapy and group approaches: The collected papers of Rudolf Dreikurs.* The Alfred Adler Institute of Chicago, 1960.

Dreikurs, R. *Psychodynamics, psychotherapy, and counseling.* The Alfred Adler Institute of Chicago, 1967.

Dreikurs, R. *Psychology in the classroom* (2nd ed.). New York: Harper & Row, 1968.

Dreikurs, R., R. Corsini, R. Lowe, and M. Sonstegard (Eds.). *Adlerian family counseling: A manual for counseling centers.* Eugene, OR: Oregon University Press, 1959.

Dreikurs, R., and M. Sonstegard. Rationale of group counseling. In D. C. Dinkmeyer (Ed.), *Guidance and counseling in the elementary school: Readings in theory and practice.* New York: Holt, Rinehart, 1968.

Durkin, H. E. *The group in depth.* New York: International Universities Press, 1964.

Ellis, A. *Reason and emotion in psychotherapy.* New York: Lyle Stuart, 1962.

Ford, D. H., and H. B. Urban. *Systems of psychotherapy: A comparative study.* New York: Wiley, 1963.

Glasser, W. *Reality therapy: A new approach to psychiatry.* New York: Harper & Row, 1965.

Goldman, G. D. Some applications of Harry Stack Sullivan's theories to group psychotherapy. *International Journal of Group Psychotherapy,* 1957, *7,* 385–91.

Grunewald, B. The application of Adlerian principles in a classroom. *The American Journal of Individual Psychology,* 1955, *2.*

Ohlsen, M. M. *Group counseling.* New York: Holt, Rinehart and Winston, 1970.

Rogers, C. R. *On becoming a person: A therapist's view of psychotherapy.* Boston: Houghton Mifflin, 1961.

Sonstegard, M., and R. Dreikurs. The Adlerian approach to group counseling of children. In M. M. Ohlsen (Ed.), *Counseling children in groups.* New York: Holt, Rinehart and Winston, 1973, 47–78.

Yalom, J. D. *The theory and practice of group psychotherapy* (2nd ed.). New York: Basic Books, 1975.

4
T-Groups and the Laboratory Approach to Sensitivity Training

The T-group represents the beginning of a new era in the small group experience. It symbolizes recent attempts to create a hybrid between psychotherapy and sociotherapy in order to deal with problems in human living. Almost equally important, however, the T-group represents the turning point of American interest toward working in small groups to solve problems. It provided a means by which the broad American public could become involved in learning how people function in groups, without the added stigma or negative connotation that they are in need of psychological help. Since their initiation, T-groups have commanded a significant amount of attention in group literature; they have been widely accepted and used by people and organizations of varying backgrounds to deal with factors that promote or hinder human relationships; and, finally, they have fathered a number of other group methods—notably sensitivity training, encounter, and personal growth groups.

All approaches to group work have their founders. Although the initial conceptualization and the development of the T-group was the work of four men (Kurt Lewin and Ronald Lippitt, social psychologists; and Leland Bradford and Kenneth Benno, educators), Kurt Lewin is seen as the single most significant figure in the development of this group type. He was one of the original founders of the model, and T-group methodology was, and still is to some extent, based on strong Lewinian concepts of group dynamics and action research (Marrow, 1969).

Although from the very beginning the T-group was practical in orientation, it had the strong theoretical background of Kurt Lewin to support it. The practical side of the T-group is its goal of producing social change. In some respects, one can say that this goal was not a decidedly new one for American people; it grew out of a climate of social concern that began to crystallize during the first half of the 20th century. Prior to the development of the T-group, for example, a number of events had taken place that indicated American society was moving in the direction of social reformulation. During the 1920s social scientists investigated "natural groups" in society. Their strong conviction was that many of the answers to social problems could be found by studying the social interactions and normal formations of these groups. From the work of some social scientists, the field of social work began to organize groups to deal with the problems of those times.

In the 1930s, John Dewey spearheaded a widespread effort to apply principles of social psychology to the classroom under the name of progressive education. Kurt Lewin, likewise, added his support to the movement with his now famous field theory and his concomitant emphasis on action research as a means to social change. Lewin's goal was to establish an academic and community task force that would not only further small group psychology but would also deal with the notion of social change. From his effort to establish this force came the development of the T-group and laboratory method as a community enterprise. Although the T-group has since taken many different courses of direction, its first mission was to construct ways in which the small-group experience could be used to teach individuals to better understand how the democratic group process could be applied to community group action. In short the emphasis was upon training groups for social action.

Since the time of Kurt Lewin, the T-group has fared fairly well. It has broadened its outlook and scope to include goals of individual and organizational change. It has also been the major setting for sensitivity training. None of this expansion has been without attendant growing pains and criticism from both the professional and public sectors.

Recently (within the last five or ten years), the terms T-group and sensitivity group have been used interchangeably, probably because the original distinctions between these two group types have become blurred. The T-group is best known as a method of laboratory training in groups. As more people became involved in T-groups, the emphasis shifted to sensitivity training, that is, to helping group members better understand themselves and others. [Further discussion of the differences between T-groups and sensitivity groups appears later in this chapter.]

Discussion has also centered around the differences between T-groups and group counseling, particularly as the latter is practiced in the schools. Ohlsen (1970a) indicates that there are both distinct differences and some similarities between group counseling and T-groups. He defines group counseling as a "therapeutic experience for persons who do not have serious emotional problems (p. 6)." According to Ohlsen, T-groups share much in common with counseling groups. In addition to using reinforcement and feedback as teaching tools, both group approaches also "focus members' attention on the here and now, changing their behavior, and both use role playing to help members learn to cope with specific situations and persons (pp. 7–8)." There are, however, some important differences between these two types of groups. T-groups are usually less carefully constructed than counseling groups; T-group leaders are inclined to direct more attention to the analysis of interactions among members, the study of group process, the examination of group effectiveness, and the achievement of insight.

Moreover, in contrast to group counseling, T-groups tend to emphasize confrontation and interpretation of behavior. Counseling groups, on the other hand, focus upon empathy and support for group members while they are expressing their feelings, planning a course of action, and implementing it (Ohlsen, 1970). Another significant difference between these two group types revolves around time. In T-group approaches, participants tend to meet in concentrated blocks of time—ten to fourteen hours as in a marathon group or over a period of several weeks for fewer hours of time. Counseling groups in the schools tend to have shorter meeting periods that are spread out over a longer time span.

If one uses Ohlsen's model as a guide, it seems evident that a T-group is not an alternate form for group counseling. Hence, the rationale for including this group approach in the book is simply that some of the principles underlying T-groups may be used in group counseling. That is to say, from studying the T-group the counselor may learn much about group interaction.

This chapter contains a discussion of the historical development of T-groups and the laboratory approach to sensitivity training. An effort is made to distinguish between T-groups and sensitivity groups. Emphasis is placed upon the key concepts of the T-group, its goals, its membership and leadership roles, and related research.

SOME DEFINITIONS

It is easier to experience a T-group than to define succinctly what it is. One might also observe that most attempts to define the T-group turn out to be descriptions of some of the goals of this group type. The T-group is best known for its introduction of the laboratory training method in group work. Therefore, three words seem crucial to understanding the T-group as it was originally constructed. These words are *educational training laboratory*.

The word *education* carries a special connotation in the T-group approach. One of Lewin's goals was to provide a new kind of educational experience as a result of one's participation in a group. As noted previously, he was mainly concerned that people would learn about the progress of democratic group formation for social change. Although the title T-group was never used by Lewin (this appellation came into being after his death), it seems clear that he agreed with many of its early principles. The T-group was to be more than a gripe session for individuals; it was designed to be a true educational experience from which participants would learn more about themselves and group dynamics.

The use of the words *laboratory training* is also essential to an understanding of the T-group. Golembiewski and Blumberg (1970) indicate that the T-group may be considered a laboratory in the following ways: (1) It attempts to create a miniature society; (2) It is geared toward working with processes that emphasize inquiry, exploration, and experimentation with behavior; (3) It is oriented toward assisting its members to learn; (4) It stresses developing a psychologically safe atmosphere to facilitate learning; and (5) Group members determine what is to be learned, even though a trainer is usually available for guidance. Summarizing some of these basic concepts, Bradford et al. (1964) define the T-group in the following manner:

> A T-group is a relatively unstructured group in which individuals participate as learners. The data for learning are not outside these individuals or remote from their immediate experience within the T-groups. The data are the transactions among members, their own behavior in the group, as they struggle to create a productive and viable organization, a miniature society (p. 1).

One of the assumptions of T-group training is that participants will become responsible for their own learning. This is a marked departure from the usual meaning of education and learning. What one learns is oftentimes a result of an individual's personal approach to the group and the types of relationships he or she establishes with others during the process of the group. T-group theory is founded upon the premise that learning is a combination of conceptualization and experience, and that individuals learn more freely and easily when they establish authentic relationships with others.

Defining sensitivity training is even more difficult than defining a T-group. There have been few efforts to even separate in any kind of meaningful manner these two group approaches.

As noted earlier, at one time these were distinct, mutually exclusive areas, but now sensitivity training has become a catchall term for almost any group concerned with human relations or personal growth. The use of standardized nomenclature to describe different group approaches would eliminate some confusion concerning the differences between these two group types.

Although few distinctions are made in the literature, this does not necessarily mean that there are no differences between T-groups and sensitivity training. Certainly, not all sensitivity training involves T-group procedures—specifically the procedure of using the transactions of group members to examine the group process. It may come down to a matter of goals. According to Egan (1970), sensitivity training is only a species of laboratory training. That is, sensitivity training is a particular kind of laboratory training "in which personal and interpersonal issues are the direct focus of the group (p. 10)." Even though this distinction is considered by most writers to be a subtle one, it does, in part, point out the major difference between these two group approaches. In the T-group, for example, goals are broader, such as "learning about group process and developing skills for diagnosing group and organizational behavior (Egan, 1970, p. 10)." These goals exist in sensitivity groups, but the focus is not primarily placed upon them. In most sensitivity groups, learning about group process or dynamics for group change is usually only incidental. A sensitivity group, then, usually has as its primary and sometimes only goal, individual personal growth. In a T-group, the personal growth that results is seen as an outgrowth of the total group's working on a particular task it has designed for itself. Partial support for this position is given by Seashore (1970), who maintains that the T-group is the primary setting for sensitivity training.

In sensitivity there has been a consistent trend toward deemphasizing the study of group process and an increasing emphasis on enhanced personal insight. Sensitivity training has come to embody for some individuals psychotherapy for normals (Weschler et al., 1962). Shepard (1964) has described the departure from T-group goals as having the following impact: "Implicit recognition that individual development was the lasting consequence of training led to increased focus on individual dynamics. Group level interventions were replaced by more personal interventions . . . and, in recent years, personal feedback has seemed to be the most important feature of the T-group (p. 380)."

HISTORICAL OBSERVATIONS

It is difficult to separate the historical events that led to T-groups and the laboratory approach to sensitivity training, partly because both were either direct or indirect outcomes of the 1946 Connecticut Workshop, and partly because the term sensitivity training was and is still now used interchangeably with T-groups. The situation is further complicated by the fact that most historical accounts of the evolution of these two approaches tend to dismiss such differences as meaningless or generally do not make any sharp distinctions between them. Even Benne's (1964) thorough and excellent review of the history of T-groups does not completely clarify how the two came to be used synonymously. It is left to the reader to infer whatever historical differences existed between the two approaches.

Birthplace of the T-Group

New Britain Teachers College in Connecticut is generally credited as the birthplace of the concepts that were later to embody the T-group movement (Benne, 1964). Although some earlier ideas provided a partial foundation for the T-group movement, it was the immediate impact of the Connecticut Workshop of 1946 that signaled the modern beginnings of the T-group movement.

What was the Connecticut Workshop, and why did it so profoundly affect the development of the T-group? It was designed and initiated for essentially practical reasons. None of its leading figures had any grandiose ideas of revolutionizing the existing group approaches to solving problems. The Workshop's purpose was to assist Frank Simpson, the executive director of the Connecticut Interracial Commission, to implement that state's new Fair Employment Practices Act. It was felt that by training community leaders and citizens of varying backgrounds—businessmon, labor leaders, and teachers—to learn how to work with intergroup tensions and to change racial attitudes, compliance with the Fair Employment Practices Act could be handled more smoothly. Kurt Lewin was to assume a major role in this work.

There were three sponsors to the Workshop: (1) the Connecticut Interracial Commission, (2) the Connecticut Department of Education, and (3) the Massachusetts Institute of Technology (M.I.T.) Research Center for Group Dynamics. At that time, Kurt Lewin was the director of M.I.T.'s new Research Center for Group Dynamics. He was given the important job of selecting group leaders to assist in the training enterprise. More importantly, however, Lewin's international reputation in the field of group dynamics made him a focal point. All eyes looked to him to make the conference work. Lewin selected as his training group leaders Kenneth D. Benne and Leland P. Bradford, both with backgrounds in adult education, and Ronald Lippitt, a social psychologist. Although these men were to become national leaders in the T-group movement, it was Kurt Lewin who became known as the father of the T-group—T symbolizing training in "educationally focused" group experiences.

At the outset, the format of the conference was relatively simple. Small groups of ten members each were established to conduct group discussions, generally centering around compliance with the Fair Employment Practices Act. Increasingly, group members related experiences that interfered with their compliance with the provisions of the act. Part of the task of the rest of the group members was to assist their peers who were experiencing problems to develop alternative solutions. Role-playing techniques were used to help individual group members diagnose problems.

Since Lewin operated on the principle of "no research without action, and no action without research (Marrow, 1969, p. 193)," a research observer was assigned to each of the small-group sessions held during the day. The task of the observer was to record and to code behavioral interactions that took place during the small-group meetings. Evening sessions were restricted to group leaders and recorders for the purpose of analyzing what happened in each of the small-group sessions.

The Accident

The real breakthrough for T-groups occurred almost by accident—when several group participants who had free time during the evenings and who had expressed an interest in the closed evening staff sessions requested permission to attend. At first, the nonstaff group members were only outside observers, listening to the perceptions of staff members concerning what had taken place in the small-group sessions. Such passivity did not last too long. As striking differences of opinion occurred between staff and group members regarding what had actually happened in the small-group discussions, heated interchanges ricocheted throughout the room.

Recognizing the potential benefit of this powerful interchange of differential perceptions among staff and group participants, Lewin, who had been initially apprehensive about group members attending the evening staff sessions, became quite excited. A new dimension in group dynamics began to unfold. Gradually, the word spread to other group participants, until all involved were attending the evening sessions.

It was no small coincidence that Lewin, coming from the engineering influences at M.I.T., borrowed that school's term of *feedback* to formulate tentative hypotheses concerning what was happening during the mixed evening sessions. For the first time group leaders, research recorders, and group participants were sharing their perceptions of each other's behavior in the small-group setting. Not having a crystal ball, no one at this time knew quite what to do with all the information gleaned from the mixed group meetings. There was general recognition, however, of the importance of feedback pertaining to how one's behavior in a group is perceived by others and what the possible educational benefits of such learnings might be. In the past, Lewin had kept separate the variables of group members' task activities and the data that researchers gathered on how group processes were affecting the functioning of the group. Now, the possibility of combining the two opened up new prospects for research and learning.

Hence, what was initially designed as human relations training in interracial matters became a much broader phenomenon. The basic problem facing Lewin, Benne, Bradford, and Lippitt was how to integrate the "back-home" content (meaning the particular task of the group) of the small-group discussion with an analysis of here-and-now data regarding the members' behavior. It was from this point on that the small-group sessions assumed the characteristics of an educational laboratory experience.

Kurt Lewin, who had provided the basic conceptual framework for what was later labeled the T-group, died in 1947. It was left up to others to implement some of his ideas. As a result of the Connecticut Workshop, another summer session of three weeks' duration was planned at Gould Academy in Bethel, Maine in 1947 to incorporate the new learnings.

Bethel, Maine: Beginnings of Sensitivity Training

With the legacy Lewin had provided, Benne, Bradford, and Lippitt, as well as a number of other individuals, planned the 1947 session. Of prime importance was the Basic Skills Training (BST) Group. The Basic Skills Training Group was a small continuing group for which an anecdotal observer was assigned to make observational data available for discussion and analysis. One of the responsibilities of the training leader was to help the group to analyze and evaluate the observational data gathered, in addition to the data coming from members and the training leader. Some of the expectations of the BST Group were as follows: (1) It would help members internalize different concepts; (2) It would give members practice in developing diagnostic and action skills of the change agent; (3) It would help participants to develop strategies for applying laboratory learnings to back-home situations; (4) It would give members a clearer understanding of democratic values; (5) It would deal with personal and interpersonal development; and (6) It would help members to acquire trainer skills. The immediate descendant of the BST Group is the T-group.

From Benne's (1964) description of the goals of the BST Group, one can well understand the present confusion over what is a T-group and what constitutes sensitivity training. For example, Benne states that one of the first objectives of the BST Group was to "sensitize" its delegates to the relationship between the growth of a group and the growth of individuals within a group. In further delineating the signs of group growth, Benne again uses the word sensitivity in different contexts. For instance, he alludes to the goals of intercommunication and semantic sensitivity and suggests that some of the responsibilities of group members are to display a sensitivity to the contribution of each member as well as to accept and to share leadership functions in a group.

That the BST Group was overloaded with learning objectives is an understatement. At the end of the summer session in Bethel, Maine (a town whose name subsequently came to be used synonymously with laboratory training), polarities had begun to develop among group participants. While some individuals wanted to focus upon discussing outside case materials, others wanted to discuss only the here-and-now happenings that stressed personal, interpersonal, and group-level materials. One can interpret this behavior as a beginning confrontation between individuals oriented more toward sensitivity groups and those persons more T-group oriented, with the latter emphasizing that the purpose of the group was to serve as a means for learning how to encourage planned changes in social systems.

The Schism

Benne (1964) outlines two basic periods in T-group evolution: 1949–1955, and 1956–1964. Within these two periods, one finds a schism between T-groups and sensitivity groups. From 1949 to 1955, an era of experimentation is evident. Those dedicated to the T-group method attempted to make a distinction between what comprises T-group and non-T-group activities. From 1956 to 1964, efforts are channeled more directly to reestablishing and reformulating T-group experiences into laboratory training.

Benne labels the first period as the "separation of 'extraneous' training functions" from the T-group. The extraneous material he refers to during this period may be largely attributed to the new training leaders introduced from the fields of psychiatry and clinical psychology. Prior to 1949, the staff of T-group trainers consisted mainly of representatives from social psychology, education, and sociology. Those individuals, who were called the "old-timers," represented the Lewinian approach to staff development and planning.

In 1949, individuals who were more clinically oriented were invited to join the staff. It was felt they could contribute to the development of a clinical model of training that could be used in conjunction with action research. The "newcomers" maintained either Freudian or Rogerian outlooks on behavioral change. With all the ingredients for a genuine conflict of interest present, the old-timers, specifically Benne, Bradford, and Lippitt, were deposed from direct leadership of the BST Group. In 1950, the BST Group was renamed the T-group.

After 1950, the objectives of the T-group underwent a type of metamorphosis. No longer was the major emphasis placed upon the Lewinian change-agents concepts in organizational and community structures. The interpersonal process of group development was the central issue. This is the period in which T-groups become essentially sensitivity groups. Here is another reason that these two group approaches are presently linked so inextricably in current literature.

As the polarities of interest evolved in the laboratory method, the BST Group was divided into two separate groups: 1) T-groups, which stressed learning about small-group dynamics and interpersonal styles of group behavior from analyzing each group's unique behavior; and 2) action (A) groups, which concentrated on the sociological approach to strategies of social action and change in large social systems. The action groups also used a traditional teaching method, with lecture-like presentations and group discussions of reading and didactic material. In reformulating what occurred, one might say that T-groups (with their emphasis on interpersonal issues) became more akin to sensitivity groups, and action groups resembled more closely the original design of the T-group as conceptualized by Lewin, Benne, Bradford, and Lippitt.

However, the sensitivity approach to T-groups proved to be such a powerful attraction to the majority of the training participants that this style of group work tended to have a carry-over effect into the A-groups. With pressure from the participants to deal with more sensitivity-related material, these groups subsequently became quite similar in format. This duplication of efforts led to the abandonment of A-groups in 1950.

The clash between sensitivity-oriented T-groups and action-oriented T-groups is revealed in the types of roles group leaders assumed. Those who were firmly entrenched in the Lewinian tradition of cooperative inquiry and action research saw their function as assisting group members in getting relevant, validated data into their discussions. Lewinian type trainers were "memberlike." They tended to express their feelings openly and participate within the group. Their dual membership in the small-group discussions and the staff group tended, however, to limit their types of group interactions.

In contrast, the psychoanalytic leader, for example, concentrated on examining sources of distortion in the data reviewed by the small group. The psychoanalytic leader functioned much like a "projection screen" for group members and was inclined not to divulge his or her true feelings. From the projections of member feelings upon her or him, the leader was able to demonstrate how members tended to distort data. For example, group members might be inclined to distort data because they were responding to the leader as they would a parent. In this case, unfinished business of the past interfered with the communication process. Psychoanalytic trainers did not become members of their group.

Reparation

In 1956, a concerted effort was made to reintegrate the T-group into the laboratory design. To accomplish this task, the schism that had come about as a result of the ineffectual separation of T-group from A-group experiences had to be repaired. A major decision had to be made as to whether the T-group was or was not a therapy group.

After seventeen years of a rather intermittently stormy evolution, the T-group had come to have the following characteristics: 1) focus upon here-and-now behavioral events; 2) observer-participant role of each group member; and 3) confrontation of members in order to bring about greater interpretive feelings and behavior on the part of group participants.

In the 1960s, two basic variations of the T-group existed: 1) the T-group as therapy for normal individuals; and 2) the instrumented T-group wherein individuals were confronted with a "dilemma" they had to remove. Variation 1 (the T-group as therapy for normals) was basically a sensitivity group. As the developers and proponents of the sensitivity model, Robert Tannenbaum, Irving Weschler, and Fred Massarik acknowledged (1961) that major similarities existed between their model of sensitivity training and other forms of group psychotherapy. The authors pointed out that sensitivity training is similar to group psychotherapy insofar as it shares the common objective of ego strengthening and improvement of the self-image. They explained that both approaches emphasize the development of insights and opportunities for reality testing in the group situation, and that both concentrated on examining an individual's life values and on replacing the ineffectual modes of behavior with more adaptive ones.

From a review of the literature, it seems relatively safe to say that T-groups and sensitivity training evolved almost concurrently, but that there existed from the very beginning a predominant emphasis on the T-group. The mix-up seems to have centered around the somewhat unbalanced symbiotic relationship of the two; specifically, one of the primary goals of the T-group as it developed through the years was greater sensitization of its group members to human relations. Although this was only one of the goals of T-groups, some individuals came to see it as the essence of the T-group movement.

The T-group, in its strictest sense, is a reformulation of the Lewinian model of action-oriented research. This model emphasizes that group participants are supposed to learn how to analyze, collect, and interpret data relevant to themselves and to the group. The T-group is basically a task-oriented group, even though throughout the years of its development it has gradually incorporated some aspects of human relations training. Yet the approach toward human relations is quite different from that of sensitivity groups. Sensitivity training is a direct descendant of the clinical approach to T-groups. While the T-group is more task-oriented, the sensitivity group is more process-oriented.

Differences Between the T-Group and the Sensitivity Model

Benne (1964) outlines three major differences between the T-group (action research model) and the clinical or sensitivity training model. The first difference deals with the type of data considered important in the group. He suggests that whereas the clinical model (renamed sensitivity model) addresses itself to problems that arise from existential encounters among group participants and between group members and leaders, the T-group or action research model makes the assumption that significant data for group inquiry can be gathered ahead of time. One does not have to wait for or rely solely on spontaneous encounters. The most important data for sensitivity groups emanates from gut level experiences of group members. On the other hand, the T-group uses the feeling level of experience as well as instruments for data gathering. These instruments do not have to be developed as the group organizes itself for action to resolve its difficulties. They may be planned in advance. In short, the sensitivity model emphasizes the collection of qualitative data only; the action research T-group model seeks both qualitative and quantitative data.

Secondly, there is the difference between outside and inside information. The action research T-group model frequently employs concepts and related skills that may arise outside of the group proper. Theory sessions may be incorporated into the action research T-group model. Conversely, the clinical or sensitivity training model restricts itself to feelings and materials that occur within the group. Proponents of this approach are inclined to view the use of outside data as fostering greater intellectualization among group members.

The third difference deals with the underlying assumptions concerning the transference of knowledge learned in the group situation. Although one of the desired outcomes of both groups is greater or better interpersonal functionings in outside associations, more importance is attached to personal growth in authentic relationships in the sensitivity group as compared with the T-group. The fundamental premise of the T-group is that as one acquires the rudiments of appropriate theory building and concepts and skills in clarifying problems in both the interpersonal and intergroup sessions, one will be at a much better advantage to help oneself and others. Disciples of sensitivity groups maintain that if personal growth occurs, all other problems will be resolved.

In addition, Back (1972) delineates three features of sensitivity training: "the concentration on the immediate group process, the emphasis on personal relations and personal remarks, and the resultant subjective experiences (p. 13)." He further propounds that sensitivity training is a procedure employing group action as an end in itself. Thus, the major thrust of sensitivity training is its adherence to strong emotional action through group process. As Back (1972) again notes: "Sensitivity training is novel in accepting the group experience as having value in itself, with recourse to any ultimate aims. It uses the present experience only (p. 78)."

There are two essential reasons that the distinctions between sensitivity groups and T-groups have blurred. First, they share a common denominator in terms of origin. A second reason for the present interchangeable use of the two words is that as T-groups have evolved, they have attempted to incorporate the concepts and procedures that were once seen as the province of sensitivity training groups. Whatever previous differences there once were between these two approaches are now mainly academic. Trying to distinguish between them on the basis of current literature is akin to searching for a needle in a haystack. The morass of confusion has continued too long for any substantive distinctions to be made after the early 1970s.

Perhaps the only meaningful way of differentiating them is to look at the modern derivatives of each approach. Esalen is the modern derivative of sensitivity groups (Back, 1972). It is one of the new personal growth movements that focus upon intensive group techniques used primarily for the development of the individual. The fact that Esalen has attempted to borrow techniques from a variety of schools has prevented it from being exclusively labeled as sensitivity training. Therefore, in the broadest sense, one could say that sensitivity groups in the 1970s are most closely related to personal growth groups, but that the many varieties of such schools prevent any direct tracing of lineage.

Modern derivatives of the T-group are even harder to trace. However, one of the direct outgrowths of this model has come to be labeled Organization Development, or just OD. The Office of Organization Development uses as its foundation the instrumented T-group or the concept of planned organizational change. While the Office of Organization Development directs its attention toward intervention strategies to help agencies and institutions to function more effectively, the instrumented T-group stresses the importance of individuals' becoming effective organization members. According to Bennis (1969), the T-group is the central activity of Organization Development interventions.

The National Training Laboratory

No historical review of the T-group and sensitivity training would be complete without mentioning the National Training Laboratory in Group Development, later shortened to the National Training Laboratory or simply NTL. Its major contribution to the laboratory method is that it supplied a formal organizational structure. The NTL began by sponsoring summer training laboratories at Bethel, Maine. Currently, the NTL offers year-round activities. Although a number of organizations have since become involved in related kinds of training activities, the NTL still assumes the major responsibility for training leaders of T-groups. It provides internships as well as accreditation for those who have completed the necessary training.

Although there are gaps in what took place, when, where, and why, the foregoing review has reported most of the major events that led to the initial differentiation and final fusion of T-groups and sensitivity groups. From this point on, however, attention is focused upon the T-group as the major setting for sensitivity training. This seems to be the only reasonable road to take in light of the current overwhelming confounding of these two approaches. To put it another way, the distinction between T-groups and sensitivity groups is now a matter of history and not one of present operational functioning.

LEWIN'S THEORETICAL CONTRIBUTIONS TO THE T-GROUP

Lewin's influence on the T-group movement has already been discussed. Here we examine his theoretical contributions to this group model. Two fundamental principles of Lewin provide the underlying rationale of T-groups as conducted by the National Training Laboratory. First is his theory of behavior change and encapsulation within a group; second is his theory of feedback.

Lewin believed that the group is an effective agent for changing an individual's behavior. He asserted that the behavior of an individual is easier to change within a group context than in a one-to-one situation. Group interaction or group dynamics produce change more readily because the individual has a greater opportunity to verify old behaviors or to try out new ones. Yet change for its own sake or fleeting change was not a major concern of Lewin. He was deeply interested in how to produce more lasting behavioral changes within a group context. To effect genuine change, Lewin postulated that one must be totally involved in the group; one must discover for oneself that one's beliefs and behaviors are unsatisfactory;

and one must be in a situation which gives one the freedom of choice to change or to do otherwise. Although all three factors are important, the process involving discovery of certain facts about oneself is crucial. When persons are able to see themselves as others see them and to discover certain facts for themselves, attitude changes are inclined to be more permanent. According to Lewin, individuals will tend to believe facts they themselves have discovered in the same way they believe in themselves (Marrow, 1969).

Moreover, Lewin hypothesized that an individual tends to act or think in an equilibrium. The environment of any group reinforces a person's sense of equilibrium. For example, if an individual is placed in a new group setting and the members of that group convince the individual to change his or her behavior, when the individual returns to the old group he or she will also revert to an old way of behaving. In order to have a more long-lasting impact on a person's behavior, Lewin proposed that one must change the nature of the group situation. He hit upon the idea of an encapsulated group, a group not bound by traditional functionings and rules of behavior. Lewin theorized that the group is not the sum of its members but a "structure that emerges from the interaction of individuals, a structure which itself produces change in individuals (Bonner, 1959, pp.19–20)." The encapsulated group was a good way to investigate how the evolving structure within the group affects a person's behavior. Later on, the encapsulated group was renamed laboratory training. The goal of laboratory training was to change an individual's behavior by establishing a different kind of group equilibrium.

In order to establish a new kind of group equilibrium, Lewin stipulated that the group must go through three stages: unfreezing, restructuring, and refreezing. Unfreezing refers to changing role expectations group members have of themselves and other participants. Lewin believed that ambiguity and the absence of any structured goals would hasten the process of unfreezing. The restructuring period is characterized by change. During this stage, group members would be encouraged to establish new relationships and to test new behaviors. As the group neared an end, a refreezing of the newly learned behavior would occur. Refreezing would tend to make more permanent whatever behavioral changes had occurred.

Lewin's theory of feedback is intimately connected to his principle of behavior change in a group situation. During the stages of unfreezing, restructuring, and refreezing, feedback would occur. The feedback that each person received would, according to theory, assist the participant in making behavioral changes.

Many of Lewin's ideas have been directly applied to the T-group and the laboratory method of training. For example, the first group at the Connecticut Workshop consisted of mainly strangers. It was felt that a group composed of strangers would not only eliminate the importance of participants' outside status, but would also force participants to establish a new identity based upon their actions in the group. Moreover, Lewin's notion of having an encapsulated group has also been used in T-groups. Generally, participants are removed from their more familiar surroundings into areas that are seen as neutral grounds. To deal with Lewin's concept of creating a new group equilibrium by unfreezing, the T-group has adopted an unstructured, ambiguous situation. Finally, the concept of feedback in the here-and-now has also been employed to help group members change. In short, the principles of behavior change and feedback form the basic theoretical underpinnings of the T-group. [These are discussed in greater detail on pp. 115–20.]

GOALS OF THE T-GROUP

As with other group approaches, the goals of the T-group are not uniform. They vary from group to group and are determined largely by the purposes of the group. What follows now is a core of goals that are generally common to most T-groups, regardless of their purposes.

Learning How to Learn

Central to all T-groups is the concept of learning. There is an underlying belief that learning is an active experience and that one learns best when one comes to accept certain facts and acts upon them. Learning within a T-group takes the form of discovery learning. People learn by discovering certain things about themselves and about others. Traditional learning and T-group learning may be differentiated in terms of the conditions under which learning takes place. In the T-group it occurs as an outgrowth of a member's participation in the development of a group. There are no answers in the back of the book. The only real answers are provided by the participants themselves.

The T-group helps a person to be more open to opportunities for learning. There is an emphasis upon freeing oneself from the conditional responses of the past. The loose structure of the T-group fosters this type of reeducation. For example, part of learning how to learn in a T-group has to do with developing a relatively high threshold for ambiguity. The ambiguous situation of the group forces participants to become more cognizant of the means by which learning becomes productive. Without the presence of familiar props, a T-group participant is inclined to develop a greater awareness of his or her own style of learning. The participant begins to understand the effect that receptiveness to new experiences has upon what is learned.

A third dimension of the "learning how to learn" concept deals with the relationship of one's peers to one's learning. One learns from interactions with others in the group. In a T-group, any member of the group who can provide data for learning is accepted as a teacher. There are multiple teachers in this kind of setting. Frequently, some participants are uncomfortable with this kind of arrangement. They feel that the concept of peers becoming teachers is like the blind leading the blind. Thus, part of T-group learning has to do with unlearning old ways of perceiving the learning process.

Mill (1972) uses a disconfirmation theory of learning to explain the process of learning in a T-group. He maintains that a member learns as some of his or her behaviors are confirmed by other members as effective and other behaviors are disconfirmed as ineffective. An individual learns more from disconfirming feedback than from confirming feedback. Mill (1972) states, "To be confirmed, to learn that one is 'O.K.' in one respect or another is rewarding, but what we really need to know in order to develop rests in the *disconfirmations* (p. 10)." Relearning how to learn, then, involves some sort of presentation by an individual, feedback from others, and experimentation with new behavior.

Self-Understanding

Self-understanding represents a special kind of learning and a desired outcome goal in T-groups. This goal is not unique to T-groups; it tends to pervade many of the group approaches to solving problems. In the T-group situation, the objective is to help a person clarify identity and increase self-esteem rather than the more therapeutic goal of discovering one's real self. Bradford (1964) outlines three aspects of identity as: (1) self-awareness; (2) the ability to play roles; and (3) the capacity to differentiate oneself from others. He states, "People gain identity partly in relationship to other people, in differentiating from them, and in relationship to position and function in the social organization (p. 196)." Individuals discover part of their identity as they interact with others. The process of increasing self-understanding is essentially one of receiving feedback and support from others. People who are acceptant of themselves and understand the basis of their actions are also inclined to be more acceptant of others.

Argyris (1962) states that the importance of self-understanding in a T-group is twofold. First, he suggests that the more individuals understand themselves, the greater the likelihood that they will be able to discuss certain aspects of themselves with minimal distortion. For example, if a person is aware and accepting of a tendency to be critical of others, he or she will tend to listen to the comments of others without distorting what they are saying. Another significant aspect of self-awareness is that the more people understand themselves, the greater the likelihood they will listen to others with minimal distortion. The person who understands that he or she tends to be critical of others, for example, will also be inclined to provide another critical individual with feedback that is minimally distorted because he or she understands that individual's problem from first-hand experience.

Increasing a person's self-esteem is seen as a companion to growth in self-understanding. Gibb (1964) affirms that individuals learn to grow as they accept themselves and others. The primary roadblocks to such acceptance are defensive feelings of fear and distrust. In a T-group members learn how to work with others to create a defense—a reductive group climate. This is to say that as an individual's fear of self and others is reduced, the individual gains self-confidence and consequently experiences greater self-esteem.

The process of increasing self-understanding in a T-group is difficult but rewarding. The typical T-group participant enters the group with a certain conception of self and others. In the early stages of group development, there is a great deal of ambiguity. This ambiguity tends to produce an identity crisis among participants. Feelings of fear and distrust pervade the group. Members are concerned about how others will see them and how they can keep their present images intact. The identity stress created by the minimal structure of the T-group spurs some individuals to examine themselves. While participants are struggling to define and to achieve group membership, they learn that they have to invest something of themselves. The process of self-investment becomes easier as members learn how to trust each other and to deal with their own fears. As the group begins to become more cohesive, a feeling of we-ness develops. Participants are now in a better position to listen to feedback. From the struggle for self-identity and the feedback of other individuals, members gain new insights into themselves, into others, and into the group itself. The satisfaction of participating with others and being accepted by members of the group helps to bolster participants' self-esteem. Martin Buber (1957) captured the importance of self-confirmation and acceptance when he said, "The basis of man's life is twofold, and it is one—the wish of every man to be confirmed as to what he is, even as what he can become, by men; and the innate capacity in man to confirm his fellowmen in this way (p. 101)."

Insight into Group Functioning

Another objective of the T-group is to help participants learn more about group functioning and effective group membership. Members first learn how to develop effective membership skills through their own participation in a group. Some important membership skills are: (1) developing diagnostic sensitivity to difficulties confronting the group; (2) increasing one's ability to communicate in order that one's diagnostic suggestions will be listened to; and (3) learning how to behave in ways that will help the group progress (Bradford, 1964). In any given T-group, participants bring with them many differences in personality and socio-economic background. For example, members may have different past experiences and current problems. Their fears and anxieties concerning the possible consequences of membership may vary. They may also have conflicting pressures to learn and change, different tolerance levels for ambiguity, and different assumptions about the nature of humanity. If a group is to function effectively, all of these differences must be accommodated by members—otherwise chaos may reign. Hence, one of the responsibilities of the participants is to learn how to become effective members in light of the differences among them. Participants are encouraged to learn how to locate and reduce group barriers to openness and trust. They must somehow learn how to resolve the different goals each participant may have. An understanding of the motivations of members, the process of communication, and group problem solving must likewise be enhanced.

Participation in a T-group helps members to learn that ineffective membership attenuates group effectiveness; that silence is not always golden, for silent and withdrawing members tend to rob the group of valuable resources needed for individual and group progress; and that a continual reevaluation of perceptions, values, and assumptions may be necessary.

Experiential learning in a T-group may also be supplemented with theory sessions on group theory and dynamics. During theory sessions, members are encouraged to become more cognizant of the needs and behavioral styles of other participants. Members are provided with information to help them analyze functional and blocking member roles.

The NTL Institute provides a number of ways of analyzing what goes on in a

T-group—some of which are discussed briefly herein. First, one may observe a group by looking at its content material—*what* the group is discussing. For example, the topic of a group may be: What is good supervisory behavior? Group process, on the other hand, refers to *how* the group is functioning. To observe group process, one examines the pattern of communications. Who talks to whom? Under what circumstances? For how long? A third way of gaining insight into group functioning is by looking at the group's decision-making procedures. Does one person tend to make the decisions? Is a decision reached by polling group members, or are decisions made by default?

A fourth approach to observing a group is to examine the amount of group task or maintenance behavior in comparison with the frequency of self-oriented behavior. Task-oriented behavior is manifested by a member's attempt to get the group task completed. When a participant attempts to improve relationships among members, that participant is said to be engaging in maintenance behavior. Self-oriented behavior is designed to satisfy a participant's personal needs or goals. Task-oriented behavior is usually exemplified by a member's effort to initiate (proposing tasks or goals); to clarify issues before the group; or to summarize suggestions the group has previously discussed. Examples of maintenance behavior are harmonizing—attempting to reconcile differences—and gatekeeping—devising ways to get the full participation of others. Self-oriented behavior tends to delimit group effectiveness. Such behavior is generally laden with emotional issues or problems. For example, some members pair up in order to establish a basis of emotional subgroup support. In these instances participants' behavior will be directed toward protecting and supporting one another. The main point is that by improving one's skills in observing what is taking place in a group, an individual will have a better understanding of groups and his or her functioning in them.

Developing Behavioral Skills

The goals of T-groups go beyond those of greater self-understanding and more effective group membership. Participants should be able to translate their understandings into specific behavioral skills. Since all interpersonal relations involve communications, it is important that participants develop "receiving" and "sending" skills. Receiving skills pertain to a person's ability to listen effectively. Listening is one of the first attending skills T-group members are taught. Sending skills refer to a person's ability to convey adequately ideas or feelings. A person may be thwarted in interpersonal relations because of inability to get ideas across. This situation may be caused by other distracting behaviors of which the person is not aware.

THE T-GROUP AS A CULTURAL ISLAND

What is the laboratory method for T-group training? Just as there exists a variety of types of T-groups, there is no one format for T-group training in the laboratory method. For example, the training period may consist of a marathon weekend program, a one- or two-week residential program, or a program that takes place for several weekends, a semester, or a year (Seashore, 1970).

The Residential Program

The residential program is perhaps one of the most common formats used, partly because this was the original design for T-group training. One of the significant features of the residential laboratory is that it takes place in a setting that removes participants from the concerns of their everyday life situations. The term *cultural island* is frequently employed to describe the residential laboratory. In addition to removing participants from their daily concerns, there are basically two other reasons given for the use of a cultural island. First, it is felt that a rather bucolic, neutral setting helps to prevent participants from coming with a ready-made package of expectations and props for behavior. A neutral setting also tends to make people more open to new types of experiences. Second, the residential laboratory functions to arouse excitement and uncertainty about the nature of the training experience. During the course of a residential laboratory, participants may be exposed to didactic sessions relating to theory development, social activities, and the regular T-group sessions.

The traditional laboratory program in the residential setting begins with a general introduction and explanation of what the T-group experience entails. Most T-group trainers allude to the idea that one of the purposes for their gathering is to learn more about themselves, and about how people behave in a group, by becoming group participants themselves. From that point on, a great deal of ambiguity may exist. The typical T-group trainer usually does not proceed with any kind of specific agenda regarding how the group should function. The lack of detailed guidelines heightens the participants' anxiety. Initially, group participants attempt to structure the session. They may suggest, for instance, that everyone should begin by giving their name and telling something about themselves. Although other suggestions for structure are also made to deal with the ambiguity of the session, few of these are followed up by group participants. Group participants may then look at the trainer for directions as to the way they should go. Finding little success in their attempts to get the trainer to structure the session for them, group participants eventually come to realize that the course the group takes is primarily dependent upon themselves.

In the average laboratory, there are approximately 40–50 participants. Large groups are then broken down into small-groups of usually ten members. There may be one, two, or three two-hour small-group sessions per day. Part of the day is also reserved for theory sessions which are designed to relate to the experiential learning that occurs in the T-group. Theory sessions concentrate on the didactic material of group process, continuous levels of communication, and observation of behavior.

The following is an example of how a typical "stranger group" in a "cultural island" setting begins. Individuals have come from a variety of places, occupations, and organizations to a secluded site for a short but intensive period of time. The participants are basically strangers to each other. The hypothetical leader begins by stating the purpose of the T-group.

"Good evening. My name is Jim Walters. We will be meeting together in the next two weeks in a T-group. Except for the general schedule that you see, there is nothing really planned. What happens here is pretty much up to us. We are going to be operating in a kind of laboratory setting, where we will have an opportunity to learn about ourselves and about groups. During the process of the group, we will examine our own behavior, feelings, thoughts, reactions, and decisions regarding what takes place in the group. My purpose is to help you try to understand what is happening in the group. Even though I assume this responsibility, I want to make it clear that I am not the teacher of the group. Your faces tell me that we have already begun the group, and I feel a sense of anticipation about what might take place."

From the time that the T-group first comes together, the group has begun. Everything that takes place within the group becomes data for observation. What the group does and does not do becomes material for discussion. The group has no formal agenda, and members may be taken aback by the fact that the usual trappings of role behavior are abolished. Participants call both the leader and other group members by their first names. Lectures and skill exercises will constitute the other part of laboratory training. Participants may be asked to keep a notebook which summarizes their reactions, observations, and theoretical formulations regarding groups.

Once the trainer makes his or her opening remarks at the first meeting, participants attempt to interact with each other and the trainer. Participants may be observed to be grappling with how they will establish their membership in the group, what roles they will assume, and how they will respond to the group leader.

A typical day, then, of participants in a T-group in a cultural or residential island is divided into several segments. During the morning, participants may meet in dyads, or groups of two. Following the dyads is usually the formal T-group, a coffee break, and a theory session. During the afternoon and evening, participants usually gather in the T-group again, have a free period, dinner, the T-group, and a social hour. It should be noted that the theory sessions are usually kept separate from experiences in the T-group, although each format is designed to improve the total learning of the individual. In some instances, theory sessions may not be used throughout the two-week session. The experiential learning component provided by the T-group experience is seen as indispensable.

By the end of the first session, group members have begun to experience what "learning how to learn" means. Participants also begin to compare notes with each other concerning their reactions to the group.

By the second or third session, participants' feedback to the trainer may become hostile. The manner in which the leader handles such feedback is crucial to the group, since his or her behavior may greatly influence the norm that is later established for dealing with conflict (Appley and Winder, 1973). During this time, members attempt to deal with the frustration of ambiguity and lack of structure. As noted previously, the group may become divided into two camps—those who desire leadership and structure and those who do not. The trainer's suggestion that the members might explore their feelings of frustration at their inability to get the group going may be ignored. Eventually, the group returns to the trainer's suggestion, and group members begin to examine each other's contributions to the lack of group process.

During this stage of the group, members may be taught how to do a "forced field analysis." Essentially, a forced field analysis is a technique used to help group participants recognize the driving and restraining forces operating to create a problem or to keep a problem from being resolved (Appley and Winder, 1973). As a result of the forced field analysis and the ongoing group experience, participants begin to raise a number of questions, such as: How are decisions made within the group? What prevents the group from making a decision? During what specific points does the group tend to falter? How is leadership distributed within the group? Is it primarily authority-centered or collaborative in nature? How are norms established? What norms have been established by the group? What procedures are used to meet individual needs?

The laboratory method also provides a means for looking at participants' usual behavior and the impact of such behavior on others. It gives individuals an opportunity to try other ways of interacting, responding, and looking at consequences. At this point, the group begins to focus on participants' behavior and interpersonal style which was manifested during the early stages as the group dealt with its concern about authority. For example, Mary, an office manager of a middle-sized company, may find that she is getting feedback about the autocratic manner in which she attempted to get the group going. Members may comment upon her tendency to establish control over others. Initially, Mary may respond defensively, indicating that her only goal was to help the group get started. Slowly, Mary may be able to explore her own behavior and the impact that it has on others. George, a college professor and previous chairman of his department, is also confronted with his need to be recognized as an authority figure. As members give George feedback, he begins to look at his need to be superior to the younger professors in his department. Insight occurs as he describes himself as "the great blond Swede," the striver who made his way simply by sheer effort and running rough-shod over graduate students and anyone else who stood in his way. His need to control others and to be superior was based upon his own, deep-set feelings of inferiority.

Gradually, other members of the group give each other feedback concerning their interpersonal behavior during the group. For example, Joe, a group member who had vacillated between supporting those who wanted structure from an authority figure and those who wanted the group to develop its own agenda (the counterdependents), is given feedback concerning his "fence-sitting." Joe comments that vacillation has been a continual problem of his. Since he hates to choose sides, he very often makes no choice at all. Joe ends his remarks by stating that one of his goals back home will be to act less wishy-washy.

The feedback that group members give each other during this period of the T-group tends to produce a high degree of group cohesiveness. Participants now feel that they know each other better, that they understand both the group process they have experienced and themselves better. During the last few sessions of the

T-group, members focus their energies on pulling together what they have learned and gained from the group. There is an attempt to integrate both formal group learning and personal information learned about oneself.

Other T-Group Formats

As noted, the residential program is only one design of the laboratory method of T-group training. Underscoring the many diversities in format, Egan (1970) categorizes four common types of laboratory design. These are: (1) the community approach; (2) the organization design; (3) the group-itself approach; and (4) the individual. The two basic factors that account for the diversity in format are the size of the group that is the focus of the laboratory and the objective or purpose of the laboratory.

The community program has as its central concern working with various citizens' groups or even entire communities. The objectives of the laboratory experience herein may be to develop leadership skills, to increase the participation of community members in the economic, cultural, and social needs and activities of the community, and to strengthen community control (Klein, 1965). The fundamental idea is that group methods may help bring about change in the communities in which people live. In this particular situation, the T-group participating may consist of representatives of a particular agency or community consultants from a variety of different types of groups. Such representatives or consultants come as units to the laboratory. Mial (1970) in his report on a leadership teamwork development laboratory demonstrates that the T-group approach may be used to establish greater collaborative problem solving among community leaders in a complex urban setting characterized by conflicting interests and rapidly changing and emerging needs and programs.

The T-group laboratory approach has also been employed in large organizations. Golembiewski and Blumberg (1970) outline three ways in which T-groups can be used within large organizations: to change work-relevant attitudes; to modify organizational styles by changing individual behaviors and group norms; and in confrontation designs. The T-group can also be used to establish organization improvement goals, team planning, and implementation of planned change.

The group design focuses upon the small group itself. Generally, this approach is used in some courses in group dynamics wherein students learn about small groups by becoming members of one. In this case, the teacher usually serves as the group leader simply because of the fact that he or she is the teacher.

T-groups have also been used in dyads, as with husband-and-wife units. Here the focus is upon the individual. T-groups that focus on the individual resemble the sensitivity model.

UNDERLYING ASSUMPTIONS OF T-GROUP TRAINING

Seashore (1970) lists five assumptions of T-group training. These assumptions deal with the nature of the learning process that differentiates T-group training from some of the other traditional models of learning. These premises relate to:

1. learning responsibility

2. staff role

3. experience and conceptualization

4. authentic relationships and learning

5. skill acquisition and values

One of the underlying assumptions in T-group training is that learning is most meaningful when people decide for themselves what they want to learn and when they are deeply involved in the process itself. Much of the learning in a T-group is, therefore, experiential. Since it is believed that individuals tend to learn best when they are most involved, each person is given responsibility for his or her own learning. The laboratory method conceptualizes learning as a transaction between learner and environment in which neither learner nor environment is fixed and in which both may undergo change. A person's style, readiness for learning, and interpersonal relationships with others determine, in large measure, what she or he will learn.

Another assumption involves the role of the leader in T-group training. It is believed that people learn best when they are not told what they must learn and when the trainer does not function as an authority figure. Thus, the early stages of T-group development are ones in which members have to wrestle with the absence of an authority figure. The trainer or leader refuses to perform the role of a typical teacher. As participants resolve their problems concerning authority figures and dependency, they are in a much better position to learn. The group leader becomes a special kind of group member. The staff or trainer's role is to help participants examine and comprehend their experiences in the group.

Seashore (1970) lists experience and conceptualization as the third underlying assumption of T-group training. This assumption is based on the belief that learning consists of both experience and conceptualization. Organizers of T-groups seek to provide a setting or atmosphere to encourage individuals to investigate their experiences as a unit in sufficient detail to be able to make valid generalizations.

The development of authentic relationships and learning is a fourth assumption underlying T-group training. According to Seashore (1970), learning is facilitated when one establishes authentic relationships with others. Authentic relationships tend to foster a person's self-esteem and to decrease defensiveness. People communicate to each other more freely when they are not on their guard.

The skill acquisition process of T-groups allows a person to develop better techniques for examining the basic motivating values behind his or her behavior. The T-group provides a setting in which a group member not only can learn but also can practice new behaviors. Through skill acquisition, a person becomes more aware of self and the motivating forces of others' behavior.

KEY CONCEPTS

As T-groups have multiplied, so have the types of laboratory experiences. But there are still some common elements to most T-group experiences. The T-group has generally gravitated toward greater emphasis on interpersonal honesty, feedback, self-disclosure, unfreezing, and observant participation.

Ambiguity

As noted in the section on laboratory method, the T-group experience has a great deal of built-in ambiguity (Egan, 1970). The ambiguity of the session often leaves participants with a feeling of being without goals; the trainer tends to use a nondirective approach and does very little to clarify or structure goals and procedures. Schein and Bennis (1965) describe the situation as follows: "The goals are unclear, the training staff provides minimal cues. . . . The general absence of expectations creates an unstructured, i.e., ambiguous situation. This serves to upset old routines and behavioral grooves and to open up new possibilities for the delegates (p. 44)."

Feedback

The concept of feedback in group dynamics was first highlighted by Lewin. He realized that an important element was missing in most of the interpersonal contacts of individuals—feedback from the early morning small-group sessions as well as from such back-home associates as employers, wives, friends, teachers, and students. Feedback is necessary for all T-groups. To be most meaningful, it should have a here-and-now rather than a then-and-there focus. To test the accuracy of feedback, one should check with other group members to establish its validity.

Feedback is the sine qua non of T-group learning. To have feedback, members must respond honestly to each other concerning their reactions to the other's behavior. The setting of the T-group encourages honest sharing of reactions regarding how one's behavior is affecting another.

Although there are many advantages to feedback, it can also have a negative effect on the group. Feedback that is delivered in a hostile or undermining tone can help strip the participant of self-esteem. There is, however, a certain readiness for feedback that can be observed in group participants. When a participant evidences a lack of this feedback readiness, group members, and particularly the leader, should weigh carefully the consequences of giving this kind of information. The group leader should discourage feedback that seeks to strip a person totally of self-esteem or should work to create group norms and sensitivity toward members' readiness for this kind of information.

Group leaders should also be aware of the concept of feedback overload. That is, a group member may be bombarded by too much feedback or information. Feedback overload normally takes place when one group participant becomes the center of attraction for too protracted a period of time. The group member who is the recipient of such feedback finds that she or he cannot absorb or integrate all the information that is being given. Feedback overload can be just as harmful as feedback can be advantageous.

The National Training Laboratory states that feedback is a way of helping a person to think about the changing of his or her behavior. The Institute stipulates the following criteria for useful feedback:

1. It should be descriptive rather than evaluative. Descriptive feedback allows the individual to use the communications as he or she sees fit. Evaluative feedback tends to foster defensive behavior.

2. To be most helpful, feedback should be specific rather than general. Global statements such as "you are aggressive" or "domineering" tend to do little good. It is better if a participant can point out in the here-and-now of the group situation how behavior is aggressive or domineering. A person might say, for example, "In the last five minutes you have not let anyone in the group talk without interrupting. You tend to attack a person whose opinion differs from yours."

3. Feedback should take into consideration the needs of both the receiver and the giver of such information. Generally, feedback is destructive if it serves only the giver's needs. The giver of feedback should be concerned with how that information is going to help the intended recipient learn more about himself or herself and facilitate the process of behavioral change within that person.

4. One should direct feedback toward behavior that the receiver can do something about. It does little good to give feedback concerning something that is beyond the recipient's control.

5. Feedback is more helpful when it is solicited rather than imposed. For example, individuals may indicate that they have some blind spots concerning the effect of their behavior on others. As noted earlier, there is a readiness for feedback and this is best manifested when people request certain information about themselves from others.

6. Good timing is another important aspect of feedback. Feedback should focus upon a person's behavior as it is currently manifested. It is of little help if the person stores up feedback and reports it when it seems to have very little relevance to the situation at hand.

7. One should check to insure that clear communication takes place in the process of giving feedback. One way of avoiding inaccurate communications is to have the receiver paraphrase the feedback to see to what extent it corresponds to what the sender had in mind.

8. Time should be given for validation of feedback from others in the group. The concern here is to check whether the feedback is just one member's perception or is shared by others in the group.

Given these criteria, feedback is a way of increasing a person's self-awareness as well as awareness of others. It is a means for the participant to check how well behavior reflects intentions. It also helps to clarify one's identity within the context of a group situation.

Here-and-Now Focus

One of the important concepts of T-groups is that learning should be rooted in the here-and-now. Essentially, the focus is on what is happening at the moment, not on early childhood experiences as in psychoanalytic groups. For many group members, it is initially difficult to focus upon here-and-now events. Their whole past learning usually has been oriented toward what other people have done, said, or written outside of the immediate learning situation (Golembiewski and Blumberg, 1970). Thus, the group leader may run into resistance if he or she maintains that members' references either to their own behavior or to that of other participants should be restricted to what is currently taking place in the group. The underlying assumption of this approach is that learning about one's method of relating to others is most beneficial when one has a chance to observe the immediate experience and to feel its subsequent impact.

Back (1972) suggests that the here-and-now method is only a myth. It is the result of the boredom with life experienced by a large, affluent, mobile middle class. Lacking any central beliefs or controlled ways to put excitement into their lives, such people reject history, especially personal history that has any kind of enduring structure. Along with Back, other individuals question the permanence of learning that focuses only on what is currently happening (Klaw, 1970). For example, what does understanding the past have to do with understanding the present?

Unfreezing

Unfreezing is another term adopted from Lewinian change theory. It refers to the process of liberating an individual from a rigid belief system and from traditional ways of viewing the self and behaving toward others. The group's encapsulation in a cultural island hastens the process of unfreezing, for it tends to encourage group participants to take a fresh look at life. Likewise, ambiguity of structure of the T-group promotes unfreezing. Without the props of conventional society and its concomitant rules and regulations, unfreezing may cause considerable discomfort. One is forced to look at today's world through today's eyes—not through those of the past or from a rear window.

Group Support and Atmosphere of Trust

Only in a group that is nonthreatening and that offers support can there be real unfreezing of group participants' old behavior patterns. Group support and an atmosphere of trust do not automatically take place because someone so pronounces. Quite the contrary; the occurrence of both of these conditions depends upon the group process. In the beginning, most participants reflect the feeling that they cannot really entrust themselves to other group members. As the group progresses, the more reluctant trusters are encouraged by the risk taking of others. Members begin to see that they do not have to present an idealized picture of themselves. The decision to take a risk often depends upon how other members who have done so have been received by the group. If other group members feel that those who first revealed their innermost thoughts are not listened to or are not generally received too well, they are not likely to follow suit.

Group support helps individuals to lower their defenses in order to communicate more honestly. However, people are not likely to lower their defenses if anxiety-arousing behavior is coupled with inadequate security measures. Here the group leader sets the tone. Symptoms of lack of trust in groups are manifested by strategy planning on the part of participants, incongruities between what is said inside and outside of the group, and impersonal behavior (Egan, 1970). Other evidences of distrust in the group are belittlement of the group powers, flattery, avoidance of conflict, and denial of group membership. The greater the degree to which an atmosphere of psychological safety pervades the group, the greater the trust that group members will experience. Moving quickly into a climate of trust formation is essential for short-term T-groups.

Self-Disclosure

T-groups are based upon the idea that self-disclosure facilitates learning because it helps one to overcome anxiety. Culbert (1970) hypothesizes that there are certain interpersonal consequences of an individual's self-disclosure. By the very fact of having revealed certain information about oneself, a person puts himself or herself in a position to influence the behavior of others. From an existential point of view, self-disclosure is seen as an individual's attempt to reduce his or her alienation from other people. Others have posited that self-disclosure is an important ingredient to a person's search for better psychological adjustment (Jourard, 1964).

Culbert (1970) outlines the interpersonal dimensions of self-disclosure as: (1) the appropriateness of self-revelation; (2) the precipitating event that motivates it; (3) the timing of the disclosure; (4) the tense, or time distinction, pertinent to it; (5) the person's wish to reveal; and (6) the relationship between the differing degrees of self-disclosure among members that symbolizes its impact or effectiveness.

The dimension of appropriateness refers to the pertinence of the self-information to the topic being discussed. Whenever an individual introduces self-information that unduly changes a topic or model without any clear or acceptable reason, the person and the information divulged are unlikely to be seen as contributing to the group. Thus, the self-revelations are considered inappropriate.

The motivations that precipitate the disclosure of personal information are also important. If an individual's motivations are viewed as incongruent, then the individual evokes responses from participants that are related to the state of incongruence. Initially, discrepant disclosures arouse a sense of self-protection from the information. Once this feeling of insulation or protection is over, group members usually bring the discrepancies to the discloser's attention. The keystone, then, is receptivity to self-disclosures. A perceived incongruence of disclosure and behavior will limit the receptivity of other group participants.

The third dimension is the timing of self-revelatory information. This aspect is closely related to appropriateness and motivation. Group participants are influenced by the point in time an individual selects for self-disclosure. If a person delays considerably in letting the group come to know her or him, group participants are likely to ask why. Is it just an attempt to get in on the bandwagon, or does it reveal other information about that person's interpersonal style of relating?

T-groups concentrate on the here-and-now. Therefore, greater significance tends to be placed upon disclosures that are present- rather than past- or future-oriented, primarily because such revelations are seen as having the highest personal relevance. They also generate the greatest amount of feedback. The general sentiment herein is, "It is easy to talk about the past, what about where you are now?"

Some self-disclosures are intentional; others are less so. Frequently, slips of the tongue or the mood of a group will prompt unintentional self-disclosures—that is, self-revelations that a group participant did not willingly wish to disclose. Group members must be sensitive to helping such a person deal with after-the-fact self-disclosures.

The sixth and final dimension deals with the complementary relationship of the members' self-disclosures. Relevant self-information is a prerequisite to a qualitatively rich interpersonal relationship. The issue of optimal self-disclosure is important. If two individuals are either responding to a low level of self-revelation or if one participant is way ahead of the other in this process, then the facilitative purpose of the self-disclosure may be hampered. The T-group leader needs to be especially aware of the latter case, for a person may reveal too much for group participants to deal with in a time-limited, nontherapeutic group. Group norms concerning self-disclosure must be developed to prevent such occurrences.

Group Norms

Group norms are usually unspoken and unexamined behavioral guidelines that indicate what is and what is not acceptable behavior in a group. The majority of members tend to act in groups according to the many subtle and indirect ways the group tells them to act. For instance, a group norm may be to engage in polite talk, to spend the first few minutes in chitchat, or to have an "anything goes" approach. Norms have a great deal of influence and power on what takes place in a group.

Trust in a group cannot be legislated, nor can it be based on rules or declarations. Group norms or unspoken ways of behaving toward each other in a group are significant in establishing an atmosphere conducive to growth.

Developing group norms that relate to feedback, group support, a climate of trust, self-disclosure, and unfreezing are essential. Typically, the norms of each T-group are peculiar to the group itself. Group leaders and members must be cognizant of counterproductive group norms or norms which militate against group process. For example, some group participants may attempt to operate on the basis of rescuing other group members from negative feedback. They may proceed on the basis that if one cannot say something positive, one should say nothing at all. In this instance, the T-group becomes a session of mutual verbal masturbation.

Porter (1972) formulates what he considers to be facilitating norms and hindering or blocking norms. Facilitative norms concentrate on collaborative behavior. They deal with the here-and-now; acceptance of one's own feelings as well as those of others; respect for the individual; describing others' behavior; and recognition that behavior has consequences. In contrast, hindering or blocking norms emphasize competitiveness. They deal with the there-and-then; censoring and/or denying one's feelings or evaluating the feelings of others; insistence upon conformity to the group; inferring the motivation behind another person's behavior; and insisting that a person "should" or "should not" behave in a certain manner.

Collaborative behavior may be seen as the opposite of competitive behavior. A group that establishes the norm of collaboration tends to work together more effectively than one that encourages competitive behavior. In a competitive group, the important question is usually "Who was right?" Whereas collaborative group norms foster a more open presentation of self-disclosure, competitive group norms reduce openness by creating polarizations—right/wrong, win/lose, attack/defense.

PHASES OF T-GROUP DEVELOPMENT

A theory of T-group development provided by Bennis and Shepard (1970) is based on the group dynamics that center around members' uncertainty of what is going to take place in the T-group. This uncertainty evokes relationships of dependence and independence within a T-group setting. The time span of the T-group may be divided into two major parts, each of which has three subphases. During each of these phases, the development of good communications is contingent upon the group members' orientations toward authority and intimacy. The typical T-group moves from the single-minded concern with authority relations to preoccupation with personal relations. The subphases are determined by the ambivalence of members' orientations in each area.

Bennis and Shepard (1970) characterize the dependence aspect as the participants' traditional patterns of relating to authority, symbolized by a leader or a structure of rules. Those participants who feel more comfortable in settings that provide a great deal of structure and guidelines for behavior are called "dependent." Members who find it difficult to relate to authority figures are labeled "counterdependent."

There is also a personal aspect to the dependence concept as offered by Bennis and Shepard. This element relates to an individual's characteristic pattern concerning interpersonal intimacy. Whereas people who require a high degree of intimacy with other group members are called "overpersonal," those who tend to shy away from intimacy with other participants are called "counterpersonal."

From a psychodynamic point of view, group members who manifest highly dependent, counterdependent, or highly personal or counterpersonal behavior are said to be "conflicted." The "independent" person is an unconflicted person. In Bennis and Shepard's opinion, the independent lacks the compulsiveness of the other psychodynamic types; therefore, he or she does not create the communication difficulties that, for example, the conflicted dependent does. The conflicted dependent's behavior may range from submission to distrust or rebellion. The independents are primarily responsible for group movement, since they are capable of dealing with the uncertainty that may typify a specific phase. Without the presence of independents, a T-group will experience great difficulty in working through problems of power and authority.

Phase I: Dependence

Subphase I—Dependence-Flight　At the beginning of a T-group, there is, as mentioned previously, a great deal of anxiety regarding the ambiguity of the group or its lack of structure and goals. Group participants tend to search for structure and common goals. They may try, for example, to define what they are supposed to be doing or saying, or they may suggest an agenda of topics. Their objective is to try to get the group trainer to provide some sort of structure that will ease their anxiety. While those with a dependent orientation search for topics that would gain the groups leader's approval, those with a counterdependent orientation watch for behavior on the part of the leader that would serve as a springboard for rebellion. In essence, group members are trying to flee from dealing with the task at hand—that is, their individual responsibility for the course of the group. Interactions among group members tend to be superficial during this phase. There is an underlying fear of having to communicate with each other in a more authentic personal and interpersonal way. Finally, members are inclined to believe that the group leader is withholding important information from them. The leader's lack of direction is usually seen as a ploy, a sort of flirtatious courting of the group.

Subphase II—Counterdependence-Fight　At this stage, the trainer rather than the ambiguity of the group becomes the central focus of concern. Discussions may revolve around the concept of leadership, with the intended purpose of pointing out how miserably the present group trainer is performing the job. Hostility is out into the open, and there may be a bid for leadership among group participants.

During this subphase, a division occurs within the group between (1) those who express a need for structure, and (2) those who maintain that there is no need for structure or leadership. Moreover, the hostility that was initially directed mainly toward the leader becomes directed toward other group members. The group is now on the brink of self-destruction. Throughout this phase, however, there is still the secret wish that the group leader will rescue the members from their predicament.

Subphase III—Resolution-Catharsis　At this stage, the role of the independents becomes more important. They are the primary source of hope for bringing the two warring factions together. Until this point the independents have not taken an active role in either of the subgroups formed—mainly because they are unconflicted in terms of their relations to authority figures.

The importance of Subphase III is that it may signal a turning point for the group. Participants come to recognize that they have to accept responsibility for what happens in the group. Thus, all of their previous behavior has led to a type of catharsis—a purging for their conflicted needs toward dependency and counter-dependency. No longer feeling a struggle for power, group members now are free to pursue common group goals. They are better able to listen to and accept each other's contributions. As dependence needs are resolved, group solidarity begins to form.

Phase II: Independence

Subphase IV—Enchantment-Flight Haunted by the memories of their past fights, group members now attempt to maintain their newfound sense of solidarity at all costs. The price that a member must pay for this fleeting state of nervous euphoria is loss of individual identity among group members. All must be sacrificed for the good of the group. There is a concerted effort to maintain harmony among group participants by careful "stroking" of the egos of other members.

Soon, however, group members begin to realize that their attempt to smooth over legitimate differences is unreal, and that their denial of problems is not resolving interpersonal issues. Near the end of this subphase, group members no longer can stand the pressures of total group enchantment. Again the group members attempt to flee the situation at hand, leading to replacement of total group enchantment with subgroup enchantment. The group now appears to be back where it started.

Subphase V—Disenchantment-Flight As in Subphase II, the group is partitioned into two polar subdivisions. But this time the divisions are based on the desired degree of intimacy necessitated by group membership. Whereas the counterpersonals join together to stave off further involvement, the overpersonals unite to demand unconditional positive regard and love. The behavior of each of the subgroups is guided by its fear of rejection by other members. The counterpersonals seek to protect themselves by not allowing anyone to get too close to them. Conversely, the demand for amnesty for the behavior of all individuals is based upon the hope that by accepting all others, they, too, will be accepted. Consequently, they can preserve their sense of self-esteem.

Subphase VI—Consensual Validation If the group has been able to overcome the hurdle of the preceding phases, they are now ready to deal realistically with the problem of interdependency. The direct motivating factor of this period is the members' acknowledgement that the group is ending. Again, the role of the independents becomes significant. At this juncture, a method of evaluation concerning the behavior of all participants must be resolved. Both the counterpersonals and the overpersonals resist any attempt to evaluate each other's behavior. The counterpersonals tend to take the stance that evaluation of group members is an invasion of their privacy and may subsequently lead to catastrophe if participants say what they really think of one another. In their attempt to shield themselves from negative remarks, the overpersonals tend to insist that any type of evaluation would unduly discriminate among group participants. The independents seek to resolve the evaluation issue by offering themselves for evaluation. They are able to do this because they have resolved their problems dealing with intimacy.

Consensus for evaluation is gradually reached as a result of rational discussion of what is at stake for each group member. This process facilitates communication and fosters a better understanding of oneself, other group members, and one's own interpersonal style of behavior.

ROLE OF THE LEADER

The role of the group leader is seen as one of facilitating learning in the laboratory method. Each group trainer, however, may interpret differently what constitutes a meaningful learning experience. (The terms trainer and leader are used interchangeably in T-group literature.) The trainer's role varies according to his or her competence, theoretical framework, and interpretation of the needs of each group as well as the nature of the group at hand (Tannenbaum, Weschler, and Massarik, 1961). Some of the more common descriptions of leadership roles are described below.

Creating a Conducive Learning Environment

The T-group leader helps to set the tone in which learning is to take place. In addition to the existential encounters that occur between group members, the T-group leader has a variety of techniques at his or her disposal to facilitate learning. For example, the leader may bring outside data into the group for analyzation of the group process. The leader may also deal with theories and concepts of group development.

Providing a Model of Behavior

The behavioral characteristics of the group leader serve as a model for other participants. A group leader should be able to accept criticism, raise pertinent questions, and express his or her own feelings. The leader's behavior helps to create a climate of trust and freedom of expression, and his or her willingness to relinquish authority allows the group to learn by sheer dint of their own effort.

Opening Channels of Communication

The group leader should be able to identify breakdowns in the flow of communication among participants. This task may be accomplished by raising questions, by delineating group and interpersonal/personal issues, and by encouraging the participation of all group members. Possessing the ability to identify problems, the group leader may be able to establish a higher level of awareness on the part of group participants. Opening up new levels of awareness is fostered by the communication skills that the group members learn.

Bradford (1964) both reaffirms the role of the T-group leader and adds some additional roles. He asserts that the type and quality of the trainer's interventions have a profound effect on the group process, the types of problems analyzed, and the learning that occurs. Nevertheless, the group leader does not determine the specific learnings of the group or direct its entire course of action. One of the leader's primary concerns is to assist the group in its method of inquiry. Bradford summarizes the trainer's purposes as follows:

1. To assist in the development of a group whose objective is to learn about the skills necessary for participation in social situations

2. To help remove barriers to a participant's learning about himself or herself, others, and the group

3. To help develop the type of group climate that facilitates learning

4. To help group members discover and utilize effectively such methods of inquiry as observation, feedback, analysis, and experimentation so as to promote group development and personal growth

5. To help group members learn how to internalize, generalize, and apply their learnings within the group to other appropriate situations.

According to Lippitt and This (1970), certain factors have a bearing upon the leader's professional competency and responsibility. They are as follows:

1. The goals of a laboratory training program have an effect upon the trainer's functioning. If, for example, the purpose of the group is more effective organizational functioning, then the training is inclined to proceed along lines that will deal with this issue.

2. The duration of the training program will likewise affect the role the trainer assumes. Training programs of short duration (three days) may require more input and directive action from the trainer.

3. Group composition is another factor that affects the way a trainer carries out his or her multiple roles. A training program involving strangers presents a different set of problems than a program containing primarily individuals who work in the same organization.

4. The trainer's professional background also has an effect upon how she or he relates to the group. A Rogerian counselor may want to focus on personal growth of participants, while a social psychologist may focus upon group dynamics.

Leadership Interventions

The role of the leader may be examined in terms of the kinds of interventions he or she uses within a group session. Dyer (1972) outlines nine different types of leadership or trainer interventions. The extent to which each of these interventions is employed will depend upon the goals and purposes of the T-group, the group composition, and the training, educational background, and theoretical position of the group leader.

Content Focus   Content interventions entail some specific introduction of information as that information relates to a specific topic the group is discussing. For example, if a group of high school students is discussing the topic "Why Young People Are Turning to Alcohol," the leader may intervene with research data, share an experience, or give an opinion concerning that topic. Frequently, the purpose of a content intervention is to help a group that is bogged down in technicalities move on to other concerns. That is, content interventions are most helpful when they provide information that group members feel they require to proceed from one point to another. While sometimes helpful, one of the dangers of content interventions is that they may encourage intellectualizing on the part of the group members, thereby keeping the group from examining its own processes.

Process Focus The purpose of a process intervention is to focus on what is happening in the group. The leader may intervene to clarify, make suggestions, or share his or her feelings with the group. For example, the leader may comment on the emphasis given to the there-and-then problems of members in comparison to the group attention given to here-and-now problems. A typical process intervention statement might be, "I feel that some group members are not ready or do not want to discuss what is taking place in the group, and perhaps to try to force them to do so would be to put them under unnecessary pressure to conform."

One of the most common process intervention statements has become known as the "I wonder" intervention. For instance, a leader might say, "I wonder what is really going on in the group now." Argyris (1962) cautions the leader against "I wonder" interventions because such statements do not encourage authentic relationships within the group. In his opinion, it is much better for a group leader to commit herself or himself more honestly. In place of the "I wonder" interventions, Argyris suggests that the group leader substitute "I believe" interventions. An example of this kind of process intervention would be, "I believe I know what is happening in the group now."

Eliciting Feelings The sharing of feelings is important in T-groups. Initially, T-group members may be hesitant to share their feelings with other participants. Such reluctance may be based on a lack of trust, lack of self-confidence, or other factors operating within the group. Some group leaders and participants maintain that the sharing of feelings tends to be one of the most beneficial aspects of T-group membership. It may not only let members know that they are not alone but may also help them see how others feel about their behavior. An example of an intervention to elicit feelings would be, "How did you feel, Mary, when the group rejected your suggestion?"

Direction Giving The use of the direction-giving intervention will depend a great deal on the philosophy of the group leader as well as on his or her perceived needs of the group. Some leaders may, for instance, provide group members with observation forms or suggest different exercises for participants to complete. The issue surrounding the use of this technique is whether or not it will reinforce dependency relations on the part of group members. There are other relevant factors to consider regarding the decision to use the direction-giving intervention. Such factors include the duration of the T-group, the level of dependency manifested by participants, the resources available to the group, and the leader's own tolerance of ambiguity.

Direct Feedback In the early stages of a T-group, members are usually anxious to know how the leader sees them. These concerns may be a legitimate request for feedback or they may be an indication that some participants have not worked through the problem of the leader as an authority figure. While some facilitators feel that to be authentic in their relationships they must give feedback to members, others believe that their feedback is no more valuable than that of other group members and consequently should carry no special weight. Some important questions regarding the feedback intervention technique are: How does the leader share his or her reactions without perpetuating the authority figure picture? How does the leader get the group to value and use feedback data from all members?

Cognitive Orientation   In some T-groups, the facilitator may offer participants a relevant theory or information in order to provide them with a conceptual framework for understanding group development. In such instances, lectures may be given, and sessions may be taped and listened to on a voluntary basis. The extent to which a group leader uses the cognitive orientation intervention will depend upon his or her own need to be seen as an expert as well as on an assessment of how best to help group members learn.

Performing Group Functions   The leader may intervene by employing task-maintenance functions. These interventions are geared toward helping the group to maintain itself as an effective system and toward promoting learning. For instance, a leader intervenes with task functions by seeking opinions or reactions to what has taken place in the group. Generally the group leader reduces such interventions as participants develop greater ability to perform these functions themselves.

Diagnostic Intervention   If a group is having difficulty getting started and jelling together, the leader may diagnose what he or she believes is happening in the group. An example of a diagnostic intervention would be, "There are a number of possible ways to explain why the group is disintegrating. One may be that the goals are too vague. Another is that we may be afraid of revealing ourselves to each other because we may be criticized. Are there any other possibilities you see?" The diagnostic intervention is designed to encourage participants to use a diagnostic approach in order to gain a better understanding of group process.

Protective Intervention   The main purpose of employing protective intervention is to keep members from "overexposure" or from revealing personal incidents and feelings that may not foster learnings appropriate to the goals of the group or that may create a situation with which the members and the leader are incapable of dealing. A leader may also protectively intervene if she or he feels that feedback directed toward a member is ill-timed or destructive.

The purpose of leader interventions is to help accomplish learning goals established with a group. The type of intervention used not only reflects the leader's theories of individual and group behavior but also "involves such factors as when and how often to intervene, around what concerns, how much of the trainer's own emotional reactions are funneled into the group, how much control he maintains, and whether he tries to become a group member, maintains his trainer status, or participates with group members outside the group (Dyer, 1972, p. 118)." It is important that a group leader examine the types of interventions he or she uses in order to ascertain if they are made primarily to satisfy the leader's own needs of responding to anxiety, conflict, and ambiguity or if they are designed primarily to foster group process and learning.

Pitfalls and Problems of T-Group Leaders

During the course of a T-group, a leader may be faced with certain dilemmas regarding how to conduct the group (Bradford, Gibb, and Benne, 1964). The dilemmas that T-group leaders face usually occur because of situations that arise among participants or because of the leader's own perspectives on group leadership. The leader's view on training may at times conflict with the goals of the traditional T-group. Likewise, participants might want to discuss certain issues that are usually held within the purview of traditionally run T-groups. In an effort to train people how to rely upon themselves, some T-group leaders may actually abdicate their leadership position. This situation raises the issue: Can the leader's role be reduced to that of just another group member? Most T-group leaders seem rather divided on whether or not the leader can ever truly become a group member. While some trainers state that the group leader is simply a more experienced group member or the best participant, others maintain such a stance signals an abdication of leadership.

It is unlikely that a T-group leader who assumes the responsibility of leadership ever truly becomes a group member, even though the apparent lack of structure tends to produce the illusion of leaderlessness. To be effective, the trainer will have to resolve the issue of leadership; otherwise, trainers are likely to confuse participants. At a very minimum, the T-group leader is responsible for: (1) keeping participants aware of what is happening in the group; (2) providing guidelines for giving or receiving feedback; (3) keeping the tension level of the group at an optimum level for learning; (4) identifying and helping break up group games which interfere with learning; and (5) helping participants differentiate between diagnosis and a mandate for change (Culbert, 1972).

The Beginning T-Group Trainer

The beginning T-group trainer faces a number of issues, including: How does one begin a T-group? What are some methods of indicating the goals of T-groups? How does one distinguish between the T-group format and other group counseling approaches? How does one deal with client expectations? How does one go about presenting oneself as a trainer? For the average beginning T-group trainer, none of these issues are clear-cut. They require the integration of both theory and practice.

As some experienced T-group leaders can attest, starting a T-group is no easy task. The T-group leader must understand the rationale upon which such groups are formed. The leader must be committed to the idea that people learn about themselves and others through the process of being in a group, that a major purpose of a T-group is to learn about group process, and that the T-group itself provides a corrective experience to help individuals ward off any insidious maneuvers that would allow others to manipulate them. The leader helps group members to learn about their responses to authority by examining their reactions to him or her in a leadership role.

The beginning T-group leader must be able to cope with a great deal of ambiguity and must be willing to wait for the democratic process to take place or to happen in the group. Such waiting may be the source of much trainer anxiety, since he or she never quite knows if the democratic process will happen or if members will become aware of their responses to authority. Essentially, then, T-group leaders must trust the group more than themselves. Group leaders of other schools take a different stance. They take the position of trusting themselves first and the group process and members secondarily. Hence, the beginning T-group leader must accept the position of being member-dependent rather than leader-dependent. This feature of T-group training provides a basic conceptual difference from some of the other group approaches. In T-groups, leaders' skills come to the forefront as a result of what clients or group participants do. As Golden (1972, p. 14) states:

> Each training group is for me like another combat flying mission, another encounter with the contingencies of the firing line. I sweat out each group because I am never really certain of myself. I do not know definitely whether my being present in a group serves any genuine purpose. Often during a group, I experience feelings of loneliness, uncertainty, and inadequacy. A training group in a sense is a happening, and so is flying at the critical moment. All the planning one has done, all the skill one has developed, all the conceptualization of strategies may or may not prove adequate to the situation one faces. Indeed, there are times when I say to myself, 'Why are you taking on this responsibility?'

Even before the T-group leader begins the training process, he or she must accept the temporary nature of relationships within the group. As Bennis and Slater (1968) point out, the T-group leader must be prepared to enter really and fully into temporary systems of relationships which have as their primary goal the learning of group participants. Temporary relationships provide no measure of real security for the group trainer. Instead, they may be the source of frustration for the beginning group trainer. If the group trainer can deal with his or her own anxiety concerning the ability of group participants to provide their own corrective group experience, and if he or she can withstand short-term, temporary human relationships that border upon intimacy, then perhaps she or he is ready to assume some of the responsibilities of becoming a T-group trainer.

It is important for the beginning T-group leader to have a clear idea of the goals of the group. Trainers may ascertain the goals of a particular T-group by asking themselves: What is my target of change? Is it the individual, the group, or a social system? If trainers find that they are focusing more on participants' personal growth needs, then they should be aware that they are crossing over the boundary of T-groups into sensitivity training.

The blurring of T-groups and sensitivity groups causes problems for both T-group leaders and participants. People who enroll in T-groups may come with the expectation that they will experience sensitivity training. A case in point is illustrated by Dyer (1972), who reports that during the course of conducting his group, one of the participants asked: "When are we going to start discussing our sexual and marital problems as they are doing in some of the other groups?" Dyer's response was that he had no intention of discussing members' marital or sexual problems. The focus of the group would be on behaviors of group members as experienced within the group, and that they would explore their development as a group and learn about group processes.

Each group leader has to decide what the focus of the group will be. Each T-group trainer must be prepared to deal with the differing expectations of group participants. The trainer should not attempt to use a model that was designed for learning about democratic group process for fulfilling participants' personal growth needs.

Strategies   Once the group leader has made some preliminary decisions about the goals of the group and how it will be run, he or she is ready to develop strategies for beginning a group. The trainer might begin indicating the purpose of the group by spelling out the logistics of the group (length of group sessions, life span of the group) and the leader's role. The group leader is responsible for making sure participants are aware of what is happening in the group (Culbert, 1972). Before a group begins, the trainer should ask the participants to let him or her know when they become confused regarding group process. This procedure helps the group leader not to mistake floundering and frustration for learning. Although floundering and frustration are often a part of the T-group growth process, they are appropriate only when they contribute to learning. People cannot learn when they are thoroughly confused and frustrated. The group should be able to help participants distinguish between necessary and unnecessary floundering and frustration.

The T-group leader is fundamentally the initiator of diagnostic observation in the group. That is, the leader works to get the group to diagnose and observe the group process that is taking place at any one given moment. For example, the group leader might say at one point: "The group seems to be bogged down concerning the role they want me to fulfill in the group. Is this an accurate observation?" If the participants' response to the group leader's question is in the affirmative, then the leader might assist participants in exploring why they are bogged down with the role they think she or he should be assuming in the group. A typical reaction might be that they are debating what should be the role of the group leader because they are concerned with authority or dependency issues. The important point is that once the group leader sets the tone for diagnostic observation, participants should be encouraged to become their own diagnosticians.

Critical Incidents   The beginning group leader should also be aware that there are certain critical incidents which tend to occur in T-groups. These critical incidents are likely to occur at different phases within the group. For example, Cohen and Smith (1972) point out that at least three critical incidents occur at the beginning, middle, and end phases of group development. During the first phase and the initial group session, participants tend to introduce themselves after brief periods of silence have taken place in the group. Group members are unsure of themselves and the direction they will take; therefore, they reflect their anxiety by falling back on familiar procedures, such as introducing themselves, and by making dependency statements. After the initial introductory exercise, group members will often turn to the group leader in an effort to get the leader to clarify his or her role. How might the leader respond to the participants' inquiries? The group leader might proceed by stating: "I feel that you feel somewhat at a loss as to where to go from here. I hear you trying to feel each other out and to establish some method for relating to each other. Introducing ourselves relieved the pressure and gave us a sense of direction. Do you think it might be appropriate for us to share with each other what we're feeling inside right now?"

Essentially, the group leader made a group-level intervention. The leader focused the group's attention on the processes that were taking place within the group and then provided another avenue of exploration the participants might take. Depending upon the phase of group life and the type of incident that occurs, the group leader might make similar or different kinds of interventions.

Cohen and Smith (1972) provide some questions to assist the beginning T-group leader in making effective interventions for critical incidents that occur within the group. According to them, trainers function most effectively when they ask themselves these questions: (1) At what point should I intervene? (2) What are the surface and underlying issues the group is attempting to tackle? (3) What level, type, and intensity of intervention would serve to get the group on the right track? (4) What are the probable effects that my intervention will have on the group?

Cohen and Smith (1972) further suggest that trainer interventions made in the beginning stages of group life should be superficial and general. The trainer who makes interventions of the one-to-one encounter type in the early stages of group life might freeze or immobolize the group, especially if members are strangers to each other and have had no prior group experience. During the early phases of the group, the trainer focuses on group-level rather than interpersonal-level type of interventions.

Once the group has established a climate of trust and sharing during the middle stages of group life, the trainer may make interventions on an interpersonal level. By this time, participants are attempting to incorporate what they learned about their own group functioning into their personal lives. They have established a certain readiness for interpersonal interventions. Interventions toward the end of a group should be made at the group level, but in a manner which helps the participants to integrate both group process and interpersonal learning that has occurred as a result of group membership.

The beginning group trainer is likely to be beset by a number of personal issues which relate to his or her suitability for T-group work. Massarik (1972) provides some guidelines that neophyte trainers might use in ascertaining their suitability for T-group leadership. According to him, trainers should manifest structure flexibility. Trainers should ask themselves: To what extent am I capable of leading a group without elaborate create structure? Conversely, can I create structure when the group situation demands it, or am I fervently opposed to structure? To be effective, trainers must also evidence what Massarik labels as *affect flexibility*. This means that trainers must be able to give and receive affection in a balanced way. Hence, neophyte counselors might ask themselves: To what degree am I comfortable in dealing with temporary, but oftentimes intense, interpersonal relationships? Third, trainers must examine their own need satisfaction system. Effective T-group trainers recognize their own personal needs and do not let them get in the way of working with the group. They do not try to use the group to satisfy their own personal needs of self-aggrandizement.

Inducing Dependency While Modeling Passivity   One of the goals of the T-group is to encourage independence among participants. Yet, very often leaders may be faced with the fact that their own behavior may encourage dependency rather than independency among group members. This situation occurs more so at the beginning of group life than at the end of the group. The dilemma trainers face is that any action they take to allay group members' discomfort may actually gratify the dependency needs of some group members. Conversely, if trainers remain relatively inactive, they are modeling a passive role for the leader. By remaining quiet, the leader may help the group to develop its own agenda and to analyze individual members' needs for an authority figure in the group. The question is: At what price does the T-group leader model passivity? Does he or she encourage group members to take a similar passive role in the group?

The effective group leader may have to cross a thin line between modeling dependency and actively encouraging independency among group members. For example, the group leader may be torn between using nonverbal exercises to demonstrate actively what is taking place within the group, or he or she may just let it happen. How the group leader resolves the issue of dependency versus independency affects the outcome of the group. A number of T-group leaders have chosen to become more active by using nonverbal exercises.

How Deep to Go   The issue of how deep the leader should go constitutes a major dilemma for some group leaders. Essentially, group leaders are torn between the time frames of the issues that group participants raise. Issues which are related to the past and which usually involve deep interpersonal problems may be appropriately labeled as there-and-then issues. Participant problems that occur as a result of the immediate involvement in a T-group may be termed here-and-now issues. Typically, the contract between T-group trainer and participants calls for an emphasis on learning in the here-and-now rather than in the there-and-then. The purpose of the T-group is not to explore deep, inter- and intrapersonal issues associated with such there-and-then, back-home issues as parental conflict, early childhood, or repressed memories. Dyer (1972) has presented arguments both for and against the introduction of there and-then data in the T-group. The arguments that Dyer presents may be summarized briefly.

There-and-then issues represent a safe retreat from what is currently happening in a group. Data from participants' personal lives are usually more interesting, but such information prevents the group from confronting problems that are presently evidenced in the group. Second, the trainer who attempts to focus on back-home situations frequently must operate with one-sided and incomplete data. The group leader should attempt to have participants focus on their back-home or personal situations but only after the group has helped them to see how they function in a group. It is unlikely that a training group can be helpful with personal problems in a one- or two-week session. Furthermore, the group leader may be irresponsible in opening up areas for examination when he or she does not have adequate follow-up opportunities for assistance. The group leader who focuses on back-home data may provide little more than catharsis or the temporary relief one obtains from releasing pent-up emotions. Moreover, unless the leader is careful, emphasis on participants' personal problems may lead to a group norm of exposure, thereby pressuring other participants to expose problems which they had no intention of exposing before entering training. Many T-group leaders do not possess the clinical training which would help them to deal effectively with personality disorders and malfunctions which individuals evidence in the group.

Conversely, one might argue that the T-group is the appropriate place for focus on interpersonal, back-home issues. The training group is an unstructured learning setting, and as such, it is a projective test onto which group participants may project or inscribe what is important to them. By focusing strictly on here-and-now issues that occur within the group, the T-group trainer may be preventing true intimacy among group members. Yet, is intimacy among group members sufficient? Intimacy for intimacy's sake is bound to lead to the worse form of bastardizing of intimacy. On the other hand, a group that evidences little intimacy is bound to be labeled as cold and unfeeling.

In essence, each T-group leader faces the dilemma of deciding how deeply he or she will explore the private lives or the intrapsychic and interpersonal functioning of group members. As noted previously, when T-group trainers delve too much into the personal lives of participants, they are leaving the realm of the T-group and crossing over into sensitivity and encounter training. It is difficult for a group leader to focus upon two competing goals: (1) learning about group process; and (2) learning about interpersonal and intrapsychic problems. One of the greatest dangers that a T-group leader faces is stressing back-home, there-and-then issues to the detriment of here-and-now, group-process issues that are occurring within the present in a group. T-group leaders who are influenced by the sensitivity and encounter movement are more likely to be torn between stressing back-home, there-and-then issues and emphasizing here-and-now issues relating to learning about group process.

Making the Experience Meaningful for Everyone   By the very nature of its unstructured learning, T-group leaders are inclined to want to make the group experience meaningful for participants. T-group leaders' emphasis on the meaningfulness of individuals' participation may be traced back to some of the elusive and sometimes personally unfulfilling goals of T-groups.

Moreover, in some instances, group leaders recognize that they are not touching some persons within the group. Failure to reach some members may cause a minor crisis within the group leader. The trainer's goal is frequently to reach all persons within a group. The trainer's sense of adequacy may be at stake if he or she does not reach all members of a group. To be effective, T-group leaders must come to terms with the fact that there will always be unfinished business which will prevent their reaching all participants. T-group leaders who place their faith in participants' ability to learn how to learn will be less disappointed than those who see as their major responsibility group participants' learning on an individual and personal basis.

The Trainer's Neurotic Needs   Trainers may either consciously or unconsciously use the T-group for their own neurotic needs. That is, they may use the group to gain praise and intimacy that is lacking within their own lives. The leader's failure to perceive accurately his or her connection with the group is one of the primary factors which contribute to this process. Another factor is the leader's sole reliance on doing what comes naturally. The trainers' neurotic needs may become more readily evident when she or he relies solely upon doing what comes naturally rather than on a repertoire of learned trainer-role behaviors (Massarik, 1972).

The leader's reliance on learned trainer-role behaviors tends to minimize the chances of not responding to the learning needs of the group or to what people should be getting out of the T-group. Two examples of learned leader-role behaviors are: (1) the purposeful intervention; and (2) training constructions. Purposeful interventions may involve intentional, nondirective paraphrasing of group members' comments or redirecting of the group process to the here-and-now. In each instance, the leader has in mind (rather than a gut-level feeling) an objective that he or she wants to accomplish based upon an assessment of the group's learning needs. Training construction is a generic heading for a host of exercises, theory sessions, and feedback forms designed to meet the learning needs of one or more group members or of the group as a whole. Both the purposeful intervention and the training construction serve as adjuncts to the trainer's doing what comes naturally.

It is important for leaders to ask themselves periodically: What needs does the T-group leadership satisfy? What am I getting out of group leadership? How do my personal needs and values get in the way of the group's learning? These kinds of questions are for the purpose of self-evaluation. They are designed to help keep group leaders and their intentions honest.

There are also other guidelines the group leader may use to avoid becoming the neurotic trainer. For instance, trainers should gauge the amount of their personal involvement within the group. This does not mean that trainers become remote but rather that they concentrate upon their special role as a professional meeting the learning needs of the group. Another approach might be to limit the back-home or interpersonal issues raised in the group. As noted previously, the use of the laboratory method should be related to participants' development purposes; and frequently the T-group leader may not be equipped to handle deep personal concerns of participants.

The T-group leader's monitoring of his or her own personal and neurotic needs is an ongoing, difficult process. This situation may be made even more difficult because of participants' tendencies to idolize the leader. In a group setting, leaders are likely to be given or invested with certain magical and superhuman powers that they do not possess. The training situation may contribute indirectly to trainers' neurotic needs.

The T-group leader faces a number of potential pitfalls that tend to occur throughout the course of the leadership role. Some of these include: inducing dependency while modeling passivity; making the experience meaningful for everyone; deciding how deep to go; and servicing the group's needs rather than those of the trainer.

Group Membership Role

There is no clearly defined group membership role. One can say that a major purpose of the T-group is to have each person decide what his or her functioning in the group will be. There are, however, certain implicit expectations of group members. For instance, participants are encouraged to learn how both to give and to receive feedback. Members are also expected to take full responsibility for their own learning. They must likewise be willing to assume responsibility for leadership in the group. Finally, members are expected to provide the data for group study. These data include their feelings, reactions, perceptions, and behaviors within the group setting.

Although T-group participants may be aware of the implicit expectations connected with their membership in the group, they may not know how to become effective group members. For some individuals, participation in a T-group may be unlike anything they have ever experienced. They may ask how they can contribute to the group and make the experience a meaningful one. Along this line, Hopkins (1964) provides some basic general points for members to consider. First, each participant must recognize that group quality or atmosphere is made by the people within the group. It is a result of the behavioral interrelations of members as they attempt to deal with the common area of need that disturbs them. Second, members must perceive themselves and other participants as referents in a similar need situation. Third, the answer to an adequate resolution of a situation or need lies in the interactions of members, and not in their responses to external objects or situations in their environment. Next, a group participant should recognize that modification of one's prior perceptions may occur as one interacts within the group. Unwillingness to restructure one's prior perceptions after interaction with other group members indicates that such restructuring is needed may tend to prevent the emergence of groupness. Fifth, participants must endeavor to reduce in themselves and others the threats that arise from earlier life experiences. Finally, a participant should be aware that all members of a group, regardless of their status in life, may have something significant to contribute.

Farson (1965) provides some suggestions for effective group membership. He presents these suggestions in the form of assumptions an individual should make on becoming a member of a sensitivity training or T-group.

1. Assume that anything and everything an individual either does or states is related to how that person is feeling at that very moment.

2. Assume that everything a member says has an element of feeling in it. Frequently, seemingly factual statements have feeling, even though the feeling being expressed may be one that indicates some measure of certainty. One should try to understand not just the content of what a person is saying but also how he or she is feeling.

3. Assume that you may not be the best judge of the impact you have on others. Try to elicit from others what kind of impact you have on them. Compare the difference between the impact you wanted to make and the impact you did make.

4. Assume that disagreement and loving are both forms of caring and that the opposites of these two behaviors are indifference and rejection.

5. Assume that you can trust your feelings, even though they may be negative. Your feelings may be giving you a great deal of helpful information about yourself.

6. Assume that you may encourage the way others react toward you, and that in some way you "set people up" to react toward you in the manner they do. Try to learn from others what it is you do to set them up. An example of this would be: Why does everyone seem to pick on me for no good reason?

7. Assume that boredom is anger and/or frustration unexpressed by an individual.

8. Assume that you and all members in the group will not be comfortable. Operate on the premise that being comfortable in the group is not the primary goal.

9. Assume that it is acceptable to experiment with how you behave in the group. Experiment with new behavior.

CONTRIBUTIONS OF THE T-GROUP AND THE LABORATORY METHOD

The laboratory method and T-groups have made several significant contributions to group theory and process. First, the laboratory method has served as a catalyst for sparking nationwide interest in the small-group approach. It supplied the format and the procedures which caught the attention of a number of researchers from a cross section of disciplines. The laboratory method can also be credited with encouraging a more extensive use of groups in a variety of settings, including the work scene, schools, regional institutes, and private practice. The T-group's emphasis on planned lack of structure and on the group's development of its own goals has become an integral part of many current group approaches.

T-groups have also generated the largest body of research of almost any group approach. Even though much of the research has left unanswered a number of important questions regarding the effects of the T-group, it has, at the very least, indicated some needed directions for future research on the small-group approach. T-group research has also generated closer scrutiny of what actually transpires in small groups designed to help individuals to gain a better understanding of themselves and of group processes.

T-groups also provided an important contribution in the area of the time duration or life span of groups. Before the advent of the T-group, group counseling and
psychotherapy were primarily oriented toward long-term results. With its residential program, the laboratory method demonstrated that participation in a group,
even for a short time, can bring about changes in individuals—however temporary
or lasting such changes may be. In many respects, the T-group and the laboratory
method ushered in the widespread practice of short-term group counseling.

The T-group is also progenitor of the encounter group, the most widespread
and popular general group approach used today. Encounter groups tend to stress
several features of the T-group, notably, its emphasis on short-term group work,
group process, and its guidelines for interpersonal feedback. Given the group
sophistication of mainly middle-class America, some people believe that the T-
group has outlived its original purpose, and therefore the search goes on for other
group approaches which will spark the imagination of the American people.

ISSUES SURROUNDING THE T-GROUP APPROACH

One of the most controversial points concerning the T-group is its relation to
psychotherapy. Golembiewski and Blumberg (1970) argue that there are major
distinctions between psychotherapy groups and T-groups. As noted above, for
example, NTL publications state explicitly that its programs are not therapy and
should not be considered as a substitute for therapy. Second, the emphasis in
T-groups is on here-and-now behavior and not on deep-seated psychological
problems. T-group trainers are not, for the most part, skilled psychotherapists and,
correlatively, do not have the background necessary to practice group psychotherapy. The NTL Institute points out that of 14,200 participants in its summer and
industrial programs held between 1947 and 1968, thirty-three people (0.02%)
found the experience stressful enough to leave. NTL maintains that even one
casualty is too many. The precautions taken to reduce stress were noted earlier
in the chapter.

On the other hand, Drotning (1966) notes that the dynamics of T-group and
sensitivity training have marked similarities to group psychotherapy. According to
him, serious emotional problems may be exposed if participants are indiscriminant-
ly stripped of their defenses. Drotning also questions the usefulness of the T-group
in work-related situations. In his estimation, group members may not be able to
transfer their learning from the T-group to the job. Drotning suggests that even if
such transferences of learning are possible, the personal exposure among co-
workers may hinder rather than help working relationships. Finally, Drotning proposes that T-groups connected with business and industry should concentrate on
group decision making and not on personal growth.

Solem (1971) maintains that the T-group method induces group pressures,
which are often experienced by the participant as a kind of devaluation of the
individual. Along these lines, he argues, T-groups also tend to encourage
conformity. They do not facilitate significant new freedom from anxiety or
frustration.

Dreyfus and Kremenliev (1970) assert that while T-groups and sensitivity groups do represent an exciting breakthrough in the traditional conservative approach to personal problems, "they can become lethal weapons in the hands of self-proclaimed facilitators or inexperienced professionals (p. 279)." The authors suggest that follow-up procedures should be instituted for those engaged in T- or sensitivity groups to see what effects the group has had on individual participants.

Both the professional and lay public have raised questions regarding the value of these group types in the educational setting. Ohlsen (1970) enumerates a variety of questions school counselors have asked pertaining to sensitivity, T-, and a third group of the same genre, the encounter group. [See Chapter 6 for a discussion of encounter group models.] He points out, for example, that school counselors want to know how group counseling differs from these other approaches. What is supposed to take place in these three groups? For what types of populations are such groups most appropriate? What kind of professional preparation is needed to lead them? How can school counselors convey to the general public what they are trying to accomplish in groups and explain how what they do differs from what less responsible individuals are doing in sensitivity, T-, and encounter groups?

In addition to parents and school officials, some state legislators have expressed their concern over the use of these group approaches in educational settings. In fact, legislation to curb group counseling in the schools has been contemplated, and action to censure its use has already been taken. At the heart of such behavior is the fear that school counselors who are improperly trained may overstep their boundaries and do more harm than good to young people. Some parents have specifically expressed concerns over losing control of their children. They see the process of group counseling as giving their children license to denigrate the family, society, and educational institutions as well as other values held in high regard by society in general.

Parents, school officials, and legislators are not the only ones who have questions about possible damage done to individuals participating in sensitivity, T-, and encounter groups. In the literature, Yalom and Lieberman (1971) have addressed themselves to encounter group casualties. Koch (1972) discusses the image of humankind underlying sensitivity and encounter group theory; he maintains that in the stampede for an authentic here-and-now confrontation, values that relate to tact, gentility, and gentleness are often trampled upon. Skousen (1970) maintains that sensitivity and T-groups are engaged in challenging and discrediting the Judeo-Christian value system.

The criticism of sensitivity and T-groups has not gone unanswered. Birnbaum (1971) asserts that sensitivity training holds a great deal of promise for fundamental improvement and reform in the schools. He posits that it may be beneficial in helping teachers to deal with the emotional factors that underlie classroom learning. Former participants point to the exhilarating experience of these groups—the freedom from the shackles of conventionalism that they provide (Klaw, 1970). Carkhuff (1969, 1970), however, addresses himself to what he labels the sensitivity fraud of T-groups. His discussion pertains to some of the more modern offshoots of T-groups. Two issues are underscored: (1) the need for behavioral objectives and research, and (2) the lack of built-in safeguards. Concerning the first issue Carkhuff (1969) states, "Unfortunately, the only evidence for change is in expressed attitudes, which are highly suspect. There is no tangible evidence for a translation of these procedures to behavior change. There is no tangible evidence for a lasting translation to human benefits." Along with Back (1972), Carkhuff (1970) proffers:

> At worst, such sensitivity training experiences are a perversion of the worst sort of a directionless middle class, aimlessly indoctrinating the naive and the vulnerable, and systematically spewing debris in their wake. At best, there is a real risk involved in trying to transfer learnings from the group atmosphere into real life, for there are no built-in safeguards for a generalization effect. At worst, the transfer from group to real life, the issues of currently dominant social values notwithstanding, is a systematically constructed design for a failure (p. 158).

Cashdan (1970) points to another potential danger in T-groups—the very real possibility that the type of reeducation that takes place among group participants may be culturally deviant. From his perspective, sensitivity learning is, by and large, remedial in nature. Given this observation, one should be aware of and investigate thoroughly what is being replaced or corrected, "since the cure may be less interpersonally adaptive than the illness (p. 218)."

Gottschalk and Pattison (1969) summarize the assets and liabilities of T-groups from a psychiatric point of view. They list the following assets of the T-group method. First, the T-group provides a means for teaching the importance of interpersonal relations within the context of natural group functioning; the T-group teaches from experience. Second, the T-group helps participants sharpen their perceptual skills to better deal with awareness of interpersonal perceptual distortions, validation procedures of verifying interpersonal perceptions, and correction of interpersonal perceptions. Third, the T-group teaches participants how to communicate better with others. Fourth, the T-groups have supplied underlying theory and method for effective intervention in organizations. Fifth, the T-group and laboratory method has served as a catalyst and support to the scientific investigation of group function and leadership, which had received little emphasis in the clinical professions. Finally, the T-group and laboratory movement has given birth to many innovations in group processes that may have clinical applicability, i.e., brief therapy groups, intensive group experiences, and the employment of nonverbal interaction methods.

The list of liabilities of the T-group supports the criticism others have made. The liabilities can be catalogued as follows: (1) lack of adequate selection criteria for participants; (2) varying competence of group leaders; (3) lack of accountability of group leaders to any professional peer group; (4) absence of clearly defined responsibility; (5) pseudoauthenticity and pseudoreality that pervade the T-group concerning the relationship between what happens in the group and what happens in everyday life; and (6) the possible encouragement of the adoption of new patterns of relationships that may be inappropriate to a group member's real-life circumstances.

RECENT TRENDS AND DEVELOPMENTS IN T-GROUPS

Since the 1960s, T-groups have undergone some changes in both philosophy and practice. Although the original emphasis on T-groups as a mechanism of learning about the democratic process continues, there is also an emphasis on other aspects of group work—for example, personal growth and organization development. As Klein (1972) has noted, comparatively little energy is now being devoted to the "engineering of new, integrative ideas in the application of group theory and research to real life problems. Theory sessions at training laboratories have gone out of style for the very good reason that as acts of communication they leave so much to be desired (p. 70)." Even in the literature, there are few studies of T-groups reported. Those studies which have been conducted are usually of an isolated nature. The period for the great tide of research on T-groups has diminished considerably.

The changes in the original focus of T-groups are also reflected in the reorganization of the National Training Laboratory (NTL). During the 1960s, NTL was organized into five centers: (1) Center for Organizational Studies; (2) Center for the Development of Educational Leadership; (3) Center for Community Affairs; (4) Center for the Development of Leadership in Government; and (5) Center for International Training. In the early 1970s, NTL was renamed the NTL Institute for Applied Behavioral Science. There was also a renaming of the centers developed in the 1960s. The centers were titled as follows: (1) Center for Organizational Studies; (2) Center for the Development of Educational Leadership; (3) Center for Black Studies; and (4) Center for a Voluntary Society. Since the early 1970s, the NTL Institute for Applied Behavioral Science has undergone several other changes, moving it toward a more personal growth and organizational development focus. Sensitivity training has become an official part of NTL.

The rapid increase in demand for group experiences also brought about changes in the professional preparation of group leaders. In the early stages of the history of T-groups, group leaders were well-trained professionals. One offshoot of this growing participant demand was a growth of ill-prepared trainers. Hence, in 1973, an organization called the International Association for Applied Social Scientists was established to accredit trainers. Much still remains to be done toward the monitoring, licensing, and accreditation of T-group leaders.

As early as 1964, Bradford, Gibb, and Benne (1964) listed four problem areas they predicted would become important for the future of laboratory education: (1) professionalization of trainers; (2) extensions and changes in the T-group method; (3) greater use of the laboratory method in nonlaboratory settings; and (4) expansion of research and theory development. In 1980, these four issues have yet to be satisfactorily resolved. There has been greater use of the laboratory method in nonlaboratory settings, but few researchers have begun to enumerate these differences and to spell out clearly what changes should be made in both theory and practice, given the extension of T-groups into organizations. Although expansion of research and theory development is necessary, little is being done in this area.

SUMMARY

In describing the historical events that led to the development of the T-group and sensitivity training, one must recognize that the beginning is never really the beginning. Like the birth of a new baby, there is always a prehistory. One of the goals in tracing the historical development of the laboratory method was to pinpoint some of the original distinctions that previously separated T-groups and sensitivity training—to try to understand how and why these two approaches have now become blurred.

One may compare some of the recent developments in the T-group to the growth of a tree that bears fruit. Although the apple tree, for instance, has only one trunk, it may have many branches. So it is with the T-group. The fruit of the T-group has fallen in different places. Presently T-groups are used in a variety of settings for a number of different reasons. One may find T-groups for personal development, for organizational change, and for more effective classroom teaching. Whatever the focus may be, the common denominator for any T-group is learning.

Much discussion has centered around the use of T-groups in the schools [see p. 137] and the applicability of this group approach to school counseling. There is not enough information available for anyone to state with any degree of confidence how frequently T-groups are used in the schools or what their effects have been in the classroom. What does seem clear is that a number of people who both oppose and support the use of T-groups in the schools may be confusing small-group discussion, which concentrates on feelings, with T-groups. It also seems reasonable to state that T-groups, as described throughout this chapter, are not equivalent forms for group counseling as customarily practiced in the schools. Some of the concepts underlying T-groups, particulary those relating to learning, may be used to great advantage in the schools by a teacher or counselor trained in the laboratory method. The objective therein would not be to turn classrooms into T-groups, but rather to sensitize teachers both to the feelings of students and to classroom dynamics.

References

American Psychological Association. Ethical standards of psychologists. *American Psychologist,* 1968, *23,* 357–61.

Appley, D. G., and A. E. Winder, *T-groups and therapy groups in a changing society.* San Francisco: Jossey-Bass Publishers, 1973.

Argyris, C. *Interpersonal competence and organizational effectiveness.* Homewood, IL: Irwin-Dorsey, 1962.

Back, K. W. *Beyond words: The story of sensitivity training and the encounter movement.* New York: Russell Sage Foundation, 1972.

Benne, K. D. History of the T-group in the laboratory setting. In L. P. Bradford, J. R. Gibb, and K. D. Benne (Eds.), *T-group theory and laboratory method: Innovation in re-education.* New York: Wiley, 1964, 80–135.

Bennis, W. G. *Organization development: Its nature, origins, and prospects.* Reading, MA: Addison-Wesley, 1969.

Bennis, W. G., and H. A. Shepard. A theory of group development. In R. T. Golembiewski and A. Blumberg (Eds.), *Sensitivity training and the laboratory approach.* Itasca, IL: Peacock Publishers, 1970, 91–115.

Bennis, W. G., and P. E. Slater. *Temporary society.* New York: Harper & Row, 1968.

Birnbaum, M. Sense and nonsense about sensitivity training. In R. W. Siroka, E. K. Siroka, and G. A. Schloss (Eds.), *Sensitivity training and group encounter.* New York: Grosset & Dunlap, 1971, 181–90.

Bonner, H. *Group dynamics: Principles and applications.* New York: Ronald Press, 1959.

Bradford, L. P. Membership and the learning process. In L. P. Bradford, J. R. Gibb, and K. B. Benne (Eds.), *T-group and laboratory method: Innovation in re-education.* New York: Wiley, 1964, 190–215.

Bradford, L., J. R. Gibb, and K. D. Benne. *T-group theory and laboratory method: Innovation in re-education.* New York: Wiley, 1964.

Buber, M. Distance and relation. *Psychiatry,* 1957, *20,* 2, 98–105.

Carkhuff, R. R. Critical perspectives on group processes. Address on growth groups presented to the Ninth Annual Conference on Personality Theory and Counseling Practice, U. of Florida, January 1969.

Carkhuff, R. R. *The development of human resources: Education and social action.* New York: Holt, Rinehart and Winston, 1970.

Cashdan, S. Sensitivity groups—problems and promise. *Professional Psychology,* Spring 1970, 217–24.

Cohen, A. M., and R. D. Smith. The critical-incident approach to leadership intervention in training groups. In W. G. Dyer (Ed.), *Modern theory and method in group training.* New York: Van Nostrand Reinhold Co., 1972, 84–106.

Cooper, C. L., and I. L. Mangham. The effectiveness of T-groups in producing on-the-job change. *Journal of Management Studies,* 1969, *6,* 53–72.

Culbert, S. A. The interpersonal process of self-disclosure: It takes two to see one. In R. T. Golembiewski and A. Blumberg (Eds.), *Sensitivity training and the laboratory approach.* Itasca, IL: Peacock Publishers, 1970, 73–86.

Culbert, S. A. Accelerating participant learning: A continuing challenge in trainer intervention. In W. G. Dyer (Ed.), *Modern theory and method in group training.* New York: Van Nostrand Reinhold Co., 1972, 116–46.

Dreyfus, E. A., and E. Kremenliev. Innovative group techniques: Handle with care. *Personnel and Guidance Journal,* 1970, *49,* 4, 279–83.

Drotning, J. E. Sensitivity training: Some critical questions. *Personnel and Guidance Journal,* 1966, *45,* 604–06.

Dyer, W. G. An Inventory of trainer interventions. In R. C. Diedrich and H. A. Dye (Eds.), *Group procedures: Purposes, processes, and outcomes.* Boston: Houghton Mifflin, 1972, 115–19.

Dyer, W. G. Here-and-now data versus back-home personal concerns: A professional and ethical decision. In W. G. Dyer (Ed.), *Modern theory and method in group training,* 1972, 233–43.

Eddy, W. B., and B. Lubin. Laboratory training and encounter groups. *Personnel and Guidance Journal,* 1971, *49,* 625–635.

Egan, G. *Encounter: Group processes for interpersonal growth:* Belmont, CA: Wadsworth, 1970.

Farson, R. E. *Science and human relations.* Palo Alto, CA: Science and Behavior Books, 1965.

Gibb, J. R. The present status of T-group theory. In L. P. Bradford, J. R. Gibb, and K. D. Benne (Eds.), *T-group theory and laboratory method.* New York: Wiley, 1964, 279–309.

Golden, W. P., Jr. On becoming a trainer. In W. G. Dyer (Ed.), *Modern theory and method in group training.* New York: Van Nostrand Reinhold Co., 1972, 3–29.

Golembiewski, R. T., and A. Blumberg. *Sensitivity training and the laboratory approach.* Itasca, IL: Peacock Publishers, 1970.

Gottschalk, L. A., and E. M. Pattison. Psychiatric perspectives on T-groups and the laboratory movement: An overview. *American Journal of Psychiatry,* 1969, *126,* 6, 91–107.

Harrison, R., and B. Lubin. Group composition models for laboratory designs. *Journal of Applied Behavioral Science,* 1965, *1,* 4, 409–32.

Hopkins, L. T. What does each member contribute? In C. G. Kemp (Ed.), *Perspectives on the group process.* Boston: Houghton Mifflin, 1964, 324–27.

Jourard, S. M. *The transparent self.* Princeton, NJ: Van Nostrand, 1964.

Klaw, S. Two weeks in a T-group. In R. T. Golembiewski and A. Blumberg (Eds.), *Sensitivity training and the laboratory approach.* Itasca, IL: Peacock Publishers, 1970, 24–37.

Klein, D. C. Sensitivity training and community development. In E. H. Schein and W. G. Bennis (Eds.), *Personal and organizational change through group methods.* New York: Wiley, 1965, 184–200.

Klein, D. C. Training for community competence. In W. G. Dyer (Ed.), *Modern theory and method in group training.* New York: Van Nostrand Reinhold Co., 1972, 68–83.

Koch, S. An implicit image of man. In C. J. Sager and H. S. Kaplan, (Eds.), *Progress in group and family therapy.* New York: Brunner/Mazel, 1972.

Lippitt, G. L., and L. E. This. Leaders for laboratory training: Selected guidelines for group trainers utilizing the laboratory method. In R. T. Golembiewski and A. Blumberg (Eds.), *Sensitivity training and the laboratory approach.* Itasca, IL.: Peacock Publishers, 1970, 157–66.

Marrow, A. J. *The practical theorist: The life and work of Kurt Lewin.* New York: Basic Books, 1969.

Massarik, F. The "natural" trainer: A systematic-normative view. In W. G. Dyer (Ed.), *Modern theory and method in group training.* New York: Van Nostrand Reinhold Co., 1972, 40–52.

Mial, H. C. Report on first leadership teamwork development laboratory for Washington, D.C. In R. T. Golembiewski and A. Blumberg (Eds.), *Sensitivity training and the laboratory approach.* Itasca, IL.: Peacock Publishers, 1970, 413–22.

Mill, C. R. A disconfirmation theory of learning. In *Reading Book for Laboratories in Human Relations Training.* Arlington, VA· NTL Institute for Applied Behavioral Science, 1972, 9–10.

NTL Institute for Applied Behavioral Science. *Standards for the use of the laboratory method.* Washington, D. C.: 1969.

Ohlsen, M. M. *Group counseling.* New York: Holt, Rinehart and Winston, 1970a.

Ohlsen, M. M. Reaction to Coulson's paper. *The Counseling Psychologist,* 1970b, *2,* 2, 38–42.

Pino, C. J. Relation of a trainability index to T-group outcomes. *Journal of Applied Psychology,* 1971, *55,* 5, 439–42.

Porter, L. D. Group norms: Some things can't be legislated. In *Reading*

Book for Laboratories in Human Relations Training. Arlington, VA: NTL Institute for Applied Behavioral Science, 1972, 34–36.

Psathas, G., and R. Hardert. Trainer interventions and normative patterns in the T-groups. *Journal of Applied Behavioral Science,* 1966, *2,* 149–70.

Schein, E. H., and W. G. Bennis. What is laboratory training: Description of a typical residential laboratory. In E. H. Schein and W. G. Bennis (Eds.), *Personal and organizational change through group methods.* New York: Wiley, 1965, 10–54.

Seashore, C. What is sensitivity training? In R. T. Golembiewski and A. Blumberg (Eds.), *Sensitivity training and the laboratory approach.* Itasca, IL: Peacock Publishers, 1970, 14–17.

Shepard, H. Explorations in observant participation. In L. P. Bradford, J. R. Gibb, and K. D. Benne (Eds.), *T-group theory and laboratory method: Innovation in re-education.* New York: Wiley, 1964, 379–94.

Skousen, W. C. Chief, watch out for those T-group promoters! In R. T. Golembiewski and A. Blumberg (Eds.), *Sensitivity training and the laboratory approach.* Itasca, IL: Peacock Publishers, 1970.

Solem, A. R. Interpersonal skills—a rejection of empathy concept and T-group methodology. In R. W. Siroka, E. K. Siroka, and G. A. Schloss (Eds.), *Sensitivity training and group encounter.* New York: Grosset & Dunlap, 1971, 191–99.

Stock, D. Research in sensitivity training. In L. P. Bradford, J. R. Gibb, and K. D. Benne (Eds.), *T-group theory and the laboratory method.* New York: Wiley, 1964.

Tannenbaum, R., I. R. Weschler, and F. Massarik. *Leadership and organization: A behavioral approach.* New York: McGraw-Hill, 1961.

Tannenbaum, R., I. Weschler, and F. Massarik. The role of the trainer. In R. T. Golembiewski and A. Blumberg (Eds.), *Sensitivity training and the laboratory approach.* Itasca, IL: Peacock Publishers, 1970, 139–40.

Weschler, F. Massarik, and R. Tannenbaum. The self in process: A sensitivity training emphasis. In I. Weschler and E. Schein (Eds.), *Issues in sensitivity training* (NTL Selected Reading Series). Washington, D.C.: National Education Association, 1962, 33–46.

Yalom, I., and M. Lieberman. A study of encounter group casualties. *Archives of General Psychiatry,* 1971, *25,* 16–30.

5

Self-Theory and Encounter Groups

Self-theory and encounter groups have had profound influences on both individual and group counseling. Much of this influence of these two approaches can be traced to the work of Carl Rogers. Rogers is not only recognized as one of the leading proponents of the self-theory approach to counseling but is also usually described as the dean of the encounter group movement. In many respects, Rogers' work has been revolutionary. His "necessary and sufficient conditions of therapeutic personality change" modified drastically the attitudes of therapists and, according to Hart (1970), ushered in the experiential period in the counseling field. Many counselors, for example, have adopted some form of the necessary and sufficient conditions for counseling espoused by Rogers, and many theorists of varying orientations have incorporated them into their own respective frameworks. It is for these reasons, as well as others, that the focus of this chapter is on Rogers' self-theory counseling approach and his basic encounter model.

Emphasis is placed first on the client-centered view on personality development and counseling. Next, early applications of self-theory to groups and recent extensions of this approach are discussed. A historical ovorview of encounter groups and Rogers' basic encounter model are also presented. Other topics discussed include the roles of group leaders and members, differences between encounter and therapy or counseling groups, recent trends in research, and contributions of encounter groups.

ROGERS' THEORY OF PERSONALITY

Rogers' theory of personality and client-centered therapy is the womb that gave birth to his basic encounter model. Originally, he did not set out to construct a theory of personality. He was more concerned with developing a theory of counseling. It was from his conception of client-centered therapy that Rogers made his formulations about personality. In explicating his theory, Rogers makes no pretense of pristine originality. He acknowledges that it is a synthesis of the concepts of a number of people—Maslow, Standal, Snygg and Combs, Rank, and Sullivan, to name a few. He was influenced primarily, however, by his own experiences as a therapist, and it is this fact that makes client-centered therapy distinctly Rogerian.

Nature of Human Beings

All theories of personality contain certain assumptions about the nature of human beings, some of which are more explicit than others. Rogers' vision of people is significant in that it serves as a launching point for his theories of client-centered therapy and personality. Throughout his writings, Rogers emphasizes the basic positive qualities of an individual. He continually refers to the dignity and worth of each person, the capability and right of each person to make decisions. Rogers also stresses the significance of the subjective nature of each individual. According to him, one can only live subjectively. Hence, learning to accept the subjective side of oneself becomes a goal of group counseling.

Moreover, Rogers posits that each person has a natural capacity for growth and development. Labeling this capacity the actualizing tendency, Rogers (1951) asserts that each individual has an innate directional tendency to develop in ways that function to maintain or enhance himself or herself. Positive growth and adjustment to life occur most readily when a person is provided with a suitable psychological environment in which the actualizing tendency can develop. Two other assumptions Rogers makes about the nature of each person are: (1) an individual is basically trustworthy; and (2) an individual is wiser than his or her intellect reveals. Thus, he rejects the destructive and antisocial nature of human beings that permeates some of the schools of psychoanalytic thought. It is society that corrupts an individual, society that turns a fundamentally positive creature into what some construe as a negative one.

It is small wonder, then, that Rogers' conception of humankind is one that has a great deal of appeal to people—particularly those who consider themselves "normal" individuals needing a modicum of help in dealing with the stresses of modern living. Through encountering one another in groups, the self-actualizing tendency of each person will begin to emerge more quickly. Free a man or woman from the inhibiting shackles of socialization and a basically positive person will emerge.

Concept of the Organism and the Phenomenal Field

Rogers' theory of personality revolves around several central concepts: (1) the organism, (2) the phenomenal field, and (3) the self. Organism refers to the total individual—in terms of physical as well as psychological well-being. The second aspect of his theory, the phenomenal field, is the private world of each individual that becomes his or her source of internal reference for viewing life. It constitutes everything that is experienced by an individual, regardless of whether or not the individual consciously symbolizes experiences into awareness. Parts of an individual's phenomenal field may be summoned into consciousness as they become associated with the satisfaction of certain needs the individual has established.

Rogers (1951) points out that each person exists and reacts in a "continuing changing world of experience of which he or she is the center (p. 483)." As an individual reacts within a phenomenal field, he or she does so as an organized whole. By responding as an organized whole, Rogers (1951) means "that the organism is at all times a total system, in which alteration of any part may produce changes in another part (p. 484)." He maintains that an individual's personality and behavior are determined by the goal of actualization. Goal directedness is, therefore, the effort to satisfy one's needs as experienced in one's phenomenal field.

Each person's phenomenal field constitutes his or her sense of reality. For example, the infant perceives all experiences as reality. A loving grandmother who attempts to embrace her grandson may find that the child responds to her overtures with episodes of frantic crying. Since he sees her as a source of threat, he reacts to her in a manner consistent with his perceptions—regardless of what the real situation may be. Thus, it is a perception of reality, rather than reality itself, that is of supreme importance. Part of group counseling may involve the opening up of and the testing of the reality of one's perceptions.

Each individual engages in what Rogers (1959) calls an organismic valuing process. Experiences that an individual perceives as satisfying needs are regarded positively, while those that are seen as not meeting needs are viewed negatively. Negatively perceived experiences lead to avoidance behavior, and positively perceived experiences lead to approach or acceptant behavior.

The Self

From interactions with others and from the total phenomenal field of experience, the infant gradually begins to differentiate a portion called the self. The self-concept is defined as the infant's differentiated elements of the experiential field which have the characteristics of the "I" or "me." Such delineation, no matter how tentative it may be, symbolizes the beginnings of the infant's conscious awareness of functioning. As a child grows older, she or he begins to receive feedback from interactions with significant others as to the type of person they perceive the child to be. From the person's evaluational interactions with others, the structure of the self begins to assume greater form, until the concept of self becomes a differentiated part of the person's phenomenal field. One may venture that complete differentiation of self from others—whether those others are parents or not—is one indication of adulthood.

Along with Freud, Rogers maintains that within each individual there is a basic craving for affection. In Rogerian terminology, this craving is labeled as a need for positive regard. The need for positive regard, in Rogers' view, is universal and reciprocal; that is, as a person satisfies another's need for positive regard, the person fulfills the same need. The individual, although a whole, is part of a greater whole (the world), wherein satisfaction of the greater whole can bring about satisfaction of the smaller whole. Hence, the introduction of the positive regard concept is significant insofar as a person now has two sources from which to evaluate behavior: (1) an innate organismic valuing process, and (2) standards, feelings, and thoughts of others concerning the person.

Positive regard is related to the socialization process, which all individuals in each society undergo in some manner or another. That is, from interactions with others in the environment, the individual internalizes certain values into the self-structure. This internalization of the values of others resembles Freud's notion of the superego. A person learns what to do as well as what not to do in order to remain in the graces of those dearest to him or her. In this respect, one can say that the self-concept is learned. According to Rogers, however, all experiences that occur in one's life do not automatically become a part of the self-structure. The individual may respond by ignoring some experiences because they do not appear to have any relationship to the perceived self-structure; by denying them symbolization into awareness; or by distorting their symbolization because they seem to be inconsistent with the individual's self-structure.

Another dimension of a person's self-structure comprises feelings of self-regard. Although it is related to positive regard, self-regard also can be distinguished from it. For example, a person may at times be more able to secure the positive regard of others than to obtain the same kinds of feelings from himself or herself. Securing other people's approval is winning only part of the battle. According to Rogers, gaining one's own self-regard is the goal a person wishes most to achieve and is the eventual end toward which behavior is knowingly or unknowingly directed. Mark Twain put it very aptly: "We can secure other people's approval if we do right and try hard; but our own is worth a hundred of it."

The resultant interaction between positive regard and self-regard is significant. If an individual feels loved by others even though he or she realizes that they do not accept certain behaviors, the individual is said to be receiving unconditional positive regard from them. Unconditional positive regard leads to unconditional self-regard. When this situation exists, the individual evaluates self-behavior as good or bad on the basis of the organismic valuing process.

In contrast, if an individual does not receive unconditional positive regard, it becomes difficult to develop positive self-regard. The desire for positive self-regard tends to make the individual work harder for the approval of others. That is, the individual who is extremely dependent on obtaining the positive regard of others may find it difficult to become his or her own person. The individual begins to like or dislike the self on the basis of others' evaluations. A person who behaves primarily in terms of the introjected values of others finds it difficult to make a positive self-evaluation unless he or she conforms to the standards of those from whom positive regard is sought.

From the interplay of positive regard and self-regard, a person develops conditions of worth. That is, an individual learns to discriminate the conditions under which the need for the positive regard of others and self-regard is most likely to be satisfied. Conditions of worth are said to exist when a person's experiences are evaluated on the basis of how others feel about them rather than by the person's own organismic valuing system; they tend to develop when the individual does not experience unconditional positive regard. Thus, conditions of worth form a second regulatory system of behavior. They may lead an individual to avoid certain activities or even thoughts because of having learned to view them as bad, or to participate in other activities because of having learned to view them as good. If the conditions of worth that an individual has learned coincide with the organismic valuing process, the individual feels a sense of congruence, and healthy behavior is likely to develop. Most of the time, however, this situation does not occur; the two regulatory systems tend to be in conflict, paving the way for maladjustment.

Maladjustment

A clearer understanding of personality maladjustment can be gained by examining what Rogers (1962) considers optimal adjustment of the fully functioning person. The optimally adjusted person is open to all experiences, even though such experiences are not always in full awareness. They are, however, available to awareness in accurately symbolized form—somewhat in the manner that Freud describes as the preconscious. The fully functioning person displays no defensiveness and has established no conditions of worth; he or she experiences unconditional positive regard. Moreover, concept of self is congruent with experiences, thereby freeing the person to respond in terms of his or her basic actualizing tendency. The openness to new experiences allows the person to be always in the process of becoming.

One of the fundamental causes of maladjustment is the incongruence between one's self-concept and one's experiences. Because this state of inconsistency may be unconscious, an individual may experience what can be designated as tension and free-floating anxiety. During such times, the individual senses the state of incongruence, but is usually not fully aware of what is wrong.

Experiences that are perceived as threatening are denied awareness. In an attempt to protect themselves from an onslaught of threatening emotions or ideas, individuals armor themselves so strongly that they create a more rigid self-structure. They tend to shy away from new experiences and to enclose themselves in a self-made prison of fear.

Gross incongruence of self, meaning the existence of a large difference between the perceived self and the actual experience, indicates maladjustment. During such times, a person feels that he or she has very few, if any, conditions of worth or self-regard. In an effort to regain a sense of balance (congruence with self), the maladjusted individual perceives experiences selectively. This kind of selective perception fosters enactment of *subception,* defined by Rogers (1951) as a defensive reaction that prevents incongruent material from coming into consciousness.

Anxiety accelerates with an increase in the amount of subception. Thus, subception, selective perception, denial of experience, distortion of experience, and rigidity are all tools the individual uses to maintain total integrity in the face of threat. Personality disorganization is now in process.

Personality reintegration occurs when unconditional positive regard and empathic understanding are communicated to the individual by others. Such communications strengthen the individual's unconditional self-regard. The defensive process previously described is now capable of being reversed, and heretofore denied or distorted experiences are symbolized into awareness and incorporated into the self-concept. The person becomes more congruent; positive regard for others is increased, and the individual's organismic valuing process becomes the basis for regulating behavior.

THE SELF-THEORY APPROACH TO COUNSELING

Rogers' approach to counseling has been labeled nondirective, self-theory, and client-centered therapy. Of all the terms used, self-theory seems to be the most appropriate, since Rogers emphasizes the effect that an individual's self-concept has on behavior. An individual experiences problems in living because of the negative statements he or she continually makes about himself or herself. One of the goals of self-theory counseling is to reverse the individual's tendency to make such negative statements. Another objective is to reestablish the individual's movement toward self-actualization by getting the individual to deal with the obstacles that block this process. Viewed from this perspective, counseling is a process of helping a person to release already existing positive forces. It is an attempt to make a person more self-directive.

The Rogerian or self-theory approach to counseling is founded on two basic hypotheses: (1) each person has the capacity to understand the circumstances that cause unhappiness and to reorganize his or her life accordingly; and (2) a person's ability to deal with these circumstances is enhanced if the therapist establishes a warm, accepting, and understanding relationship (Rogers, 1951). Therefore, Rogers maintains, it is the quality of the interpersonal encounter that is the most significant element in determining the outcome of any counseling relationship. Scholarly knowledge, training, counseling orientation, or techniques are secondary (Rogers, 1962). Thus, from Rogers' point of view, the most important question a counselor can ask is: How can I establish a relationship that will facilitate the personal growth of this client? Once a facilitative relationship has been established, the client is in a better position to reorganize self-structure in accordance with reality and his or her own needs.

Conditions of Therapy

To establish a facilitative relationship, certain conditions of counseling must exist. If the counselor establishes and maintains these conditions, then successful therapy has a greater chance of taking place. Rogers lists six necessary conditions for therapy. One can say that establishing these counseling conditions are part of self-theory techniques.

The first condition requires that two people should be in a state of psychological contact. In his earlier theoretical statements, Rogers used the word *relationship* to express the notion of psychological contact between two people. Being in a state of psychological contact means that the client and the counselor see their experience together as a relationship.

The second condition is that the client be incongruent. The state of incongruence on the part of the client refers to unsuccessful attempts to cope with life's problems. Rogers (1961) describes this condition thus: "He is, in short, faced with a problem with which he has tried to cope, and found himself unsuccessful (p. 282)."

Third, in contrast to the client, the counselor should be in a state of congruence. Facades and role playing on the counselor's part tend to inhibit learning. The congruent counselor is one who is in touch with what he or she is experiencing. The congruent counselor can also communicate these feelings to the client when they are appropriate to the encounter. Rogers asserts that unless the counselor is genuine, the client will find it difficult to be himself in the counseling relationship. Rogers' research, as well as that of others, has provided some confirmation of the idea that the more genuine and congruent the therapist is in the relationship, the more likely that change will take place in the client's personality structure.

Unconditional positive regard for the client by the counselor is the fourth necessary condition for therapy. Seeing each client as a separate entity, the counselor attaches no strings to acceptance of the client. It is the counselor's acceptance of the client that promotes the client's acceptance of self. In essence, unconditional positive regard means that the counselor experiences a warm, positive, acceptant attitude toward the client.

The fifth important condition necessary for the success of the relationship is counselor empathy. Rogers (1961) defines empathy as the counselor's ability to sense the client's private world as if it were his or her own but without ever losing the "as if" quality.

The final condition for therapy is that the client should recognize the counselor's congruence, acceptance, and empathy. Without a perception of these qualities, the client will not feel free; the client will not feel in a nonthreatening relationship. It is part of the counselor's responsibility to make sure that his or her intended behavior is perceived accurately.

Any theory of counseling is related to a concept of behavioral change. Many of the changes desired in client-centered therapy have been expressed in terms of the goals of counseling. As noted, the major behavioral change sought is a change in the person's self-concept. As this occurs, the client is inclined to become more receptive of others and more open to experiences and feelings both inside and outside the counseling relationship. Becoming more self-confident and self-directive, the individual gradually moves toward becoming the type of person he or she would like to be. Often this will bring about a more realistic adoption of goals; a greater maturity in behavior; more flexibility in one's perception of reality; and a more subjective experience of the self in the present rather than in the past. Although the techniques used may differ according to theoretical orientation, most counselors support, in some measure, Rogers' necessary and sufficient conditions of therapy.

Carkhuff's Applications of Self-Theory to Individual and Group Counseling

Rogers' client-centered therapy has been extended and modified by a number of individuals, including Carkhuff (1971), Truax (1961), Gendlin (1968, 1969), and Patterson (1969). Carkhuff (1969, 1971) has borrowed the most heavily from Rogers but has avoided or eluded the client-centered label. In his two-volume text, *Helping and Human Relations: A Primer for Lay and Professional Helpers*, Carkhuff developed a model which put forth the primary core dimensions of the interpersonal process. Much of Carkhuff's model is based on the necessary and sufficient conditions for counseling which Rogers had described earlier. Carkhuff also renamed some of Rogers' conditions, added new ones of his own, and developed scales to measure the level of these conditions offered by counselors and other helping individuals. As a result of his research and writings about the core dimensions of a helping relationship and his overall model for systematic human resources development, Carkhuff has profoundly influenced the direction that both individual and group counseling is taking.

In many respects, Carkhuff's model is more comprehensive than the client-centered approach. Carkhuff has tended to expand the client-centered approach by using such methods and procedures as confrontation, interpretation, behavior modification, and information giving. Carkhuff (1969) also introduces new factors in client-centered therapy by using different levels of the facilitative conditions at different stages of counseling, and by stressing that his preferred method of treatment is to teach the client directly the interpersonal behaviors put forth in client-centered therapy.

Carkhuff's (1971) model states three fundamental goals for the helping or counseling process. They are paraphrased as follows:

1. *Client self-exploration.* The first goal of counseling is to provide therapeutic conditions that promote the client's self-exploration. Before anything can take place, both the counselor and the client must examine all aspects of the difficulty which the client presents.

2. *Client self-understanding.* After being helped to explore problems and feelings in depth, the client will be able to understand what is causing the present difficulty.

3. *Client action.* Once the client achieves understanding, he or she is ready to begin taking action. Taking action is perhaps the most difficult aspect of the counseling process. Understanding without appropriate action is generally viewed as nonproductive. During this stage, the counselor helps the client to examine the available alternatives, and then helps the client plan a series of steps that will hopefully lead to a successful outcome.

Hence, the counseling process which Carkhuff (1971) proposes is divided into two basic stages: a facilitation stage and an action stage. The facilitation stage constitutes the first part of the counseling process. Its primary objective is to establish a therapeutic relationship with the client so that the client feels secure and safe enough to explore himself or herself and to eventually search for and develop self-understanding. Although Carkhuff's counseling process uses six conditions or dimensions of counseling that are provided to the client, these dimensions assume either greater or less prepotency in each of the two stages of counseling. For example, during the facilitation stage, the conditions of empathy, respect, concreteness, and genuineness are crucial. During the action stage, the dimensions of confrontation and immediacy tend to become most crucial. These conditions are described to show how Carkhuff has extended and revised Rogers' early theory regarding the conditions of therapy.

Empathy   Carkhuff (1969) describes empathy along the same lines as did Rogers. Basically, empathy means that the counselor tries to see the client's world as the client sees it and to convey this understanding to the client. Carkhuff and Berenson (1977, p. 8) have asserted: "We must emphasize that empathy is not the client-centered mode of reflection with which it is most often confused." Carkhuff and Berenson go on to state that their view of empathy represents an integration of the client-centered notion of the reflection of client feelings and the psychoanalytic emphasis upon the importance of diagnostic accuracy. This fact seems to be best exemplifed by Carkhuff's (1969) five-point scales which have been developed to measure the core conditions of a facilitative relationship. The empathic understanding scale measures, for example, levels of a counselor's or helper's empathic expression. The emphasis is on movement from low levels to high levels of empathic understanding. The high levels of empathic understanding (4 and 5) reflect the influence of the psychoanalytic school, whereas level 3 tends to characterize the client-centered notion of reflection of feelings to demonstrate empathy. Carkhuff and Berenson (1977) also posit that "the helper's final, not his initial, level of empathic understanding is related to patient improvement in therapy .... The implication is that, ultimately, the helper's effectiveness is related to his continuing depth of understanding rather than to his ability to 'technique it' during early phases of therapy (p. 8)." These investigators maintain that too much empathy too early in the counseling relationship may have a negative effect upon the client's development.

Respect   Carkhuff (1971, p. 170) has defined respect as "the ability to respond to the other person in such a way as to let him know that you care for him and that you believe in his ability to do something about his problem." In many ways, Carkhuff's definition of respect is similar to Rogers' concept of positive regard. In fact, Carkhuff uses the term positive regard interchangeably with respect. He notes, however, that it is erroneous to subsume his concept of respect under Rogers' notions of unconditional positive regard or nonpossessive warmth. According to Carkhuff and Berenson (1977), the terms unconditional positive regard or nonpossessive warmth are superfluous and misnomers. Carkhuff and Berenson (1977, p. 10) state: "Unconditionality would, instead, appear to be nothing more than the initial suspension of potentially psychonoxious feelings, attitudes, and judgments by the helper in all significant interactions with helpees." Carkhuff's concept of positive regard goes beyond the counselor's initial suspension of negative feelings toward a client (unconditional positive regard); it (respect) continues throughout the counseling relationship. Moreover, Carkhuff maintains that there are different levels at which a counselor or helping person may demonstrate or communicate respect to a client. Rogers does not deal with the levels at which positive regard may be communicated; positive regard is presented as a unidimensional and an all-or-nothing concept.

Genuineness   Carkhuff's concept of genuineness bears much resemblance to Rogers' concept of therapist congruency. In fact, Truax and Carkhuff (1967) have affirmed that the foundation for the entire helping relationship is the establishment of a genuine relationship between the counselor and the client. Similar to Rogers, Carkhuff defines genuineness in terms of the counselor's ability to be honest with self and with the client. Carkhuff differs from Rogers in that he makes one important qualification regarding the counselor's genuineness: negative counselor genuineness is nonfacilitative. Counselor genuineness should not be confused with counselor license to say and do what one feels at any given moment. The counselor must be guided by what is effective for the client, and in doing so, the counselor may have to withhold some very genuine responses. Carkhuff's concept of counselor genuineness differs from Rogers' concept of therapist congruency in that Carkhuff places limitations on the counselor's display of genuineness in the helping relationship and provides a scale to describe the counselor's level of genuineness. As Carkhuff and Berenson (1977) have stated, at level 5 (the highest level), the counselor's responses indicate that the counselor is freely and deeply himself or herself in the therapeutic relationship; the counselor is completely spontaneous but makes responses that may be hurtful to the client in a constructive manner so as to open additional areas of inquiry for both the counselor and the client.

Concreteness   This concept refers to the counselor's ability to get the client to be more specific about his or her concerns. Concreteness is a variable primarily under the therapist's control; it pertains to the counselor's ability to help the client pinpoint his or her feelings and experiences. The dimension of concreteness represents a departure from Rogers' self-theory approach, since the counselor does not merely wade in the client's general and sometimes vague expressions of what's bothering the client. A study by Truax and Carkhuff (1967) has indicated that concreteness is the most significant contributor to effective counseling, far outweighing the importance of empathy, positive regard, and genuineness. As with the other dimensions described, there is a scale to measure the counselor's degree or level of concreteness displayed in the counseling relationship.

Confrontation   This dimension represents an attempt on the part of counselors to help clients crystallize and hopefully reconcile their inconsistencies of expression and behavior. Confrontation implies that the counselor must take some risks to help clients bring into awareness their own discrepancies. Carkhuff (1969) has conceptualized confrontations into three broad categories:

1. Confrontation of a discrepancy between a client's expression of what he or she wishes to be and how the client actually experiences himself or herself to be (the ideal versus the real self in Rogerian terms)

2. Confrontation of a discrepancy between the client's verbal expression of self-awareness (in Rogerian terms, insight) and observable and/or reported behavior

3. Confrontation of a discrepancy between how the counselor or helper experiences the client and the client's expression of self-experience

Carkhuff (1969) suggests that it is better to initiate mild confrontations at first and to build gradually into more direct and forceful confrontations. A single confrontation will not permanently or effectively change a client's view of self or behavior pattern. However, a series of well-executed confrontations that are consistent in nature and delivery, and are based on client readiness, will have greater therapeutic potency and will lead to greater client self-exploration. Counselor confrontation of clients has been more emphasized by Rogers in his basic encounter model than in his early conceptualizations of client-centered therapy. Carkhuff's notion of counselor confrontation is based on the belief that a counselor will recognize and note the discrepancies between client statements or between what the client is doing and saying. Regardless of which situation exists, the counselor must be able to point out these discrepancies to the client.

Confrontation entails an active combination of immediacy, empathy, and interpretation. According to Carkhuff and Berenson (1977), only those counselors who evidence deep levels of understanding that go far beyond what is being said should be entitled to confront. Other qualifications are: the counselor must demonstrate deep and appropriate changing levels of regard and respect for the client; the counselor should be physically robust and "live fully from a high level of energy"; and "only those who love what they respect and respect those whom they love are potential sources of nourishment" should be entitled to confront. Carkhuff and Berenson lists five ways in which confrontation may be used by the helper: (1) to deal with discrepant helpee behaviors; (2) to expand the counseling process by creating various levels of crisis in the relationship; (3) to make interaction between counselor and client more immediate by dealing fully with the here-and-now of the relationship; (4) to show that the counselor will respond by taking risks; and (5) to open up new areas to explore and to reexplore previously unresolved problem areas.

Immediacy This concept refers to the counselor's ability to deal with the situation at hand in the counseling relationship. It suggests that the counselor or helper should have a sound understanding of the dynamics of what is taking place in the here-and-now with clients. Similar to other group counseling or therapy approaches, the counseling relationship is viewed as a social microcosm of the client's outside world, and clients' behaviors in the counseling situation represent their strategies for coping in life. Carkhuff (1969) presents four guidelines to assist counselors in focusing upon the central issue of what the client is trying to say that he or she cannot express directly. Accordingly, he suggests the following guide-lines concerning immediacy:

1. The counselor should focus upon experiencing the immediacy of the client-counselor relationship.

2. The counselor should disregard or hold in suspension the verbalized or actual content of the client's statements.

3. The counselor should try to analyze what the client is doing to slow down the counseling process.

4. The counselor should intermittently become a participant observer and try to sense and feel the immediate situation in the counseling relationship by asking himself or herself what is going on at that moment.

Focusing on immediacy helps the counselor respond to clients' dependency, manipulation, trust transference, resistance, and other interpersonal issues. The risk in responding to immediacy is admittedly high but necessary if the counselor is to reach the client. In responding to the immediacy of the moment of the therapeutic relationship, the counselor evidences a certain degree of confidence in his or her approach in deciphering the client's ploy of therapeutic encountering.

HISTORICAL OVERVIEW OF ENCOUNTER GROUPS

The primary goal of the following historical overview is to capture the spirit within which encounter groups developed. This seems essential, since the encounter movement is as much a social phenomenon as it is a psychological one.

Although the encounter group movement is a relatively recent development, the germination of the concept can be traced as far back as 1914, when J. L. Moreno provided the first literary definition of the term in a series of poetic writings, translated as *Invitation to an Encounter.* In describing the essence of an encounter, Moreno depicted two people exchanging eyes in an effort to understand and to get to know each other. The description is dramatic. The initial confrontation between the two individuals is fundamentally destructive, with each trying to tear out the other's eyes and to substitute them for his own. Yet, as each person begins to realize the futility of his acts, he no longer needs to destroy or impose his perceptions upon the other. Understanding of both themselves and one another comes when each can look at the other through the other's eyes. Concerning the impact of the encounter, Moreno (1969) states:

> A meeting of two: eye to eye, face to face. And when you are near I will tear your eyes out and place them instead of mine, and you will tear my eyes out and will place them instead of yours, then I will look at you with your eyes and you will look at me with mine (p. 7).

Moreno's poetic definition of an encounter has never become the official definition of encounter groups. There is none. Rather, the spirit of his definition has lingered on throughout the years—the picture of two people or a group of people trying to get to know each other by breaking down the artificial, self-imposed barriers individuals create. Moreno's interest in psychodrama ended what might have been his involvement in the development of encounter groups. Yet, ideas about human involvement do not just die; sometimes they are deservedly reincarnated. Such was the case with Moreno's concept of encounter. After lying dormant for a while, the actual reincarnation of the concept of encounter in terms of groups took place forcefully in the 1960s. The techniques Moreno developed in psychodrama were later incorporated into the encounter group approach—specifically those using a therapy group to act out emotionally significant feelings for the purpose of catharsis and the acquisition of new behaviors. Experience in action is another common touchstone for both psychodrama and encounter groups.

The T-Group as Progenitor of the Encounter Group

To look for more substantial beginnings of the encounter movement, one must go back to the annals of the T-group movement and the schism that occurred when clinical modifications were introduced in the design of that group orientation. As noted in the preceding chapter, Freudian and Rogerian approaches clashed sharply with those of the Lewinian-oriented T-group staff members. The emphasis of the clinical staff on personal feedback in the here-and-now setting proved to be too great a rival for the Basic Skills Training Group, which attended to theory, group dynamics, and general back-home issues. Thus, by the early sixties the trend that had started in 1949 became embodied in the phrase "group therapy for normals (Weschler, Massarik, and Tannenbaum, 1962)." That is, the goals of the T-group were refashioned, and the stage was set for a more forceful emergence of the encounter group as a separate approach.

At this point, two major developments in the evolution of the encounter group can be distinguished: (1) the shift from the social change emphasis of the T-group to a clinical emphasis, and (2) the inclusion of the encounter group within the framework of psychotherapy for normal individuals. Concomitantly, the beginning of a change can be seen in the role of the group leader. The leader was now given, or, perhaps more accurately, now came to assume, additional freedom to be himself or herself and to use a wider variety of techniques that entailed more direct physical contact and confrontation with group members.

Along the way, there was also a geographical shift in centers for small-group laboratories from Bethel, Maine, and the East Coast to the West Coast. Although no single source of the encounter movement can be identified, most of the recent developments emanated from the Western Behavioral Institute at La Jolla, California. It was there that Rogers coined the phrase "basic encounter group" to differentiate this new group experience from that of the traditional T-group. Already a giant in individual psychotherapy, Rogers began to accommodate and to modify his theory of client-centered therapy to groups. To a great extent, it was Rogers' fundamentally positive humanistic views, rather than his formulations in client-centered therapy, that provided the impetus for the personal growth aspect of encounter groups. In his approach to encounter groups, little attention is directed to the analysis of group dynamics or the learning of such dynamics by participants. Instead, the Rogerian encounter group leader focuses on interpersonal or intrapersonal dynamics. Most of the proponents of this school make little distinction between personal growth and psychotherapy. In brief, as a result of Rogers' efforts, the institute became a breeding ground for encounter groups (Back, 1972).

One cannot stress sufficiently the significance of the shift in geographical location to the wild flower growth of encounter groups. California, with all of its emphasis on the youthful culture, was ripe for a group experience that advertised a promise of intimacy and a sense of belongingness (Lieberman, Yalom, and Miles, 1973). Having traveled hundreds of miles for the land of sunshine and honey, people came to California uprooted from their background of nuclear and extended family ties. They were, essentially, strangers in a new land who had discarded the proverbial worn-out but, nevertheless, familiar shoes of the past for new ones that required a certain amount of breaking in and adjustment. Some individuals saw in the encounter group approach the creation of a forum that would allow them to air personal problems that were often interwoven with their adjustment efforts. Rogers' basically positive philosophy gave hope to those who felt a loss of intimacy in interpersonal relations and who were experiencing low self-regard.

Almost simultaneously, but independently, other schools of psychotherapy added their support to the encounter group movement. For some, their support was mainly a matter of joining the lucrative bandwagon; for others, it was a matter of belief in the efficacy of the encounter method. Psychoanalysts like Mintz and Schultz, who were somewhat disenchanted with the traditional psychoanalytic approach to group therapy, saw in the encounter approach a new, more efficient method of conducting group work. For instance, Schultz stresses the experiencing and deepening of interpersonal relationships through the liberation of bodily restrictions. By freeing oneself from bodily restrictions, participants learn how to get in touch with their own bodies and with other people in a fuller sense. Significance is placed upon experiencing, while understanding the underlying causes of these inhibitions is a minor concern.

In Gestalt encounter groups, weight is given to heightened emotionality and body linguistics—what the body tells one by its posture and gestures. The leader assumes a prominent role in Gestalt-oriented encounter, and the participation of other members is minimal. Yet Gestalt therapists, while joining the swelling throng of encounter group supporters, have maintained some measure of their own identity. Each school of thought, whether Rogerian, psychoanalytic, or Gestalt-oriented, seems to be united around the general notion that people need help to deal with a society that appears bent on a technocratic, dehumanistic collision course with self.

The Social History Context

When the social context of the evolution of the encounter group is considered, it becomes more than just a matter of modification of the T-group. Encounter groups developed mainly as a response to a number of broad societal forces operating in American culture. These factors were not unique to California; they were only accentuated there. California was a pacesetter in its acceptance of encounter groups, much as it has been in other areas. With the precedent set, people in other parts of the country also latched onto the encounter group format.

One might ask how social occurrences affect the encounter movement. Riesman (1962) provides some possible answers. He notes in *The Lonely Crowd* that the days of the legendary inner-directed frontiersman struggling fiercely on his own are now a thing of the past and that Americans are becoming more outer-directed than inner-directed. One can say that the encounter group provides just one more outlet for the trend toward outer-directedness.

The gravitation toward what has been labeled the permissive society has also had its effects. More and more Americans seem attracted to the concept underlying the phrase "do your own thing." Polite talk and conversation are seen as artificial and middle-class in the worst possible sense. "Tell it like it is" is the slogan that swept the country in the late 1960s. For some people, the encounter group provides an opportunity to "tell it like it is."

Ruitenbeek (1970) relates the general appeal of the encounter group to what he calls the American character. According to him, Americans tend to adopt a pragmatic view of life. They are geared towards getting things done in the quickest fashion possible. The short time duration of the encounter group is consonant with this attitude. Why go through the long process of working through unconscious motivators of behavior when one can obtain what is perceived as a quick cure that deals with the here-and-now?

Blanchard (1972) provides still another way of analyzing the encounter group movement. He postulates that it is essentially a third force movement—a counterculture created as a reaction to some of the socialized anxiety of a highly mobile middle-class population. Throughout history, members of the middle class have been the most consistent patrons of psychotherapists; their support for the encounter group movement continues the pattern of involvement already started. The social changes manifested in these groups are both implicit and explicit. In terms of the counterculture concept, such groups emphasize direct action, freedom from restraint, growth, and overt expression of feelings.

Agreeing with Blanchard's thesis of the counterculture element in encounter groups, Parloff (1972) sees the movement as an attempt to define humankind as it should be and possibly could be if only given the opportunity. According to Parloff, this attempt is not a new one; every age seeks to define humanity in a manner that is consistent with the dominant feelings of that period. Presently, the humanistic-existentialist view has taken hold. The culture is denounced for thwarting an individual's desire for self-actualization, love, and intimacy. The more affluent our society has become, the more keenly aware the middle-class individual has become of alienation. He or she has been able to satisfy lower-order needs for basic survival; now the individual seeks to satisfy higher-order needs. The middle-class individual is suffering from a hitherto unnoted kind of deprivation—

what Parloff (1972) calls *residual deprivation.* "He experiences a sense of mean-inglessness in the mere attainment of what had earlier been touted as the good life. Man's attention has shifted from his belly to his belly button and, now, to that of his neighbor (p. 179)."

Viewed by some as the dean of this new therapeutic social movement, Rogers (1967) affirms that he is offering participants a package of distinctly counterposed values. He sees these counterposed values as "becoming more spontaneous, flexible, closely related to their feelings, open to their experience, and closer and more expressively intimate in their interpersonal relationships (p. 275)."

The encounter movement, then, is labeled counterculture for a number of reasons, such as its disdain for the overly rational, the tendency of group members to bare their burdens publicly rather than privately, and its distrust of professionally trained psychotherapists.

Back (1972) sees some negative offshoots of this third force in American society. According to him, the encounter movement has created the "groupie junkie," the person who seems to live for the weekly, weekend, or yearly encounter experiences and who proceeds from one session to another searching for a new type of group experience high. For some people the groupie habit is costly—both psychologically and monetarily. Yet, it is the psychological addiction, Back theorizes, which is the more difficult one to break. It produces a nation of psycho-logical cripples. In his opinion, such groups foster the very kind of dependency behavior that they try to help the participant overcome.Back states that inherent in most encounter movements is the danger of aftereffects and withdrawal symp-toms. For instance, when former encounter group participants go back into the everyday world, some find it difficult to cope with their daily existence. Their cultural island, with all of its emphasis on honesty, intimacy, and openness, is hard to reproduce in the real world. These factors, from Back's perspective, weaken the potential positive effects of the encounter group movement.

To summarize, one of the first significant factors that led to the rise of encounter groups was the revision of the T-group to include a more personal focus. The encounter group emerged out of the sensitivity focus of the T-group. From this point on, it began to go through a separation and individuation period from the T-group. A greater emphasis was placed upon touching, hugging, and other forms of physical contact. A second major factor was the technological and sociological developments of the times. People began to feel, more than ever before, out of touch with themselves and others around them. The net result seemed to be a society of people on the fringes. To reduce their sense of marginality, individuals joined encounter groups. They saw the group situation as a means to change both their external and internal states.

The history of encounter groups seems to change each day. Using Rogers' terminology, one might say that they are in the process of becoming. What encoun-ter groups are actually becoming is still largely unknown. Until the social conditions from which they developed change or until one finds a substitute for them, it seems that encounter groups will continue to grow in number.

ROGERS' BASIC ENCOUNTER GROUP MODEL

Although Rogers' affiliation with the small-group experience dates as far back as 1946, when he was involved at the University of Chicago with an intensive, experiential course of training for counselors of returning GIs, it has only been since the mid-1960s that the small-group experience has become a primary focus of his work. His reason for becoming involved with such groups was quite simple: by his own account, he saw the potency of a group in bringing about changes in attitudes and behaviors of individuals. Rogers underscores, for example, the idea that both acceptance and understanding of group members among and between themselves have a greater effect and meaning than acceptance by a therapist. Part of the powerfulness of the group—and specifically the encounter group—lies in the notion that the kind of peer acceptance that occurs traditionally in childhood and adolescence may be a missing element for individuals. Hence, acceptance or validation of one's worth by other group members constitutes a vital experience for some people.

It has been said that in creating the basic encounter model, Rogers did more than develop a new *form* of group work. He has essentially tried to develop a new *kind* of life and civilization based on short encounters and an individual's ability to share deep feelings with people whom he or she tends to see only rarely (Back, 1972). That is, whether intended to or not, the impact of the basic encounter model has caused people to examine the lives they lead in society and the implicit rationale upon which that society seems based. In terms of American society at large, this is seen as the potential potency of the encounter model.

Some changes can be observed in Rogers' approach to individual counseling, his initial involvement with small groups, and his later involvement with encounter groups. These changes center largely around his more active and confronting interaction with group members. In his revised approach to groups, more attention is focused on the contribution of participants. Much of what people previously labeled as nondirective counseling is missing. Before discussing other shifts in Rogers' orientation, a clear understanding must be obtained of what is meant by a basic encounter.

There are a number of definitions of encounter groups. Despite the proliferation of definitions, however, most interested people tend to use Rogers' definition as a foundation. Rogers defines an encounter group as one that stresses personal growth through the development and improvement of interpersonal relationships via an experiential group process (Rogers, 1970). Using some of Rogers' basic concepts, Thomas (1969) defines an encounter group as simply a group of people committed to the task of becoming more fully human in their daily lives. Stoller (1969) visualizes the encounter group as a meeting place to which individuals come to learn about themselves without the underlying implication that they are sick or in serious psychological difficulty. In his opinion, through the experiencing of each other, participants ultimately experience themselves more fully. Each of these definitions underlines the importance of spontaneity and unfreezing of human potential. Accordingly, the encounter movement symbolizes a war against unused human potential.

In his book, *Carl Rogers on Encounter Groups* (1970), Rogers makes few distinctions between T-groups and encounter groups. He merely notes that although the T-group was originally intended to focus upon human relations skills, it has become much broader in scope. That there are many points of overlap between these two group types seems evident. For instance, similarities are apparent in the key concepts of both of these group types. What, then, distinguishes a T-group from an encounter group? First, although both models emphasize ambiguity, the T-group is fundamentally more structured and has a more theoretical learning foundation than does the encounter group. The encounter model, as yet, has no single acceptable theoretical framework. Second, the term feedback is sometimes used in different ways for each of these models. Feedback in the encounter group tradition is more akin to confrontation. Whereas T-group leaders tend to restrict feedback to observable or identifiable behaviors, encounter group facilitators make no such restrictions. In the encounter model, feedback occurs during the process of confrontation between various participants.

Another difference is in the T-group's strict adherence to the here-and-now focus on material presented to the group. Members are asked to deal with what is happening in the group itself and not to introduce material that relates to their lives outside of the group. Even though the here-and-now of group participants' behavior is likewise of prime importance in the encounter model, the content of any member's expressions may be related to the past. In fact, Rogers (1970) notes in his description of the process of the basic encounter that participants' early personal revelations frequently deal with past occurrences in their lives.

Furthermore, the T-group appears to be more task-oriented than the encounter group. The task is essentially that of learning more about group dynamics and how participants themselves function in a group setting. In contrast, the encounter model is more process-oriented; it stresses intimacy among group members as a goal in itself. Although the T-group also addresses itself to the intimacy issue, it usually does so within the context of the group's working on the task of understanding the dynamics of the group process.

The differences between T- and encounter groups may be viewed as those that occur along a continuum. In some respects the T-group represents the more conservative or traditional wing of the human-potential movement. Encounter groups, on the other hand, are customarily associated with the more liberal or radical wing of this movement. Yet, perhaps one of the greatest distinctions between these two group types is not in the expressed purposes of the models or even in what happens in each one of them, but rather in the reasons for which participants join either of these two group types. That is, individuals who join the personal growth encounter groups as described by Rogers attend such groups for the avowed purpose of broadening their own personal growth, and those who join T-groups do so for personal growth plus other types of learning experiences, such as for educational purposes and organizational development.

In summary, both encounter and T-groups are part of a larger human-potential movement. Since both group approaches have been frequently confused and used interchangeably, a concerted effort has been made here to delineate some of the specific differences between the two. Attention is now directed toward the key concepts of encounter groups, recognizing that some overlap may occur with the key concepts previously presented in terms of T-groups.

Key Concepts of the Basic Encounter Model

Some individuals might go so far as to say that there are no key concepts associated with encounter groups, that they spring from spontaneous generation—having no past or future. But despite the many types of encounter groups and their lack of solid theoretical foundation, it is nevertheless possible to extract certain commonalities of thought. For example, Frank (1961) suggests that there exists a set of necessary conditions for any encounter group experience to occur. These conditions are:

1. an acknowledgment of a situation that causes an individual to feel different from (usually inferior to) the rest of society

2 the availability in a society of a group of qualified individuals who, by special training or experience, have attained a recognized competence in dealing with this condition

3. a socially reinforced belief by the individual sufferer that these practitioners and their techniques will help him or her

4 a separation of the individual from the customary environment and status as preparatory steps to treatment

5 a recognition by the sufferer as a result of the encounter between sufferer and practitioner that a reintegration into more effective living has now become possible

Most of the aforementioned concepts are espoused by Rogers (1970). However, to broaden the scope of this delineation, an effort also has been made to outline ideas that seem to cut across the various encounter models. Moreover, in describing Rogers' basic encounter model, it is important to recognize that Rogers was not interested in constructing a high-level abstract theory of group psychology. On the contrary, he was more concerned with sharing his experiences as an encounter group member and facilitator.

Common External Characteristics The external characteristics of encounter groups generally refer to their size and composition. The size of most encounter groups is fairly standard—ranging from eight to eighteen members. One of the reasons for limiting group size is to give each person an opportunity to contribute to the ongoing interaction. Hence, such groups should be large enough to meet most of the needs of the participants so that the absence of one or two individuals does not seriously hamper the group, yet small enough so that absences of members are actually felt (Egan, 1970).

Group composition varies according to the nature of the group. To a great extent, self-selection determines group membership. Generally, encounter groups are composed of strangers who have come voluntarily together for a session that may last from a weekend to a few weeks, or may be a course taken for a few hours each week. Most participants are usually strangers to each other, have not selected each other for coming together, and commonly assume that they will not see each other again. Even for groups of individuals who know each other—such as the cases where individuals are selected from the same organization and work environment—there is also a feeling of the ephemeral nature of the group. For instance, in the encountering situation that contains members of the same organization, there is a separation of what occurs in the group experience from the members' other experiences together—or so the theory goes. The feeling is that members will not see each other under these same conditions again. Back (1972) points out that in the latter case, this may be an erroneous assumption. There are inherent difficulties in having such a group—difficulties that tend to linger on long after the encountering experience is over.

Encounter groups are unstructured, leaving members to find their own directions. The leader's role, in its broadest sense, is to facilitate the expression of group members' thoughts and feelings.

Group Goals Rogers maintains that he usually does not have any specific goals for the groups with which he works. Putting his faith in the group's ability to move, or what one might label the "group actualizing tendency," he stresses the negative aspects of setting specific goals. From interactions within the group, he posits that participants will forge their own individualized goals rather than any predetermined goals of the group leader. Although the concept of self-determination of goals seems ideal, it also raises some questions. One might ask, for example: Does the absence of group goals serve to make the group more cohesive or more destructive? To what extent do individual goals militate against the total development or growth of the group?

Moreover, despite Rogers' protestation that he does not have any specific goals for any particular group, inherent in all that he seems to say are certain implicit, if not explicit, goals. As noted previously, the primary focus of such groups is upon developing members' awareness, expression, and acceptance of feelings. This is a goal. Even the term *basic encounter* suggests that the group has within it certain goals. The group is expected to create an atmosphere in which participants can deal with each other with more depth than is generally experienced in traditional personal interactions. Broadly speaking, the goal of any encounter group may be seen as one that helps individuals to free the frozen assets within by exposing themselves to an experience that requires emotional investments. The expected return rate of these investments is that people will come to realize their growth potential. In this sense, the ultimate goal is a person's encounter with self.

Personal Growth and Psychotherapy for Normals In general, Rogers does not make clear-cut distinctions between personal growth goals of an encounter group and therapy goals. Rogers prefers to say that each group has psychologically growth-promoting effects, thus avoiding any other implications of the term *therapeutic*. One possible reason for his lack of careful differentiation between the two terms is that he sees them as being intimately related. Some measure of support for this interpretation is given by Rogers in his writings. For example, he asserts that the purpose of counseling is to enhance the individual's personal development and psychological growth. He also maintains that a counselor's ability to help an individual enhance personal growth is not something that can be accomplished by the technical knowledge of the counselor. He states: "Constructive personal growth is associated with the counselor's realness, with his genuine and unconditional liking for his client, with his sensitive understanding of his client's private world, and with his ability to communicate these qualities in himself to his client (Rogers, 1962, p. 428)."

Not all theorists agree with Rogers' lack of distinction between a personal growth encounter group and psychotherapy. From a review of the literature on encounter groups, one can distinguish three points of view concerning this issue. First is the stance that encounter groups, although similar, are not equivalent to psychotherapy groups and potential participants should be told so at the very beginning (Golembiewski and Blumberg, 1970). Second, there is the view that encounter groups are potentially psychologically dangerous rather than therapeutic (Yalom and Lieberman, 1971). To strengthen their position, Yalom and Lieberman point to the encounter group casualties that occur when individuals who should not use encounter groups as therapy groups do so anyway. Third, the encounter group is seen by some writers as a special variant of psychotherapy; it is intended to augment, not to replace, the latter.

Burton (1969) declares that encounter groups are a special variant of psychotherapy that should be undertaken mainly by individuals trained in the psychotherapeutic method. Instead of conceiving of encounter groups as abbreviated or as a less expensive way of providing therapy, he suggests that they contain the seed for a new psychological approach to suffering, growth, and self-actualization. According to Burton (1969), "Psychotherapy is no longer for the diseased (pp. 8–9)." It is also for normal individuals who suffer from what he terms the existential neuroses—alienation, loneliness, despair, and anxiety. He posits that some of the same concepts and techniques of helping the diseased can be used with the nondiseased person. When viewed from this perspective, then, encounter groups either now constitute or will soon constitute a "secularized psychotherapy for Everyman (Burton, 1969, p. 8)." The importance of the encounter as a psychotherapeutic force is that the process of encountering allows one to experience one's missed subself as one interacts with other group participants who symbolize that subself. Thus the encountering experience "makes up for both the inadequate introject and the false one (Burton, 1969, p. 20)."

Partial support for Burton's position is given by Maslow (1968), who states that "what we call 'normal' in psychology is really a psychopathology of the average, so undramatic and so widely spread that we don't even notice it ordinarily (p. 16)." Given the present turmoil in psychotherapy as to what constitutes mental illness or what constitutes therapy, Rogers may be wise in not addressing this issue in terms of encounter groups. Undoubtedly, for some individuals the encounter group experience may constitute psychotherapy, for others it may be only a stepping-stone to more traditional forms of counseling, and for still others it may only be another type of social group. Whether rightfully or wrongfully, the concept of psychotherapy for normal individuals is and probably will continue to be linked with encounter groups. For this reason alone, it merits consideration as one of the key concepts of encounter groups.

Psychological Climate Some of the conditions Rogers originally established for individually oriented client-centered therapy are still evident in his approach to encounter groups. The major difference is that these concepts have been updated to take into consideration the presence of other individuals in the counseling situation. When Rogers uses the term *psychological climate,* he is referring to the type of group atmosphere that fosters freedom of expression and reduces participants' defensiveness. In Rogers' estimation, a trusting and cohesive group climate is one of the most necessary therapeutic requirements of the basic encounter.

Concurring with Rogers, Frank (1961) affirms that the greatest potential drawback of therapy groups is the tendency, especially in beginning meetings, to supply insufficient support for members to cope with the stresses such groups generate. One of the most prevalent fears of participants is of taking risks, of disclosing themselves, and of dealing with emotional issues. Erikson (1959) conceptualizes this fear in terms of a shame experience. He states: "Shame supposes that one is completely exposed and conscious of being looked at.... One is visible and ready to be visible.... Shame is early expressed in an impulse to bury one's face, or to sink, right then and there, into the ground. But this, I think, is essentially rage turned against the self (pp. 142–43)."

The psychological climate is of great importance to any kind of personal encounter group. Rogers addresses the notion of psychological safety from both the group leader's and participants' roles. The group leader establishes the psychological climate by role-modeling behavior. Participants do so by demonstrating their caring for each other. [The specifics of each of these roles are discussed more fully later in this chapter.]

Mutual Trust The development of mutual trust is necessary for the success of any encounter group. Once trust has been established among group members, participants find it easier to express both negative and positive feelings. The freedom of expression that pervades the group helps each member to become more self-acceptant. In earlier Rogerian terminology, one would say that it facilitates the development of self-regard.

Gibb and Gibb (1969) have applied their TORI (trust-openness-realization-independence) theory of organization development to encounter groups. They propose that growth is universal to all human beings and, furthermore, that it is a progression from fear to trust, from censored to open communication, from dependence to self-determination, and from dependence to interdependence. From their perspective, the most significant barriers to growth are an individual's fears, distrusts, and inaccurate life theories. Thus, the TORI theory is founded upon the premise that the deepest needs of human beings are to trust and to be trusted, to be intimate in communication, to self-actualize, and to be genuinely independent. In order to change a rate of growth, a person must have deep experiences that help to disconfirm fears and distrust so that the person can rebuild his or her life theory in a way that is more congruent with trust experiences and trust assumptions. A good encounter group should provide an opportunity for this type of fear reduction.

Feedback and Communication   No real encounter can occur between two people without feedback and communication. In some respects, the communication exchange that occurs during an encounter group forms part of the nucleus of encountering. An underlying assumption of an encounter group is that somewhere along the way, people have lost the art of communication. The encounter group is one means of opening up the channels of communication that individuals tend to close down because of the fear of what others will think about them and, perhaps more importantly, of what they will think about themselves. The general notion is that the feedback each participant receives will help the participant understand how he or she is perceived by others and what impact his or her behavior has on interpersonal relationships.

Confrontation   There is a tendency on the part of some individuals to use the terms *feedback* and *confrontation* interchangeably. Although feedback may be given in the process of confrontation, it is not the equivalent of confrontation. Feedback is too mild a term to convey the type of interchange that occurs in encountering. Confrontation challenges a person to become more totally integrated. It usually focuses on discrepancies within an individual (between the ideal self and the real self) and between the person's verbal expressions and actions. From a therapeutic view, confrontation, when used appropriately, forces a person to engage in self-examination.

It is hypothesized that some measure of confrontation is necessary in any kind of meaningful human and growth-oriented interaction. Douds, Berenson, Carkhuff, and Pierce (1967) assert that life "without confrontation is directionless, passive, and impotent (p. 172)." In the absence of confrontation, an individual may gravitate into what Maslow (1968) termed *psychopathology of the average.* Rogers does not explicitly define confrontation. Instead, he uses the word to connote a kind of intense interaction between individuals that occurs during the process of each giving the other feedback.

Rogers' use of confrontation in the group situation represents one of his major departures from his earlier nondirective approach. Describing how he uses confrontation in groups, he stresses that he mainly confronts participants on the specifics of their behavior, using only those feelings that he is willing to claim as his own. Rather than saying to a group member, "Your attempt to intellectualize your problems away is a sign of avoidance," Rogers would confront the participant with the feelings that this intellectualization aroused in him.

The research of Berenson, Mitchell, and Laney (1968) indicates that effective therapists tend to confront their clients more frequently than less effective therapists, but that they also provide the conditions under which confrontation is likely to be received positively. That is, they confront with empathy and positive regard.

Egan (1970) suggests certain guidelines for making confrontation a constructive group process. Some of his suggestions are as follows:

1. Confrontation should be done to demonstrate one's concern for another.

2. Confrontation should be a way of becoming involved with another person.

3. Confrontation should address itself primarily to another's behavior and only tangentially to that person's motivation.

4. Each person should be willing to confront himself or herself honestly in the group.

Experiencing Experiencing is another major concept pervading most encounter group literature. According to Rogers (1959), it refers to the "unity of emotion and cognition as they are experienced inseparably in the moment (p. 198)." It is important in an encounter group that a participant experiencing a feeling be aware of that feeling and express it. Since part of maladjustment is associated with the lack of openness to experiencing and a rigid self-structure, one of the goals of Rogerian-oriented encounter groups is to help a person get in contact with what he or she is feeling at any given moment.

One of the drawbacks of the encounter movement for some individuals is that it puts too much faith in experiencing for experiencing's sake. Back (1972) postulates that an overemphasis on experiencing promotes a distrust of the cognitive and the intellectual, even when these things are positive in nature. When primary stress is placed upon experiencing, participants come to feel that only feelings and personal experience are of any value or can be trusted. One point in Rogers' favor is that he does not use gimmicks, as some encounter group leaders do, to get the participants more quickly at a feeling or experiencing level. He theorizes that this phenomenon will occur naturally during the process of most encounter groups.

Intimacy Another common touchstone of most encounter groups is the emphasis placed on intimacy. The lack of an ability to engage in human relations that involve intimacy or some sort of self-realization is construed as another example of psychopathology of the average. One of the central questions surrounding the push toward greater intimacy in human relations is: Do encounter groups foster real or pseudo-intimacy? And secondly, to what extent is the sense of intimacy reached in any encounter group an indication of a person's continued ability to engage in such relationships? That is, the opponents of encounter groups maintain that these groups foster fleeting pseudo-intimate relationships, which in the long run do more harm than good.

The Process of the Basic Encounter

Although Rogers outlines what he considers the process of the basic encounter group, he points out that none of the stages are in a clear-cut sequence. Much depends upon the different composition of groups. Describing the process of group interaction as "a rich and varied tapestry," he depicts the stages he believes are most common to the encounter groups in which he has participated. These stages are summarized below.

Milling Around   Basically, this concept refers to group members' attempts to avoid taking directional responsibility and to use techniques such as small talk and superficial interpersonal interactions as defensive measures to prevent them from "getting down to business." Milling around is largely a warm-up activity that grows out of the uneasiness of group members in an unstructured situation. Rogers' account of this initial phase is similar to that described by Bennis and Shepard (1970) as a stage in the beginning T-group. That is, in the absence of a preestablished group goal, participants flounder. A certain discontinuity exists in the personal expressions of group members. After one person has stopped talking, another might start off on a completely different topic, as if oblivious of what the first person expressed. During the milling around period, participants are prone to ask what the actual purpose of the group is.

Resistance to Personal Revelations   Usually during the milling around period, some individual reveals something personal. Such self-disclosure is met with mixed reactions from the group. There is an approach-avoidance complex involved with self-disclosure. Some members may respond by trying to protect another person from personal expressions of feelings, or prevent such expressions, since self-revelations tend to make them uncomfortable. They become concerned about protecting their public selves. Yet, these very same individuals who shy away from self-disclosure also feel the greatest need to be intimate with others. It is the risk involved that takes the group into flight action and resistance. However, as an atmosphere of psychological safety and mutual trust begins to pervade, resistance to self-disclosure declines.

Concern with the Past   The first type of personal revelation that occurs in a group usually deals with the past, possibly because it is a great deal safer to talk about the past and possibly because some people feel that others can understand them better by knowing what their life experiences have been. Moreover, a participant may speak of a present feeling as though it were in the past. For example, an individual might say: "I know how you feel because I had a similar feeling when I was in your position." In this case, the individual may be trying to give the appearance that all is well, when, in reality, he or she is still struggling with the same problem. A maxim of beginning encounter group participants seems to be: when in doubt, talk about a present feeling as though it were a part of the past.

Voicing of Negative Feelings   As the group moves from being absorbed with past feelings and occurrences, participants are inclined to move to here-and-now expressions of feelings that are likely to deal with negative reactions to other group members. Rogers theorizes that this shift occurs because (1) members want to test the freedom and trustworthiness of the group; and (2) it is generally easier to express negative feelings, since deeply positive ones leave one vulnerable to rejection. To demonstrate the latter case, Rogers points out that if a person says that he or she hates someone, then at least the recipient of the attack can respond in a similar attack fashion. However, if a person states that he or she loves another, the person is taking a greater risk, for the recipient may respond with dislike.

Personal Exploration The catharsis that occurs with the expression of negative feelings of one group member toward another frees the individual to proceed with an exploration of present feelings, which are usually about self. For example, a person might talk about the struggle to become an adult and to extricate himself or herself from parental influence. Another participant might attempt to answer the question of who he or she is. In the beginning stages, personal evaluation tends to emphasize the negative, since most people are more keenly aware of the negative things about themselves than the positive ones.

Communication of Immediate Interpersonal Feelings From an absorption with themselves and their own personal struggles, group members move to a concern with their interpersonal relations with each other. They indicate in the here-and-now how the behaviors of other group participants affect them. Although Rogers does not specifically label it as such, transference relations are likely to occur in this interpersonal feedback period. A person might say: "I like you because you remind me of my mother," or "I resent you because you try to dominate the group, just the way my father dominated our family," or, even more simply, "I can't stand the way you respond to others and me." This phase of expression of here-and-now interpersonal feelings in the group represents the core of the encounter, even though other stages are to follow. Participants are now ready to deal with each other. As Moreno imaginatively expressed it [see p. 156], members have passed through the phase of wanting to tear each other's eyes out and to substitute each other's eyes for their own.

The Group Healing Capacity At this point, group members understand the fellowship of pain and suffering. They realize that many wounds have been opened —some that perhaps needed to be and others that perhaps were better left alone. They offer each other warmth and compassion, which up to this stage they seemed to have forgotten about. Participants attempt to enter into the life-space or phenomenal field of each other. They are inclined to reach out to one another— to demonstrate their caring and understanding. It is the caring attitude of group members more than the expertise of the group facilitator that Rogers believes is of the utmost importance. For instance, in describing the case of Joe, Rogers (1970) points out how group members try to help Joe deal with his marital problems. While one participant attempts to help Joe get in touch with his true feelings about his wife, another tries to present alternate ways of dealing with the problem. These efforts, in Rogers' opinion, demonstrate the healing capacity of group membership.

Self-acceptance People who come to encounter groups tend to rate low on the scale of self-acceptance. From an acceptance of self, Rogers maintains that a person is in a better position to change behavior. During the process of gaining self-acceptance, a participant may reveal his or her innermost fears as well as the conditions of worth upon which he or she has built self-acceptance. For example, a company executive expresses the feeling that he is still a little boy, but in the work situation he is able to wield power. He begins to understand that his conditions of worth are based mainly upon external factors and that in order to truly accept himself, he must extricate himself from some of the conditions of worth he has established for himself.

The Cracking of Facades   One of the reasons individuals become members of an encounter group is to learn how to relate to others more honestly. People get tired of carrying the weight of the masks they wear. Despite this goal, however, many find it difficult to take off their masks. During the course of an encounter group, the masks that participants wear may be dropped. Rogers refers to this as the "cracking of facades." In the beginning of an encounter group, participants make requests that the masks of polite social intercourse no longer be worn. As the group continues, such requests may become a group demand. For example, one group member demands of another: "Why do you always seem so cool? You're the woman with all the answers. Why don't you stop playing Miss Cool and just be you?" As a result of this confrontation, other members also ask the participant to stop wearing a mask.

The cracking of facades occurs throughout an encounter group. Depending upon what happens in a group, it may occur early for some individuals. The significant point is that the preceding phases of Rogers' basic encounter group model set the stage for group readiness for the cracking of facades.

Feedback   Members may give each other feedback throughout the duration of an encounter group. At this stage in the group, however, members are more inclined to give constructive feedback. Constructive feedback does not necessarily mean positive feedback. Quite the contrary, it may emphasize an individual's negative points. It is the manner, tone, and delivery of feedback that helps to make it constructive or destructive.

Confrontation   The momentum toward confrontation is not continuous in an encounter group. Like the waters of an ocean, confrontations in a group are characterized by ebbs and flows. During this stage in the sequence, confrontations are inclined to be more pronounced, as group members sense that the climax is near.

The Relationship Outside the Group   One of the major benefits of being a member of an encounter group is that relationships are established or strengthened in outside events and meetings. Rogers maintains that contacts made outside the group may strengthen an individual for the next group meeting. Participants have an opportunity to resolve misunderstandings and to build bridges for new relationships.

The Basic Encounter   One can best understand the basic encounter stage by examining its outcomes. According to Rogers, group participants come into closer contact with each other than is customary in everyday life. Group cohesion is now at its height, as most members no longer have to cling to their protective facades, no longer seem bent upon destroying one another, and can, therefore, relate to each other more effectively.

Expressions of Closeness   As the group nears an end, members express positive feelings about their experience; they discuss their feelings of closeness for one another. People sense a certain realness of their experience. Somehow, all the pain they have suffered now seems well worth it. Feelings of warmth, trust, and group spirit are at their apex. The end is in sight, and group members may be wondering how they can apply and transfer what they have learned in the group to their daily lives.

Behavior Changes Although behavior changes usually have been occurring both before and after the basic encounter phase, they are more pronounced toward the end of the group. Rogers notes, for example, that such observable behavior changes as gestures, tone of voice, spontaneity, less artificiality in inter-personal relations and more verbal expressions at the feeling level tend to take place. Rogers also comments that not all behavior changes are positive, but these other changes, in his judgment, are minimal compared to the overwhelmingly positive aspects of encounter group participation.

The Group Facilitator

Rogers does not generalize about what the role of the encounter group leader should be. Instead, he limits himself to his own function as an encounter group facilitator. In this respect, Rogers' comments are deeply personal; they are an outgrowth of his experiences rather than a summary of the different roles encounter group leaders have assumed. One of the major points Rogers stresses is his continual effort to combine the roles of group participant and facilitator without making it appear that he is consciously trying to do so. Acknowledging his own dilemma, Rogers delineates what he considers essential in facilitating an encounter group: establishing a group climate. The facilitator sets the tone for the group. Rogers tends to begin most encounter groups in a very unstructured and nonassuming manner. For instance, at the outset of the group he might say something like: "Here we are. What happens in this group is largely up to us." Rogers also maintains that in setting the climate of the group, the facilitator attempts to make each group member feel that the facilitator is psychologically in tune with the member. Although Rogers might not agree with a participant's particular views, he feels it is important that the facilitator listen to what each person has to say and that the facilitator be psychologically in touch with the feelings the person is expressing, no matter how superficial or significant the statements might be. Note that this is a restatement of his earlier assumptions concerning human beings. That is, each individual is worthwhile and worth understanding.

Acceptance of Where the Group Is Rogers adheres to the old maxim: Begin where the learner is, not where you would like the learner to be. He does not attempt to move the group when it appears bogged down in superficial talk, primarily because he feels that each group has its own readiness-for-growth barometer. Acceptance of where the group is does not mean, however, approval of the group members' actions. To illustrate this point, Rogers (1970) cites the example of an encounter group experience involving high-level educational administrators. For the first evening of a weekend session, the administrators engaged mainly in social chatter. Although Rogers felt annoyed with the group's focus on trivia, he also believed that trying to redirect its course by the use of intervention techniques dealing with the here-and-now of their behavior would have been a contradiction of the idea he had expressed in the opening session—specifically, that it was up to the group to decide what it wanted to do with its time. But it was up to him to decide whether to endure it any longer. Having reached this decision, Rogers walked out and went to bed. He reports that after this point, the participants' interactions with each other were more meaningful. In essence, acceptance of the group does not necessarily mean approval of what transpires.

Operating in Terms of the Group Leader's Feelings   In typical nondirective therapy, the counselor is inclined to ignore personal feelings in deference to those of the clients. In his work with encounter groups, one sees a shift in Rogers' philosophy. He emphasizes revealing or making use of his own feelings regardless of whether or not such feelings relate to the group as an entity, to one individual, or to himself. Rogers also notes that there is a certain amount of risk when he operates in terms of his own feelings as a group facilitator, since he attempts to express both positive and negative feelings. Expressing his own feelings is Rogers' way of completing an I-Thou relationship. He states that he is a much more facilitative person when he "owns" his own feelings in the process of immediate interaction with a participant.

Avoidance of Interpretive or Process-Oriented Comments   Rogers acknowledges that he makes very few comments on the group process of encountering. To do so would, in his opinion, make the group more self-conscious and thus retard its progress. Instead, he relies upon other members to comment upon the group process—mainly because such happenings tend to occur more naturally.

In contrast to Freudian psychotherapists, Rogers does not make interpretations of a participant's behavior. If a group member is angry, it is more important that that person is open to and aware of his or her anger than that the group facilitator interpret the source of the anger. Rogers conceptualizes an interpretation as to the cause of a person's behavior as little more than an educated guess. The only real weight it carries is that associated with the authority of the therapist. In encounter groups, Rogers wishes to avoid such authoritative behavior as a group leader.

Physical Contact   While Rogers does not belittle the more physically oriented branches of encounter groups, neither does he seem to hold such techniques in high regard. In his estimation, any type of physical movement or contact should be that with which the facilitator is comfortable. Admitting that his own personal background has created certain reservations within him concerning the more overt kinds of behavioral contact with group participants, Rogers indicates that he does not consciously try to promote such behavior within his participants. Occasionally, he might get up, walk around, change places with a participant, or hug and embrace members who seem to be suffering, but these are spontaneous rather than planned responses. To this extent, one might say that Rogers represents the more conservative element of encounter groups.

Techniques of the Basic Encounter Facilitator   Remaining fairly consistent with his theory of individually oriented client-centered therapy, Rogers does not propose any specific techniques for encounter groups. Whatever techniques he uses are couched in his description of a facilitative leader. In other words, one cannot separate the techniques of encounter group facilitators from what it takes to become a facilitative leader. The two are intricately interwoven. The lack of specific techniques seems to be both the downfall and the advantage of the basic encounter model. Rogers' approach to groups does not encourage the counselor to use more directive techniques, even when such techniques appear to be more appropriate to the problem at hand. One finds tremendous variety in the types of techniques used in encounter groups, defying any neat categorization.

Group Member Roles Each member of an encounter group is expected to assume a certain amount of responsibility for setting the directions and the goals of the group. Confrontation and feedback are also responsibilities of group members. Generally, as in client-centered therapy, much is left up to the encounter group participants. They decide, they direct, and they, in the final analysis, assume a greater responsibility for what happens in the group than does the facilitator.

EARLY RESEARCH FINDINGS

The research findings concerning self-theory contributions to counseling can be divided into three categories: (1) those that refer to individual counseling; (2) those that deal with early applications of self-theory concepts to counseling; and (3) those that deal with the Rogerian basic encounter model. Of the three categories, research on encounter groups is least available.

Studies on the self-theory approach to individual and group counseling constitute significant contributions to the counseling profession. The most important findings of this body of research deal with Rogers' necessary and sufficient conditions for therapy. Research by Truax (1961), Carkhuff (1967), and Carkhuff and Berenson (1977) demonstrate that these conditions help to bring about change in clients. Truax and Carkhuff (1967) found that counselors who communicate warmth, genuineness, and accurate empathy are more effective in helping their clients. Moreover, clients who perceive these conditions tend to engage in greater self-exploration. In short, much of Rogers' theory concerning the facilitative conditions of therapy has been supported (Carkhuff and Berenson, 1977).

Lieberman, Yalom, and Miles (1973) have provided the most extensive investigation of encounter groups and, according to them, also the most scientific study of the movement. Although the authors included in their investigation seventeen different encounter groups—Gestalt therapy, personal growth, and T-groups, to mention a few—attention is focused here primarily on the findings with regard to encounter groups associated with Rogers. It should be noted that Rogers himself did not lead any of the groups in the study, although the findings of the investigation reported herein refer to a Rogerian marathon group. Reviewing how participants felt about their group, Lieberman, Yalom, and Miles (1973) state:

> The members of this group were dissatisfied customers. They did not find it a pleasant experience (tied for eleventh place among the seventeen groups), they were not turned on by the group (sixteenth place), they did not find it a particularly constructive experience (tied for twelfth place), they did not feel that they had learned very much (tied for thirteenth place). The overall testimony ranked this group thirteenth. They felt

less negative about the leader, rating him midway among the leaders. They felt he was too passive and slightly remote (p. 68).

ISSUES SURROUNDING ENCOUNTER GROUPS

The encounter group movement is largely responsible for the resurgence of interest in the small-group experience. Yet in the process of reviving professional and public interest in this experience, it has also generated a great deal of controversy. While there are those who place a garland around the movement, there are others who charge quackery and fraud, and still others who label it a communist plot. Opponents warn that encounter groups will bring about the decay of the small-group experience, while proponents say that it is creating a renaissance. It seems clear that polarities of interest and thought have evolved within the encounter movement, and it seems equally clear that these same polarities have clouded, rather than elucidated, the issues at hand.

The purpose here is not to provide a chorus of either support or denunciation, but rather to investigate the salient issues as they have been discussed in the literature. These issues can be divided into three categories: (1) the goals of encounter groups, (2) encounter group casualties, and (3) standards for group leadership.

Goals

Central to much of the debate about encounter groups are their goals. Some of the questions raised concerning this issue may be stated as follows: Are the objectives of the encounter groups worthwhile and meaningful? Are these goals attainable or do they represent attractive promises never really meant to be achieved—sirens luring the innocent into their snare? What is the significance of these goals for society at large?

Broadly speaking, the goals of encounter groups are to develop an individual's self-awareness as well as an awareness of others; to facilitate personal growth and self-actualization; to engage in intimate and meaningful interactions with others; to foster greater openness to experience and experiencing; and to attenuate the alienation from other people suffered by modern men and women. Proponents of encounter groups argue that their objectives get to the very core of today's human problems. These problems include low feelings of worth, estrangement from oneself, and alienation from others. The feelings of intimacy created in encountering with others in a safe psychological environment are an essential way of reducing such feelings. It is a way of attending to the psychopathology of the normal—the overlooked silent majority frequently neglected by psychotherapists (Coulson, 1970).

Partial support of the claims of encounter group leaders is given by the participants themselves. On the average, members tend to report satisfaction with their group experience and indicate that it has helped them to be closer to themselves and to others.

Conversely, opponents of the encounter model question both the meaningfulness of these goals and the ability of encounter group participation to meet these goals. Kagan (1970) suggests that becoming one's real self and obtaining greater intimacy do not constitute meaningful goals because they lack specific content and substance. Back (1972) postulates that encounter models equate openness of expression of one's feelings with intimacy. He maintains that openness, or what one reveals to another about oneself, does not indicate mutual caring. Perfect strangers will reveal certain aspects of their lives to each other; this does not necessarily mean that an intimate relationship has taken place. Beyond this, however, Back (1972) takes the position that the encounter approach to intimacy produces the very opposite of what it is supposed to achieve. That is, in its audiencelike approach to intimacy, it functions to dehumanize participants. An encounter group tends to impersonalize intimacy by demanding that each person should learn how to be intimate with people whom he or she is not likely to have seen before or will ever be likely to see again.

In his criticism of encounter groups and their goals, Woodman (1970) refers to "norming" in encounter groups. He states that techniques that were once designed to be facilitative in encounter groups have now become norms of behavior for successful membership. Since it is expected that encounter group members deal with their feelings in the here-and-now, some participants experience greater constraints than before they entered the group. What was genuine open communication becomes a type of false open communication. To satisfy the requirements of encounter group membership, participants may tend to bypass real experience, thereby sacrificing congruence for outward appearances.

The difference of opinions surrounding encounter group goals does not appear to be irreconcilable. As Parloff (1972) indicates, one of the major contributions of encounter groups is their demonstration that it is possible to facilitate rapid group formation and cohesion. Encounter group goals in themselves are not inherently bad. The real issue seems to focus around group techniques and group norming of these goals.

Casualties

The issue of encounter group casualties is significant because it addresses a very thorny question: How psychologically dangerous can encounter participation be? The term encounter group casualties refers to the severe psychological decompensation participants undergo following an encounter group experience (Yalom and Lieberman, 1971). Proponents of encounter groups declare that the whole casualty issue has been blown out of proportion and that it is merely a scare tactic used to undermine the human-potential movement (Rogers, 1970; Mintz, 1971; Back, 1972). To buttress his point of view, Rogers (1970) notes that out of a total sample of 587 subjects with whom he worked in forty groups, only 2 members manifested a psychotic reaction during or immediately following the encountering experience.

Yalom and Lieberman's (1971) study of encounter group casualties among a sample of 209 university students does not present quite as bright a picture. Of the 170 people who completed the experience, 16 individuals were considered casualties—defined as "an enduring, significant, negative outcome which was caused by their participation in the group (Yalom and Lieberman, 1971, p. 16)." They also report that "the most vulnerable individuals were those with low self-concept and unrealistically high expectations and anticipations of change (p. 16)." In the 1972 follow-up of this sample report, Lieberman, Yalom, and Miles indicate that at the termination of the encounter groups, slightly over 60 percent of those who remained in the groups saw themselves as having benefited. However, six months later, approximately 10 to 20 percent of this group indicated that they were less enthusiastic about the positive change they previously saw. Lieberman, Yalom, and Miles (1973) conclude that "overall, encounter groups show a modest positive impact, an impact much less than has been portrayed by their supporters and an impact significantly lower than participants' view of their own change would lead them to assume (p. 130)."

In reviewing the debate concerning encounter group casualties, it seems clear that some participants have undergone psychological damage that can be associated with participation in an encounter group. On this point, both opponents and proponents agree. What they do not concur upon, however, is the percentage of these encounter casualties and their relative importance. Proponents of encounter groups point out that casualties may and do occur in many forms of psychotherapy, including individual and group work. Yet very few people, in their opinion, are up in arms when such casualties occur under the label of psychotherapy. There is, in other words, a prejudicial focus upon casualties that take place as a result of encounter group membership. In addition, encounter group advocates maintain that the psychiatric label of adverse effects may actually be a blessing rather than a negative outcome. It may symbolize the first stage toward true personal growth. Moreover, group facilitators who take responsibility for what happens to participants as a result of their being in an encounter group only further infantilize them and impede their personal development.

Opponents of encounter groups, on the other hand, maintain that the real number of casualties is unknown and may very likely be even greater than the figures reported. They reject the philosophical position that since encounter group participants come of their own accord, group leaders should have no direct responsibility. The laws of the marketplace, they contend, should not be invoked or used in encounter group situations. They also reject what they consider to be the flippant attitude of encounter group leaders toward psychological breakdowns. Personal growth may occur when an individual does receive adequate assistance from a concerned psychotherapist, but breakdowns in themselves do not necessarily mean a step forward for personal growth. What opponents seem to object to most is that such groups lack adequate built-in follow-up procedures to ascertain if casualties have occurred, and that group leaders seemingly accept little responsibility for postencounter group care for those who, in fact, do experience psychological damage from their participation in an encounter group.

The points raised by both sides concerning encounter group casualties are important. It would appear, however, that a middle ground might be taken. That is, better screening procedures and postgroup care follow-up could reduce both some of the concerns and some of the incidence of encounter group casualties. Likewise, it would seem appropriate for other forms of group psychotherapy to examine more closely the entire casualty question.

Group Leadership

The third major issue is the controversy surrounding group leadership standards. The primary argument against encounter group facilitators is that they lack proper training for the mission they undertake (Goodstein, 1970; Ohlsen, 1970). Encounter group leaders come from all walks of life. They may be psychiatrists, social workers, guidance counselors, educators, clergymen, people who have only one or two experiences in encounter group participation, or anyone who wants to work in a group situation. Even those "qualified" individuals within the encounter movement tend to devalue the importance of graduate training in psychotherapy. For instance, concerning graduate training as a prerequisite for engaging in psychotherapy, Rogers (1965) states:

> Often, he (the student) becomes so burdened with theoretical and diagnostic baggage that he becomes *less* able to understand the inner world of another person as it seems to that person. Also, as his professional training continues, it all too often occurs that his initial warm liking for other persons is submerged in a sea of psychiatric evaluation, and hidden under an all-enveloping profession role (p. 106).

Despite Rogers' argument, it would seem that some kind of training is appropriate for encounter group leaders. But what should that training consist of? Tannenbaum, Weschler, and Massarik (1970) offer four general areas of competency that encounter group leaders should possess. These areas are:

1. conceptual knowledge of the field of human nature and psychology

2. training experience in group work under the supervision of qualified group leaders

3. technical skill in self-examination and group intervention methods

4. humanness and sufficient resilience under stress

Similarities and Differences Between Encounter and Therapy or Counseling Groups

Much of the criticism surrounding encounter groups has not dealt with the differences concerning encounter and group counseling approaches. On the contrary, the criticisms have tended to focus on the excesses or the abuses of the encounter movement. Such a focus has tended to obsure rather than reveal important similarities and differences that do exist between these two group approaches.

Moreover, there has been a continual blurring of encounter groups with therapy groups. As Yalom (1975) and Lieberman (1977) have pointed out, many critics of encounter groups use encounter techniques, and confusion exists over just how these two approaches differ from each other. The fact that both highly trained clinicians and paraprofessionals use encounter techniques of necessity raises questions about the differences between encounter and group therapy models.

At the outset, it should be pointed out that both therapy and encounter groups share certain similarities. For example, both emphasize the development of an individual's positive potential. Both stress similar outcome goals, such as awareness of one's behavior, sensitivity to others, acceptance of others, and insight to oneself. Moreover, both therapy and encounter groups place a high value on self-disclosure. They also share the fundamental assumption that the group is a social microcosm which reflects the interpersonal issues that confront people in the larger society.

Despite the overlap in the areas specified, there are fundamental differences between encounter and group counseling models. These differences may be placed into two categories: extrinsic and intrinsic. Extrinsic differences refer to the outward appearances of the two group models; they constitute what Yalom (1975) calls the "front," or the specialized language and techniques which are not basic to the group process. Conversely, intrinsic differences are those which constitute the "core" of the treatment process or the basic mechanisms of a group approach. Throughout this section, the differences between encounter and therapy groups are discussed primarily, although not exclusively, in terms of the core. Encounter groups are differentiated from other group counseling models in terms of their respective origins, theoretical foundations, goals, participants, leadership, group procedures and techniques for change, and time duration.

Origin The encounter approach to groups stands out from most group models in terms of origin and reason for being. For instance, most encounterists attribute the popularity of the movement to the common social malaise of a highly technological and impersonal American society (Rogers, 1970). No other group model has so emphasized or based its reason for existence on these conditions.

Instead, most counseling group models (the T-group is a notable exception) trace their origin to models of individual counseling and personality development. In other words, the roots of encounter and counseling groups are just not the same. Therapy groups have roots that are anchored deeply in various schools of individual counseling, while the roots of encounter groups are attached more strongly to social issues and commonly perceived social problems.

The origin of the encounter movement has tended not only to define the problem but also to stipulate the treatment process necessary to remedy the situation. Because of its emphasis on the common social malaise of American society, patienthood is ubiquitous. As Lieberman (1977) has posited: "Unlike group therapy, which emphasizes patienthood, or self-help programs, which emphasize a common problem, the Human Potential Movement (encounter movement) emphasizes the relevance of its activities to all who want to change, grow, and develop.... A major distinction between the previously mentioned activities and encounter or growth groups is that the latter view themselves as having universal applicability (p. 22)." If patienthood is ubiquitous, then all potential group members, all individuals either need or can profit from its services.

In therapy groups, patienthood is limited to an underlying theory of individual maladjustment. Not all individuals are seen to need therapy. Most therapy groups tend to stress that each person is different in history, development, and psychody-namics—the things that make the person happy or sad, that cause the person to climb mountains or just sit at their feet. The type of human sameness, or human homogeneity, that some encounterists emphasize is quite different from that which most group therapists stress. The encounter movement, as a result of its same-ness of people origins, tends to homogenize human life, putting all people and their problems under the common denominator of social malaise, estrangement, loneli-ness, and the like.

Theoretical Foundations The difference in theoretical foundations provides another means to compare and contrast encounter and therapy groups. Most group models are based on a major body of theoretical knowledge, even though in doing so, the theorist may have borrowed from several other theories. For example, the teleoanalytic approach to group counseling is based on the theory of Adler's individual pyschology, the psychoanalytic on Freudian psychology, and the rational-emotive on that of Ellis' rational-emotive psychotherapy for individual treatment.

With the exception of Rogers' client-centered therapy, encounter groups have no major theoretical foundation to guide their activities. The basic belief that pervades the encounter school is that people are basically good, and that their goodness will surely rise to the surface in encounter groups—if it is only facilitated. This belief alone is insufficient to serve as a foundation for an entire group ap-proach. As Rosenbaum (1970–1971,p. 42) has stated: "Carl Rogers is committed to the concept that man is basically good. Therefore his concept of unconditional positive regard makes sense—at least from his point of view. The Rogerian thera-pist accepts completely the client he is treating, since the individual is seen as someone who merely needs acceptance so that he becomes the really good person he is fundamentally. This also accounts for Rogers' enthusiasm for en-counter groups since they are supposed to promote the basic goodness which resides within the individual."

The encounter movement is, then, based on an implicit view of people. That view is basically positive and accounts in part for the movement's lack of emphasis on screening clients, diagnosing them, or developing a specific treatment plan for individual participants. There is no need to screen participants if their basic good-ness will rise to the surface. There is no need to diagnose encounter participants if all suffer from the same common social malaise. There is no need to have separate, individual treatment plans for participants if all one needs to do is to provide each with unconditional positive regard or the other conditions of therapy which Rogers (1951, 1970) espouses.

Besides this view of people, encounter groups have no major theoretical foun-dation. As Maliver (1973, p. 137) has stated: "Aside from a simple-minded human-ism, most encounterists have no theory of behavior to guide their activities. In its absence, encounterists are left with no standard to judge and set goals for begin-ning players, no means of determining a player's progress, no model for the finished player, and no rationale against which group interactions may be tested. Each of these is a significant factor in professional psychotherapy, and each is substantially ignored in the encounter game."

Most therapy group models are based, then, on a theory of personality development which delineates what constitutes normal or maladjusted behavioral development, what therapeutic counseling procedures should be used, what the goals of therapy are, and the desired changes needed in order for an individual to experience a healthy psychological development. In other words, there are guidelines for leader behavior, member behavior, and the treatment process.

Denes-Radomisli (1974) presents a slightly different view concerning the theoretical foundations of encounter groups. According to her, the encounter culture is and admits to being atheoretical on the whole, but it presents its image as being primarily existential and humanistic. This image, from Denes-Radomisli's perspective, is erroneous. It is built upon false similarities, illusions which give the appearance of sameness. She posits that the encounter model lacks the depth of existentialism and states: "Encountering reflects an adequate understanding of Existentialism about to the same degree that Astrology reflects an adequate understanding of Astronomy (Denes-Randomisli, 1974, p. 110)."

In Denes-Radomisli's opinion, the apparent similarities between existentialism and the encounter movement result from three general factors: (1) the adoption of the existential vocabulary; (2) the apparent incorporation of the existential conception of the importance of person-to-person relatedness; and (3) the use of existential techniques of phenomenological observation. Since encounter groups are sometimes linked to the existential school, her comments merit additional consideration.

Denes-Radomisli (1974) posits that encounter group leaders have adopted the existential vocabulary—for example, the discovery of the authentic individual, I-Thou, and the term existential loneliness—without giving adequate attention to the manner in which existentialists originally and currently define these terms. Concurring with this perspective, Rosenbaum (1974) likewise affirms that Rogers' use of Buber's term I-Thou is a far cry from the way Buber (1964) presented it in his book *The Worlds of Existentialism.* Buber (1964) used the term I-Thou to refer to the fact that an individual's identity develops from true sharing with other persons. Basic trust takes place in a living partnership in which each person identifies the particular real personality of the other in his or her wholeness, unity, and uniqueness. From Rosebaum's perspective, the mere transitory and sometimes gimmicky and theatrical reaching out that frequently occurs in encounter groups is more akin to the I-It type of relationship that Buber describes. I-It relations occur when an individual treats self or another person exclusively as an object rather than as a person. As Rosenbaum (1971) has stated regarding the I-Thou and I-It relationships in encounter groups, encounterists never engage in a meaningful dialogue with one another. "Their so-called humanness is impersonal. People are brought together to experience—whatever that means—and they really don't give a damn about one another after their abreactive experience. They weep, scream, shout—a combined Holy Roller and Pentecostal meeting—and this is called psychotherapy? . . . It is my belief that they engaged in a mass deception. . . . The king is naked."

Similarly, Maliver (1973) questions whether Rogers or most encounter leaders ever actually deal with true existential loneliness. According to him, the existential loneliness described by existentialists is a much more pervasive condition which cannot be reduced by instant contacts provided by encounter groups. From his perspective, existential loneliness may be at its height when one is in the company of others. About the only areas in which encounterists and existentialists truly meet (the third factor of similarity) is on the technique of phenomenological observation, or the idea that the group leader makes observations about a participant's behavior without preconceived ideas about such behavior.

Goals   Since issues surrounding the types of goals are discussed in another section, they are not dealt with here. This section focuses primarily on how encounter and therapy group goals differ. The goals of encounter groups differ from therapy groups in several significant ways. First, the goals of encounter groups are obscure and lack specificity. As Yalom (1975, p. 456) has asserted: "The goals of the group are often vague. Occasionally, they stress merely the provision of an experience—joy, a state of being 'turned on,' entertainment—but more often they implicitly or explicitly strive for some type of change—change in behavior, attitudes, values, life-style, degree of self-actualization, change in one's relations to others, to nature, to one's physical being, or change in one's way of being in the world."

Unlike therapy groups, the goals of encounter groups are not related to an underlying theory of personality or group development. For instance, a major goal of rational-emotive therapy is to help the individual give up the irrational beliefs that cause his or her psychological disturbance. In Adlerian psychology, the therapist strives to analyze an individual's life goals and to change them to more productive ones. Psychoanalytic group leaders generally work toward the goal of personality maturation of individuals.

Both encounter and therapy group leaders differ on the importance they place on the need to set specific goals. Almost all major group counseling models discussed in this book agree on the need to set specific goals for either individual members or the group as a whole. Encounterists maintain that such a procedure is unnecessary. Setting different goals for individuals would mean that there are basic differences among people and that all people should not be treated alike in therapy. Rogers, for example, has not only defended the encounter position of not setting specific goals for individual participants, he has also gone one step further. He has denied that he would treat clients differently based upon their respective problems. For example, during a historic confrontation between Buber and Rogers, Rogers has been quoted as saying: "I would say that there is no difference in the relationship that I form with a normal person, a schizophrenic, a paranoid (Maliver, 1973, p. 232)." Few traditional group therapists would venture such a statement. Goals would be based on the types of problems individuals would be facing. Not all clients would be treated alike.

Even when encounterists and traditional group therapists share common outcome objectives, there is a difference in the emphasis that they place upon certain goals and how such goals are to be accomplished. For example, both encounter and counseling groups stress the importance of individuals' being able to experience and express greater intimacy in their lives, especially with those whom the participants or clients consider important in their lives. The difference is, however, that in encounter groups the individuals' increased capacity to express and experience intimacy in their lives is seen as a goal in itself—one that is paramount and that supersedes all others. In therapy groups, greater intimacy, particularly among participants or group members, is generally not pursued as a goal or end in itself. In encounter groups, intimacy is often equated with participants' openness with each other in the group; the more participants attempt to be open and honest with each other (even though such openness and honesty may be premature and detrimental to the individual), the more the group leader assumes that intimacy is taking place. In therapy groups, intimacy occurs as a result of group members' trying to resolve their own problems—as an offshoot of deep, personal sharing of their concerns and life problems. The manner in which intimacy is accomplished in therapy groups and the primacy with which group leaders rate this as an important goal are decidedly different from encounter groups.

Participants The differences between participants in encounter groups and those in therapy groups are difficult to describe accurately, primarily because there is so little reliable data that exist on participants in either of these two group models.

Basically, encounter group participants have been distinguished from group counseling clients in terms of their respective psychological health or their level of individual functioning. On the average, participants in encounter groups have been described as psychologically healthier than individuals in counseling groups. Members of encounter groups constitute the so-called normal people in American and Western society. Such individuals theoretically come to encounter groups because they are experiencing the psychopathology of everyday living. Encounter participants suffer from what Burton (1969) terms existential neuroses—alienation, loneliness, despair, and anxiety.

Moreover, the encounter group has an appeal for individuals because it is cheaper and faster than most forms of traditional group counseling and because it does not carry the same stigma as does traditional group counseling or therapy. As Maliver (1973, p. 219) has suggested: "Most encounter participants feel they have a 'hang-up' they want to get rid of, such as 'relating to the opposite sex,' 'dealing with anger,' 'experiencing feelings,' and 'self-assertion.' In the view of most professionals, each of these statements is likely to reflect a deeper emotional disturbance."

Moreover, despite the differences that have been mentioned concerning the psychological functioning of encounter versus counseling group members and the reasons that individuals choose one group format over the other, Lieberman (1977) has posited that the composition of encounter and therapy groups has become increasingly similar. In a study of individuals seeking clinic or direct group psychotherapy, growth-centered (encounter) experiences, NTL group experiences, or consciousness raising in women's groups, Lieberman (1977) found that the participantlike characteristics of the samples were remarkably similar in the reasons for joining a group. Participants in encounter groups tended to choose such groups for the very same reasons as did participants in therapy groups. Both encounter group and clinic or therapy clients were similar in that they entered with direct psychotherapeutic or help-seeking goals. Those entering group psychotherapy provided by clinics had 98 percent direct psychotherapeutic or help-seeking goals; those in encounter groups had 70 percent such therapy-related goals.

Commenting upon the similarities of goals between individuals who seek psychotherapy and those who seek encounter groups, Lieberman (1977, p. 24) has concluded that: "The Human Potential (or encounter) movement's appeal is not primarily for hedonistic, playful seekers after joy. Rather, participant goals are instrumental and focus primarily around issues of obtaining help with personal problems." In other words, encounter group participants are not just seeking personal growth. Like the people who select therapy groups, encounter participants choose such groups because they feel they need or want therapeutic assistance with their personal problems in life.

Leadership   Differences in leadership vary greatly in both therapy and encounter groups. Generally speaking, however, leaders of counseling and encounter groups differ widely on the responsibilities of leadership and on the type of training or professional preparation needed for adequate group leadership. Encounterists tend to accept less responsibility for treatment of individuals within their groups. This situation may be attributed, in part, to the issue of offering professional care. Since some encounter group leaders maintain that they are offering opportunities for personal growth rather than therapy, they limit the areas of their responsibilities. Some encounter leaders have adopted the stance of: "You do your thing, and I'll do mine. I am not responsible for what happens to you in this group." This position has led to much of the criticism of encounter group leaders.

Many therapy group leaders see themselves as accepting greater responsibility for treatment of group members, and treatment is rightfully the issue here. In therapy groups, treatment is usually based upon clients' needs or therapists' diagnosis of clients' problems. The counselor assumes professional responsibility for the change or group process that individuals experience. Among other things, professional care implies not doing harm and continuing treatment for as long as the individuals' needs require, plus follow-up. Moreover, most therapy group leaders take a case history and make some kind of tentative diagnosis to obtain a basic understanding of an individual's personality. Most leaders of counseling groups also set specific treatment goals. According to Maliver (1973, p. 135), encounter group leaders differ on all these points: "They hold that they are not responsible for the change process, that every individual is entirely responsible for himself. For the most part, they deny any special status, or even authority, contrary to their actual behavior in the group session." In their view, diagnosis, specific treatment plans, and follow-up are expendable procedures.

Regardless of these issues, there are basic differences in the way that encounter group leaders present themselves. Generally speaking, there is greater leader transparency in encounter groups. Encounter group leaders are inclined to stress less informality and, consequently, there is usually less of a leader-membership gap between them and their participants (Yalom, 1975; Lieberman, 1977). Furthermore, some encounter group leaders also emphasize that they try to become group members during the life course of the group. In most therapy groups, the leader rarely has becoming a group member as a major goal.

Group Procedures and Techniques for Change   There is no one group format for either therapy groups or encounter groups. Overall, however, encounter groups tend to have a looser group format and less structuring than most counseling groups. Emphasis is placed on experiencing, and there is greater reliance on exercise (such as the trust exercises) than in counseling groups. In encounter groups, there is little conscious consideration of how a particular group member's emotional reactions and needs are integrated with the group process. The major technique for change in encountering is the expression of emotion, regardless of how short-lived such emotion may be.

Leaders of therapy groups differ on all of these points. Group format is usually defined for participants ahead of time. Both group procedures and techniques for change are tied to a central theory of personality development. Although participants may experience strong emotional reactions, the leader typically analyzes such emotions in terms of the participant's life history and psychological needs.

Time Duration   Encounter groups are noted for their time-limited, rapid-fire approach to group members. Whereas encounter groups are usually short-term (ranging from a weekend to several weeks and sometimes longer), therapy groups are much longer. The short time span of encounter groups has led some theorists to question the efficacy of this approach in assisting the psychologically normal. The concern is that problems may be opened up within the encounter group which require more time for the participant to work through successfully. Because of their longer time span, therapy groups offer a greater likelihood that clients' intra- and interpersonal problems which surface in the group will be recognized and dealt with by the group leader.

CONTRIBUTIONS OF ENCOUNTER GROUPS

The contributions of encounter groups have often been submerged or forgotten because of the excesses of certain segments of the field. Many of these excesses have resulted from what Yalom (1975) calls a "crash-program mentality," that is, if intimacy is good, then increased and instant intimacy must be even better. If touching is good, then kissing, feeling, and hugging indiscriminately must be even better. If self-disclosure is good, then total, immediate, and indiscriminate self-disclosure must surely be desirable. If a small group experience is good, then it must be good for everyone—regardless of a person's life stage, problems, or life situation. These excesses have been cited as not only having negative effects on some participants but also being a bastardization of such concepts as intimacy, self-disclosure, and involvement.

Frequently, Carl Rogers and the self-approach to groups have been identified with such excesses, even though Rogers himself has eschewed these practices for his basic encounter model. There is a need for a more balanced view of encounter groups.

A more balanced view of encounter groups and the basic encounter model would take into account the contributions as well as the limitations of this group approach. For example, Maliver (1973), one of the most fervent critics of encounter groups, has conceded that such groups may serve some useful purposes. He acknowledges that many people may at least feel briefly that they have changed as a result of their encounter experiences, and that this in itself may be a significant benefit. Moreover, another benefit is that many people who have participated in encounter groups undergo some form of psychotherapy—if only, as Maliver (1973) suggests, to "pick up the pieces after a shattering encounter trip."

Perhaps more important is the fact that encounter group experiences may lead to individuals' general improvement in communication skills. As Maliver (1973) has indicated, encounter participants often become aware of irritating mannerisms, such as interrupting or not listening to others, and they may subsequently try to change such behaviors.

The impact of the encounter group movement on traditional forms of therapy appears to be widespread. For example, Lieberman (1977) has noted that encounter group participants' experiences have led to a certain degree of "group-wiseness among individuals. As a result of their contact with encounter groups, participants have begun to demand greater therapist transparency in groups." Lieberman (1977, p. 26) has stated: "The probable increase in therapist transparency among most practitioners is more likely a product of patient expectation than of any radical shifts in theoretical perspective." Such expectations may be attributed to the greater openness of encounter group leaders.

Greater therapist transparency has gone a long way to change the belief that a good group leader should assume the posture of the proverbial blank screen. As Lieberman (1977, p. 26) has noted: "The traditional 'blank screen' demeanor is just not possible any more with most clients." In other words, the experiences and expectations of individuals in encounter groups have exerted a considerable influence on what therapists currently do.

Furthermore, some encounter techniques have been adopted by group leaders of varying theoretical orientations. For example, many of the more traditional approaches to group counseling have adopted an increased emphasis on the here-and-now, the use of structured group exercises, leader transparency, and the time-limited approach to group therapy. These techniques and changes in thought regarding how group counseling should be conducted can be attributed to the impact of the encounter movement. Encounter groups are noted for their excesses, but they have also made fundamental contributions to the small-group experience.

RECENT TRENDS IN ENCOUNTER RESEARCH

Research on encounter groups has lost some of its initial impetus. The controversy that was engendered by the 1973 publication of Lieberman, Yalom, and Miles' *Encounter Groups: First Facts* has begun to wane. Encounter groups have become less of a novelty and more of an accepted, although still heavily criticized, part of the small-group experience.

From 1976 on, the group literature reflects a considerable reduction in the number of articles published on encounter groups. This may be attributed to several important developments, two of which are: (1) in their pure form, fewer encounter groups are being conducted; and (2) encounter group techniques have been modified greatly or incorporated into the more traditional approaches to group therapy so that they no longer have the distinctiveness they previously had. In other words, encounter groups may be undergoing the process of incorporation into the broader field of group psychotherapy and counseling, and research that might earlier have been placed under the banner of encounter is published under Gestalt, transactional analysis, or, in some instances, just small-group experience. Some of the research conducted under the banner of encounter groups is presented below. To obtain a feeling of the direction of encounter group research, some of the earlier studies are cited.

McCardel and Murray (1974) investigated the influence of structural aspects on weekend encounter groups. Of the three groups involved, one was highly structured, another used exercise-oriented techniques, and the third used nonstructured basic instruction. These three groups were compared with an at-home control group on self-report measures. In contrast with the at-home control group, the three encounter groups demonstrated significant improvement on self-report measures, but they did not differ significantly among themselves. Moreover, the encounter groups did not differ significantly from an on-site control group that led participants to believe that they were also in an encounter group but gave them only recreational activities. McCardel and Murray (1974) concluded that the favorable outcomes of encounter group experiences reported in the literature may be attributed to nonspecific therapeutic factors, such as participants' expectancy of favorable outcomes, group enthusiasm, and the reactive nature of outcome measures.

Conyne (1974) reported no significant differences between treatments in a group experience of five selected Bell and Howell Personal Growth Encounter Tapes and five unstructured sections for six groups of participants enrolled in a counselor education course in group procedures. Hoerl (1974) found that people who signed up for encounter groups were generally more flexible than individuals who did not volunteer.

In 1977, Weigel produced one of the most provocative articles on encounter groups. He theorized that the encounter movement had peaked in 1974, and what some encounter leaders were now experiencing was a "requiem for a social movement." He noted the decline in research and in scholarly articles on both marathon and encounter groups. In analyzing the decline of the encounter movement, Weigel pointed out leaders' sensationalism, exploitations, and extremism. As Weigel (1977, p. 215) has stated: "Another closely related factor affecting the group movement has been the exploitations and the ripoffs of group members, and the subsequent bad publicity (either through the media or word of mouth) that has followed. Here I'm referring to inordinately high fees, inappropriately large groups, lack of leader responsibility for group follow-up (or casualties), and what I'd call 'absent leadership.' " He noted that fadism seemed to be another cause. The work of Robert Carkhuff, which was noted earlier in this chapter on extensions of the self-theory of Carl Rogers, is cited by Weigel as the new fad in individual and group counseling. According to Weigel (1977, p. 214), "the wholesale adoption of the position and techniques of Robert Carkhuff appears to reflect a very similar trend" to that of encounter groups.

Much encounter group research has been conducted with undergraduate or graduate students as subjects. Many of these investigations used widely different methods of subject recruitment and compensation—for example, solicitation through introductory psychology classes, newspaper ads, and advertisement through counseling centers. Dies (1978) conducted a study on the implications of encounter group volunteering for research and practice. Analyzing the studies that have been completed on encounter groups, Dies (1978, p. 23) noted: "In just over one-half of these research projects, students were recruited from classroom contexts in which substantially different methods of compensation were utilized. Some students were paid volunteers, others received extra experimental credit for their participation, some were strictly voluntary, while still others were required to participate in their groups as part of their formal course requirements. In some instances, methods of subject compensation were unclear." In his study of encounter group volunteering, Dies (1978) found that students who received extra experimental credit for their participation in encounter groups tended to manifest different attitudes, personalities, and interaction styles from students who participated on a strictly voluntary basis. Dies' study also raised several other issues regarding the influence of subject recruitment and compensation on encounter group research.

Shawver and Pines (1978) examined the issue of value-attribution patterns found in encounter groups. The authors raised two basic questions: (1) What are the patterns of value-attributions that will be shown in encounter group transcripts? (2) How do encounter groups use value-laden language in an effort to promote their stated goals of personal growth and enrichment? The investigators analyze four transcripts—two of them were random samples taken from published transcripts and two were taken from private recordings. Shawver and Pines (1978) found that when group participants talked about themselves, they "primarily engaged in neutralizing negative valuations, implying that they are not 'cold,' 'stupid,' or 'rigid.' The second highest self-valuation was negative (p. 20)." These findings appeared to contradict the very positive interpersonal growth goal of encounter groups and the supportive manner in which such growth is supposed to occur in encounter groups. The investigators also found that group members were largely negative in their descriptions of other group members. The authors concluded that encounter groups use very negative value-laden language during the course of promoting change in participants.

The research on encounter groups seems to be characterized by several trends. There is a dearth of carefully designed and executed research. There has been a continual blurring of therapeutic and encounter group research. There has been a dramatic reduction in the published research involving encounter groups. Encounter groups have almost been subsumed under the broad heading of small-group experience and other therapeutic approaches. There is evidence of both the harmful and the beneficial aspects of encounter groups on participants, but lack of well-controlled studies makes it difficult to state definitively the absolute harmful effects of this group format. Much of the success or failure of encounter groups depends upon a number of factors, some of which have been identified—such as the nature and type of leadership and the ego-coping skills of participants—while other factors have yet to be identified.

SUMMARY

This chapter has traced the development of Rogers' basic encounter model and, correlatively, the encounter movement. Although encounter groups have gone beyond Rogers' model and have had an effect upon virtually every major theoretical school of psychotherapy, Rogers' model still serves as a foundation for all other variant approaches.

Some of the arguments for and against encounter groups have been raised. It is evident that encounter groups have had a profound effect on the intensive group experience, but it seems equally as evident that they have lost some of the attraction they initially held for individuals. Reduced numbers of research publications and declining attendance at Esalen and many of the growth centers in both the East and West are just a few of the indicators of the lessening attraction of encounter groups. There are, of course, other indicators, such as the incorporation of encounter group techniques by other theoretical schools and the backlash against encounter leaders' exploitations and extremism. It is still too early to write a requiem for the encounter group movement. The fact that encounter group techniques have been incorporated by the more traditional schools is both a positive and negative sign for the movement—negative in the sense that the movement may die from incorporation, and positive from the perspective that the value of encountering techniques has been implicitly acknowledged.

There may also be other factors contributing to the lessening attraction of encounter groups that operate in the broader American society. That is, American society is now in a "back to basics" movement. From the world of small-group behavior, this may signal the desire to return to more traditional approaches of group psychotherapy and counseling.

Before one dismisses the encounter group movement as a passing fad, it would be wise to consider the American Psychiatric Association's Task Force Report I on *Encounter Groups and Psychiatry*. This report acknowledges that a number of innovative techniques developed under the encounter group format are now being applied to traditional schools of therapy and that some therapists and counselors are currently using encounter groups as an adjunct technique to accelerate traditional modes of group counseling. The Association's 1970 prediction appears to summarize aptly some of the current developments noted in the counseling field. It states:

> In summary, it seems apparent that the small group field is a rapidly expanding one, that it has a broad interface with the mental health field, and that, though the bizarre aspects may fade, the encounter group is based on a solid foundation and appears to be destined to survive for some time to come (p. 9).

Likewise, Lakin (1969, p. 31), a fervent critic of encounter groups, has commented on the future of experiential and encounter groups.

> The mainspring of conviction remains the fact that interpersonal effectiveness can be increased if the group experience is properly managed. The central concern of the experiential group movement remains the transmission and sharpening of methods of understanding interactional processes. These assets can, of course, be diluted, even destroyed, by the over-claim, poor leadership, or indefensible leader practices.

In short, there has been a recent decline in the attractiveness or relevance of encounter group experiences. Given the backlash of responses to this movement, there may also develop a reduction of the bizarre practices originally posited by this group approach. More and more, encounter group techniques seem to be applied in group counseling and group psychotherapy. The future of encounter group techniques seems to be that they will be incorporated, almost imperceptibly, into the mainstream of group counseling and psychotherapy. It is likewise predicted that encounter techniques will be used chiefly to intensify and accelerate the more traditional approaches to group counseling and psychotherapy. The entire self-help approach to groups is viewed as every person's answer to the encounter group. As more and more people become "practical practitioners" in the group counseling approach, they will eventually supplant the once popular encounter group format. Through the vehicle of incorporation, encounter groups are currently receiving pressures from both traditional modes of psychotherapy and self-help groups.

References

American Psychiatric Association. *Task force report I: Encounter groups and psychiatry.* Washington, DC 1970.

Back, K. W. *Beyond words: The story of sensitivity training and the encounter movement.* New York: Russell Sage Foundation, 1972.

Bennis, W. G., and H. A. Shepard. A theory of group development. In R. T. Golembiewski and A. Blumberg (Eds.), *Sensitivity training and the laboratory approach.* Itasca, IL: Peacock, 1970, 91–115.

Berenson, B. G., K. M. Mitchell, and R. C. Laney. Therapeutic conditions after therapist-initiated confrontation. *Journal of Clinical Psychology,* 1968, *24,* 363–64.

Blanchard, W. H. Encounter group and society. In R. N. Solomon and B. B. Berzon (Eds.), *New perspectives on encounter groups.* San Francisco: Jossey-Bass, 1972, 13–29.

Buber, M. I and Thou. In M. Friedman (Ed.), *The worlds of existentialism.* New York: Random House, 1964.

Burton, A. Encounter, existence, and psychotherapy. In A. Burton (Ed.), *Encounter: The theory and practice of encounter groups.* San Francisco: Jossey-Bass, 1969, 7–26.

Carkhuff, R. R. *The counselor's contribution to facilitative processes.* Urbana, IL: Parkinson, 1967.

Carkhuff, R. R. *Helping and human relations: A primer for lay and professional helpers, Vol. 1. Selection and training.* New York: Holt, Rinehart and Winston, 1969.

Carkhuff, R. R. *Helping and human relations: A primer for lay and professional helpers. Vol. II. Practice and research.* New York: Holt, Rinehart and Winston, 1969.

Carkhuff, R. R. Critical perspectives on group processes. Address on growth groups presented at the Ninth Annual Conference, Personality Theory and Counseling Practice, U. of Florida, January 1969.

Carkhuff, R. R. Helping and human relations: A brief guide for training lay helpers. *Journal of Research and Development in Education,* 1971, *4,* 17–27.

Carkhuff, R. R., and B. G. Berenson. *Beyond counseling and therapy* (2nd ed.). New York: Holt, Rinehart and Winston, 1977.

Conyne, R. K. Effects of facilitator-directed and self-directed group experiences. *Counselor Education and Supervision*, 1974, *13*, 184–89.

Coulson, W. Inside a basic encounter group. *The Counseling Psychologist*, 1970, *2*, 1–27.

Denes-Radomisli, M. Gestalt group therapy: Sense in sensitivity. In D. S. Milman and G. D. Goldman (Eds.), *Group process today*. Springfield, IL: Charles C Thomas, 1974, 108–19.

Dies, R. R. Encounter group volunteering: Implications for research and practice. *Small Group Behavior*, 1978, *9*, 23–48.

Douds, J., B. G. Berenson, R. R. Carkhuff, and R. Pierce. In search of an honest experience: Confrontation in counseling and life. In R. R. Carkhuff and B. G. Berenson (Eds.), *Beyond counseling and therapy* (1st ed.). New York: Holt, Rinehart and Winston, 1967.

Egan, G. *Encounter: Group processes for interpersonal growth*. Belmont, CA: Wadsworth, 1970.

Erikson, E. H. *Identity and the life cycle*. New York: International Universities Press, 1959.

Frank. J. D. *Persuasion and healing*. Baltimore: Johns Hopkins Press, 1961.

Gendlin, E. T. Focusing. *Psychotherapy, Theory, Research, and Practice*, 1969, *6*, 4–15.

Gendlin, E. T., J. Beebe, M. Cassens, and M. Oberlander. Focusing ability in psychotherapy, personality, and creativity. In J. M. Shlien (Ed.), *Research in psychotherapy*. Washington, D.C.: American Psychological Association, 1968, *1*, 217–41.

Gibb, J. R., and L. M. Gibb. Role freedom in a TORI group. In A. Burton (Ed.), *Encounter: The theory and practice of encounter groups*. San Francisco: Jossey-Bass, 1969, 42–57.

Golembiewski, R. T., and A. Blumberg. *Sensitivity training and the laboratory approach*. Itasca, IL: Peacock, 1970.

Goodstein, L. D. Some issues involved in intensive group experiences. *The Counseling Psychologist*, 1970, *2*, 50–55.

Hart, J. T. The development of client-centered therapy. In J. T. Hart and T. M. Tomlinson (Eds.), *New directions in client-centered therapy*. Boston: Houghton Mifflin, 1970.

Hoerl, R. T. Encounter groups: Their effect on rigidity. *Human Relations*, 1974. *27*, 431–38.

Kagan, N. Issues in encounter. *The Counseling Psychologist*, 1970, *2*, 43–49.

Koch, S. An implicit image of man. In L. N. Solomon and B. Berzon (Eds.), *New perspectives on encounter groups*. San Francisco: Jossey-Bass, 1972, 30–52.

Lakin, M. Experiential groups: Some ethical issues in sensitivity training. *American Psychologist*, 1969, *126*, 954–57.

Lakin, M. Response to Coulson. *The Counseling Psychologist*, 1970, *2*, 34–37.

Levitsky, A., and J. S. Simkin. Gestalt therapy. In L. N. Solomon and B. Berzon (Eds.), *New perspectives on encounter groups.* San Francisco: Jossey-Bass, 1972, 245–54.

Lieberman, M. A. Problems in integrating traditional group therapies with new forms. *Journal of International Group Psychotherapy*, 1977, *27*, 19–33.

Lieberman, M. A., I. D. Yalom, and M. Miles. *Encounter groups: First facts.* New York: Basic Books, 1973.

Lifton, W. *Working with groups* (2nd ed.). New York: Wiley, 1966.

Lifton, W. Group-centered counseling. In G. M. Gazda (Ed.), *Basic approaches to group psychotherapy and group counseling.* Springfield, IL: Charles C Thomas, 1968, 234–35.

Luria, A. A semantic analysis of a normal and neurotic therapy group. *Journal of Abnormal Social Psychology*, 1959, *58*, 216–20.

Maliver, B. L. *The encounter game.* New York: Stein and Day, 1973.

Maslow, A. H. *Toward a psychology of being* (2nd ed.). Princeton, NJ: Van Nostrand, 1968.

Massarik, F. Standards for group leadership. In R. N. Solomon and B. Berzon (Eds.), *New perspectives on encounter groups.* San Francisco: Jossey-Bass, 1972, 68–82.

McCardel, J., and E. J. Murray. Nonspecific factors in weekend encounter groups. *Journal of Clinical Psychology*, 1974, *42*, 337–45.

Mintz, E. E. *Marathon groups: Reality and symbol.* New York: Appleton-Century-Crofts, 1971.

Moreno, J. L. The Viennese origins of the encounter movement, paving the way for existentialism, group psychotherapy, and psychodrama. *Group Psychotherapy*, 1969, *22*, 7–16.

Ohlsen, M. Reaction to Coulson's paper. *The Counseling Psychologist*, 1970, *2*, 38–42.

Parloff, M. B. Group therapy and the small-group field: An encounter. In C. J. Sager and H. S. Kaplan (Eds.), *Progress in group and family therapy.* New York: Brunner/Mazel, 1972, 174–207.

Patterson, C. H. A current view of client-centered or relationship therapy. *The Counseling Psychologist*, 1969, *1*, 2–27.

Riesman, D. *The lonely crowd: A study of the changing American character.* New Haven: Yale University Press, 1962.

Rogers, C. R. *Client-centered therapy: Its current practice, implications, and theory.* Boston: Houghton Mifflin, 1951.

Rogers, C. R. Significant learning: In therapy and in education. *Educational Leadership*, 1959, *16*, 232–42.

Rogers, C. R. A theory of therapy, personality, and interpersonal relationships, as developed in the client-centered framework. In S. Koch (Ed.), *Psychology—a study of science: Volume III. Formulations of the person and the social context.* New York: McGraw-Hill, 1959.

Rogers, C. R. *On becoming a person: A therapist's view of psychotherapy.* Boston: Houghton Mifflin, 1961.

Rogers, C. R. The interpersonal relationship: The core of guidance. *Harvard Educational Review,* 1962, *32,* 416–29.

Rogers, C. R. The therapeutic relationship: Recent theory and research. *Australian Journal of Psychology,* 1965, *17,* 95–108.

Rogers, C. R. The process of the basic encounter groups. In J. F. G. Bugental (Ed.), *Challenges of Humanistic Psychology.* New York: McGraw-Hill, 1967, 267–77.

Rogers, C. R. The interpersonal relationship in the facilitation of learning. In R. Leeper (Ed.), *Humanizing Education.* Association for Supervision and Curriculum Development, NEA, 1967.

Rogers, C. R. Interpersonal relationships—Year 2000. *Journal of Applied Behavioral Science,* 1968, *4,* 265–80.

Rogers, C. R. *Freedom to learn: A view of what education might become.* Columbus, OH: Charles E. Merrill, 1969.

Rogers, C. R. *Carl Rogers on encounter groups.* New York: Harper & Row, 1970.

Rosenbaum, M. The responsibility of the psychotherapy practitioner for a therapeutic rationale. *Journal of Group Psychoanalysis and Process,* 1969–1970, *2,* 5–17.

Rosenbaum, M. Responsibility of the therapist for a theoretic rationale. *Group Process,* 1970–1971, *3,* 41–47.

Rosenbaum, M. An overview of group psychotherapy. In D. S. Milman and G. D. Goldman (Eds.), *Group process today.* Springfield, IL: Charles C Thomas, 1974, 15–35.

Ruitenbeek, H. *The new group therapies.* New York: Avon Books, 1970.

Semon, R. G., and W. Goldstein. Verbal participation and perceived benefit from group psychotherapy. *International Journal of Group Psychotherapy,* 1961, *11,* 49–59.

Shawver, L., and A. Pines. Value attribution in encounter groups. *Small Group Behavior,* 1978, *9,* 14–21.

Stoller, F. H. A stage for trust. In A. Burton (Ed.), *Encounter: The theory and practice of encounter groups.* San Francisco: Jossey-Bass, 1969, 81–96.

Tannenbaum, R., I. Weschler, and F. Massarik. The role of the trainer. In R. T. Golembiewski and A. Blumberg (Eds.), *Sensitivity training and the laboratory approach.* Itasca, IL: Peacock, 1970, 139–40.

Thomas, H. F. Encounter—the game of no game. In A. Burton (Ed.), *Encounter: The theory and practice of encounter groups.* San Francisco: Jossey-Bass, 1969, 69–80.

Truax, C. B. The process of group psychotherapy. *Psychological Monographs,* 1961, *75,* (7, Whole No. 511).

Truax, C. B., and R. R. Carkhuff. *Toward effective counseling and psychotherapy: Training and practices.* Chicago: Aldine, 1967.

Truax, C. B., R. R. Carkhuff, and F. Kodman, Jr. Relationships between therapist-offered conditions and patient change in group psychotherapy. *Journal of Clinical Psychology,* 1965, *21,* 327–29.

Truax, C. B., J. G. Shapiro, and D. G. Wargo. Effects of alternate sessions and vicarious therapy pretraining on group psychotherapy. *International Journal of Group Psychotherapy,* 1968, *18,* 186–98.

Weigel, R. G. The marathon encounter: Requiem for a social movement. *Small Group Behavior,* 1977, *8,* 201–22.

Weschler, I. R., F. Massarik, and R. Tannenbaum. The self in process: A sensitivity training emphasis. In I. Weschler and E. Schein (Eds.), *Issues in sensitivity training.* (NTL Selected Reading Series) Washington, DC: National Education Association, 1962, 33–46.

Woodman, L. Some thoughts on norms and other pressures in encounter groups. La Jolla, CA: The Project on Community Center for Studies of the Person, 1970.

Yalom, I. D. *The theory and practice of group psychotherapy* (2nd ed.). New York: Basic Books, 1975.

Yalom, I. D., and M. A. Lieberman. A study of encounter group casualties. *Archives of General Psychiatry,* 1971, *25,* 16–30.

6
Gestalt Approach to Groups

Much of what we know as Gestalt therapy has come about through the work of one man—Fritz Perls. Fritz Perls not only gave Gestalt therapy its current name; he also can be credited with much of the popularization of this counseling approach. Originally, Perls did not set out to construct a theory of counseling. His efforts grew out of his dissatisfaction with psychoanalysis and out of his need to express his experiences with clients. The road to creating Gestalt therapy was a long one. In 1921, Perls received his M.D. degree from Friedrich Wilhelm University. With the rise of Nazism, he fled Germany in 1933 and Amsterdam in 1935. He was a man on the run for his life, and much later he was to say of this period, "To suffer one's death and to be reborn is not easy (Perls, 1969)." Little is written on how much of Perls' own history affected his development of Gestalt therapy. After working in South Africa from 1935 to 1946, Perls moved to the United States in 1946 and established a private practice.

It was in the United States that Perls was to piece together the disparate parts of his life and to develop Gestalt therapy, a task at which he had been at work for some time. In 1947, he published "Ego, Hunger, and Aggression," wherein he pointed out the significance of Gestalt psychology in psychotherapeutic procedures and leveled criticism at psychoanalysis. Four years later, Perls, Hefferline, and Goodman published *Gestalt Therapy* and Perls predicted that there would be an explosion of interest in Gestalt therapy within twenty years. By the 1960s, however, Gestalt therapy had already caught on; the interest that Perls had predicted had come sooner than he had thought.

One of the key factors in Gestalt therapy's achievement of national recognition was Perls' move to California and his joining the staff of the Esalen Institute in 1966. It was at the Esalen Institute that Gestalt therapy became intimately connected with the human potential movement and, accordingly, the "in thing" in small-group behavior and individual counseling. One of the basic goals of the founders of Esalen has been to incorporate Eastern modes of thought into Western science. Psychotherapy is *not* one of Esalen's major goals. The staff of Esalen tend to view psychotherapy as a means to adjust people to the social environment; this is the antithesis of their goal to release the "too well-adjusted," the too tightly controlled people for growth and greater integration (Ruitenbeek, 1970). In 1969, Perls published *Gestalt Therapy Verbatim,* a book of selected and edited audiotapes completed at weekend dreamwork seminars he conducted at Esalen from 1966 through 1968. Esalen became the home of Perls toward the end of his life. He died in 1970, at the age of seventy-six, after a brief illness.

Throughout his life, Perls exuded a certain mystique, an aura of honesty which most people praised because they lacked it in themselves. A biography of Fritz Perls written by Martin Shepard (1975) paints a different view of Perls. According to Shepard (1975), Perls was a Bauhaus bohemian who was self-driving, doubting, but lovable and brilliant. In some fundamental ways, he was almost completely dishonest in his personal life and in his closest personal relationships. Shepard pictures Perls as suffering from a "neediness paradox." He states: "Fritz Perls wanted, but wouldn't ask. And so he condemned the wantingness of others." To those who were emotionally attached to him, he manifested impenetrable defenses and was contradictory in nature. As a detached "taker," however, he displayed a brilliant genius in his professional life in ferreting out and helping others to work on their defenses. Like Freud, Perls minimized contact with his clients. Whereas Freud sat behind his clients, Perls hid behind the empty chair, across from his clients. Both men sought relief from their clients; both men were brilliant manipulators in that they got not only their clients but other therapists as well to buy into the correctness and efficacy of their own needs for detachment and distance from others. Commenting on Shepard's biography of Perls, Ryback (1975) has stated: "This holistic view of Fritz, his neurotic rootlessness, his chronic self-doubts and, above all, his driving destiny to become a great master in the world of psychotherapy, reveals a human, lovable person. It leaves me feeling glad that Fritz did his thing, and that Martin Shepard did his, too."

GESTALT PSYCHOLOGY: THE FORERUNNER OF GESTALT THERAPY

Although Perls borrowed heavily from Freud and others, much of the impetus of Gestalt therapy can be traced from Gestalt psychology. Gestalt psychology provided a number of contributions to Gestalt therapy. Foremost among these were the concepts of figure and ground, unfinished situation, and Gestalt.

Gestalt psychology found its origins in Germany and Europe in general. Max Wertheimer, Wolfgang Kohler, and Kurt Koffka were the leading proponents of this new branch of psychology as it was developed during the 1920s. The most well known of the Gestalt contributions are in the fields of perception and learning. According to Helson (1968), Gestalt psychologists caught the imagination of people. They were contrasted with the drab experimentalists (behaviorialists who were later to emerge). Helson (1968, p. 1006) has commented as follows regarding the success of Gestalt psychologists:

> Those who experienced the first two and a half decades of the Gestalt movement and followed its various developments will remember the excitement and enthusiasm it engendered. More than any other movement in experimental psychology, it appeared like a bright meteor lighting up the otherwise dim sky of perceptual theory.

Without the contributions of Fritz Perls, Gestalt psychology would have remained a meteor that burned itself out. As Wallen (1970) has noted, Gestalt psychologists stopped far short of applying their insights to the realm of the interpersonal and therapeutic process. According to Wallen (1970, p. 13), Perls made a unique contribution in that he extended the academic boundaries of Gestalt psychologists:

> This approach represents an extension of academic Gestalt psychology by adding needs and bodily awareness to the gestalt-forming process and then utilizing these insights in therapy to help unblock the need-fulfillment pattern.

Wallen's comments provide the necessary backgrond from which to view the contributions of Gestalt psychology to Fritz Perls' rendition of Gestalt therapy.

The Concept of the Gestalt

Gestalt therapy derived its name from the German school of Gestalt psychology. Although there is no precise English equivalent of the German word *Gestalt,* the term is used to connote an individual's attempt to construct meaningful organized wholes. English and English (1958, p. 225) have defined a Gestalt as: "a form, a configuration or a totality that has, as a unified whole, properties which cannot be derived by the summation from the parts and their relationships. . . . It may refer to physical structures, to physiological and psychological functions, or to symbolic units." In other words, Gestalt psychologists posit that the whole is more than the sum of its parts; indeed, the whole determines the parts. Gestalt psychologists used the term *Gestalt* to refer generally to an individual's perceptual organization. Perls used the term to connote the entire being or wholeness of an individual. Gestalt therapists posit, therefore, a holistic concept of human beings. They do not divide human beings into different parts, as do some theorists, who tend to focus only on the cognitive aspects of human existence and who ignore the sensory and emotional modes of experiencing (Harman, 1974). Just as Gestalt psychologists emphasized that people tend to perceive things in terms of wholes rather than fragmented parts, Perls stressed the unity and integration of a "normal" person's personality. One of the goals of Gestalt therapy is to help individuals reown and integrate the parts of themselves that they have previously rejected.

The Concept of Figure-Ground

Gestalt psychologists maintained that during the process of perceiving objects, an individual tends to form figures and grounds. A figure is an object, element, or person which emerges (becomes foreground) and stands out against a background. In terms of perception, a figure is that which a person is paying attention to; it constitutes a person's center of attentive awareness. A ground is the context in which a figure appears and against which the figure stands out. For example, an individual may look at a painting twice and comment that each time he or she saw something different. This situation exists because the first time, the individual was paying attention only to certain objects in the painting—a woman's face, for instance. When the individual looked at the painting the second time, the importance of the original figure (the woman's face) receded into the background, and thus the individual was able to pay attention to another object within the painting— the child next to the woman.

The fact that different objects may become the focus of an individual's attention and then fade into the background is an important principle in Gestalt psychology. This principle may be labeled the principle of shifting attention or figure-ground formations. That is, as a shift of emphasis occurs in what a person is paying attention to, the figure and ground change positions, and a new gestalt is formed.

Perls extended the Gestalt psychologists' concept of figure-ground as it relates to human visual perception of activities to other dimensions of people's lives. He affirmed that figure-ground relationships tend to occur in almost all aspects of human life. For example, an individual's thoughts, feelings, and senses in general are governed by figure-ground relationships. Individuals tend to hear, feel, and think certain thoughts because certain sounds or experiences have become figured in their lives. A mother might sleep through a loud thunderstorm, but she awakens when she hears the faint cry of her child. The child's cry became figured against the background of the noise of the thunderstorm and whatever else was happening. People feel certain ways about themselves because some events have become figured in their memory. For instance, individuals may describe themselves as lazy because they have formed this type of rigid, figure-ground perception of themselves. Their life experiences, such as parents calling them lazy or their failure to complete specific tasks, constitute the background against which their view of themselves as lazy is figured.

Perls used the concept of figure-ground in Gestalt therapy in several important ways. First, he posited that prior experiences constitute the background (ground) against which the individual figures a present experience. Second, an individual's most pressing need becomes figured. For example, an individual's immediate need of safety from a dangerous situation becomes more prominently figured than a need for love. People who have faced dangerous situations have usually been quoted as saying: "All I could think of was how to get out of there; I couldn't think about anything else." This statement illustrates Perls' belief that in an individual's struggle for survival, the most pressing need not only becomes figured but also organizes the individual's behavior until it is satisfied. As this need is satisfied, it tends to recede into the background, making room for the next most significant need. This change of need dominance, according to Perls, is necessary for both an individual's survival and healthy development.

The destruction of gestalts and the formation of new figure-ground relationships are important concepts in Gestalt therapy. According to Perls, Hefferline, and Goodman (1951), the destruction of gestalts is necessary for the healthy survival of an individual. When an individual is unable to destroy old gestalts and move on to new ones, he or she tends to live in the past. Moreover, interference with the formation and destruction of gestalts may mean that the individual clings compulsively to the unfinished situation; this results in other needs going unmet. For instance, Polster and Polster (1973) describe how an incomplete gestalt blocked a young woman's current relationship with men. During the therapy session, Peggy stated that she had never again sat on her father's lap after her mother had screamed at her for sitting there when she was a little girl. From that point on, Peggy accustomed herself to distance in her relationships with men and eventually chose a husband whom she knew did not want physical closeness. In spite of her defenses and beliefs about getting close to men, Polster and Polster (1973, p. 30) state: "The surge toward completing that early interrupted act—probably a whole series of them, since sitting on (her) father's lap only begins a sequence of closeness—is a force about which she must remain vigilant. The Gestalt view is that Peggy will feel dissatisfied until she has the opportunity, perhaps several opportunities, to allow that surge to take its course and reach completion."

Hence, one goal of Gestalt therapy is to help a person regain his or her former elastic figure-ground formation. According to Perls, Hefferline, and Goodman (1951), the healthy person experiences a continually emerging and receding interplay between figure and ground. A person who is suffering from neurosis, for example, may manifest a rigidity of figure-ground formation. Part of the process of Gestalt therapy involves helping the individual to make contact with both environment and self so that he or she makes less rigid or incomplete figure-ground relationships.

Perls also used the concept of figure-ground to emphasize the importance of awareness. In fact, what the Gestalt psychologists had designated as perception was relabeled awareness. Individuals who have elastic figure-ground formations are generally more aware of themselves and of what is happening around them. This situation occurs because the individual is experiencing a dynamic, free-flowing relationship between figure and ground. For example, while walking to a car, the individual who has an elastic figure-ground relationship observes trees, birds, and people. Attention shifts spontaneously to whatever appears in the foreground. The individual is, in essence, aware of the environment and of what he or she is doing. In contrast, the person who does not have an elastic figure-ground relationship is usually unaware of all the things going on. The individual may not see people or birds or the trees, only the parking lot. The level of awareness of environment and self is reduced. One of the goals of Gestalt therapy is to help individuals restore their awareness.

According to Polster and Polster (1973), figure-ground formation is the basic dynamic of awareness. In taking this position, the authors address indirectly the issue of the accessibility of ground or life experiences. Contrary to the psychoanalytic school which stresses the importance of the unconscious, Gestalt therapists maintain that there is a free flow between an individual's accessible and inaccessible information about self. The most important information about an individual does not necessarily lie, as Freud posited, in an unconscious realm that is largely inaccessible to the person without therapeutic assistance. Information in an individual's unconscious may become assessible by the individual's forming new figure-ground relationships and by staying in the here-and-now in group therapy.

The Concept of Closure

Individuals are inclined to organize their perceptions in a complete manner so as to reduce tensions that would arise from a sense of incompleteness. For instance, if one sees an incomplete drawing of a familiar object—a house for example—one tends to complete the drawing in one's mind and to label it a house. This concept illustrates the principle of closure, which may be summarized to mean that a person's mind acts to finish a figure and to perceive it as complete. When looking at Figure 1, most individuals would perceive a house instead of a series of lines.

Figure 1 Principle of Closure

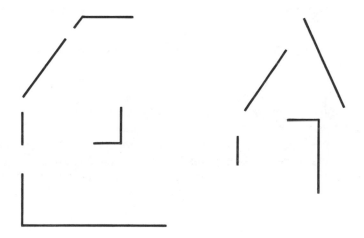

In contrast to Gestalt psychologists who dealt with the principle of closure primarily in terms of visual perception, Perls (1969) applied it primarily to an individual's thoughts, feelings, and total senses. In Gestalt therapy, lack of closure represents almost all unfinished business or life experiences. If unfinished life experiences are powerful enough, the individual is in deflected directions, regardless of how successful he or she appears to be. As Polster and Polster (1973. p. 37) have stated:

> Closure must come either through a return to the old business or by relating to parallel circumstances in the present. Thus, a person who has never been able to sit on her father's lap may find closure through doing it with someone else ... or perhaps through *fantasying* doing it again. Once closure has been reached and can be fully experienced in the present, the preoccupation with the old incompletion is resolved and one can move on to current possibilities.

The contributions of Gestalt psychology to Gestalt therapy as articulated initially by Perls, Hefferline, and Goodman (1951) and later summarized by Passons (1975) are as follows:

1. An individual's behavior is a gestalt, a whole that is greater than the sum of its parts.

2. An individual experiences the world according to the principles of a figure-ground relationship.

3. An individual will tend to seek closure of an incomplete gestalt. An incomplete gestalt draws an individual's attention until it is unified and stabilized.

4. An individual will tend to complete gestalts on the basis of his or her most prevalent need.

5. A person's behavior can be most meaningfully understood only in its immediate context.

THE CONTRIBUTIONS OF EXISTENTIALISM TO GESTALT THERAPY

Existentialism also exerted a considerable influence on Perls' development of Gestalt therapy. As Emerson and Smith (1974) have pointed out, Perls "adopted the existentialists' dictum that one must take responsibility for one's own life (p. 8)." Although Perls accepted the existential concept of personal responsibility, he felt that the major drawback of existentialism was that it needed some form of external conceptual support, such as psychoanalysis enjoyed from the work of Freud and his followers. According to Perls (1969, p. 16): "Gestalt therapy is the first existential philosophy to stand on its own two feet." In some respects, Perls reproached the existentialist school for its failure to concretize its ideas and to develop an external conceptual support system. Commenting upon existentialism and Gestalt therapy, Perls (1969, p. 16) stated: "Existentialism wants to do away with concepts, and to work on the awareness principle, on phenomenology. The setback with the present existentialist philosophies is that they need their support from somewhere else. If you look at the existentialists, they say that they are non-conceptual, but if you look at the people, they all borrow concepts from other sources. Buber from Judaism, Tillich from Protestantism, Sartre from Socialism, Heidegger from language, Binswanger from psychoanalysis, and so on. . . . Gestalt therapy has its support in its own formation because the gestalt formation, the emergence of needs, is a primary biological phenomenon."

Despite Perls' criticism, Gestalt therapy does use some of the concepts with which existentialism has come to be identified. For example, Gestalt therapists emphasize one's being in terms of the present moment. They tend to pay little attention to past events. Moreover, Perls has posited that one of the goals of this approach is to create a "continuum of awareness." It is felt that by creating this moment-to-moment awareness, the client will inevitably become cognizant of the unfinished business of the past. Perls also has elaborated on the idea that unless one is asleep, one is always aware of something. When such awareness becomes unpleasant, an individual is inclined to interrupt it by intellectualizing, by taking flight to the past, or by "jumping like a grasshopper from experience to experience . . . just a kind of flash, which leaves all the available material unassimilated and unused (Perls, 1969, 1. 51)."

To help the client become more aware of what he or she is experiencing at any given moment, Gestalt therapists pay strict attention to bodily movements and voice intonations. As Perls (1969, p. 53) has stated: "A good therapist doesn't listen to the content of the bullshit the patient produces, but to the sound, to the music, to the hesitations." From observing the body cues, the Gestalt therapist points out inconsistencies in verbal and nonverbal behavior. The therapist might say, for example, "You say that you are angry, but you are smiling" or "An angry person does not smile." These kinds of statements compel a person to make his or her own interpretation, since discrepant behavior is brought to the present.

Gestalt therapists are more concerned with the *now* of behavior than with interpreting unconscious motivators of behavior. To focus on awareness of behavior, Perls asks *what* questions, such as: "What are you doing now?" He avoids the *why,* or cause, questions. Similar to existential therapists, Gestalt counselors emphasize the Eigenwelt (the relations to one's self) rather than the past. To direct an individual's attention to awareness of here-and-now behavior, Perls' famous dictum is "Lose your mind and come to your senses." In this instance, he is trying to get the person to become aware of the totality of experiences.

Gestalt therapy does have existential origins; however, many of the contributions have been minimized or incorporated so thoroughly that they are often forgotten. Polster and Polster in their book *Gestalt Therapy Integrated: Contours of Theory and Practice* devote only one paragraph to the contributions of existentialism to Gestalt therapy. The authors state:

> Existentialism's primary contribution to psychotherapy has been through the develop-
> ment of a new—and broadly inclusive—ethos. It has brought relativity into the social
> and behavioral sciences by defining fresh views of authority, truth, participant experi-
> ence and the application of psychotherapy principles for personal growth. . . . Though
> the existentialists offer little in the way of practical prescriptions, their concepts of
> experience, authenticity, confrontation . . . have encouraged psychotherapeutic in-
> ventiveness aimed at giving substance to these otherwise abstract goals (1973, p.
> 316).

GESTALT THEORY OF PERSONALITY DEVELOPMENT

Gestalt therapy distinguishes itself from both existentialism and Gestalt psychology by its development of a theory of personality and human behavioral development. Neither Gestalt psychology nor existentialism have focused on creating an
explicit theory of personality development. The effort of Perls in this area represents, in part, his belief that a system of therapeutic help should have as its

foundation an external conceptual framework that describes the theoretical bases of its techniques.

The Nature of Human Beings

According to Passons (1975), Gestalt therapists maintain eight assumptions about the nature of human existence. These are as follows:

1. People constitute a holistic functioning. Bodily functions, emotions, thoughts, sensations, and perceptions of all kinds function interrelatedly. None of these parts can be understood adequately outside the context of the whole person.

2. People are a part of their environment, and they cannot be understood appropriately apart from their environment. This principle corresponds to the Gestalt view that an individual's behavior can only be meaningfully understood in context.

3. People choose how they respond to external events by the movement and placement of the limbs. People are actors rather than just reactors.

4. People are capable of being fully aware of their sensations, thoughts, emotions, and perceptions.

5. People are capable of making choices and are thus responsible for their behavior because of the process of self-awareness.

6. People have the capacity to live effectively and to govern themselves by their own assets.

7. People experience themselves primarily in the present. They are able to experience the past and the future in the here-and-now through the process of remembering and anticipating.

8. Individuals, by their nature, are neither basically good or basically evil.

The Gestalt approach to human nature represents a deeply humanistic view of people; however, it should not be confused with the self-actualization theory of Rogers. Rogers posited that people are basically good, but he construed their self-actualization ability in terms of future satisfaction of goals. From Rogers' perspective, people were in the process of becoming, they were striving to become self-actualized. In essence, self-actualization is what one is striving to become. In contrast, in Gestalt therapy, "Becoming is the process of being what one is and not a process of striving to become (Kempler, 1973, p. 262)." Gestalt therapy emphasizes the now rather than the process of becoming.

Normal Personality Development

Unlike some of the other theorists discussed in this book, Perls does not present a systematic theory of personality development that is readily comprehensible.

Although he talks about different dimensions of human functioning and development, he fails to unify these dimensions so that they present a logical, systematic, and sequential view of human development. Following Perls' tradition, this section, then, presents briefly some of the key elements he stressed regarding the healthy functioning and growth of human beings. The terms *contact, ego boundary, self-actualization,* and *need fulfillment* are central in Perls' description of human development.

As a child develops, it discovers that there is a difference between itself and the world. The child recognizes that there is a place where it ends and the rest of the world begins. This differentiation of the self from other human beings is an important element in personality development. The moment that the child begins to differentiate itself from its surroundings, it has made contact with its environment and has begun to establish what Perls calls "ego boundary." Contact may be defined as a child's awareness of and behavior toward assimilating the novelties in its environment and its rejection of the unassimilable novelties. As Perls, Hefferline, and Goodman (1951) have stated: "The organism grows by assimilating from the environment what it needs for its very growth (p. viii)." In further describing the importance of contact to human development, Perls, Hefferline, and Goodman assert:

> We must conclude that all contact is creative and dynamic. It cannot be routine, stereotyped, or merely conservative because it must cope with the novel, for only the novel is nourishing. . . . On the other hand, contact cannot passively accept or merely adjust to the novelty, because the novelty must be assimilated. All contact is creative adjustment of the organism and environment. . . . Growth is the function of the contact-boundary in the organism/environment field; it is by means of creative adjustment, change, and growth that the complicated organic unities live on in the larger unity of the world. . . . Contact, the work that results in assimilation and growth, is the forming of a figure of interest against a ground or context of the organism/environment field (1951, pp. 230–31).

Making contact is, then, the way that a child grows. The child grows by assimilating some novelties and rejecting unassimilable novelties. All experience of the child is ultimately contact, which may be described as the awareness of the field or motor response in the field. Contact boundary is where the experience occurs; it does not separate the organism and its environment, but instead limits the organism and contains and protects it at the time of touching.

Through contact, the child forms figure-and-ground relationships. It is important that as a child makes contact with its environment, it makes strong figures and grounds, for such relationships in turn lead to strong gestalts. For example, in Gestalt therapy, the counselor works to remake the dynamic relationships of the figure and ground until the individual's contact is heightened. Heightened contact in the present of the therapy session allows the client to work through unfinished business.

During the process of normal personality development, a child develops a self and a self-image. According to Perls, Hefferline, and Goodman, the self is defined as the system of contacts the child has made at any given moment. "As such, the self is flexibly various, for it varies with the dominant organic needs and the pressing environmental stimuli; it is the system of responses; it diminishes in sleep when there is less need to respond. The self is the contact-boundary at work; its activity is forming figures and grounds . . . it is the artist of life. It is only a small factor in the total organism/environment interaction, but it plays the crucial role of finding and making the meanings that we grow by (1951, p. 235)."

The self is what an individual actually is, whereas the self-image is what the individual feels he or she should be according to the expectations of others. The self moves the individual toward self-actualization, while the self-image tends to retard this process. Self-actualization is the motivating force in personality development.

Frustration is important in the development of the self. According to Perls: "Without frustrations there is no need, no reason, to mobilize your resources, to discover that you might be able to do something on your own (1969, p. 32)." Frustration in life helps a person to become more self-supporting, since the experiences that one undergoes teach a person that he or she can do and endure certain setbacks in life. When an individual maintains a self-image that is inconsistent with the self, the individual experiences tension and internal conflict between what the self wants to do and what the self-image says should be done. In normal personality development, people achieve some balance between the self and the self-image.

As noted previously, Perls did not believe that it was necessary to have theories of "normal behavior." In his opinion, what people called normal behavior was in actuality adjustment to the reality of others. Perls, Hefferline, and Goodman (1951) have summarized the functioning of the psychologically healthy person as follows:

> The description of psychological health and disease is a simple one. It is a matter of the identifications and alienations of the self. If a man identifies with his forming self, does not inhibit his own creative excitement; and conversely, if he alienates what is not organically his own and therefore cannot be vitally interesting, but rather disrupts the figure/ground, then he is psychologically healthy, for he is exercising his best power and will to do the best he can in the difficult circumstances of the world. But on the contrary, if he alienates himself and because of false identifications tries to conquer his own spontaneity, then he creates his life dull, confused, and painful (p. 235).

Maladaptive Behavior

Perls was much more explicit about maladaptive functioning than he was about normal personality development. The healthy person sees himself or herself as an ever changing process rather than as something that is static. He or she functions as a "systemic whole comprised of feelings, perceptions, thoughts, and a physical body whose processes cannot be divorced from the more psychological components. When the person's inner state and behavior match, there is little energy wasted within his organism and he is more capable of responding appropriately (for him) to meet his needs. The less-well-integrated person has voids or splits in his self that inhibit full mobilization of his resources (Passons, 1975, p. 20)."

The person who is suffering from maladjustment experiences a split between what the person is and what the person believes he or she should be. The individual alienates or disowns large aspects of personality. Such disowning results in the individual's having personality "holes" which are usually covered over with identifications that were initially based on external demands.

In maladaptive functioning, the individual lives for the self-image rather than the self. Instead of trying to actualize the self, the individual tries to actualize the self-image, which is usually a distorted and unrealistic view (Ward and Rouzer, 1974). The individual has lost or temporarily abandoned self-regulation. He or she is regulated by the opinions of others and the external demands of the environment.

Projection, retroflection, and introjection are the three most common means individuals use to maintain their maladaptive behavior. Projection may be defined as an individual's placing in the outside world those parts of the personality which he or she either refuses to accept or is unable to identify with. The projecting person has difficulty distinguishing between the inside and the outside world. Those features of an individual's personality (such as attitudes, feelings, and actions) which are inconsistent with self-image are disowned and placed onto objects or persons in the environment. For example, if a neurotic person cannot love, he or she may place this unwillingness to love on others. From the neurotic person's perspective, the world does not love the person. Projecting an attribute onto others allows the individual to avoid taking responsibility for his or her own feelings.

Retroflection may be defined as the means an individual uses to give himself or herself what the individual was unable to obtain from the environment. What was originally directed toward the world changes its course of direction and is bent backward toward the individual. For example, an individual who wants to hurt another individual may commit suicide. The narcissistic individual falls in love with herself or himself, so to speak, because she or he does not receive the love that was sought from others. The individual receives partial satisfaction from retroflective behavior by giving himself or herself what the individual was unsuccessful in obtaining from the environment. Retroflections are characterized by an internal personality split into "doer" and "done to" (Ward and Rouzer, 1974).

Introjection is the swallowing whole of things that must be destroyed before they can be assimilated into a person's behavior repertoire. Introjection, then, "involves a lack of assimilation such that the structure of what is taken in is preserved rather than destroyed and transformed" (Ward and Rouzer, 1974, p. 25). For instance, a person who meets someone whom he or she admires may adopt the other person's behavior, mannerisms, speech, and beliefs so as to become as much like the other person as possible. The individual becomes a phony because he or she has swallowed another person's behavior wholesale without transforming it to meet his or her own personality needs and self-actualization tendency. As a result, the introjected behavior stands out like a sore thumb.

Maladaptive functioning occurs out of the individual's consistent and unaware use of self-manipulation. The person tries to manipulate himself or herself in some devious way to meet needs that were previously unsatisfied. The maladaptive person has lost his or her original and spontaneous self-regulatory system. The person is no longer flexible in dealing with the environment or the self.

GESTALT GROUP COUNSELING

Gestalt counseling is usually conducted in groups, although, as pointed out later, group process per se is not given a great deal of attention. Gestalt group counseling frequently employs a concentrated workshop format. Counseling is a part of participants' total living experience for brief periods of time. Gestalt therapy groups may also meet over a sustained period of time.

Fritz Perls became most identified with the Gestalt therapy workshop as a result of his work at Esalen. The groups that Perls conducted were usually noncontinuous, ranging from a day to several weeks, and participants' formal contact with each other ended at the conclusion of the workshop. Perls conducted Gestalt group counseling by focusing on a single client or participant at a time. By not focusing on the group itself, Perls diverted each client's attention away from the reality of the group and the processes that may have been taking place within the group. The most important reality was the individual's reality rather than that of the group. Perls' approach represents Gestalt group counseling in its purest form, and it is this form which is described in the rest of the chapter.

Before doing so, it is significant to point out the differences between Gestalt group therapy and using Gestalt approaches in groups. Passons (1975) makes several distinctions between Gestalt group counseling and using Gestalt techniques. In a counseling group that uses Gestalt techniques, not all of the interventions used by the group leader will be of a Gestalt nature. The counselor may employ a number of techniques outside the realm of traditional Gestalt group counseling. The counselor will use Gestalt approaches selectively, as they are appropriate in the development and focus of the group. In the non-Gestalt counseling group, the leader is not the principal figure in the group, and the counselor pays attention to group process. There is multiple interaction between the group leader and group members as well as among the members themselves. In the Gestalt counseling group, the counselor is not concerned with facilitating interaction among group members; the opposite of this statement is true for counseling groups which use Gestalt techniques. The roles of group members, leaders, the emphasis on group process, and the use of other counseling interventions are distinguishing features of the counseling group which uses Gestalt approaches.

Unlike some of the other group approaches described in this book, the Gestalt counseling group stresses the significance of a client's nonverbal experience. Gestalt group therapy denies the special status most theorists attribute to the mind. This therapeutic approach puts the body on the same level as the mind.

Instead of a client's only talking about problems, the Gestalt therapist helps the client reenact problems. The therapist helps the client get in contact with the split parts of himself or herself by talking to these parts and taking their roles. The goal is to help the client reown the various parts of his or her personality and to become an integrated person.

Confrontation is a key element in the Gestalt approach to counseling. Perls labels his no-nonsense confrontation approach as "cutting through the garbage." That is, in any kind of counseling situation, Gestalt therapists come quickly to the point. They do not allow the individual to meander around the problem. They confront the client by pointing out discrepancies in verbal and nonverbal behavior, and continually attempt to make the client aware of feelings and actions at any given moment.

Goals of Gestalt Counseling Groups

A primary goal of Gestalt counseling groups is to help group members grow up. As Perls (1969, p. 28) has stated: "We have a very specific aim in Gestalt Therapy, and this is the same aim that exists at least verbally in other forms of therapy, in other forms of discovering life. The aim is to mature, to grow up." Gestalt group counselors promote client maturity by having clients take responsibility for their own lives. Such leaders tend not to coddle group members. They push them, at times almost relentlessly, to assume ownership of the feelings they have and the statements they make. Gestalt therapists believe that some individuals, under the guise of becoming self-actualized, try to disown parts of their personality. Responsibility, then, from the Gestalt position means that a person is willing to say "I am what I am" or "I am I." It means that the individual is able to free the self from the "shoulds" of society and parents. The individual learns to own what he or she is and to disown what he or she is not. Maturing is transcendence from the environmental support of others to self-support. In Gestalt therapy, the counselor helps clients to discover that they can do many things they never thought they could do.

Individual awareness is the second goal of Gestalt group counseling. As noted previously, Perls has affirmed that everything that happens to an individual is grounded in awareness, and that awareness is the only basis for knowledge and communication. Awareness implies a state of individual consciousness that develops spontaneously whenever the individual pays attention to whatever becomes foreground. It implies that the individual is in touch with self and environment—with what he or she is doing, thinking, planning, and feeling. Gestalt therapists help clients recognize how they block and distort their awareness. Gestalt therapists believe that when individuals become aware of what they are doing in the here-and-now, they are able to make more meaningful choices and to take direct action.

According to Perls (1969), awareness in and of itself can be curative. As he has stated: "And I believe that this is the great thing to understand: *that awareness per se—by and of itself*—can be curative. Because with full awareness you become aware of this organismic self-regulation, you can let the organism take over without interfering, without interrupting; we can rely on the wisdom of the organism (Perls, 1969, p. 17)."

Another goal in Gestalt group counseling is to help the individual achieve integration. Integration means to unite the various parts of an individual to form a complete whole. The Gestalt therapist stresses the importance of integrating opposing forces within the individual—for example, love and hate, top-dog and underdog, or one's "shoulds" and one's "wants." Perls has cautioned against the idea that total integration and total maturity are ever achieved. One can only approximate the achievement of these goals. "Now there is no such thing as total integration. Integration is never completed; maturation is never completed. It's an ongoing process for ever and ever. . . . There's always something to be integrated; always something to be learned (Perls, 1969, p. 64)."

Another goal of Gestalt group counseling is to help a person deal with and accept anxiety as part of the natural order of life (Levitsky and Simkin, 1972). A participant must be willing to take risks, to confront, and to try to assimilate experiences into a whole. In order to truly be oneself, one must learn to function as a total communicating unit, that is, to be aware of one's thoughts, feelings, and sensory sensations. People know they are alive because they are experiencing life, not just going through the motions of living. They are able to taste the food they eat, to feel the laughter in their bodies, to own up to their anger, resentments, and happiness.

Key Concepts and Technigues

It is difficult to separate Gestalt concepts from its techniques. In fact, all techniques of this school of thought are seen as extensions of the basic concepts—as a means of implementing its fundamental tenets. Techniques in and of themselves have no sacrosanct qualities from the Gestalt perspective. They are convenient means to achieve the previously outlined goals. Some of the more common approaches used to attain these goals are described below.

Assuming Responsibility   As indicated previously, one of the goals of Gestalt encounter groups is to get participants to assume responsibility for their feelings and behavior. Gestalt therapists maintain that language is frequently used to disguise an individual's unwillingness to assume responsibility. For example, the word *can't* is often employed to camouflage a person's refusal to do certain things. That is, the word *can't* may mean "won't." A common technique of the Gestalt encounter leader is to have an individual experiment with *won't* as a substitute for *can't*. For instance, a group member once complained to the leader, saying "I can't make friends." The leader, in turn, asked the member to experiment with substituting the word *won't* for *can't*. "How does it feel," he asked, "when you change your statement to 'I won't make friends'?" The group member responded that substituting *won't* for *can't* made her feel as if she were in the driver's seat; it put her in control, as it were. All her life she had felt pushed to make friends and rejected when individuals didn't seem to want to become friends with her. Now she more clearly understood some of the underlying dynamics of her own behavior. In reacting against the self-imposed pressure, she frequently did things to make others not like her. Her own behavior created a self-fulfilling prophecy. In essence, the substitution of the word *won't* for *can't* may at times be a more genuine expression of feelings. By owning and accepting the strength implied in the word *won't,* a person learns to become more responsible for his or her own behavior.

Gestalt encounter group leaders see the statement "I feel guilty" as another example of how participants use language to avoid taking responsibility. According to them, hidden behind expressions of guilt are feelings of resentment. The woman who says she feels guilty about working because it takes her away from her children too much might be concealing feelings of resentment about either the children or the work she does. Guilt feelings are usually an individual's attempt to show good intentions or compliance with the mode of behavior society considers appropriate when in reality the person does not want to do what society deems acceptable. To get at the heart of guilt feelings, the Gestalt encounter leader may ask a participant to experiment with substituting *I resent* or *I demand* for *I feel guilty*. As the participant uses these substitute words, the leader asks if the participant feels more comfortable. The underlying belief here is that unexpressed resentment prevents an individual from dealing adequately with a situation. The person is inclined to hang onto feelings of resentment, thereby letting them interfere with functioning.

The Hot Seat   This technique is a commonly used approach to bring about greater self-awareness on the part of an individual. Usually, a session begins with the leader's explanation of the "hot seat" concept. Members are simply told that anyone who wants "to work" may sit in a chair facing the leader. The person who decides to sit in the chair is told to begin by stating a specific life problem. All references to the problem should be made in terms of present feelings—the here-and-now. The group leader explains that other members may be asked to help in some sort of structured way, but that unless specifically asked to do so they are not to interfere. The individual usually sits in the hot seat anywhere from ten to thirty minutes or until both the individual and the leader feel they have reached closure. During a member's stay in the hot seat, the leader interacts directly and aggressively in order to get to the problem. If no one comes forward to work after the leader's explanation of the hot seat approach, the leader may decide to wait it out until someone comes forward or to initiate warm-up games.

Polster and Polster (1973) delineate some of the advantages of the one-to-one hot seat technique in a group setting. First, the individual in the hot seat, although apart from the group, may experience a heightened sense of community. The presence of other people watching an individual react tends to add greater significance to what that person is doing. Second, the individual in the hot seat has an opportunity to reveal himself or herself not only to the leader but also to the group members. Third, group members may be able to learn something about themselves from watching another person deal with his or her concern in the hot seat.

Polster and Polster (1973) also point out that a "floating" hot seat technique may be used to elicit greater group participation and interaction. The authors describe the floating hot seat approach as the interaction of one individual with all other members of a group. For example, one individual may decide to sit in the hot seat in order to deal with a fear of taking risks. The group leader as well as the members would then respond to that individual as he or she attempted to work on the fear.

Making Rounds   In this warm-up game, confrontation is at its height. Frequently, making the rounds is precipitated by a person saying something that the leader feels should be expressed to other members in the group (Ruitenbeek, 1970). For instance, a participant may have said, "I hate everyone in this room." The facilitator might respond by saying, "Make that statement to each person here and, in doing so, express your feelings about each person." Making rounds may also take the form of asking a person, "What are you in touch with?" This question attempts to help the participant become aware of his or her particular mood, feeling, and body sensation at a given moment. During the course of this exercise, a participant may feel like working through some unfinished materials of the past, in which case rounds would be suspended and the individual and therapist would work together. The intent of the exercises is that a person will gradually learn to discover different aspects of the self. Self-discovery is emphasized throughout Gestalt group work.

Now and How Fritz Perls (1969) once said that the Gestalt therapy stands on two legs: now and how. *Now* refers to a person's immediate awareness of experiencing. *How* refers to a person's description of the manner in which certain feelings are experienced. A now statement brings the past and the present together. For instance, instead of talking about past experiences with significant others that caused unhappiness, a group member would state, "Now I am feeling like a hopeless child, still clinging to my mother's apron strings." In order to get the individual to deal with the how of this feeling, the leader would ask the individual to demonstrate behaviorally what this statement means. The group leader might ask: "What are the sensations you experience when you feel like a child, still clinging to your mother's apron strings?" If the person responds by expressing feelings of unhappiness or anger when demonstrating the how, the leader would try to encourage the individual not to leave the feeling behind. This method is called "staying with it." The Gestalt leader would say, "Can you stay with this feeling?" In essence, the stay with it technique demonstrates Perls' belief that neurotic behavior is sustained by a person's phobic avoidance. By asking the person to try to continue experiencing fears, Perls is trying to help the person deal with the neurosis. Concerning the importance of now and how in Gestalt therapy, Perls (1969) states:

> These are the two legs upon which Gestalt therapy works: now and how. The essence of the theory of Gestalt therapy is in the understanding of these two words. Now covers all that exists. The past is no more, the future is not yet. Now includes the balance of being here, is experiencing involvement, phenomenon, awareness. How covers everything that is structure, behavior, all that is actually going on—the ongoing process. All the rest is irrelevant—computing, apprehending, and so on (p. 44).

> Gestalt therapy uses eyes and ears and the therapist stays absolutely in the now. He avoids interpretation [and] verbiage production. . . . But what is there is there. Gestalt therapy is being in touch with the obvious (p. 54).

Body Language Gestalt therapy stresses the use of body language or cues in helping a participant deal with a problem. If a person is tapping the side of a chair, for example, the group leader might ask, "What is your hand saying to the chair?" By phrasing the question in this manner, the leader avoids interpreting the person's tapping. The participant tells the leader what the tapping means. The emphasis on the body movements is related to Gestalt therapists' belief in the wholeness of an individual. It is a way of saying that what goes on in a person's mind is a reflection of what goes on in the body. Hence, there is a concerted effort to integrate body with mind. Since the Gestalt therapists are convinced that important messages are sent via body language, encounter group leaders should be able to demonstrate skill in reading body language.

The Empty Chair   This is a common technique used in Gestalt-oriented encounter groups. The empty chair technique is designed to help a group member deal with different parts of the psyche. The participant accomplishes this task by projecting onto the chair aspects of self of which he or she is aware. For example, if a person is feeling angry with himself or herself because of aggressive behavior, the group leader would direct the person to "put into the chair" the feelings of aggressiveness and then to go to the empty chair and assume the role of this aggressiveness. This technique forces the person to get in touch with his or her aggressiveness—to become it, rather than to intellectualize or talk about it. The dialogues that occur between that portion of an individual's perceived self and the individual promote the integration of feelings and thoughts.

Top-dog and Underdog Introjections   Borrowing from the psychoanalytic tradition, Perls (1951) uses the concept of introjection to refer to the process by which individuals take into themselves aspects of other people, particularly parents. As children grow, they tend to learn by absorbing what is around them, that is, they are inclined to swallow whole their parents' values as well as those of school and society. They operate on the basis of introjected standards of rightness and wrongness. According to Perls, some sort of taking-in process is both inevitable and perhaps even necessary. The critical point is the degree to which individuals discriminate in their taking in of others. In an effort to deal with the world, the introjector usually attempts to minimize differences between what he or she has swallowed from parents and society during the process of growing up and what he or she truly wants to do by simply not making any distinctions between these two forces. The introjector refuses to discriminate between parental desires and personal desires because to do so would require some restructuring and would elicit anxiety.

When individuals introject uncritically, they may fail to assimilate adequately that which they have introjected. There may be a split between what they want to do and what they feel they should do. Perls labeled "should" introjections as top-dog. Top-dog is, in many respects, the rough equivalent of the psychoanalytic superego. Top-dog operates upon shoulds. He or she has a righteous and authoritarian nature. Top-dog is usually a bully who backs up shoulds with manipulative demands and threats of catastrophe. "If you don't eat your food, Mommy won't love you anymore" and "If you don't act like a good girl, then you'll be called cheap trash, and nobody will ever respect you."

Underdog attempts to control top-dog by reacting defensively, apologizing, and playing the role of "nobody likes me." He or she is usually passively aggressive, makes excuses for behavior, and has countless reasons for delay.

The importance of top-dog and underdog is that they tend to be two conflicting components contained within the same individual. The struggle between top-dog and underdog is easily demonstrated by an individual's frequently unfulfilled promises to himself or herself. The recriminations of the top-dog lead to self-torture games, games which demand impossible perfection. The perfectionist cannot enjoy other people or life because he or she is trying to live up to idealized versions of what life should be like.

One of the techniques used to deal with introjections is to have the group member learn to differentiate between *I* and *you*. A participant might be asked to make up sentences beginning with I. I sentences give the individual a feeling of self. Another intervention technique is to have a participant go to each person in the group and say "I am tortured by . . . ." Finally, an individual might be asked to carry on a dialogue between top-dog and underdog. In this instance, the person would imagine that the significant person were there and would furnish statements and responses for both himself or herself and the other person.

Expressing Resentment and Appreciation Gestalt counselors maintain that resentments cannot exist without appreciations. An individual clings to resentments because he or she also appreciates something about another person or a situation. This is to say, without appreciations a person would simply forget about the other person. The counselor can promote growth in a group by having members express both their resentments and appreciations of each other.

There are certain advantages to using the resentment and appreciation intervention technique. First, it may be employed to deal with the unfinished business of a current or previous group meeting. For example, at the end of a meeting the counselor might suggest, "Maybe we can clear the air by having those of you who feel as if you were left hanging express your appreciations and resentments of our meeting today." Or, a counselor might state, "At the end of our last meeting, some of you seemed to have left upset. My hunch is that we should deal with the unfinished business of our last meeting by expressing our resentments and appreciations of what went on."

Second, participants learn that contact made with one another is not an either-or situation. Any one participant may express both resentments and appreciations of another group member. Participants learn to understand what others like and dislike about them.

Third, the resentment and appreciation technique may be used to counteract the tendency toward negative feedback in an encounter group. Individuals are inclined to find it easier to express negative feelings. They can tell you what is wrong with the world, the society, and their own group, but they are inclined to find it difficult to say what is right about each one of these concerns. By expressing appreciations and resentments, one learns at least to look at two aspects of an individual or a situation.

Changing Questions to Statements Gestalt counselors focus a great deal of attention on an individual's need to ask questions. Often one will learn that a person who tends to ask questions is not really seeking information. A tendency to respond in this manner may indicate laziness, passivity, or an unwillingness to state declaratively what he or she is feeling. An individual who asks a question frequently wants to make a statement. For example, one group participant blurted out, "I'm having problems at school just because I'm supposed to be a brain. Nobody likes to be around a brain. That's the same kind of feeling I'm getting about people in this group." In response, another participant asked, "Do you really believe that's the cause of your problem?" Behind this seemingly innocent question was the statement, "I don't feel that's the cause of your problem."

According to Gestalt counselors, the problem with questions is that they tend to send mixed messages and block honest communication. Both the person who poses a question and the intended receiver may profit from explicit statements. The receiver is less likely to be sent a mixed message, and the questioner learns how to express feelings more explicitly and honestly.

Part of the counselor's task is to distinguish genuine questions from those that are used for other reasons. A case in point is the hypocritical question, wherein the poser of the question tries to manipulate people into doing or seeing things his or her way—for example, "Don't you think we should change the topic of this discussion?" Not all questions are bad, and some may actually provide support; the person who asks, "How are you feeling?" may be showing concern for another individual. One rule of thumb the counselor may employ to distinguish genuineness among the different types of questions is to ask the person to change his question into a statement. The rapidity and the ease with which the questioner can do this gives the counselor additional insight as to the type of question asked. The participant who feels more comfortable when he changes a question into a statement most likely was not asking a question at all.

I and Thou   As with other encounter group leaders, Gestalt counselors focus upon developing I-Thou relationships within the group setting. Basically, *I* and *Thou* refer to Martin Buber's belief that an individual's identity develops from true sharing with other people. Trust among people occurs as each person seeks to identify the personality of another individual in his or her wholeness, unity, and uniqueness. To promote I-Thou relationships within a group, Gestalt counselors work to have group members make contact with each other in their communications. They emphasize that members must indicate to whom they are talking. Participants are also encouraged to be aware of the difference between "talking to" and "talking at" a person. Thus, a counselor may direct individuals in a group to use the name of the intended receiver at the beginning of a sentence. The counselor may point out that the sender's voice tone and verbal behavior indicate that the sender is trying to avoid making genuine contact with others. Failure to establish I-Thou relationships leads to feelings of alienation and aloneness, while the development of such relations promotes group warmth, cohesiveness, and group process.

Sharing Hunches   Gestalt counselors do not tend to encourage group members to offer interpretations of one another's behavior. They consider interpretation as merely verbiage—as a technique that covers rather than reveals. In place of interpretations, group members are asked to share their hunches. For instance, a participant may preface a statement with the words, "My hunch is . . . ." By stating one's feelings in terms of hunches, the individual does not create as much defensiveness in the other person. He or she allows the person greater latitude for accepting or rejecting the hunch. He or she also acknowledges that what one may know about another's behavior is at best a hunch.

Role Reversals   The Gestalt group leader uses reversals to help participants understand that overt behavior may represent the opposite of their latent impulses. A participant may, therefore, be asked to role play a specific feeling or behavior that she or he seems to be demonstrating to excess. A case in point is the person who may purport to suffer from extreme timidity. In a group setting, such a person might be asked to play the role of an exhibitionist. By assuming this role, the individual may make contact with a part of the self that has been previously denied.

Unfinished Business   Although this concept is central to Gestalt therapy, its origins can be traced to the psychoanalytic school of thought. Unfinished business refers to the tendency of an individual to relive in the present thoughts and feelings that belong more appropriately to the past. That is to say, those things that lie in the death of the past are still affecting one's behavior in the present. Generally speaking, such unfinished business of the past is denied awareness and, therefore, never really becomes "figured" in one's continuum of awareness [see pp. 198–201]. It still remains in the background, interfering with one's "contact functioning" —a present-oriented, reality-bound awareness of both oneself and of others. It was Perls' belief that a person's unfinished business of the past should be dealt with to the extent it is affecting present behavior. Acknowledgement, acceptance, and owning of feelings were seen as essential. According to Gestalt therapy, once a feeling is owned in the present, then it can become figured. Feelings that are figured by an individual no longer become the central organizers of behavior. Perls believed that unacknowledged grief, anger, or loss of a loved object constitute the bulk of unfinished business. Therefore, very often he would ask a participant to place a lost loved object in an empty chair and to say good-bye to this person.

Authenticity   The development of authenticity pervades all Gestalt encounter groups. This refers to an individual's state of truly being himself or herself. In order to attain this goal, a person's continuum of awareness must be systematically expanded and figured.

Withdrawal   Unlike some other encounter group approaches, the Gestalt school emphasizes an individual's right to withdraw from contact. Pointing out the polarities in life, Perls (1969) suggests that just as there can be no left direction without a right, there can be no real contact without a withdrawal. Each individual must establish effective, personal contact boundaries so that his or her feelings may become fully figured. Likewise each person must allow his or her withdrawal from a group to become fully figured. Withdrawal is significant because it symbolizes the organismic regulation of an individual. People decide for themselves whether or not they want to be left alone or in contact with other people.

The Gestalt counselor may help a participant to withdraw psychologically from a group if that individual indicates that he or she wants to do so. Here the counselor takes into consideration the principle of saturation. That is, the participant may have become saturated with making contact with other members. Typically, if a person expresses a need to withdraw, the counselor might say, "Try to relax and imagine that you're going to leave this group. What are you experiencing now? Can you try to put yourself into what you are experiencing now?" Gradually, the participant breaks contact and withdraws into whatever he or she is experiencing at that moment. The individual's own organismic regulation system would determine when contact should again be made.

Role of the Leader   The Gestalt-oriented encounter group leader is central to the group. In fact, one could go so far as to say that in the Gestalt encounter group, it is the leader who determines much of what will take place, and with whom and when such interactions will occur. In many instances, a group leader's work with one participant takes precedence over the group. This is clearly demonstrated in the hot seat approach, where the role of the group members has been likened to that of the Greek chorus in drama. Group initiative is considerably diminished, and interrelationships among participants are underplayed. The Gestalt group leader designs techniques, games, or exercises to help the participant intensify the total experience. The leader attempts to create greater awareness of nonverbal cues and contact-avoiding behaviors. The leader emphasizes the importance of risk and confrontation, and of chewing over and assimilating emotional experiences. Furthermore, the Gestalt group leader serves as a role model. He or she is frequently very open with the group members about personal feelings and does not attempt to hide behind the role of therapist group leader. The goal is to demonstrate authenticity in relationships with participants. Because of the prominent role of the group leader, it has been said that Gestalt therapy in encounter groups is actually individual therapy that takes place in the presence of a group. Perls agrees in part with this view, but he also points out what he sees as the advantage of Gestalt group work.

When the group leader works with one participant in the presence of other group members, the participant cannot use his or her usual phobic way of disowning or manipulating the leader. Now, in place of the individual opinion of the leader, there are the collective opinions of other group members concerning the existence or nonexistence of certain maladaptive behaviors. Or the Gestalt group leader may likewise use the group for performing such collective experiments as talking gibberish together or engaging in withdrawal exercises designed to help group members understand the importance of the group atmosphere. By observing the manipulative games of other group members (playing helpless, stupid, wailing, or other seductive roles), participants may see their own neurotic behavior more clearly.

The Gestalt group counselor must be both willing and able to reveal himself or herself as an authentic person. This means accepting responsibility for his or her behavior in the group experience, rather than playing the role of "Aw shucks, I'm just like every other member of this group." Such behavior would be unauthentic. The Gestalt group counselor openly acknowledges and assumes responsibility for being a combined leader-facilitator-person. This is perhaps best demonstrated by a willingness to take risks within the group. The Gestalt counselor leans heavily on intuitive processes. The asking of a seemingly simple question such as "What are you experiencing at this moment?" may embark the counselor, the participant, and the group on a journey into virgin territory that is rich and fascinating.

The Gestalt leader does not try to assume responsibility for members of the group. Each person is expected to assume responsibility for his or her own behavior. Group members are offered an experience in living, nothing more and nothing less. Each member does his or her "own thing" and does not try to live up to the expectations of others.

Levin and Shepherd (1974) have posited that the Gestalt counselor assumes several roles, those of: (1) expert-helper; (2) see-er, linguist, and communications expert; (3) frustrator; (4) creative agent; and (5) teacher. Upon entering counseling, the client tends to view the counselor as an expert-helper, as someone who has the training and power which is supposed to help one achieve health and balance. Because of the role and expectations the client has of the counselor, obstacles to contact and communication initially take place. The counselor realizes that many of the positive characteristics that the client attributes to the counselor may be based on the client's desire to relinquish part of his or her responsibility as client in the therapeutic relationship. The counselor cannot make the discoveries which the client so desires. The counselor can only facilitate or promote those discoveries and expressions which lead eventually to the client's healthy development.

As a linguist and communications expert, the Gestalt counselor must be sensitive to the subtle discrepancies between the client's verbal and physical expressions (Levin and Shepherd, 1974). The counselor examines the client's language and verbal messages not only for content but also for context, quality, the client's tone, usage of pronouns, tenses, and slips of the tongue. During this phase of group counseling, the counselor may ask a client: "What are you feeling right now? Are you aware of the tone of your voice? Are you aware that you spoke of your anger, not in the past but in the present?" These techniques give the client the responsibility for self-awareness and his or her own discoveries. By the counselor's focusing on the client's awareness of self, the client gradually becomes aware of his or her style of responding and how he or she either interrupts or blocks the flow of awareness and contact. The counselor attempts to help the client reduce these blocks and experience feelings and sensations. The counselor's emphasis on client awareness serves three essential therapeutic functions: (1) accentuating the steps that have to be taken for possible client fulfillment; (2) promoting the client's working-through process; and (3) helping the client to recover old experiences. The therapist uses his or her own awareness in facilitating these therapeutic functions for the client.

In Gestalt therapy, neurosis is conceptualized as an individual's maintenance of incomplete or unfinished situations of the past in the present. The neurotic individual comes to therapy lacking an adequate support system. To get the client to develop and rely on an internal support system, the counselor may frustrate the client. Frustration of the client essentially means that the counselor interrupts the client's pattern of self-defeating and neurotic behavior and attempts to change the client's manipulative devices. As Levin and Shepherd have maintained:

> Frustration comes as a result of the patient's wanting from his therapist what he has gotten, or has not gotten from his environment, and the therapist, refusing to give that, thus prevents the payoff to the patient. What comes is out of the inevitability of the therapist's responding differently to the patient than people in his past have done, thus creating a new situation where the patient is thrown back on his own resources. This is a natural consequence of the therapist's not wanting to support the patient's pathology and continued confluence, but wanting instead to foster greater differentiation and responsibility in the patient (1974, pp. 28–29).

The Gestalt counselor also works as a creative agent and drama coach. For instance, the counselor helps the client to "set the stage and get clear on which characters are in his play and what seats they occupy (Levin and Shepherd, 1974, p. 29)."

Role of Group Members   As with some of the other group approaches, there is no single clearly defined role for group members except that they are expected to assume responsibility for their own behavior. Each individual has a right to exercise personal choice concerning the degree to which he or she wants to participate in the group. An individual has the right to decide, for example, whether or not to sit on the hot seat. He or she is not forced to do so. An individual also has the right to withdraw. The major confrontation a group member experiences is with herself or himself. Group members provide support for one another. They learn, however, that some of their methods of intended "helpfulness" may block growth in another person. Hence, Gestalt encounter groups are cautioned against exerting group pressure on a person to become something other than what he or she is.

Rating Gestalt-Oriented Encounter Groups   That concepts from Gestalt therapy have permeated most types of encounter groups is an inescapable conclusion. On the other hand, it also seems clear that to label Gestalt-oriented groups as encounter groups is somewhat misleading. In contrast with others, the Gestalt-oriented group does not have the type of encountering that normally takes place among participants in such groups. Lieberman, Yalom, and Miles (1973), in their now popular study of encounter groups, give a favorable review of the Gestalt-oriented encounter group. In their "looking back" section, the authors compare how members of a Gestalt-oriented group rated their experience in the group to the seventeen groups studied:

> At the end of the group, the members were exceedingly enthusiastic. They found their group a pleasant experience (first among the seventeen), they were "turned on" by the group (first among the seventeen); they considered it to be a constructive experience (tied for first among the seventeen); they felt that they learned a great deal (second among the seventeen groups). Overall, he (the group leader) was rated second (pp. 31–32).

SUMMARY

Gestalt techniques have been incorporated into the various theoretical schools of counseling. Few counselors practice Gestalt therapy in its purest form. Gestalt group counseling is different from other group approaches in that the interactions between group members and the development of the group as a whole are not emphasized. The group exerts its influence primarily by establishing an atmosphere of approval for individual emotional expression.

References

Emerson, P., and W. L. Smith. Contributions of Gestalt psychology to Gestalt therapy. *The Counseling Psychologist*, 1974, *3*, 8–12.

English, H. B., and A. C. English. *A comprehensive dictionary of psychological and psychoanalytic terms.* New York: David McKay Co., 1958.

Harman, R. Goals of Gestalt therapy. *Professional Psychology*, 1974, *5*, 178–84.

Helson, H. Why did their procedures fail and the Gestalt psychologists succeed? *American Psychologist*, 1968, 1006–11.

Kempler, W. Gestalt therapy. In R. Corsini (Ed.), *Current psychotherapies.* Itasca, IL: Peacock, 1973, 251–86.

Levin, L. S., and I. L. Shepherd. The role of the therapist in Gestalt therapy. *The Counseling Psychologist*, 1974, *4*, 27–30.

Levitsky, A., and J. Simkin. Gestalt therapy. In L. N. Solomon and B. Berzon (Eds.), *New perspectives on encounter groups.* San Francisco: Jossey-Bass, 1972.

Lieberman, M. A., I. D. Yalom, and M. B. Miles. *Encounter groups: First facts.* New York: Basic Books, 1973.

Passons, W. R. *Gestalt approaches in counseling.* New York: Holt, Rinehart and Winston, 1975.

Perls, F. S. Workshop vs. individual therapy. *Journal of Long Island Consultation Center*, 1967, *5*, 305–10.

Perls, F. S., *Gestalt therapy verbatim.* Lafayette, CA: Real People Press, 1969. (Paperback, Bantam, 1971)

Perls, F. S., R. Hefferline, and P. Goodman. *Gestalt therapy.* New York: Julian Press, 1951. (Paperback, Dell, 1965)

Perls, L. One Gestalt therapist's approach. In J. Fagen and I. L. Shephard (Eds.), *Gestalt therapy now.* Palo Alto, CA: Science and Behavior Books, 1970, 120–30.

Polster, E., and M. Polster. *Gestalt therapy integrated: Contours of theory and practice.* New York: Brunner/Mazel Publishers, 1973.

Ruitenbeek, H. *The new group therapies.* New York: Avon, 1970.

Ryback, D. Books: The Fritz Perls Mystique. *Psychology Today,* 1975, *9,* 75–76.

Shepard, M. *Fritz: An intimate portrait of Fritz Perls and Gestalt therapy.* New York: Saturday Review Press, 1975.

Wallen, R. Gestalt therapy and Gestalt psychology. In J. Fagen and I. Shepherd (Eds.), *Gestalt therapy now.* Palo Alto, CA: Science and Behavior Books, 1970.

Ward, P., and D. L. Rouzer. The nature of pathological functioning from a Gestalt perspective. *The Counseling Psychologist,* 1974, *4,* 24–26.

7

Rational Approaches to Groups

Rational approaches to group counseling represent an orientation that is gaining increasing recognition in the counseling literature. Although there are several theories which might have been included under rational approaches to counseling, two have been singled out for presentation in this chapter. These are Rational-Emotive Therapy (RET), as developed by Albert Ellis, and Reality Therapy, as conceptualized by William Glasser.

Reality Therapy and Rational-Emotive Therapy share a number of similarities. Both, for example, use a cognitive or primarily intellectual approach in working with clients. Both the Rational-Emotive therapist and the Reality therapist are usually quite active; they tend to be eclectic and to adopt a variety of counseling techniques in working with clients. During the counseling process, the counselor assumes the stance of a teacher, which entails confronting the client with what she or he is currently doing and then teaching the client to think and act in a more appropriate way that will help satisfy basic needs. Both Rational-Emotive and Reality Therapy emphasize the client's ability to solve problems based upon his or her cognitive or reasoning ability; and both counseling approaches can be taught to clients, teachers, and counselors in a relatively short time. In describing their theories, Ellis and Glasser have spent little time discussing the etiology of normal and abnormal personality development. Instead, they focus on the counseling process. The two approaches are presented separately in this chapter and are summarized in the concluding section.

REALITY THERAPY

As with some of the other theoretical approaches discussed in this book, Reality Therapy grew out of disenchantment, in this case, that of Glasser with some of the basic tenets of his training in Freudian psychoanalytic counseling procedures. Although now used with a variety of clients in a number of different settings, Reality Therapy was originally used in the treatment of office patients, mental hospital patients, and adult and juvenile lawbreakers. Much of Glasser's work with juvenile offenders grew out of his years of work at the Ventura School for Girls of the California Youth Authority.

What is Reality Therapy? Reality Therapy is an approach to counseling which stresses that people are normal or experience healthy psychological development to the extent that they are able to deal with the real world. A basic goal of this approach is to help the client deal appropriately with the real world.

Principles of Personality Development

Reality Therapy posits that everyone has two constant psychological needs: "the need to love and be loved and the need to feel that we are worthwhile to ourselves and to others (Glasser, 1965, p. 9)." Healthy or normal personality development is a function of the degree to which individuals have been able to meet their needs appropriately. In order for individuals to fulfill their needs, they must have at least one person with whom they are emotionally involved. They should feel that such a person really cares about them and thinks that they are worthwhile. For the young child, this person is usually the mother. Through interaction with the mother or other persons, a child gains a sense of human involvement, closeness, psychological warmth, and emotional ties. Glasser (1965) assumes that when a person is unable to fulfill these two basic psychological needs, the person suffers in his or her own particular way. As Glasser (1965, p. 12) has stated: "We know, therefore, that at the time any person comes for psychiatric help he is lacking the most critical factor for fulfilling his needs, a person whom he genuinely cares about and who he feels cares about him. Learning to fulfill one's needs appropriately begins in infancy." According to Glasser (1965, p. 11): "A person who does not learn as a little child to give and receive love may spend the rest of his life unsuccessfully trying to love."

Learning responsible behavior during childhood is one of the keys to being able to satisfy one's psychological needs to love and be loved, to feel that one is worthwhile to self and to others. Glasser (1965) defines responsible behavior as the ability to fulfill one's needs in a manner that does not deprive others of their ability to fulfill their needs. For example, a young child who is overindulged by parents may receive an abundance of love, but the parents may not make the critical distinction between loving the child and accepting its behavior, which may be both good and bad. Unless these distinctions are made by the parents, the child may not feel loved or worthwhile. The child may feel unloved by being rewarded for behavior that he or she believes is wrong or unworthy of love. Loving a child while not demanding responsible behavior not only deprives the child but also damages the parents' basic need to feel a sense of self-worth.

Learning responsible behavior is crucial to a child's development of a "success identity." Conversely, irresponsible behavior leads to a personality with "failure identity." The child achieves a success identity by being involved in activities that satisfy basic needs. Individuals who develop a success identity do so as a result of a loving relationship with responsible parents. Responsible parents are those who establish an involvement with their children through teaching, role modeling, discipline, and love. As noted previously, children want to be responsible, but they generally do not "accept discipline and learn better ways unless they feel the parents care enough to show them actively the responsible way to behave (Glasser, 1965, p.18)." A child's feeling of self-worth comes from being able to do things for herself or himself and carry out tasks to a successful completion.

Conversely, children with failure identities do not meet their needs for love and self-worth and, accordingly, they experience pain (Wubbolding, 1975). People with failure identities attempt to meet their needs for love and self-worth through one or more substitutes. They tend to be absorbed in: (1) their own thinking, which if excessive leads to psychosis; (2) their own emotions, which may lead to depression or loneliness; and (3) their physical reactions which may result in ulcers, headaches, or other sickness. A failure identity often leads to juvenile delinquency and addiction to drugs or alcohol (Glasser, 1972).

The responsible and healthy child has parents who enforce discipline with an element of love. By their actions, such parents convey to the child something of the message: "I care enough about you to force you to act in a better way, in a way you will learn through experience to know, and I already know, is the right way (Glasser, 1965, p. 19)." Normal personal development comes about as a result of a child's learning of the three basic Rs of Reality Therapy: right, responsibility, and reality.

The term *right* is used to refer to Glasser's belief that there is an accepted standard against which an individual's behavior can be compared. As Glasser (1965, p. xiii) has stated:

> To be worthwhile we must maintain a satisfactory standard of behavior. To do so we must learn to correct ourselves when we do wrong and to credit ourselves when we do right. If we do not evaluate our own behavior or, having evaluated it, if we do not act to improve our conduct where it is below our standards, we will not fulfill our needs to be worthwhile and will suffer as acutely as when we fail to love or to be loved. Morals, standards, values, or right and wrong behavior are all intimately related to the fulfillment of our needs for self-worth and (are) ... a necessary part of Reality Therapy.

As noted previously, responsibility is the process by which a child meets his or her needs for love and self-worth without infringing upon the rights of others. Such needs must be met within a given social and cultural context. A child does not act irresponsibly because he or she is ill but rather is ill because he or she acts irresponsibly. Acting responsibly implies a sense of right and wrong. It suggests that there are moral standards to which we all adhere. Glasser (1965) posits that people who are not exposed intimately to others who care enough about them "both to love and discipline them will not learn to be responsible. For that failure they suffer all their lives (p. 16)." The earlier that people are exposed to love and discipline, the easier and more quickly they will learn responsibility. In short, children learn responsibility through their involvements with responsible people, preferably loving parents who discipline them but who allow them enough freedom to try out new responsibilities.

The concept of reality assumes a pivotal role in Glasser's views on personality development. Reality Therapy maintains that a real world exists beyond an individual's subjective views of the world. Such a world consists of the hard facts of everyday living, such as the fact that one does not get everything one wants or desires. Glasser emphasizes the importance of objective rather than subjective reality. A fully functioning individual operates within the constraints of the real world and attempts to meet his or her needs within those constraints.

In sum, then, personality is formed as the individual strives to meet physiological and psychological needs. The most important needs are to love and be loved, and to feel worthwhile to oneself and to others. A child learns how to meet these needs effectively through having one intimate person who teaches the child what is right, to behave responsibly, and to face reality. A child who has been raised in this manner develops a success identity which is critical to healthy functioning.

Maladaptive Behavior

According to Glasser (1965), the traditional terms which counselors use to describe maladaptive functioning, such as neurosis or psychosis, have very little meaning or utility in helping a person develop more appropriate behavior. The basic motivating factor behind an individual's inappropriate behavior is that he or she is unable to fulfill the two basic psychological needs.

According to Glasser, the manner in which an individual expresses problems may only reflect the degree to which an individual is unable to fulfill needs. As Glasser (1965, p. 5) has stated: "We believe that, regardless of how he expresses his problem, everyone who needs psychiatric treatment suffers from one basic inadequacy: he is unable to fulfill his essential needs. The severity of the symptom reflects the degree to which the individual is unable to fulfill his needs."

Glasser asserts that people who evidence maladaptive behavior have one common characteristic: "They all deny the reality of the world around them (1965, p. 6)." Until such individuals can face up to the "real world" and accept its constraints, the therapist will not be able to help them.

Maladaptive behavior may begin at any point in an individual's life, but usually its roots are found in early childhood. The individual who manifests maladaptive behavior never learned how to fulfill needs through involvement with another caring and loving person. They not only deny the reality of the real world, but also they have not learned how to live responsibly.

REALITY GROUP COUNSELING

As with most other group approaches described in this book, Reality Therapy has its beginning in individual rather than group treatment. Reality group counseling consists, in large measure, of principles and counseling procedures adopted from individual treatment. Although Reality Therapy is used in a variety of settings, it is currently most frequently used in the schools, in juvenile delinquent centers, and in private practice. The group approach described here has been used primarily with young people in schools and in corrective institutions.

Goals of Group Counseling

Whether in the schools or in corrective institutions, the goal of Reality group counseling is to help individuals learn how to satisfy their psychological needs to love and be loved and to feel worthwhile to themselves and others. The Reality-oriented group counselor is essentially a teacher who helps people to become more responsible and to deal more effectively with the real world.

Differences between Reality and Traditional Counseling

According to Glasser (1965), Reality Therapy differs from traditional counseling in six important ways. These differ primarily from the standpoint of the counselor's involvement in group counseling.

1. Reality Therapy does not accept the concept of mental illness. This theory assumes the position that the counselor cannot become involved with a mentally ill person who has no responsibility for his or her behavior.

2. The Reality therapist works in the present and toward the future. The therapist does not become involved with a client's history because the therapist cannot change what has happened to the client nor does the therapist accept the fact that the client is limited by the past.

3. The counselor does not relate to the client as a transference figure but rather as himself or herself.

4. The Reality-oriented counselor does not look for the client's unconscious conflicts or the reasons for those conflicts. Such a counselor takes the position that by looking into the client's past, the counselor encourages the client to excuse behavior on the basis of unconscious motivations.

5. Reality therapists stress the morality of a person's behavior. They face and deal with the issue of right and wrong, and deal directly with how they feel about a client's behavior.

6. Reality counselors teach clients better ways to fulfill their needs in a responsible manner. A primary goal is to help clients find more satisfactory patterns of behavior.

Most of the above points differ sharply with psychoanalysis in groups and client-centered group counseling. The Reality therapist is active in groups.

Group Process

Reality group counseling views counseling as a rational process that stresses the here-and-now in behavioral terms. It seeks to treat group members' observable behavior rather than their expressed attitudes. "Group members work toward goals mutually defined with the counselor, and, through continuous behavioral commitments, actively seek to establish new behavioral habit patterns (Bigelow and Thorne, 1969, p. 191)." The counselor makes it clear that group counseling itself cannot cure an individual of his or her problems. The client's resolution of difficulties can only come about by facing up to reality and taking responsibility for oneself.

Glasser and Zunin (1973) have described eight major counseling steps that comprise either individual or group counseling. These steps form the cornerstone of Reality Therapy and are summarized below.

Counselor Involvement First and foremost, the counselor must demonstrate that he or she is involved to a meaningful degree with each group member. Involvement entails the building of a strong emotional relationship between each group member and the counselor. In doing so, the counselor attempts to show the client that he or she really cares about the client and will stay with the client until the client gets better. In becoming involved with a group member, the counselor is often affected by the group member's problems and may even suffer with the member until the problems are resolved. The counselor shows group members that he or she is willing to self-disclose when it is in the best interests of group members, and conveys to each person a belief in their ability to help themselves.

Emphasizing Clients' Present Behavior Instead of Feelings As noted previously, Reality-oriented counselors deal only with current issues. They do not analyze the past or the reasons that group members adopted present forms of behavior (Wubbolding, 1975). Moreover, unlike the client-centered counselor, the Reality-oriented counselor does not spend a great deal of time eliciting a group member's feelings about behavior. Instead of saying, "Can you tell me more about why you feel angry?" the Reality-oriented therapist asks, "What are you doing that makes you feel angry?" The focus is on the client's behavior rather than on the feelings surrounding that behavior. Changing the negative or undesirable behavior is considered more important than talking about feelings about such behavior. To illustrate his point, Glasser (1965) gives the example of an adolescent girl who had experienced continual temper tantrums over her mother's unwillingness to let her date a particular boy. The girl had stated on several occasions that she could not talk with her mother about this subject without an argument ensuing. Rather than discussing the girl's relationship and feelings toward her mother, Glasser suggested that she discuss the subject with her mother just once without losing her temper. The change in the girl's behavior had a dramatic effect on her mother. The mother not only saw her daughter in a different light but also grew calmer in discussing the situation with her daughter. As the mother grew calmer, the daughter found that she could discuss dating the young man on its own merits, and the conflict between mother and daughter gradually disappeared. The important principle learned is that the counselor did not wait for a change in either the client's or the mother's attitude. A behavioral change was sought first, and attitudinal changes occurred as a result of the client's change in behavior. During the process of counseling, the group is used to help group members try out new behavior.

Emphasis on the Now Rather Than the Past Reality Therapy stresses the importance of current client functioning. Past events in a person's life are discussed only to the extent that they have a bearing on the client's current ability to fulfill needs or to develop alternative strategies for behaving. In discussing the client's behavior, the counselor stresses the client's assets as well as liabilities. It is assumed that clients are more aware of the weaknesses than they are cognizant of their strengths. Group members' individual strengths are viewed as the building blocks for later changes in behavior.

Making Value Judgments   One of the counselor's tasks is to help group members make value judgments regarding their own behavior. During this stage, group members are forced to reevaluate their behavior. The counselor attempts to get each group participant to evaluate their behavior in terms of whether it is responsible or irresponsible. For the most part, the counselor does not make such decisions for group members, even though the counselor makes it clear that irresponsible behavior is not condoned. The counselor does make value judgments, but the most important value judgments are those which come from group members themselves.

Developing a Positive Plan of Action   After helping group members evaluate their irresponsible behavior, the counselor is ready to help them develop a positive plan of action. This plan should be based upon reality and should adhere to a step-by-step procedure designed to ensure group members' success. As Glasser and Zunin (1973, pp. 301–2) have stated: "It is much better to have client success in small stages than to try to effect a large change and experience failure. Successes breed successes and failures breed gloom and defeatism."

Client Commitment   Reality-oriented group counselors emphasize the importance of having group members commit themselves to their plans of action for dealing with self-defeating behavior. As Barr (1974, p. 67) has affirmed, "a plan that does not have the client's firm commitment is likely to fail." In making a commitment, the group member takes responsibility for his or her own actions. Commitment means that group members' plans are contingent on their own behavior rather than on that of others, regardless of how central others' behavior might be viewed in resolving their problems.

No Excuses   Sometimes group members may fail in their efforts to complete their plans of action. When group members report to the group that they have not been able to carry out their plans of action, the counselor does not spend a great deal of time asking or exploring why a particular member's plan failed. Instead, the Reality counselor helps the group member to draw up and to make a commitment to another plan that is largely a modification of the original one. The new plan may entail smaller, more manageable steps which will help ensure the group member's success rather than failure. During this phase of counseling, the group leader must be careful to refrain from dwelling on why a particular member's plan of action failed. Instead, the counselor says to the client: "We all agree that your plan of action failed. The important point, however, is not to dwell upon *why* your plan failed but rather on how you are going to accomplish what you desire now." By this statement, the counselor communicates to the client a faith in the client's ability to develop and to carry out a reasonable course of action that will help fulfill basic needs and change behavior. The group member is, therefore, encouraged rather than discouraged to try a different approach toward resolving difficulties.

Eliminate Punishment   Similar to the Adlerian approach, Glasser and Zunin (1973) affirm that clients learn better by the law of natural consequences than they do by punishment. Punishment only tends to reinforce an individual's negative or self-defeating behavior and to support a client's failure identity. During the counseling process, the counselor lets the client experience the natural consequences of failure to carry out a plan of action. When a client fails to enact a course of action, the counselor helps the client go back to an earlier step.

Difficulties In Implementation   Wubbolding (1975) cites four reasons why a counselor may experience difficulty in proceeding through the eight counseling stages. First, the counselor may not take sufficient time to establish involvement with the client. This situation usually occurs when the counselor is so bent on dealing with the client's problems that she or he ignores the everyday little things, such as small talk and finding out about individual interests. Very often, these types of discussions form the basis for developing a deep relationship between client and counselor. By establishing a deep involvement with the client, the counselor conveys the idea that the client is not just another human problem to be worked upon but is a total human being, who has assets as well as liabilities.

The second reason that some counselors may experience difficulty with Reality Therapy is that they establish vague plans with clients, such as "I will try to establish a better relationship with my parents," or "I will study harder in school." Instead of making such general goals, the counselor would do better to help the client develop specific but attainable small goals. Plans which require broad or sweeping changes within the client may be doomed to failure. It is better to begin with one step that is attainable than to fail at enacting one's long-range goals.

A third pitfall the Reality therapist may face is forcing a plan upon group members before they have made a value judgment to change their behavior. Before a plan is made, the group member must sincerely desire to change the behavior which does not meet needs for love and self-worth. Without such a commitment from group members, the plan of action that is formulated may have little chance of success. As Wubbolding (1975, p. 165) has stated: "Counselors should not impose a plan on clients but rather assist them to make their own plans by presenting various alternatives and consequences to the possible choices."

Fourth, the counselor may proceed too quickly toward obtaining group members' commitment. People commit themselves when they are ready to do so and not before then. Counselors who attempt to force a sense of commitment upon group members may only obtain a type of pseudocommitment.

Reality Therapy demands a great deal from the counselor since she or he must evidence more than just empathy. The counselor must be involved with the client and be willing to suffer with the client. Equally important and difficult is the fact that the counselor must relinquish traditional doctor and counselor roles and must meet the client as a person who is willing to struggle with the client as long as the client evidences by behavior a commitment to change faulty ways of behaving.

Guided Group Interaction

Much of Reality Therapy, particularly as it is practiced in the schools and in corrective institutions, can be labeled guided group interaction. Guided group interaction is a term used by Mowrer (1973) to indicate how relatively large groups of people (fifteen to thirty) can be counseled in a group using Reality Therapy. The term is used to describe much of Glasser's work at the Ventura School for Girls (actually a reformatory school) and in the public schools in Los Angeles and, indeed, across the nation. Mowrer uses the term guided group interaction to distinguish Glasser's approach to groups from that of the more traditional approaches to group counseling, for example psychoanalysis and client-centered group counseling. Guided group interaction tends to emphasize group discussion techniques more than it does group analysis or individual analysis within a group. Under the Reality Therapy approach, there is considerably less focus on the process that the group is experiencing at any one particular time. For example, the counselor does not usually make such statements as "I feel that the group is dealing with issues of its own," or "The group seems to be bogged down with the issue of how to relate to authority figures." The process of the group is important only insofar as it helps foster a sense of involvement, commitment, and a plan of action for each group member. There is less of an emphasis on the pathology of individual group members, their history, and transference relations than in some of the more traditional approaches to group counseling. The focus of the discussion in Reality-oriented groups tends to revolve around individual members' progress with their plans of action to rectify the lack of fulfillment of their psychological needs.

To illustrate the nature of guided group interaction, Glasser and Iverson (1966) give the following account of a session that took place at the Ventura School for Girls in California:

> The one technique which seems to weaken and eventually break down negative peer group sub-culture is the technique of insisting upon, or demanding, *sharing of responsibility for behavior* by the girls. It is this same requirement that is the most often and most bitterly resented and rejected by the newly arrived girls. . . .
>
> The matter of peer group sub-culture has been a major "thorn in the side" of correctional institutions since their inception. Through the use of Large Group Counseling, and the "share the care" ground rule, major constructive breaks in the peer group sub-culture are possible. . . . Wards who protest that they "would rather die than fink" quickly become adept at informing staff against other wards who, by their negative resistance to the program, threaten group privileges. . . .
>
> At deeper psychological levels, wards also learn, through "sharing the care," that they can have rewarding, stable experiences in their interpersonal relationships. Wards who have never experienced genuine "care" from others discover that it is possible to profit, in a non-delinquent manner, from close and empathetic associations with others (p. 11).

Many of the basic tenets of Reality Therapy as used with delinquent girls have also been applied to public schools. Reality Therapy in the schools is a part of the daily curriculum and is practiced by teachers as well as counselors. Glasser

(1969) maintains, for example, that children can be taught methods of satisfying their needs for love and self-worth in the school. In the school situation, love is conceptualized in terms of social responsibility. Teachers and children alike must learn how to care enough to help each other with the social and educational problems of schools. These goals can be accomplished if the schools correct their errors of noninvolvement, irrelevance, and 'memorizing the right answers' and instead promote involvement between teacher and student, and between students.

Guided interaction in the schools takes the format of classroom meetings or discussions. On such occasions, the teacher leads the entire class in a nonjudgmental discussion about what is important and meaningful to them. The discussions are usually one of three types: (1) social problem-solving, which deal with students' social behavior in school; (2) open-ended, which center on intellectually important topics; and (3) educational-diagnostic, which focus on how well the students understand the concepts of the curriculum. Glasser (1965, 1969) maintains that classroom meetings, using the concept of guided group interaction, should be a part of the regular school curriculum. Such meetings should occur every day in the elementary school and two or three times a week in high school. A major goal is to demonstrate to young people that the classroom can be a working, problem-solving unit and that each person has both individual and group responsibilities in the school. In *Schools Without Failure* (1969), Glasser gives detailed descriptions of how to conduct classroom meetings, covering such topics as the seating arrangement (a circle), the length of sessions, and methods of stimulating discussion.

Role of the Group Leader

The role of the Reality-oriented group leader has, in some respects, been described in earlier sections of this chapter and therefore will not be dealt with at length here. Glasser (1965) posits that an effective counselor should meet four essential requirements. First, the counselor must be a responsible individual who is able to fulfill his or her own needs. Second, the counselor must be strong and able to withstand the client's pleas for sympathy or justification of behavior. The counselor does not accept client excuses for irresponsible behavior. As Glasser (1965, p. 32) has stated:

> We never sympathize with, or excuse him for anything he does, nor do we let him excuse himself. We never agree that his irresponsibility is justified no matter how much he may have suffered at the hands of others. . . . We never blame others for the patient's irresponsibility or censure mother, father, or anyone deeply involved with the patient no matter how irresponsible they are or were. The patient cannot change them; he can only learn better ways to live with them or without them. We never encourage hostility or acting out irresponsible impulses, for that only compounds the problem.

Third, the counselor must in the beginning accept the client as is. Fourth, the group leader must be able to become emotionally involved with each group member. To some degree, the counselor must be affected by the client and his or her problems, and must even suffer with the client in the course of counseling. "The therapist who can work with seriously irresponsible people and not be affected by their suffering will never become sufficiently involved to do successful therapy (Glasser, 1965, pp. 23–24)."

The Reality-oriented group leader is a warm, active, confronting person who strives to become involved with group members. A major task of the counselor is to point out the reality of what the client is currently doing and not to search for reasons for the behavior. The counselor is interested in the client as a person with wide potential and not just as a person with problems. "In fact, one of the best ways not to become involved is to discuss his problems over and over. Although continually listening to misery is one way of giving the patient sympathy, he soon discovers that with all the talk the therapist can do nothing directly to solve his problems (Glasser, 1965, p. 31)."

Reality-oriented group leaders are generally eclectic in the techniques they use. Most of the techniques which have become associated with Reality Therapy have been discussed in terms of the stages of group counseling.

Role of Group Members

Glasser (1965, 1969) describes the role of group members in terms of their sharing of responsibility. Through the norming process, group members encourage each other to accept responsibility for their actions. Group members help one another by becoming involved and showing that they care. Group members tend to focus on the irrational and irresponsible behavior of fellow participants rather than on the process interactions that occur between them. In Reality group counseling, group members do have a powerful role in getting others to conform to the group's standards of behavior, but the group leader is still clearly in control of the direction that the group takes.

Summary of Reality Therapy

Reality Therapy posits that people have problems because they lack a meaningful involvement with others and because they are not acting in ways to meet their needs. The task of the Reality counselor is to become involved with the client, get the client to face reality, and encourage the client to behave responsibly. Facing reality and acting responsibly may be difficult for many clients, but Glasser maintains that in the long run such behavior will be well worth the pain.

RATIONAL-EMOTIVE GROUP THERAPY

The Rational-Emotive (RET) approach to counseling was founded by Albert Ellis in 1955. Originally trained in the classical psychoanalytic method, Ellis developed Rational-Emotive Therapy because of his increasing dissatisfaction with psychoanalysis. Rational-Emotive counseling is based on the belief that human emotions and problems are largely a product of an individual's irrational thinking. It operates on the principle that if one can change an individual's faulty or irrational thinking about what life should be all about, then one has taken the first step toward helping that person alter those emotions that occur in support of such irrational thinking. As Ellis (1973, p. 79) has stated, Rational-Emotive counseling "stresses a cognitive-rational-persuasive approach toward helping the client discover exactly his other basic values, how they create so-called emotional problems, and what he or she can do to question, challenge, and change them and to become more realistic and thoroughly self-accepting."

Rational-Emotive counseling was developed by using an eclectic approach. For example, in constructing Rational-Emotive Therapy, Ellis (1962) acknowledges that he used some of the tenets of the neo-Freudians—especially those of Alfred Adler, Carl Rogers, the existentialists, the learning theorists, and the General Semanticists. Ellis maintains, however, that despite the many strands of Rational-Emotive counseling, RET is not a thoroughly eclectic approach, "since it does have and rests upon a centralized *theory* of human disturbance and of psychotherapy (Ellis, 1962, p. 329)."

Moreover, as with some of the other theoretical approaches, it is difficult to separate Rational-Emotive counseling from the personality of its founder. The distinctively energetic, hard-hitting, no-nonsense approach of Ellis has become almost the trademark of Rational-Emotive Therapy.

This section explores the Rational-Emotive approach to group counseling. A brief overview of Ellis' theory of personality development and maladjustment is presented. Two Rational-Emotive group approaches are singled out for discussion: (1) traditional RET group counseling approaches; and (2) group counseling at the Living School. Other topics include Rational-Emotive group counseling techniques, group leader and member behaviors, and research related to RET.

Personality Development

Basically, Rational-Emotive Therapy does not present an explicit theory of personality development. In fact, in Ellis' major work, *Reason and Emotion and Psychotherapy,* he provides only a two-page reference to personality change. Rational-Emotive Therapy is first and foremost a theory of human disturbance and counseling techniques. Ellis spends much more time discussing the development of maladaptive behavior than that of normal personality development. The Rational-Emotive approach discusses personality development primarily in terms of human acquisition of primarily irrational behavior.

The basic theme of the Rational-Emotive approach to personality development is that people are both uniquely rational and irrational. The degree to which people are either rational or irrational in their dealings with self and others determines the extent to which there will be healthy or maladaptive personality development. Since Ellis (1962) maintains that individuals' emotions or psychological disturbances are largely a result of their thinking illogically or irrationally, individuals can rid themselves of their emotional or mental unhappiness and disturbance if they learn how to maximize their rational ability and minimize their irrational thinking.

Nature of People

According to Ellis (1973, 1962), people are uniquely suggestible and, at the same time, uniquely rational human beings. Ellis further posits that people have the unusual potential to build or rebuild their own emotions and behavior. Although irrational thinking may be increased by parental upbringing and social learning, it is essentially "deeply rooted in the mere state of being human and living with other people (Ellis, 1962a, p. 1)." Moreover, people are fallible, limited, and biologically rooted.

Ellis does not state whether the nature of people is basically good or bad. He does state, however, that all people, through their upbringing and social learning, have a tendency to blame or excoriate themselves, especially when they are children. Such a tendency toward self-blame inevitably leads to individuals' development of irrational and sometimes maladaptive behavior.

Furthermore, Ellis (1973) maintains that a person enters the world with two strong, opposite predispositions: (1) to be self-preserving, pleasure-producing, and self-actualizing; and (2) to be self-destructive and hedonistic and to avoid actualizing his or her potentials for positive growth. These competing bipolar tendencies exist within all individuals; however, each person has certain inborn tendencies in one direction more than in the other.

The A-B-C Theory of Personality and Emotional Disturbance

Ellis (1962, 1974, 1973) uses an A-B-C model to explain an individual's acquisition of irrational behavior. The A-B-C model is based on the assumption that human emotions are mainly either a form of thinking or a result of thinking, and that one may control one's emotions by controlling one's thoughts. Thinking and feeling, then, are not two different processes; instead they overlap considerably and are, for all practical purposes, essentially the same thing.

The A-B-C theory of personality disturbance may be described as follows. A person experiences A, an activating event or problem. The person's beliefs, or B, about the problem or activating event are aroused. At this juncture, the person's beliefs may take one of two courses: they may be rational or irrational. The consequences of a person's irrational or rational beliefs are represented by C. In the case where an individual has irrational beliefs about an activating event, C may take the form of that person's experiencing of disturbing feelings or behavior, such as depression, anger, or hostility.

An illustration of the A-B-C theory of personality disturbance may help to clarify what takes place. For example, Jane is criticized unfairly at work for something which she did not do. The criticism that she receives represents A, the activating event. Jane's beliefs (B) about the criticism now enter the picture. Her belief system consists of the "self-talk," or the internalized sentences, that she tells herself about how she should react to the criticism. Jane's belief system will cause her to respond rationally or irrationally about the event at work. She may respond irrationally and say to herself that it is horrible or awful that she should have been criticized so unjustly. She may also tell herself that she needs the approval of her supervisor and that, therefore, she feels bad about the event. A more rational approach for Jane would be to say to herself that it was unfortunate for her to be criticized unfairly at work, that she will seek to redress such criticism, but that it isn't horrible or catastrophic that she should be criticized. The emotional consequence (C) of Jane's beliefs will vary, depending on whether they were rational or irrational. If her beliefs were irrational, she may become very upset and nervous;

if they were rational, she may view the incident as just another unfortunate happening which needs correcting.

Children are inundated by B types of statements from parents. That is, parents tend to convey to their children that it is awful or horrible that they are not the first in their class or that they are not liked by everyone. These kinds of moral dictums tend to be reinforced by the society at large. For example, American society tends to elevate the all-American person who is at the top of the class, a good athlete, and liked by teachers and students alike. As each young person strives to reach this golden ideal, he or she may become frustrated. The all-American wife is one who encourages her husband, works at a paid job, manages effectively to run the house and raise the children in the "good old" American way. Anything short of this miracle might suggest that the woman is lacking in some way. It matters little that belief systems may be based on illogical or irrational thinking. It is difficult to fulfill all the roles a woman is supposed to coordinate smoothly. Likewise, it is difficult to be a masculine, successful, intellectual, athletic, and handsome man.

Most individuals develop personalities that are based largely on belief systems of what they should be like. Those who have healthy personality development, according to Rational-Emotive formulations, operate most of the time on their rational belief systems. Those individuals who experience great difficulty or maladjustment operate on the basis of a faulty or irrational belief system. Ellis (1962) maintains that the events in a person's life are not the cause of psychological disturbances in and of themselves, but rather it is the postulates one develops about oneself and the world in connection with the events which cause maladaptive behavior.

Ellis does not neglect early causal experiences. Instead he refuses to dwell upon them. Moreover, the counselor's emphasis on the individual's early childhood or past events tends to indicate to the client that he or she is bound by the events that took place rather than capable of transcending them.

In essence, the Rational-Emotive approach to personality development and counseling is based on the belief that people become emotionally disturbed or develop maladaptive behavior through their acquisition of irrational and illogical thoughts, philosophies, or attitudes. The counselor helps the client by analyzing feelings and by demonstrating to the client how emotions arise not from past events but from present irrational attitudes or illogical fears about such events or situations.

Irrational Ideas

Ellis (1962) had identified eleven major illogical ideas or philosophies which lead to widespread neurosis in Western civilization. These eleven ideas, as presented in *Reason and Emotion in Psychotherapy* in 1962, are paraphrased as follows:

1. It is absolutely essential or a dire necessity for a person to be loved or approved by almost everyone in the environment.
   This idea is irrational because it is impossible to be loved by all the people one comes in contact with, even family members and significant others,

all of the time. Demanding that one be approved and loved by all those whose approval one seeks is perfectionistic and, therefore, unattainable. It also makes one continually dependent on the approval of others rather than that of oneself. Being approved might be more appropriately defined as a preference rather than as a necessity.

2. It is irrational to believe that one should be completely competent, adequate, and achieving in all areas if one is to consider oneself worthwhile. To demand that one be thoroughly successful or masterful in all or most respects is to open oneself to anxiety and feelings of personal worthlessness. No one can be completely competent and masterful in all or even most areas. The person who strives to be thoroughly competent is, in reality, often striving to best others; he or she is inclined to become other-directed rather than self-directed. One does not have complete control over one's achievement in even restricted or selected areas, and such overconcern can result in acquiring great fears of failure or of taking risks. Hence, the person who tries to be thoroughly competent is doomed to failure.

3. It is irrational to believe some people are wicked, bad, or villainous and that, therefore, they should be severely blamed and punished for their acts.
Everyone makes mistakes, and blame and punishment will not necessarily change that person's behavior. One should recognize that people may commit wrong acts out of stupidity, ignorance, or emotional disturbance. People are fallible and are prone to committing errors. To err is human.

4. It is irrational to believe that it is terrible and catastrophic when things are not the way one would like them to be.
Life will never be "a rose garden." One might as well realize this fact. The reality of life is that many things will not be as one would like. It is better not to agonize over how we would like life to be and how it actually is in reality. When things go wrong, one should view such events as bothersome; treating an event as a catastrophe does not change it. One should try to change situations that are not to one's liking. It does not make sense to become or remain illogically upset over the frustrating events of life or the injustices of the world.

5. It is irrational to believe that human unhappiness is caused by external events and that people have little or no ability to control their unhappiness and disturbances.
Many people believe that they are shaped by other people and events and that if they could only change those people and events in their lives, they would be happy. They believe that they cannot help getting upset when certain situations occur in their lives. These beliefs are illogical in that one person can rarely do harm to another, except for physical assault or deprivation of certain tangible items such as money or food. What people

are really responding to are the psychological onslaughts or attempts to hurt them, such as ostracizing them or attacking them verbally. Nasty remarks by others only hurt if one tells oneself that one should be hurt. In other words, it is the attitude that one has toward certain events more than the event itself which bothers an individual. People can control their own happiness and disturbances by refusing to get upset over certain events. People can control their emotions.

6. It is irrational to be terribly concerned about something that is or may be dangerous or fearsome.
   Worrying over an event will not prevent it from happening. It is more logical to take steps to prevent a dangerous event from taking place. Likewise, overconcern about an event taking place may lead to needless exaggeration of the possibility of the situation's occurring.

7. It is irrational to believe that it is easier to run away from or avoid life's difficulties and self-responsibilities than it is to face them.
   Facing up to life's difficulties and responsibilities often leads to an individual's gaining self-confidence and self-respect. People cannot solve their problems by running away from them. Usually, the problem must be dealt with at some point in time.

8. It is irrational to believe that one should be dependent on others or that one needs a person to rely on who is stronger than oneself.
   The more a person depends upon others, the more he or she is at those persons' mercy. Individuals who are self-reliant usually feel better about themselves. While individuals should not foolishly refuse all help from others, they should be able to stand on their own two feet.

9. It is irrational to believe that past events in one's life completely control or determine one's present behavior and that because an event or a situation strongly affected one's life, it will indefinitely continue to have the same effect as it once did.
   Events of the past do not necessarily control one's present life. People who cling too strongly to the importance of past events as determiners of their current behavior often use the past as an excuse not to change. Things continue to affect individuals' lives primarily because such individuals allow them to have an influence.

10. It is irrational for one to become unduly upset about other people's problems or difficulties.
    Getting upset over other people's problems may not help those individuals or oneself. If a person is harming others, it might be wise to take appropriate steps, but worrying about the situation will not help. If one worries about other people's problems too much, their problems may become one's own.

11. It is irrational to believe that there is always a correct and precise answer

to every problem, and that it is catastrophic if such an answer is not found. Searching for the perfect solution to life or to every problem can become a futile and frustrating activity. Oftentimes, there is no perfect solution or precise answer. The quest for perfection may limit an individual's ability to solve a problem, since no one approach or solution will provide all the answers or remedy the situation. A person should accept the fact that to err is human and that people learn by trial and error rather than by searching for the perfect solution to every problem.

Ellis (1962, 1974, 1973) maintains that these eleven irrational ideas constitute the major causes of emotional problems and maladaptive behavior. Many of these ideas are taught to children by their parents and the general culture in which they live. The net effect of this two-pronged teaching is that many people in American society have become what Ellis (1972) labels neurotics who are statistically normal. By its own propagation and indoctrination of people, American society unfortunately gives birth to people who are almost doomed to become emotionally disturbed if they accept the correctness or sanctity of these eleven irrational beliefs. The counselor's task is to help individuals recognize their own illogical thinking and to develop more rational methods for living.

More recently, Ellis (1974) has summarized most of the eleven irrational ideas which cause the major forms of human disturbance under the rubric or heading of childish demandingness. From his perspective: "Demandingness or dictating seems to be, in fact, the essence of virtually all of what we normally call emotional upsetness. While the less disturbed individual strongly desires what he wants and makes himself appropriately sorry or annoyed if his desires are unfulfilled, the more disturbed person dogmatically demands, insists, commands, or dictates that his desires be granted and makes himself inappropriately anxious, depressed, or hostile when they are not (pp. 80–81)."

The person who evidences maladaptive behavior, then, tends to make three major kinds of demands: (1) that he or she receive the approval of virtually all the people whom he or she deems significant in life and that he perform consistently well; (2) that all people should treat him or her with the appropriate degree of fairness, consideration, and, sometimes, love; and (3) that the world should be an easily and personally gratifying place in which to live.

A Rational Philosophy of Living

In lieu of the irrational ideas about life or the demandingness of people, Ellis (1958, 1962, and 1974) has developed postulates for a more rational philosophy of living. These postulates may be paraphrased as follows:

1. Focus on your own self-respect rather than other people's approval.

2. Almost all human unhappiness is caused by or maintained by the view individuals take of situations rather than by situations themselves.

3. Acts performed by others should not be viewed as wrong, wicked, or bad,

but rather as inappropriate to the situation and antisocial. The people who perform such acts should be viewed as deficient, ignorant, or psychologically disturbed.

4. It is unfortunate when things are not the way one would like or prefer them to be, and one should attempt to try to change or control them. But if it is almost impossible to change such things, it would be better to acknowledge their existence and quit telling oneself how awful or horrible they are.

5. When events or situations may be dangerous or fearsome, it is better to face them frankly and try to render them nondangerous or nonfearsome. If this becomes impossible or unrealistic, it would be better to think of other things and to stop saying to oneself what a terrible or horrible situation one is either in or may be in.

6. The easy way out of a situation becomes, in the long run, the much harder way. The only way to solve problems and to gain our own self-respect is to face up to problems and tackle them squarely.

7. It is generally better to stand on one's own two feet and gain faith in oneself and one's ability to deal with the difficult circumstances of life than to be dependent and rely on someone stronger than oneself to save or rescue one from dealing with life's problems.

8. A person should accept himself or herself as imperfect, with normal human limitations and fallibilities rather than continually strive for unreachable perfection in every area. While doing well is important, emphasis should be placed on action and moving toward a goal rather than on doing well. An individual's goal to do well is often based on doing well for others rather than for oneself or what is appropriate for a given situation.

9. A person should learn from past experiences, but he or she should not be overly attached or prejudiced by past events or situations that have previously had an important effect on his or her life. Learning from past experiences is one thing; being governed by them is quite a different case.

10. The deficiencies of other people are largely their problem and require first their own efforts to change. Putting undue and unreasonable pressure on people to change may actually encourage them to cling tenaciously to their old, inefficient ways.

11. People tend to be happiest when they are actively involved in charting their own destinies and absorbed in developing their creative pursuits or devoting their attention to people or projects outside of themselves. People have enormous control over their emotions if they choose to work at controlling such emotions.

To think and respond rationally, an individual must stop trying to defeat himself or herself. The person should plan his or her life so as to have more growth-enhancing than retarding experiences. This is not an easy task to accomplish, and it is one of the reasons why Rational-Emotive therapists posit that so many people are unhappy. To be honest with oneself is a basic first step in Rational-Emotive Therapy. Being less than honest and rational with one's decisions encourages maladaptive rather than healthy behavior. Healthy personality development requires a rational approach to life. Rational-Emotive Therapy is as much a philosophy of life as it is a theory of normal and maladaptive behavior development.

INDIVIDUAL RATIONAL-EMOTIVE COUNSELING: GOALS AND PROCEDURES

As with most group approaches, rational-emotive counseling was initially designed for and employed in individual treatment. It is important to review individual RET counseling for several reasons, foremost of which is that the individual format provides the necessary background for understanding the Rational-Emotive approach to group counseling.

Ellis (1962, 1973) describes Rational-Emotive counseling as an active-directive, behavioral approach which stresses rational views of the world and of the self. The counselor's primary task is to help the client develop and internalize a rational philosophy of life. The counselor deals with the individual's underlying pattern of illogical thinking rather than just the presenting concern that the person originally brings to counseling. For example, a person may come to counseling with the presenting concern that she or he feels anxious and nervous most of the time. While the presenting concern is important, the real problem may be that the individual is telling herself or himself a series of illogical statements about how the world should be.

The primary objectives of Rational-Emotive counseling are to: (1) show the client that internalized sentences, self-talk, or beliefs are the real source of difficulty; and (2) help the client examine and eliminate illogical beliefs. The Rational-Emotive approach uses primarily an educational model of counseling and personality change. RET counselors maintain that teaching is an important part of the counseling process.

In RET counseling, the counselor largely directs the counseling process in an authoritative fashion. Initially, however, clients are approached in a warm, supportive fashion, and they are encouraged to express their feelings. Ellis (1962) maintains, however, that Rational-Emotive counselors do not delude themselves into thinking that such relationship-building and expressive-emotive methods are likely to really get at the core of an individual's illogical thinking. Relationship techniques are considered merely as preliminary techniques.

The counselor uses the A-B-C model of psychological disturbance to work with clients' irrational ideas. However, the main therapeutic technique is for the counselor to dispute (D) the client's irrational beliefs. The counselor challenges, questions, and confronts the individual's irrational beliefs in order to change them to more rational attitudes.

In short, individual treatment using the Rational-Emotive approach to counseling entails three phases: (1) the establishment of a therapeutic relationship; (2) the cognitive phase, in which the counselor attempts to help the client identify and explain the problem, including the consequences of the person's irrational beliefs; and (3) the behavior phase, during which the counselor stresses techniques for behavior modification and uses homework assignments with the client.

RATIONAL-EMOTIVE APPROACHES TO GROUPS

Ellis (1962) formed his first Rational-Emotive Therapy group in 1958. From that point on, Ellis has continued to use RET in groups. The Rational-Emotive counseling group uses basically the same approach outlined for individual counseling. The counselor emphasizes the A-B-C method for analyzing disturbing behavior. The main objective is to teach individuals how to become more rational in their behavior and to control their disturbing emotive responses to life events.

In the early years of RET group counseling, Ellis (1974) tended to use more restrictive techniques. Since that time, however, he has incorporated almost all the major theoretical innovations of the past two decades. Rational-Emotive counselors now use such techniques as nonverbal exercises, weekend marathons, and personal encountering.

The incorporation of more sensitivity-oriented and nonverbal techniques has tended to raise questions concerning the theoretical compatability of Rational-Emotive group counseling with these newer group methods. Ellis (1974) has defended the use of these techniques on the grounds that it is not the use of specific techniques which is important but rather the rationality of group goals and procedures. Ellis points out that although he uses techniques similar to those used by other group theorists, basic differences exist between his approach and that of other theorists. One may understand the differences that exist by examining what Ellis calls rational and irrational goals and methods of group counseling.

Rational and Irrational Goals

Rational goals in groups help participants to grow up, accept reality, and become more tolerant of themselves and others. As noted previously, they help individuals rid themselves of irrational beliefs about life. Rational group counseling goals may be achieved by using methods which on the surface appear to be nonrational, such as touching or personal encountering.

Conversely, irrational group counseling goals have two major features. The group leader: (1) believes that a rational approach is undesirable and therefore strives for nonrational or irrational goals; or (2) believes that rationality is desirable but tries to achieve rationality in group counseling by irrational means. According to Ellis (1974), group counseling tends to become irrational when participants are allowed to stew in their own emotional juices with little constructive help from the counselor, or when the counselor places an undue emphasis on participants' expression of emotions just for the sake of emoting. Counseling groups also become irrational when exercises or games are used indiscriminately or without adequate planning or worthwhile behavioral goals in mind.

Group counseling becomes rational when the counselor chooses goals which are designed to help group members correct or undo their self-defeating behavior and when the counselor goes about trying to achieve such goals in logical, empirical, and efficient procedures. Rational counseling procedures help participants to reconstruct their basic self-destructive philosophies.

Group Process and Procedures

The Rational-Emotive group process varies slightly depending upon the type of group one is leading—for example, a weekend encounter as opposed to a counseling group in an educational setting. There remains, however, a set of core procedures which are found in most Rational-Emotive groups. Compared to other counseling group approaches, the Rational-Emotive group is considerably more didactically oriented. The RET counselor assumes the role of a teacher.

The first session of an RET counseling group usually begins with the counselor's asking one of the participants to present a troubling problem. Group members are then asked to respond to the person, using the A-B-C model of therapeutic intervention. Participants function as auxiliary counselors to the client who presents a problem. For example, a client might state that he feels "up tight" most of the time and cannot seem to relax. Consequently, he spends most of the time working—not because he enjoys working but because he feels guilty when he is not working. His absorption in work is creating problems in his marriage.

Group members question and challenge the presenter concerning his feelings and the underlying statements he is telling himself. For instance, group members might ask him why he feels he has to work all the time, especially when he dislikes doing so. What kinds of statements is he telling himself about the necessity to work so intensely? Is he telling himself that he only feels worthwhile when he is working? As in individual counseling, the goal is to help the person discover and articulate the illogical belief that is at the source of the emotional disturbance.

The counselor may then give the client a homework assignment, such as spending an hour each day with his family in a nonwork activity or reserving at least a half-hour each day for physical activity. During the next group session, the client is asked to report the results of his homework assignments and to examine his belief systems again. These procedures are repeated until the client has changed his irrational beliefs concerning his compulsive need to work and has adopted more healthy or less emotionally disturbing behavior.

Usually two to three individuals may present their problems during one session of a Rational-Emotive counseling group. Each individual is therapeutically interviewed by the other members of the group in the same Rational-Emotive manner. On some occasions, a group session may be devoted to the problems of one individual.

RET group counseling uses a no holds barred approach, and no restrictions are placed on the types of subjects that can be discussed. Although catharsis for its own sake is not encouraged, members are encouraged to share their feelings with each other. This is in order to show them on a philosophical level that there really is nothing frightful about revealing themselves to others and that the world will not stop if they do so (Ellis, 1962).

RET group counseling is philosophically and cognitively centered, but group leaders may use a wide variety of techniques; for example, role playing, exercises, and assertion training. The group itself may also give participants homework assignments. During the course of a group session, the group leader may engage in direct teaching of group members to help them become better auxiliary counselors. For example, when a participant challenges and disputes other group members' irrationalities, that participant is observed and corrected by the leader and the remaining group members. The group leader may indicate to the participant or auxiliary counselor how he or she challenged another incorrectly, how to correct such wrong challenges, and what cognitive steps can be taken to develop more appropriate challenges that would benefit both the group and the participant or auxiliary counselor.

Group Counseling at the Living School

Given the hard-hitting approach of Ellis and the earthy language that he is sometimes noted for using in RET group counseling, one would not normally associate him or his method of group counseling with young children. Moreover, the criticism that Rational-Emotive counseling is designed for highly intelligent, educated, and verbal individuals also adds to the belief that RET group counseling may be inappropriate for young children and adolescents. Ellis' (1973) group counseling approach at the Living School challenges these notions. Emotional education and group counseling at the Living School not only tends to present another side of Ellis the man but also demonstrates the utility of RET group counseling with younger populations in educational settings. It is for these reasons, as well as others (primarily the attempt to present a more thorough review of Rational-Emotive group counseling), that group counseling at the Living School is presented.

The Living School is a private school established by Ellis that functions as an integral part of the Institute for Advanced Study in Rational Psychotherapy (Ellis, 1973). Whereas the Institute is a training institute for therapists and teachers founded in 1968, the Living School is designed to provide both emotional and academic education for young people from the first grade through high school. Children from a variety of racial-ethnic backgrounds attend the Living School, which is located in New York City.

According to Ellis (1973, pp. 80–81), the Living School is "perhaps the only school in the world where all children receive group counseling continually in spite of (and, indeed, because of) the fact that they are *not* emotionally disturbed. The Living School, in other words, gives preventive counseling, on a regular and systematic basis, to all its pupils, whether or not they have behavior problems. It is an emotional education which has as its goal to reduce the likelihood of children later developing mild or severe personality maladjustment problems that they might have otherwise developed."

Group counseling at the Living School is both similar to and different from traditional RET group counseling or therapy. It is like all other RET group counseling sessions in that groups are organized and run in almost exactly the same manner as are regular adolescent or adult group counseling. It is different in that the essentials of rational living are taught in the classroom, on the playgrounds, and, in general, in the normal course of teachers' interacting with children through a variety of means. The primary differences lie, then, in the emphasis on prevention rather than remedial treatment and in its incorporation into the total educational setting of young people.

Group Counseling Goals at the Living School   The primary goal of group counseling at the Living School is to teach children the main principles of Rational-Emotive counseling. Children are taught the A-B-C of Rational-Emotive psychology from the first grade on. They are taught that people become disturbed because of their irrational beliefs and philosophies and that it is these beliefs rather than the events which happen to them which really upset them and have to be changed if they are to live happily. Children are taught to dispute their irrational beliefs, such as, that it is awful if they failed math or did not receive an A in a course. The goal of teaching a child to dispute irrational beliefs is to have the child arrive at two main cognitive and behavioral effects, or E. For example, if a child has disputed an irrational belief successfully—in this instance, that it is horrible that he did not receive an A in math—then he should first experience a cognitive effect, which would help him change his basic philosophy to the following: "It is unfortunate that I did not receive an A in math, but it is hardly awful that I received a C, even though there are several good reasons that I should have received a B." A second effect, an emotive-behavioral one, is achieved when the child loses his distress and depresssion and more calmly proceeds to try again to succeed at achieving in math. In other words, the child decides that he is not a worthless person for having received a C and then not only proceeds to acquire a rational outlook on his failure but also no longer experiences the negative emotional and behavioral consequences of his earlier irrational belief that it is catastrophic not to achieve a much higher grade. In essence, the child retrieves himself from emotionally debilitating beliefs to more rational and productive action. Rational-Emotive group counseling at the Living School seeks to free children from what Ellis (1973) calls "silly ego games" and to help them become more self-directive than previously.

Rational-Emotive group counseling at the Living School does not emphasize an "anything goes" policy. It stresses that children should be helped to learn how to: (1) accommodate themselves to prevailing realities (such as family, friends, and associates who may treat them unfairly) when they cannot very easily escape from such realities; and (2) modify their own basic attitudes and philosophies, especially their need or desire to obtain others' approval so that they do not feel they have to conform to existing circumstances. Healthy children must decide for themselves what position they will take in life. As Ellis (1973) has posited, the major treatment goal of the Living School's group counseling program is to prevent rather than to remediate children from becoming seriously anxious, depressed, hostile, or self-defeating. Preventive treatment in the early grades is set for children largely in consultation with their parents.

The RET Group Leader

The Rational-Emotive group is leader-centered. It is the leader's task to make sure that the group is philosophically and cognitively based. As noted previously, the RET group counselor is usually very active, probing, and challenging to group participants and uses the contributions of group members adroitly. Most frequently, the RET group leader is a teacher who continually forces group members to evaluate their irrational ideas. The RET group leader does not place a great deal of stock in group members' history, nor does the leader attempt to become acquainted with an individual's history except as it relates to an individual's illogical beliefs. To a large extent, Rational-Emotive counseling ignores the transference relationship unless it is important and attacks its irrationalities when it does assume a pivotal role in the counseling relationship. Resistance is usually construed as the client's refusal to learn the A-B-C model of Rational-Emotive psychology and/or the client's refusal to apply this methodology once it has been learned. The RET group counselor maintains that the client is not truly improved or "cured" until he or she is able to put into practice what has been learned in group counseling. The group leader normally holds sessions of two and a quarter hours, followed by an after-group session consisting of an hour. The group leader is expected to be thoroughly trained in RET counseling procedures.

Group Members' Role

To a large degree, the group member's role has already been described. Group participants provide each other with several kinds of feedback. They show each other that they are likewise troubled by irrational and illogical ideas. They provide each other with honest observations concerning how they come across to each other, how they relate, and how they can improve their human relationships. Group members may provide each other with social participation and valuable feedback outside the normal confines of the counseling group. Group members who are severely disturbed hold on so tenaciously to their irrational ideas that they usually require persistent interventions from the therapist and other participants.

SUMMARY OF RATIONAL-EMOTIVE AND REALITY THERAPY

Rational-Emotive and Reality Therapy share a number of commonalities. Both Ellis and Glasser point out the centrality of irrational beliefs in promoting maladaptive behavior. People are unhappy because of what they tell themselves about how life should be. The idea that people need to face up to reality pervades both theories. Both Ellis and Glasser attack peoples' irrational beliefs, but they do so from slightly different perspectives. For example, Ellis clearly labels the irrational ways in which people deal with life: they expect to be loved and approved by all and they think it is easier to run away from problems and self-responsibility than it is to face up to them. Glasser, on the other hand, does not present a list of the most common beliefs that lead to unhappiness. He never really adequately defines reality or lack of reality. However, both Glasser and Ellis are clearly saying that in order for people to be happy, they will have to take a more realistic, rational approach to life.

The two men also differ on the degree of counselor involvement necessary for client change. Glasser places a great deal of emphasis on counselor involvement, even stating that the counselor must suffer with the client in the process of helping. In contrast, Ellis gives only passing attention to the nature of the counseling relationship. He states that counselor involvement is necessary but not sufficient for change. One might even venture to say that Ellis would consider it irrational for the counselor to suffer with the client in the process of helping.

Both Ellis and Glasser also differ on their approach to what constitutes right and wrong. For example, Ellis takes a more existential view. In his opinion, such terms as right and wrong are relative; therefore, individual group members are encouraged to develop their own individual criteria for determining if their behavior is right or wrong. Glasser, on the other hand, asserts that there is an external standard of morality and that a client's behavior should be evaluated against this standard. It is unclear what laws comprise such a standard of reality or, perhaps more importantly, who determines what it should be. The counselor's role in both Reality and Rational-Emotive Therapy is one of confronting group members with what they are doing and then teaching them to think and behave in a healthier fashion.

Neither Ellis nor Glasser pays much attention to group process per se. The main focus is on the progress of individual members within a group rather than on the stage of group development. Both Ellis and Glasser have applied their method of group counseling in educational settings. In applying their work to such settings, they have emphasized that their approach to counseling can be used in both a preventive and a remedial manner. Glasser maintains that his guided interaction approach to classroom settings can help promote schools without failure. Ellis stresses a similar point in the Living School. Both Ellis' and Glasser's emphasis on the utility of their counseling approaches for prevention of maladjustment represents a decided departure from most theorists' emphasis on remedial treatment.

CONTRIBUTIONS OF RATIONAL APPROACHES

A major contribution of Reality Therapy and Rational-Emotive Therapy has been their emphasis on the importance of cognition in counseling. The majority of other group counseling approaches have stressed the importance of the clients' emotions rather than their cognitive ability. Both Rational-Emotive and Reality Therapy serve as prime examples of the increasing recognition of and attention to cognition in psychology.

Ellis, in particular, has contributed to our understanding about the relation between individuals' thinking and their emotions. His belief that people suffer from their irrational beliefs about events and situations has gained increasing recognition and acceptance in the counseling literature. The fact that Ellis places the responsibility for correcting such irrational beliefs on the clients themselves represents another departure from traditional counseling approaches and is a contribution of Rational-Emotive Therapy. In many respects, Ellis has demystified the process of counseling. The essentials of Rational-Emotive Therapy can be taught relatively quickly to counselors and clients alike.

The strength of Reality Therapy lies in the fact that it can be used in a number of settings with varying numbers of individuals. For example, Reality Therapy has proved most successful in adolescent corrective institutions and in public schools. It can be used with small groups of people (as in the traditional counseling groups) or with thirty individuals, as in the case of classrooms. Both teachers and counselor can be trained to use Reality Therapy within a relatively short time. The emphasis placed on client responsibility is a major attraction of Reality Therapy, especially during an age that tends to stress that everything is relative and that people should do "their own thing." Both Ellis and Glasser can be credited with modernizing or simplifying the theoretical position of Adlerian group counseling.

References

Barr, N. I. The responsible world of reality therapy. *Psychology Today,* 1974, *7,* 64–68.

Bigelow, G. S., and J. W. Thorne. Reality versus client-centered models in group counseling. *The School Counselor,* 1969, *1,* 191–94.

Davison, G. C. Relative contributions of differential relaxation and graded exposure in vivo desensitization of a neurotic fear. *Proceedings of the 72nd Annual Convention of the American Psychological Association,* 1965, 209–10.

Di Loreto, A. O. A comparison of the relative effectiveness of systematic desensitization, rational-emotive and client-centered group psychotherapy in the reduction of interpersonal anxiety in introverts and extroverts. (Unpublished doctoral dissertation, Michigan State University, 1969). Dissertation Abstracts 1970 (June) V 30 (12-A) 5230. Also published in *Comparative Psychotherapy.* Chicago: Aldine-Atherton, 1971.

Ellis, A. Rational psychotherapy. *The Journal of General Psychology,* 1958, *59,* 35–49.

Ellis, A. *Reason and emotion in psychotherapy.* New York: Lyle Stuart, 1962. (Sixth Printing, 1971).

Ellis, A. A weekend of rational encounter. In A. Burton (Ed.), *Encounter.* San Francisco: Jossey-Bass, 1969, 112–27.

Ellis, A. Rational-emotive psychotherapy. In R. Corsini (Ed.), *Current psychotherapies.* Itasca, IL: Peacock, 1972, 169–206.

Ellis, A. Emotional education at the Living School. In M. M. Ohlsen (Ed.), *Counseling children in groups.* New York: Holt, Rinehart and Winston, 1973, 79–94.

Ellis, A. Rationality and irrationality in the group therapy process. In D. S. Milman and G. D. Goldman (Eds.), *Group process today.* Springfield, IL: Charles C Thomas, 1974, 78–96.

Ellis, A., and R. A. Harper. *A guide to rational living.* Hollywood: Wilshire Books, 1971.

Glasser, W. *Reality therapy: A new approach to psychiatry.* New York: Harper and Row, 1965.

Glasser, W. *Schools without failure.* Harper and Row, 1969.

Glasser, W. *The identity society.* New York: Harper and Row, 1972.

Glasser, W., and N. Iverson. *Reality therapy in large group counseling.* Los Angeles: The Reality Press, 1966.

Glasser, W., and L. M. Zunin. Reality therapy. In R. Corsini (Ed.), *Current psychotherapies.* Itasca, IL: Peacock, 1973, 287–315.

Lynn, D. B. Personal philosophies in psychotherapy. *Journal of Individual and Group Psychology,* 1961, *17,* 49–55. (Reprinted by Institute for Rational Living.)

Mowrer, O. H. Group counseling in the elementary school: The professional versus peer-group model. In M. M. Ohlsen (Ed.), *Counseling children in groups.* Holt, Rinehart and Winton, 1973, 243–70.

Ritter, B. The group desensitization of children's snake phobias using various vicarious and contact desensitization procedures. *Behavior Research and Therapy,* 1968, *8,* 127–32.

Tolsi, D. J., and W. A. Carlson. Client dogmatism and perceived counselor attitudes. *Personnel and Guidance Journal,* 1970, *48,* 657–60.

Velten, C. A. A laboratory task for the induction of mood states. *Behavior Research and Therapy,* 1968, *6,* 473–82.

Wubbolding, R. E. Practicing reality therapy. *Personnel and Guidance Journal,* 1975, *11,* 164–66.

8

Transactional Analysis in Groups

A theoretical approach to group counseling that has developed rapidly over the last twenty years is transactional analysis. TA, as it is commonly called, was developed by Eric Berne beginning in the early 1950s. Like many other theorists, Berne developed his new theoretical formulations from his own therapeutic practice.

Berne observed that within each of his clients there existed differing patterns of behavior, speech, and movement. These observations led him to conclude that each individual was in reality a combination of several individuals. Each of these differing individuals within an individual could be described as possessing a unique pattern of behavior, and at various times these separate individuals are in control of the individual's total personality. These separate individuals within the total individual were to become known as "ego states" and form an integral part of TA theory.

With these preliminary ideas, as well as others, Berne began a series of weekly meetings with other professionals in the Carmel, California area in the early 1950s (James, 1977). In 1958, Berne organized a seminar group in San Francisco similar to the one in Carmel. The group was originally called Social Psychiatry Seminar and was incorporated in the state of California on May 19, 1960 (Barnes, 1977). The group later changed its name to the San Francisco Transactional Analysis Seminar. Meetings were held almost weekly at Berne's home until his sudden death in 1970. During the short span of time between 1958 and 1970, the major portions of transactional analysis were developed. Since Berne's death, the work has been further developed by many individuals and by the many transactional analysis groups spread across the United States and other countries. "As interest in TA developed, some of the people who were originally supervised by Eric Berne moved to other locations and formed seminars and institutes of their own. Because of this dispersal, the growing number of institutes, and the increasing interest in TA, the International Transactional Analysis Association was established in 1964 (James, 1977, p. 27)." It is now estimated that there are over 10,000 individuals who are members of ITAA. While ITAA is open to all individuals, there are differing classifications of membership. Any individual may become a member by completing the ITAA introductory course 101. Other classifications of membership, which include special field members, clinical members, and teaching members, require extensive advanced training (James, 1977).

While Berne and many of his associates felt that TA was an entirely new approach to personality and therapy, there is little question that many of its ideas are directly related to basic psychoanalytic concepts. Harry Stack Sullivan, a neo-Freudian, had a tremendous influence on TA notions about interpersonal communications. Sullivan's concepts of interpersonal transactions have become a basic unit with TA theory. As shall be seen, there is also some relationship between ego states of Parent, Adult, and Child and the Freudian concepts of super ego, ego, and id. None of this is to take away from the unique contribution of TA, both to the public and to the helping professions.

It is particularly appropriate to include a chapter on Transactional Analysis in a text focusing on group counseling, because the greater part of Transactional Analysis utilizes a group modality. No single chapter, however, can be an exhaustive treatment of any approach to counseling. Hence, the aim here is to try to present material that will first give the reader a basic understanding of the TA position on personality development and abnormal development, then shift the focus to the ways in which TA concepts are utilized in the group process. Among topics discussed will be the TA view of other group processes, appropriate techniques, group leader behaviors, and research on the approach. Readers who wish to go beyond this basic introductory chapter are urged to read the original material as written by Berne and other individuals such as Steiner, Cartman, Grossman, English, James, Kupfer, Jongeward, Dusay, and others.

PERSONALITY DEVELOPMENT

The total personality of the individual is a product of the psychological and physiological needs that an individual is born with or acquires through transactions with others. A child comes into this world with two prior needs: physiological and psychological nurturing. The physiological nurturing consists of providing the child those physical elements necessary for survival—food, air, water. The need for psychological nurturing is met at this stage simply by holding the infant and keeping the infant comfortable. The important point here is that to satisfy either one of these basic needs, the infant must be involved with another individual. That is, some transaction must take place between the rather helpless child and some adult. At this point personality begins to develop, and its total development is a product of life-long interaction between needs and transactions to meet those needs.

Motivation

Beyond the basic physiological needs for survival, TA theorists hold that the motivating force within individuals is generated from the concepts of stimulus hunger, structure hunger, and position hunger.

Stimulus Hunger and Strokes   Based on an examination of the research, Berne concluded that stimulation is a primary need of individuals. Stimulation can be defined as a need for some form of attention, either physical or psychological, from the individual's environment. "The work of Renee Spitz and H. F. Harlow has shown that without adequate stroking, the organism, infant or monkey, shows retarded growth in all areas, physical, emotional, and mental (Kambly, 1971, p. 9)."

The primary way in which stimulus hunger can be satisfied is through strokes. Strokes are recognition given by one person to another. Strokes are essential for survival and much of an individual's behavior is motivated by attempts to receive them. In infancy this need is met through actual physical stroking, which later, for the most part, is replaced by symbolic stroking of various kinds: words, facial expressions and other nonverbal cues.

It is important to understand that strokes have several characteristics. They can be either conditional or unconditional and they can take on positive, negative, or mixed valences. Conditional strokes are given to an individual in recognition of a particular behavior. Unconditional strokes are those that are received by an individual from another simply for being. Either conditional or unconditional strokes, however, may take on positive, negative, or mixed (crooked) valences. A father praising his daughter for running a good race is a conditional positive stroke. A conditional negative stroke is a mother slapping her son for disobeying. In both examples, the individual is receiving the strokes, either positive or negative, on the basis of what he or she did. A conditional stroke with a mixed valence is one that carries both a negative and a positive message. A teacher telling a student that her paper is so good he doesn't know how she did it is sending a conditional mixed (crooked) stroke. In the case of the mixed, or crooked, stroke, most often the overt stroke is positive, but it is accompanied by a covert negative stroke. Examples of unconditional strokes are: "I really like you" (positive) or "I really don't like you" (negative). Unconditional strokes are strokes that are given to the individual for what they are, not for what they accomplish.

While one might conclude that an individual would seek only positive strokes, such is not the case. Individuals learn to seek the kinds of strokes that they originally received as children. A child whose parents provided negative strokes would come to believe that negative strokes were the only ones worth seeking. This feeling becomes a primary motivation for behaviors that others might consider maladaptive. The point here is that the search for the type of strokes the individual received in childhood is a primary motivating force for the individual, and his or her transactions with others will be utilized to receive the necessary strokes for survival.

Structure Hunger   A second motivating force is termed structure hunger.

"Structure hunger recognizes a dilemma of man through the ages—what to do with 24 hours a day, 168 hours a week (Holland, 1973, p. 359)." Structure hunger is often thought of as an extension of stimulus hunger. In effect, it is the need for an individual to structure his or her life so that the potential for receiving the necessary strokes is enhanced. To satisfy structure hunger, the individual engages in social situations in which time is organized for the purpose of receiving strokes. Berne (1966) writes, "People are willing to pay almost any price to have their time structured for them, since few are capable of structuring their own time autonomously for very long (p. 230)." Hence, individuals seek ways to structure their time with a minimum of effort and, most importantly, with a minimum of risk. The risk in an unstructured situation is that the individual will not receive the strokes needed for survival. The ways in which an individual can structure time to receive the strokes needed in a relative order of safeness are:

1. *Withdrawal* is an autistic attempt to provide oneself strokes through the use of fantasy. An individual who uses withdrawal as a means for receiving strokes is generally unable to find the strokes needed in the external world. Risk to the individual is minimal, unless withdrawal is used exclusively to receive strokes, but strokes received utilizing withdrawal are of minimal value

2. *Rituals* are most often termed the social amenities. They take us through the day and allow us to give and receive strokes with a minimum of effort. The morning interchange at the office, which may sound like the following, is a ritual:

Dick	Mary
–Good morning.	–Good morning.
–How goes it?	–Fine, and with you?
–Good, see you later.	–Yeah, later.

    Here both individuals gave and received strokes or recognition with a minimum effort.

3. *Pastimes* are similar to rituals except that the form of the transaction is less stereotyped. "When people are not trying to accomplish a goal but are only 'talking about' something, usually one of their favorite subjects they are engaging in a pastime (Woollams, Brown, Huige, 1977, p. 505)." Examples of pastimes are a group of parents discussing their children; a group of adults discussing the current sports scene; and a group of young adults discussing automobiles. They are transactions utilizing external events or subjects which enable individuals to interact without really revealing much about themselves.

4. *Activity* generally is considered to be work that deals with external reality. "When one's energy is directed to external sources (objects, tasks, ideas, etc.), the person is engaged in an activity. Work, hobbies, and chores are

common examples; hence, most people spend a great deal of their waking hours involved in activities (Woollams, Brown, and Huige, 1977, p. 505)." Activity is a major source of strokes for many individuals. An individual described as a workaholic is an individual who receives necessary strokes primarily through activity.

5. *Games* are probably the most publicized way individuals have of obtaining strokes. As the TA movement has grown, the list of games individuals utilize has also grown. Games are an orderly series of transactions, with both overt and covert messages being exchanged simultaneously, providing an ultimate payoff in strokes for both participants. The payoff from a game is often referred to as a trading stamp, and individuals collect trading stamps and store them. The particular kinds of stamps (payoffs) individuals seek in their games defines their basic "racket" or basic life-style. People who are in an angry racket will engage in games in which they can end up angry at the opposite party in the transaction. This, of course, requires an individual with the complementary racket of "everyone is angry with me." Thus, a game is only played when both parties to the transaction can be winners. In effect, there are no real losers in games that people play with one another; both partners receive the payoff they seek.

6. "*Intimacy* is a game-free exchange of internally programmed, affective expressions (Berne, 1966, 231)." Intimacy has the potential for occurring in the absence of the other forms of time structuring. "Intimacy is the most rewarding of all the ways of structuring time. It is also the most difficult to define. Intimacy involves the sharing of feelings, thoughts, and experiences in a relationship of honesty and trust (Woollams, Brown, and Huige, 1977, p. 505)."

To some extent, at least, all individuals use these six methods of obtaining strokes through time structuring. Difficulties arise when there is an overreliance on one method to the exclusion of others, particularly the exclusion of intimacy.

Position Hunger   A third motivating force is position hunger, which is the need for individuals to have their life-long patterns confirmed. The need is related to the particular racket of the individual. The racket is most often established in childhood through the kinds of strokes the child receives and thus comes to accept as the kind needed. One can think of position hunger as the need to continually reaffirm who we are in our chosen life position. To develop a better understanding of the motivating power of position hunger, we need to examine the concepts of life position, life script, and counterscript.

Life Position   Berne (1973) suggests that the destiny of every human being is determined by what happens inside one's head when one is confronted with what goes on externally. Each individual makes his or her own decisions as to how to live, and the TA position is that this decision is made very early in development. "Before children are eight years old they develop a concept about their own worth. They also formulate ideas about the worth of others. They crystalize their experiences and decide what it all means to them, what parts they're going to play, and how they are going to play them (James and Jongeward, 1971, p. 34)." From a TA perspective there are four potential life positions that a child can adopt.

1. I'm OK—You're OK. This is the basic trust position with which all individuals are born. It is also the ultimate goal of living. It is the best position for productive life but, unfortunately, it is the least maintained one. To hold the "I'm OK—You're OK" position means to feel secure in your own worth as a human being and in the worth of those around you.

2. I'm OK—You're not OK. This position is held by those who either look down on everyone else or who are suspicious of the motives of everyone else. Harris (1969) feels that this position develops from an overreaction to being treated as not OK. The child who is beaten repeatedly by parents originally thought to be OK may reverse positions as a self-defense. Individuals who adopt such a position are unable to be objective about themselves. They are individuals who feel they are always right and everyone else is wrong. Criminal behavior is often a result of having chosen this particular life position.

3. I'm not OK—you're OK. Berne (1973) describes this as the depressive self-abasement position. Harris (1969) states that it is the universal position forced on children. It derives from the Adlerian belief that almost everything that occurs in a young child's life tells the child that she or he is inferior, or not OK. An individual who adopts this position is in a constant search for strokes. Such an individual will be deferential in manner and eager to follow the lead of others. This position may lead to a very productive but unsatisfying life. The position often leads to withdrawal, depression, and, in severe cases, suicide (James and Jongeward, 1971).

4. I'm not OK—you're not OK. This is life's hopeless position. It is adopted by those individuals who have learned first that they are not OK, but their parents are. However, as soon as they are old enough to take care of themselves, even to a minimal degree, their parents begin to shun them. Because they receive no strokes from their parents, they soon adopt the idea that no one is OK. Such persons seek only to get through each day and through life in general. This futile position, when adopted by individuals, often leads to schizoid-type behavior and, in extreme cases, suicide or homicide (James and Jongeward, 1971).

The position chosen by the child is determined by the number and type of injunctions and permissions given to the child through transactions with parents and other authority figures prior to the age of eight.

Injunctions   Injunctions are commands from the parents of the individual to behave in certain ways. The degree of impact on the child depends on both the form of the injunction and the severity with which it is enforced. Berne (1973) describes three levels of injunction:

1. First degree injunctions are straight commands that are reinforced either through approval or nonapproval. They are relatively mild and their use does not prohibit the individual from developing a fairly positive life position.

2. Second degree injunctions are crooked commands which contain contradicting covert and overt messages that are enforced through blackmail and threats. Because of the confusion they cause within the individual, such injunctions tend to produce individuals who simply move through life existing from day to day.

3. Third degree injunctions are commands that are enforced through the use of severe punishment. Such injunctions produce the acceptance of a negative life position and an accompanying life script that dooms the individual to the life of a loser.

Injunctions, regardless of the degree, are all negative in nature. While they do not by themselves prohibit the development of the "I'm OK" position, the more they are used by those around the child, the greater the probability that the child will adopt the "I'm not OK" position.

Permissions   Permissions, unlike injunctions, are permits to make one's own choices given by the parents to the child. The more permissions that are given, the more likely it is that the child will develop both the positive life position and a life script that is productive. Permissions are recognitions of the child's ability to make his or her own decisions. As such, they increase the probability of the child's developing the notion that "I'm OK."

Life Script   Having chosen a life position, regardless of how premature or faulty that decision, the individual will then attempt to plan his or her life so that it will fit within the life position. Such a plan or script permits individuals to meet their basic needs for confirmation of their chosen position in life, for structuring of their time, and for obtaining the recognition and strokes that they need for existence. In short, very early in life children make the decisions that set the courses for their lives. Similar to a script for a stage play, this life script sets the guidelines for all that is to occur in life. It is important to remember that because the life position and life script are chosen very early in life, they are often unrealistic. "They're likely to be somewhat distorted and irrational, because children perceive life through the small peekhole of their existence. These distortions can create some degree of pathology ranging from inconsequential to serious. However, they seem logical and make sense at the time the child makes them (James and Jongeward, 1971, p. 34)."

Counterscript   In addition to the chosen life script, many individuals who have received crooked injunctions from their parents will develop, at least for some period in their life, a counterscript. Dusay and Steiner (1971) describe a case where a child had been given a message from his mother's Child ego state to be violent, and at the same time a message from the mother's Parent ego state to be a good boy. The result of this crooked message was that the child's life script became one of violence, which ended in his being incarcerated. During incarceration, the individual lived his counterscript by being a model prisoner, which got him released. His life became a constant repetition of this cycle. Many individuals' lives show a similar pattern of opposing behaviors operating at various times. Understanding individual scripts and counterscripts is an essential requirement of Transactional Analysis. They will reveal the reasons for the ways in which individuals seek to maintain their positions, structure their time, and seek their necessary strokes. In short, they explain why individuals behave as they do.

Ego States

Having examined the basic motivating forces important in personality development, we should now turn our attention to an examination of an equally important concept in Transactional Analysis: ego states. Berne (1966) believed that every individual contained three separate, albeit related, ego states: Parent, Adult, and Child. Each of these ego states is distinguished from the other by possessing its own gestures, mannerisms, intonations, and content of verbal behavior. At any given period of time one of these ego states is in charge of the individual, and it is that personality which is seen.

While having some relationship with the Freudian concepts of id, ego, and superego, the Child, Adult, and Parent are conceived to be quite different by TA theorists. Berne (1966) maintains that "superego, ego, and id are inferential concepts, while ego states are experiential and social realities (p. 220)." Thus, a key difference to keep in mind is that Transactional Analysis is concerned about observable, conscious behavior as opposed to the traditional Freudian concern with the unconscious.

Child Ego State   The Child ego state is basically characterized by joy, creativity, charm, and spontaneity. It is extremely important for normal functioning because it is the only part of the individual that can really enjoy itself. The Child ego state may be further divided into component parts known as the Natural Child, the Adapted Child, and the Little Professor. The Natural Child is that part of the child which is relatively untrained and free of parental injunctions; the Adapted Child is formed as the child interacts with those around her or him; and the Little Professor is the initial adult-like thinking of the child. In adults the Child ego state is a representation of the actual child until approximately age seven.

A person who is operating in the Child ego state will use child-like words such as "gee" or "golly." He or she will be fidgety, laugh loudly, scream, jump up and down, and cry. Since society tends to frown on child-like behavior in an adult, individuals search for situations in which this behavior is permitted, such as parties and sporting events.

The Child ego state in each individual is a product of inherent factors and the social, economic, and emotional environments. Much of its formation occurs either before the individual has any vocabulary or during the time when there is a very limited vocabulary; hence, much of the child is composed of emotions. During the formation of the Child ego state, the individual is confronted on the one hand by needs to explore, to know, to act, and to experience pleasure and on the other hand by the demands of the environment, principally in the form of parental demands. These demands are often in conflict, since to gain parental approval the child must discard some behaviors which bring the child pleasure. This is the development of that part of the Child ego state known as the Adapted Child. "The predominant by-product of the frustrating, civilizing process is negative feelings. On the basis of these feelings, the little person early concludes, 'I'm not OK' (Harris, 1969, p. 48)."

The Child ego state, however, is not composed solely of negative or "I'm not OK" feelings. It is also composed of all those exciting, pleasurable feelings generated by first discoveries such as the first touch and smell of a flower, the first step, the first turning of a faucet. This is the happy, carefree part of the Child ego state known as the Natural Child.

Yet a third part of the Child ego state is that part which begins to develop as the child reasons, even in a limited way, about the world. It is that part of the child that begins to respond to nonverbal cues from the environment, that is intuitive and creative. In effect, the child is able to reason out some of the child's own solutions to circumstances that confront the child. That is that part of the Child ego state known as the Little Professor.

All three of these components make up the Child ego state and it is the foundation upon which the individual builds a self-image. Berne (1973) stresses that the individual must understand his or her Child, not only because it will be there throughout life but also because it is the single most important part of the personality.

Parent Ego State   The Parent ego state is basically composed of traditions, beliefs, and values transmitted to an individual by his or her parents. It is a collection of recordings from the external world, without any exclusion of their content being made. It makes no difference whether these recordings are accurate representations of the way it is; they are recorded as truths.

In the Parent ego state one feels, talks, and behaves in the same manner as one's parents did when one was a small child. Even when not actually operating from this ego state, the individual is influenced by it. The Parent ego state is similar in action to what is commonly referred to as a conscience.

The individual, when operating from the Parent ego state, can be characterized as behaving in a nonperceptive and nonthinking fashion. Decisions are based on edicts handed down from the past. Many of these "how to do this" edicts come equipped with the commands "never" and "always" and "never forget about that (Harris, 1969)." Hence, in this ego state the person behaves not on the basis of current data from the environment but upon the basis of all the rules for living and behaving that were incorporated from parents.

Such an ego state is necessary for the survival of the culture as well as for permitting each individual to move through each day without having to invest a great deal of energy in evaluating each and every situation. It can be destructive, however, when the ideas within the Parent ego state are so strong that they preclude the inclusion of new appropriate data. In normal development, much of the material in the Parent ego state is subject to updating, but when this process of updating fails to occur, the individual is likely to experience difficulty in managing life. Just as the Child ego state is composed of differing parts, so too is the Parent ego state. Because the Parent ego state is a direct recording from the actual parents, it registers material from all three ego states of each parent. Children record into their Parent ego state the injunctions or rules from their parents' Parent ego states, such as "Always tell the truth," "Christians are the best kind of people," "Respect the law." Children also record their parents' behavior when the parents are behaving as children. Perhaps most important, children record the inconsistencies in behavior within one parent and between parents. A parent tells the child that one should always keep one's word, but often the parent does not keep promises made to the child. The father tells the child one thing and the mother tells the child the opposite. These inconsistencies can lead to a malfunctioning Parent ego state in the child.

In normal growth and development, we can expect much of the parent to be formed by the time the individual first attends school. In normal development, however, it will continue to be modified as the individual continually interacts with authority figures from whom new "parent" behavior can be incorporated. In fact, the extent to which the Parent ego state is productive in the life of the individual depends on how appropriate to the current situation is the information stored there. In short, if the Parent ego state remains static, it will become a nonfunctional part of the individual. If, however, it is open to updating from the Adult ego state, the Parent ego state can be an important part of a fully functioning individual.

Adult Ego State   The Adult ego state is that part of the individual which acts as an assimilator, instructor, and evaluator of information. It might be favorably compared to a regulatory agency that makes decisions about the whole system. As such, it is devoid of feeling though it has the capacity to evaluate the feelings of the Child and Parent ego states. "It is organized, adaptable, intelligent, and functions by testing reality, estimating probabilities, and computing dispassionately (James and Jongeward, 1977, p. 18)."

When operating in the Adult ego state, the individual can be characterized as essentially factual. Questions are concerned not with feelings, but with facts; "What is the purpose of the meeting?" Answers are similarly factual: "The purpose is to plan a course of action for our group." Behavior is purposeful and directional.

The reader will recall that one subpart of the Child ego state was termed the Little Professor. In actuality the Little Professor is the forerunner of the Adult ego state. It begins to form around ten months of age. As the infant develops the physical ability to move both itself and other objects in its world, it begins to separate itself from its world. This realization of self is the beginning of the adult.

As the infant develops and actually experiences more and more of the world, it begins to accumulate and evaluate its own data against that which it has been taught (its Parent) and that which it feels (its Child). At this stage the Adult is fragile and easily overridden by the injunctions from the Parent and the emotions from the Child. Given proper nurturing, the Adult will continue to grow as the Child tests out information. For example, the young child may be told not to touch the stove because he or she will get burned. Invariably, the child will touch the stove at least once in an attempt to check the information. Quite obviously, then, the Adult ego state, given normal development, is unlike both the Child and Parent ego states in that it is less static. The Parent and Child are largely products of the past, while the Adult is concerned with present data. Its efficiency is a product of how well it developed from infancy onward, but it is not directly tied to the past.

A fully functioning Adult is able to evaluate experiences in a rational way. It can examine the data in the Parent ego state and either substantiate the material there or update it. It can also examine the feelings associated with the Child ego state and evaluate whether or not they are appropriate to the present situation. It does not attempt to rid the individual of the Parent and Child ego states, but it does attempt to keep them current, appropriate, and in check.

Transactions

TA theory "holds that a person's behavior is best understood if examined in terms of ego state, and that the behavior between two or more persons is best understood if examined in terms of transactions. A transaction consists of a stimulus and a response between two specific ego states (Steiner, 1974, p. 34)." From infancy onward, transactions are sought in order to meet the basic needs of the individual. It is through transactions between the child and its parents that the foundations for the individual's personality are formed, and they become the means through which the individual attempts to receive the strokes needed for existence.

As shown in Figure 2, each individual in a social interaction has the potential of entering that transaction in any one of the three ego states available. In any interaction, the communication will continue if the stimulus and response are complementary. Such a transaction might be:

1. Jack: What time is it?
   Helen: It is 12:35.

This is a complementary message from one Adult ego state to another Adult ego state. A complementary message could also go from the Child of one individual to the Parent of the second:

2. Jack: May I go out and play?
   Helen: Yes, you may

The message is complementary as long as the ego state of any individual being addressed is the ego state that responds. Any other response creates a crossed transaction, and communication stops. Figure 3 demonstrates the following crossed transaction:

Jack: What time is it?
Helen: You are a real clock watcher.

Figure 2   Complementary Transaction (adapted from Berne, 1964)

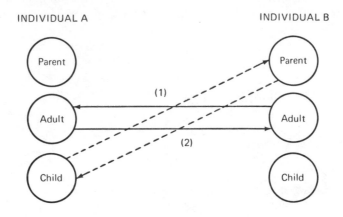

Figure 3   Crossed Transaction (adapted from Berne, 1964)

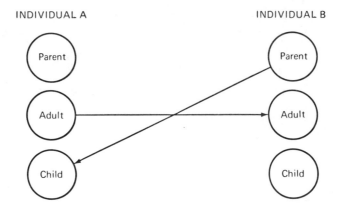

The question was asked from an Adult ego state and addressed to an Adult ego state; however, instead of the Adult responding, the Parent ego state of B responded to the Child ego state of A. In this transaction, the ego state that was addressed in the original statement was not the ego state that responded. Thus, it is an example of a crossed transaction which interrupts communication. Yet a third kind of transaction is the ulterior transaction, in which there is a message at two different levels, psychological and social. The following transaction is diagrammed in Figure 4:

Figure 4   Ulterior Transaction (adapted from Berne, 1964)

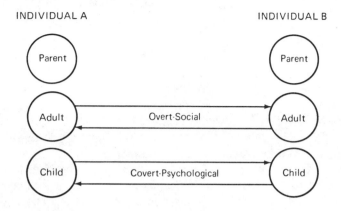

Debbie: Would you like to see my new apartment?
Rick: Sure.

At first glance this may seem like a transaction between two Adult ego states. On further inspection, however, the message may be between two Child ego states:

Debbie: Let's go where we can be alone and have some fun.
Rick: I'm all for that.

In many transactions it is important to understand the covert rather than the overt part of the message. This type of transaction is also termed crooked, in that the covert message may be quite different from the overt. Such transactions between parents and their children cause much frustration in children.

Transactions, then, take three basic forms: complementary, crossed, and ulterior or crooked. They are the building blocks of personality and through them the needs of individuals are met. That is, the transactions are a result of an individual's motivation to meet his or her needs.

DEVELOPMENT OF PERSONALITY

Transactional Analysis holds that each individual is born with a positive potential which needs only to be nurtured to become a reality (Dusay and Steiner, 1971). Certainly there are physiological, psychological, and sociocultural factors that place differing limits on each individual, but within those limits there is the potential for positive growth and development, and the adoption of the desirable "I'm OK—you're OK" position.

Even prior to conception, however, there are factors operating that may affect the potential of the child. In some cases these factors will enhance the positive development of the child, such as in the case of a child who is really a welcomed addition to the family. In other cases, such as an unwanted child, the factors can have a detrimental effect.

As mentioned previously, at birth the child adopts the natural position of trust, "I'm OK—you're OK." Given positive prebirth factors, there is a possibility that this position can be maintained in transactions with the parents. In large measure this calls for the parents to provide unconditional, positive strokes to the child. During the critical stages of life, up until about the age of six months, the provision of these unconditional strokes, as well as the caring for the infant's physiological needs, are all that are needed for continued normal development.

After the age of six months, the task of helping the child maintain at least a partial feeling of "I'm OK" through healthy parenting behavior becomes more difficult. Falzett and Maxwell (1974) have described the kinds of healthy parenting that need to be provided to the child from the age of six months through twelve years. While their description of healthy and unhealthy parenting behavior shown in Table 1 does not describe all possible behaviors, it does provide a general guideline for behaviors that will act to enhance or hinder normal development. Healthy parenting behaviors at all stages of development facilitate the child's development of means for receiving strokes that are not based on games and rituals. Unhealthy parenting, on the other hand, increases the probability that the child will develop the "I'm not OK" life position and will turn to games and rituals for most of its necessary strokes.

Obviously, the behaviors shown in Table 1 do not include all the healthy or unhealthy parenting behaviors. However, Table 1 does provide a general guideline —a guideline that places emphasis on respecting the child, encouraging the full development of its own Adult ego state, and the development of necessary psychomotor skills. Given healthy parenting, the child will develop ego states that are functional and will develop means of receiving strokes that do not rely solely on games and rituals. Rather, there will be a balance of means ranging across intimacy, games, activities, pastimes, and rituals, and the child's chosen life position will enable it to live a relatively script-free life.

Given healthy parenting, each ego state of the individual will have the capacity to function on its own. In a healthy adult, each ego state can be subdivided into three parts based upon where the particular data came from during ego state formation. Subdivision of the ego states are shown in Figure 5. Each of these ego states has the potential for acting as the administrator of the physical and psychological functioning of the individual. However, only one of the ego states can be in charge at any one point in time, "that is, imbued with the energy necessary to activate muscular complexes involved in behavior (Dusay and Steiner, 1971, p. 201)." There are times, however, when the individual may have one ego state cathected and a second ego state cathected sufficiently so as to be aware of the behavior of the first ego state. The reader may best be able to grasp this concept

Table 1 Falzett and Maxwell's Developmental Process

Age Range	Healthy Parenting	Unhealthy Parenting
6–18 months	During this period it is essential that the parents provide an atmosphere where the child feels free to explore its world. At the same time the parents must also provide a degree of protection such that the child will not be harmed by that exploration. Transactions between parent and child should concentrate on communication from the parents Child to the child's Child.	Parents may be overprotective and refuse to permit the child to explore its world. At the other extreme, they may behave in a way that does not provide the child any protection from the environment.
18 months–3 years	While the majority of the transactions between parent and child still should take place from the Child ego state of the parent to the Child ego state of the child, some Adult transactions should begin during this period. The child should be encouraged to develop some self-control and some consideration of the needs and feelings of others.	Unhealthy parenting at this stage of development is characterized by either excessive demands on the child, or by the complete absence of demands. Generally, Adult to adult transactions do not take place. The child is given little encouragement to solve its own problems.
3–6 years	Parents continue facilitating the development of problem-solving skills in the child. Parents act to encourage the development of appropriate and consistent ways to receive strokes rather than the development of game playing. They focus on helping the child understand its own feelings and behaviors.	Parents continue to discourage the child's problem-solving behavior. Indeed, they often act to tease the child for expressed ideas or fantasies.
6–12 years	Parents should enter into Adult-Adult transactions with the child regarding values and social rules. This requires parents to really listen to the child's ideas and to respect the child's right to hold its ideas. Parents should provide as many doing experiences for the child as they can in order to facilitate skill development.	Parents do not permit value exploration but rather impose a rigid set of rules and values. Adult-Adult transactions are avoided as parents continue to demean the child's own reasoning powers.

by thinking about his or her behavior at a recent social gathering. In such a circumstance, you may have been caught up in the activities and your Child ego state became cathected. While you were enjoying your child-like behavior, a part of you was perhaps saying, "Behave yourself" (Parent), or "If I drink any more, I will have a headache tomorrow" (Adult). The statement from the Parent or the Adult may, in fact, have been so strong as to decathect the Child and fully cathect the second ego state. The point here is that this dialogue-like behavior between two ego states within the individual frequently takes place; it is necessary for normal functioning and is tremendously important in counseling.

The Parent and Child ego states, because they are often less acceptable than the Adult, often attempt to pass themselves off as the Adult. The husband who asks his wife, "Why aren't you ready to go yet?" may be asking an Adult question but most probably is asking the question from his Parent. In effect, he is saying, "You are bad because you are not ready." Similarly, the verbal communications of an individual may indicate an Adult ego state, but careful observation of the nonverbal behavior may indicate a Child or Parent ego state operating.

In normal functioning it is necessary that an individual have the capacity to operate from all three ego states. This means that there has to be enough permeability among the three ego states so that an individual can move from one to another when appropriate. The Parent is most appropriate when the individual must control either some situation or some individuals such as children. The Adult is appropriate when some situation must be dealt with through a rational decision-making process. Finally, the Child is appropriate in situations calling for creativity or the expression of natural emotion (Dusay and Steiner, 1971).

MALADAPTIVE PERSONALITY DEVELOPMENT

Maladaptive behavior in TA terms is a product of an individual's having chosen a life position other than "I'm OK—You're OK," the selection of a life script that is designed to confirm that position, and the lack of fully developed and uncontaminated ego states. The severity of the difficulty experienced by the individual is in direct proportion to the amount of unhealthy parenting that took place during the individual's developmental years. The kind of parenting received will affect the actual life position chosen by the individual, and will determine how deeply entrenched the position has become through punishment from parents, and how severely contaminated are the ego states.

Maladaptive Life Positions

As discussed earlier, the "I'm not OK—You're OK" position may be the least maladaptive position in that the individual can lead a productive, albeit not very joyful, life. Such a position, while not desirable, is the norm. Hence, in TA terms, most individuals are not behaving in ways that lead to true self-fulfillment. In TA

Figure 5   Ego States and Subdivisions

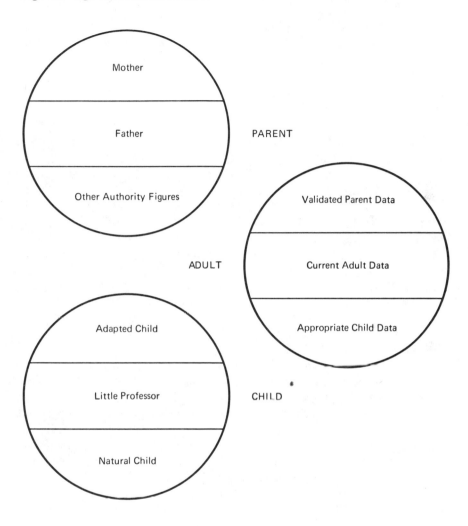

terms most of us during our developmental process move from the natural position of "I'm OK—You're OK" to the adapted life position of "I'm not OK—You're OK."

The two positions of "I'm OK—You're not OK," and "I'm not OK—You're not OK" are the most maladaptive life positions. The former position leads to a life script dominated by paranoid thinking. Individuals choosing this stance are the ones most likely to engage in antisocial behaviors. The latter position is one of hopelessness and despair. While such individuals will generally not cause anyone else difficulty, their lives can be characterized as boring and joyless.

Maladaptive Ego State Structure

Besides selecting a life position that can lead to inappropriate behavior, the individual, through an inappropriate developmental process, may develop two maladaptations in the structure of the ego states: exclusions and contaminations.

Exclusions In a healthy individual, ego state boundaries are really semipermeable, and psychic energy can move from one ego state to another as the situation demands. In some individuals, however, the ego state boundaries become too flexible, while in others they become too rigid.

An individual with lax ego state boundaries appears to lack identity and gives the impression of being haphazard in behavior. His or her psychic energy slips continually from one ego state to another in response to very minor stimuli. Such individuals may have great difficulty functioning in the real world; they can be described as never knowing what they are going to do next. They become people who are avoided by others because their behavior is completely unpredictable.

The development of rigid ego state boundaries, on the other hand, does not permit the free movement of psychic energy based on the requirements of the situation. The boundaries are like thick walls, holding energy within one ego state, while excluding the other two. The behavior of persons with this problem appears rigid because they tend to respond to most stimuli with the same ego state. Such individuals appear to have only one ego state, whether it be a Parent, an Adult, or a Child. Such individuals are unable to respond to new situations and are generally out of touch with what is going on around them.

Contamination Contamination is the intrusion of one ego state, usually the Parent or the Child, into another ego state, usually the Adult. "Contamination occurs when the Adult accepts as true some unfounded Parent beliefs or Child distortions and rationalizes and justifies these attitudes (James and Jongeward, 1971, p. 231)." Contamination from the Parent is most often found in the form of prejudices which have been expressed to the child with such force that they are treated as fact. "In extreme cases, contamination from the Parent is experienced as hallucinations, the sensory perception of things that are not real (James and Jongeward, 1971, p. 231)." An individual whose Adult ego state is contaminated by his or her Child is generally one that distorts reality. In more severe cases, the contamination of the Adult from the Child ego state can cause delusions. The most common delusion created by this contamination is the delusion of grandeur and/or persecution.

In large measure the development of a maladaptive life position and the development of poorly functioning ego states, whether through exclusions or contaminations, are products of unhealthy parenting. Instead of providing the child unconditional positive strokes, the parents make their strokes conditional on the child's doing what the parents want. Such parenting behavior leads to the selection of the "I'm not OK" position.

The lives of such children are also full of parental injunctions against certain behaviors. Children are given few permissions to explore, to develop their own solutions, or to express their ideas or feelings. Such behavior of the parents causes the child's ego state to become dominated by the Adapted Child rather than the Natural Child; it both hinders the development of the Adult ego state and leads to its contamination; and, finally, it causes the development of a severe and rigid Parent ego state.

Thus, just as appropriate behavior or normal development is the product of parent behavior toward the child so, too, is abnormal or maladaptive behavior. In the former case, the parents provide an atmosphere of love and respect where the child is encouraged to develop, while in the latter case the child experiences negation and is permitted to grow only in prescribed and narrow directions.

TRANSACTIONAL ANALYSIS IN GROUPS

As indicated earlier in this chapter, the growth of Transactional Analysis has produced at least three major branches of TA thinking. Barnes (1977) terms these three schools the Classical School, the Cathexis School, and the Redecision School. The Classical School, founded by Berne, can be further subdivided into three distinctive branches known as the Eric Berne Seminars, the Radical Psychiatry Movement, and the Asklepieion Foundation (Barnes, 1977). The Radical Psychiatry Movement was founded by Claude Steiner; the Asklepieion Foundation was founded by Martin Groder. The Cathexis School was founded by Jacqui Lee Schiff. The Redecision School is directed by Robert and Mary Goulding. The practices recommended by each of these branches of Transactional Analysis are somewhat different. Thus, it is difficult within any single chapter to capture the thinking of such a diverse group of individuals. Nonetheless, most individuals in these various schools do agree on the basic TA approach to group counseling. Thus, the remainder of this chapter will examine the basic concepts of TA as applied to group counseling. It will examine the objectives of TA, its notion of the group process, group leader characteristics and behaviors, and levels of counseling. Readers should keep in mind that as TA has grown and expanded, it has become even more action oriented. In many cases, TA group leaders utilize Gestalt techniques within a TA framework.

Objectives

Berne (1966) describes four general objectives that are needed to a greater or lesser degree for most clients. The first objective is to help clients decontaminate their ego states. The second objective is to help clients to develop the capacity to use all their ego states as situations warrant. Third, the counselor helps each individual discard an inappropriate life script and replace it with a productive script. Fourth, the counselor and the client spell out the specific objectives for the client in the form of a contract.

Counselor-Client Contracts. The counselor-client contract is a specific statement of objectives to be attained in the group. It comprises three levels: administrative, professional, and psychological. At the administrative level, the counselor needs to explain to the potential group members the relationship between counselor, organization (i.e., the school, mental health agency, etc.), and the group (Berne, 1966). Often this means spelling out the restrictions that the particular organization places on all of them. For example, the school may limit the length of time they will be permitted to meet. At the professional level, the prime question of concern is whether the goals of counseling will conflict with other goals of the clients. If, for instance, a group member is receiving some form of aid from an agency and the goal of the group counseling is to help the participants to become self-supporting, some persons may not choose to enter counseling. Both the administrative and professional levels of the contract have a direct bearing on the psychological level. It is at the psychological level that the counselor and the client state their objectives and commitment to the process. The objectives and the commitments by both counselor and group members need to be stated in such a way as to avoid any possible misunderstanding. Dusay and Steiner (1971) report that retrospective analysis of contracts from TA groups demonstrates the following four requirements:

Mutual Consent   Both the group member and the counselor, through Adult-Adult transactions, must agree on their mutual objective. In achieving mutual consent, it is imperative that the Adults of both the counselor and the participant are the parties to the contract. Indeed, from the TA perspective, no actual counseling takes place until such a transaction occurs. If the member is unable to use his or her Adult, then the counselor acts from his or her Parent. Most often such a relationship is a Parent (counselor)-Child (group member) relationship and is not counseling. Only after an Adult-Adult transaction is established does counseling begin.

Consideration   Each of the two individuals involved in the contract gives something to the other for their efforts. The counselor gives professional skill, time, and knowledge. In private settings in some agencies, the group member gives money. In situations where that is not possible (i.e., schools), the only consideration may be to have the participant sign a contract to give time and effort to the counseling process. This may be in the form of an agreement that states the time, place, and duration of each meeting and the minimum number of sessions.

Competency   As it relates to counselors, competency means that counselors have the requisite training and experience to fulfill their part of the contract. In establishing contracts with group members, counselors must decide if they have the tools to help individuals reach their objectives. As it relates to clients, competency means being able to enter into a contract. If clients cannot use their Adult, they cannot make a valid contract. Furthermore, in the case of minors or incarcerated individuals, the persons responsible for them must also agree to the contract or the individual might be forced to terminate the counseling right in the middle of the process.

Legality   This simply means that the objective to be achieved through counseling is legal and within ethical guidelines to which the counselor adheres.

Given these four requirements, contracts must be written in simple terms with the desired objectives clearly stated. For example, an individual member cannot enter into a contract that states, "I want to improve my self-concept"; rather, the contract must call for a specific behavior, "I want to be able to date two different people by the end of the quarter." Contracts can be worked out either individually or in the group. The advantage of working them out within the context of the group is that everyone then knows exactly why everyone is there. This cuts down on the playing of games within the group. While the contracts may be written in the first session, it is permissible, and sometimes advisable, to wait a while longer. During the initial group meetings, both the participants and the counselor have an opportunity to observe each other and decide whether in fact they are parties who can enter into valid contracts.

A second distinct advantage of contractual group counseling is its built-in accountability. Using a contract system makes it difficult for a group member to say after four or five sessions, "I don't know why I am here." The contract means that counselor and group members both know why they are there and, more importantly, whether they are moving toward achievement of the objectives they have set out to accomplish. Once the original contract has been fulfilled, the relationship may either terminate or a new contract may be entered into in order to achieve a subsequent goal.

It should not be concluded from the preceding that contracts are rigid, for in the life of a group it may become apparent to both the group members and the counselor that some changes may need to be made. Possibly the goals were originally set too high or too low. It may be that the original contract called for dealing with symptoms of anxiety and, when these are resolved, individuals may wish to shift their attention to a resolution of the underlying dynamics that are causing the anxiety. In such cases, it is both appropriate and necessary that the contract be rewritten.

The objectives of TA, then, can be conceptualized as global goals which transcend most groups and group members, and as very specific objectives in the form of counselor-member contracts.

The Group Process

Transactional Analysis is best viewed as a contractual treatment of individuals within a group. While group dynamics are considered important, the primary focus remains on the transaction between and among group members. "The group serves as a setting in which people can become more aware of themselves, the structure of their individual personality, how they transact with others, the games they play, and the scripts they act out (James and Jongeward, 1977, p. 11)."

TA, perhaps more than any other approach, stresses the proper physical, as well as psychological, setting for the group. Berne (1966) emphasizes the need for a comfortable setting in which there is little possibility of interruption—phone calls, for example. The suggested seating plan is a circle with the counselor seated where he or she can clearly see the faces of all participants. Finally, the leader needs to have a chalkboard available for everyone's use.

Berne (1966) recommends careful preparation of group members before the actual counseling situation begins. Many TA counselors meet individually with clients for from one to four sessions prior to placement in a group. Other counselors utilize what are termed preparatory group meetings before the actual counseling process begins. In either case, the functions of these preparatory meetings, whether individual or group, are to present the prospective group members with information about Transactional Analysis, the group process, and the expectations placed on them. These initial preparatory meetings also provide an opportunity for both the counselor and the potential group member to get to know one another.

Berne held the belief that almost any individual could participate in a group. He suggested that only on rare occasions should anyone be excluded from the group process. Even then it should be done only after the counselor has carefully examined the motives for the exclusion. This belief was based on his findings that TA could be effective with all types of participants and individual problems. A word of caution is added here by the current authors: a group counselor must be aware of his or her own limitations, and some of these limitations will preclude the counselor from working with the vast array of clients with which Berne worked. Such being the case, most group counselors should carefully consider and evaluate perspective members for any group.

The Group Structure   TA groups are seen as having a simple structure composed of an external boundary that separates the group from other individuals and an internal boundary that separates the counselor from the group members. The external boundary is what separates the group members from outside influences, but it is not always as complete as it may seem. Generally, any member of a group is subject to forces, both personal and social, which are external to the group but which have direct influence on the feelings and behavior of the individual within the group. The more cohesive the group becomes, however, the stronger the external boundary becomes and the less subject the individual is to external forces.

The internal boundary clearly separates the counselor from the members. The leader can never fully become a member; to try to accomplish that task would be to give up some leadership responsibilities. The group leader, according to Berne (1966), behaves in two ways within this structure. When acting as a group leader, he or she is engaged in transactions with group members directly related to the goals of counseling. In the second role, he or she is acting as an internal apparatus of the group by keeping internal order. This second function is similar to what other approaches would refer to as facilitating group process behavior, and while it is important in TA groups, it is secondary to the counselor's role in Transactional Analysis.

Within the internal structure of the group, there may also be subgroups. This is often the case in family and marriage counseling. In such circumstances, the group leader must be keenly aware of whether he or she is transacting with an individual member of the total group or a representative of a subgroup. Non-awareness of the subgroup dynamics can cause severe damage to the group process.

Group Dynamics   The process of a TA group centers around the major and minor internal boundaries where transactions take place within the group. Figure

6 illustrates the types of boundaries that might be expected in a normal TA group. Any transaction that takes place between the counselor and one of the members is considered a major transaction. Transactions between members are considered minor transactions. Through the use of a diagram, such as represented by Figure 6, it is possible to examine the total group process. In a fully functioning group, all individuals should be involved in both major and minor transactions. If the transaction patterns indicate that individuals are not taking part in one or both types of transactions, then the group is not functioning as it should. For example, if the subgroup represented by members Paige and Scott only interacts with the counselor and does not enter into minor transactions with other members, then the group process is not operating at optimum levels.

Figure 6   Group Structure (adapted from Berne, 1966)

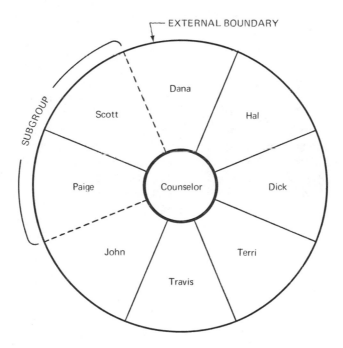

It is graphically clear from the diagram and from Berne's (1966) distinction between what are major and minor transactions that he believed that the TA group process should be leader-centered. Berne appeared to place more emphasis on the transactions between leader and member and less emphasis on the member-member interactions. Steiner (1974), however, places more emphasis on the transactions between group members. "In effective group work the relationships that are highlighted are the relationships between the group members rather than the relationships between the group members and leader; in Transactional Analysis, the leader is an advisor who tends to stay out of the interactions (Steiner, 1974, p. 229)." The safest conclusion from this discussion is that all transactions within the group are important, whether they are leader-member or member-member transactions. Member-member transactions provide important data for the analysis of the participants' means for receiving necessary strokes and for the determination of the ways they go about maintaining their life positions. While leader-member transactions may provide similar data, they also provide the leader an opportunity to share perceptions of an individual member's behavior or to make an analysis of what is really going on in the transactions between members. This is extremely important in the TA group process and is the reason why the leader is the key to success in any TA group.

The TA Group Leader

It is expected that a group leader of Transactional Analysis will be fully aware of the dynamics of group interaction. In TA terms, however, he or she is much more than a facilitator of the group process. She or he is, in effect, the leader and in no way can ever hope to become one of the group members. In short, the leader has a function to perform that is different from that of members. Given this key position within the group, there is a danger that a group leader will attempt to fulfill the role of rescuer. Steiner (1974) believes that every helping situation has the potential for leading individuals into the roles of rescuer and victim. "The role of rescuer is a role in which one person, in a one-up position, denies to, or diminishes in another person, the victim, the power of helping himself by accepting a request for help without making demands for equal participation or by imposing help without a request for it (p. 240)." A good group leader avoids accepting the role of rescuer by seeing the group members "as complete human beings capable of taking power over their lives (Steiner, 1974, p. 237)." Thus, given that the group leader has an in-depth knowledge of group dynamics and of the principles of Transactional Analysis, the most important ingredient for group leader effectiveness is the belief in the capacity of the group members to adopt an "I'm OK" life position and to develop appropriate means for receiving their necessary strokes.

Leader Preparation The first and foremost prerequisite for a TA group leader is being skilled in the analysis of ego states, transactions, games, and scripts. It is perhaps not so obvious that a leader must be able to be himself or herself in the group situation. While it is expected that the leader is the individual within the group who possesses certain skills that will help others, these skills are not to be applied mechanically. As a contractual approach to group counseling, TA holds that the group leader and the members are equal partners in the experience. Furthermore, at all times in the process, the group members have the right to know and understand whatever the group leader knows about them. Thus, the group leader is expected to interact with the members on an open basis, sharing his or her perceptions of their behavior. In essence, while the counselor is the leader, he or she is anything but a mysterious figure who hides self, feelings, and knowledges from the group members.

To be this kind of leader, the counselor must have gone through a program which helped develop an understanding of his or her own ego states and own life script. Leaders must have an understanding of their own motivations and behaviors. They must be able to recognize their Parent, Adult, and Child so that they can tell from which of those ego states they are operating at any point in time during the group process. To put it simply, TA group leaders must have a complete understanding of themselves from a TA perspective.

Initial Leader Behaviors   Early behaviors of the TA group counselor are little different from other approaches if the group participants have completed an introduction to the concepts of Transactional Analysis. If, however, the group participants have not been introduced to the concepts of Transactional Analysis, the TA group counselor will often spend from one to three sessions giving the participants an introduction to these concepts. Given this didactic experience, the TA group leader is then ready to proceed with the actual process of group counseling. In the initial stages, the key to success is the counselor's ability to listen to and observe the participants. Good observational skills are far more important than any particular technique. "Any well-read student or properly programmed computer can make correct interpretations, given properly weighted findings; the real skill lies in collecting and evaluating data (Berne, 1966, p. 66)." The group counselor must be attuned to both the verbal and nonverbal messages being communicated by members through a sense of each group member's ego states, transactions, games, and scripts.

It is also important, particularly in the early stages, for the counselor to demonstrate commitment to the process—a belief that the group members and counselor are there for a purpose and that he or she will do his utmost to let nothing interfere with that process. This calls for the counselor to convey to the group participants a strong belief in their capacity to resolve their difficulties. By such behavior, the counselor must also indicate quickly to the group that side trips into nonmeaningful conversations of a purely social nature will not be tolerated. The counselor can convey to the participants the importance of the group time, not only through words, but by establishing set meeting times and length for meetings and holding to those established times.

Techniques of Leadership   Beyond the initial behavior of the group leader, there are four classifications of counselor behaviors that are important in TA groups: protection, permission, potency, and operations. The first three of these characteristics are related directly to the establishment of the required atmosphere in a productive TA group, while the last classification is more directly concerned with specific counselor behaviors.

Protection   The TA group counselor must offer each client adequate protection from physical and psychological harm. "An offer of protection implies that the therapist is qualified and willing to effect cure, and that he will be available if or when needed throughout the course of treatment (Wollams, Brown, and Huige,

1977, p. 522).'' Providing supportive statements from the Parent of the counselor to the Child of the group member(s) is protection. When a group member is about to give up a lifelong game, change a script, or in some way make some change in behavior, there is bound to be some anxiety. The behavior about to be given up has provided some strokes to the individual, and to give that up for an untried behavior is threatening. In these instances the counselor must convey to the individual the feeling that the group is a safe environment for the individual to try the new behavior. In effect, the counselor assures the group member that he or she will not get punished for the new behavior. Group members must feel the presence of this protection or they will never try new behaviors. In this instance the counselor acts as a Parent providing support to the Child in a time of crisis.

Permission Individuals who are experiencing difficulty are, at least in part, still behaving on the basis of injunctions placed by their parents. "Since the client arrived at his script decisions under pressure of parental injunctions and since he continues to respond to the pressure of his Parent ego state, permission to change from a new Parent source is very useful and perhaps even necessary (Wollams, Brown, and Huige, 1977, p. 522).'' Permissions are given in four areas: (1) to use the group time effectively; (2) to experience all ego states; (3) to not play games; and (4) to overcome parental injunctions (Dusay and Steiner, 1971).

1. The counselor gives the group members permission to use their group time effectively by not allowing them to utilize time-structuring procedures that are nonproductive. Earlier in this chapter, ways in which people attempt to structure time were discussed, and these same procedures are attempted in groups. While time structuring such as pastimes and games can lead to group members' understanding of themselves, the counselor needs to focus the group as much as possible on work activity that involves Adult to Adult transactions. If, for example, a group member continually uses the Child, the counselor may need to be very directive in trying to get the group member to use the Adult. A statement such as "That is what your Child is feeling, but what does your Adult think?" is one example of an attempt to structure time effectively by the counselor.

2. The counselor also gives permission for the group members to experience all their ego states. Permission to use the Adult is facilitated by the use of a chalkboard. The presence of a chalkboard indicates that any of the members or the leader can at any time diagram the transactions that are occurring in the group. In effect, this means that all transactions, whether from Parent to Child, Child to Child, and so forth, can be subjected to Adult analysis. A chalkboard forces thinking, which is an Adult activity. Permission is also given to experience the Child. An individual who has been taught not to trust the feelings from his or her Natural Child often must be encouraged by the counselor to let these feelings out. This sometimes can be accomplished by role playing of situations or by asking the individual to imagine being a child again and act out what he or she is feeling as a Child.

Actual permission to use a Parent is generally not necessary, since most individuals experiencing difficulty have a highly developed Parent.

3. Permission not to play games is given by the counselor by actually interrupting games. When two or more members of a group continually engage in a particular game, the counselor diagnoses the game being played by the members and then gives the other members permission not to play that game with the individuals in question. In this way, the game players no longer receive the strokes that were the payoff for the game and the game loses its importance.

4. Most often injunctions given by the group members' Parents are the reasons for the adoption of a maladaptive life script. The counselor must give each group member the permission to overcome these injunctions. Dusay and Steiner (1971) use the example of an alcoholic who is under an injunction to drink. The permission from the counselor to overcome this injunction has two parts: first, a Parent (counselor) to Child (group member) statement: "Do not drink"; second, an Adult to Adult transaction which rationally examines the reasons for not drinking. Both transactions must occur or the permission will not be accepted. A group member who cannot use the Adult will not understand why he or she should not drink, and if the counselor only uses the Parent command, the Child of the member may merely rebel at the command.

Wollams, Brown, and Huige (1977) suggest that the most powerful permissions are permissions that are simultaneously given from all three ego states of the counselor.

Potency   The use of the appropriate counseling technique in given situations is called potency. The TA group leader must recognize that the maladaptive life script of an individual was formed because of very powerful injunctions applied by the parents. To counter these very powerful injunctions, the TA group leader must use his or her skills in a maximally effective and powerful fashion. This means that the counselor times interventions so that they are maximally effective, keeping in mind what the group members are ready and able to handle. The degree of potency of a counselor is directly related to his or her competence in diagnosing ego states, transactions, and games and to the ability to use these diagnostic skills at the appropriate time in the group process. For example, it is not always appropriate to expose the game a group member may be playing. If the game is taken away before the group participant is ready, or if the counselor tries to enter an Adult-Adult transaction before the individual can energize the Adult, the group member may pull completely into a shell. The ultimate test of counseling potency is the sweeping away of the client's parental injunctions (Dusay and Steiner, 1971).

Operations   These are rather specific techniques used by TA group leaders. The following list of eight such techniques is not all-inclusive, but it does include those found useful by Berne (1966) in conducting Transactional Analysis.

1. Interrogation.   This is the process by which the counselor questions the group members in such a way as to obtain an Adult response. It is specifically used with members who have difficulty using their Adult and to clarify material presented. Its overuse must be avoided or the group interaction will be limited to the leader's asking questions which are answered by group members.

2. Specification.   When the counselor and the group member can clearly identify some behavior, it is placed in its appropriate category. This only occurs in Adult-Adult transactions between counselor and group member. For example, both may agree that a certain statement made by the group member came from the Adapted Child. This process is particularly useful in helping group members understand the operations of their three ego states.

3. Confrontation.   The counselor uses confrontation to point out inconsistencies in group members' behaviors. It is particularly useful for pointing out discrepancies between verbal expressions by group members and their nonverbal behavior.

4. Explanation.   This operation is best thought of as a teaching behavior on the part of the counselor. It is a procedure whereby the Adult of the counselor explains to the Adult of the group member either why the member has been doing something or what the member has been doing. If the counselor receives an Adult response, then the explanation has been accepted.

5. Illustration.   The counselor uses illustrations to clarify material for the Adult of a group member, while at the same time trying to break some tension in the group by using humor that pleases the Child. Such a procedure indicates to the group that the use of both the Adult and the Child is appropriate in certain situations.

6. Confirmation.   Generally, after the first time a group member is confronted with a certain behavior, the behavior will disappear for a while but then will return. Confirmation is an attempt by the counselor to help the individual recognize how the behavior has reappeared. This points out to the group member that he or she has not yet really given up the particular behavior and needs to work harder at getting rid of it.

7. Interpretation.   When the Child of a group member attempts to distort a situation, the counselor needs to interpret this behavior to the member. As used in TA, interpretation takes a form very similar to more traditional analytic procedures. It is an attempt to help the group members see the reasons behind their behavior. To be successful the interpretation must come from the Adult of the counselor and be received by the Adult of the group member.

8. Crystallization. In this last step in the process, the counselor presents to the group member the fact that the member is now ready to quit playing the game in which she or he has been involved.

As was pointed out earlier, the preceding list is not all-inclusive. Counselors may also use operational techniques that they feel have been effective for them. It is vital, however, that the counselor in some manner provide protection to the group members and give them permission to experience and grow. Success will also depend on the counselor's relative potency in diagnosing ego states, transactions, games, and scripts and, finally, in the timing of interventions to maximize effectiveness. All of these procedures are designed to help the group members achieve both the general objectives of Transactional Analysis and their individual specific objectives.

In addition to the techniques outlined by Berne, two followers of Berne have developed procedures that are useful in helping the counselor and the clients develop an understanding of ego states and of the games that they are playing. These two procedures are referred to as Ego Grams and the Karpman Triangle.

Ego Grams   "The ego gram was created in order to symbolize the amount of energy that a person exudes in each of his or her ego states at any time. After considering his or her ego gram, a person becomes clear about what he or she wants to change, raise, lower, or develop in certain ego states (Dusay, 1977, p. 40)." The ego gram concept is based on the belief that each individual tends to spend differing amounts of time and energy in different ego states. Thus, the ego gram as shown in Figure 7 gives an individual profile.

Figure 7 Ego Gram

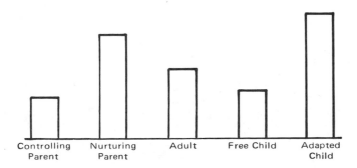

Dusay, the developer of the ego gram, believes that the amount of energy possessed by any one individual is a constant. Thus, if a person reduces energy from one ego state, then there is more energy available for a second ego state.

Through the ego gram process, for example, a client may see that he or she is spending far more time and energy in the controlling Parent ego state than in the Adult. Having perceived this situation, the client can then choose to begin the process of moving energy from the controlling Parent ego state to the Adult. Dusay (1977) states that "the ego gram is highly advantageous when it is constructed in groups, in that it is a valid measurement of how an individual's energies line up. There is usually 80 to 90 percent agreement about the way a person's ego gram lines up when an informed group is constructing it (1977, p. 40)." It is apparent that the ego gram can be a useful tool for the group counselor to help participants understand their own ego state structure. It is obvious that in order to use this procedure, the counselor must have a thorough knowledge of Transactional Analysis such that an accurate ego gram can be constructed from an observation of the client's behavior.

The Karpman Triangle   The Karpman Triangle is a useful procedure for developing an understanding of games. The Karpman Triangle is illustrated in Figure 8. The triangle is based on the assumption that individuals who play games are assuming one of three roles: persecutor, rescuer, or victim. While individuals who play games know all the roles and may move from one role to another as the game progresses, most individuals have a favorite role that they wish to fulfill (Wollams, Brown, and Huige, 1977). The persecutor role is most often filled by an individual who feels that he or she is better than anyone else. The rescuer role is played by individuals who feel they know more than someone else, and the victim role is played by someone who wishes to feel helpless. Knowing that these are the three basic roles found in most games, the counselors can use the triangle to help analyze a game being played by group members. As was the case with ego grams, the Karpman Triangle should be utilized only by those individuals who have had extensive training in Transactional Analysis.

Figure 8   Karpman Triangle

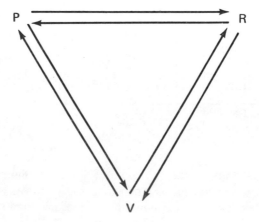

P   R

V

Levels of Counseling

Berne (1966) states that the objective of TA in groups is to help each participant move through a progression of stages. Such a process implies that an individual comes to counseling in order to reorient or restructure his or her entire life-style or goals. Quite clearly, not all persons who come to the group situation have a desire to reorient their entire lives; often they simply may be interested in and need work at the structural level. Hence, counselors need to be aware of both the levels and the expected outcomes of each of the four levels of counseling.

The Level of Structural Analysis Each individual has the capacity to oper- ate from three distinct ego states: Parent, Adult, and Child. In normal functioning an individual has the capacity to move from one ego state to another as the situation warrants. As noted in the earlier discussion on maladaptive development, however, individuals often suffer from the fact that their ego boundaries are either too loosely or too rigidly defined. In the first instance the individual cannot maintain an ego state; in the second instance one or more ego states are nonoperable because they are excluded. It often happens, too, that an ego state, usually the Adult, is contaminated by material from the Parent or the Child. This contamination keeps the Adult from functioning at optimum levels.

Structural analysis is the process of trying to help the individual examine the structure of his or her ego states. The goal is to help the individual establish the predominance of reality-tested ego states that are free from contamination by material from the past (Berne, 1966). This requires the counselor to be aware of the behavioral characteristics of each ego state and how its malfunctioning is manifested. In the group setting an individual who constantly shifts ego states, regardless of the inappropriateness of the behavior, is most probably suffering weak ego boundaries. Exclusion is manifested by a group member who constantly maintains a particular ego state regardless of the situation. The exclusion is an attempt to deny the existence of a particular ego state. The constant Parent, for example, is most often attempting to deny the existence of the Child.

Contamination of an ego state can be seen in prejudiced attitudes and in delusions (Berne, 1961). In the case of prejudice or unwarranted beliefs, the contamination involves material from the Parent intruding into the Adult; in the case of delusions it is generally material from the Child intruding into the Adult. In each case the goal of counseling at the structural level is, first, to help the individual recognize the attitudes and behaviors from each ego state through the use of the organizational techniques discussed earlier. After having either decontaminated or established the boundaries, the counselor then strives to have the individual place his or her Adult in overall charge of functioning.

The Level of Transactional Analysis This level is concerned with determin- ing the nature of transactions that individuals enter into. At this level the counselor must be able to identify from which ego state a group member is communicating either to the counselor or to another member. The reader will recall from the earlier discussion of transactions between ego states that these transactions can take three forms: complementary, crossed, and ulterior. Complementary transactions are those in which the response is appropriate to the stimulus. A crossed transaction occurs when the response is not appropriate to the stimulus, and ulterior transactions are ones in which both overt and covert messages are communicated.

In the group situation the counselor must help members examine the nature of their transactions. Most often this process is facilitated by the use of a chalkboard when communication has broken down (crossed transaction) or when the counselor feels she or he has identified an ulterior transaction. Through the use of the chalkboard, the counselor and then group members can diagram the transactions that have taken place. After diagramming the transaction, the group can then process the material produced. This step is extremely important, particularly if the group is to progress to the next level—game analysis. For it is only when group members can analyze many of their own transactions that they can enter into the stage of game analysis. This is not to say that this level does not have some benefits in and of itself. Often the analysis of transactions provides individuals with valuable skills which can help them improve their interpersonal interactions. Being aware of the nature of transactions enables an individual to discard communication behaviors that are ineffective and concentrate on developing more productive transaction patterns. Such a process may be particularly helpful for teachers, parents, families, and marriage partners.

The Level of Game Analysis   Games are a series of ulterior transactions designed to lead to a concealed but well-defined payoff (Berne, 1966). Readers who desire a full discussion of games should read Berne's *Games People Play* (1964). Individuals who have found little success in structuring their time in more productive ways rely heavily on games to receive the strokes they need. The difficulty is that such behaviors are false and keep the individual from interacting with the world in a meaningful fashion.

Beyond the ability to assess ego states and the nature of transactions, this level of counseling requires the counselor to have the ability to determine the payoff that the individual receives from the games. Because ulterior or covert messages are involved, this determination takes careful observation and listening by the counselor. Once the payoff has been determined, the counselor can use the operational techniques of confrontation, confirmation, illustration, and, finally, crystallization to help the client see the game and then to give the client permission to give it up. Often this permission involves the other group members in that they are instructed not to play the game with their fellow group member. Since the game no longer has a payoff, the group member is forced to develop a new way of interacting.

The Level of Script Analysis   This stage of counseling may be achieved by only the most advanced groups (Berne, 1966). The life script is the life plan of the individual and is based on his or her basic life decision. In persons who are experiencing difficulty, this decision was usually made in the form of an acceptance of one of the "I'm not OK" positions. Because these decisions are unconscious, they are very difficult to bring to light, and most counseling groups would not venture into this area. If entered into at all, it should only be after the progression through the other three levels, and the counselor must be prepared to provide the protection needed when a group member in effect says, "My whole way of life is a mistake." At this point depression with all its manifestations is at its height in an individual. Because of this, the current authors recommend that only a highly trained professional enter this level of counseling.

SUMMARY

As can be seen in this brief overview of Transactional Analysis, it is by and large a leader-oriented approach which, at least in part, has grown out of analytic thought. TA is somewhat unique in that it places equal importance on insight and actual behavior change. As the years progress, more and more emphasis is being placed on the group process. In many ways its emphasis on behavior exhibited in the group is very similar to a Gestalt therapeutic approach.

As with most approaches discussed in this text, the reader who is interested in pursuing Transactional Analysis in groups is urged to do further reading in the area. In addition to the books listed in the reference section of this chapter, the reader is encouraged to examine the *Transactional Analysis Journal.* Specific training in Transactional Analysis is offered by many TA institutes or societies throughout the country and around the world.

References

Barnes, G. (Ed.) *Transactional analysis after Eric Berne: Teachings and practices in three TA schools.* New York: Harper's College Press, 1977.

Berne, E. *Games people play.* New York: Grove Press, 1964.

Berne, E. *Principles of group treatment.* New York: Oxford University Press, 1966.

Berne, E. *What do you say after you say hello?* New York: Bantam, 1973.

Dusay, J. The evolution of transactional analysis. In G. Barnes (Ed.), *Transactional analysis after Eric Berne: Teachings and practices in three TA schools.* New York: Harper's College Press, 1977, 32–52.

Dusay, J., and C. Steiner. Transactional analysis in groups. In H. I. Kaplan and B. J. Sadock (Eds.), *Comprehensive group psychotherapy.* Baltimore: Williams & Wilkins, 1971, 198–240.

Falzett, B., and J. Maxwell. *O. K. childing and parenting.* El Paso, TX: Transactional Analysis Institute of El Paso, 1974.

Harris, T. A. *I'm OK, you're OK: A practical guide to transactional analysis.* New York: Harper & Row, 1969.

Holland, G. Transactional analysis. In R. Corsini (Ed.), *Current psychotherapies.* Itasca, IL: Peacock Publishers, 1973, 353–99.

James, M. *Techniques in transactional analysis for psychotherapists and counselors.* Reading, MA: Addison-Wesley, 1977.

James, M., and D. Jongeward. *Born to win: Transactional analysis with Gestalt experiments.* Reading, MA: Addison-Wesley, 1971.

Kambly, A. *An introduction to transactional analysis made simple.* Ann Arbor, MI: The University Center, 1971.

Steiner, C. *Scripts people live.* New York: Grove Press, 1974.

Wollams, S., M. Brown, and K. Huige. What transactional analysts want their clients to know. In G. Barnes (Ed.), *Transactional analysis after Eric Berne: Teachings and practices in three TA schools.* New York: Harper's College Press, 1977, 487–526.

9

Behavioral Counseling in Groups

Behavioral psychology has a long history, but its extensive use in the process of group counseling is a phenomenon of the last two decades. Individuals who adhere to a behavioral approach to group counseling believe that behaviors for which people seek counseling are learned behaviors, and that the most effective means of changing behavior is through the utilization of the principles of learning (Heckel and Salzberg, 1976). Franks (1969) states that the behavioral approach to counseling is a matter of response modification involving the application of some type of learning theory. He defines behavioral counseling as the beneficial modification of behavior in accordance with experimentally validated principles of learning and the biophysical properties of the individual. While this early definition of behavioral counseling was appropriate in 1969, it is now much too narrow to encompass all the techniques utilized by a behavioral counselor. Behavioral counseling is now "conceptualized as a teaching-learning process in which counselors, using a variety of learning techniques, help clients learn the behaviors necessary for the solution of their problems. A counselor, teacher, or parent working with clients who wish to change their behavior is not limited to any one technique. Indeed, any procedure or combination of procedures which have been shown to be effective in helping others may be used (Hosford and deVisser, 1974, p. 9)." Hence, the behavioral group counselor is viewed as a special kind of learning specialist (Krumboltz, 1966), even though behavioral approaches to group counseling have gone beyond the basic principles of learning. Their adherence to basing their techniques on empirical evidence from the behavioral sciences remains central to the approach.

A key difference between a behavioral approach to group counseling and most other approaches is its emphasis on behavioral outcomes. Most approaches to group counseling seek to clear up the client problem through the process of helping the client gain insight. These insight-oriented approaches attempt to bypass the symptom and to focus on the internal mechanisms of the individual. The behavioral counselor functions as though the symptom were the difficulty and tries to remove it. The insight-oriented counselor wants to enable clients to understand the character of their symptoms and the relationship to their lives so that they can exercise better control over both. The behavioral counselor will try more directly to eliminate the undesired behavior so the client will feel better regardless of whether or not the client understands. Simply stated, insight-oriented approaches believe that the client must develop self-understanding before behavioral change can take place. The behavioral counselor, however, believes that understanding is not necessary for behavioral change to occur. This is not to say that modern behavioral counselors believe that there is no place for understanding. They simply believe that changes in behavior can occur prior to self-understanding and indeed the changes in behavior may facilitate the clients' developing a better understanding of themselves and their own behavior.

It is indeed unfortunate that many critics of behavioral approaches to counseling still base their criticism on the writings of such individuals as Skinner. Many of these critics base their arguments on the now classic debate in 1956 between Carl Rogers and B. F. Skinner. During that debate Skinner argued that the environment of the individual was the sole determiner of the individual's behavior. Rogers argued that individuals were the sole determiners of their own behavior. Clearly, these two individuals were at opposite ends of the continuum between viewing people as reactive beings and as actors. It is worth noting that the approaches represented by both men have moved closer to a middle ground over the last twenty years. Increasingly one hears such individuals as Carkhuff, Truax, and others calling for more behavioral-change techniques in counseling. At the other extreme, one also hears from the behaviorists more and more emphasis on the internal feelings of individuals. The development of self-management procedures and the techniques of covert reinforcement are but two examples of behavioral techniques that have as a focus the internal feelings of individuals.

Despite this move away from the extreme position of Skinner and the early behaviorists, the behavioral approach to counseling still relies on a basic assumption that most problems encountered by individuals are problems in learning. They also place a heavy emphasis on a systematic approach to the process of counseling. Most modern behavioral counselors would agree with Hosford and deVisser's definition of behavioral counseling as "a learning process in which counselors employ a systematic procedure to help clients accomplish a particular change in behavior (1974, p. 15)." Most behavioral theorists would also accept the six characteristics of behavioral counseling outlined by Hosford and deVisser. These are:

1. Behavioral counseling is a planned, systematic process.

2. Human problems are generally the result of deficits in learning or inaccurate learning, and therefore counseling is viewed as a teaching-learning process.

3. The goal of counseling is to help the client make specific changes in behavior desired by the client.

4. The one-to-one interaction between counselor and client is only one way to bring about changes in behavior. The counselor must be able to utilize procedures in the client's environment, such as working with parents, teachers, and peers in order to facilitate client improvement.

5. No one set of techniques or procedures is appropriate for every client. Different clients with different problems call for different procedures.

6. A key element to the behavioral approach is the scientific method. This includes problem identification, systematic observation of the client, careful control, the careful gathering of data, and the replication of results when possible.

These six steps are the general framework for a behavioral approach to counseling. While it is impossible here to describe all the techniques and beliefs of those who call themselves behaviorists, this chapter will focus on the central concepts and techniques that will flesh out the framework just presented as it applies to group counseling. Readers interested in pursuing the field of behavioral counseling in depth are encouraged to read the works of such individuals as Ullman and Krasner (1965), Bandura (1969), Lazarus (1972), Wolpe (1959), Krumboltz and Thoreson (1969), Mahoney and Thoreson (1974), and Krumboltz and Thoreson (1976). Of particular interest to those interested in pursuing behavioral approaches in the context of the group are publications by Rose (1977), Harris (1977), and Heckel and Salzberg (1976).

The central concepts utilized by most modern behavioral counselors are still founded in social learning theory. Hence, the concept of personality development presented in this chapter is in accordance with that position. Consistent with that position, the process of learning maladaptive or unacceptable behavior patterns is then explored. To understand more fully the learning of behavioral patterns that make up the personality, some general assumptions and principles of learning are examined. These represent the foundation upon which the process of behavioral counseling is founded—a foundation that is appropriate for groups as well as for individual counseling. Later, the process of behavioral counseling is described, including initial interviews with the client, establishing behavioral goals, and establishing strategies of behavioral modifications. Several strategies that are appropriate for group counseling are presented, with examples selected from the research literature.

THE PRINCIPLES OF LEARNING

Prior to examining the behavioral position in relation to the development of personality, both normal and abnormal, it is necessary to examine the basic principles of learning that underlie those processes. As noted earlier, the individual's personality or behavior pattern is learned through interaction with other people. How does this learning actually occur? What are the variables in the process of learning and how can they be examined to better understand the complex learning of behavior? There is no single theory that covers all learning phenomena. No one theory has been developed and experimentally supported to handle the social, perceptual, verbal, and interpersonal processes. However, there are some assumptions about human behavior that are shared to a large extent by all learning approaches and that form the bases of the behavioral approach to personality development and to counseling.

Kanfer and Phillips (1970) present a procedure for analyzing the learning process which provides a useful framework for understanding the basic principles of learning. For convenience of analysis, the continuous behavior of a person can be partitioned into segments and studied without losing the key elements of the behavior and the environmental conditions. Ordering of events is essential for uniform observation and classification of independent and dependent variables. The essential components for analysis of behavior include stimuli (S), the biological condition of the organism (O), response repertoire (R), and the consequence of the behavior for the organism's environment or for self (C).

An understanding of the behavioral process requires specification of each of the elements and their interaction with each other. This is dependent upon a detailed analysis of each element that can affect the learning and execution of the act, and a summarizing of all the conditions acting at the time of the response that may have relevance to the probability of the response occuring.

The Organism

It is a misunderstanding to believe that behaviorists place no significance on the biological factors in human behavior. Although a few psychologists believe that biological factors influence only a few cases of behavioral problems, most behaviorists recognize that an interaction exists between the biological variables and social learning conditions. In addition to damage to or the malfunction of biological systems, particularly the brain, other biological problems play a significant role in determining behavior. "Schizophrenia, alcohol and drug addictions, sexual deviations, and antisocial behavior have been particularly singled out for attention of investigators holding the biogenetic hypotheses of behavior deviation (Kanfer and Phillips, 1970, p. 65)."

Other commonly encountered conditions that need to be observed in behavior patterns include various organic diseases, nutritional deficiencies, age, genetically determined characteristics, and physical deformities. These variables, which influence the parameters of an individual's response to environmental stimuli, may influence one's ability to change responses or one's reactions to the consequences of one's behavior. An individual's anatomical structures, physical capacities, and emotional responsiveness influence the response system and the individual's attempts to change behavior.

Drug-induced inhibition or acceleration of physiological variables has been utilized to affect complex behavior patterns. Such procedures have been effective in influencing the behavior patterns of hyperactive children in school. This type of change in the child's behavior may lead other people to respond more favorably to the child, thereby creating a more conducive environment for learning more adequate behaviors.

The Response

A person's responses may be classified into two categories: respondent or unlearned behaviors, and operant or learned behaviors. Respondent behavior is frequently considered reflexive, since it occurs automatically in response to a specific stimulus, like shedding tears in response to peeling onions. Respondent behavior is always elicited automatically to a specific stimulus and is not under voluntary control of the person. The capacity of the person to make this type of response is dependent upon the innate equipment of the organism. Respondent behavior formed the basis of classical conditioning theory developed by Pavlov. Classical conditioning makes use of the fact that some events in an individual's environment are related to certain automatic muscle responses (Michael and Myerson, 1962). In a classic study conducted by Watson and Rayner (1921), it was demonstrated that a fear response could be elicited by a previously neutral response when it was paired often enough with an aversive stimulus. In this situation the original respondent behavior generated by an aversive stimulus is now produced by a previously neutral stimulus. The previously neutral stimulus is now referred to as a conditioned stimulus and the response which it produces is a conditioned response.

The type of response that is under voluntary control is called an operant behavior. It is influenced by the reinforcing events or consequences that follow its occurrences. Operant responses include all behaviors that "operate on" the outside environment. Almost any movement under the voluntary control of an individual may be classified as an operant response, such as picking up a book, writing a letter, or talking with a friend. Because human behavior is much less instinct control, human beings exhibit more operant behavior than respondent behavior; therefore operant responses and learning assume a more significant role in the development of human behavior.

Consequences

The basic principles of operant behavior are outlined by B. F. Skinner (1938). Skinner postulated that if a behavior were followed by some event in the individual's environment that brought satisfaction to the individual, then the probability that the behavior would occur in the future would be increased. In other words, operant behavior is influenced by the reinforcing conditions or consequences that follow it. The consequences of a response that increases the probability of its reoccurrence are referred to as reinforcers. A reinforcer can be material, such as something edible, or social, like a smile, if it increases the probability that the response it follows will be emitted again. A response is strengthened by an increase in the frequency of its appearance, and when the consequences that follow a response have increased the frequency of the response, conditioning has occurred.

Primary and Secondary Reinforcement Primary reinforcers are stimuli that are rewarding because they satisfy basic biological needs such as food, water, air, and sexual stimulation. These are called primary reinforcers because the reinforcing properties of the stimuli do not have to be learned. Beyond early childhood, however, very few of the reinforcements an individual receives are classified as primary reinforcements. Through the developmental process each of us learns that other stimuli are reinforcing. Examples of very potent secondary reinforcers for most individuals are praise, high grades, and money. These stimuli do not satisfy a biological need and are, therefore, considered secondary or learned reinforcers. In most cases, to make a reinforcing stimulus out of a previously nonreinforcing, or neutral, stimulus, it is necessary only that obtaining a more primary reinforcement is contingent upon having obtained the neutral stimulus— such as using money to buy food. By this process the previously neutral stimulus becomes learned or conditioned, and it in turn can be used as a backup reinforcer for making other neutral stimuli learned reinforcements. It is indeed unfortunate that the word secondary is used to describe reinforcers such as praise, for from early childhood on most behavior is directed toward secondary reinforcers.

Schedules of Reinforcement When or how often a correct response is reinforced is called the schedule of reinforcement. Continuous reinforcement is the schedule used when a reinforcement is given each time the correct response occurs. Continuous reinforcement is an extremely efficient procedure for developing new behaviors; therefore, in beginning to learn a new behavior, continuous reinforcement of a correct response or an approximation of the response is the preferred mode of reinforcement.

Continuous reinforcement is not, however, the best procedure for maintaining a response once it has been developed. To maintain a response so that it will resist extinction, one or more of several types of intermittent reinforcement schedules may be used. Intermittent schedules do not deliver reinforcement after each correct response, but only after some of the correct responses. There are two basic types of intermittent schedules: ratio and interval.

A ratio reinforcement schedule occurs when a reinforcement is made contingent upon a certain number of correct responses, irrespective of the time taken to perform these responses. A fixed ratio schedule is used as a reinforcement following a fixed number of correct responses, while a variable ratio is used after a variable number of correct responses. In contrast to ratio schedules, interval schedules deliver reinforcement on the basis of time elapsed since the last reinforcement, irrespective of the number of responses. With a fixed interval schedule, the first correct response following a specified period of time is reinforced, while the variable interval schedule delivers a reinforcement following the performance of the next correct response, following the passage of a specific period of time.

Positive and Negative Reinforcement Reinforcements may be classified as either positive or negative according to the state of the individual after the reinforcement has been employed. "The operation of presenting a positive reinforcer contingent upon a response is called positive reinforcement. The operation of removing an aversive stimulus contingent upon a response is called negative reinforcement (Michael and Myerson, 1962, p. 4)." To put it another way, in positive reinforcement the response is strengthened by the addition of something, while in negative reinforcement the response is strengthened because something is removed or withdrawn. Contrary to popular belief, negative reinforcement is not the same as punishment. Negative reinforcement is the removal of an aversive stimulus as a consequence of performing the response, while punishment is the presentation of an aversive stimulus as a consequence of the behavior. Negative reinforcement can be effective, but punishment is generally not effective over long periods of time.

Putting It Together

How do the laws of learning just outlined act together to cause the formation of complex behavior patterns in individuals? The complex behavior is shaped through a number of successive approximations. During each of these approximations, certain behaviors are reinforced and others are not. The general processes of generalization, discrimination, extinction, and shaping are involved in this process.

Generalization Behavior that is learned in one stimulus situation tends to be repeated in similar situations. The spreading or transfer of a learned response from one stimulus to another similar stimulus is called generalization. The more similar the two stimulus situations, the more likely the response is to be repeated. Although the process of generalization is beneficial in a learning process, it may have some disadvantages in some situations. For example, to the extent that a fear generalizes to other objects or situations, a person may be inhibited and restrict his or her behavior in exploring unfamiliar situations. A child that is bitten by the neighbor's dog may generalize and come to believe that all dogs will bite. Thus, the child becomes fearful of all dogs. The advantage of generalization is that an individual can take a behavior that has served well in one situation and transfer it to other similar situations with the assurance that this behavior will probably work. This enables an individual to move from one situation to a new but similar situation without having to learn a completely new set of behaviors.

Discrimination While it is very helpful that individuals learn to generalize from one situation to another similar situation, it is quite obvious that individuals also need to develop a capacity for discriminating between similar but different situations. Discrimination is developed through the process of differential reinforcement. In this process the appropriate response to a given stimulus is reinforced, while the inappropriate response is not reinforced. Through this pattern of differential reinforcement, the individual learns to make the correct response only in the presence of the correct stimulus. In effect, the individual learns to tell the difference between two similar but different situations. The level of discriminative ability of an individual depends on how important a particular situation is for that individual. A portrait photographer, for example, must know a great deal about cameras, lighting, and film while the average camera buff may need to know much less. There is no question, however, that the ability to discriminate between situations is an important tool for all individuals.

Extinction   Behavior will occur as long as that behavior receives some form of intermittent reinforcement. Behavior that ceases to be reinforced (either positively or negatively) will eventually disappear. The rate of disappearance of the response is directly proportional to the length of the time that the response has been reinforced on an intermittent basis. Extinction is important in the process of development, for it enables us to eliminate behaviors that are no longer useful. An infant that cries learns that such behavior most often brings some form of reinforcement. As the child grows older, however, crying does not produce the same results. This is true of many behaviors that we learn; they are useful at one developmental stage of our lives but become useless—they do not bring the desired results—in later stages of development.

Shaping   The processes of extinction, generalization, and discrimination interact together and produce shaping. Shaping is the name given to the process of moving from a vague approximation of the desired behavior to the final desired behavior. Many of our complex behaviors, such as riding a bike or driving a car, are a result of the process of shaping. Our initial attempts at riding a bike or driving a car are indeed vague approximations of the final desired behavior. Through the process of differential reinforcement in which correct responses are reinforced and incorrect responses are not, the final desired behavior is achieved. This is the process of shaping.

Higher Order Learning Processes   Laws of learning outlined on the previous pages account for a great many of the behaviors exhibited by human beings. Before examining how all these laws interact in the process of personality development, we need to examine two other basic concepts important in learning theory: mediating responses and imitative learning.

Mediating Responses   One of the clear differences between human beings and other animals is the ability of human beings to delay gratification. For example, we often become hungry at times other than the prescribed time for eating. Most often, through a mental process referred to originally by Dollard and Miller (1950) as "higher mental processes," we are able to delay gratification until the appropriate time. Such is the case in many situations encountered by human beings. Through the utilization of language and other symbols, we are able to recognize the fact that we will receive the desired reinforcement at some time in the future. Thus, we are not forced to seek reinforcement every time a stimulus situation cues us to do so. Homme (1965) refers to these internal mediating responses as covariants. "Covariants are events the laymen call mental. These include thinking, imagining, reflecting, ruminating, relaxing, daydreaming, fantasizing, etc. (p. 502)." However we refer to these internal events, their importance is that they enable us to evaluate the situation and to delay our response until a more appropriate or convenient time.

Imitative Learning   Learning theorists maintain that the process of learning is often shortened in human beings because a large part of human behavior is learned through imitation. Introduction of models for imitation is a vital part of social learning. According to this concept, behavior is learned because a model, having the power to mediate rewards for the individual, exhibits behavior which then becomes paired with positive reinforcement. Such behavior is learned through imitation.

Some of an individual's behavior is learned through a process that does not involve direct reinforcement. This learning is said to take place through a process of vicarious learning. In this process the observer learns a particular response by observing some other individual perform the behavior. Miller and Dollard (1941) called this "matched dependent behavior" and believed that the individual learned the response only if he or she matched the behavior of the model. Mowrer (1960) states that the response of the model could be learned by an observer simply by rewarding the model. In this process it is assumed that the reward given to the model is a vicarious reward for the observer. Bandura (1969) has attempted to formulate a comprehensive theory of observational learning that relates both acquisition and performance of the model to behavior. His theory requires neither that the observer perform overt responses, nor that reinforcement be administered to either the observer or the model. Bandura calls his theory a contiguity-mediational theory. Contiguity between the stimuli and the model's response is regarded as a necessary but not sufficient condition for observational learning. According to Bandura, observational learning requires two representational systems—imaginal and verbal—by which the modeling stimuli are coded for memory representation. These representations function as mediators for subsequent response, retrieval, and reproduction. Apparently "in the course of observation, transitory perceptual phenomena produce relatively enduring, retrievable images of model sequences of behavior. Later, reinstatement of imaginal mediators serve as a guide for reproduction of the matching responses (p. 133)."

This section has attempted to outline many of the basic concepts involved in behavioral theory. Because many of these principles form the basis for techniques used in behavioral counseling, it is important that the reader understand these concepts. Given an understanding of these concepts, we can now turn our attention to how these various principles of learning interact in the development of an individual's personality.

CONCEPT OF PERSONALITY DEVELOPMENT

The basic assumption of a behavioral approach to personality development is that behavior is learned, and an individual's personality develops through maturation and the learning process. While Havighurst is frequently quoted in terms of the developmental task concept, writers seldom present his foundation. Havighurst (1952) stated that the developmental tasks are all learning tasks. "To understand human development, one must understand learning. The human individual learns his way through life (p. 12)." Living is a series of tasks to learn, where learning well brings satisfaction while learning poorly brings unhappiness and social disapproval. The behavior the person learns is a result of interaction with the environment, particularly with meaningful individuals. One does not come into the world as innately good or bad, but neutral, rather like the Lockean notion of a tabula rasa. The manner in which one's personality is developed depends upon interaction with the environment. From a learning theory point of view, men and women are reactive beings. They react to stimuli as they are presented and, as they react, patterns of behavior and, ultimately, personality are formed.

Learning theorists do believe that some behavior is a result of innate characteristics and the interaction of these characteristics with the environment. However, innate characteristics cannot be controlled; hence, attention should be focused on those things that can be controlled or explained, i.e., the observable interaction between the individual and his or her environment.

The concept of personality development presented in this chapter is in accordance with the social learning theory. Consistent with that position, the process of learning maladaptive or unacceptable behavior patterns is then explored. To understand more fully the learning of behavioral patterns that make up the personality, some general assumptions are outlined. These represent the foundation upon which the process of behavioral counseling is founded—a foundation that is appropriate for group as well as individual counseling. Later, the process of behavioral counseling will be described, including initial interviews with the client, establishing behavioral goals, and establishing strategies of behavioral modifications. An individual's behavior is determined by the goals she or he sets and sometimes by goals imposed by society. "An individual responds with those behaviors that he has learned will lead to the greatest satisfaction in a given situation (Rotter, 1964, p. 57)." That is, an individual behaves in ways he or she has learned will lead to the greatest satisfaction. A reward or reinforcement is any action or condition that affects the behavior toward the goal. The individual's motives for behaving are developed through experience, and gradually a set of differentiated motives or needs is built up.

Most needs of an individual are learned. Early goals arise from association with a reinforcement of physiological needs. As individuals mature and interact with their environment, other goals become important. Nonetheless, behavior is always goal-directed, and new goals derive importance from their association with earlier goals. Through this process, a set of differentiated needs gradually develops in the individual, varying from specific to general. The more specific the category of the need, the greater the possibility of predicting and understanding the individual's behavior.

The process may be illustrated by examining the interaction between mother and child. The initial interaction with the mother results in meeting the child's need for food. This satisfaction gradually becomes generalized to the extent that the child receives pleasure simply by being in the presence of its mother. It learns to want attention from its mother, a goal which is separate from the first goal of reducing its feeling of hunger. Through their continuing interaction the child learns that some of its behaviors result in pleasurable attention from its mother, while other behaviors do not. In order to receive pleasurable attention, the child strives to do things that will please its mother and focus its mother's attention on itself. Finally, this process may generalize to the extent that the child behaves in certain ways even though its mother is not present, because the child has learned that its mother would approve of these behaviors and this has become self-satisfying to the child. This illustrates the process of moving from basic physiological needs to secondary learned needs.

Rotter (1964) has outlined three general characteristics of learned needs: need potential, freedom of movement, and need value.

Need potential is the term Rotter uses to describe a set of behaviors that are directed toward meeting a particular need, such as receiving positive feedback from others, and the probability of those behaviors occuring in a given situation. For example, a lawyer may be confronted with a choice of going to the golf course with some friends or of staying in the office late and preparing for an upcoming case. In this situation, the lawyer has the option of responding to either the need to be with friends or the need to prepare an airtight case. If the need to be with friends has a higher need potential than the need to prepare the airtight case, then the behavior of going to the golf course is the one most likely to occur. In most situations, individuals are confronted by such conflicting need situations, and a choice process is required.

The second characteristic of learned needs referred to by Rotter is freedom of movement. This is the belief on the part of the individual that certain patterns of behavior will lead to certain desired outcomes. Although behavior is directed toward certain goals, the individual is not a robot; he or she has some control. A person frequently behaves in accordance with anticipated future rewards. Besides need satisfaction or reinforcements, behavior is determined by the individual's expectation that reinforcement will occur. This expectation results from previous experience. Children behave as they do because they expect that unique behavior will lead to satisfaction of a goal that they value. They may know other behaviors that have led to the goal, for example, of gaining attention, but at the present time they may have little expectation that these other behaviors will lead to satisfaction. For instance, crying will gain attention and care for a young child, but this behavior in a teenager will likely result in rejection.

Another general component of understanding behavior is the value (need value) attached to the goal, that is, the degree to which the individual prefers one satisfaction to another (Rotter, 1954). In any given situation, one need or goal may have more value than another. A student may have a need to please the teacher but may also have a need to be seen in a favorable light by his or her peers. The relative value the student attaches to these two needs in a given situation will in part determine which pattern the student chooses to use.

From a learning theory framework, then, each individual is born with innate needs, but most needs are learned through interactions with the environment. As individuals grow and mature, they learn that certain patterns of behavior bring certain satisfactions, and these experiences lead to the development of different patterns of behavior. Individuals differ in their behavioral patterns because they perceive specific situations somewhat differently. The female child who receives positive feedback for engaging in behaviors that were traditionally associated with male children is more likely to engage in those behaviors in the future than a female child who receives negative feedback for engaging in those behaviors. In each case the female child learns through experience what a given situation means to her and reacts to the situation on that basis. Quite obviously, much of this learning takes place in early childhood; thus, the learning theory approach to personality development is similar to other approaches in that it recognizes the importance of early experiences in the process of development.

While childhood experiences are very important in the development of a need hierarchy in the child, the particular hierarchy of an individual is constantly under revision as one moves through life. As each individual continues to interact with the environment, some behaviors are strengthened or newly learned, while others are weakened or extinguished. It is also important to recognize that as individuals mature, they move from a reliance on external reinforcements for their behavior to a greater reliance on self-reinforcement. In early childhood we may use external reinforcement in order to get a child to read, but once the child has taken on the reading behavior, the simple joy of reading a good story becomes a powerful self-reinforcement for continued reading. In adulthood self-reinforcement is often most powerful.

In understanding the importance of reinforcement in developing personality, we must remember that reinforcement can only be understood in terms of the individual. Simply stated, what is reinforcing for one individual may not be reinforcing for another. Premack (1965) suggested that almost any event has the potential to be reinforcing to someone. He further stated that in order to understand what would be reinforcing for an individual, we need to observe the activities in which that individual normally takes part. We can assume that those behaviors in which the individual engages most frequently are the behaviors which bring the most reward or satisfaction.

In summary, an individual's personality develops as that individual interacts with the environment. Essentially, this interaction is governed by the laws of learning outlined in this chapter. As this interaction occurs, the individual begins to develop a series of needs, and these needs within each individual begin to be placed in a hierarchical form. For each individual this hierarchical form will differ somewhat depending on the value placed on various learned needs. Initially, the individual is largely dependent on external sources for satisfaction and/or rewards, but as the individual matures the power of self-reinforcement becomes much more important. In addition, as the maturation process takes place, each individual develops the capacity for mediating responses largely through the use of symbols, particularly language. This human characteristic permits individuals to delay their responses to a particular stimulus and to plan and formulate responses in anticipation of other stimuli. It is this characteristic more than any other that separates the development of human beings from the development of other animals. It should be kept in mind that, even with this ability to mediate responses, personality development as seen from a learning theory perspective is still basically a process that is subject to the laws of learning.

INAPPROPRIATE BEHAVIOR DEVELOPMENT

Those behaviors that are inappropriate—that is, they either cause the individual or those around the individual difficulty—are learned in much the same way as are appropriate behaviors. The behaviors have been learned because they were re-warded at various times in the individual's development. Students who act out in class may behave in that manner because they have learned it is their most effective way of receiving attention. When the teacher disciplines such students, they are receiving the satisfaction or reward they sought. Although others may consider this behavior inappropriate, it has brought the reward that the student values, i.e., attention. In the same manner, a person who is withdrawn, who might be considered a social isolate, has learned to behave in that manner. The reward for withdrawing is not having to participate in a situation that induces fear, fear that may also have been learned because of past unsatisfactory experiences.

Maladaptive behavior differs from adaptive behavior only to the degree that the behavior is not satisfying to the individual or to the others in the environment. In a very large part, the culture in which the individual lives determines what is appropriate or inappropriate behavior. It is from interaction with this culture that individuals also learn to rank what is satisfying or not satisfying to themselves as well as to other individuals, and to place it in their behavioral hierarchy.

The learning theorists believe that one can explain maladaptive behavior with the same principles as adaptive patterns of behavior; in fact, all behaviors are the individual's attempt to modify the situation so that it will bring the highest degree of satisfaction. All behavior is formed through a learning process, whether the end result is adaptive or maladaptive. The individual has established a pattern of behavior because it has brought some reinforcement—some satisfaction. As shall be seen, one of the real keys to the behavioral counseling process is the ability of the counselor to help the client determine what satisfaction is being achieved by certain behaviors.

BEHAVIORAL COUNSELING

The learning theory position is that counseling is a special learning situation. Any changes that occur in the client's behavior as a result of the counseling process are a direct result of the same principles of learning that apply outside the counsel-ing situation. Therefore, the process of counseling is concerned with the appli-cation of these same principles of learning.

Learning is an individual process and, even in group counseling, individual variables must be considered. As noted earlier, the vast majority of behavioral counseling has been conducted individually; however, application to group settings has been increasing. Harris (1977) lists five reasons for the rapid and successful expansion of behavioral counseling procedures within the context of group coun-seling.

1. In group counseling, the counselor is not the only individual who dictates or suggests possible behaviors to the individual. Group members are able to provide an additional source of positive reinforcement to other group members, as well as suggestions as to possible alternative methods of behaving.

2. The group situation provides an opportunity for individual members to try out new behaviors. Often the group situation provides an opportunity for the members to act as models for one another. This modeling behavior can lead to

a more rapid acquisition of appropriate behaviors by the other group members.

3. In a group situation, every member has the opportunity to operate in a leadership or teaching role. If one member of the group has some skills which other members do not have, the individual is given the opportunity to teach these skills to the other members.

4. The group as a microcosm of life provides an opportunity for the group counselor to evaluate the effectiveness of the treatment process through observation of the individual clients within the group interaction.

5. Individuals who begin to change behaviors as a result of the counseling process often encounter difficulty with their family and friends who are not involved in the change process. This lack of support from significant others in the client's world is often the reason that client behaviors changed in counseling are not sustained in the real world. The group process, however, provides a ready-made support system for individuals attempting to make real changes in their lives in the outside world.

It is for these reasons that more and more behavioral counselors are turning to the use of groups, particularly for clients whose problems are based on social interactions with other individuals. It should be remembered, however, that behavioral group counseling is focused on individuals collected into a group setting rather than on the dynamics of the group interaction. Behavioral group counseling does not deemphasize the importance of the counselor's utilization of the principles of learning. It simply changes the setting in which those principles are utilized.

Counselor Role

The behavioral group counselor works to eliminate specific problems and to increase the clients' productive behaviors and pleasurable interpersonal relationships. Wolpe (1958) emphasizes the need for the counselor to be accepting, to try to understand the client and what he or she is communicating, and to be nonjudgmental. "All that the patient says is accepted without question or criticism. He is given the feeling that the therapist is on his side (p. 106)." Krumboltz (1966) believes that it is essential for the counselor not only to be understanding but to communicate this understanding to the client. The counselor must be warm and empathic and hold each individual in high regard. If these conditions are not present, it is impossible for the counselor to determine the client's difficulty and to gain the necessary cooperation from the client. This preliminary relationship is an important step in the counseling process. The counselor can become an important reinforcing agent only if the client sees the counselor as someone who gives the client the freedom to express concerns in an atmosphere that is nonjudgmental. Once this relationship has been established, the counselor and client can begin to work toward resolving specific problem behavior. Unless the problem is clearly defined with a clear understanding of its antecedents and consequences by both the counselor and the client, the counseling process will not progress.

The counselor's behavior throughout the group process is that of participant-observer. At times in the process, the behavioral group counselor may be very active in leading and at other times may be relatively passive and observing the group interactions. The counselor may ask questions to learn the antecedents of problem behavior, the specifics of the behavior, and the reinforcements that have maintained it. The counselor may also lecture to inform the group members about the origin of the problem and to explain the process they need to go through to bring about change. The counselor may utilize such techniques as role playing, role rehearsal, and psychodrama. However, "Most procedures are derived from operant and respondent conditioning and modeling theories. Reinforcement, shaping, extension, and time out from reinforcement are examples of operantly derived procedures commonly used in group treatment. . . . Systematic desensitization, used either with individuals in the group or with the whole group, is an example of a commonly used respondent conditioning procedure. The presentation of high status models, the reinforcement of models in the presence of the imitator, and the use of role played model presentations are examples of procedures used in group treatment that are derived from modeling theory (Rose, 1977, p. 10)." The counselor will also utilize cue statements which elicit from the client the discussion of desired behaviors. The counselor is always quick to reinforce progress made by the client. Verbalization is a part of the process, but the counselor does not work for expression of all impulses.

The behavioral counselor exerts pressure on clients to transfer the new behaviors to life situations and reinforces their descriptions of success when they return to the group. This is an important part of the process because such success makes the client a model for other members of the group. Success is eventually dependent upon the reinforcement the clients receive in the life situation and the ability of the client to utilize self-reinforcement.

The behavioral counselor is active in the group by directing much of the activity and reinforcing the goal-oriented behaviors. The counselor's actions are always focused on helping group members move toward their own specific goals. The counselor is generally concerned with the individual rather than the group interaction.

Member Role

Behavioral group counseling is generally conducted with groups of individuals with similar presenting problems. Because the members share similar concerns, they can offer reinforcement to each other as they make therapeutic progress. Group interaction among members in a behavioral group tends to be more goal directed than is true in other group approaches. Thus, the interaction pattern at any particular moment in the group process might reflect a focus on one particular individual as the group is helping that individual work on his or her concern. This interaction pattern is a reflection of the fact that behavioral group counseling tends to be a treatment of an individual within the group context rather than the treatment of a group. Thus, each member's role in a behavioral group is primarily concerned with his or her own behavior. Members describe their problems as specifically as possible, explore the environmental variables and internal variables that may stimulate and reinforce them, and state the desired new behaviors. Once the particular goal for each individual client has been defined, it is largely the counselor who describes and leads the plan of action designed to change the behavior in the desired direction. As can be seen, then, the behavioral approach to group counseling places much less emphasis on the dynamics of member-member interactions within the group.

The Process

Two useful frameworks for examining the process of behavioral group counseling have been developed by Blackham and Silberman (1971) and by Rose (1977). The Blackham and Silberman model suggests four stages in the behavioral group counseling process. First, the problem behavior is defined and analyzed. Second, a developmental and social history is secured to further delineate the problem and its present adaptation. Third, specific goals for behavior change are established. Fourth, methods of modifying the behavior are identified and implemented. The Rose model lists functions that take place in the behavioral group process rather than stages. The Rose model includes beginning the group, assessment, monitoring and evaluation, treatment planning and implementation, and transfer and maintenance of behavioral change. The authors believe that an amalgamation of these two frameworks is a helpful way to examine the behavioral group counseling process.

Beginning the Group

The initial activities in behavioral group counseling are very similar to other more traditional group counseling approaches. It is assumed that the counselor has met with each individual prior to the initial group session to determine the individual's suitability for the group process and willingness to participate. Initial activities in the first group meeting are concerned with organizing the group, orienting the clients to the group process, and beginning the process of building group cohesion. Orientation to the group process should include establishing initial group norms for behavior in the group and rather specific references to what the group process will entail and what is expected of the members of the group. A unique part of the orientation for behavioral groups is the establishment of the general treatment contract for each member (Rose, 1977). The organizational part of the orientation process is simply one of deciding such things as time for meeting, duration of meeting, whether the group will be an open or closed group, and so on. To initiate the process of building group cohesion, the behavioral group counselor may utilize techniques borrowed from the more traditional group dynamic approaches. These may include specific exercises designed to enhance interpersonal relations and communications among group members.

Definition of the Problem   While the analysis of the individual member's problem begins with the individual interview prior to the initial group session, it is expected that this preliminary statement made by the group member will be refined in the early stages of the group process. Rose (1977) describes this clarifying process as the assessment stage. "Assessment is the group activity concerned with determining the problem to be modified and the resources of the individual and his or her environment that will facilitate remediation of the problem (Rose, 1977, p. 8)." Once the problem has been stated by the client to the other group members, it is desirable to expand the analysis. When, where, and with whom is the problem behavior exhibited? The counselor wishes to identify the antecedents of the behavior as well as the consequences of the behavior. By making a systematic analysis of the problem behavior, the counselor is able to determine the stimuli or events that may be evoking the behavior. Even though the group member may perceive this as a problem behavior, it has persisted because the member has been receiving some type of reward. Therefore, the counselor explores possible reinforcing elements in the problem situation. Whenever it is possible, careful observation of the problem behavior in the appropriate situation helps to determine the reinforcing contingencies. If the group member is in a school situation, it may be possible to observe the classroom behavior. In family situations, a family group counseling process may permit an analysis of the situation.

It is important to know how pervasive the problem behavior is, that is, does it occur frequently, is it a new behavior the client wishes to initiate, or does it occur only in specific situations with specific people? It is also important to determine who else in the client situation is helping to maintain the behavior or could be helpful in modifying the behavior. It is of central importance in this stage of the process that the counselor help group members learn how to specify their problems in terms of overt behaviors.

The reader should not infer that the assessment or definition of problem stage is a one-time occurrence. While it is extremely important that the problem be defined in terms of observable behavior early in the group process, this problem definition should be kept open to revision and modification as the group process unfolds. As the group develops and new data is collected, it may be that the group member, with the assistance of the counselor and other group members, may redefine his or her problem or may subdivide it into smaller, more specific problem areas.

The Developmental and Social History   Related to the need for the client to specify a problem in concrete terms is the need for information about the individual which will be useful in identifying health status and physical deficiencies, as well as obtaining a picture of the client's general developmental pattern in areas of intellectual, social, and emotional development. Through a developmental and social history the counselor should gain a comprehensive picture of the client. The client should reveal areas of success and failure, competencies and deficiencies, social relationships, coping behavior, and areas of conflict.

There are some clients whose problem behavior may not be exclusively the result of reinforcing conditions, but may have physical or organic determinants. These conditions must be identified and considered in behavior analysis. The social history reveals the social reinforcement history of the problem area and includes the stimuli, events, and conditions that serve as the reinforcers. These may be obtained by inquiring about the activities or things that the client selects when free choice is possible. The counselor will then examine the extent to which the problem behavior may be resistant to change and the social reinforcements which the client prefers. The counselor should be alert to the relative reinforcement properties of significant individuals in the client's life and how they might be utilized in formulating a strategy to modify the behavior. In many instances it may be useful to interview other individuals in addition to the client. Obviously, the counselor must secure the client's permission to do so.

Stating Behavioral Goals   Just as clients must state their problem in behavioral terms, they must also state their goals for the counseling process in behavioral terms. Rotter has stated his goals of counseling as "helping the patient to live a more constructive life, to contribute to society, to maximize his potential for achievement, to maximize his feelings of affections or contributions to others (1962, p. 1)." His goal is to help an individual reach a state of happiness and pleasure, which on the surface is not very different from goals of any approach to counseling. This is a long-term goal, however, rather than a specific behavioral goal which will eventually lead to the long-term goal.

Krumboltz (1966) states that the goals of counseling must be stated in specific terms. These are particular behaviors that are in need of modification. Individuals come to counseling with a particular problem that they have been unable to resolve.

Because the goals of counseling are stated in specific terms, they will be different for each individual member of the group. The critical element in establishing the behavioral goal for counseling is that it is the basis for a strategy to modify all behaviors and to develop new behaviors. The methods the counselor will use to help each client may be different depending upon the client and the problem.

Strategies for Behavioral Change   When specific short- or long-term behavioral goals have been stated, change strategies can be formulated. "Treatment planning involves choosing from a number of highly specific procedures that have been demonstrated to be related to achieving behavioral change goals (Rose, 1977, pp. 9–10)." Once the goals have been clearly defined, the form of treatment intervention as specified in the roles of other group members and significant others outside the group are delineated. In this stage of the process, it is helpful for the group counselor to develop specific, weekly behavioral contracts with each individual group member. These behavioral contracts provide excellent vehicles for both the counselor and the group members to monitor progress toward the desired outcomes. They also provide the counselor immediate feedback as to whether the particular intervention strategy chosen is being effective and if not, provides ample opportunity for revision in treatment strategies. It is important during this process that the counselor provide adequate opportunities for the client to raise questions, to express his or her attitudes and feelings about the procedures and the process. It is also important to utilize the feedback from the other group members in helping to evaluate the progress being made by a particular group member.

Transfer and Maintenance of Desired Behavior   The general goal of all counseling is to help clients engage in their desired behaviors outside the counseling situation and maintain these desired behaviors after the termination of counseling. It is often the case, however, that clients will demonstrate the desired behavior in counseling but are either unable to translate that behavior into action in their real life situation or find themselves unable to maintain the new behavior. Because of these inherent problems, the behavioral group counselor pays particularly close attention to the concepts of transfer and maintenance.

A transfer of behavioral change can be facilitated through the use of the group as a microcosm of the real world. The counselor should establish situations in which group members can try out new desired behaviors in the group situation such that they can receive feedback on their efforts. This feedback should enable each member to refine and shape behavior so that it will actually work in the outside world. Activities such as role playing, behavioral rehearsal, and behavioral reversal can be very helpful in facilitating the transfer of learning.

Several procedures are helpful in facilitating the client's maintenance of desired behavior after the termination of treatment. A helpful procedure in both initiating transfer of behavior and the maintenance of behavior is the utilization of homework assignments. These assignments must clearly specify the desired behavior and conditions under which the behavior is to be exhibited during the interim between sessions. The client is then asked to bring back to the group session a report in relation to the outcomes of the homework assignment. A second procedure useful in enhancing maintenance is the gradual termination of the counseling process. When a group has been meeting on a once-a-week basis, the group might change its schedule to every other week and then to an intermittent schedule which allows individuals to experience their new behaviors over longer and longer periods of time but still provides the necessary support system. Rose (1977) points out that the procedures of gradual fading of the treatment process and the thinning of the reinforcement schedule lend themselves to the process of group termination. The individual members feel increasingly comfortable with the behaviors that they have been able to transfer to the outside world, and with their ability to maintain those behaviors there becomes less of a need for the support group. This developing independence on the part of the client provides the framework through which the counselor can terminate the group process. In this stage the client is characterized most often as being motivated by self-reinforcement as opposed to the need for external reinforcement from either the counselor or the other group members.

INTERVENTION STRATEGIES

As indicated earlier in this chapter, behavioral counseling has gone far beyond the rather narrow definitions of behaviorism typified by Skinnerian psychology. Certainly there are those who follow a basically traditional model with a reliance on techniques that are rooted in the laws of learning. There are many others, however, who, while operating from a basically behavioral position, utilize techniques from a wide variety of approaches. As Lazarus states, "In the practical details of my day-to-day work with clients, I have found it necessary to broaden the base of conventional behavior therapy (1972, vi)." Two other individuals representing a broad-based behavioral approach, Krumboltz and Thoreson, state, "There is no 'approved list' of techniques the use of which enables one to call himself a behavioral counselor. The door must be kept open to all procedures that might be helpful (1969, p. 3)." While these and other similar theorists are calling for what might be termed a behavioral eclecticism, the base from which they operate is behavioral. This means that despite the utilization of techniques which might not be based on learning theory, the focus remains on overt behavioral change in the client. In some cases these changes are related to the development and strengthening of new behaviors, while in other cases they may be focused on the weakening or extinction of undesirable behaviors. The intervention strategies outlined in this section of the chapter focus on techniques designed to accomplish one and/or the other of these general goals. Strategies which will strengthen or develop new behaviors include shaping techniques, contingency contracting, assertive behaviors, modeling, behavioral rehearsal, cognitive restructuring, and covert reinforcement. Strategies designed to weaken or eliminate maladaptive behaviors include extinction, reinforcing incompatible behaviors, desensitization, and satiation.

Strengthening Behaviors

Shaping This is a method of teaching behaviors through successive approximation and chaining. Behavior that has never been exhibited by the individual cannot be reinforced. Therefore, to teach the behavior, we must reward behaviors that are close to or that approximate the desired behavior.

A complex behavior is also shaped through a number of successive approximations, during which certain behaviors are reinforced and others are not. Through this process the behavior gradually becomes closer to what is the desired behavior.

To shape a behavior that is not in the individual repertoire, it is first necessary to specify in clear behavioral terms the desired final behavior. The next step is to analyze the component parts to determine the necessary sequential steps. In achieving the final behavior, the counselor must start with the level of proficiency that an individual has already attained; then begin shaping the desired behavior by reinforcing each approximation of the desired behavior; then raise the criterion and make the reinforcement contingent upon closer approximation of the desired behavior.

While shaping may appear to be simple, this is far from the case, and it requires that certain precautions be recognized. Hosford (1969) outlined four crucial considerations in the process of using reinforcement as a technique to shape behavior. First, the counselor needs to be certain that the reinforcement to be utilized is strong enough to produce the necessary motivation to engage in the desired behavior. In effect, the counselor must discover what is reinforcing for each individual client. The reinforcement that will work for one group member may not have any effect on a second group member. The Premack principle outlined earlier in this chapter is of critical significance in this process of determining the appropriate reinforcer. Utilizing the Premack principle, the counselor must determine those things which bring satisfaction to the client and make those things contingent upon completing the desired behavior. Suppose, for example, a male client has the desire to improve his interactions with females. Suppose, further, that this client is a relatively heavy smoker. The group counselor might utilize the smoking behavior to reinforce appropriate interpersonal behaviors. That is, the client might be forbidden to smoke until such time as he engaged in an interpersonal interaction with a female member of the group. After successfully completing this exercise, the client might be permitted a cigarette. While one can argue the advantage of using smoking behavior as a reinforcer, in this case the client obviously gains pleasure from smoking, and the Premack principle calls for the utilization of something that brings satisfaction to the individual as a reward for engaging in desired behavior.

A second point cited by Hosford is that the reinforcement utilized must be used in a systematic manner. As Krumboltz (1966) has stated, the question for a behavioral counselor is not whether to use reinforcement but how to use it in a systematic fashion. To shape a behavior of a client that is not in the client's initial behavioral repertoire, it is first necessary to specify in clear behavioral terms the desired final behavior. Initially, it is important that the counselor reinforce every client response which indicates movement in the desired direction. As counseling progresses, the client should be required to exhibit closer and closer approximations of the desired behavior before reinforcement is given. Additionally, the space between reinforcements should become longer and longer and be intermittent. An intermittent schedule will facilitate the retention of the desired behavior in the outside world.

The third element outlined by Hosford is the relationship between the desired behavior and the application of the reward. If the reward is to be effective, the contingency between the desired response and the reward must be clearly evident to the client. The fourth consideration outlined by Hosford is that the counselor must be able to elicit an approximation of the desired response from the client. This involves the use of statements by the counselor which are designed such that the client can hardly avoid responding in the desired direction. These counselor statements, called cue statements, are really a verbal prompting of the client by the counselor.

Certain cautions in shaping should be recognized. The desired approximation must be reinforced immediately upon its execution; otherwise, a different response would be reinforced. Also, the successive approximations of the desired behavior must be reinforced. If an approximation is reinforced too long, it may become too well established to move on to the final desired behavior. It is apparent that effective shaping involves appropriate selection and reinforcement of responses as well as determining the length of time to reinforce each approximation before moving on to the next. Hence, the counselor must have clearly in mind the response sequence that is most likely and necessary to lead to the desired behavior.

Behavior Contracts   Dustin and George (1973) suggest that behavioral contracts are a simple extension of behavioral principles in that the contract sets forth the contingencies between reinforcement and desired behaviors. In effect, a behavioral contract is an agreement between two or more individuals to behave in certain ways and to receive certain rewards for that behavior. The contract defines the expectations and responsibilities that must be carried out and the consequences. It is a means of scheduling the exchange of positive reinforcements between the individuals involved. The contract structure specifies who is to do what, for whom, under what conditions. Therefore, the contract makes explicit the expectations of every party to an interaction and permits each to determine the relative benefits and costs of remaining in the relationship. The contract simply spells out in advance under what conditions the rewards will be given to the client and under what conditions those rewards will be withdrawn.

Behavior Contract Assumptions In discussing behavioral contracting within families, Stuart (1971) described four assumptions upon which the contract is predicated. First, it is assumed that receiving positive reinforcements in interpersonal exchanges is a privilege rather than a right. It is a privilege in the sense that it is a special prerogative which one may enjoy at the will of another person upon having performed some qualifying task. Frequently it is the responsibility of one person to grant the privileges requested by another on a reciprocal basis. A second assumption is that effective interpersonal agreements are governed by the norm of reciprocity. Reciprocity implies that each individual has rights and duties and that the items of value in an exchange must be exchanged on an equitable basis. It is important that everyone accept the notion of compensating others fairly for everything that is received. A third assumption states that the value of an interpersonal exchange is a direct function of the rate, range, and magnitude of the positive reinforcements mediated by that exchange. Each individual should seek to offer the other the maximum possible rate of positive reinforcement, because the more positive reinforcement the person emits, the more will be received. The final assumption states that rules create freedom in interpersonal exchanges. While rules delimit the scope of a person's behavior, they also create the freedom with which he or she may take advantage of the privilege.

Prerequisite to establishing a behavioral contract is the careful definition of the client's problems, the situations in which they are expressed, and the client's willingness to try the procedure. It is important that an achievable task be specified so that each person understands the task to be performed. The criterion for success must be stated and then one must identify a reinforcer. When this is done, a contract may be established in which the reinforcement is contingent upon meeting the task and the criterion expectation.

A few suggestions for contracting would include: stating the contract in positive terms; setting achievable tasks and criteria; reinforcing as quickly as possible; encouraging self-contracting; and using a series of contracts. (A contract leads to a task, followed by a reward which leads to a new contract, followed by a task and then a reward.)

To enhance the ease with which reinforcement is given, tokens or points may be given for the performance of the desired behavior and removed for undesirable behavior. When tokens or points are used, it is important that the clients have opportunities to exchange them for reinforcing stimuli or events that they have previously stated. In reality, then, token economies are a series of behavioral contracts.

Contingency Elements of a Good Contract   First, the contract should detail the privileges that each person expects to gain after fulfilling his or her responsibilities. Second, the responsibilities specified in the contract must be monitored by the counselor or other group members so they may determine when the responsibility has been fulfilled and reward can be granted. The third element in the contract is a system of sanctions for failure to meet the responsibility. At times the existence of sanctions may make the difference in moving toward compliance with a contract obligation. A fourth element in the contract provides a bonus clause which assures positive reinforcement for compliance with the terms of the contract. To counteract the sanctions clause, bonuses which call for permission to remain out longer or to receive extraordinary privileges are built into contracts as contingencies for extended periods of compliance with the responsibilities. Fifth, each individual should be provided with a means of responding to contract violations, and each is reinforced for long chains of desirable responses. The contract is not complete unless a means is established for keeping track of the rates of positive reinforcement given and received. This is accomplished through a feedback system, which permits each individual to cue each other person on how to respond in order to earn additional inducement, and to signal when to reinforce the other.

Assertive Training   This strategy is appropriate with individuals who have nonadaptive anxiety-response habits in interpersonal relationships; the anxiety inhibits their expression of appropriate assertive feelings and the appropriate assertive act. When such anxiety inhibits the appropriate behavior in the interpersonal relationship, individuals may be left at an objective disadvantage and may find themselves short-changed, if not empty handed, with respect to their goals. Such people continue to have the unexpressed impulses reverberating within them, and in many cases these lead to somatic symptoms. The most frequent assertive responses are the expression of anger and resentment.

Wolpe and Lazarus (1966) state that assertive behavior counterconditions such responses as anger, with the result that any anxiety raised by the situation is also inhibited. Carrying out assertive acts is usually followed by rewarding consequences that will continue to inhibit the anxiety. Operant conditioning principles may be used when assertive behavior has to be shaped with an individual who lacks it, not because of anxiety but because the individual has apparently never had the opportunity to acquire assertive habits. There may be cases in which operant conditioning is used in combination with counterconditioning concepts.

The counselor is guided by information obtained from the group member's statement of the problem and analysis of his or her social and developmental history. Assertive training seems appropriate with individuals who describe anxiety in situations from exploitation and/or domination from other people, and from indignities and feelings of degradation.

Assertive training begins by informing the person, frequently by illustrative examples, that the outward expression of feelings will reciprocally inhibit anxiety and that such expression on repeated occasions will lead to a cumulative conditioning that will inhibit the anxiety responses. They then discuss this topic and examine easy assignments that might be carried out. Easy assignments should precede major ones so that the individual can receive a reinforcement from a positive experience. Getting instructions to the individual is important because the conquest of anxiety depends on the occurrence of overt acts of assertion, and the development of assertive patterns will be determined by the consequences of these acts. Role playing of situations within the group provides an opportunity for practice in asserting oneself and an opportunity to receive reinforcement. In the initial stages of assertive training, it is helpful to achieve any expression of assertion. Gradually the group member gains the feeling of control in the relationship, and self-assurance grows until she or he is able to carry through successfully the direct expression whenever it may be necessary.

Members may keep careful notes of their significant interpersonal encounters and discuss them in the group. It is important to examine the circumstances around the situation, the individual's feelings at the time, the manner in which the individual reacted and how he or she felt immediately afterward, and the individual's own subsequent appraisal of the situation. Group members may help each other in identifying their own reasonable rights in given situations and in determining an appropriate assertive stance.

Wolpe and Lazarus (1966) suggest that there is a pattern in assertive training. First, the group member becomes more aware of his or her assertiveness and its negative repercussions to self and others. This is followed by an intellectual understanding of assertive behavior and its positive effect, followed by unhappiness about his or her ineffectiveness in assertive responses. If there are positive consequences to this training, the probability of engaging in more assertive behavior increases. There are times when success leads previously timid and dominated individuals to overassert themselves. However, negative feedback from the environment and some assistance from the counselor or group members would assist the person in toning down such responses. The group member needs to learn to be assertive without dominating. As the client becomes aware of a growing effectiveness in interpersonal situations, he or she develops a genuine and fitting indifference to minor slights and small irritations. Appropriate behavior usually elicits positive feedback from other individuals, and this will improve the client's self-concept as well.

Modeling

Group counseling has generally been used with a number of individuals sharing a common problem. However, the gathering of a group of people with similar problems may lead to a pool of ignorance about how to deal with the problem or to a peer reinforcement of socially inappropriate behaviors. If the group members are to learn more appropriate behaviors, it may be necessary to inject examples of the desired responses into their world. Models can be presented as examples of the desired behavior or as examples of ways in which problems can be solved. The basic assumption of modeling is that most learning resulting from direct experience can also be learned through vicarious reinforcement or imitative learning.

Mediation Process Bandura (1969) has formulated the most complete theory explaining both the acquisition and performance of modeling behavior. In order for the observer to reproduce a response under similar stimulus conditions subsequently, there must be a mediational system for retention and retrieval of the stimulus response association. Bandura presents four aspects of this mediation process: (1) attention; (2) retention; (3) motor reproduction; and (4) incentive. Attention to the responses of the model is an obvious prerequisite for observational learning since its absence would result in failure to recognize or differentiate the distinctive feature of the model's response. If social behavior is to be reproduced, especially after extended periods of time, there must be a retention of the observational inputs in some symbolic form. Obviously, if an observer is to reproduce responses of a model, he or she must have the physical attributes necessary for motor reproduction. Finally, if the modeled response has been incorporated into the repertoire of the observer, it will not be a chosen response to a set of stimuli unless suitable incentives are contingent upon the performance of that response.

There are two requisites for using models in group counseling. First, it is necessary to identify problems and to specify behavioral outcomes of counseling in a manner that allows for assessment. The outcome may vary from having the group member seek occupational-educational information to having the member become more socially acceptable. The second requisite is the necessity of being able to provide examples of the behavior that is to be emulated. These samples of behaviors might be film, audio tape, video tape, live, or possibly written. While theoretically any of these forms of modeled behavior could be effective with the cognitive or personal-social problems, it should be evident that it is easier to capture a specific observable response than to record subtle examples of complex psychological and sociological functioning. Hence, films and tape models have been more prominent in dealing with cognitive problems, while live models seem to be effective in helping members solve personal and social problems. Obviously, it is important to select and present models that are acceptable to the group members.

One approach to using the model in the group would involve tapes or filmed models in order to demonstrate desired behavior. The group counseling continues after this presentation with a discussion of how the members can implement the kind of behavior demonstrated by the model. Note that the model in this situation is used only as a demonstration of desired behavior; there is no opportunity for interaction between the model and the participants. The model may, however, act as a stimulator of discussion in the desired directions. The probability of group members performing the desired behavior can be greatly enhanced by introducing incentives for these responses and by reinforcing them when they occur in the model as well as in the observers. If the group sees the model's behavior being rewarded, this also will increase the amount of imitative behavior. Although, as noted above, the audio and filmed models have been employed mainly with cognitive problems, they may also be used with personal and social problems. This, obviously, involves identifying the problem areas and finding models ahead of time, thus making model selection a complex problem. Another approach to using models is to involve live peer models in the counseling situation. Here the models are considered part of the group and are encouraged to participate in discussions. They are not exposed to the members as a paradigm of model behavior but are allowed to present themselves and their solutions to the problems. This opportunity for the members to interact on a personal basis with the live models appears to be a definite aid in the problem of solving personal and social problems. Appropriate thinking is stated about the behavior and appropriate acts are initiated, receiving reinforcement in the group. Needless to say, each successive approximation that is modeled should be immediately reinforced in the group. As the group members initiate the modeled behavior outside the group, it is important that they receive reinforcement in their environment. The reinforcement received in the environment will probably be more of a variable reinforcement schedule.

Live Peer Models   Several studies have been conducted which illustrate the use of live peer models in group counseling. One of those studies is utilized here for illustrative purposes.

Warner and Hansen (1970) found that reinforcement of live peer models in group counseling reduced students' feelings of alienation. Juniors in high school who were identified as having strong feelings of alienation were selected for group counseling. The models in this study were peers selected by students and teachers as having good overall adjustment to the school and society. The clients and models participated in a group discussion involving feelings of normlessness, powerlessness, and meaninglessness. The counselors reinforced feelings and ideas of how to overcome these feelings and how to implement the behaviors that would make it possible for the students to participate in school in such a way as to alleviate feelings of alienation.

Filmed or taped models may be used as a stimulus for discussion and modeling behavior. Krumboltz, Varenhorst, and Thoreson (1967) found that exposure to audio-taped interviews in which the model received reinforcement for information-seeking behavior, followed by a live discussion in which the counselor reinforced information-seeking behaviors in the group participants, resulted in an increased level of information seeking.

Behavioral Rehearsal   Behavioral rehearsal is generally used in combination with other behavioral approaches. It may be utilized as part of the shaping process or after the presentation of some model to the group. In behavioral rehearsal, the group member is able to try out a particular behavior within the safe environment of the group. In this way the client is actually able to practice the desired behavior and to receive feedback from the other group members as well as the counselor. As Rose (1977) indicates, behavioral rehearsal also enables the counselor to move the group members successively through more difficult trials until they master a complex behavioral pattern. Behavioral rehearsal in the group setting also has the distinct advantage of enabling an individual engaging in the behavioral rehearsal to act as a model for the other group members.

Cognitive Restructuring   As behavioral counselors turn more and more attention to the cognitive thought process involved in human behavior, there has been a corresponding increase in techniques designed to work with a cognitive process. It is increasingly apparent that in some situations clients come to counseling knowing the particular behaviors that they wish to engage in or the behaviors that they wish to eliminate. Their problem is not one of defining desired or undesirable behaviors but in learning how to accomplish the particular objective. In many such cases, it may be appropriate for the counselor simply to advise the client of the proper course of action. In other cases it may mean that the counselor has to help the client restructure his or her thinking process. Rose (1977) presents an excellent overview of specific, cognitive restructuring procedures which includes corrective information, thought stopping, the dispelling of irrational beliefs, relabeling, and systematic problem solving. Readers interested in pursuing these cognitive procedures are urged to examine the book by Rose.

Covert Reinforcement Covert reinforcement is a process somewhat similar to cognitive restructuring in that it involves individuals using imagery to reward themselves. It involves clients pairing an image of their undesired behavior with a second image that is extremely negative, or pairing an image of a desirable behavior with an image of an extremely positive consequence. Used in a positive fashion, we might have individuals who desire to stop smoking imagine themselves turning down the offer of a cigarette with an image of their lungs as being very clear and pure. With those same individuals, we could use covert reinforcement in a negative fashion by pairing an image of themselves accepting the cigarette with all the undesirable effects of smoking: very black lungs, a strong body odor, and perhaps even holes in their clothes from the ashes. Covert reinforcement is based on the classical conditioning model. The belief is that eventually the images have been paired together long enough that the actual behavior will produce the paired image. Mahoney and Thoresen (1974) suggest, and the authors agree, that negative covert reinforcement can be a very aversive procedure. While the procedure is very new and needs further study, the authors do believe that covert, positive reinforcement may be an effective behavioral change technique.

Weakening Behaviors

Extinction Extinction is the process of lowering the frequency of a behavior by eliminating the reinforcements that are maintaining it. An obvious example would be to ignore a specific behavior when it is found that one's attention to it, even though negative, is really reinforcing the behavior. Usually, when beginning a program of extinction, the client will try even harder to gain attention so the maladaptive behavior may increase before a decrease is seen. For this approach to be successful, the reinforcement must continue to be withheld.

A counselor would probably not use this approach as the sole method for weakening behaviors of group members. However, it would serve as a tool to use within the group to weaken exhibited inappropriate behaviors. For example, when a group member discusses irrelevant material, the counselor may look away and not react until that individual makes an appropriate response. Ignoring the behavior and getting group members to ignore it is very useful in helping a participant eliminate a behavior.

Reinforcing Incompatible Behaviors   By reinforcing positive behaviors, one can lessen the amount of deviant behavior. For example, if the counselor wants participants to talk about themselves, reinforcing types of responses about themselves while ignoring non-self statements may lead the persons to reduce the non-self talk. Although the two behaviors are incompatible, one can reinforce positive behaviors even while trying to eliminate undesirable behavior. This approach to altering maladaptive behavior involves two basic elements: unlearning a maladaptive behavior and learning an adaptive behavior. Although these two are not entirely separate processes, they must both be achieved. The use of extinction procedures (see above) may eliminate some undesired behaviors; but if the counselor also uses a systematic reinforcement of a desirable behavior, it may be a more efficient procedure. By reinforcing an incompatible behavior, the maladaptive behavior may be eliminated and a desirable behavior develop simultaneously.

Wolpe (1967) describes the situation somewhat differently. He believes that all neurotic behaviors are expressions of anxiety in one form or another. He also believes that there are numerous psychological states that are antagonistic or inhibitory to anxiety so that when behaviors conducive to these states occur in the person, he or she does not experience anxiety at the same time. This is called reciprocal inhibition. If the counselor can discover which anxiety-inhibiting response would serve to counter a given symptom and teach the client to produce that response regularly, the symptom will gradually disappear. It may even be replaced altogether by a generally better behavioral manifestation. The object, however, is not to teach a preselected new pattern of behavior but to break the old pattern. Where a particular stimulus once elicited an anxiety-laden response, the therapeutic procedure, by inhibiting the occurrence of that response, loosens its connection with the stimulus. Eventually that stimulus loses its power to create anxiety and the symptom will disappear. The new behavior that was originally used to inhibit the anxiety is no longer needed. It may or may not be maintained for other reasons.

To use this strategy by reinforcing a specific incompatible behavior, it is necessary first to identify the behavior to be eliminated and the desirable behavior to be promoted. This should be followed by a systematic observation and recording of the behaviors to obtain a baseline. The recording should be continued throughout the treatment to determine the extent to which the procedures are effective and to make necessary adjustments. Once the behavior to be eliminated and the behavior to be established have been specified, extinction and positive reinforcement are used simultaneously. When the desired behavior has attained sufficient strength, a change to a variable schedule is advised in order to make the adaptive behavior more resistant to extinction.

Systematic Desensitization   This is a specific form of reinforcing incompatible behaviors based upon the principles of relaxation. Relaxation is used to countercondition an anxiety situation. The term reciprocal inhibition is borrowed from physiology and refers to the phenomenon in which one set of nerves or muscles functions antagonistically to another so that they cannot function simultaneously.

Wolpe and Lazarus (1966) apply this concept to counseling by proposing a variety of techniques for antagonistic responses selected by the client and counselor to be systematic behaviors in a manner that would prevent the symptoms from being expressed. Wolpe assumes that the client's symptoms are learned or conditioned habits, and since the responses the counselor selects to suppress may be new habits that are learned or conditioned, it is appropriate to describe this form of treatment as counterconditioning.

An extensive analysis of the behavior of the person is necessary before beginning the technique of systematic desensitization. The technique involves three separate sets of operation: (1) training in deep muscle relaxation; (2) the construction of anxiety hierarchies; and (3) the counterposing of relaxation and anxiety-evoking stimuli from the hierarchies. Wolpe and Lazarus (1966) propose a series of twenty-minute interviews devoted to training in deep-muscle relaxation. Although this training could be established in any sequence, beginning with the arms is most convenient to demonstrate and to check on. The next session focuses on relaxation of muscles around the head, followed by sessions on biting the teeth and tensing the *masseter* and *in temporalis* muscles, sessions dealing with the neck and shoulders, and finally sessions dealing with the muscles of the back, abdomen, and thorax. The second phase of treatment involves the construction of anxiety hierarchies. This requires accurate recognition of the stimulus sources of the maladaptive responses, painstaking itemization, and careful grading of the items. The final anxiety hierarchy is a graded list of stimuli incorporating differing degrees of a feature that evokes anxiety in the client. A feature common to the listed stimuli is known as a theme of the hierarchy. Some themes are easy to recognize, such as a phobia. When all of the identified sources of anxiety have been listed, the counselor classifies them into themes. Usually there is more than one theme. After the client has learned to become calm by relaxation and the counselor has established appropriate hierarchies, the procedure of desensitization is begun. The client is asked to relax and to lift a hand to indicate when a theme is disturbing. The client is then asked to imagine himself or herself in scenes in the lowest level of the hierarchical list. Slightly disturbing scenes are presented several times, alternating with relaxation until the scenes cease to be disturbing. The counselor must be careful not to present scenes with high anxiety-evoking potential too soon. As sensitivity to scenes is lowered, the scenes higher on the hierarchy become less provoking and can be imagined. Further desensitization can then occur.

Satiation   This is a process of presenting reinforcement at such a high rate that it loses its reinforcing value and may become adversative. Satiation can be induced either by providing such an abundance of a stimulus that its reinforcement values are lost or by continuously reinforcing a response until it is no longer performed. It is a simple technique that brings to mind the folklore of eliminating a young person's interest in smoking by plying the youngster with cigars. After the youngster has smoked enough to turn green, his or her appetite for smoking generally tends to decrease.

SUMMARY

Behavioral counseling in groups involves a broad range of short-term procedures founded on the premise that acts are more potent than thoughts and words for influencing human behavior. The counseling strategies have been employed in a wide range of problem areas with all ages and in all settings. The cited research illustrates the strategies applied in a variety of schools, clinics, and hospital settings with children, adolescents, and adults. The behavioral techniques are designed for the individual.

The research examples suggest that the use of behavioral counseling in groups has primarily been individual counseling within the group setting rather than a group process. That is, the counselor has provided individual counseling to more than one person at a time; however, there has been very little reliance on the group members interacting with each other. It seems possible that the interaction of group members could be used in the process of reinforcement to help a member learn new behaviors.

References

Bandura, A. *Principles of behavior modification.* New York: Holt, Rinehart and Winston, 1969.

Blackham, G., and A. Silberman, *Modification of child behavior.* Belmont, CA: Wadsworth, 1971.

Dollard, J., and N. Miller, *Personality and psychotherapy.* New York: McGraw-Hill, 1950.

Dustin, R., and R. George, *Action counseling for behavior change.* New York: Intext, 1973.

Harris, G. G. (Ed.). *The group treatment of human problems, a social learning approach.* New York: Grune & Stratton, Inc., 1977.

Havighurst, R. *Developmental tasks and education.* New York: David McKay, 1952.

Heckel, R. V. and H. C. Salzberg. *Group psychotherapy, a behavioral approach.* Columbia, SC: University of South Carolina Press, 1976.

Homme, L. E. Perspectives in psychology: XXIV. Control of coverants, the operants of the mind. *Psychological Record,* 1965, *15,* 501–11.

Hosford, R. E. Behavioral counseling—a contemporary overview. *The Counseling Psychologist,* 1969, *1,* 1–33.

Hosford, R. E., and L. A. J. M. deVisser. *Behavioral approaches to counseling: An introduction.* Washington, DC: APGA Press, 1974.

Kanfer, F., and J. Phillips. *Learning foundations and behavior therapy.* New York: Wiley, 1970.

Krumboltz, J. *Revolution in counseling.* Boston: Houghton Mifflin, 1966.

Krumboltz, J., and C. E. Thoresen (Eds.). *Behavioral counseling: Cases and techniques.* New York: Holt, Rinehart and Winston, 1969.

Krumboltz, J., and C. E. Thoresen (Eds.). *Counseling methods.* New York: Holt, Rinehart and Winston, 1976.

Krumboltz, J. D., B. B. Varenhorst, and C. E. Thoresen. Nonverbal factors in the effectiveness of models in counseling. *Journal of Counseling Psychology,* 1967, *14,* 412–18.

Lazarus, A. A. Clinical behavior therapy. New York: Brunner/Mazel, 1972.

Mahoney, M. F., and C. E. Thoresen. *Self-control: Power to the person.* Monterey, CA: Brooks-Cole, 1974.

Michael, J., and L. Meyerson. A behavioral approach to counseling and guidance. *Harvard Educational Review,* 1962, *32,* 382–402.

Miller, N. E., and J. Dollard. *Social learning and imitation.* New Haven: Yale University Press, 1941.

Mowrer, O. H. *Learning theory and the symbolic processes.* New York: Wiley, 1960.

Premack, D. Reinforcement theory. In D. Levine (Ed.), *Nebraska symposium on motivation: 1965.* Lincoln Nebraska Press, 1965, 123–80.

Rose, S. D. *Group therapy: A behavioral approach.* Englewood Cliffs, NJ: Prentice-Hall, 1977.

Rotter, J. B. *Social learning and clinical psychology.* Englewood Cliffs, NJ: Prentice-Hall, 1954.

Rotter, J. B. Some implications of social learning theory for the practice of psychotherapy, 1962. (mimeo)

Rotter, J. B. *Clinical psychology.* Englewood Cliffs, NJ: Prentice-Hall, 1964.

Skinner, B. F. *The behavior of organisms.* New York: Appelton-Century-Crofts, 1938.

Stuart, R. B. Behavioral contracting within the families of adolescents. *Journal of Behavior Therapy and Experimental Psychiatry,* 1971, *2*(1), 1–11.

Ullman, L., and L. Krasner (Eds.). *Case studies in behavior modification.* New York: Holt, Rinehart and Winston, 1965.

Warner, R. W., and J. C. Hansen. Verbal-reinforcement and model-reinforcement group counseling with alienated students. *Journal of Counseling Psychology,* 1970, *17,* 168–72.

Watson, J. B., and R. Rayner. Conditioned emotional reaction. *Journal of Experimental Psychology,* 1920, *3*(1), 1–14.

Wolpe, J. *Psychotherapy by reciprocal inhibition.* Stanford, CA: Stanford University Press, 1958.

Wolpe, J. *The practice of behavior therapy.* New York: Pergamon Press, 1969.

10

Counseling Theories: Synthesis, Conceptual Models, and Techniques

In 1968 George Gazda, first president of the Association for Specialists in Group Work, wrote: "Group counseling has not reached the stage in its development, as has its sister discipline on group psychotherapy, where numerous labels have been applied to a variety of practices (p. 263)." In the relatively few years since that statement was made, the group counseling movement has grown to such proportions that it is difficult to sort out all the different approaches that are being advocated in the literature. While recognizing that there are additional approaches to group counseling not covered in this text, the authors believe that the approaches discussed in the preceding chapters are sufficient to provide the reader a base from which to begin to formulate a personal theoretical approach to group counseling.

Quite obviously, any attempt to synthesize theories is influenced by one's own biases. That being the case, it is appropriate at this juncture to state that the current authors adhere to an eclectic position. This does not mean that counselors should operate by picking first from this approach and then from that approach on a whimsical basis. Rather, it means that each group counselor must develop an approach that works for him or her and that provides the best possible service to clients.

Robinson (1965), in discussing eclecticism, described four different orientations to counseling: pragmatic, syncretic, personality theorist, and eclectic. The *pragmatic counselor* is one who does not believe in any theory. Rationale for this position is that theory is something conceived in an ivory tower which has no relationship to actual counseling practice. Such a counselor feels that personal experience is the only thing on which he or she can rely. The *syncretic counselor* is one who uses various ideas from several theories. This counselor makes no attempt to blend these ideas into a consistent framework, and his or her counseling practice is a conglomeration of techniques with no inherent rhyme or reason for their use. The third type of counselor described by Robinson is the *personality theorist*. This category is comprised of counselors who fall in love with a particular approach and advocate its use for everything and everybody. The final category is—in Robinson's view—the *true eclectic*. The eclectic counselor attempts to pull valid and testable ideas from various approaches and blends them together into a consistent whole. Many who call themselves eclectic counselors really belong to the *pragmatic* or *syncretic* categories, while a few counselors belong in the *personality theorist* group. There is increasing evidence that the *true eclectic* position should be the choice of most, if not all, counselors. "As treatments useful in one area of human disturbance are found to be less valuable in another, efforts are made to arrive at better criteria for selecting patients for particular forms of therapy and for modifying existing forms. Here the stated task for the future is to achieve greater specificity concerning the effects of particular kinds of interventions (Karasu, 1977, p. 852)." Clearly, the true eclectic chooses techniques based on some evidence that those techniques will be effective with a particular group of clients.

It is the true eclectic category that is advocated here. A true eclectic approach means that the counselor has a reason for choosing a technique from the behavioral approaches on one occasion and a technique from the relationship theorist on another. Hence, we are not advocating a hodge-podge; rather, we are asking counselors to develop a consistent and systematic personal approach to group counseling. This chapter, as well as the preceding ones, has been designed to provide theoretical foundation for such development. Beginning with this chapter, the focus shifts from the theoretical foundations to an examination of the techniques which may be utilized in the group counseling process. This examination of the group process is designed to build a framework on the theoretical foundations already presented. It is up to you, the reader, to finish your own structure.

This synthesis of group counseling theories, then, has as its purpose an examination of both the commonalities and the divergencies in thought presented in the earlier chapters. To facilitate this process, a conceptual model will first be presented through which the relationship among the basic theoretical approaches to counseling can be examined. From this base model will be presented a second model which will illustrate how these orientations are related to group counseling. Using both of these models as a foundation, interrelationships among the theories will be analyzed in terms of group process, expected member behaviors, leadership style, and generalized techniques.

GROUP COUNSELING THEORIES

Attempts to develop an overriding model that would provide a meaningful framework for understanding the relationships among differing approaches to counseling are not new. Individuals such as London (1964), Ullman and Krasner (1965), Patterson (1966), Swenson (1967), Barclay (1968), Frank (1971), Frey (1972), Marmor (1975), and Karasu (1977) have all studied the similarities and differences in therapeutic approaches and have attempted to develop various systems for understanding the interrelationships among these approaches. These models range in complexity from Patterson's single dimension of rational-affective through Karasu's three-theme model to Barclay's four-celled model. In examining the complexity of group counseling theory, it would seem that no single-dimension model can be satisfactory. At the same time, a model like Barclay's, which is based on philosophical orientations removed from actual counseling practice, deepens the dichotomy between theory and practice already too prevalent in our profession. What is needed, then, is a conceptual model that has more relationship to actual counseling practice. The model developed by Frey (1972) appears to meet that standard.

Conceptual Model Number One

Frey (1972) combined the two unidimensional models of London (1964) and Patterson (1966) into a two-dimensional model. The Patterson linear model, which places differing theoretical approaches to counseling on a rational-affective dimension, was used to examine the actual process of counseling. The London model, which classified counseling on the basis of its emphasis on insight-action, was used as a second dimension to examine the goals of counseling. The result of this combination is a four-celled model which is capable of showing the relationship among counseling approaches both in terms of what actually occurs during counseling and in terms of the goals of counseling.

Insight-Action Dimension   As used here, insight-action dimension is used to define the emphasis placed by a particular counseling approach on the internal frame of reference of the individual or on the behavior of the individual. Those who adhere to the position that insight is a necessary prerequisite to behavior change and who adhere to the view that counseling must be involved with the total individual are placed toward the insight end of the dimension. Theorists who view counseling as being concerned about specific behavioral outcomes from counseling are placed toward the action dimension.

Rational-Affective Dimensions   The second dimension, rational-affective refers to the emphasis given by a particular approach to the expected nature of activity in counseling. There are those who place more emphasis on counseling as a reasoning cognitive process, while others see the necessity for placing emphasis on the emotions being experienced by the individual. In the first instance, the belief is that more rational thinking leads to feeling better, while the latter believes that only after the emotions are sorted out can one reason more effectively.

Figure 9 is a graphic presentation of the model. The basic dimensions are those proposed by Frey (1972). In examining the model, the reader should keep in mind that the farther from the intersection of the axis a particular position is located, the more different it is from the theoretical positions located in other quadrants. The closer to the center a theoretical position is located, the more similar it is to positions located in other quadrants.

Quadrants   In Figure 9, it can be seen that Transactional Analysis and T-

Figure 9 Counseling: Conceptual Model Number One

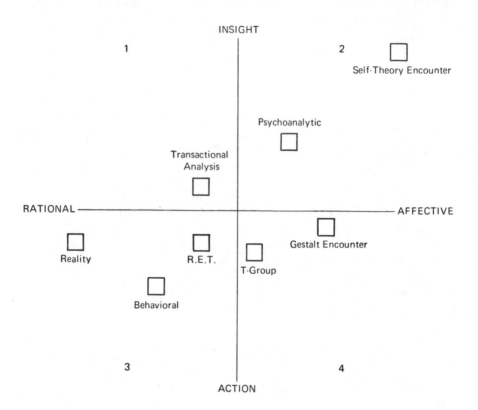

group theory, while in different quadrants, are both close to the axis, as is the R.E.T. position. This illustrates that even though they may use slightly different terminology and methods, they have a great deal of similarity in terms of their views of both the process of counseling and the outcomes that are seen as the objectives of the process. The Transactional Analysis position is the only theoretical position shown in the rational-insight quadrant, thus indicating that TA places a somewhat greater emphasis on a rational process, which leads first to insight, then to changes in emotion or affect, and finally to changes in specific behaviors. The R.E.T. position is located closest to the intersection of the two dimensions, thus indicating that R.E.T., while generally considered a rational approach, places a rather balanced emphasis on insight and action. It does emphasize a slightly more rational than affective approach. But, as the name of the approach implies, there is also emphasis on the affective areas. The T-group people see reasoning and insight as part of the process, but they are slightly more concerned with affect and action in the form of direct behavioral changes.

In quadrant II, insight-affective, are found both the psychoanalytic and the self-theory encounter theorists. The emphasis here is on the need for clients first to understand their feelings, their inner motivations and needs, and their responsibility for themselves. Emphasis is on feeling, knowing, and understanding (Frey, 1972). While the actual method used to achieve the objectives in these two approaches is quite different, both the self-theorists and the psychoanalytic theorists see counseling as an affective process, with insight into oneself as the primary objective. Certainly the psychoanalytic position places more emphasis on exploration of the past than does the basically here-and-now position of self-theory. But if one considers the general beliefs of both, it is clear that they share very similar notions about both the process and the objectives of counseling.

Before leaving the discussion of quadrant II, a word of caution is needed. The self-theory encounter position in the quadrant is based primarily on the theoretical writings of Carl Rogers. Other writers, notably Carkhuff (1969a, 1969b, 1971), discuss the basic position of Rogers, but they also discuss more action-oriented factors. Hence, the more an individual counselor adheres to the notions of Carkhuff, the closer to the intersection of the four quadrants he or she would be located.

In quadrant III, affective-action, are found both the T-group theorists and the Gestalt encounter theorists. The T-group position was previously discussed. The Gestalt position, however, is somewhat unique in that it places the heaviest emphasis on the affective or feeling dimension. In terms of the insight-action dimension it leans toward action, but there is almost equal emphasis on the necessity for insight. As such, it strikes more of a balance between insight and action than do the self-theorists, behaviorists, or psychoanalysts, and is close to the TA, R.E.T., Reality, and T-group theorists on this dimension.

Finally, in quadrant IV, action-rational, are located those that adhere to a reality therapy orientation, a group of counselors collectively called behaviorists, and the previously discussed R.E.T. position. As is shown in Figure 9, the behaviorists as a group tend to be much more action oriented than do other approaches. They hold to the belief that changes in behavior brought about through a largely learning theory position must develop before one can feel better about oneself. The recent emphasis placed on the internal functioning of the human mind by some behaviorists would move this position closer to the axis of the dimensions. The reality therapy position places more emphasis on the rational thought process involved in counseling than other approaches shown in Figure 9. There is in this approach, however, a rather good balance between insight into one's behavior and emphasis on specific behavioral changes.

In examining Figure 9, it becomes clear that many of the differing theoretical positions fall in rather close proximity to each other in terms of a general outlook toward the process of counseling and toward the objectives of that process. Not surprisingly, the behaviorists and self-theorists show up at the extremes, followed closely by the Gestaltists, Psychoanalysts, and Reality Therapists. It *is* important to note, however, that, as this model suggests, most approaches to counseling have more basic similarities than they do differences.

If this were the only model used, an adequate understanding of the interrelationships among the general orientations toward the counseling process and out-comes could be developed. But since we are primarily interested in how these general orientations are applied to the group process, a second conceptual model is needed which, while directly related to the first, is more specific to the group situation (Figure 10).

Figure 10   Counseling: Conceptual Model Number Two

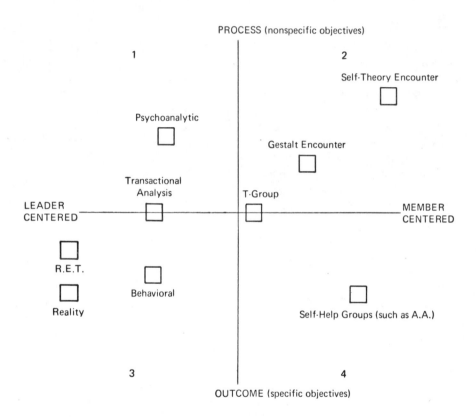

Conceptual Model Number Two

One of the crucial dimensions along which various group theorists can be placed is a continuum running from leader-centered to member-centered. Leader-cen-tered represents an orientation toward the group leader as expert. With such an orientation, much of what happens is determined by the behavior of the group leader. A member-centered orientation leads to a view of the group leader as a facilitator of member-member interactions. Much of what happens is a product of the group members' interactions, not the leader's direction.

A second dimension which is most difficult to define using a single word is what we refer to here as a process outcome continuum. Process, as defined here, refers to an emphasis on the use of group dynamics principles, on the benefits of the group situation itself, and on the holistic approach to individuals. Outcomes as defined here means more emphasis on what happens after counseling, on specific behavioral changes, and on the concept that group counseling is actually individual counseling occurring in a group setting.

Dimensions and Quadrants   While the four dimensions of this group model are not completely compatible with the basic orientation model shown in Figure 9, there is a great deal of overlap. The leader-process, member-process, member-outcome, and leader-outcome quadrants are roughly equivalent to the rational-insight, insight-affective, affective-action, and action-rational quadrants. As an example, those who adhere to a basic counseling orientation of insight-affective will hold to the view that group counseling should be concerned about process factors and should be member centered. As will be seen, however, the models are not completely interchangeable.

As with the basic orientation model, the group model shows both the TA and T-group approaches located at the intersection of the quadrants. In this model, it is conceivable that the T-group approach could have been placed directly in the center. While the traditional TA people are very leader-centered, most neo-TA theorists are quite balanced in their approach. It is the neo-TA people that are reflected in this diagram; thus both of these approaches tend to have a balance between leader-centered and member-centered emphasis, and a balance between a concern for process and outcome variables. Certainly the T-group, with its semistructured activities, and TA, with its contracts, have elements of leader-centered behavior, but both are also concerned about facilitating member-member interactions within the group. Likewise, both are concerned about the total individual and the transfer of group learning to outcomes outside of counseling.

One change in quadrants between this model and the previous model involves the psychoanalytic position. The reader will recall that the psychoanalytic position fell in the insight-affective quadrant of the first model. In the group counseling model, it moves to quadrant I because of its reliance on the concept of group leader as expert. It is also important to note that, while it is located in a process-oriented quadrant, the process emphasized is different from the process emphasized by the Gestalt and self-theorists located in quadrant II. The dynamics of psychoanalytic groups are involved with what might be termed as there-and-then themes, as opposed to the here-and-now perspective of the Gestalt and self-theory groups. The major dynamics of psychoanalytic groups are the working through of transferences and countertransferences. The psychoanalytic position moves closer to quadrant II when the psychoanalytic group focuses on the group members as a reconstruction of a family. In this case, the focus of the psychoanalytic group is also on the interactions with other group members. The objective of this particular psychoanalytic approach is to help the individual see how interactions with others are based on faulty perceptions formed early in life through interactions with family members.

The Gestalt and self-theory positions located in quadrant II tend to be concerned with what is going on either in the group or in actual life at that time. The Gestalt encounter groups tend to have more of a balance between leader-centered and member-centered activities than does the self-theory encounter approach. Both positions, however, place a great reliance on the importance of the actual group process. They believe that it is the interactions of group members that lead to therapeutic change. The third quadrant, outcome-leader, contains those adhering to behavioral, reality, and R.E.T. positions. Of all the positions shown in Figure 10, those shown in quadrant III have the least concern for group dynamics and the most concern for specific outcomes from counseling. They also place more importance on the leader's engaging in specific behaviors designed to bring about changes in the group members. While they do not ignore the importance of member-member interaction, they place more importance on the group counselor as leader of the group process.

While no specific approach discussed here falls into quadrant IV, it is the quadrant where self-help or leaderless groups that come together for a specific purpose could be placed. Alcoholics Anonymous would be a good example of an approach located in this quadrant. Here the interpersonal process is utilized to help each individual abstain from alcohol. Hence, it is process oriented, but toward a specified objective.

Using the two models, specifically the group model as a base, a more detailed description can be given of the actual process of the group; that is, what events are likely to occur? As can be expected, those approaches within a particular quadrant have more in common with each other than they do with approaches in other quadrants. However, there are some basic beliefs about group counseling that transcend the model. Such are, by and large, the factors that influence the counselor to choose the group modality instead of individual counseling in certain situations. Before proceeding with a discussion of leader behaviors and techniques common to each of the four quadrants, it is necessary to examine the commonalities that cut across all the quadrants.

THERAPEUTIC FACTORS IN THE GROUP PROCESS

Ohlsen (1974) has suggested that a successful group counselor must recognize, understand, and know how to release the facilitative potential of the group itself. Similarly, Corsini (1957) has suggested that, while the group leader may be of the greatest value to the group process because of training, he or she is far from the only ingredient, and it would be erroneous not to consider the importance of the group members themselves. If some central factors that are common to the process of group counseling can be established, then it is possible to obtain some central notion of the process which can help to develop strategies for selecting clients, for composing the group, and for developing leader behaviors and techniques that will enhance these facilitative factors (Yalom, 1975).

A classic attempt to define the common therapeutic or facilitative factors that cut across various theoretical approaches to group work was conducted by Corsini and Rosenberg in 1955. From a review of over three hundred articles on group work, they produced a list of nine therapeutic factors which they felt were present in all groups. In a more limited study, Gottschalk (1966) examined T-groups and found that there was a great deal of similarity between what actually went on and what would be expected to take place in psychoanalytic groups. Similar studies by Berzon, Pious, and Parson (1963) and by Yalom, Tinklenberg, and Gilula (Yalom, 1975) also demonstrated that the clients of differing types of therapy groups identified therapeutic elements that cut across the groups. While it is clear that there is general agreement about the existence of common therapeutic factors in group counseling, the reader should not assume that all factors are equally important, or even present in all groups. Rohrbaugh and Bartels (1975), in an investigation utilizing thirteen therapy and human relations groups, found some variation in therapeutic factors dependent upon the type of group and the type of participants. Finally, Hill (1975) analyzed the list of common facilitative factors developed by Corsini and Rosenberg (1955), Yalom (1975), and Hill (1957). He reported that there was clear consensus on four factors: catharsis, acceptance or cohesion, spectator therapy, and intellectualization or information. He found four other factors about which there was general agreement that the factors were present in all groups: universalization, reality testing, altruism, and socialization. Finally, he found some support for the factors called installation of hope and imitative behavior. Hill's analysis provides a framework for presenting common therapeutic factors. We begin by presenting those about which there is clear consensus that they are common factors, and finish with those about which there is less agreement. The factors as presented are a synthesis of the list developed by Corsini and Rosenberg (1955), Yalom (1975), Guttmacher and Birk (1971), and Hill (1975).

Acceptance or Cohesion

"The feeling of true acceptance, cohesion, and sense of belonging which develops in a group therapeutically engaged often enables parties to work on issues they would not really grapple with in individual therapy (Guttmacher and Birk, 1971, p. 553)." Cohesion does not necessarily mean that all members are friends. Rather, it is a feeling shared by all group members that each individual has a place in the group. There develops a sense of oneness of purpose, and it is this purpose that binds them together. If a group is to function in an effective way, this feeling must be developed. It is this feeling of being part of something special, and the feeling of individual importance within the group structure, that permit individuals to deal with material that otherwise might provoke such high levels of anxiety that it could not be dealt with. Of all the therapeutic factors, this one is at the core of a successful group; without it there really is no group. A leader, through modeling behavior, can do much to enhance the development of this feeling in members.

Catharsis or Ventilation

Catharsis is the expression of either repressed or stored-up emotion; it often releases the tension created by the emotion within the individual. The fact that the group provides a safe environment in which an individual can freely express deep feelings is a benefit in and of itself. This is generally one of the first goals of many group leaders, and many theorists feel that catharsis is one of the primary factors in developing group cohesion. It should be noted, however, that seldom is the ventilation of one's feelings enough. While it has great benefit in releasing bottled-up material, it is only one step in the counseling process. It is indeed unfortunate that, in many groups run by leaders who are not appropriately trained, catharsis is looked upon as the ultimate goal, and there is no attempt to help the individual reintegrate after the ventilating experience. It is also true that the group leader must be sure the entire group is ready to deal with a single individual's catharsis. If the phenomenon takes place prior to a group's development of the ability to handle it, the individual will most likely be harmed by the experience. If the group members treat the individual with warmth, acceptance, and respect during and after the catharsis, the process most likely will be beneficial. If, however, they reject or in some way show hostility toward the individual because of material revealed, then the experience can be a negative one.

Spectator Therapy or Imitative Behavior

All individuals within a group have the opportunity of being spectators, and "it is while being a spectator that one might inculcate behaviors of others to be tried out subsequently as a participant and thus while being a spectator thereby make a therapeutic advance (Hill, 1975, p. 425)." Yalom (1975) refers to spectator therapy as imitative behavior. Bandura (1969) has demonstrated in numerous investigations that learning does take place through imitation, and the group process provides each member with many potential models. In the individual setting, the only model provided to the client is the counselor. In a group situation, the members can examine the behaviors of many different individuals. In some cases, group members will observe behaviors which seem more effective than their own and will attempt to take on those behaviors. Members also have the opportunity to see behaviors that are similar to their own, and the reasons why those behaviors are ineffective or inappropriate. Because a group is composed of so many different types of individuals, there is potential for both positive learning (i.e., taking on a new behavior) and negative learning (i.e., doing away with behavior that is inappropriate).

The introduction of specific types of models in the group counseling process is a specified form of this natural group phenomenon. In short, this involves the counselor's presenting to the group in some fashion a model who demonstrates the desired behavior. This concept and the concept of leader as model both receive more detailed attention in the leadership chapter. Here we are simply referring to the natural process that occurs because the group represents a microcosm of real life.

Information or Intellectualization

In almost any problem situation that can be brought to mind, an element in solving that problem is information and intellectualization. The group situation, simply because it is a group, has the potential for providing each member with a vast storehouse of information about self, others, institutions, and a variety of other circumstances. It is difficult to conceptualize many human difficulties that do not involve both an emotional ill and a cognitive or intellectual level. Group leaders, therefore, must make sure that each member in the group has dealt with both the emotional and the intellectual level of his or her concern. In short, information is an important therapeutic variable, and the visceral processing of that information is often as important as the processing of emotion.

Universalization

To seek out counseling is a very difficult step for many individuals. Such a step means dealing with the fact that there are some things that the individual simply is unable to deal with alone. Such a feeling leads to the conviction that no one else could experience what one is experiencing. Individual counseling offers very little opportunity for an individual to discover that he or she is not alone in having problems. The group situation, however, provides the unique opportunity for the individual to experience the fact that having problems is not unique. Yes, each member is a unique individual with a particular life pattern and behaviors that are causing difficulty. But in the group, the individual is often confronted with the fact that other individuals have similar problems. In simple terms, there is relief in knowing that you are not all alone in a boat in the sea of unknown faces. Yalom (1975) found in his own group work that there are two general feelings of group members that approach universality. One is the general feeling of inadequacy. Quite obviously, such a feeling can relate to many specific situations (i.e., job, marriage, peer relations), but there is a similar general feeling experienced by group members. The second universality described by Yalom is a feeling of interpersonal alienation. In many ways, individuals experience a sense of being cut off from other people. Once again, the exact form of this feeling can be related to many different kinds of situations.

The feeling of not being alone in one's misery acts to reduce the individual's personal anxiety. It also lends itself to the establishment of the feeling of cohesiveness among the group members. If other people also have difficulties, then it is not as hard for the individual to express personal concerns. There is less fear that the other members will reject the individual for being weak. Rather, the feelings of similarity allow the individual to share in the group process.

Reality Testing

The group, because it represents a microcosm of real life, also presents a relatively safe environment in which members have the opportunity to express feelings and attitudes, to try new behaviors, and to receive accurate feedback. An individual who has had difficulty being assertive has the opportunity in the group situation to try various forms of assertive behavior in a situation where he or she will not get hurt. The group setup also provides a situation in which problems, particularly of an interpersonal nature, exist as in life in the outside world. An individual who is aggressive in real life will tend to be aggressive in the group situation. Thus, the group provides for the direct observation of the participant's behavior, perceptions, and feelings, and enables the counselor to understand more fully the individual's needs and problems (Guttmacher and Birk, 1971). In this way, both the counselor and the other members of the group can deal with the behavior directly, rather than as discussed in abstract terms by a client in individual counseling. The difference is being able to deal directly with behavior as opposed to having to deal with behavior through the client's verbalizations, which tend to be filtered through the client's eyes. In effect, the client is confronted with the reality of behavior.

Guttmacher and Birk (1971) point to the strong advantage of reality testing in the group for those individuals with what they term ego-syntonic problems. These are individuals with subtle character problems that are peculiar to them. Often these individuals do not feel that they really have a problem; the problem is in their environment. The student who always blames personal difficulties on those "bad" teachers is one example. In individual counseling, it is difficult to get such a client to really examine personal behavior. In the group situation, however, the client is confronted with his or her behavior by other group members.

Altruism or Peers as Co-Counselors

In group counseling, unlike individual counseling, there is the potential for group members to help each other. Group members can offer support, reassurance, and insight to other members, and they can also point out strengths and weaknesses to each other (Yalom, 1975). Both Yalom (1975) and Corsini and Rosenberg (1955) refer to this therapeutic factor in the group as altruism. It has long been recognized that one of the most powerful influences on any individual's behavior is the influence generated by peers. In the group situation, peers are often able to make criticisms, confront, and question other group members much more effectively than is the counselor. Group counseling facilitates this phenomenon because of the natural tendency of individuals to want to help their fellows. The group generates the feeling of "I help you and you help me," and it is this kind of reciprocal process on which such self-help groups as Alcoholics Anonymous are based.

Socialization or Interpersonal Skill Learning

While the self-theorists, T-group/sensitivity group theorists, and the encounter theorists tend to place more emphasis on interpersonal learning and the group process than do other approaches, all groups enhance the development of these skills. For many individuals, the group provides one of the very few opportunities in their lives to form meaningful relationships with other individuals. This lack of socialization is at the heart of many client difficulties. Thus the sense of openness, honesty, and feedback that is encouraged in most groups lends itself to helping individuals see those behaviors they engage in that turn people off, and to improve on these behaviors that are conducive to good social relationships. In this atmosphere they feel encouraged to try to make contact with others, and they have the opportunity to observe others' interpersonal skills and to try those behaviors (imitative learning). As they attempt these new behaviors, they have the opportunity to receive feedback on their appropriateness. While the development of interpersonal skills is not the sole purpose of counseling for many group counselors, few would argue that it is an important outcome that well may influence whether anything else productive occurs.

Transference

While not all theorists discuss the transference phenomenon, most acknowledge that the past interpersonal experiences of an individual group member will affect his or her interactions with other group members. The more traditional counselors will talk about the group as becoming a representation of the primary family unit, while others will discuss it in terms of past learning affecting the present. Regardless of the reason given for the phenomenon, or what it is called, clients in a group situation do ascribe attitudes, feelings, and behaviors to other group members that are not based on the actual behavior of these individuals. That is, in some way the individual member forms a distorted perception of fellow group members. The advantage of this taking place in the group counseling situation is that such behaviors are not permitted to become fixed, as they are in the outside world. Rather, this stereotyping behavior or transference behavior is dealt with in the group. Either the counselor will challenge the behavior or, hopefully, the group members themselves will confront the individual with what he or she is doing. In either case, the individual with the distorted perceptions is helped first to see how these perceptions are distorted, and then to work them through so that he or she can interact with people as they are.

The elements in the group counseling process dealt with here cut across the various approaches to groups. These are elements that take place in the group process to a greater or lesser degree, depending on the particular group and the manner in which it is being led. Their importance cannot be overemphasized, because they provide therapeutic benefits to group members irrespective of other group procedures being used. They are, in effect, some of the prime reasons for using the group process instead of individual counseling. Except for catharsis, information, and to a lesser extent transference, the therapeutic factors discussed are ones that take place in the group situation and not in an individual counseling situation. Having examined, then, the common core of therapeutic factors in the group process, it is now appropriate to turn to the ways in which the various theorists view the leader's function and the techniques appropriate to the group process. This involves the various positions as they appear in the four quadrants on the group model.

BEHAVIOR OF GROUP MEMBERS

As has been shown in Figure 10, membership factors are a major dimension of the group model, and the importance attributed to the behavior of members within the group setting varies in proportion to the amount of importance given to the counselor as leader of the group. The more reliance that is placed on the concept of counselor as expert, the less reliance is placed on the importance of membership behaviors. In general, those theorists shown in quadrant II of Figure 10 place more emphasis on member behaviors, while those theorists shown in quadrants I and III are somewhat less concerned with member behaviors and characteristics. Nonetheless, there are certain characteristics of members and member behaviors which are relatively consistent across theoretical positions, and it is to these commonalities that we now direct our attention.

Group Composition

The composition of the group is certainly an influential factor in member behavior, especially in ultimate behavior. Most group theorists, with the possible exception of some theorists in quadrant III, favor a group composed of heterogeneous individuals as opposed to a homogeneous population, except in the case of severe behavioral disturbances, which would be treated in group psychotherapy. The heterogeneous group is preferred because it provides a much more realistic representation of the real world, thus enhancing the possibilities of more interaction among members and of more reality testing. Some theorists in quadrant III lean to a relatively homogeneous group, such as a group of individuals who are experiencing the general problem of interpersonal relations. They would argue, however, that while the members share the common general concern, there would exist a great many variations of that problem within the group membership. Hence, their position is that all groups are really heterogeneous groups.

Group Norms

These, like group composition, are not specific behaviors, but their formation is a result of member behavior. Once again there is general agreement across theoretical positions that there is a need to establish norms which permit each individual within the group to express himself or herself in a free and open fashion. The self-theorists talk about these norms in terms of each individual member's behaving in a minimally facilitative fashion. In this view, the norms of behavior that are established place all members in a helping role as well as a role needing help. The basis for the establishment of these norms springs from the group counselor's modeling the appropriate behavior. The Gestalt group leaders also place a great deal of reliance on the group members to establish the proper facilitative norms. In both cases, the leader will also try to get the group to examine any norms that appear to be nonfacilitative, but for the most part there is faith in the ability of the members to establish the appropriate norms.

T-group and TA group leaders place a similar emphasis on the establishment of norms which facilitate feedback, group support, a climate of trust, self-disclosures, and the unfreezing of past modes of behavior. As with the self-theorists, there is somewhat of a belief in the group's ability to establish these norms, but if necessary the leader will provide the appropriate direction.

The more analytically oriented counselor shown in quadrant I of Figure 10 expresses less faith in the group's ability to establish norms; hence, such a counselor will attempt to structure the group's behavior along appropriate lines. In general, however, analytic counselors do believe that each individual must give up some ego identity for the sake of group identity, an identity which they feel is necessary if the group is to function therapeutically.

While those theorists in quadrant III place the least emphasis on the establishment of group norms, they do advocate the establishment of modes of behavior in which everyone can participate freely.

Despite these minor differences, there is an emphasis in all approaches on the establishment of group norms that permit an open, honest, threat-free atmosphere. The only question is how much confidence is placed in the group members to do this themselves, and how much reliance there is on the leader to guide the establishment of these norms. It is also true that, beyond the establishment of norms for the initial group behaviors, each theorist tries to establish norms of behavior that are consistent with the underlying theoretical approach. In the T-group situation, the emphasis is on the here-and-now material and such a norm is established, while quite the contrary is encouraged in the analytic group. The behaviorist is concerned about discussing actual behavior; the reality therapist is concerned about discussing true reality and commitment; the self-theorist is more concerned with an individual's feelings; and the TA counselor encourages exploration of game playing and scripts. In each case, the group leader encourages those behaviors which she or he believes will lead to a facilitative atmosphere and discourages those that do not. The group members will quickly learn these behaviors and will move to establish norms that conform to them. When these norms are established, the members themselves will generally act to enforce them, so that when a member begins to behave in ways that are not in agreement with the norms, that member will be censored. In this way norms, once established, do control group member behavior.

Role Behavior of Members

The behavior taken on by individual members as they fulfill certain roles within the group is defined as role behavior. For example, one member may at one time during the group act as a conciliator between warring factions within the group, or may act in a blocking role by negating whatever the group discusses.

The relative importance attributed to the role behavior of group members depends in large part on the extent to which a particular approach relies on the dynamics of the group process as part of the therapeutic process. It is not surprising that theorists in quadrant II pay a great deal of attention to the effects of membership roles on both individual and group performances, while those in quadrants I and III place much less emphasis on member roles. Despite the position of this latter group, there is a great deal of evidence that individual group members do take on certain roles within the group process, and the nature of these roles has a great deal to do with the success of any group. The area is so important that an entire chapter is devoted to the topic of membership roles. It is hard to conceive that individuals do not adopt certain roles within the group and that these roles do not affect group behavior. Every individual, before coming to group counseling, has been a member of a number of groups, and in each one of these groups there were certain roles which the individual performed. In the family, the individual may fulfill the role of parent and spouse; at work, the individual may be the low person on the staff. Each position calls for differing kinds of behavior, even though there is a common core. It is to be expected, then, that such an individual would come to the group with certain role expectations for self and others, and these expectations are going to affect the roles the individual adopts in the group, which in turn are going to affect the behavior of the group as a whole.

In general, a member of any group can choose to move in and out of any one of three broad categories of roles. The person can perform in a role that serves the function of facilitating the communication and feeling of trust; the person can fulfill a role which acts to move the group toward the accomplishment of its task; the person may take on a role which acts to hinder the process of the group. It is hoped, of course, that most members will operate in the first two areas, as they are appropriate in the group process; that is, they will develop flexible role behavior. It is to be expected, however, that in most groups some individuals, at least for a period of time, will take on blocking roles.

Transference and Member Behavior

Earlier in this chapter, transference within the group was discussed as a therapeutic factor common to most groups. It should be apparent that such a phenomenon plays an important function in determining the behavior of members. The analytically oriented counselor, in particular, places a great deal of importance on the fact that the group has the potential for becoming a recapitulation of each individual's family. Thus a multiple transference occurs, which is going to affect the way each member behaves toward both the group leader (father or mother) and the other members of the group (siblings). While other approaches do not place this degree of emphasis on transference, there is general agreement that group members tend to behave towards one another as they behave toward similar people in the outside world. This is particularly true in TA groups, where it is felt that the group member will engage in the same games in the group that he or she does in the outside world. In either case, the member is behaving in ways which are not consistent with the actual situation, and this behavior can become the base for helping individuals look at themselves.

LEADER FUNCTIONING: A SYNTHESIS OF TECHNIQUES

Any attempt to synthesize the thinking of many individuals runs the risk of oversimplification. However, given our position that no one theoretical approach to group counseling provides the best therapeutic modality for all clients, such a synthesis is mandatory. This section will first examine the general leader behaviors and techniques as found in each of the quadrants in Figure 10. We will then turn our attention to an examination of the interrelationships between and among the expected leader behaviors as represented by the four quadrants in Figure 10.

Quadrant I: Leader-Process

As its name implies, the emphasis in this quadrant is on a group process under the expert direction of the group leader. There are two basic approaches to group counseling located in this quadrant, psychoanalytic and Transactional Analysis. As pointed out earlier, it is somewhat misleading to place TA in this quadrant, because of the many differences among those who call themselves TA counselors. The classical TA leaders are very leader-centered, but many of the neo-TA leaders are quite process-oriented. It is placed here because much of its focus is on analysis of life positions and life scripts of group members. Hence, in terms of the process dimension, it tends to share with psychoanalysis a there-and-then orientation and a focus on the total individual. It needs to be pointed out that this emphasis in TA shifts to more of a here-and-now orientation once the there-and-then material is understood. It should also be pointed out that the more traditional TA theorists will be more closely aligned with the psychoanalytic position while those neo-TA theorists who have taken on a decidedly Gestalt orientation will move closer to the kinds of leader behaviors typically found in theorists in quadrant II.

The traditional TA group leader's primary responsibility within the group is to establish conditions that enable the leader to study the ways in which people interact. As such, there is some relationship to the kind of group process representative of quadrant II. During the initial period of group counseling, the leader is developing an understanding of the characteristic games of each group member, which leads to an understanding of their individual life scripts and the nature of their ego states. The accrued material is then interpreted to each group member as appropriate. This constitutes the there-and-then part of the process.

The TA counselor then attempts to move the group members toward action by first giving each group member the feeling that he or she has the group leader's and the other group members' protection and permission to try new behaviors. Hence, the first stage of traditional TA group counseling shows a strong resemblance to psychoanalytic groups. However, in its contractual agreements between leader and group members and its focus at later stages on process, it moves very close to the behavioral position. It should be reemphasized that the newer schools of Transactional Analysis place much more emphasis on the importance of member-member interaction which is characteristic of quadrant II.

Counselors who adhere to the more traditional psychoanalytic position hold that the counselor, as the professionally trained individual in the relationship, has the responsibility of directing the group counseling toward the accomplishment of its goals. Most often, theorists of an analytic persuasion who utilize group procedures do so in an attempt to recreate the family situation for their clients. The purpose of this procedure is not so much to gather information about the current family situation, but rather to gain insight into the childhood development of each of the clients. The analytic leader in a group situation is expected to engage in the same general behaviors that he or she would exhibit in individual therapy. The leader's direction is designed to facilitate free association and transference phenomenon among all members, which in turn enables the leader to develop an understanding of the clients' early development and current difficulties. Based on this understanding, the counselor, as the acknowledged expert, is able to make tentative diagnoses of the problems and to present the diagnoses to the clients through the use of interpretations.

By facilitating the uncovering of repressed material, the counselor helps the clients to see and understand what has been causing their difficulties. Having seen the causes of their behavior, it is assumed that they will be able to develop new modes of behaving, free of the previously repressed material. It is clear that the psychoanalytically oriented group leader feels the need to fulfill a responsible leadership role. While believing that some form of relationship is necessary, the psychoanalysts view the relationship with group members as similar to the relationship between enlightened despots and their subjects. Whatever the dynamics of the group, it is still the leader who is in charge. This is in clear contrast to the group leaders in quadrant II, who see their role as part of a democratic process, a sharing of leadership and responsibility. A further differential between the two quadrants is that, in the psychoanalytic view, it is the leader who holds most of the therapeutic potential. It is the leader's behavior that will enable individuals to rid themselves of repressed material and move to more adaptive ways of living. Those theorists shown in quadrant II have much more faith in both the therapeutic potential of the group and in its individual members' abilities to guide their own lives. In both cases, however, the emphasis is more on insight rather than on specific behavioral outcomes.

As has been indicated, the dynamics of the group from an analytic position are largely concerned with the re-creation of the family, or multiple transferences. These transferences are facilitated if very little structure is provided by the counselor in the initial group sessions. The group is encouraged to free associate, to say anything that comes to mind. As was noted in the psychoanalytic chapter, there is some difference of opinion as to how effective this is in the group setting, but there does seem to be general agreement that, at the very least, the group discussion can approach the level of true free association. Through the free association or group discussion and the transference relationships, the counselor develops an understanding of the group members. The counselor then uses interpretations to help each member of the group understand the repressed material that has been affecting his or her present behavior. Having led the clients to self-awareness, the therapist's assumption is that they will now develop new modes of behavior. The key to this quadrant is the amount of responsibility given to the group leader for the activities occurring in the group. As Brackelman and Berkovitz indicate, "Too little activity on the part of the group therapist allows the group to avoid dealing with him by escaping into the group, and identifying with the group's dysfunctional behavior (1972, p. 39)."

Quadrant II: Member-Process

The group leaders in this quadrant, regardless of particular theoretical orientation, basically view their role as facilitators of the group process. Those group leaders who adhere to the self-theory, Gestalt, and T-group positions believe that the prime responsibility of the leader is to establish the proper group conditions. In large part, they believe that the group counselor does this by modeling behavior that is appropriate for all members of the group. They attempt to make it clear that they are not accepting full responsibility for the process of the group. In effect, they demonstrate through their behavior that in their view leadership is shared by all members. Nonetheless, the very fact that they model behaviors they believe are necessary does give some structure to the group. Their groups are not leaderless. The Gestalt group leader will tend to be more active during this period and is particularly concerned about focusing the group on the here-and-now dynamics of the group. The self-theorists tend to open the group in very unstructured fashion, thus indicating from the first that they are not there to lead the group in any particular direction. For both the self-theorists and the Gestalt theorists, the opening will usually consist of only a summary of the reasons for the members being there. If the group has been established because of a specific need of the group members, this statement will generally be directed toward the therapeutic outcome for which the group members joined the group. If the group is more of a personal growth experience, then the statement may be much more open ended.

After the opening, the counselor in both the Gestalt and self-theory positions will attempt to model the desired behaviors. The first is to make all individuals feel safe in the group situation. As Rogers states, "I want him to feel from the first that if he risks saying something highly personal, or absurd, or hostile, or cynical, there will be at least one person in the circle who respects him enough to hear him clearly (1970, p. 47)." The goal of the leader, through the modeling of appropriate behaviors, is to establish a threat-free, nonjudgmental atmosphere with an emphasis on the collaborative nature of the relationship among all participants, including the leader.

Leader behaviors as seen by the Gestalt and self-theorists, then, are designed to release the therapeutic potential of the group. Group members are believed to have at least as much therapeutic power as does the counselor. The leader seeks to provide the conditions that will facilitate the development of self-understanding in each individual. The focus is on here-and-now feelings, attitudes, and behaviors. The leader does not attempt to get individuals to explore their pasts or the possible underlying causes of behavior. Rather, the leader is concerned with present functioning and how to make that functioning more adaptive. Given such a relationship, the belief is that the individual will be brought to an understanding of self and behavior and, because the individual group member has the ability to plan in a rational fashion, he or she will be able to engage in new, more appropriate behaviors without any further assistance from the group leader.

By and large, the T-group/sensitivity group leader is very similar to the self-theory group leader. The principal difference lies in the importance of the members of the group further transferring the learning of fairly specific skills to the outside world. While the emphasis is on leader as facilitator, it is as facilitator of both the group process and of the learning of specific material. The more the leader is oriented toward the traditional NTL-group position, the more reliance there will be on transfer of learning and on activities that are designed to facilitate that learning. In such cases the leader will often use structured exercises which the members go through; the leader then helps the group members process that material and translate the new learning to situations outside the group. In this sense, the leader goes through a fairly prescribed procedure and does function in the traditional sense of leader. The more he or she moves toward the encounter end of this continuum, the more emphasis there will be on leader as member, and the less emphasis there will be on structured procedures and transfer of learning.

In terms of techniques used by the group leader, the self-theorist and Gestalt group leaders advocate an essentially technique-free process. In both cases, the emphasis is primarily on counselor behaviors that enhance member-member interactions, basic group trust, the expression of feeling, and the development of insight on the part of each member. The emphasis of the self-theorist is on the counselor's ability to convey the dimensions of empathy, respect, genuineness, concreteness, immediacy, relevant counselor self-revelation, and confrontation. The last three of these dimensions go beyond the establishment of a facilitative relationship and are more action oriented. Self-theorists who adhere to the use of these last three dimensions really are taking an eclectic position and would show up closer to the axis of Figure 10. They are dimensions that go beyond the original position of Rogers and are designed to move the clients toward behavioral changes based on the insights they have developed during the first phase. Beyond the counselor's providing these conditions, modeling the conditions for the group members, and encouraging their use of the dimensions, few specific techniques are advocated.

While the Gestalt group leaders do not necessarily talk about the provision of the dimensions just discussed, the behavior they advocate for the leader is very similar. As with the self-theorists, their primary concerns are with the facilitation of an understanding of the dynamics going on in the group, and with helping individuals recognize that they can maintain control over their own lives.

The T-group leaders' approach is also similar to the self-theory approach, but many of them advocate the use of interaction exercises that are designed to facilitate interpersonal understanding. The T-group leader has as the chief goal the facilitation of an environment conducive to learning. Data in the form of problem situations or simulations brought to the group may facilitate the development as such as environment. The T-group leader also attempts to model desirable behavior for all group members by raising questions, expressing feelings, and accepting criticism. The group leader is profoundly concerned with keeping the flow of communication between members open and will be quick to point out blocks to that communication process. Finally, the leader is very concerned about the transfer of learning from the group to the outside. Hence, a chief technique is processing the material produced in the group and focusing the group's attention on the application of this learning to the outside.

Quadrant III: Leader-Outcome

Group counselors in quadrant III place an emphasis on leader-directed activities and on specific outcomes of the counseling process. They are similar to counselors in quadrant I in that they believe that the counselor must be an active leader of the group process, but they differ from those in quadrant I in that their focus is on behavioral change rather than on the development of understanding. This difference is a difference in degree, for counselors who are in quadrant III do not say that understanding is not necessary or desirable. Rather, they believe that understanding does not necessarily lead to changes in behavior. Therefore, they have a tendency to spend much more time in the group process working on specific behavioral changes to be made by the clients in the world outside of the group. Theorists in quadrant III also have some similarity to those in quadrant II. In particular, during the initial stages of the group process, theorists in quadrant III will utilize many of the group-building techniques so important to theorists in quadrant II. Unlike the theorists in quadrant II, however, the theorists in quadrant III believe it is necessary to move beyond a focus on member-member interactions and the dynamics that those interactions produce to a focus on specific behavioral outcomes desired by each individual member of the group.

The behaviorists believe that the first step in the group process is the establishment of a sound counseling relationship. As Krumboltz and Potter (1973, p. 71) state, "Group members must learn to trust each other and work together to help each member accomplish his own goals." The crucial question for the behaviorists, however, is: What behaviors can the group leader utilize to develop such a feeling of trust and openness within the group? This implies that it is the responsibility of the group leader to "define operationally exactly what behaviors indicate the presence of trust, openness, and cohesiveness. In this way the counselor knows precisely what behaviors he wants to increase or decrease" (Krumboltz and Potter, 1973, p. 71) through reinforcement. Given the establishment of the relationship, the counselor and the group members can then come to an understanding of the particular problem each group member is experiencing. At this stage, the counselor and each of the group members define the particular behaviors that each desires either to achieve, to eliminate, or to attain in combination. A key difference between this and the approaches in quadrant II occurs at this point, for now the goal of counseling is defined in terms of specific outcome behaviors desired by the clients.

Having defined the problem, the role of the group leader shifts. The counselor now chooses from a wide variety of behavioral techniques those strategies that will help each group member resolve a particular concern. As can be seen, the behavioral counselor tends to shift his or her behaviors as the group moves through the early stages of self-exploration to the later stages of developing more adaptive modes of behavior. Depending on orientation, the counselor will make use of reinforcement, modeling, shaping, extinction, counterconditioning, cognitive learning, covert reinforcement, and contracting. It is, however, the group leader who decides which one of these techniques is appropriate and then uses it to help each client achieve a goal. The group situation for the behavioral counselor also has the benefit of providing the possibility of added reinforcements from other group members as each member moves toward a particular goal. These reinforcements are often more powerful than any reinforcements coming from the counselor. The group situation also has the benefit of providing for the use of modeling procedures. It has been demonstrated that the use of models who actually take part in the group process can be a beneficial addition to the counseling process (Hansen, Niland, and Zanni, 1969; Warner and Hansen, 1970; Warner, 1971). This is one of the most action-oriented or specific outcome-oriented approaches, and it stands almost by itself as a group approach. It does, however, have some rather close allies in the two other theories listed in this quadrant, those of the Reality theorists and the R.E.T. theorists.

Both the R.E.T. and Reality Therapy positions place more emphasis on the ability of the clients to shape their own destinies. Because they tend to view people more as actors than as reactors, as do the behaviorists, these two approaches place more emphasis on developing the cognitive abilities of the group members. Like the behaviorists, they place some importance on the development of a sound counseling relationship and therefore will rely on similar group-building techniques to those used by theorists in quadrant II. Like the behaviorists, their emphasis beyond the point of establishing a good group relationship is also on specific behavioral changes for each client.

Rational Emotive Therapy is essentially a teaching procedure designed to help clients develop a rational understanding of their behaviors. The role of the R.E.T. group leader is to confront clients' expressions of irrational thinking which lead to inappropriate and self-defeating behaviors. Through this process, each client is helped to develop an understanding of his or her irrational thought process. Once this understanding is developed, the client is helped to develop new, rational ways of thinking and behaving. At this stage the R.E.T. group counselor may use such things as homework and even some behavioral reinforcement techniques. Of the three approaches in quadrant III, the R.E.T. approach comes closest to being an eclectic position in that it places some emphasis on insight. Its primary emphasis, however, is on behavioral change and, like other positions in quadrant III, it places a heavy reliance on leader behaviors.

The most cognitively oriented approach in the entire model is Reality Therapy. A key element in this approach is the importance placed on reality—not reality as perceived, but reality as it exists. Glasser states, "The therapist must not only be able to help the client accept the real world, but he must then further help him fulfill his needs in the real world so that he will have no inclination in the future to deny its existence (1965, p. 9)." The goal of the group counselor, from a Reality Therapy perspective, is to become involved with each group member and to get each group member to face reality. As members are confronted with reality, they are forced to make decisions as to whether their current behavior is responsible or irresponsible. Responsible behavior leads to normal functioning, while irresponsible behavior leads to maladaptive behaviors. As Glasser states, "Reality may be painful, it may be harsh, it may be dangerous, but it changes slowly. All any man can hope to do is struggle with it in a responsible way by doing right and enjoying the pleasure or suffering the pain that may follow (1965, p. 41)." As with the behaviorists, the focus is on specific behaviors which are in need of change by group members. It is different from the behaviorists in that it places much more reliance on the members' abilities to develop an understanding of their current functioning —not how they got where they are, but how they are going about doing what they are currently doing. While believing in the importance of the group members' perceiving the counselor's caring for them, the counselor exhibits no sympathy for their current plight, nor does the counselor accept any excuses from them for not engaging in the behavior which they desire. The clear message given to group members is that they, and they alone, are responsible for their behavior and therefore it is only they themselves who can change their behavior. Feeling that one wants to change a behavior is not enough. The clients must make active commitments to change and then proceed to engage in the new behaviors.

Quadrant IV: Member-Outcome

The reader will recall that this quadrant is best represented by groups of a self-help or leaderless orientation. As such, no counselor is involved in the ongoing operation of the group, but it is possible that a counselor will refer individuals to such groups. The most obvious examples are such self-help groups as Alcoholics Anonymous, Weight Watchers, and groups involved in the problem of drug abuse. In general, these groups come together for a very specific purpose (i.e., to eliminate alcohol consumption), and the means for achieving this aim are largely through member-member interaction and support.

The Quadrants: A Sequential Model

A close examination of the literature on the group counseling process reveals that no single quadrant shown in Figure 10 really represents the entire group process. Rather, it is apparent that for most counselors the group process reflects a movement from one quadrant to another in a rather predictable sequence. As has been seen, some theorists place more emphasis on activities and/or techniques representative of a particular quadrant, but we believe that most theorists and practitioners utilize techniques from at least three of the four quadrants. The sequence in question begins with leader behaviors generally associated with quadrant I, then moves to leader behaviors associated with quadrant II, and generally ends with behaviors consistent with quadrant III. It is also clear that there are certain conditions generally referred to as facilitative behaviors of the group leader which are deemed important for all group leaders, regardless of the quadrant from which they operate. Having examined each of the quadrants separately, we will now turn our attention to an examination of those counselor behaviors seen as the heart of the counseling relationship. Then we will examine those leader behaviors and techniques representative of each quadrant in the sequence generally used by most group leaders.

Core Conditions   Almost any examination of group counseling literature indicates a wide acceptance of, and research support for, the need for the group leader to engage in behaviors that establish a good working relationship with group members. As with the common facilitative factors previously discussed, these behaviors on the part of the leader transcend the whole spectrum of approaches to group counseling. Tyler (1969) suggested that the first and most important goal of counseling must be the establishment of a relationship between the counselor and the client. From a psychoanalytic position, Horney (1942) has written that it is necessary for the counselor to provide the client with a great deal of friendly interest. Sullivan (1954) used the words "awareness" and "respect," and Adler (Ansbacher and Ansbacher, 1956) talked about the counseling relationship as being similar to a mother-child relationship. From a behavioral perspective, Dollar and Miller (1950) suggest the need for empathy, acceptance, and mental freedom for the client. Similarly, Wolpe and Lazarus (1966) described the need for the counselor to communicate to the client the desire to serve, as well as empathy and respect. Krumboltz (1966) suggests that the counselor must communicate an understanding and caring for the client. Certainly the T-group and the Encounter Group theorists also place a great deal of importance on the relationship, as do the R.E.T. theorists and the Reality therapists.

Rogers (1957) was one of the first individuals to call attention to the importance of what he termed the necessary and sufficient conditions for therapeutic change in counseling. Since that time, the conditions described by Rogers have been subjected to a great deal of research and modification. Truax (1963), in a study that was to have tremendous impact on the profession, found that counselors who provided high levels of accurate empathy, understanding, nonpossessive warmth, and genuineness induced greater self-exploration and behavioral changes in individuals than did counselors who offered low levels of these conditions. Since that time, the importance of the relationship dimension in counseling has been substantiated in a multitude of research investigations. Rogers et al. (1957), Truax and Carkhuff (1967), Carkhuff and Berenson (1967), and Carkhuff (1969a, 1969b, 1971) have all demonstrated the importance of the relationship. Carkhuff (1969a, 1969b) has now refined these dimensions, renamed them, and refined a scale for measuring the level of counselor-offered dimensions. The importance of these scales are that they measure conditions for counseling that most counseling theorists believe are necessary in both individual and group counseling.

While much of the previously cited research has been conducted with individual counseling, several studies have been conducted which demonstrate the importance of the facilitative conditions in the group process. Rogers, Gendlin, Kiesler, and Truax (1967), in an extensive study covering nine years, found that group members who participated in groups led by counselors rated high on the facilitative dimensions were released from hospitals in a shorter time than group members who participated with group leaders rated low on the conditions. Parloff (1961) found a strong relationship between the quality of relationship exhibited by the group leader and retention in the group counseling process. Finally, Caligor (1977), in a study of twenty-eight groups, found a strong relationship between retention and the group leader's being perceived by the group members as empathic, congruent, and nondefensive.

In large part, then, the forming of a cohesive group is attributed by many individuals to the establishment of a necessary counseling relationship. The key difference between theorists is that while most feel the conditions are necessary, some believe that the conditions are not sufficient in and of themselves to produce therapeutic change. More specific discussion on these general conditions will be found in the chapter entitled "Establishing the Group."

Structuring Given the necessary conditions which cut across theoretical lines, it is our position, as stated earlier, that most successful group counselors begin the group process with techniques associated with quadrant I, gradually move to techniques associated with quadrant II, and end with techniques associated with quadrant III. In the initial group session or sessions, even when the counselor has met individually with each group member prior to the first session, the group members often are uncertain about the process they are about to begin. In this stage, it is extremely important for the group leader to provide a general framework for the group members. Muro and Dinkmeyer (1977) refer to this process as structuring. It is clearly a technique or behavior of the group leader which is directive in nature. It is of particular importance with inexperienced group members and with younger-aged children. Structuring involves defining the goals for which the group was brought together. It is not enough to have stated these goals in the individual meetings with members prior to the first group session. The group leader has the responsibility of making sure that all group members in the presence of each other understand the purposes for which they were brought together.

The first step in establishing general goals is for the leader to make sure there is a clear understanding of the problem. Napier and Gershenfeld (1973) list the following steps in clarifying the problem:

1. The counselor should make a general statement relative to the reason the individuals were brought together in the group. The counselor should then solicit comments from the members relative to their understanding of the reasons they are there. The purpose here is to make sure there is some general concern shared by the group members, even if each member may have a specific concern related to the larger one.

2. The counselor should then lead the group to a discussion of specific factors that the group members believe contribute to the problem.

3. Once the factors have been identified, the counselor should restate the problem and subproblems as specifically as possible.

Having clarified the problem(s) with the group, the group leader should now turn these problem statements into goals. That is, what are the group members going to try to accomplish through the group process? The position taken here is that the more specific these goals are, the more likely the goals will be achieved. The goal of having each member feel better about himself or herself is nice, but it is too global. The question really is: In what specific ways do the members want to do things differently so that they will feel better about themselves?

A second part of structuring is communicating to all group members the basic rules and regulations that will govern at least the initial stages of the group. While these rules and regulations should not be cast in stone, they should clearly set the limits under which the group operates. Such things as time of meeting, whether the group will be open or closed, the confidentiality of the material discussed, and the amount of physical behavior which will be permitted are all possible items for inclusion in the initial group norms. As Ohlsen (1977) indicates, "Effective structuring contributes to the therapeutic climate; over-structuring and rigid rules interfere with it (p. 25)." Given this caution, it is imperative that you, as a group leader, provide the minimum of structure which will permit the group to begin the group process. Perhaps the largest single reason for the failure of groups among beginning group counselors is that they do not provide the necessary framework for the initial group process.

A form of structuring which should not be overlooked is your own behavior as the group leader. Particularly in the initial stages of the group, the group members will be looking to you as a model for the appropriate group behavior. The initial goal-setting activity provides an excellent opportunity for you to model good group behavior. As you show a willingness to listen to other group members, to express your own feelings, to respond to others in an empathic and genuine way, the group members will see these as desirable and expected behaviors. As the clients begin engaging in these desirable group behaviors, it is important that you provide positive reinforcement for their actions. This can be a simple nod of the head, a smile of approval, or a positive statement made to the individual engaging in the desired behavior. In the same way, it is important that you do not reinforce behaviors which are inappropriate in the group process. Most often this is accomplished best, except in severe cases, by ignoring the undesirable behavior.

The Group Process   Having established the goals of the group and at least the initial norms, the focus of the leader can now shift to the group process. To an extent, some guidelines for the group process have already been established by the counselor modeling the desired behaviors. Up to this point, however, the group members have been able to operate at a rather safe level. If the group is to cohere into a true group, the members must develop a level of trust and openness. Of prime importance at this stage is developing the appropriate member-member interactions. Thus begins the transition from leader behaviors associated with quadrant I to behaviors that are more closely aligned with quadrant II. At least initially, the leader provides some direction, but the focus is clearly on the principles of group dynamics characteristic of quadrant II.

Regardless of theoretical orientation most, if not all, group counselors believe that a feeling of trust among members which leads to free expression of both cognitive and affective material must be developed early in the group process. Several factors make it necessary that the group counselor pay particular attention to the development of this feeling of trust. First, even with the careful screening interview and careful structuring by the group leader, most group members, especially inexperienced ones, come to the initial meetings unsure of themselves and of what to expect in the group process. A second factor is that our society tends to discourage the expression of feelings and attitudes. Thus, individuals come to the group situation having been conditioned to do the opposite of what is necessary for a good therapeutic group. Third, in the initial group sessions individual members do not know one another, even though they may have been told that the other group members share similar concerns. Thus, they have no data about each other to help begin meaningful discussion. Finally, all of us, even in those times when we are in need of help, have a natural tendency to defend ourselves against outside attacks. Therefore our initial meetings with other individuals are often characterized by defensive and protective behaviors.

Semistructured Activities   In order to counteract these factors, many group leaders utilize a variety of semistructured activities designed to initiate the group process. The feeling here is that these activities are very useful in the initial sessions because they offer the advantage of being relatively threat free. They have the further advantage of generating data among individuals that can provide for the initial member-member interaction. Following are some brief descriptions of simple semi-structured exercises designed to facilitate the development of trust and openness in groups. These experiences are atheoretical and can be utilized by counselors with a variety of backgrounds. It should be kept in mind by the group leader that these exercises are not simply games but are activities designed specifically to provide experienced-based learning. As Pfeiffer and Jones state, "Experience-based learning is facilitated by adherence to a model that begins with experience and ends with an answer to the question, 'So what?' The experiential model includes five cyclical steps (1977, p. 1)." The five steps outlined by Pfeiffer and Jones include experiencing, publishing, processing, generalizing, and applying. Experiencing is the actual process of completing the specified activity or exercise. It is unfortunate that some group leaders who use structured exercises to initiate groups stop at this point, for, if the full five-step process outlined by Pfeiffer and Jones is not followed, the exercises become nothing more than an enjoyable activity rather than an activity with a specified purpose. A second stage outlined by Pfeiffer and Jones is what they term publishing reactions to the actual activity. It is simply the process of having the group members share their reactions to the activity. This logically leads to the third stage, which is the processing of these reactions among the group members. It is often at this point that the group members can be helped to see the relationship between the kinds of behaviors going on during the activity phase and the kinds of behaviors needed in the group process. The fourth stage consists of generalizing from the activity to the ongoing group process. This then leads to the final stage of the learning experience model, which is "applied." In the context used here, applying the material that was learned means utilizing the skills developed in the activity in the ongoing group process.

Getting acquainted exercises　The following are examples of simple exercises that can be used to set the members of your group interacting with one another.

1. *Who am I?*　This exercise is designed to help the group members get to know each other in a relatively fast and nonthreatening way. Group members simply are given cards on which they answer the question "Who am I?" They do this by writing a series of adjectives or words that describe their values. These cards are then pinned on, and the members are instructed to circulate until each member has had a chance to look at the others' cards. There is no talking. At the end of this brief period, the members are instructed to find one of the individuals with whom they feel they would have something in common based on what they saw on the cards. The individuals then pair off and discuss what is on each other's cards.

2. *Introductions.*　Have the members of the group pair off and talk with each other in the dyad for a period of five to ten minutes. Tell them that after this period, they will come back to the group and introduce each other to the rest of the group. This exercise is quite threat free, but it does provide a

very good vehicle for helping group members examine the kinds of things that people generally share with each other in early stages of interaction.

3. *Discovering similarities.*   In a similar fashion to exercise 2, individuals are broken into dyads, told to find out as much about each other in terms of similarities as they can, and then return to the group and share those similarities with the rest of the group.

Even with these ice-breaker exercises, it is important to go through the five-stage process outlined by Pfeiffer and Jones. Much valuable learning can be lost if these exercises are not processed in this fashion. Beyond these initial ice-breaker exercises are exercises designed to focus more directly on the group process. These are usually designed to facilitate self-disclosure, appropriate listening skills, and appropriate feedback techniques among members.

Four-Corner Exercise   This exercise is designed specifically to build group cohesion. A secondary purpose is to provide a relatively safe manner for participants to begin the self-disclosure process with one another. Finally, the exercise can be used to demonstrate the importance of good listening skills. The procedures are as follows:

1. Pass out a blank 4×7 card to each participant.

2. Ask participants to fill in the following information.
   a. Upper right-hand corner of the card
      (1) The most difficult decision you've made in the last two years.
      (2) The most important thing you've learned about yourself in the last year.
      (3) The most exciting learning experience you've had in the last two years.
   b. Upper left-hand corner of the card
      (1) The place where you feel the most loved.
      (2) The place with the most beautiful view.
      (3) The place you last spent three consecutive happy days.
   c. Lower right-hand corner of card
      (1) Two people who have been your teachers.
      (2) People with whom you have unfinished business.
      (3) A person with whom you find it hard to communicate.
   d. Lower left-hand corner of card
      (1) The last time you cried.
      (2) The year your life changed the most.
      (3) The first time you became aware of yourself as an adult.
   Note: The information in the four corners need not be the information just outlined. You may find it more appropriate to seek information of your own choosing.

3. After all four corners have been completed, have the group members

separate into dyads. Each individual in the dyad must discuss one corner of his or her card with the partner. The corner to be discussed is self-chosen, and it is important to make that clear to all members. After both members of the dyad have shared one of their corners, move to step four.

4. Bring all the group members together. Ask members to discuss one corner of their cards with the whole group. After each group member has talked about his or her corner, the rest of the group must respond to something they said (validate the speaker). Examples:
    a. I felt good when you said _____.
    b. You are really happy/sad when _____.
    This sequence should be repeated until the whole group has participated and each member has been validated.

5. The next step is to process the experience. The key process questions are:
    a. How do the participants feel about the experience?
    b. What kinds of things do people initially share with one another? Note: Usually they share more facts than feelings. Discuss how people's feelings tell more about them than do facts.
    c. What process was necessary to validate the speaker? (Listen.) This answer is key because it is a necessary behavior in the group process.

Agree-Disagree Exercise   This exercise also is designed to build group cohesion and to begin the process of self-disclosure. It may be more appropriate than the four-corner exercise when the group has been brought together around a central topic. The exercise is particularly appropriate for building good listening skills and teaching proper group behaviors. The procedures are as follows:

1. Construct a minimum of ten statements related to the problem area for which the group members were brought together. These statements should be worded in ambiguous fashion so that there is no right or wrong answer to the statement. In front of the statement should appear a place to place a check mark under one of three columns—an agree column, a neutral column, and a disagree column. Examples of statements for a group of young girls brought together to discuss premarital sexual relations are as follows:

    A N D
    ___ ___ ___ a. A 15-year-old girl should be required to have parental consent before an abortion is performed.
    ___ ___ ___ b. Teenagers should always be required to have permission from their parents before obtaining birth control materials.
    ___ ___ ___ c. Abortions should be made available only in case of rape or when there is a danger to the teenager's health.

2. Give each group member the agree-disagree sheet. For each statement, ask them to check whether they agree, are neutral, or disagree. They

should not think about the statement but simply check their initial response.

3. When all participants have completed the form, have them pair up with another member of the group whom they do not know well.

    a. Once they have paired up, tell them that the two of them must come to an agreement on each item, and that there is no longer any neutral column.

    General time frame for this part of the activity is fifteen to twenty minutes.

    b. Have participants come back to the entire group. Now all the members must come to a consensus on each item. When your group has completed about three or four items, or worked for ten to fifteen minutes, stop them and institute the following rule. The person who was talking when you stopped them should continue after you give the rule.

    > *Rule: Before anyone speaks, they must repeat the essence of what the previous person said to that speaker's satisfaction. They then can say what they want to.*

    Let the group continue after instituting this rule for another ten to fifteen minutes.

4. Once again, it is important that the group members process their reactions to the experience. Of particular importance is getting them to focus on what happened when the listening rule was put into effect. Depending on the items you included in the agree-disagree exercise, you may also have generated a great deal of data for future discussions around the problem area.

It is impossible within the context of this chapter to list all possible techniques designed to facilitate the building of trust and openness in the group. The exercises listed above are but examples of the type of semistructured exercises that can be used by group leaders in almost any therapeutic situation. As was pointed out earlier, the importance of the exercise is heightened when it goes beyond fun-and-games and is taken through the complete cycle recommended by Pfeiffer and Jones. In this way the exercise is fun, but it also provides meaningful learning for the group and thereby avoids the trap of becoming an end in itself. Rather, it becomes a vehicle through which more important outcomes are achieved.

Further examples of semistructured activities to be utilized in groups may be found in Pfeiffer and Jones (1969–77) and in Napier and Gershenfeld (1973).

Many group leaders who adhere to a theoretical orientation representative of the process-member quadrant will continue to utilize semistructured activities throughout the group process. Individuals who adhere to this particular approach more often than not are working with groups from a developmental or human relations perspective rather than a remediation perspective. Group leaders who adhere to the continued use of exercises such as have been outlined really share characteristics of quadrant I, leader dominated, and quadrant II process oriented.

The key, however, is that their focus is on process and member-member interaction even though the exercise itself is leader directed.

Process Interventions   Individuals who can be identified more clearly with quadrant II may utilize the kinds of activities/exercises outlined here and in the manuals by Pfeiffer and Jones, but they quickly move beyond this to an emphasis on process interventions. In other words, they simply use the exercises to begin the group process, and then pull back from direct leadership of the group activities. Rather, they turn to the utilization of process interventions designed to facilitate the group's own growth and development and the development of its therapeutic potential. Vriend and Dyer (1973) and Muro and Dinkmeyer (1977) have outlined several types of process interventions useful for group counselors regardless of theoretical approach. The list of suggested process interventions presented here is an amalgamation of the two lists.

1. *Universalizing.*   This is the process whereby the group leader tries to help each member become aware that his or her feelings and concerns are similar to those of other group members. This usually can be accomplished by the counselor's intervening after a group member has stated a feeling about a particular situation. For example, group member A states, "I really get angry when my parents question me about what I do." A group leader could then intervene with the following statement: "Susan seems to get pretty angry when her parents question her. Do others have a similar feeling when your parents question you?" Here the clear attempt is to make the group members feel more comfortable with each other as they recognize shared feelings.

2. *Linking.*   Related to the ability to universalize is the ability of the group leader to provide a linking mechanism between the expressions of feelings and contents expressed by group members. The intuitive ability of the counselor needs to come into play at this point, for the counselor is piecing together bits of information expressed both verbally and nonverbally by a variety of group members. In many cases the group members themselves will not see the linkage until the counselor presents an analysis to them. Having seen the linkages as interpreted by the group leader, members will have a tendency to develop a greater feeling of cohesion among themselves. A specific example of a linking statement is· "John and Martha seem to get really uptight when they feel that teachers are putting them down, and I see a lot of the rest of you nodding your heads that this seems to bother you also."

3. *Dealing with here-and-now interaction.*   "This refers to the ability to sense the meaning and form the feelings, actions, and thoughts being expressed at a given moment in the group, thus involving what the total group seems to be experiencing, as well as the individual group members (Muro and Dinkmeyer, 1977, p. 283)." This intervention is extremely important for the

counselor because often in the group process, it is the dynamics of what is going on rather than the words being expressed that is important. For example, if the group had begun to deal with a very sensitive issue in an emotional kind of way and then suddenly changed the topic and moved to a very cognitive level, it would be important for the group counselor to try to get the group members to recognize the defensive behavior in which they had just engaged. At this point, then, an intervention which asks the group to look at what is happening right now is an important intervention. In and of itself, it may be the single most important process intervention used by group counselors.

4. *Promoting cohesion.*   Cohesion within a group is built as members really begin to interact with one another in a deeply interpersonal level. "In early sessions, the members may 'talk about' each other instead of talking directly 'to' each other. The group counselor will merely redirect by asking the member to speak directly to the person, e.g., 'I get very angry when you monopolize our time,' instead of 'some of us take up too much time' (Muro and Dinkmeyer, 1977, p. 283)." Another way of promoting cohesion is to ask group members how they feel about what someone else in the group is saying, but attempt to get them to direct their responses to the individual rather than to you as the group leader.

5. *Blocking.*   In the role of gatekeeper, the group counselor must be able to block inappropriate group behaviors. "This involves intervening in any communication that is distractive to the group or the growth of the individual members. Blocking checks communication that hinders the growth of a member (Muro and Dinkmeyer, 1977, p. 283)." As Muro and Dinkmeyer indicate, one of the most effective blocking statements is for the leader to say "I feel _____ because _____" (for example, "I feel upset because you continually butt in and tell people what they should do.")

The techniques outlined in this section are techniques designed to facilitate the group process. They are characteristic of leader behaviors designed to facilitate the member-member interaction so important in quadrant II types of activities. Certainly other techniques are appropriate and important to the group process, such as questioning, identifying, labeling, clarifying, reflecting, summarizing, reviewing, restating, interpreting, reassuring, encouraging, and supporting. As these latter techniques are also important in individual counseling, they have not been highlighted in this section. Rather, our attempt has been to highlight those process interventions peculiar to the group situation.

Action-Oriented Techniques   Once again, some counselors, who believe that the member-member interaction and the group dynamics thus produced will lead to therapeutic change, will not utilize more action-oriented techniques. Counselors who go beyond a reliance on the member-member interaction and the group dynamic process will then turn to activities more associated with quadrant III. Activities in this quadrant are characterized as being leader-initiated and action-oriented. Each of the particular theories associated with quadrant III will have its own peculiar set of techniques which are action-oriented. There are, however, some techniques associated with the action quadrant that cut across theoretical lines.

1. *Confronting.*   Confronting is a technique utilized by the group counselor to get the group and/or individual members to see discrepancies between what they are saying and what they are doing, or between their behavior and what they claim their intentions are. The degree of confrontation can cover a wide continuum, from the group leader simply saying "I'm not sure I understand. You seem to be saying _____ but on the other hand I hear you saying _____" to a more direct "You told me you want to do this, but I just saw you do this." The group counselor must have a fine sense of judgment and timing in order for the confrontation to be effective. The confrontation that is so direct as to completely threaten or turn off the recipient is nontherapeutic. Thus, a safe practice is to begin with rather mild confrontations, with a movement toward more severe confrontations as time and circumstances warrant.

2. *Modeling procedures.*   The counselor may use himself or herself, other persons, characters from fiction, tapes, or video models. Regardless of type, the goal is to prepare the individual to engage in specific behaviors demonstrated by the model. Modeling procedures, per se, have been discussed in great depth in the behavioral chapter, and the reader may wish to review those procedures now.

3. *Setting up hypothetical situations and role playing.*   The key here is to establish realistic situations in which the clients can act out a particular situation they may wish to engage in outside of counseling. Role reversal, in which the client must take the part of someone he or she will be forced to interact with on the outside, is also an important procedure. In either case, the focus is on getting the client to act out the anticipated behavior of self or others and then having the group as a whole examine the results and reactions to that behavior. In a very real sense, role playing takes advantage of the group as representing a microcosm of the real world.

4. *Homework.*   This technique is used particularly by cognitive directive oriented counselors associated with quadrant III. Specific assignments are given for activities to be conducted by the group members outside of the group. They are designed to provide actual success experiences as well as data for future group discussions.

5. *Persuasion, exhortation, pressure, and coercion.*   "There may be times, not only in emergencies, when all counselors may use different degrees and kinds of nonphysical force on a counselee (Vriend and Dyer, 1977, p. 283)." Some individuals, such as Ellis, see persuasion and related techniques as useful with almost all group members. While generally not

recommending such extreme measures, we do believe there are times when, certainly, clients need to be persuaded or cajoled into attempting particular behaviors.

SUMMARY

The techniques outlined in this section under each of the quadrants are not intended to be exhaustive. Rather, they are indicative of the types of techniques which may be utilized at a particular time during the process. We also believe that throughout the process it is apparent that group counselors, regardless of theoretical orientation, begin with activities related to quadrant I, move to activities associated with quadrant II, and then shift to the action-oriented techniques representative of quadrant III. As counselors operate in each of these stages of development of the group, they obviously utilize techniques consistent with their own particular theories. The point made here is that, as the conceptual model illustrates, group counselors have more in common than is apparent or often realized. In keeping with our eclectic position, we believe that what may be more important is the recognition of the process of movement from quadrant I through quadrant III rather than adhering blindly to a particular therapeutic approach. It is our belief that for some clients a self-theory orientation to groups may be very productive, while for other clients a Behavioral or Reality or R.E.T. approach may be the better one to utilize. Indeed, some early research into the relationship between characteristics of clients and therapeutic approach has indicated that there is some relationship between certain client characteristics and the advisability of using certain therapeutic modalities.

This chapter has attempted to synthesize the various approaches to group counseling. It has attempted to further develop a conceptual model which would facilitate an understanding of the group process, regardless of theoretical position. Finally, it has attempted to illustrate some general techniques associated with various parts of the conceptual model. The next chapter will take a look at more specific techniques related to the conceptual model and particular clients and settings.

References

Ansbacher, H., and R. Ansbacher. *The individual psychology of Alfred Adler.* New York: Basic Books, 1956.

Bandura, A. *Principles of behavior modification.* New York: Holt, Rinehart and Winston, 1969.

Barclay, J. Counseling and philosophy: A theoretical exposition. In B. Shertzer and S. C. Stone (Eds.), *Guidance monograph series.* Boston: Houghton Mifflin, 1968.

Berzon, B., C. Pious, and R. Parson. The therapeutic event in group psychotherapy: A study of subjective reports by group members. *Journal of Individual Psychology,* 1963, *19,* 204–12.

Brackelmann, M. D., and I. H. Berkovitz. Younger adolescents in group psychotherapy: A reparative superego experience. In I. H. Berkovitz (Ed.), *Adolescents grow in groups.* New York: Brunner/Mazel, 1972.

Caligar, J. Perceptions of the group therapist and the dropout from the group. In L. R. Wolberg and M. L. Aronson (Eds.), *Group therapy 1977: An overview.* New York: Stratton Intercontinental Medical Book Corporation, 1977.

Carkhuff, R. R. *Helping and human relations, Vol. 1.* New York: Holt, Rinehart and Winston, 1969a.

Carkhuff, R. R. *Helping and human relations, Vol. 2.* New York: Holt, Rinehart and Winston, 1969b.

Carkhuff, R. R. *The development of human resources: Education, psychology and social change.* New York: Holt, Rinehart and Winston, 1971.

Carkhuff, R. R., and B. G. Berenson. *Beyond counseling and psychotherapy.* New York: Holt, Rinehart and Winston, 1967.

Corsini, R., *Methods of group psychotherapy.* New York: McGraw-Hill, 1957.

Corsini, R., and B. Rosenberg. Mechanisms of group psychotherapy: Processes and dynamics. *Journal of Abnormal and Social Psychology,* 1955, *51,* 406–11.

Dollard, J., and N. Miller. *Personality and psychotherapy.* New York: McGraw-Hill, 1950.

Frank, J. Therapeutic factors in psychotherapy. *American Journal of Psychotherapy,* 1971, *25,* 350–61.

Frey, D. H. Conceptualizing counseling theories: A content analysis of process and goal statements. *Counselor Education and Supervision,* 1972, *11,* 143–250.

Gazda, G. M. A functional approach to group counseling. In G. M. Gazda (Ed.), *Basic approaches to group psychotherapy and group counseling.* Springfield, IL: Charles C. Thomas, 1968.

Glasser, W. *Reality therapy, a new approach to psychiatry.* New York: Harper & Row, 1965.

Gottschalk, L. Psychoanalytic notes on T-groups at the Human Relations Laboratory, Bethel, Maine. *Comprehensive Psychiatry,* 1966, *7,* 472–87.

Guttmacher, J. A., and L. Birk. Group therapy: What specific therapeutic advantages? *Comprehensive Psychiatry,* 1971, *12,* 546–56.

Hansen, J. C., T. M. Niland, and L. P. Zani. Model-reinforcement in group counseling with elementary school children. *Personnel and Guidance Journal,* 1969, *47,* 741–44.

Hill, W. F. Analysis of interviews of group therapists. *Provo Papers,* 1957, *1,* 1.

Hill, W. F. Further consideration of therapeutic mechanism in group therapy. *Small Group Behavior,* 1975, *16.*

Horney, K. *Self-analysis.* New York: Norton, 1942.

Karasu, T. B. Psychotherapies: An overview. *The American Journal of Psychiatry,* 1977, *134.*

Krumboltz, J. D. *Revolution in Counseling.* Boston: Houghton Mifflin, 1966.

Krumboltz, J. D., and B. Potter. Behavioral techniques for developing trust, cohesiveoess, and goal accomplishment. *Educational Technology,* 1973, *13,* 26–30.

London, P. The modes and morals of psychotherapy. New York: Holt, Rinehart and Winston, 1964.

Marmor, Marmor cites common factors in therapies. *Psychiatric News,* 1975, 1–15.

Muro, J. J., and D. Dinkmeyer. *Counseling children in the elementary and middle schools.* Dubuque, IA: Wm. C. Brown, 1977.

Napier, R. W., and M. K. Gershenfeld. *Groups: Theory and experience.* Boston: Houghton Mifflin, 1973.

Ohlsen, M. M. *Guidance services in the modern schools.* New York: Harcourt, 1974.

Ohlsen, M. M. *Group counseling, second edition.* New York: Holt, Rinehart and Winston, 1977.

Parloff, N. Therapist-patient relationship and outcome of psychotherapy. *Journal of Consulting Psychology,* 1961, *25,* 29–38.

Patterson, C. *Theories of counseling and psychotherapy.* New York: Harper & Row, 1966.

Pfeiffer, W. J., and J. E. Jones. *The handbook of structured experiences for human relations training,* Vols. 1–6 and annual handbooks. La Jolla, CA: University Associates, 1969%N1977.

Robinson, F. P. Counseling orientations and labels. *Journal of Counseling Psychology,* 1965, *12,* 338.

Rogers, C. R. The necessary and sufficient conditions of therapeutic personality change. *Journal of Consulting Psychology,* 1957, *21,* 95–103.

Rogers, C. R. *Carl Rogers on encounter groups.* New York: Harper & Row, 1970.

Rogers, C. R., E. L. Gendlin, D. J. Kiesler, and C. B. Truax. *The therapeutic relationship and its impact: A study of psychotherapy with schizophrenics.* Madison: University of Wisconsin Press, 1967.

Rohrbaugh, M., and B. D. Bartel. Participants' perceptions of "curative factors" in therapy and growth groups. *Small Group Behavior,* 1975, *6,* 430–56.

Sullivan, H. *The psychiatric interview.* New York: Norton, 1954.

Swenson, C. Psychotherapy as a special case of dyadic interaction: Some suggestions for theory and research. *Psychotherapy: Theory, Research and Practice,* 1967, *4,* 7–13.

Truax, C. R., and R. R. Carkhuff. *Toward effective counseling and psychotherapy: Training and practice.* Chicago: Aldine, 1967.

Tyler, L. E. *The work of the counselor.* (2nd Ed.) New York: Appleton-Century-Crofts, 1969.

Ullman, L., and L. Krasner (Eds.). *Case studies in behavior modification.* New York: Holt, Rinehart and Winston, 1965.

Vriend, J., and W. W. Dyer (Eds.). *Counseling effectively in groups.* Englewood Cliffs, NJ: Educational Technology Publications, 1973.

Warner, R. W., Jr. Alienated students: Six months after receiving behavioral counseling. *Journal of Counseling Psychology,* 1971, *18,* 426–30.

Warner, R. W., Jr., and J. C. Hansen. Verbal reinforcement and model reinforcement group counseling with alienated students. *Journal of Counseling Psychology,* 1970, *17,* 168–72.

Wolpe, J., and M. Lazarus. *Behavior therapy techniques.* New York: Pergamon Press, 1966.

Yalom, I. D. *The theory and practice of group psychotherapy.* (2nd Ed.) New York: Basic Books, 1975.

PART TWO

GROUP COUNSELING: PROCESS

11

Group Counseling Process: Application of Techniques

It is beyond the scope of this book, and perhaps of any book, to describe completely all the possible interactions between the various theoretical approaches to
counseling. It is possible, however, to develop a general model which, given a
certain situation, may provide a general direction for the group counselor. Even in
providing a general model, however, we run the risk of implying that counselor
characteristics are not important. This, of course, is far from the truth, and it is
exactly the reason why the model presented here will not deal with specific
theoretical approaches but will deal rather with the four quadrants used as a base
in Chapter 10.

While the whole subject of the group process is a complex matter, it is hoped
that the conceptual models presented in Chapter 10 have provided the beginning
of the framework for the reader to develop a personal position. It should be clear
at this point that, in terms of general group atmosphere, leader behaviors, and
member behaviors, there are a great many commonalities, particularly among
theorists located in similar quadrants of the model. There are, of course, differences, but they are often those of degree rather than of kind. We have also tried
to indicate that most group counselors, regardless of theoretical orientation, use
general techniques from at least three of the four quadrants.

Given this background, it is probably apparent to the reader that we believe that
each of the theoretical positions presented in Chapters 1 through 9 are in many
ways only partial theories. Despite some claims to the contrary, it is unlikely that
any single approach is the best one for every participant. Given that assumption,
it is important to examine those settings and types of member difficulties in which
the various positions discussed in the earlier chapters appear to have the highest
probability for producing successful outcomes. Such an examination is in line with
the eclectic position of this book: differing individuals and differing situations re-

quire different approaches. The purpose of this chapter, then, will be to operation-
alize that belief by taking the conceptual models developed in Chapter 10 and
applying those models to a systematic examination of a variety of settings and
client concerns. Included in this presentation will be a discussion of specific techniques that we believe are appropriate in particular settings for particular kinds of
concerns.

The material presented in Figure 11 is an attempt to show the relationship
between probable age of clients in a setting and the general classification of client
concern. As one moves from the bottom of the figure to the top, the focus shifts
from a concern with rather specific outcomes to a focus on the total individual. As
one moves from left to right across the figure, the focus shifts from what traditionally has been called guidance types of activities, through activities generally described as counseling, and ends with techniques that are often referred to as
therapy. Each circle shown in Figure 11 represents the four quadrants discussed
in Chapter 10. The different circles reflect changes in the type of concern which
might be the focus of a particular group counseling activity. The bottommost circle
in the figure represents those groups put together for obtaining information. This
is a rather specific concern with a rather specific desired outcome. We could
consider groups represented in this area of the figure as being concerned with a
very small segment of their clients' behaviors, while the circle at the top of the
figure represents those more concerned with the total individual and more involved
in a total therapeutic process. In short, as the focus of concern moves from the
bottom to the top in Figure 11, the degree of emphasis on affective or process
factors increases. The degree of emphasis also shifts from specific, detailed
outcomes of a particular nature to a more generalized goal related to total reorganization of the individual personality. This is not to say that there is no affect in
the group process when an informational concern is the focus, but the specific
content receives more emphasis than does the affect. At the other end of the
model, the reverse is true. The small circles shown in the figure represent those
work settings in which the majority of counselors operate. Built into this dimension
is the factor of age of group members, at least through the first three categories.
In categories three and four, we can expect that most clients will come from an
adult population. Because the age level of clients is so important, some additional
factors will be presented here before further examining the model.

In general, the relative age of group members should be taken into account in
four specific areas:

1. The younger the group, the smaller the size. In most cases group size, even
   with adults, should not exceed eight to ten, and this number should be
   reduced to four to six at elementary age levels.

2. The length of any one session should also vary directly with age level. At
   the youngest ages, sessions should generally run from fifteen to thirty
   minutes, while with adults the usual time frame is one-and-one-half to two
   hours, extending upwards to what are termed marathon sessions of varying lengths.

Figure 11   Group Process by Setting and Type of Concern

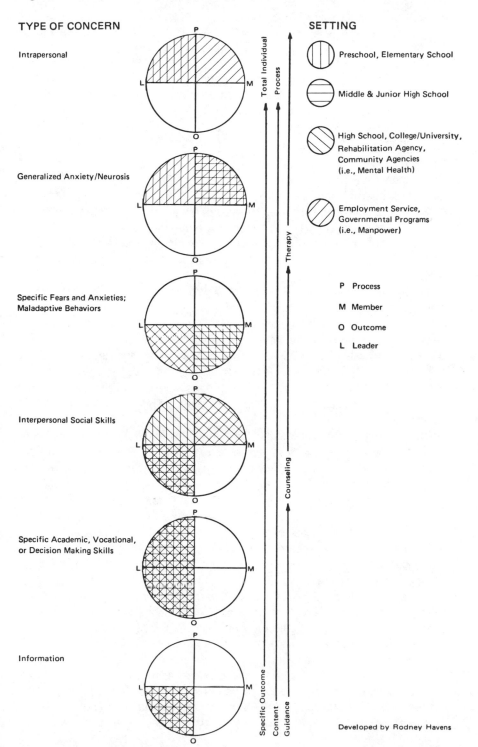

TYPE OF CONCERN

Intrapersonal

Generalized Anxiety/Neurosis

Specific Fears and Anxieties;
Maladaptive Behaviors

Interpersonal Social Skills

Specific Academic, Vocational,
or Decision Making Skills

Information

SETTING

Preschool, Elementary School

Middle & Junior High School

High School, College/University,
Rehabilitation Agency,
Community Agencies
(i.e., Mental Health)

Employment Service,
Governmental Programs
(i.e., Manpower)

P   Process

M   Member

O   Outcome

L   Leader

Total Individual
Process

Therapy

Counseling

Specific Outcome

Content

Guidance

Developed by Rodney Havens

3. The younger the group members, the more reliance should be placed on counseling procedures of an activity nature. With young children, the use of play techniques, puppets, and the like is most appropriate.

4. The younger the group, the more need there is for the counselor to structure activities. A possible exception is what is often referred to as unstructured play therapy, but even here the counselor is structuring in the sense that the room is set up for play and the children are encouraged to engage in those activities.

As shown in Figure 11, then, the younger the client population and the more content- or specific outcome-oriented the concern, the more likely it is that group processes that place emphasis on the kinds of dynamics represented by quadrant III will be successful. On the other hand, as one moves toward a group composed of adults with concerns in the interpersonal domain, the probability is that those group processes represented by quadrant II will be the ones that produce the most successful results.

In using the model represented by the figure, one can note that each circle is keyed to indicate from which quadrant we believe group counselors should select techniques for that particular setting and type of concern. In many cases, there will be overlap between and among the four quadrants. In cases in which two or more quadrants are listed as possible sources of techniques, the counselor has the option of choosing the quadrant that most closely matches his or her theoretical orientation. It should be clear, however, that for some settings and for some client concerns, certain quadrants are, in our judgment, inappropriate as a source of techniques.

The model presented is eclectic in that given different sets of circumstances, different group counseling procedures representing different theoretical viewpoints are recommended. Certainly this model is not perfect, but we believe that it provides general guidelines. The tendency in using any model is to consider each category a discrete entity, but that is not the case in real life. In real life, the lines between categories are often blurred. For example, a group may be formed for the purposes of improving decision-making skills, but in the course of the group process it may become apparent that the improvement of interpersonal skills is also a desired goal. In such a case, the dynamics of the group process need to change to meet these new demands.

It is also true that the model does not speak directly to the differing external factors impinging on groups in different settings. A school situation, for example, is certainly going to present different external restraints, especially in the difficult area of scheduling, than would be found in a rehabilitation agency. What can be said here is that each counselor must be aware of, and make adjustments to, the external factors emanating from the particular work setting.

Each setting also provides a population of clients that differ in more than age. Rehabilitation agencies and the Employment Service have been established to work with rather specified populations. Each of these populations has unique characteristics that must be taken into account in planning a group. It is expected that counselors working in each of the settings described in the model will have had special training in the characteristics of the general population with which they will be working.

The remainder of this chapter will utilize the model presented in Figure 11 as a base. We will examine, in turn, each of the areas of concern as these concerns might be presented in particular settings. In each section, we shall examine and present techniques found in the literature that we believe are representative of the kinds of techniques that hold the most promise for the particular concern and setting.

The reader will find that, as the chapter moves from a discussion of the client concerns at the bottom of the figure to concerns at the top, fewer specific techniques are outlined. The reason is that we believe that the more severe and generalized the client concerns, the more emphasis should be given to the process factors. When a client concern is deep seated, long lasting, and general in nature, no single specific technique is going to solve the concern. What is needed in such circumstances is an intensive therapeutic relationship between the group counselor and the members of the group. A great deal of group counseling, particularly in nonschool settings, deals with client concerns represented at the top of Figure 11, and readers should pay close attention to the material presented in the chapters on establishing and maintaining the group.

The specific techniques presented are not intended to be exhaustive, but rather are representative of techniques that we feel are most productive with that concern in that setting. In most cases, the techniques will be atheoretical, though in a few cases they will be closely aligned to a particular therapeutic approach. Even in those few cases, we believe the techniques can be used by counselors who adhere to differing therapeutic modalities.

INFORMATION SEEKING—ALL SETTINGS

As shown in Figure 11, there is a distinct relationship between the content of a particular group and the process used with that particular group. A point originally raised by Goldman (1962)—that groups that had information as their focus often failed because counselors did not pay enough attention to the process variables— was reemphasized and expanded upon in an excellent article by Cramer and Herr (1971). Groups that have information dissemination as their primary focus have usually been referred to as guidance groups rather than counseling groups. Cramer and Herr make the point that many group guidance activities handled by counselors have failed because they were treated as an academic subject. They state: "What is necessary is a view of process variables which does not exclude content. Process and content are not either/or dimensions; they must interact if group guidance activities are to be meaningful to the students involved (1971, p. 152)."

Cramer and Herr (1971) suggest that in the area of information dissemination, there are two basic questions that must be answered. First, what kind of information necessary for sound decision making is best presented in a group situation?

Second, what specific group methods can be utilized best to help the group members internalize the information? They suggest, and we agree, that two kinds of knowledge are necessary. Information isolated from consideration of personal variables is most often useless. Therefore, groups that focus on information dissemination with the goal of helping the members make better decisions need to help the individuals look at the particular situation about which the information is being presented in light of knowledge of self. "Knowledge of self and interaction to one's social environment can rarely be achieved by relying solely on intellective and didactic methods. Hence, a term such as 'affective discussion' may be used to describe a type of activity which bridges the gap between purely intellective emphasis within a tight structure—the stereotype of group guidance—and 'gut-level' responses emphasized in group counseling (Cramer and Herr, 1971, p. 153)."

Affective Discussion Groups

The affective discussion group described by Cramer and Herr is our idea of the type of group that is most effective when the area of concern is related to information. As described by Cramer and Herr, affective groups are characterized in several ways:

1. The role of the group leader is very structured and directive, with a clear focus on specific desired outcomes.

2. While other concerns may be raised by group members, these concerns are not permitted to become the focus of the group. They will be followed up later by the counselor in individual settings.

3. By their very nature, affective groups are largely preventive and developmental in nature.

4. Affective groups usually are designed to meet for shorter lengths of time than counseling groups.

5. Affective groups can be characterized as having some particular piece or kind of information around which the group discussion may occur.

In considering the utilization of affective groups for purposes of information dissemination, counselors' "preplanning should focus on the vehicles which generate affective discussion: case study materials, role playing, expectancy tables, audio visual materials and other written material. A flexible use of such materials must include attention to how students learn and how they internalize what they have learned (Cramer and Herr, 1971, p. 154)." In short, the counselor planning to utilize affective groups must consider which particular vehicle will provide the best avenue for generating discussion around the particular issue of concern. Utilizing the case study approach, group participants may be asked to examine and discuss a set of data about a situation. Possible alternatives arising out of the particular situation may be presented and the group asked to choose the best alternative. The leader may choose not to provide alternatives but to ask the group to generalize the alternatives.

A second vehicle suggested by Cramer and Herr for affective discussions is role playing. Generally, role playing can be utilized in conjunction with other material. For example, a situation with background data may be presented to the group and then two or three members of the group may be asked to act out this situation. Once the short role-playing session is completed, all the group is involved in discussing what took place.

An especially effective tool with young children is presenting the information in story form using written, visual, and audio material. Various game formats can also be used with young children. In either case, it is important to follow the activity with an open discussion of the material presented.

An often overlooked source of information for affective groups is probability tables. Such tables are an excellent vehicle for helping individuals see the relationship between self and environmental settings or circumstances. The tables in effect help them to weigh the odds of their achieving desired outcomes under specified circumstances.

Affective groups are, in our estimation, an excellent approach to be utilized when the area of concern relates specifically to information. They can be characterized as leader-directed and thus are associated with activities in quadrant III. The variables attributable to setting might affect the type of information being utilized in the group but, more than likely, the setting will have no other effect on groups in this area. The important advantage of groups over individual counseling for information-related concerns is that they provide a vehicle through which the group members can process the information in terms of themselves and their environment. If the group counselor does not provide the opportunity for the group members to engage in the processing of the information, the counselor has lost the advantage of a group format.

SPECIFIC ACADEMIC/VOCATIONAL DECISION-MAKING SKILLS—ALL SETTINGS

As shown in Figure 11, we believe that two quadrants provide possible techniques for group counselors working with individuals who have concerns related to academic career, vocational, and/or decision-making skills. As was the case with information seeking, we believe that two quadrants provide techniques that are applicable regardless of the particular setting in which the clients may be found. Our first choice is quadrant III. In certain circumstances, group leaders may wish to utilize techniques from quadrant I.

The position taken here is that quadrant I activities are appropriate when individuals come to counseling not really sure of what specific skills they need to work on. It is often the case, for example, that individuals do not recognize a need for improving decision-making skills. In such circumstances, therefore, the first task of the group leader is to help the individuals explore their situation in such a way that they come to a determination that, indeed, they are in need of specific skill training. Whether the skill training required is in the area of decision-making or academic or vocational areas is not as important as coming to the realization that they indeed do need some skill training.

Following this realization, the group members are ready for more specific activities that would be typically associated with quadrant III. Thus, we are saying that in some circumstances, there is a sequential relationship between activities carried on in quadrant I and those appropriate to quadrant III. We also recognize that some individuals will come to counseling fully recognizing the specific skill training they need. In such circumstances, it may be appropriate for the group counselor to move rather quickly to techniques or activities associated with quadrant III. In general, we make the assumption that individuals in preschool, elementary, middle, and junior high and some individuals in senior high, colleges, and universities will be in the former group. Older individuals more characteristically found in rehabilitation agencies, community agencies, and employment settings will usually be in the latter category.

In the case of younger clients, counselors more often than not make a priori decisions that a certain group of individuals need to be involved in developmental groups focusing on the development of skills in a particular area. In this case, the first task of the group leader is to help the group develop an awareness of their need for the particular skill or skills in question. As Varenhorst and Gelatt (1971) point out, counselors need to admit openly that certain skills are not only a good thing for clients, they are necessary for life survival. Often in a group, then, the counselor's task is to convince the participants that "without the skill in question they 'will experience less freedom in their lives and will fail to develop into independent, responsible, mature adults' (Varenhorst and Gelatt, 1971, p. 109)." When dealing with specific skills, it is imperative that the counselor include in the group programs: persuasion related to a point of view about the skill in question, the teaching of the skill itself, practice in the skill and, finally, help in clarifying values and recognizing the emotional factors attached to the process (Varenhorst and Gelatt, 1971).

The Decision-Making Process

A classic group procedure appropriate for the development of specific skills is the group procedure originally outlined by Clark, Gelatt, and Levine (1967), amplified by Varenhorst and Gelatt (1968), and further amplified by Varenhorst and Gelatt (1971). This process includes five basic steps.

Step One: Recognizing the Importance of Decision Making   The first step is to help the group members recognize the importance of decision making in their own lives. This can be done by helping them brainstorm the number of decisions they must make every day, ranging from rather inconsequential decisions to very important ones that have implications for their later life. In taking the students through this process, the counselor must make each participant aware of three particular prerequisites outlined by Varenhorst and Gelatt: (1) they must make accurate analyses of themselves, others, and their environment; (2) they must acknowledge that any decisions they make are their own; and (3) they must accept responsibility for their own decisions.

Step Two: Finding Alternatives   Once the participants have recognized the importance of decisions and the number of decisions they make, the second step involves having the group select a decision they all must make in the near future. The counselor then helps the group explore possible outcomes. Often the group at this stage will find that they need additional information in order to move to the third step in the group decision-making process.

Step Three: Evaluating Consequences   The third stage involves the group leader's helping the group members evaluate each of the alternatives developed in Step Two. At this point, it is important to recognize that the various members of the group may evaluate alternatives in slightly different priority orders. This fact can be used by the group leader to illustrate to the group the importance of values in making decisions. As each group member has a particular set of values, it is highly likely that a heterogeneous group will evaluate alternatives in different priority orders. Thus the group members can be helped to see that in many circumstances there are several possible correct answers to a given dilemma.

Step Four: Developing Strategies   Once each participant has selected an alternative he or she wishes to pursue, the group leader then helps them develop a specific strategy for obtaining that outcome. "Because each person wants to increase the probability that what he wants to happen will occur, he must decide the best way of exercising what control he does have to bring about those desired results (Varenhorst and Gelatt, 1971, p. 113)."

Step Five: Implementing the Decision   The final step in teaching the decision-making process is for the group leader to help each group member implement the strategy developed.

We would add a sixth step to this process by suggesting that, once the strategy is implemented or at least attempted, each group member may wish to bring a report back to the group and discuss the process of implementation. Such a discussion can help each group member to see the importance of weighing alternatives carefully and to realize that, even in the best circumstances, not all decisions work out in the way they were planned.

Similar group procedures have been outlined by Schroeder (1964), Krumboltz and Thoreson (1964), and Aiken and Johnston (1973). In all cases, it has been found that a structured program used in combination with verbal reinforcement from the counselor is an effective way of teaching specific skills to group members. We believe that the process is enhanced through the use of reinforcement procedures, but that the structured format is the most important part of the process.

Simulation Games

Another important source for counselors is a book by Boocock and Schild, *Simulation Games in Learning* (1968). This text discusses how simulation games may be utilized to teach a variety of life-coping skills to individuals. Included in the text is a discussion of the original game developed by Boocock and modified by Varenhorst entitled "The Life Career Game: Practice in Decision Making." As with the decision-making process outlined by Varenhorst and Gelatt, a life career game has the advantage of following a structured format.

INTERPERSONAL SOCIAL SKILLS

Elementary Settings

As Figure 11 illustrates, we believe that activities associated with the two quadrants that are leader directed are most appropriate for working with elementary children experiencing interpersonal or social difficulties. Our first preference is for those activities associated with the leader-outcome quadrant. We do believe, however, that at least initially some activities may be selected from the leader-process quadrant.

SIPA Robert Tyra (1979) has outlined an excellent way of organizing elementary groups that he refers to as SIPA. SIPA refers to Structure, Involvement, Process, and Awareness. We believe that this four-step process is a good model for counselors to use with elementary school children.

The first step, Structure, is especially important for elementary school children. Dinkmeyer and Muro (1971) suggest that the group rules originally proposed by Ginott in 1961 be adapted for most elementary groups. The four simple rules which have been shown to be useful are: (1) no toys are to be taken from the room; (2) no physical attacks are to be made on the counselor or on other children; (3) no one is to leave the room; and (4) there is a definite time limit (Dinkmeyer and Muro, 1971, p. 215). Regardless of the rules that you establish, it is important that you state clearly your expectations for group behavior and indicate to the group members the reasons for their participation in the group.

The second stage of the group process as described by Tyra is Involvement. "The counselor, as the initiator of the activity, should become involved with the group and participate fully in the activity (Tyra, 1979, p. 270)." Dinkmeyer and Muro refer to this as playfulness. They state that "being a little playful, whether you use toys or not, helps you into the world of the child.... The counselor, however, must not become just another child (Dinkmeyer and Muro, 1971, p. 216)." Beyond the notion of playfulness, the stage of Involvement is that stage in the process where the counselor involves the young participants in some form of activity. The exact nature of the activity will depend both on the purposes of the group and on the orientation of the counselor. Keat, in his excellent book entitled *Fundamentals of Child Counseling* (1974), describes a variety of activities which may be used with young children in groups. He discusses activity group counseling, bibliotherapy procedures, modeling procedures, behavioral rehearsal, the utilization of mirrors, the use of the incomplete sentence, the use of music, the use of toy rooms, and the use of games. It is impossible, and indeed unnecessary, to repeat all of his suggestions here. We strongly recommend that counselors who will do a great bulk of their work with elementary-aged children examine this text in detail.

Keat does depart from the recommendations of Tyra by stating that he believes that, in most groups with elementary children, the discussion section should come prior to the activity. He states: "They are usually willing to sit down for a while to discuss things, and then to move to some activity. If the children immediately begin an activity, it is sometimes difficult to lure them to sit down and talk about things (especially with behaviorally disordered boys). Also, by following talk with activities, the counselor can make some desirable activities contingent upon the child's performance during the talk session (Keat, 1974, p. 111)." While agreeing with Keat that it may be difficult to get young people to sit down and discuss something after a period of activity, we believe that the best utilization of activities is prior to the discussion. It appears to us that discussion followed by play is just that. That is, the play may have no relationship to the material that was discussed by the group. When the activity comes first, however, the counselor is able to relate the group discussion to the activity that preceded it. In either case, however, what is most important is that the activity utilized by the counselor be processed by the group members. In this way, any learning that did occur during the activity may be enhanced.

The final stage of Tyra's model is Awareness. We believe that this stage is critical because it focuses the group members' attention on how they can apply what they have learned in the group to their life outside the group. Tyra suggests that at this point, the group may be ready to sign contracts with the counselor to initiate certain specified activities outside of counseling.

As stated earlier, we believe the SIPA model as proposed by Tyra provides the counselor with an excellent framework for elementary group counseling. We believe that the general techniques outlined by Keat in his book are excellent and, despite their minor differences over when the activity should occur, we believe that the activities outlined by Keat fit well within the model.

Initiating the Group Process   In addition to general format, one of the initial concerns experienced by most counselors is the initiation of the group process. Particularly among inexperienced counselors, the question often is: What happens if they don't talk? In an excellent article, Kissiah (1975) describes several procedures that he found helpful in working with elementary children. He suggests using name tags in which the children list any three things about themselves they want, and then asking the children to circulate and discuss each other's cards. He also suggests providing children with hypothetical situations which are nonthreatening but which elicit feelings and emotions. In discussing these and other techniques used to initiate the group process, he points out very clearly that "completion of an activity is really irrelevant except insofar as it contributes to establishing a productive climate. Some groups will not need any structure, even at the beginning, but the activities described are found valuable for most groups (1975, p. 19)."

Keat and Maki (1975) also describe an excellent activity for working with young children in a group setting. This activity is of particular importance when the group is composed of inhibited or uncooperative children.

> The talking, feeling, and doing game combines a variety of gaming procedures that make it enticing for children. The children roll dice and move a marker over the

indicated number of spaces on the playing board. The child draws a color card corresponding to the color of the space landed upon. If the color is white, the child draws a talking card (e.g., "Of all the things you learned in school what do you like learning about least? Why?"). When the marker lands on a yellow space, the child takes a feeling card (e.g., "How do you feel when a person you are playing with starts to cheat?") These feeling cards are probably the most meaningful ones, therapeutically. There are also blue doing cards (e.g., "nod your head, clap your hands, stamp your feet—all at the same time"). The game has therapeutic as well as diagnostic aspects. To an astute school counselor, the doing cards can be useful for informally determining strengths and weaknesses in the child's gross motor coordination, emotional development, and cognitive functioning (p. 59).

In addition to the preceding, it would appear to us that the talking, feeling, and doing game has the potential for initiating a group process in a rather nonthreatening but productive way. An article written by Bender (1973) also lists some activities which we believe will facilitate group discussion about feelings and emotions. We believe that the kinds of activities discussed by Bender in the talking, feeling, and doing game described by Keat and Maki not only have the advantage of eliciting affect, but they also have the distinct by-product of building group cohesion.

A Communication Lab   A specific procedure designed to help elementary students with their communication skills and interpersonal relations was described by Cross, Myrick, and Wilkinson (1977). They describe a six-session communication lab. In abbreviated form, the six sessions are structured as follows:

Session One: Member Introductions   Participants are paired and asked to talk together for a period of three minutes and then to introduce each other to the rest of the group.

Next, participants are asked to figure out what feelings are being expressed by certain nonverbal behaviors. The group leader may have to engage in some nonverbal behavior to get this process started.

Each member is asked to describe something that happened to him or her in the past week without describing personal feelings about it. Have participants listen for the feeling that is being expressed.

Session Two: Self-Disclosure   Each participant is asked to draw on a sheet of paper a shield consisting of four parts. In each part, they are to place something which is a symbol about themselves. For example, in one quadrant they can place something they do or do not like about school; in another quadrant, what foods they don't like to eat, and so on. Any self-disclosing symbol will do. When members have finished the shields, they place them in front of themselves. Then they are asked to share with the rest of the group one of the four quadrants on their shield. Allow the participants time to share their feelings about the experience.

Session Three: Self-Disclosure and Feedback   Participants write on pieces of paper three words which they think their classmates might use to describe them. Papers are collected and shuffled, then read out loud one at a time. Participants try to match the sheets with the correct person.

Session Four: Feedback   Members are asked to describe each other through metaphors. For example, the following model may be helpful: "William (or other first name), I see you as a (object) (p. 189)."

Session Five: Unstructured   This group is left open so that any concerns developed during the group process may be discussed.

Session Six: Termination and Positive Feedback   Every participant gets a turn at sitting in the middle of the circle and having the other members tell his or her best qualities or strengths. Once each member has had an opportunity to be in the center of the circle, the group is asked to process how they have felt and what they have learned over the six sessions.

Assertiveness Training   A similarly structured format is suggested by Rashbaum-Selig (1976) for teaching young people assertiveness behavior. Her program is a ten-session program with the specific purpose of having students learn to discriminate between nonassertive, assertive, and aggressive behavior, and to engage in appropriate behaviors through behavioral rehearsal. The similarity between this program and the one just described in more detail is that each session is planned in advance. As one reviews the elementary counseling literature as it relates to groups, it becomes very clear that the structured format is the preferred mode of operating.

Cognitive Dissonance   A technique which holds some promise for getting elementary children to engage in new behaviors has been described by Mayer, Rohen, and Whitley (1972). Their approach, based on Festinger's theory of cognitive dissonance, has been used in a group situation with a variety of young people. Mayer, Rohen, and Whitley state that "counselors, then, can foster dissonant-enhancing situations from which attitudinal and/or behavioral changes are likely to occur by providing opportunities for their clients to observe contradictory items of information. The items can relate to behaviors, feelings, opinions, or events in the environment (1972, p. 279)." They go on to list several examples of the kinds of situation to which they are referring.

1. A student holds the opinion that adults tell him or her what to do. In group counseling, the student observes that the counselor and/or counselors do not tell him or her what to do.

2. Another student has the opinion that adults do not listen to young people. During group counseling, the student observes that indeed the counselors do listen.

3. A student constantly interrupts others when they are talking. Apparently making the assumption that others did not mind being interrupted during the group process, the student is given feedback that indeed members do mind when the student interrupts.

These are but three examples listed by Mayer, Rohen, and Whitley of creating dissonance in the group. They go on to describe how bibliotherapy may be used to create dissonance. They cite an example of a third-grade client who felt no remorse about stealing. However, when the group read a story that dealt with the immorality of stealing and discussed it in the group situation, dissonance was created in the third grader. Also discussed as a procedure for creating dissonance is role playing. In a role-playing situation, clients can be asked to engage in behaviors that they have stated they will not engage in. By engaging in the behavior, they are automatically setting up a dissonance-inducing situation.

Once the dissonance has been created in the clients, regardless of the particular method used, the counselor can help the group members process their feelings and move toward a reduction of dissonance by changing behaviors or feelings and attitudes. As Festinger's theory points out, when dissonance is created in any of us, we move to reduce that dissonance. Through careful structuring, the counselor can create dissonance and then help the clients reduce that dissonance by moving in a positive direction. Quite obviously, this procedure is a very structured and leader-directed activity and, as such, should be used with great caution and care by group counselors.

Middle and Junior High Settings

Probably no other stage of develoment is as fraught with potential for conflict as the stage of development found in young people in middle and junior high school. The literature is replete with accounts of the developmental anxieties that young people of this age experience. Because many of these anxieties are directly related to interpersonal and social concerns, the group process is a natural avenue for counseling in the middle and junior high schools. Rachman (1975), in his excellent book *Identity Group Psychotherapy With Adolescents,* suggests that the group process is uniquely relevant to adolescent behavior and to the adolescent quest for identity. Rachman goes on to say that the group counselor working with adolescents must first of all be willing to utilize himself or herself as a major instrument in the counseling relationship. He states: "A flexible, innovative, creative approach where all meaningful techniques are considered is also necessary. But, above all, technology is always secondary to human needs and concerns (1975, p. 111)."

Perhaps even more than elementary groups, groups that operate with middle and junior high school youngsters need a fairly detailed structure. More than most, "adolescent groups usually spend a period of time testing the limits . . . . They try out a variety of feelings, thoughts, and behaviors in an attempt to understand and establish the limits or boundaries of acceptable and meaningful functioning" within the context of group counseling (Rachman, 1975, p. 114).

We believe that most of the techniques discussed in the preceding section on elementary children are also generally applicable in the middle and junior high schools. It is important, however, that the group counselor recognize that the different developmental level of the middle and junior high school adolescent will create interpersonal difficulties and concerns beyond those normally experienced by elementary school children.

The Hutchins and Cole Model   In addition to the techniques discussed earlier, Hutchins and Cole (1977) have outlined a model for improving interpersonal relations for middle and junior high school students. Their five-step model takes advantage of several generalized techniques and has the distinct advantage of following a fairly structured format. The model is designed to improve interpersonal relationships of adolescents by teaching them how to reduce conflict with their peers. Any individual who has worked with this age youngster knows how important this particular skill is at this age level.

Hutchins and Cole (1977) suggest that the counselor first meet with each individual separately to determine whether the individual is indeed committed to the group process and to learning something about his or her own behavior and ways of improving it. After this initial step, the students are brought together in a group of four to eight students. The five-step process is then instituted.

Step One   The first step is designed to help the students clearly identify what kinds of individuals they value. Each student is asked to list the names of individuals "whom he or she contacts socially and categorizes data about these people to see if friends are the same or different and whether friendships are of long or short duration (Hutchins and Cole, 1977, p. 135)." The remainder of Step One focuses on a discussion of the data generated in the first part of the session.

Step Two   An exercise that utilizes behavioral rehearsal is introduced into the group. Participants are presented with open-ended conflict situations and are asked to list their solutions. The group then discusses the alternatives and the consequences of each solution listed by each member. The purpose of this exercise is to teach the group members that alternatives and consequences should be considered before actually engaging in particular behaviors.

Step Three   In this step, a role-playing exercise is utilized to help the participants discover how people within a conflict situation feel. Each group member is asked to play a role in a particular middle or junior high school conflict. They are instructed to give feedback and talk about the feelings they experienced while in the roles.

Step Four   In many ways, this is a culminating experience for the group process in that each student is asked to prepare a written statement about every other group member. These statements are given to the group leader and are then read aloud by the group facilitator. This is a critical exercise, and the group counselor must be very careful to exercise excellent judgment in reading the statements. The exercise can, however, provide useful feedback to all group participants. The group should not be terminated without processing the information generated in this feedback session. We believe that this feedback session can lead to several other sessions dealing with the material generated.

Step Five   Step Five, the behavior contract, is an individual contract between each group participant and the group counselor. As was stated earlier, we believe that such steps as behavioral contracts, which translate the learning that takes place within the group into the actual life situation, are an integral part of the counseling process. Too often, we believe, learning in counseling is left inside the counseling office and not taken home.

The key to operating groups at the middle and junior high school level, we believe, is first of all to have a deep understanding of the developmental process that these young people are going through. The second essential ingredient is for the counselor to utilize self in bringing a warm, compassionate, and understanding adult into the lives of these adolescents. Finally, we recommend activities drawn from quadrant III which rely on leader direction in a fairly structured format.

High School Through Adult Settings

It may be argued that individuals who are in high school and older adults who come to counseling with interpersonal or social skill deficits come closer to suffering characterological disorders than do younger clients with the same problems. With younger clients, the assumption may be made that their problem is related to a deficit in learning. However, the older client who has a history of interpersonal and social difficulties has a more deep-seated problem. For this reason, we believe that some techniques associated with either quadrant I or quadrant II may be very beneficial, particularly in the early stages of counseling. It is probable that older adult clients need to make a systematic evaluation of their feelings, attitudes, and behaviors. For these clients, understanding their problems and their antecedents may be a necessary prerequisite to the learning of new, more appropriate behaviors.

ALPHA Program   One program that recognizes the importance of self-understanding prior to the elimination of self-defeating behaviors or the learning of new behaviors is a program called ALPHA. Program ALPHA was described in an article by Sparks which appeared in *The School Counselor,* March 1978. A central part of the ALPHA program is a two-hour group session which meets each day and focuses on communication skills, self-understanding, and the elimination of self-defeating behaviors and subsequent development of new behaviors (Sparks, 1978).

Sparks makes a strong point, and we concur, that the first step of any successful counseling program must be to help the group participants develop a strong and realistic set of goals. Students in the ALPHA program are told that the purpose of the group process is to provide an opportunity for them to begin acting on some of the things they are learning about themselves, their values, interests, strengths, and behaviors. They are told that the first step in instituting changes in a desired direction is to learn how to establish goals which maximize the probability of success.

Sparks' program for helping individuals clarify their goals involves asking group members the following questions:

1. Is the stated goal achievable within the proposed time span?
2. Is the attainment of the goal dependent upon people over whom the individual has no control?
3. Do the participants really believe they can achieve the goal and, too, do they really want to?
4. Is the goal stated in such a way as to be measurable?
5. Is the goal stated without any alternative?

6. Will the attainment of the goal be physically or emotionally harmful to the participant or to anyone else? (1978)

Sparks believes that all these questions are critical, for in some cases participants will select goals which are not reasonable in the time frame they have chosen. They may also select goals over which they really have no control. The achievement of any goal is also dependent upon how badly someone wants to achieve the goal and whether, in fact, the person really believes that he or she can achieve the goal. If participants list some alternative to the goal, that indicates either that the goal is not that important or that they do not believe they can achieve the goal they have selected. Finally, the goal needs to be stated in such a way that one can determine whether or not one has achieved the goal. And certainly goals should not be achieved at the expense of someone else.

We believe that the goal-setting program outlined by Sparks can be an important early step in the group counseling process with high school students and older adults who are experiencing interpersonal or social concerns. In many cases, these individuals first need to understand what it is they are trying to accomplish by coming to counseling. Once this decision is made, they are ready to proceed to some skill development. But a shy individual who really does not believe that he or she can change behavior or does not really want to change behavior, will not benefit from any amount of skill training.

The Pannor and Nicosia Format   Somewhat similar to the program outlined by Sparks is a general group counseling format outlined by Pannor and Nicosia (1975). They initiated this system because of the general problem of getting a group focused within a rather limited time frame. As they state, "Without being heavy handed, one of the leaders intervened to subdivide the limited time into certain basic areas (Pannor and Nicosia, 1975, p. 207)." They subdivided each session into seven sections. First, they asked the group members to specify what it was they would like to discuss that day. A second time frame was a period of clarification of the specific problem under discussion. Third, members were asked to discuss similar situations relating to the clarified problem statement. Fourth, the participants were asked to think about alternative ways of dealing with the problem situation. Fifth, a discussion was held about how the group members felt after they had selected appropriate alternatives. The sixth stage was described as stroking time. This period was utilized "to pull together significant ideas and strengths, reinforcing and validating successful coping behavior alluded to by members during the session (1975, p. 208)." Step seven was the follow-through and was actually carried out at the beginning of the next session, when the counselor asked the individual participants how they did with what they had discussed in the previous session. While this format may be too structured for many counselors, we believe that it may provide a useful framework for managing group counseling.

The Baldwin SAM   Baldwin (1976) describes yet another method for structuring group activities. Baldwin refers to his model as the Structured Activity Model (SAM). He states that the "Structured Activity Model for designing group learning activities enhances the generation of relevant data for group exploration in a nonthreatening manner when the content area is personally threatening or controversial (1976, p. 431)." The SAM model has three basic stages: activity focusing, generating data, and data processing.

During the activity-focusing stage, the first goal of the group leader is to help the group develop a premise statement. The premise statement is a description of the reason for the group's being together. Baldwin believes that to be effective, premise statements must be behaviorally descriptive. A second activity during the activity-focusing stage is to develop goal statements related to the purpose of the group. As with the premise statement, the goal statements need to be as behaviorally oriented as possible. Following the establishment of the goal statements, the group leader engages in some orientation remarks related to the goal statements developed by the group and to the process that the group is about to enter.

The second stage, generating data, is also leader-directed. In this stage, the leader has designed some activities which are related to generating data pertinent to the goal statements. For example, a group that is dealing with relationship barriers between members of the opposite sex might be asked to complete the following sentence on a 3 $\times$ 5 card: "The most important skill I can possess that will assist me in maintaining a good relationship with someone of the opposite sex is _____ (Baldwin, 1976)."

The group members can then use these cards as springboards for discussions. This moves into stage three, data processing. In this stage, the emphasis is on processing the information that was generated by the specific activity designed by the group leader. As Baldwin indicates, the structured activity format provides an avenue for everyone to be involved in the group process while carefully defining limits which may reduce the feeling of personal risk. It also produces a task orientation. We believe that this task orientation is often missing from the group process.

The Importance of Structure   It is apparent that we believe that the orientation of group process, in dealing with high-school age and older clients who suffer some interpersonal or social skill difficulty, should be somewhat less structured than similar groups with younger clients. Nonetheless, the models described in this section do provide some structured framework within which the group leader can operate. We believe that with this age client, there is some need for self-exploration and self-understanding which leads to the development of a commitment to change or to work on the development of specific skills. The ingredient most often missing in groups brought together for the purpose of working on interpersonal or social skills is the task orientation. Many group leaders whose orientation is to focus on process and generation of feelings and emotions in a group lose sight of the reasons why the group was brought together. We believe that the models outlined in this section permit the group counselor to focus on the process and generation of affect, while at the same time maintaining a desired orientation toward task accomplishment. It has been clearly documented that one of the chief reasons for dropouts from counseling is clients' feelings of lack of progress toward the achievement of their goals. Providing some structure enhances the client's awareness of movement toward the achievement of goals, and thereby reduces the risk of client dropout.

SPECIFIC FEARS AND ANXIETIES: MALADAPTIVE BEHAVIOR

Preschool and Elementary Settings

The preponderance of the literature related to working with preschool and elementary school children with specific fears and anxieties or with specific behavioral problems supports leader-directed group procedures designed to produce specific outcomes, activities and techniques which are most often associated with quadrant III. There are, however, some individuals who write about techniques that are more closely associated with quadrant I.

Rhodes' Approach Rhodes (1973), in an article entitled "Short-Term Groups of Latency-Age Children in a School Setting," describes an approach that is leader-directed and insight-oriented. While the model she describes is concerned about specific outcomes, its first focus is on developing children's insight into their difficulties. According the Rhodes, a group process is designed "to free the child's resources, to enlarge on the child's repertoire of coping patterns, and to draw on the reservoir of ego strength which the child had accumulated (1973, p. 204)." She believes that the leadership style of a group leader needs to be directive if constructive work is to occur in a relatively limited number of sessions. Thus, she places strong emphasis on the development of a clear focus for the group, clear goals, and a group leader who is active and provides direction and who puts limits on both group behavior and content produced.

Rhodes believes that the first step of the group leader is to develop an understanding of the symbolic language being expressed by the children in the group and to interpret this behavior to them in the here-and-now. This is the basic generation of data for group discussion. As the group participants learn that it is an okay thing to experience negative feelings in the group, they become more free in expressing their feelings in relation to situations outside the group process. As this feeling of comfortableness with the group process develops in group participants, the leaders encourage group members to express their feelings and to share their fantasies with the rest of the group. More often than not, the fantasies are a mixture of actual fact and fantasy. As these fantasies are discussed in the group process, the individual members are helped to sort out what is fact and what is fantasy. The group leader can encourage the participants to act out or to role play certain situations. "The child who dramatized the violent anger toward a teacher, for instance, might evolve to a point where he could play out a better way of expressing his resentment (Rhodes, 1973, p. 211)."

While Rhodes' approach is clearly based on analytic theory, it may provide a useful beginning procedure for counselors working with young children with specific behavioral problems or fears. By being allowed to be themselves and to use fantasy and role-playing activities, the children may overcome their natural fear of adult authority. Rhodes' approach also can give the group counselor a better understanding of the specific dynamics underlying each individual member's behavioral disturbance. Given this understanding, the group counselor may be in a better position to utilize specific techniques to help each child modify his or her behavior.

Tidwell and Bachus' Approach   Another approach associated with quadrant I has been described by Tidwell and Bachus (1977). Tidwell and Bachus developed their approach specifically for working with aggressive school children. The purpose of their program was to reduce fighting and injurious physical contact among elementary school males. The program consisted of eight bimonthly, hour-long sessions. The focus of the program was on the teaching of values and decision making. Tidwell and Bachus argue that aggressive behavior can be diminished by instilling in participants "the values of helping others, cooperation, empathy, and respect for the feelings of others while we taught them several decision making skills (1977, p. 3)." The outline of their eight-session program is as follows:

Session 1—Helping Others   The first part of this session involves presenting a situation to the participants which requires them to discuss suggestions they might give to someone trying to help someone else. The second part of the session focuses on completing the worksheet which describes how they help at home, whom they help, what the person they help gets from their help, and, finally, what they get from helping.

Session 2—Group Decision Making   Following a review of the first session, a second hypothetical situation is given to the group members. This hypothetical situation involves making a decision about who should be protected if humanity's survival were in question.

Session 3—The Empathic Helper   This session focuses on the importance of understanding each other. To start this session, participants are asked to role play in dyads. One individual is blindfolded and then led around the room by his or her empathic helper. The group is then asked to discuss how it felt to be led and to lead.

Session 4—Experiencing Empathy   The focus of this group session is on what it feels like to have someone really understand you.

Session 5—The Aggressive Experience   In this session, participants are asked to describe fights in which they have been involved, to consider the consequences of their decision to fight, and, finally, to consider what alternatives to fighting they had.

Session 6—A Fictional Fight   In this session, a fictional fight is described for the participants to analyze. They are asked to consider the antecedents, the alternatives, and the consequences.

Session 7—Finding Alternatives   This session is a continuation of the discussion that began in session 6.

Session 8—The Culminating Experience   The focus of this session is on trying to reinforce the notion that each participant "has the responsibility first to consider reasons, alternatives, consequences, and feelings when facing potential aggression, and then to make active, pro-social decisions (1977, p. 6)." The key element to the program described by Tidwell and Bachus is that it is a structured attempt to combine the teaching of values and the importance of decision making as it relates to a specific behavioral problem. It is unique in that it has a specific objective, the reduction of aggressive behavior, but its focus is on the development of insight in combination with the development of a specific skill: making sound decisions. We believe that any program that focuses on the development of sound decision-making skills has strong merit.

Culbertson's Approach   An interesting approach that cuts across quadrants II and III is described by Culbertson in an article entitled "An Effective, Low-Cost Approach to the Treatment of Disruptive School Children," which appeared in *Psychology in the Schools.* In this program, therapy is seen as a two-level model. "The outer form of therapy was one of behavior modification with a reinforcement pattern for any given day determined by performance in the previous session. . . . The reinforced behaviors in the therapy meetings (defined by the teachers as those needed to improve the student's adjustment in the classroom) were: (a) sitting on one's seat; (b) listening to someone else speak; and (c) taking turns talking during the discussion periods (1974, p. 185)." A second level of therapy related to the development of a highly personal and special relationship between the group counselor and the children participating in the group. The emphasis was on the counselor's interest, concern, and caring for the children. It was designed to provide an opportunity for the children to vent their feelings about home and school.

Culbertson reports that the outcomes from this two-level approach to group therapy with disruptive school children have been very productive. It is unique in that it combines a very structured behavior modification program designed to focus on very specific outcomes with the provision of an opportunity for children to express their anger and frustrations comfortably.

Other Approaches   Several articles describe specific behavioral procedures to be utilized in a group setting with elementary school children. The approaches described share the common denominator of being designed to deal with the specific problem in an individualized way within a group context. In one form or another, all of these approaches emphasize the necessity of the group counselor's first clearly developing an understanding of each participant's particular problem. A second step is clear definition of the specific behavioral goal for each participant. Given the selection of the goal, the counselor then must choose the particular behavioral technique that will be utilized to modify the individual's behavior. The specific behavioral procedures have been outlined in the chapter on behavioral counseling and need not be reviewed here. It is important, however, to remind the reader that not all reinforcements or behavioral procedures work the same for all individuals. Four articles which are examples of the utilization of behavioral procedures with elementary school children are:

1. "Activity Group Therapy Model" by Cermak, Stein, and Abelson (1973)
2. "Individualizing Behavior Therapy for Children in Group Settings" by McInnis and Marholin (1977)

3. "Behavioral Group Counseling with Disruptive Children" by Gumaer and Myrick (1974)

4. "Group Desensitization of Test Anxiety in Elementary School" by Barabasz (1973)

Adolescence Through Adulthood

In many ways, there is little difference between activities described in the preceding section and activities and techniques appropriate for clients from adolescence through adulthood. In dealing with concerns related to specific fears and anxieties or to specific maladaptive behaviors, the participants in a group, particularly as they approach adulthood, are very aware of the reasons why they come to counseling or have been brought to counseling. Most often, therefore, the early stages of counseling can focus on developing cohesion in the group and on sharpening each participant's understanding of the specifics of his or her difficulty. There is very often, however, a key difference between working with elementary school children and working with adolescents and adults with specific behavior problems. In many cases, the adolescents and adults will not be located in school settings but in other institutions or in noneducational settings. It is imperative that counselors who operate in these settings develop a complete understanding of how the nature of the setting will influence the operation of the group. The counselor in a high-security correctional facility, for example, will operate with many more restrictions than the counselor in an elementary school. On the other hand, a counselor in a low-security correctional facility may have more freedom than a counselor operating in an educational setting. The same may be said for counselors operating in rehabilitation agencies and other adult facilities. That is, the rules and operating procedures of the particular agency or facility may affect such things as who can be in a group, how long the group may meet, for what purposes the group may meet, the confidential nature of the group, and where the group may meet. These are just some of the factors that each counselor must consider in working in these various settings.

   Working in the Correctional Facility   One setting in which counselors find themselves more and more involved with clients is the correctional facility. In that setting, more often than not, "group treatment has been described by many clinicians as the optimal therapeutic approach (Julian and Kilmann, 1979, p. 4)." Julian and Kilmann undertook an extensive review of the outcome literature related to group work in correctional facilities. Their excellent article, which appeared in the *Journal of Group Psychotherapy,* reviewed thirty-two outcome studies. From that review, they concluded that "overall, behavioral and modeling groups appeared the most effective. Fifty percent of these groups obtained positive change when specific outcome categories were examined (1979, p. 33)." They also noted that group procedures that took place within the context of the correctional facility rather than outside the facility appeared to achieve superior results. Their extensive review lends clear support to the utilization of techniques associated with quadrant III when working with individuals in a correctional facility. It appears that groups operating in such settings are most beneficial when they have a specific outcome as a goal of the therapeutic process and when the therapeutic process is fairly well structured. Groups that have no clear focus and rely on member-member interaction appear not to function well in a correctional facility.

In contrast to the findings reported by Julian and Kilmann is a program reported on by Kahnweiler in the November 1978 issue of the *Personnel and Guidance Journal.* Kahnweiler describes a model of group counseling that he utilizes in the Federal Correctional Institution in Tallahassee, Florida, in which the group members assume the responsibility for what occurs in the group. He describes the typical group goals as being increased self-understanding, increased ability to help others, and increased ability to communicate effectively. His article goes on to describe the typical stages that he believes the groups go through. They are very similar to the stages found in any group process. He states that stage one is a period of testing the counselor, and stage two is a period of complaining about the circumstances of being in prison. At about the fifth or sixth session, the group members begin to confront one another with their behaviors. The group then moves to the fourth stage of mutual trust and helping. Kahnweiler believes that the most important element in the success of his groups at Tallahassee is the counselor, not the specific techniques involved. The first quality he lists is that the counselor must be aware of the correctional facility environment and its potential effect on the inmates' mental and physical health. He states that counselors who operate in a correctional facility must have a high degree of self-awareness and interpersonal sensitivity and respect. Finally, he says that a counselor in a correctional setting must be both self-confident and assertive. This last point is particularly important during the phase of testing by the inmates. As Kahnweiler states, "A correctional facility is but one of many settings that exemplifies the discrepancy between working realities and textbook descriptions of counseling roles (1978, p. 164)." It is for that very reason that the counselor who operates groups in a correctional facility must have a high degree of self-confidence and self-reliance. The counselor who does not have these characteristics is subject to manipulation and deception by the inmates (Kahnweiler, 1978).

Working in the V.A.   Yet another setting in which many counselors work with adults in a group situation is the Veterans' Administration. A unique program for working with veterans with self-defeating behaviors has been described by Banks, Grimmer, Hardy, Hiatt, and Lowe (1979). They describe the operation of what they refer to as a self-defeating behavior workshop (SDB). The SDB workshop is a highly structured group process which meets twice a week for a four-week period. Generally, the groups are led by co-counselors who have been trained in SDB theory. In the first session, the counselors describe SDB theory to the participants, and each participant is asked to identify and then describe a self-defeating behavior that he or she wishes to eliminate during the group sessions. The unique aspect of the group process in the SDB workshop is that the only interaction that can take place is between the person talking and the group leader or leaders. No interaction is permitted from the group members. The next six sessions cover in sequence: fears—past problems that have led to the development of the SDB; choices—how the individuals maintain the SDB from moment to moment; techniques—how the individuals maintain the SDB; disowning—how the individual gives responsibility for the SDB to someone else; prices—what it costs the individual to maintain the SDB; and non-SDB life roads—positive alternatives to self-defeating behaviors. The last of the eight sessions is left open for group discussion, and in this session members are permitted to discuss the group process with one another (Banks, Grimmer, Hardy, Hiatt, and Lowe, 1979). Each of the first seven sessions begins with the leader presenting a lecture on the topic for that night and then giving each group member some reading material related to the topic. What follows is a rapid-fire interaction between the group leaders and each participant. The results of this program appear to be very promising. Readers who are interested in working with veterans are encouraged to examine this article and the SDB approach in more depth.

Working in a Family Service Agency   Much of the literature related to group work with adult populations refers to the utilization of more traditional therapeutic modalities such as Gestalt, Existential, Transactional Analysis, or Self-Theory. Relatively little, until the most recent past, has been written about the utilization of behavioral procedures in a group setting for adults. Sundel and Lawrence (1974) describe a rather systematic behavioral approach to the group treatment of adults in a family service agency. They suggest a model which utilizes behavior modification principles in time-limited group counseling. "The major features of this model include developing pro-treatment group norms; teaching effective problem-solving skills that can be employed during and after group treatment; maximizing the therapeutic effects of social reinforcement by members for each other; developing desired client behavior within the group which a member can then apply in his natural environment (Sundel and Lawrence, 1974, p. 327)." In the program they describe, little attention is given to group composition. They believe that there is no need to try to balance groups in terms of age, sex, marital status, social class, or type of problem. They do believe that it is an advantage to have at least two members of the same sex in each group. The following carefully constructed format is utilized in this time-limited group process.

Intake   An intake interview is held with each client prior to the group's formation. During this intake interview, the counselor elicits certain statements from each potential participant: (1) a specific statement of the problem the individual wishes to work on in the group in behavioral terms; (2) tentative specification of the goals the individual has for the therapeutic process; (3) a statement as to whether the individual will participate in a group; and (4) a verbal contract regarding the rules for participation in the group. The goals selected by the participant are ranked and a tentative treatment contract is established.

Group Development and Treatment   In the actual group process, the counselor is responsible for directing the activities and the relationships between and among the group members. During this part of the process, five rules must be followed by group participants. The rules are as follows:

1. Members are expected to attend every meeting of the group.

2. Members should refrain from socializing outside of the meeting until the series of meetings is concluded.

3. Group discussion must be focused on a contemporary event that relates to the members' problems.

4. Members are to refrain from hostile confrontations.

5. Members should work on assigned tasks between group meetings (Sundel and Lawrence, 1974, p. 332–33).

Sundel and Lawrence point out that it is extremely important that these five rules be enforced from the beginning of the group.

During the actual group process, one of the early tasks is to teach group participants the process of behavioral assessment. This includes teaching participants the concepts of response, antecedents, consequences, and frequency, and then teaching them the actual assessment procedure. The next step is to teach participants a problem-solving process which includes five steps:

1. Defining the problem, its antecedents, and its consequences

2. Determining the frequency of the problem

3. Stating goals

4. Developing alternative behaviors

5. Deciding on the best alternative

One of the tools suggested by Sundel and Lawrence in helping individuals develop a clear understanding of their difficulties is behavioral reenactment. "In behavioral reenactment, the member gives a clear description of what occurred in one of the problematic interchanges. He is then asked to reenact the situation with group members performing the roles of significant others. After the reenactment, members indicate to him what they observed about his behavior (Sundel and Lawrence, 1974, 335)." Once a clear understanding of the problem is developed, either using behavioral reenactment or other procedures, the group counselor and members help the participant develop an intervention plan. Of particular importance during this process is utilizing group members, as well as the counselors, as social reinforcers of the individual's attempt to change behavior.

While Sundel and Lawrence have not developed any new techniques, they have put together what we believe is a very usable package for working with adults in a group setting. We believe that it has the distinct advantage of not only helping participants solve the immediate concern but also teaching them two very important skills to be utilized in later life: behavioral assessment and problem solving. These are two skills missing in many people who come to counseling.

Marriage Counseling   Another area in which counselors are increasingly using the group process with adults is the area of marriage counseling. Blinder and Kirschenbaum (1976) point out that most objections to the treatment of married couples in a group setting stemmed from a narrow commitment to the utilization of psychoanalytic theory. Their point is that more here-and-now oriented therapeutic approaches may be beneficial in treating married couples in groups. In particular, they discuss the advantage of utilizing transactional analysis procedures in the process of group therapy with married couples.

Their approach is based on the assumption that marital discord can be expected when any of the following exists between the partners:

1. *Perceptual distortions*   Partners who are suffering marital discord see each other as they expect each other to be, rather than as they really are.

2. *Disturbances in communication*   The marriage partners act upon assumptions rather than reality.

3. *Frustrated dependency needs*   Each partner's need for unconditional love is not being met.

4. *Threats to adaptive defenses*   A good marriage provides the partners a measure of security they cannot achieve by themselves. If, however, one partner does not receive the support that he or she needs, the marriage may become dysfunctional.

5. *Fear of the unfamiliar*   If either partner changes the familiar pattern, it creates a new situation which can produce fear.

Given these assumptions, Blinder and Kirschenbaum recommend that a minimum of four couples be selected for each group. Prior to the initial group session, each couple is seen separately for four or five conjoint interviews, as well as some individual interviews with each partner. These individual and conjoint meetings provide the counselor with the background data necessary to understand the particular areas of dysfunction within each of the marriages.

At the initial group session the counselor asks each of the couples to describe their "previous day's fears and fantasies as they contemplated coming to their first group session (1976, p. 232)." This techniques leads to an exploration of how each couple views their particular problems and what prompted them to seek marriage counseling.

A second technique utilized to develop group cohesion is for the group counselor to choose one couple as the group's initial focus. The counselor does this on the basis of selecting a relatively nonthreatening situation that the couple has presented to the counselor in one of the individual interviews. They use the example of a couple having difficulty sitting down to eat and having an enjoyable meal. In exploring their problems with this relatively simple situation, the couple's characteristic pattern of misunderstanding each other can be pointed out. This exploration becomes meaningful not only to that couple but also to the rest of the group, as they see how miscommunication can cause difficulty for the focus couple as well as for themselves.

A major technique utilized throughout the group process, then, is for the group counselor to demonstrate continually how poor communication and acting on unverified assumptions can cause difficulty in the marital situation. As the various spouses interact within the group process, the counselor stops the interaction and asks the group to respond to the couple's behavior. This process of correcting poor communication patterns and moving people away from acting on unverified assumptions will lead to a healthier marriage.

The procedures outlined in this section generally can be described as techniques and/or procedures consistent with the theoretical position represented by quadrant III. As stated at the beginning of this section, it is our belief that most adults come to counseling with an awareness, at least at one level, of what their difficulties may be. Thus, the task of the counselor is to help the clients clarify and specify those difficulties and then to provide a treatment procedure for the resolution of the difficulties. As shown in Figure 11, there may be times when self-help groups can also operate with individuals experiencing particular fears, anxieties, or maladaptive behaviors. Certainly, alcoholic groups that function to help people stay dry, or other similar groups, are self-help groups designed not so much to solve a problem as to maintain a pattern of behavior that is nonmaladaptive. Such groups are clearly necessary in some circumstances, but the reader should not confuse them with groups that are designed to help clients solve particular problems.

GENERALIZED ANXIETIES/NEUROSES—ALL SETTINGS

As indicated in Figure 11, we believe the techniques associated with quadrants I and II are most appropriate when individuals come to counseling being unsure of what is causing their feelings of discomfort. For the younger child, we recommend techniques that are clearly associated with quadrant I. Many of the procedures described earlier in this chapter for young children are appropriate in this area. We believe that one of the best sources for detailed procedures for working with young children is the book by Keat referred to earlier.

When working with older clients, regardless of setting, who are experiencing general diffuse anxiety, we believe that the group counselor must provide an atmosphere very similar to that described by Rogers and his followers. That is, the focus must be on developing an atmosphere in the group in which the individuals feel comfortable in letting themselves go. In these cases the emphasis must be on providing a therapeutic environment where the clients can explore themselves in depth and gradually come to understand themselves such that they might make some specific changes. We believe that the process described by Carkhuff and others as necessary for therapeutic change is very applicable for at least initiating the process. When an individual is experiencing diffuse anxiety, the first step in the therapeutic process must be to help him or her to get a handle on where that anxiety is coming from. It may well be that, after a period of using a process compatible with quadrant II, clients will be ready for techniques associated with quadrant III, but counselors should be careful to avoid moving to quadrant III before clients are ready.

GROUP PROCESS: INTRAPERSONAL DIFFICULTIES—ALL SETTINGS

While we believe that most counselors will not be operating with clients who are experiencing intrapersonal difficulties in a school setting, there are increasing numbers of counselors who are finding themselves in work situations such as mental health agencies. There individuals must be highly skilled in the development of an intense therapeutic atmosphere which is conducive to the group members looking into themselves. Counselors who are trained at this level may also utilize similar techniques to those used in the case of general diffuse anxiety. As with the diffuse anxiety, the first step with individuals who are experiencing intrapersonal difficulties must be to help them develop an understanding of the antecedents of their difficulties. In the case of intrapersonal difficulties, these antecedents are often deeply entrenched and far out of the individual's awareness. Thus, a group counselor must have a great deal of skill, patience, and understanding in order to move group participants slowing toward an understanding of their particular difficulties.

SUMMARY

In this chapter we have attempted to outline techniques and procedures that we feel are generally applicable to the kinds of problems and settings represented by Figure 11. Consistent with our general belief in an eclectic position, we have tried to present techniques which are atheoretical in nature. However, we are sure it is obvious that in many cases we tend to adhere to an action-oriented approach. In so doing, however, we do not discount the benefits of techniques associated with quadrants I and II. Rather, our belief is that often activities associated with quadrants I and II are initial steps toward final resolution of problems, which can be accomplished through techniques associated with quadrant III. As client problems become more severe and long lasting, however, the group counselor must shift from the utilization of specific techniques to an emphasis on process variables.

We also make no claim that the techniques described in this chapter are the only techniques that are appropriate. They are listed in this chapter as illustrative rather than exhaustive. By necessity our descriptions of the techniques and procedures are also rather brief, and our hope is that the reader whose interest has been heightened by reading about a particular technique will go to the original source for more detail on the procedure. In short, our attempt has been to provide a stimulus that will help our readers form a base for their own particular procedures.

References

Aiken, J., and J. Johnston. Promoting career information seeking behaviors in college students. *Journal of Vocational Behavior,* 1973, *3,* 81–87.

Baldwin, B. A. A structured activity model for personal exploration and discussion groups. *Journal of College Student Personnel,* 1976, *17,* 431–36.

Banks, J., J. Grimmer, R. Hardy, D. Hiatt, and J. Lowe. Self-defeating behavior workshops: Systems approach for hard-to-serve veterans. *Personnel and Guidance Journal,* 1979, *57,* 313–15.

Barabasz, A. F. Group desensitization of test anxiety in elementary school. *The Journal of Psychology,* 1973, *83,* 295–301.

Bender, R. C. Structured group experiences. *Elementary School Guidance and Counseling,* 1973, *8,* 71–73.

Blinder, M. G., and M. Kirschenbaum. The technique of married couple therapy. In Ard and Ard (Eds.), *Handbook of Marriage Counseling.* Palo Alto, CA: Science and Behavior Books, Inc., 1976.

Boocock, S. C., and E. O. Schild (Eds.). *Simulation games in learning.* Beverly Hills, CA: Sage Publications, 1968.

Cermak, S., F. Stein, and C. Ableson. Hyperactive children and an activity group therapy model. *American Journal of Occupational Therapy,* 1973, *26,* 311–15.

Clarke, R., H. B. Gelatt, and L. Levine. A decision-making paradigm for local guidance research. *Personnel and Guidance Journal,* 1965, *44,* 40–51.

Cramer, S. H., and E. L. Herr. Effecting a rapproachment between group guidance and group counseling in the schools. In J. C. Hansen and S. H. Cramer (Eds.), *Group Guidance and Counseling in the Schools.* New York: Appleton-Century-Crofts, 1971.

Cross, G., R. Myrick, and G. Wilkinson. Communication labs: A developmental approach. *The School Counselor,* 1977, *24,* 186–91.

Culbertson, F. M. An effective, low-cost approach to the treatment of disruptive school children. *Psychology in the Schools,* 1974, *11,* 183–87.

Dinkmeyer D. C., and J. J. Muro. *Group counseling: Theory and practice.* Itasca, IL: Peacock, 1971.

Gelatt, H. C., and B. Varenhorst. A decision-making approach to guidance. *Bulletin of National Association of Secondary School Principals,* 1968, *52,* 88–98.

Goldman, L. Group guidance: Content and process. *Personnel and Guidance Journal,* 1962, 518–22.

Gumaer, J., and R. D. Myrick. Behavioral group counseling with disruptive children. *The School Counselor,* 1974, *21,* 313–17.

Hutchins, D. E., and C. G. Cole. A model for improving middle school students' interpersonal relationships. *The School Counselor,* 1977, *25,* 134–36.

Julian, A., and P. Kilmann. Group treatment of juvenile delinquents: A review of the outcome literature. *The International Journal of Group Psychotherapy,* 1979, *29,* 3–37.

Kahnweiler, W. M. Group counseling in a correctional setting. *Personnel and Guidance Journal,* 1978, *57,* 162–64.

Keat, D. C. *Fundamentals of child counseling.* Boston: Houghton Mifflin, 1974, 96–131.

Keat, D. C., and D. Maki. The talking, feeling, and doing game. *Elementary School Guidance and Counseling,* 1975, *10,* 58–62.

Kissiah, R. K. Beginning group counseling: A practical approach. *Elementary School Guidance and Counseling,* 1975, *10,* 14–20.

Krumboltz, J. D., and C. E. Thoresen. The effect of behavioral counseling in group and individual settings on information-seeking behavior. *Journal of Counseling Psychology,* 1964, *11,* 324–33.

Mayer, G. R., T. M. Rohen, and A. D. Whitley. Group counseling with children: A cognitive-behavioral approach. In Diedrich and, Dye (Eds.), *Group procedures: Purposes, processes, and outcomes.* Boston: Houghton Mifflin, 1972.

McInnis, E. T., and D. Marholin. Individualizing behavior therapy for children in group settings. *Child Welfare,* 1977, *56,* 449–62.

Pannor, H., and N. Nicosia. Structured problem solving to improve participation in a large high school group. In Berkovitz (Ed.), *When schools care.* New York: Brunner/Mazel, 1975.

Rachman, A. W. *Identity group psychotherapy with adolescents.* Springfield IL: Charles C Thomas, 1975.

Rashbaum-Selig, M. Assertive training for young people. *The School Counselor,* 1976, *24,* 115–21.

Rhodes, S. L. Short-term groups of latency-age children in a school setting. *International Journal of Group Psychotherapy,* 1973, *23,* 204–16.

Schroeder W. W. The effect of reinforcement counseling and model-reinforcement counseling on information-seeking behavior of high school students. Unpublished doctoral dissertation, Stanford University, 1964.

Sparks, D. C. Group goal setting. *The School Counselor,* 1978, *25,* 235–38.

Sundel, M., and H. Lawrence. Behavioral group treatment with adults in a family service agency. In Glasser, Sarri, and Vinter (Eds.), *Individual change through small groups.* New York: The Free Press, 1974.

Tidwell R., and V. Bachus. Group counseling for aggressive school children. *Elementary School Guidance and Counseling,* 1977, *12,* 2–7.

Tyra, R. P. Group guidance and the SIPA model. *Elementary School Guidance and Counseling,* 1979, *13,* 269–71.

Varenhorst, B., and H. D. Gelatt. Group guidance decision making. In J. C. Hansen and S. H. Cramer (Eds.), *Group guidance and counseling in the schools.* New York: Appleton-Century-Crofts, 1971.

12
Group Leadership

The success of any group endeavor is a function of many variables, including the particular situation, the membership, and the leader. The most important of the variables is leadership, for even with a good situation and "good" membership, a group with a poor leader will not function at optimum effectiveness. Hence, a first order of business in examining group process is an examination of leadership: What are the various leadership styles? What are the personal characteristics that are needed for effective leadership? What are the general goals of leadership? What are the specific techniques that can be utilized within the general role of leader that will facilitate the achievement of counseling goals for the group members?

LEADERSHIP STYLES

The process of leadership in groups has been the subject of considerable attention from the disciplines of sociology, psychology, counseling, and other related fields during the last twenty years. In particular, those individuals working with task and T-groups, such as the National Training Laboratory, have been concerned with the effects of various forms of leadership on participants. Much of this research continues to be concerned, at least in part, with the effects of three general styles of leadership. These were identified by Kurt Lewin (1944) as authoritarian, democratic, and laissez-faire. Other theorists list four or five different styles, using terms such as "leader-centered," "group-centered," "planless," "directive," "nondirective," "autocratic," and "anarchic." Despite this proliferation of types and names, it appears that most writers are simply talking about refinements or finer distinctions within the more general classification system developed by Lewin. These general styles have received much attention, and a brief discussion of them can be used to form a basic understanding of leadership style for a prospective group counselor.

Authoritarian Leader

The leader who adopts this stance is one who feels that the group members, by themselves, are not able to develop the necessary insights or group behaviors that will bring about necessary changes. The belief is that the members got themselves into their particular difficulty because they could not direct themselves; therefore, it is to be expected that they need expert advice. Because of the leader's superior knowledge and expertise in group dynamics, it is the leader who directs the process. It is the leader, as the expert in human behavior, who is able to explain the behavior of the group and the individual members. The authoritarian leader "assumes that integration results from his explanation, that is, from something external added to the internal reality of the group members (Kemp, 1964, p. 229)." As the process unfolds, the authoritarian leader holds that he or she is the one person able to understand the significance of the material presented, and it is through his or her interpretive feedback to the group members that the individuals will develop an understanding of their own behavior. Quite clearly, this view of leadership behavior is compatible with those theoretical positions emanating from a psychoanalytic model, but counselors who state allegiances to other theories may still have some authoritarian attitudes. It is also a position often advocated by counselors fresh from a teaching situation who mistakenly equate group counseling with the teaching situation. While some leaders adhere to this position on theoretical grounds, many also adopt it because it appears to be a form of leadership in which the counselor is protected from self-disclosure to the group.

Democratic Leader

A second form of leadership is what has been referred to as democratic, group-centered, or nondirective. The democratic leader, unlike the authoritarian, refuses to accept sole responsibility for either the direction of the group or the final solution of member concerns. Rather than a complete reliance on their own expertise, leaders who operate from this perspective rely on the ability of the participants to develop self-understanding. As Rogers (1971) has stated, "I trust the group, given a reasonably facilitating climate, to develop its own potential and the potential of its members (p. 275)." The democratic leader uses clarification, synthesis, feedback, and evaluation of process as the chief tools. The aim of this leader is to involve members to such an extent that each participant contributes to the welfare of other individuals within the group. The implication here is not that the democratic leader lets the group go anywhere it desires. Rather, it means that the democratic leader works in cooperation with the group in establishing goals, directions, and procedures. Unlike the authoritarian leader, the democratic leader does not accept full responsibility for the group, but shares the responsibility with group members. The democratic leader views himself or herself not as an expert with all the answers, but rather as an individual who can facilitate the process of human development. Those who adhere to a more humanistic or phenomenological theoretical position tend to operate from this end of the leadership continuum.

Laissez-Faire Leader

A laissez-faire leader is in fact no leader at all. The few individuals who adhere to this position hold that it is the sole responsibility of the group members to direct themselves in whatever directions they feel necessary. The leader is simply another member of the group. There are no plans or procedures unless they evolve from the membership. Many who advocate a "let it all hang out" atmosphere in the group will not accept any form of leadership. It is a freewheeling experience and the pieces drop where they may. Beginning counselors often fall into this leadership style in an attempt to be nondirective. There is also a tendancy for leaders who have a strong need to be liked to use this style. This is generally unfortunate, for as Mahler (1969) describes it, it is a sort of catch-as-catch-can approach and in most groups of this type no one catches anything.

A Continuum

In examining the brief discussion of leadership styles, it should be apparent to the reader that they fall along a continuum of leader responsibility and control. Moving from total control and responsibility of the authoritarian to the no-control, no-responsibility position of the laissez-faire leader, Figure 12 illustrates the communication pattern or the expected dynamics of a group operating under each of these leadership styles.

In the authoritarian group it can be expected that almost all the communication and dynamics will center on the leader. In the democratic group the leader still occupies a central position but "aims at replacing a single leader with as many potential leaders as there are group members (Gordon, 1972, p. 72)." In the laissez-faire group the leader abdicates the leadership position and the group is left to its own often limited resources.

As mentioned earlier, much of the research has centered on comparative studies of these three or similar styles of leadership. The results of these investigations have demonstrated that groups under a laissez-faire leader tend to be more concerned about having a good time and about the social behavior of group members. The group sessions can be described as discussions of an intellectual nature, but cannot be characterized as counseling (Berzon and Solomon, 1966; Rothaus, Johnson, Hanson, and Lyle, 1966; Shaw and Blum, 1966; Bednar and Lawlis, 1971). That is, members tend not to reveal themselves or to deal with any real concerns. Any work that is done on a group concern or task tends to be of very poor quality. The group with an authoritarian or directive leader will develop a high level of energy dealing with their concerns as identified by the leader, but much of this work is not internalized by group members. These groups also are characterized by feelings of hostility among members and toward the leader, dissatisfaction with the group experience, scapegoating, and competition among members. While the democratically led group may not spend as much time actually focused on a group concern, the quality of the time they do spend is more productive than it is in the authoritarian led group. Even more important, those in a democratically led group are more satisfied by the experience, more original, and develop a stronger interpersonal bond with other group members. As a gen-

Figure 12 Communication Patterns under Three Leadership Styles

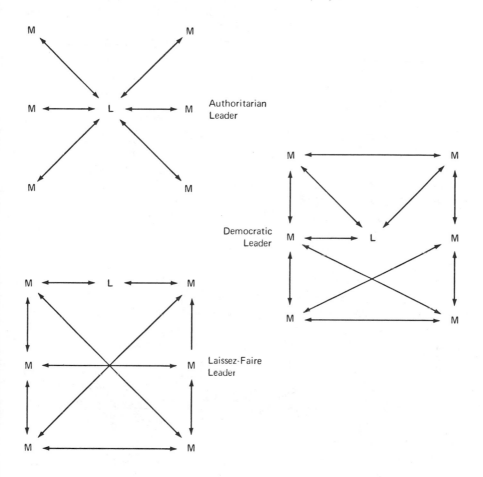

eral rule, one of the prime goals of group counseling is improved interpersonal skills, and it appears that the accomplishment of such a goal is much more likely in a democratic group than in an authoritarian group. Thus, the research seems to suggest that as a general style of leadership the democratic style is most productive, with the authoritarian style finishing a poor second and the laissez-faire style a distant last.

LEADERSHIP FUNCTIONS

The three leadership styles are broad descriptions that continue to be used. However, more specific leadership functions have been identified. Lieberman, Yalom, and Miles (1973) identified basic leadership functions: emotional stimulation, caring, meaning-attribution, and executive function. These four dimensions were derived from their research on leadership in encounter groups. However, they suggest that these dimensions are capable of discriminating among leaders of highly varied orientations whether in counseling or personal growth groups. These four dimensions have also led to a leadership typology of more specific leadership styles.

Emotional Stimulation

Emotional stimulation involves a leader's behavior that emphasizes revelation of feeling, revelation of personal attitudes and values, frequent participation as a member, and drawing attention to self. The leader's behavior emphasizes the release of emotions by demonstration. The leader is a risk taker who expresses anger, warmth, or love and shows how it is done. It is the leader's personality that stimulates the members and moves the group experiences.

The emotional stimulation style also emphasizes challenges. The leader is frequently involved in dialogues with individual members, and a high value is placed on personal confrontation. Unsettling is considered a primary condition to learning. This style includes challenging assumptions the members hold about themselves.

Another aspect of this leadership style is the emphasis on intrusive modeling. The leader stimulates the members to model in terms of style, values, behavior, and beliefs. A leader who is high on stimulation is generally described as charismatic.

Caring

Caring as a leadership function and style involves protecting; offering friendship, love, or affection; and inviting members to seek feedback as well as support, praise, and encouragement. The leader expresses considerable warmth, acceptance, genuineness, and concern for the other members of the group.

Meaning-Attribution

The meaning-attribution function involves techniques of cognition. The leader provides the members with concepts for how to understand what is happening and with frameworks for how to change. The leader is an interpreter of reality. Leaders who are high on meaning-attribution would have understanding of how it is and how people are feeling as the major goal.

Some leaders who emphasize meaning-attribution are most concerned with emphasizing aspects of the group as a whole; others are primarily concerned with the individual. Therefore, some leaders would use interpretations which focus on the group and emphasize cognitive recognition of the group climate, raising issues or asking the group to reflect on its behavior. Other leaders would direct attention at individual behavior and request similar information relative to interpersonal issues.

The meaning-attribution function involves the leader's giving names to experiences that members undergo. It involves translating the feelings and behaviors into ideas.

Executive Function

The executive function involves limit setting, suggesting or setting rules and norms, setting goals or direction of movement, managing time, pacing, blocking, and interceding, as well as inviting, questioning, and suggesting procedures for a person or the group. Leaders who are high on this function emphasize the expression of emotion through suggestion rather than through demonstration. They may be described as movie directors, stopping the action and focusing on a particular behavior of an individual or the group. The intent of this behavior is to have the members learn about particular cues, emotions, or personal behaviors. The leader is asking the group to reflect upon some action but different from the interpretative reality. The leader is more likely to ask the group to provide the answers than to give answers to them. The executive function is directed primarily toward management of the group as a social system that may use structured material as a mechanism for goal achievement.

Effect of Functions

Lieberman et al. (1973) evaluated the relationship of the four basic dimensions of behavior to group outcome. From their tabulations, they concluded that the most effective styles of leadership are displayed by leaders who are moderate in the amount of stimulation, high in caring, and moderate in expression of executive functions, and who utilize meaning-attribution. Conversely, less effective leaders use very low or very high stimulation, are low in caring, do very little meaning-attribution, and use too little or too much executive behavior.

Another way they demonstrated their findings was to examine the relationship between the four basic leader functions and outcome by using correlations. Their final rank order correlations indicate that outcomes related to stimulation rho = .24, caring rho = .60, meaning-attribution rho = .70, and executive function rho = .20. The authors concluded from the analysis that stimulation and executive function are associated with outcome in a curvilinear fashion. That is, leaders who have too much or too little are unsuccessful. The caring dimensions had a linear relationship, with overall success related with high caring. Meaning-attribution had a linear relationship, with high meaning-attribution associated with success and low level associated with failure.

From the patterns of effective and ineffective leadership styles, it is apparent that the two central functions without which leaders are rarely successful are sufficient levels of caring and meaning-attribution. The combination of high levels of affection and cognitive behaviors are critical.

Lieberman et al. also analyzed their data to assess whether encounter group leaders of different conventional theoretical label had methodological differences. Their findings did not support the view that leaders who were labeled similarly behaved similarly when leading encounter groups. They concluded that some of these differences existed in how leaders approached the task of running the group, but the similarities and differences were not associated with a particular school of thought.

LEADERSHIP TYPOLOGIES

Lieberman et al. (1973) developed an empirical typology of leaders derived from the behavioral variables in their study. Six leader types were identified from their research methods: energizers, providers, social engineers, impersonals, laissez-faires, and managers.

Energizers

The definitive characteristic of energizers is intense emotional stimulation. These leaders have a high to moderate attention to the executive function, and they are also relatively high on caring. These leaders are generally perceived as the most charismatic. In the Lieberman et al. study, only the energizers were strongly attached to a belief system and emotionally tied to a founder of a particular school of thought. Parallels were drawn between these leaders and their behaviors in "religiostic" movements. The religious quality of their behavior was dominant in the charismatic style, allowing them to feel assured in taking over for members and asserting firm control. The leaders felt able to guide members forward and lead them in the right direction. The level of proselytizing behavior was highest for members in groups with such leaders.

Providers

The providers are leaders specializing in caring and meaning-attribution. They use a moderate level of emotional stimulation and executive function. As leaders they focused on individuals, giving love as well as information and ideas about how to change. They projected a quality of enlightened fraternalism. They used a systematic theory about how individuals learn behaviors but did not press it on the group members.

Social Engineers

The distinctive characteristic of social engineers is their use of group-oriented meaning-attribution. They are group focused and concerned with how members relate to the social system. They provide a moderate amount of caring, indicating relatively high levels of support and affection, are quite low on emotional stimulation, and varied from little to frequent use of the executive function. They are perceived as low in charisma. They offered the communication of support and the steering of the work of the group as a whole rather than aid on individual or interpersonal issues; hence the title of social engineers.

Impersonals

These leaders are described as impersonal because they are distant and aggressive stimulators. They are low on caring and executive function, relatively high on emotional stimulation, and not particularly high on meaning-attribution. Their behavior is simply described as impersonal.

Laissez-Faires

The laissez-faire!leaders are moderate to high on meaning-attribution but obtain low scores on the other three basic dimensions of leadership. They exhibit the classical descriptions of laissez-faire leadership in providing low levels of input, not stimulating emotions or controlling certain conditions or offering support. The leaders had views about how members learn in group situations and communicated some ideas to the members. However, this communication is not worked through by the other three leadership functions.

Managers

The manager style of leadership is characterized by extremely high scores on the executive function. The manager style of leadership controls how, about what, and for how long members interact with one another. In the Lieberman et al. study, the use of structured exercises was the major form of control the leaders used. The observer labeled such leaders as "top sergeant."

Effective Typologies

From the analysis of leadership behaviors, Lieberman et al. concluded that how leaders conduct themselves makes a substantial difference in the relative benefit or harm members expesience. The four basic dimensions of leadership were found to underlie a variety of leader behaviors. Caring and meaning-attribution were associated with beneficial effects, while excessive stimulation or inordinate executive functions were associated with negative outcomes. In analyzing the leadership typologies, the provider, social engineer, and energizer styles were found to be successful, while the laissez-faire, manager, and impersonal styles were found to be unsuccessful.

THE LEADERLESS GROUP

Before leaving this discussion of general leadership style, another form needs to be examined. There is a growing interest in the effects of so-called leaderless groups, first proposed by Abrahm Wolf in the 1940s. Wolf's strategy was to use the leaderless group in alternate fashion, that is, group members meet alternatively with and without a leader. Wolf (1963) met with his groups for one and one-half hours a week for at least a dozen sessions. After the members had sufficient exposure to each other and to the general procedures of the group, he urged the group to meet two or three times a week without his presence in addition to his regular sessions. The members frequently volunteered their homes for meeting places for such alternate sessions. He stated that these meetings added materially to the friendly and sympathetic atmosphere and that uninhibited participation was stimulated.

Wolf and Schwartz (1962) differ from the earlier position and suggest that alternative sessions may begin immediately after the first regular session. They state that the therapists' reluctance to introduce the alternative session early reflects the leaders' need to play the role of an overprotective parent, and may necessitate working through a considerable amount of resistance in the members prior to the procedure not present during the early session.

The leaderless group procedure is not without opposition. Yalom (1975) believes that groups meeting regularly without a leader may be potentially destructive. However, he does advocate leaderless meetings occasionally. He adds that groups should have developed to a productive stage before embarking on leaderless meetings. Members may resist the group meeting without a group leader by questioning the practicality or productiveness of such a meeting. The use of a number of regular sessions before starting leaderless alternate meetings is a typical recommendation. Kadis (1956) recommended that group members should have developed intercontrols and a stage of cohesiveness to help handle outbursts prior to using the alternate session. Similarly, Mullan and Rosenbaum (1962) suggested that it is appropriate to allow the group to experience "one explosive situation" prior to an alternate session.

In addition to Wolf's concept of an alternate meeting, Kadis (1963) discussed two types of coordinated leadesless meetings. A pre-meeting is held in the group as an opportunity to warm up before the counselor joins the group. Post-meetings are characterized by a reduction in tension and are held anywhere after the regular group meetings. The post-sessions frequently reflect the group's level of cohesiveness and permit the group to continue member interaction regarding issues that arose during the group meeting. There is some concern that the pre- and/or post-sessions turn into unproductive social gatherings.

Mullan and Rosenbaum (1962) list the advantages of employing alternate sessions: (1) an increase in the creativity potential of the members and the group as a whole; (2) ego building for each member and the development of cohesiveness within the group; (3) development of the cotherapeutic function of each member and the therapeutic function of the total group; (4) a testing of each individual's need to act out; (5) a relocation of all ties, that is, transference and countertransference; (6) new appraisal of the leader and other authorities as well as oneself and other group members; and (7) a denial of the leader role with a resulting increase in group centeredness and each member's sense of responsibility.

Bieber (1957) listed several reasons for opposing the use of alternate sessions: (1) when a leader is absent, there is a blurring of lines between members' socializing and therapy which may prove confusing and disruptive to the group members; (2) the members' disclosures are not interpreted but merely serve a cathartic purpose which is of less therapeutic value; (3) the counselor must retain the leadership in the group since she or he is the only skilled person; (4) during the leaderless meetings, the therapist is unable to provide protection against exaggerated acting out of antisocial or masochistic behaviors.

During the late 1960s and early 1970s, other forms of leaderless groups were developed. The self-directed groups use technology to stimulate group interactions. Self-directed groups usually employed stimulus materials with tape recorded instructions. The group engaged in exercises followed by a discussion of the interaction, after which the group continued with the next instruction from the tape. Generally, self-directed groups are designed for individuals whose goals are developmental as well as therapeutic.

Berzon (1969) organized leaderless groups for an empirical study. She organized a group of disabled volunteers with no instructions beyond the request to meet for twelve to eighteen weeks. There was a buzzer placed in the room so members could sequest assistance; however, it was seldom utilized. The group seemed to lose direction, and confusion and frustration were evidenced. Berzon concluded that the group needed some additional form of leadership. As a result, the program Planned Experiences for Effective Relating was developed. Berzon et al. (1969) concluded that self-directed groups, using carefully planned program materials, can be an effective means of personal growth for individuals who participate in them.

Seligman and Desmond (1975), after a review of the leaderless group phenomenon, conclude that although the future looks promising, it bears careful watching. Everly (1975) also offers a word of caution regarding leaderless therapy groups. We might conclude that the leaderless group may be a productive vehicle for those individuals who generally live effective lives but desire an opportunity to form meaningful human contacts and to learn more about themselves in the process. The research in this area remains somewhat sparse, and it is not recommended that groups be constituted of individuals with moderate or severe disturbances. Counselors who are interested in using leaderless techniques in conducting groups should be aware of the disadvantages in an effort to provide effective treatment for the group members.

PERSONAL CHARACTERISTICS OF GROUP LEADERS

One of the most common misconceptions regarding counseling is that a well-trained one-to-one counselor who is good at it, will automatically be an effective counselor in a group setting. This idea is unfortunately fostered, covertly if not overtly, in many programs of counselor preparation. Far too many programs offer a didactic course in group work but do not offer any practicum training or experiential learning in group procedures. Happily, this practice is changing as a result of the growing recognition that both special characteristics and training are needed if counselors are to be effective in group settings.

Slavson (1962) listed the following personal qualities of the group leader as essential: poise, judgment, maturity, ego-strength, freedom from excessive anxiety, perceptiveness, intuition, empathy, imaginativeness, ability to avoid self-preoccupation, desire to help people, and tolerance of frustration. One could argue, quite correctly, that these are necessary attributes for any counselor, yet within the context of group leadership these personal qualities are magnified. In individual counseling the counselor needs to demonstrate those qualities to only one person at a time, while the group process calls for dealing with a number of individuals concurrently.

The counselor may be confronted with resistance, loss of control, open hostility, transference, dependency, and threat of exposure—all these not from just one individual but from many at one time. Simultaneously he or she needs to be able to invest in and care for each individual, to understand the reactions of all members as part of the group process, to be open to a variety of opinions, to be attuned to the feelings of all members, and to maintain a perspective of his or her position in the group (Dye, 1972). Quite clearly, group leaders must understand themselves at a deeper level than is perhaps necessary for counselors operating on a one-to-one basis. Above all, group leaders must be willing to invest of themselves in the process without fear of what the group will learn about them. They must be able to relinquish control without fear of letting the group get out of their grasp. In short, group leaders must not only trust and respect themselves; they must care about and trust in the group members' desire and ability to work toward goals in a mutual effort. Group leaders who feel their role is a lonely one place the whole burden on themselves, a burden that will inhibit their ability as leaders.

Garetz and Fix (1972) suggest that the counselor base his or her approach on four principles of leadership: (1) practically applying a solid theory of group dynamics; (2) encouraging maximum group self-direction; (3) showing high respect for the group members and being emotionally honest with them; and (4) serving as a behavioral model. The latter two principles certainly emphasize the counselor as a person.

Members frequently ascribe power and authority to the leader to increase their own feelings of security as they test the group situation. The members' response to the leader's position allows the leader to use authority to help them work through their interpersonal conflicts. However, leaders who are diluted by their position of authority may view the conflicts in the group as struggles between the members and themselves as persons rather than the role conflict that exists during that stage. If leaders are aware of themselves as persons, they will be able to help members to recognize that the conflicts are not primarily with the leader and come to a more satisfactory growth-producing resolution of the issue.

The counselor's use of respect, warmth, empathy, and genuineness has been shown to be effective in establishing a relationship conducive to personal growth. A leader who is emotionally honest with the members and shows high levels of respect for them can establish an atmosphere in which the members feel free to interact. Although most counseling approaches emphasize the need for warmth and empathy in the counseling relationship, many leaders seem to fear becoming really involved. Their aloofness is similar to the reticence they are attempting to overcome in the group members. In addition, many counselors are cautious of expressing a full range of their emotions and are more apt to play a professional role than to be real persons. The counselor's communication of an honest emotion in the context of a warm relationship can be a constructive therapeutic force. Counselors who avoid full emotional participation in the group may be expecting more of their clients than they are asking of themselves. It would seem that if leaders expect emotional honesty from the group members, they should be first to demonstrate it in their own behavior. Hence, the importance of the counselor's personal behavior as a model.

Parker (1972) outlines some personal qualities enhancing the group counselor's effectiveness. His outline described five personal qualities: broad personal experience, self-awareness, accepting attitudes, emotional expressiveness, and personal security.

The counselor should be able to comprehend and be empathic with a variety of life-styles and be able to relate to clients who express their personalities in various ways. The counselor should be aware of current events in business, science, and social and political areas that affect the well-being of clients. The counselor must know his or her own needs, sensitivities, motivations, frustrations, deprivations, and vulnerabilities. The counselor must know how to defend against anxiety and be capable of spontaneous participation with minimal countertransferences. The counselor should be aware of the social impression he or she makes. The counselor must communicate an accepting attitude. The counselor should be free of prejudices and permit others to express doubts and anger toward her or him. Group therapists should not become unduly frustrated when clients are slow to change because of resistances or are overly sensitive to members' criticism and complaints. The group counselor serves as a model and, therefore, should be emotionally expressive. The counselor should be able to experience and express warmth, caring, respect, support, as well as negative feelings of anger, fear, and resentment. When expressing negative feelings, counselors have to have insight into themselves and the impact of such expressions on helping the group resolve issues. The counselor must maintain personal security and identity apart from his or her need for group support. This permits the group members to develop identity and independence as well as to rely on the group as a vehicle for that process. It is implied that the counselor has an adequate emotional adjustment and can function with some confidence in social and professional areas.

Consistent with the Lieberman et al. research (1973), leaders of groups who experience the most positive change provide high caring, high feedback, a medium amount of structure, and a medium level of emotional, aggressive stimulation. That study suggested that leaders did not behave differentially according to theoretical approaches to counseling. Although the leaders certainly learned techniques and had some adherence to a position in leading groups, it is more likely the variance in personality that affects the leader in these major dimensions.

Another personal consideration in leadership is the acceptability of the leader by different class, race, and age groups. Many authors have asserted that group members from low-income groups relate more easily to a leader from a similar background, and in some areas, racial groups are unwilling to work with alien leaders. However, Vontress (1971) stated that there is great variability in the attitude within each race and class, and Mackler (1971) described how he used stereotyping in rationalizing his fears of nonacceptance. MacLennan (1975) suggested that the problem is likely to be enhanced in homogeneous groups where there is a wide difference between the leader and the members. Heterogeneous groups concerned with personal change are needed to help group members to understand each other's humanness and to identify common dynamic problems.

Berger (1974) discusses the impact of the counselor's personality on group process. He suggests the counselor's use of self in the therapeutic process, referring to the dynamic, constantly changing, integrated utilization of the total person for constructive therapeutic purposes. The use of the person includes utilizing physical behaviors and sensations, emotional states, reactions to self and others, cognitive awareness, and all other ways of feeling—thinking—knowing which are referred to as intuitive. The way a counselor uses his or her personality is a reflection of a whole life history as well as a professional technique. In other words, the counselor's use of self involves what he or she does and who he or she is.

The counselor's personality will be expressed in the selection of a theoretical position. The personality would be expressed differently by a counselor using a behavior modification approach from the counselor using a Gestalt approach in working with the group. The counselor's use of personality will influence how a group is initiated. The counselor's personality will also influence the use of self in establishing intimacy with members of the group. Intimacy does not develop as a result of technical strategy but because of the personal involvement which has significant meaning for the members.

Berger also addresses himself to the concern of the counselor about assuming omnipotence and superiority. He suggests that the counselor and group members can be protected from the notion of omnipotence by the counselor's having received some type of counseling; professional training which includes adequate supervision; a desire and ability to acknowledge errors, frailties, and overreactions; involvement in seminars, workshops, and professional organizations; adherence to a democratic type of interpersonal relationship with all people; and, when appropriate, acknowledgment to the group members that they have seen what the counselor has not.

STRATEGY OF LEADERSHIP

Primary Goal of Leadership

In individual counseling, the counselor is the chief agent of therapeutic change. In the group counseling situation, however, the leader is only one of many possible agents for change. In a group situation the counselor can be assisted by the group members who provide the acceptance and support, the hope, the experience of universality, the opportunities for altruistic behavior, and the interpersonal feedback, testing, and learning (Yalom, 1975). It is the counselor's primary task to release this facilitative potential. Simply bringing together a group of individuals into a common meeting will not release this potential. A collection of individuals is not necessarily a group. It is the counselor's goal to help the group develop into a cohesive unit with an atmosphere maximally conducive to the operation of these therapeutic factors. Group cohesion comes about as members develop a sense of personal involvement, as they feel an atmosphere of warmth and unity, and respond to a feeling of personal acceptance from both the leader and other group members (Bednar and Lawlis, 1971). The leader meets goals by providing a facilitative base, modeling appropriate behaviors, and becoming a member-leader of the group.

In part, the leader can provide the climate for group cohesiveness prior to the first group meeting. The importance of selection of members to establish a balanced group, meeting each prospective member individually to deal with purposes of the group, and qreplanning by the counselor are leader behaviors that have a direct bearing on the probability that group cohesion will develop.

Of prime importance in the initial group meeting is the leader's task of establishing a general goal for the group process to which all the members can agree. This is necessary even if the leader has followed the recommendation of meeting individual members separately prior to the first session. Such a procedure allows members and the leader to clarify why they are there.

While the above tasks are important in establishing the group as a therapeutic agent, the most important role of the counselor at this juncture is to promote the facilitative atmosphere, which will enable the group process to proceed. Gazda (1973), in describing the process of helping, likens the process to the preparation for a space shot. No matter how complex the rocket itself, the rocket would go nowhere without a strong concrete and steel launching base. So, too, the group leader may have all kinds of sophisticated techniques, but unless he or she has provided a facilitative base which enables the group to cohere, the group will go nowhere.

Developing the Group

To provide the most meaningful experience for members in the group, the counselor assumes responsibility for selecting members for the group and establishing the group composition. He or she is also responsible for establishing a location for the group that is conducive to their work, deciding if it is to be an open or closed group, and if closed, determining the duration. In other words, the counselor establishes the group and the beginning structure from which the group atmosphere and culture will develop. Initially the members are strangers and know only the counselor through the preliminary interview. Therefore, the counselor serves as the main focus point, and members will relate primarily to the leader until they are able to form into a group. When the group begins, the members are often insecure, apprehensive, and unsure about the behavior and the group organization. They are therefore dependent upon the counselor for direction. During this stage, the members start to engage in the counseling process by accepting influence first from the counselor and later from the others in order to gain a favorable reaction. During this early stage, the counselor tries to shape the group into a therapeutic social system. The counselor structures the group with a code of behavioral rules which will exist until the group members establish their own unique norms for the group. The norms for the group are developed from the expectations the members bring to the group and from the specific structure established by the leader. The pre-counseling interview conducted by the counselor with each individual member will be a major force in establishing expectations of norms. However, previous experience and other social expectations will also determine members' behaviors in establishing norms. It is important that the counselor design the group culture to be optimally therapeutic and therefore influence the group by establishing appropriate rules of behavior. Because these early norms are significant in the manner in which the members will continue to behave, the counselor should be deliberate in establishing the norms he or she thinks will be therapeutic for group behavior.

Yalom (1975) discusses how the leader shapes norms. He suggests that two basic roles the counselor can assume are those of a technical expert or a model-setting participant. Leaders who work as technical experts deliberately employ a variety of techniques to move the group in the direction they consider desirable. They attempt to shape the norms exclusively during the pre-session interviews with members, and then reinforce their instructions by the weight of their authority and experience and by providing a rationale behind their suggested mode of procedure. The second manner of influencing norms in the group is to have the counselor model the desired behaviors. For example, the leader may use some self-disclosure as a form of modeling self-disclosure for the group members. The leader's nonjudgmental acceptance of others' strengths and weaknesses will help the members accept each other. In most groups, the counselor will use both technical expertise and modeling to help shape the norms of the group.

Although the leader helps shape the norms of the group, the true group norms are negotiated among the members through the life of the group. A second stage of the group generally involves a period of conflict. Often the conflict involves members reacting to norms of the group that are imposed by the leader or expected from other members; therefore, the second stage of the group is frequently a working out of appropriate behaviors which are accepted for the group functioning. It is not until after the group has worked through the norming behavior that it can move into the third stage of the group—cohesiveness. Once the norms have been established, the group can develop sensitivity to one another and a spirit of working together.

The Facilitative Base

The group counselor's chief variables in establishing a facilitative base with the group members have grown out of the theoretical position espoused by Rogers and extended by Carkhuff, Truax, Gazda, and others. Essentially, the counselor promotes a facilitative atmosphere by providing certain conditions to the group members. Rogers (1957) postulated that: (1) the counselor and participants need to be in psychological contact; (2) the group members feel anxious and in a state of incongruence; (3) the counselor is congruent; (4) the counselor feels the members are deserving of unconditional positive regard; (5) the counselor has empathic understanding of them; and (6) the clients are aware of these counselor conditions.

Psychological contact means that the group members and counselor have come together and the members perceive the active listening on the part of the counselor. The second condition simply means that participants must come to counseling perceiving some discrepancy between what they are and what they would like to be. In counseling, they meet a congruent counselor who is aware of his or her own feelings and is unafraid of communicating himself or herself to others. The fourth condition refers to a belief that each counselor must hold that every individual is worthwhile, even when that individual's behavior is not worthwhile. The fifth condition is related to the first in that the first requirement of empathy is active listening. In this sense, empathy means really trying to understand the client at the deepest possible level. The last condition refers to the essential fact that the client must perceive the other five conditions as being present. If not, the conditions really do not exist for the client.

To these dimensions, Carkhuff (1969a, 1969b) has added concreteness, confrontation, and immediacy. Concreteness is the ability of the counselor to get the members of the group to be specific about their feelings. "Specifically, concreteness refers to the helpee pinpointing or accurately labeling his feeling and experiences (Gazda, 1973, p. 26)." The counselor accomplishes this largely by being concrete with his or her own statements. An element of being genuine is the ability to tell it like it is; in effect, to confront a group member when that is appropriate. Confrontation is simply the counselor's telling the client what it is the counselor is hearing. It generally occurs when the counselor notices a discrepancy between what the group member is saying and doing, or it may be that the counselor simply perceives something different from the group member (Carkhuff, 1969a, 1969b). Immediacy is the ability to focus on what is happening between the counselor and a participant, or it may be something that is going on in the group. The group member "can gain a better understanding of himself, especially how he affects others (in this case, the helper), when the helper appropriately uses the immediacy dimension (Gazda, 1973, p. 28)."

Levels of Facilitative Dimensions   To make these conditions less abstract and more measurable, Carkhuff (1969a, 1969b) developed a five-point scale to assess the level of the facilitative dimensions. This permits the operationalization of the dimensions and relates improved functioning of the participant to higher offered conditions by the counselor. On all scales, Level 3 is defined as minimally facilitative interpersonal functioning. At Level 3, the counselor's response of empathic understanding is essentially interchangeable with those of the group members in that they express essentially the same affect and meaning. The positive respect and communication for the members' feelings, experiences, and potentials are communicated, and the counselor provides no discrepancies between what he or she verbally states and the nonverbal cues indicating his or her feelings. The counselor's response to the relevant concreteness of the group member is defined as the counselor's enabling the member to discuss personally relevant material in a specific and concrete terminology.

Below Level 3 the responses of the counselor detract from those of the members of the group. At Level 2 the counselor does respond to the expressed feeling of a member but in such a way as to subtract noticeably from affective communication. Also, the counselor's response exhibits little respect or concern for the feelings and experiences of the member. There are some indications that the counselor's responses are slightly interrelated to what other cues indicate the member is feeling at the moment. The counselor frequently leads or allows the discussion of relevant material to be dealt with on a somewhat vague or abstract level. At the first level there is communication of a clear lack of respect or negative regard for the individual member, and the counselor's expressions are clearly unrelated to other cues which indicate what the individual is feeling. The counselor's general responses at the first level are negative in regard to the client's expressions; the responses either do not attend to, or distract significantly from, the expression of the client. The counselor leads or allows the discussion with the client to deal only with vague and anonymous generalizations.

Above Level 3, the counselor's responses are additive in nature. Hence, at Level 4 the responses of the counselor add noticeably to the expression of the group member in such a way as to express feelings of a deeper level than the member is expressing. The counselor's communications create a deep respect for the group member, and the counselor presents positive cues indicating a human response, whether it is positive or negative, in a nondestructive manner to the individual. The counselor is frequently helpful, enabling the member to develop more fully in concrete and specific words his or her emphasis of concern. At the fifth level, the counselor's responses add significantly to the feelings and meaning of the individual in such a way as to express accurate feelings beyond what the group member is able to express. The counselor communicates a very deep respect for the client's worth as a person and his or her potential as a free individual. The counselor's expressions indicate a free and deep involvement in the relationship with the client. The counselor is completely spontaneous in action and open to all of his or her experiences. The counselor's communications are always helpful in that they assist the participant in discussing specific feelings and experiences fluently, directly, and completely.

Model of Dimensions These five levels are present across the dimensions of empathy, positive regard, concreteness, genuineness, confrontation, and immediacy. The first three dimensions are chiefly concerned with the establishment of a facilitative, or rapport-building, relationship. The last three dimensions come into action after the relationship has been well established. This does not mean that in the initial phases of counseling the counselor focuses only on the first three dimensions and in the later phases of counseling concentrates on the last three. If counseling is to be most effective, the first three dimensions are present throughout the counseling, and the more action-oriented dimensions are used when the counselor perceives that the group members are ready. For example, a counselor cannot use the dimension of confrontation until such a time as a grouq member perceives the counselor's empathic understanding, respect, and concreteness. In effect, the counselor must demonstrate caring to the member of the group before he or she has the right to try to help this person solve a difficulty.

The applicability of this model to the group counseling process is strongly supported through four propositions developed by Carkhuff (1969b, pp. 130–31):

1. The core of functioning or dysfunctioning (health or psychopathology) is interpersonal.

2. The core of the helping process (learning or relearning) is interpersonal.

3. Group processes are the preferred modes of working with difficulties in interpersonal functioning.

4. Systematic training in interpersonal functioning is the preferred mode of work with difficulties in interpersonal functioning.

The four propositions developed by Carkhuff recognize that as individuals, we do not develop in a vacuum. Rather, we are the products of our own individual differences in interaction with our particular environment. Much of that environment is composed of other individuals. Hence, it is to be expected that much of our behavior, good and bad, is a product of that interaction. It follows, then, that the most effective way of dealing with difficulties that arise is through the group process, and that individuals who wish to be helping persons through the use of groups should be trained through the group process.

Carkhuff (1969b) emphasizes that in all group situations designed to provide assistance to members, the key to success is the level of functioning of the leader. In effect, it can be stated that the facilitative base, if provided by the counselor, will help the individual members to develop into a cohesive group. Rather than feeling separated from the leader and other members, they will feel a kinship. This feeling of kinship will spread and deepen as the leader continues to model those behaviors that are necessary for group success. The leader as model may well be the most important technique of leadership and, as such, is deserving of special attention.

Anticipation

Gruen (1977) demonstrated that relevant leader input influences the group process toward movement and working through. A leader's accurate anticipation provides a climate in which the members can move toward problem solving. The leader's anticipation involves expectations about members' behavior and problems in themes that emerge in a particular group session. The leader bases his or her functions on a theory about the group, a theory about personality as it is revealed in the group, a knowledge of group dynamics, and knowledge about and interest in the particular members of the group.

The leader's knowledge and anticipation provide a basis for accurate empathy. This in turn provides a measure of security for the clients to explore their problems. Gruen points out that anticipation is never complete. If the group is structured for the members, they will have a lot to say about the things that emerge, and the days between meetings provide important life experiences which will influence the material in the next session. Also, the counselor should not play his or her role as a prepared script but should proceed with a general set of guidelines and principles.

The opposite of accurate anticipation occurs when the leader is surprised, and his or her efforts to revive accurate anticipation hold the group back. Gruen's findings suggest that a good theory is important for the promotion of movement.

Gruen also found that leader control in the meeting promotes movement. He did not find a linear relationship, and does not mean that an authoritarian or laissez-faire leader moves the group. His conclusion compares favorably with the executive function described by Lieberman et al. (1973).

Boundaries

Gurowitz (1975) discusses the importance of group boundaries and leadership potency. He describes the group as an aggregation of members which has an external boundary separating it from the world at large. The group is divided into members and leaders who are separated by an internal boundary. Gurowitz believes that both barriers are necessary to define the aggregation of the group, that the strength of the external boundary is a measure of the cohesion of the group, and that the strength of the external boundary is largely a function of the internal boundary. Firm internal boundaries provide a feeling of safety for the members by making it clear that the group process is under control. In a single-leader group, the internal boundary is a fairly direct function of the leader's potency. In a two-leader group, the internal boundary involves a collective potency and is influenced by the function of the group members' understanding of the relationship between the leaders and the degree of clarity between the leaders themselves. He suggests that where great disparity exists between the training, experience, and responsibility of the two leaders, and the effects of this disparity is not resolved, the strength of the internal boundaries will be diminished. Gurowitz believes that where the internal boundary is weak, the external boundary is experienced as a fence confining the members in an unsafe place. In a group where there are strong internal boundaries, the external boundary is a wall keeping out the external threat.

Here-and-Now or There-and-Then

Many leaders in group counseling emphasize the group's focusing on the here-and-now rather than the outside and/or past experiences. This indicates that the group interaction is an ahistoric one. Focusing on the here-and-now facilitates the development of each group member into this social microcosm. It emphasizes feedback to each other, immediate catharsis, immediate self-disclosure, and an acquisition of new socializing behaviors. By focusing on the here-and-now, the group becomes more vital and the members become intensely involved in the meeting. Yalom (1975) suggests that the here-and-now focus will rapidly reach the limits of usefulness without a second step which is the illumination of the process. The group must examine itself, study its own interactions, and integrate that experience. Therefore, the effectiveness of the here-and-now involves the group's living in the present and also examining and reflecting its behaviors that have just occurred. Accordingly, the counselor has two functions: to involve the group in a here-and-now interaction and to guide the self-reflective commentary.

Many counselors believe that to find the basic cause of behavior, one must refer to the past. Therefore, part of the working-through process in the group is to have individuals refer from the here-and-now experience to the past. It is assumed that by understanding the relationship of past to present behavior from the feedback of group members, the individual can better understand the causes of the behavior, and with that insight can develop more appropriate behaviors both in and outside the group. Yalom (1975) suggests that the future is also a powerful determinant of behaviors. Members have an idealized self and a series of goals toward which they strive; therefore, the future strivings as well as the past influence the members' behaviors. Maintaining a here-and-now interaction is never fully attainable in a group. A discussion of past experiences and future anticipations are an important part of group discussions. However, leaders generally try to emphasize group discussion and feedback remaining as much as possible between members in the group. This group interaction is a training and rehearsal for behaviors that can be done by the individual in outside life. Therefore, the working-through process involving the past may be done by the individual outside the group meeting, leaving more time for the group to interact and practice their behaviors in the here-and-now.

Gruen (1977) reports that when a leader makes an interpretation which covers a number of instances of behavior manifestations, or when a leader connects past with present behavior, this has a significant effect on the group process. This is an important leader function in group movement. It is assumed that interpretation resolves group issues and provides closure, permitting the group to move on to new territory. It is also important to note that the leader behavior also influences the emergence of interpretation by other group members. Through their interpretations, they attempt to help each other and share in the leadership function. Gruen also found that group cohesion was related to the leader's use of interpretation. When a leader ventured beyond reflection of feelings to more connective interpretation, members became more involved with each other.

Two studies compared the effectiveness of there-and-then versus here-and-now counselor interpretations in group counseling. Roback (1972) compared the impact of four group counseling approaches with in-patient populations. The conditions were insight only, interaction only, combined insight and interaction, and a control group. A trend toward more global positive change in the combined insight and interaction group than in any of the other three was found, suggesting that the benefit of insight and interaction techniques may be additive. Abramowitz and Jackson (1974) reported that the combined there-and-then with here-and-now interpretations group tended to demonstrate more consistently positive outcomes than did other groups. A possible reason for their success could lie in the greater freedom of expression the leaders afforded. An obvious dual advantage of such a context to group members is that more problems can be worked through in different ways and that more outlets are available for release and resolution. These studies indicate that rather than a separation of here-and-now leadership styles, or an interpretation of past to present, a combination of these approaches may be the most effective form of leadership.

Structured Exercises

Structured exercises are sometimes used to accelerate group interaction. Assigning tasks to individuals circumvents the usual introductory behaviors. The exercises also speed up individual work by helping members get in touch with suppressed emotions, unknown parts of themselves, and their physical bodies. Structured exercises may be used at other times when the group is having difficulty working through a particular issue. The directed exercise helps the individuals get in touch with the conflicting issues.

Some structured exercises last only a few minutes while others may use the whole group time. The exercises may be verbal or nonverbal. However, the discussion of what occurred in the interaction and the feelings that arose are important aspects in using structured group exercises.

The popularity of structured groups has grown to the point that they may be misused. An exercise may be selected to do a specific task within the group. The entire group counseling experience should not be made up of a series of structured group exercises. The Leiberman, Yalom, and Miles encounter group project (1973) studied the impact of structured exercises. They report that leaders who used large numbers of exercises were popular with their group. However, the members of high-exercise groups had a significantly lower outcome level than did members of low-exercise groups. Yalom (1975) poses two drawbacks in using structured exercises. First, it is questioned whether or not the acceleration and bypassing of the early stages of group interaction is really therapeutic. In a short-term group, it may be appropriate to employ techniques to speed the stages and to help the group move through an impasse. However, in long-term counseling, the bypass of the early stages is not thought to be as therapeutic. A second caution in using structured exercises concerns the leader's establishing himself or herself as the director of the group. Members then feel that help comes only from the leader. They wait their turn to work with the leader and cease to use other members of the group or give enough help to other members of the group. The cautions indicate that using structured exercises should be selective and that the leader should use them deliberately to help a group for a specific purpose.

Leader Model

While the leader cannot take sole responsibility for what takes place within the group, neither can he or she ignore some responsibility for what takes place. As Beymer (1970) indicates, the leader functions as a model of behavior independent of personal willingness to assume that function. In communications to members, both verbal and nonverbal, the leader acts to establish the norms of behavior for all group members. To the degree the leader attends to any of the statements expressed by the members, he or she is contributing to the establishment of the group's agenda (Mahler, 1969). If the group process is to be maximally effective, the group members must interact with each other in an open, forthright, nondefensive, nonjudgmental, and confrontive manner, and the counselor must model this behavior (Yalom, 1975). If the leader continually attends to expressions of factual material and does not attend to expressions of feelings, he or she can expect that the group members will also focus on factual material to the exclusion of feeling material. Therefore, it is extremely important that group leaders identify their major behavioral assets and liabilities in terms of the impact of these behaviors on group members, and that they guide their behavior within the group appropriately (Bednar and Lawlis, 1971).

The modeling function of the leader is a technique that is always in operation, while other specific techniques are used by the leader at various points within the process. The counselor must always be sensitive to the ways in which the behavior of members is a direct result of those behaviors that the leader has modeled. This requires that prior to the group meeting, the leader thinks about those behaviors that he or she wishes to model in the group. Chances are that if the leader pays no attention to this, he or she will end up modeling as many inappropriate as appropriate behaviors.

Of prime importance is the ability of the leader to model good communication skills. The leader must demonstrate the ability to really listen to group members, to accurately perceive the meaning and feeling in messages, and to communicate perceptions to others. If one recognizes that many human problems are a direct result of a breakdown in communication, either within an individual or between individuals, the importance of modeling good communication skills for the group members becomes apparent.

A second benefit of modeling these procedures for the leader is that, as he or she carries out these behaviors, the distance between the members and the leader begins to lessen. Members become more aware of the leader's true humanness, and as this occurs, the members come to see themselves as co-workers with the group leader. This process of identification with the leader has been shown to be related to positive outcomes in group situations (Cooper, 1969; Smith, 1971; Bolman, 1971; Simmons, 1972). The identification and humanizing of the group leader leads to the natural question, "Should the counselor be leader or member?"

Leader Member

The question of whether to maintain some distance from the group membership or to attempt to become simply another member in the process is one that causes difficulty for many group leaders. As noted from the discussions on theoretical positions in Part One of this text, there are supporters on both sides of the question. Those who adhere to the counselor in the position of leader point out that the counselor must act in ways to both maintain and develop the group process. That is, in effect, the leader must fill a sort of directorship role. The advantage of such a position is that the group does generally move in a smoother fashion with fewer side trips. The disadvantages are that such a position creates feelings of dependency in the group members, and acts to establish a definite barrier between leader and members.

It is to these disadvantages that those who adhere to a leader in the position as member point. They feel that the leader as member allows the membership more of an opportunity to develop their own strengths, rather than depending on the leader. It also lessens the possibility of barriers developing between leader and members. Unfortunately, such a position often leads the group into a wandering kind of pattern. With no leader, groups often have a tendency to become easily sidetracked and bogged down in trivia.

In short, there are positive and negative aspects on both ends of the continuum. The position taken here is: first, it is not, nor should it be, an either/or question; and second, it is almost impossible to give up one's leadership position even if one desires to do so. The individual who is responsible for bringing together the group will almost always be viewed by the group members as someone with some kind of authority. This is particularly true in institutions, such as school settings, where there may be a large age difference between counselor and group members. Even when such a leader tries to abdicate the position, the group members may be more inclined to see her or him as an ineffective leader rather than as a true member of the group.

While it is true that the leader can never fully shed the role, he or she can engage in behaviors that facilitate a human interaction between himself or herself and other group members. As was discussed earlier in this chapter, this process is facilitated by the counselor's success as a model, ability to demonstrate interpersonal honesty and spontaneity, and ability to accept and admit fallibility.

Of special interest in the leader-member issue is the role of self-disclosure on the part of the counselor. As indicated by Gazda (1973), self-disclosure on the part of the counselor can lead to greater closeness between the group leader and the group members. However, self-disclosure can be a double-edged sword, in that inappropriate self-disclosure on the part of the leader may confuse the group members and actually shift the focus from them to the leader. Self-disclosure on the part of the leader may be appropriate if the leader has really experienced a situation relevant to what the group is concerned about, and they seem to be floundering in their own ignorance about what to do. A second, more important type of self-disclosure on the leader's part is that which deals with the actual process of the group. This has elements of both the immediacy and genuineness dimensions described by Carkhuff (1969a, 1969b, 1971) and discussed earlier. In early group meetings, there is usually some anxiety in both the group members and the leader. As the leader perceives this anxiety, it can be very helpful to state, "I sense many of you feeling a little anxious about what is going to happen in this group, and I am feeling a little anxious about it myself." This type of self-disclosure deals with a current feeling, allowing the group members to see the leader as someone who has feelings similar to their own. Such self-disclosure has a better chance of being relevant to the members than does self-disclosure which deals with the leader's past. Process-oriented self-disclosure enables the members to see the leader as genuine and congruent, and this has been found to be related to group members working on their own congruence (Cooper, 1969). The need for cautious use of this procedure has been illustrated in a study by Weigel (1972). He found that group members may perceive counselor self-disclosure as a negative indication of counselor mental health. Group members may see such self-disclosures as a means by which the counselor is asking them for help. In summary, then, leader self-disclosure, particularly of a process nature, can be beneficial to the group process, but it must be used with judicious restraint.

Coleading

Many leaders in the group counseling field are encouraging the use of two counselors in the group situation. The interest in coleaders was generated in large part as a result of its being used as a training device. In training, one experienced counselor actually directed the group, with an inexperienced counselor acting as an observer. This was found to be an effective training device for inexperienced counselors. More importantly, some of the counselors involved began to feel that there were also definite benefits to the clients in the group. In more traditional theoretical approaches, the practice of "multiple therapy is frequently seen as the creation of a symbolic family, in which the therapists serve as mother and father figures (or authority figures in general) for the sick client-child (Zimpfer, 1971, p. 306)." Others, such as Lundin and Aronow (1952), simply feel that two counselors provide a broader area of interaction for the group members. In general, there is a feeling that coleaders can enhance the process, for as one counselor is actively involved in the process, the other counselor can be more observant of the dynamics going on in the group. There is also agreement that in cocounseling there will develop a general division of the leadership functions. Often this entails one of the counselors filling primarily the supporting role, while the other counselor may behave in a more confronting or active manner. Some counselors will establish these roles before the group starts, but the feeling here is that if two counselors are involved, they should not set the roles ahead of time but should interact in a free fashion. This allows the therapists "to agree, disagree, have different feelings for the client and for themselves at any moment of the therapy (Mullan and Sangiuliano, 1964, p. 319)." In effect, this sets up a participant-observer situation, and each leader can slip in and out of several roles.

While the process of cocounseling can be beneficial, counselors need to be very careful in selecting a cocounselor. Zimpfer (1971) indicates that the literature strongly suggests that not every pair of counselors will work well together. Gans (1957) listed six conditions that are necessary for two counselors to work together:

1. Each counselor must know his or her own strengths and weaknesses and must work within those limits.

2. Each counselor needs to utilize the strengths and minimize the weaknesses of the partner.

3. Each counselor must avoid a conflict over who really controls the group.

4. They must not permit the dominant counselor-passive counselor hierarchy to stabilize and cause resentment within the group.

5. Both counselors should be experienced in group procedures.

6. Each counselor needs the ability to be flexible in his or her approach.

Weinstein (1971) presents some prerequisites such as trust, understanding, recognition of personality differences, and equal ability as factors necessary for effective cotherapy. Trust requires that the cocounselors be constructive in their comments and behavior toward each other inside and outside the group meetings. Trust provides the foundation for the counselors to accept each other and explore the effects of their relationship on the group. Understanding and recognizing differences in personality allows each leader to acknowledge that the other has personal and professional strengths and weaknesses which affect the therapeutic leadership style. The therapeutic partnership should be a model of respected

differences, in which the cocounselors struggle together to grow, work out differences, and remain supportive but separate.

The use of coleaders can benefit the group by increasing the validity and
objectivity in observance of transference and countertransference. Balgopal and
Hull (1970) state that one of the hazards in group counseling is competition for the
counselor to respond to the subtle pressures of the transference situation and
unwittingly gratify the clients' expectations. An advantage of having coleaders is
that seldom do both leaders become involved in the same web of unrealistic
expectations at the same time. Balgopal and Hull suggest that most effective
coleading occurs when the leaders are compatible, flexible, know each other's
assets and liabilities, are able to resolve issues of dominance and submission, and
speak to each other freely about their observations and feelings. By doing so,
countertransference reactions may be understood, group resistance overcome,
and group goals realized.

Probably the most important aspect of coleadership is the working alliance
which involves the interaction between two counselors where trust is implicit and
impediments to the equanimity of the relationship can be worked through. In order
for a working alliance to develop, certain issues must be worked through. Major
issues between coleaders involve anxiety about trusting, competition over who is
the better leader, concerns over who is in control or in charge of the interview, and,
when it is appropriate, issues of a male and a female coleader.

In short, the coleaders need to be compatible individuals who will use each
other's abilities and will not get involved in a power struggle within the group. If the
coleaders unintentionally get into a pattern of competition, the group's will be
destroyed. Coleaders must also guard against the possibility of the group's split-
ting as some give their loyalty to one leader and some to the other. If this begins
to happen, the leaders must be able to bring this out for discussion in the group.

Zimpfer (1971), in his extensive review of the literature, listed the following nine
areas where cocounseling could be enhancing:

1. For students who come from split homes, it can provide some positive adult
    identification.

2. Individuals who need to modify their attitudes toward authority figures will
    have two adults with whom to interact in a rather free atmosphere.

3. Clients who tend to try to split and conquer their parents will often be
    confronted with this behavior as they try to repeat it with the counselors.

4. The presence of two counselors increases the possibility that every group
    member will be able to identify with at least one of the counselors.

5. An opportunity is provided for the group members to observe the free way
    in which two adults can interact, have differences, and resolve those differ-
    ences.

6. Cocounselors can contribute a deeper and broader level of experience to
    group members than can a single counselor.

7. Clients can experience the fact that there are at least two individuals who are concerned about them.

8. Cocounseling enhances the opportunity to examine the individual differences within the group and to plan for those differences.

9. Cocounseling, when composed of two counselors from different levels within an institution, can enhance the transition from one level to another.

It is clear, then, that cocounseling can be a beneficial technique, but, just as it may increase the potential for growth of group members, it also increases the possibilities of problems within the group. Hence, counselors planning to use such an approach need to pay careful attention to the selection of the coleader and the group and should, during the actual process of counseling, continually review the dynamics of each session. In this way, some of the pitfalls may be avoided and the added potential of coleadership will be released.

THE TECHNIQUES OF GROUP LEADERSHIP WITHIN THE PROCESS

General leadership styles and leadership behaviors which need to transcend the entire group process have been examined. Keeping these overall behaviors in mind, we focus here on more specific leader behaviors that are needed at various points within the process.

Planning

Structuring presents a unique problem to the group leader. The need is to provide general direction and, at the same time, provide an opportunity for the group members to take some responsibility for the direction of the group. The type of planning or structuring that is called for is one that establishes the proper social milieu: a milieu that enables each member to feel that he or she is an active participant in the process, and one in which each member who desires to make a contribution can do so. Planning, as such, then, is concerned with (1) thinking about ways to enhance the group environment as opposed to planning what precise events will take place in that environment; (2) being aware of the expectations and feelings of individuals as they enter the group for the first time; (3) being aware of the group dynamics that can be expected; (4) being aware of one's own expectations and needs; and, most importantly, (5) being aware of those leadership behaviors that can respond to the expectations and feelings of the group members and to the expected dynamics of a beginning session.

While planning is extremely important in the early stages of group counseling, it is also important that the group counselor review each session in terms of where the group is; what the particular dynamics are that occur; where the various individual members are in this process; and how his or her own behaviors are enhancing or hindering the process. Such a review can provide a great deal of useful information which may be helpful in leading the next session. It is during such planning that a counselor can develop ideas for dealing with a resistant or blocking group member; can take a second look at interaction patterns; and can decide where he or she might focus the group a little better. Such sessions on the part of the leader are as essential as any particular behavior during the group process.

Getting Started

The success of almost any group will depend in large part on the success of the first session. That the counselor be a model of desired behaviors is extremely important at this beginning stage. It is also important to reduce the tension, anxiety, shyness, and insecurity of the individuals in the group by getting them involved in the process. One method of dealing with the initial feelings of group members, discussed earlier in the context of the dimensions of genuineness and immediacy, is some self-disclosure on the part of the leader. For example, a leader may indicate that she or he shares many of the members' uncertainties about the group, although at the same time being excited about the potential for growth in the group.

Of at least equal moment is the need for the leader to provide some means for the group to begin interacting. The leader may attempt this by presenting some open-ended questions such as: "What kind of thoughts do you have about being here?" or "What kinds of expectations do you have about this process?" Another approach, particularly for the less experienced counselor, is to begin the first session using a somewhat structured exercise. One such exercise is to have the members pair off in dyads with the instruction to get to know one another well enough to introduce each other to the rest of the group. After about five minutes, have everyone introduce each other. When this is completed, ask the group to consider the kinds of data each member shared. More often than not, the data will be factual rather than of an affective or feeling nature. The leader now needs to have the group discuss (process) this in terms of what implications it has in their lives and for the group. Such things as defensiveness, unwillingness to invest in each other, and social habits are all areas of discussion which may flow from this beginning exercise.

"The purpose of using a communication activity such as this to initiate a group is to give the participants a common experience that brings them together with a common focus and then establishes a basis on which the group process can build (Trotzer, 1973, p. 374)." The exercise by itself is only an exercise. It is in the processing of the material generated that the counselor can get the group members to focus on themselves. This is, of course, one of the primary purposes for which the individuals were brought together in the group.

In using this procedure, one caution is in order: the exercise is allowing the leader to structure the situation. This, in turn, may cast the leader in the authoritarian position and increase the members' dependency on the leader. This is why it is dangerous to decide to simply use an exercise—any exercise. The importance of the exercise is in the processing and, by processing, some of both the feelings of structure and the notion of leader as authoritarian are removed. Exercises, if relied on exclusively, also have a tendency to create a game atmosphere among the members, thus creating a way for them to avoid their real concerns. Hence, it is recommended that they be used, if at all, simply to get the group going and then be dropped.

Dealing with Resistance

"Every effective leader tries to understand forces within his group that contribute to and interfere with the group's goals (Ohlsen, 1970, p. 49)." One of the most potent forces that interfere with the group process is resistance. Individuals attempt to organize their lives in such a way as to reduce the possible occurrences of stress and anxiety. This is recognized as the much-discussed need for individuals to maintain homeostasis, or to reduce the amount of dissonance. Through the use of habits, rituals, and normal routine, individuals attempt to bring their lives into a state of control by their ability to predict most events. Think of how one's own equilibrium is thrown off when a new situation arises; when a late Sunday evening routine is suddenly interrupted by the unexpected arrival of people from out of town. In such situations, feelings of dissonance are heightened; one's state of homeostasis is thrown out of balance. Individuals coming to a group for the first time experience similar feelings. They find themselves in a situation where they cannot predict events; hence, they desire to protect themselves. The individuals feel vulnerable and fear being seen as inadequate or incompetent. To avoid this, there is a tendency to withdraw, to not participate, and certainly to avoid risking any real involvement with other group members.

Resistance may also occur later in the group process when individuals or the group as a whole do not want to deal with material that may make them uncomfortable. Once again, in an attempt to reduce the dissonance created by the unpleasant or unprepared-for material, they resist through withdrawal, changing of topics, or a flight into hostility toward the leader. Regardless of when it takes place in the life of the group, the leader must recognize the phenomenon. The resistance may occur within a particular group member or it may be a group resistance. It may take the form of withdrawal, intellectualization, hostility toward the leader or other members, or any behavior that attempts to move the group away from areas that are causing discomfort. In any case, resistance on the part of either the individual or the group must be overcome if the group is to move forward.

If it is group resistance, the leader needs to focus the group on what is happening. It is an intervention on the part of the leader designed to force members to look at the way they are behaving without supplying the why. An example of such an intervention might be: "A few minutes ago we were discussing how we felt about being here, and now we seem to be talking about how people feel in new situations, and I am wondering how that relates to us." This question could be enough to refocus the group on themselves; but if the pattern of resistance continues, the leader may need to intervene by interpreting the group's recurrent behavior to them. For instance: "It seems very difficult for us to deal with anyone else's feelings. Every time one of us begins to talk about something that really concerns us, someone changes the subject and everyone else joins in." In both of these examples, the counselor is attempting to focus the group's attention on their avoidance behavior. The counselor may also do this by commenting on his or her confusion or uncertainty about what is going on in the group by asking, "Is there something going on here I don't understand? It seems the group is avoiding something." In any case, the counselor is saying to the group, "We are avoiding why we are here. I'm aware of it, and I do not feel it is most productive for us to continue such behavior. Shouldn't we examine why we are engaging in such behavior?"

In cases of individual resistance within the group, the counselor must be sure that an interpretation of resistance behavior will not drive the individual deeper into a shell. In most cases it should not be a direct confrontation of the resistance. Rather, the counselor may try to get at it by placing the responsibility with himself or herself. For example, the counselor might say to an individual: "I have a feeling that I am doing something you are uncomfortable with," or "We are doing something that makes you uncomfortable" or "that you don't agree with." The group must be at a stage where it will help the individual work through the difficulty of self-examination rather than jumping on the individual for his or her behavior. Thus, the timing and the type of intervention are extremely significant.

Counselors must learn to trust their feelings that something is going on which is interfering with the process. The actual form and timing of the intervention are generally an individual matter. Some counselors may wait longer; others, and this is the feeling of the current authors, will intervene whenever they sense some group resistance, even though the resistance might not be completely understood (Yalom, 1975). Either way, the counselor must constantly use an intervention strategy which keeps both the individual's and the group's attention on the central issues. As the counselor continues to engage in this behavior, she or he is also modeling it for the group members. Hopefully, as a result of this, the group members themselves will intervene when resistance is evident in either individuals or the group as a whole.

Dealing with Transference

The transference phenomenon, first described by Freud (see Chapter 2), is the transferring of repressed experiences from the past onto some similar figure in the present. While all therapists or counselors will not accept the complete Freudian notion of transference, there is some consensus that past experiences of individuals will affect their present experiences either positively or negatively. Thus, an individual's behavior toward the group leader or other group members may be a function of past interpersonal encounters and, in particular, encounters with others who have had some authority relationship with the client.

Unlike individual counseling, the client's distortions are not limited to the counselor; they involve all the group members. Not only may the leader be seen as representing someone from past experience, but each member may be seen the same way. The individual not only perceives the leader and the members in this distorted fashion, but his or her behavior will be directed at them as though they actually were those others from the past. Hence, the counselor must be aware of the member's double distortions (Yalom, 1975). Each group member will to some degree perceive the counselor and other members incorrectly because of past experiences. In this state, the member misunderstands the present situation in terms of the past. The member then tries to relive the past without dealing with the present. Somehow the client must be helped to see this behavior and to deal with it.

If transference-like behaviors do occur, it is important to help the individual work through these distortions. This is true regardless of whether they are distortions directed toward the leader or other members. Rather than deal with these distortions in a traditional analytic interpretive mode, the leader should attempt to deal with the distortions by trying to engage the client in an interpersonal encounter (Yalom, 1975).

The group leader, when he or she feels distortion is occurring, must try to feed back to the client what the client seems to be doing. An example might be: "I'm a little confused by your reaction to me. You seem to be ascribing some authority powers to me I don't feel I possess." Or, "I'm not sure why you are acting toward Lois as you are." In effect, the counselor attempts to get the participant to look at current behavior in terms of whether it is valid or is a product of the past. It is often these transference-like behaviors that are causing individuals difficulty in their lives. By being confronted with them, individuals may come to see just how inappropriate they are.

Countertransference

Countertransference is the conscious or unconscious emotional response of the counselor to group members. It stems from the counselor's needs rather than the needs of the other participants (Kaplan and Sadock, 1971). In the event that a counselor has countertransference involvement with a group member, the counselor will experience difficulty in attempts to understand the client and see the client objectively. In the group situation, the counselor's behavior may be observed by the other group members, who will demand more appropriate responses.

Just as with transference, there is considerable disagreement between group counselors as to how to deal with countertransference (see Chapter 2). The more tranditional Freudians simply urge the group leader to be aware of the possibility of countertransference. Encounter group leaders, however, strongly recommend that the counselor verbalize his or her feelings. They hold that the group members will perceive these feelings regardless of whether they are expressed by the counselor or not, and it is better to bring them out in the open (Kaplan and Sadock, 1971). The position taken here is that certainly the counselor must be aware of reactions to the group participant; whether they are caused by the past or present may be relatively unimportant. What is crucial is how these feelings may be adversely affecting the counselor's ability to deal with an individual in an objective fashion. Hence, at the very least, counselors need to be aware of these feelings and, if the feelings are strong enough, the counselor may need to articulate them. The authors would agree with Kaplan and Sadock that these feelings will be perceived by the group members, regardless of whether the counselor acknowledges them. Self-disclosing in this manner may be a good modeling procedure which will help the other group members deal with their own transference feelings.

Self-disclosure

Self-disclosure is an important aspect in an interpersonal relationship. Sidney Jourard (1958) coined the term self-disclosure and defined it as a process of making one's self known to others by revealing personal information. The clients' self-disclosure has traditionally been considered a significant part of counseling. However, the counselor's self-disclosure is as important as the group members' self-disclosure. The importance of the counselor's self-disclosure has been established by research indicating that the process of self-disclosure occurs in a reciprocal fashion. There is a high correlation between self-disclosure output given to a person and the amount of disclosure received from that person (Jourard, 1964). Lazarus (1971) stated that in the counseling interview, the verbal self-disclosure of the counselor opens the therapeutic communication chanoels. Jourard and Jaffe (1970) also demonstrated that the counselor's self-disclosure promotes client self-disclosure.

The counselor's personal disclosures serve as a model for members' revealing personal information (Vondrachek and Vondrachek, 1971; and Blackburn, 1970). Vondrachek and Vondrachek (1971) suggest that counselors' personal disclosures may serve as a stimulus for immediate recall of personal experiences of the clients and thus increase the self-disclosing behavior.

A counselor's personal disclosure may also act as a reinforcement for the clients' disclosure. Worthy (1969) states that the reception of personal disclosure from a counselor can act as a reinforcement, thereby increasing the likelihood of reciprocal self-disclosure. He also found that the more intimate the disclosure, the more potent it was as a reinforcer. Graff (1970) also found that self-disclosing counselors were more effective than other counselors because their personal disclosures served as reinforcements for the clients' behavior.

Although the importance of the counselor's self-disclosure is well established, there is a difference of opinion regarding the number and amount of counselor self-disclosure. There is evidence that self-disclosure can be detrimental in the counseling relationship. Weigel et al. (1972) investigated the relationship of perceived self-disclosure of both group members and counselors, their liking for each other, and their evaluation of each other's mental health. The findings suggest that members' and counselors' role images of clients were in agreement on a positive relationship between liking and mental health and liking and self-disclosure. However, clieots perceived the counselor's self-disclosure as a negative indicator of the counselor's mental health. Dies (1973) also reported that openly disclosing counselors were viewed by their clients as being less relaxed, strong, stable, and sensitive than less transparent counselors. Some clients may feel that the counselor is guilty of unprofessional conduct by not remaining in a professional role. The self-disclosing counselor may violate the client's role expectations for a counselor's behavior.

It is possible that group members with low levels of self-disclosure might be threatened by leaders who are high in self-disclosing. Therefore, such members might rate the leaders lower on mental health and helpfulness. However, May and

Thompson (1973) found that there was a positive relationship between group leaders' personal levels of self-disclosure, mental health, and the group ratings of their effectiveness. These findings are in favor of higher levels of counselor self-disclosure and are at variance with the findings of Weigel et al.

The best explanation seems to be Jourard's hypothesis that the relationship between self-disclosure and mental health is nonlinear (Jourard, 1971). He suggests there is an optimal level for self-disclosure beyond which point it may be destructive either in terms of the individual's feelings or the interpersonal relationship. While too little counselor self-disclosure may fail to produce client disclosures, too much counselor disclosure may decrease the time available for the group members or may cause them to be concerned for the counselor. Even so, most research indicates that there is a reciprocal effect in the interpersonal relationship suggesting that counselors using personal disclosures will be effective in stimulating group self-disclosures.

Timing

One of the most important skills a group counselor needs to develop is a sense of timing. No interventions, whether they are self-disclosures, interpretations, clarifications, or whatever, will be beneficial unless the timing is appropriate. The skill of timing interventions is enhanced by being aware of the general dynamics or life-stages of a group, discussed in Chapters 14 and 15. It is also, however, dependent on the leader's awareness of where each indiviual group member is in his or her own growth process. This, of course, is more difficult in an open group where members are constantly coming and going. But even in a closed group, different members will be at different stages of development.

Mahler (1969) suggests that timing on the part of the leader needs to be influenced by four factors. First, the counselor needs to be aware of the readiness of each individual member to share feelings with the group. Premature disclosure can cause individuals a great deal of anxiety and can increase withdrawal behavior. Second, the counselor needs to be cognizant of the member's ability to forego defenses. If the counselor asks this before the member is ready, the member is likely to become even more defensive. A third area described by Mahler is the readiness of the individual member to deal with material that is more than surface behavior. Once again, if the counselor forces the issue, the individual may retreat. On the other hand, if the counselor always holds back, the individual may never progress beyond surface material. A final area of consideration is the readiness of the group member to discuss behavior or attitudes that are socially disapproved. This is an extremely critical area in that the member must discuss them if there are to be any changes. The counselor needs to be aware of both the individual's readiness to engage in this behavior and the group's ability to respond to the individual in a facilitative fashion. Timing, then, is a crucial factor in leader behavior regardless of the particular kind of counselor intervention involved.

Feedback

Feedback from the counselor can take many forms (see discussion in Chapter 4), but here it refers to the counselor's providing a kind of summary of either the content of the group's discussion or of the process that is occurring within the group. It means simply presenting the facts without any form of interpretation, saying to the group, "This seems to be the essence of what you have been discussing" (content) or "These seem to be the feelings you have been expressing" (affect) or "These are the kinds of things that seem to be happening right now in the group" (process). The purpose of doing this is to try to get the group to focus on one of these areas. One of the chief roles of the leader is to keep the group focused, as well as to keep a balance between and among content, affect, and process. In essence, by providing feedback the counselor is acting as the ego of the group—that part of the group which administrates and filters all that is occurring within the group. The counselor does not make judgments but simply states that this is the way it is. The counselor trusts in the group's ability to deal with the material. Clarification, confrontation, and interpretation are also forms of feedback, but because of their special nature they will be discussed separately.

One further area where feedback can be effective is in the area of nonverbal communications. The counselor must be acutely aware of the nonverbal communications that take place among members, and between the counselor and the group. This is particularly important when the leader perceives an individual sending one verbal message, "I really am enjoying the group," while at the same time sending a conflicting nonverbal message through body movements such as undue shifting in the chair or other nervous mannerisms. In such cases, the counselor should provide feedback to the individual about the conflicting messages that are being sent, such as, "I'm a little confused; you are saying how much you enjoy being here, but you appear to be a little nervous." In such cases, the nonverbal message is probably the true message, and feedback may help the member bring this true feeling out.

General feedback is important throughout the process, but it is of particular importance in the early stages of the group when the goal is to have the group open up and participate with each other. The more specific forms of feedback to be discussed next are best used as the group moves into a stage of development where it is prepared to work on the reasons for which the group was constituted.

Clarification A slightly more directive form of feedback is a clarification statement by the counselor. Here the counselor is trying to sort out for the group what appears to be the central issue or theme. In many cases the group members may be discussing the same thing but do not seem to be understanding each other. In effect, they are playing a semantics game. In other cases they may be discussing the superficial aspects of some concern. In either case the counselor, by clarifying, is attempting to focus their attention on what he or she perceives to be really happening. In doing so, even if the counselor misses slightly, the attempt may help or encourage other group members to clarify what is being discussed or what is going on in the group.

A clarifying statement can also be used quite effectively by a group leader to summarize the content, the feeling, or the process of what has been transpiring in the group. Such a statement can be used after a long interaction among group members, at the end of a session, or as a stimulus to begin a new session. As with the simple clarification, the summarizing attempt is to focus the group on what the leader perceives as the central theme of the group. In effect, the leader, through careful listening, develops an understanding of the relationship between differing statements and then presents an analysis of the relationship to the group. Such a process facilitates the forward movement of the group as each statement is related to previous material (Gordon, 1972).

Confrontation   A strong type of feedback is confrontation. There are times within the group process when individual members or the total group engage in behaviors that are conflicting, or are blocking group movement. In these cases, it is often necessary for the counselor to point out this behavior to the individual or the group. A member, for example, may be stating that he really wants to work on certain concerns, but at the same time is engaging in behaviors that are blocking. Whenever the focus of the group begins to get at these concerns, the member does whatever he can to change the focus. At these times the counselor needs to feed back this material to the member. In order for this confrontation to be successful, the counselor must also communicate caring for the member. Thus, the confrontation might be worded, "John, I am really trying to help you work through your concern, but I feel that every time I get close to you, you put me off, and I am confused by that." In effect, the confrontation is a statement that lets the group member or the total group know that the counselor is aware of what is going on. Because there is the high risk in confrontation that the individual or group confronted will further retreat, it should be used very carefully; it is essential that the individuals who are confronted understand that it is done out of caring orientation.

Interpretations   Interpretive statements by the counselor represent another technique which has been the subject of considerable controversy. On the one hand, those theorists who adhere to a self-theory phenomenological position hold that interpretations should be used sparingly. They focus largely on here-and-now processes either within the individual or the group. On the other hand, theorists who adhere to a more traditional or analytic approach hold that the counselor must interpret to individuals perceptions of how past, often unconscious, material is affecting the present life of the individual. The position held here is that in counseling situations, interpretations can facilitate understanding on the part of either individuals or the group as a whole. For the most part these interpretations will deal with present behavior; however, it is often necessary to try to help individuals see how their past is affecting their current behavior, as in the case of transference or transference-like behaviors. A counselor does not need to adhere to an analytic position to see the viability of the notion that past events can color present behavior.

Interpretive statements by the counselor are most effective in helping individuals see the manner in which they are using defenses such as projection or displacement, or to help them see the pattern of their maladaptive behavior. Through making interpretations, the counselor can focus the group on its defenses, such as intellectualization and avoidance, or on antitherapeutic patterns of behaviors that have become established within the group (Yalom, 1975). In either case, the key to the success of an interpretation is the ability of individuals or the group to use the material. The effective counselor is one who can make the kind of interpretations that the participants can assimilate, verify, and utilize (Parloff, 1968). Interpretations that go too far beyond what the individual or the group is ready or able to deal with will at best fall on deaf ears and at worst cause resistance and hostility. Thus, while interpretive statements are a necessary and potentially powerful tool, the counselor must use them with caution.

Reinforcement

Yet another technique over which there is some disagreement is the use of reinforcement by the counselor. The question does not seem to be whether or not reinforcement procedures should be used in counseling; the question rather is how they can be used to greatest advantage (Krumboltz, 1966). Studies by Krumboltz and Thoresen (1964), Hansen, Niland, and Zani (1969), Warner and Hansen (1970), and Warner, Swisher, and Horan (1973), as well as others, have demonstrated that reinforcement by the counselor in a group situation can be an effective tool for bringing about behavioral changes in group members.

Reinforcement is a verbal or nonverbal response by the counselor that is designed to give positive feedback to a statement made by a participant. In counseling, reinforcement can be used first simply to establish the appropriate group atmosphere. The counselor, through positive attention to client behaviors and through statements that establish a positive therapeutic atmosphere, will increase the likelihood of a good atmosphere being formed. Later in the process, when the group and the counselor have clarified the goals they are working toward, the counselor can begin positively reinforcing those statements by group members that indicate some movement toward accomplishment of the desired goal.

Reinforcements take the form of positive attention by the counselor to the speaker. Some examples are verbal responses: "that sounds great," "yes," "you seem to have a good idea there," or nonverbal responses: smiling, physically leaning toward the speaker, and good eye contact. The potency of any of these responses will depend on the strength of the relationship. The group member may care little about what the counselor responds to positively. In fact, if the member is hostile to the group leader, the member may take the positive attention as a negative reinforcement and move in a direction opposite to the desired goal. Hence, reinforcement is not something that can be applied in a mechanical fashion. Any reinforcement, to be effective, is contingent on the member's feeling positively toward the group leader.

Modeling

The leader as model concept was discussed earlier in this chapter. An extension of that concept is the use of other models in counseling. These models are presented to the group members as examples of the desired behavior, or as examples of ways in which the clients' problems can be solved. The basic assumption of social modeling is that much learning that results from direct experience can also be learned through vicarious reinforcement or imitative learning (Hosford, 1969; also see Chapter 9). While this approach has developed out of social learning theory and much of the research on the use of models in counseling has been done in conjunction with verbal reinforcement counseling, models may be effective in group counseling using differing theoretical positions.

The principle involved in the use of models is to present models to the clients with which they can easily identify and which demonstrate the desired behavioral outcome. The client, through a desire to receive the same rewards as the model, will imitate the behavior that caused the model to receive rewards. The models themselves, then, may act as reinforcing agents or simply as stimuli for the desired responses.

A number of studies demonstrate that the use of models can be an effective technique in group counseling. Truax and Carkhuff (1967) found that clients who listen to taped excerpts exemplifying self-exploration prior to treatment showed greater positive change than control clients. Krumboltz and Thoresen (1964) found models effective in increasing information-seeking behavior of high school students. Krumboltz and Schroeder (1965) found modeling effective in increasing the amount of career planning done by high school students. These studies used models either on tape or film and presented them to the clients once early in the counseling process. Two studies, however, have examined the effectiveness of peer models who actually take part in the counseling sessions. Hansen, Niland, and Zani (1969) found peer models to be effective in increasing the social acceptance of low sociometric elementary school children. Warner and Hansen (1970) found that participating peer models were effective in reducing high school students' feelings of alienation.

While most of the research on the use of models in counseling has been done in conjunction with research on reinforcement counseling, this does not preclude models being used by counselors under a different theoretical framework. The models need not be thought of as strictly reinforcement agents, but simply as additional stimuli to produce interaction among the group members. When all of the clients in a particular group exhibit the same problem, it may be difficult for them to learn a solution to their problem from each other. Perhaps this is why much past research on the effects of group counseling has generally shown insignificant results. Many behaviors are learned by people through interacting with others, and the use of models in a group counseling situation gives the members of the group an opportunity to interact with and learn new desired behaviors from the models. In everyday life we expect people to learn from each other through interaction, the naive learning from the experienced. We refer to this as the process of socialization, and group counseling using models merely utilizes the socialization concept in a miniature and controlled setting. With this assumption as a guide, it appears that models would be appropriate for most theoretical approaches to group counseling.

A crucial question on the use of the models in group counseling is: How and what types of models should be used? The evidence thus far accumulated seems to indicate that the nature of the problem to be discussed in group counseling may influence the type of model utilized.

Type of Model   Taped or filmed models have been successful when the problem is centered at the cognitive end of the continuum, such as information seeking or career planning. The presentation to the clients in the group counseling situation involves the model demonstrating the desired behavior via tape or film. A one-shot presentation of a taped or filmed model may be all that is needed. Problem areas that might fall into this category could be such things as vocational or educational decision making, study skills, work habits, and the like. The group counseling continues after this presentation with a discussion of how the participants can implement the kind of behavior demonstrated by the model.

Live peer models have been effective in helping clients resolve problems of a more personal or social nature. In this situation, the models are considered part of the group and are encouraged to participate in the discussions. They are not presented as some paragon of model behavior, but are allowed to display themselves and their solutions to the problems through interacting with other group members. The clients may not always accept the model, because of an inability to identify the model as someone they would like to be like. But when the model is present in the ongoing process of counseling, there is greater likelihood that identification will take place. For a problem that is centered more in the affective or feeling end of the continuum, it appears that the live peer model can be effective. Problems that would fall into this area might deal with such things as interpersonal relationships, parent relationships, and prejudice.

Selection of Models   The actual selection of the models to be used is an essential function of the counselor. The concepts of relevancy and identification must be kept in mind if the models are to be effective stimuli for interaction or effective reinforcing agents for the desired behaviors. A young male who has found his solution to the parent relationship may not be at all relevant to a group of female high school students with a similar problem, and vice versa. Then the chances for the identification process to occur are very slim. As stated earlier, it is this identification process which must take place in order for the model to be an effective aid in the counseling process. The model must be someone similar enough to the group member so that he or she feels able to adopt this new behavior pattern into his or her own life-style. Hence, the method of selecting either a taped or live model to be used with the counseling must be based on the type of problem and the composition of the group. For some problems, such as interpersonal relations, a sociogram filled out by students may be an appropriate way to select the models. For problems concerning educational matters, such as study skills, it may be more appropriate to select models through teacher ratings. Regardless of the selection procedures, the key concepts to keep in mind are the type of problem and the nature of the group membership.

Role Techniques

The group counselor is frequently confronted with one of the following situations: (1) the group is discussing an issue in abstract terms; (2) there is a sharp difference of opinion among group members; (3) an individual is holding to a position or a behavioral pattern despite verbal attempts by the counselor or other members to get the member to look at his or her behavior; and (4) individuals see the need for new behavior but are afraid to try it under real conditions. In these kinds of cases, the counselor may wish to introduce one of the varieties of role techniques. These techniques enable participants to experience a lifelike situation in concrete terms rather than in an intellectual discussion. They enable the group members to engage in behaviors that are different for them, to analyze these roles, and to try out several different forms of behavior that might be used in dealing with a specific situation. Several specific role techniques have grown out of the work of Moreno (1946), four of which seem most appropriate for group counseling.

Sociodrama   In this technique, some of the group members act out a social situation which the group has been discussing. Often with young people this involves some conflict with authority figures, such as parents or teachers. Whatever the case, members take the various roles in the situation under discussion and act them out. The leader must break off the sociodrama whenever the actors come to a solution or when it becomes apparent that they are going around in circles. The leader's task at this point is to get the entire group to process the information produced by the insight in terms of what it means to them in the real situation they had been discussing. This technique often moves a group beyond an impasse that they had reached in group discussion.

Role Playing   This technique is very similar to sociodrama, the prime difference being that the leader actually provides each member with a brief description of the role the member will play in the situation. Otherwise, the process is the same as in sociodrama. The roles provided to the members are designed to help them understand their own behavior, as well as the behaviors of others with whom they may be in conflict. The roles can be devised to establish an abstract interpersonal situation that enables the participants to interact without seemingly risking any disclosure on their part. Of course, in the acting out of the roles they do reveal themselves, and it is this data which is then processed in the discussion following the role playing.

Role Reversal   The technique of role reversal is used to get members to see circumstances from a different perspective. A child who cannot understand the behavior of a parent may be asked to take the role of the parent, while the leader or another group member will act out the child's role. Or, two group members may be arguing over some matter, and the leader can ask them to switch roles and continue their discussion from the new point of view. This technique is excellent for helping individuals understand the other's point of view, and for helping open communication between individuals who have stopped listening to each other.

Role Rehearsal   After individuals in a group have expressed the desire for new behaviors, there is either some fear as to how this new behavior will be perceived by others, or fear of not actually being able to carry out the behavior. A young man who has been extremely shy with women may, after a time in the group, recognize the behaviors in which he needs to engage, but is fearful of carrying them out. In such a situation, it may be helpful for the group leader to let him "practice" the role with a female group member and then let the group and the female member give him feedback on his behavior. The technique has the advantage of letting a group member try some behavior within the safety of the group.

In using all these role techniques, the leader must be sure that the group is ready to deal with the role playing in a serious fashion and that the material produced by the role playing is processed by the group in a productive fashion. If the group approaches the situation with frivolity, or if the material is not processed, then the exercise will most probably not be beneficial.

SUMMARY

For the most part, the leader behaviors and techniques that are necessary in the group process cut across theoretical lines, and individual counselors will place more reliance on some of the behaviors and less on others.

In general, the current authors are advocating a form of leadership that is participatory and eclectic in nature. The leader can perhaps be best thought of as comparable to the ego of the group. The leader attempts to establish an atmosphere which enables the group to deal with its conflicts and interpersonal needs, and helps them translate insights into action in the outer reality of the real world. The leader facilitates the members' movements through the processes of disclosing self to others, of gaining feedback from others, of developing self-understanding, and then of attempting new behaviors, first in the group situation and finally in the outside world (Lazarus, 1971).

For each counselor, the exact method used must be his or her own. As stated earlier in this chapter, the exact form of leadership will be dependent on the group composition, the particular situation, and, perhaps most importantly, the knowledge and personal characteristics of the counselor.

References

Abramowitz, S., and C. Jackson. Comparative effectiveness of there-and-then versus here-and-now therapists' interpretations in group psychotherapy. *Journal of Counseling Psychology,* 1974, *21,* 288–93.

Balgopal, P., and R. Hull. Keeping secrets: Group resistance for patients and therapists. *Psychotherapy, Theory, Research and Practice,* 1970, *10,* 234–36.

Bednar, R. L., and F. G. Lawlis. Empirical research in group psychotherapy. In A. E. Bergin and S. L. Garfield (Eds.), *Handbook of psychotherapy and behavior change.* New York: Wiley, 1971.

Benne, K. D., and P. Sheats. Functional roles of group members. In J. C. Hansen and S. H Cramer (Eds.), *Group guidance and counseling in the schools: Selected readings.* New York: Appleton-Century-Crofts, 1971, 218–26.

Berger, M. The impact of the therapist's personality on group process. *American Journal of Psychoanalysis,* 1974, *34,* 213–19.

Berzon, B., and L. N. Solomon. The self-directed therapeutic group: Three studies. *Journal of Counseling Psychology,* 1966, *13,* 491–97.

Berzon, B., L. Solomon, and J. Reisel. Audio tape programs for self-directed groups. In L. Solomon and B. Berzon (Eds.), *New perspectives on encounter groups.* San Francisco: Josey-Bass, Inc., 1972, 321†23.

Beymer, L. Confrontauion groups: Hula hoops? *Counselor Education and Supervision,* 1970, *9,* 75–86.

Bieber, D. The emphasis on the individual in psychoanalytic group therapy. *International Journal of Social Psychiatry,* 1957, *2,* 275–80.

Blackburn, J. The efficacy of modeled self-disclosure on subject's response in an interview situation. *Dissertation Abstracts,* 1970, *31* (3-B), 1529, 1530.

Bolman, L. Some effects of trainers on their T-groups. *Journal of Applied Behavioral Science,* 1971, *7,* 309–25.

Bolman, L. Some effects of trainers on their groups: A partial replication. *Journal of Applied Behavioral Sciences,* 1973, *9,* 534–39.

Burke, W. W. Leadership behavior as a function of the leader, the follower, and the situation. *Journal of Personality,* 1965, *33,* 60–81.

Carkhuff, R. R. *Helping and human relations: A primer for lay and professional helpers. Vol. 1: Selection and training.* New York: Holt, 1969a.

Carkhuff, R. R. *Helping and human relations: A primer for lay and professional helpers. Vol 2.* New York: Holt, 1969b.

Carkhuff, R. R. *The development of human resources, education, psychology, and social change.* New York: Holt, 1971.

Carkhuff, R. R. *The art of helping: A guide for developing helping skills for parents, teachers, and counselors.* Amherst, MA: Human Resources Development Press, 1972.

Cooper, C. L. The influence of the trainer on participants' change in T-groups. *Human Relations,* 1969, *22,* 515–30.

Dies, R. Group therapists' self-disclosure: An evaluation by clients. *Journal of Counseling Psychology,* 1973, *20,* 344–48.

Dye, H. A. Some considerations for school counselors who work with groups. In R. C. Diedrich and H. A. Dye (Eds.), *Group procedures, purposes, processes, and outcomes: Selected readings for the counselor.* Boston: Houghton Mifflin, 1972, 120–25.

Everly, G. Leaderless therapy groups: A word of caution. *Group Psychotherapy and Psychodrama,* 1975, *28,* 180–83.

Gans, R. The use of group co-therapists in the teaching of psychotherapy. *American Journal of Psychotherapy,* 1957, *11,* 618–25.

Garetz, C., and A. J. Fix. Difficult problems in therapy group leadership. *Hospital and Community Psychiatry,* 1972, *23,* 248–50.

Gazda, G. M. *Human relations development: A manual for educators.* Boston: Allyn and Bacon, 1973.

Gibb, C. A. The principles and traits of leadership. In A. P. Hare, E. F. Borgatta, and R.F. Bales (Eds.), *Small groups: Studies in social interaction.* New York: Knopf, 1967, 87–95.

Gordon, T. A. Description of the group-centered leader. In R. C. Diedrich and H. A. Dye (Eds.), *Group procedures, purposes, processes, and outcomes: Selected readings for the counselor.* Boston: Houghton Mifflin, 1972, 70–101.

Graff, R. The relationship of counselor's self-disclosure to counselor effectiveness. *Journal of Experimental Education,* 1970, *38,* 19–22.

Gruen, W. The effects of executive and cognitive control of the therapist on the work climate in the group therapy. *International Journal of Group Therapy,* 1977, *27,* 139–52.

Gurowitz, E. Group boundaries and leadership potency. *Transactional Analysis Journal,* 1975, *5,* 183–85.

Hansen, J. C., T. M. Niland, and L. P. Zani. Model reinforcement in group counseling with elementary school children. *Personnel and Guidance Journal,* 1969, *47,* 741–44.

Hardy, R. C. Effect of leadership style on the performance of small classroom groups: A test of the contingency model. *Journal of Personality and Social Psychology,* 1971, *19,* 367–74.

Hosford, R. E. Behavioral counseling—A contemporary overview. *The Counseling Psychologist,* 1969, *1,* 1–32.

Jourard, S. *Personal adjustment: An approach through the study of healthy personality.* New York: Macmillan, 1958.

Jourard, S. *The transparent self.* Princeton, NJ: Van Nostrand, 1964, 1971 Revised.

Jourard, S. *Self-disclosure: An experimental analysis of the transparent self.* New York: Wiley, 1971.

Jourard, S., and P. Jaffe. Influence of an interviewer's disclosure on the self-disclosing behavior of interviewees. *Journal of Counseling Psychology,* 1970, *17,* 252–57.

Kadis, A. The ultimate meeting in group psychotherapy. *American Journal of Psychotherapy,* 1956, *10,* 275–91.

Kadis, A. Co-ordinated meetings and group psychotherapy. In M. Rosenbaum and M. Berger (Eds.), *Group psychotherapy and group function.* New York: Basic Books, 1973, 437–48.

Kaplan, H. I., and B. J. Sadock (Eds.). *Comprehensive group psychotherapy.* Baltimore: Williams and Williams, 1971.

Kemp. G. C. Bases of group leadership. *Personnel and Guidance Journal,* April 1964, 760–66. Also in J. C. Hansen, and S. H. Cramer (Eds.), *Group guidance and counseling in the schools: Selected readings.* New York: Appleton-Century-Crofts, 1971, 227–35.

Krumboltz, J. D. *Revolution in counseling.* Boston: Houghton Mifflin, 1966.

Krumboltz, J. D., and W. W. Schroeder. Promoting career explorations through reinforcement. *Personnel and Guidance Journal,* 1965, *44,* 19–26.

Krumboltz, J. D., and C. E. Thoresen. The effect of behavioral counseling in group and individual settings on information-seeking behavior. *Journal of Counseling Psychology,* 1964, *11,* 324–33.

Larson, C. U. The verbal response of groups to the absence or presence of leadership. *Speech Monographs,* 1971, *38,* 177–81.

Lazarus, A. A. *Behavior therapy and beyond.* New York: McGraw-Hill, 1971.

Lewin, Kurt. The dynamics of group action. *Educational Leadership,* 1944, *1,* 195–200.

Lieberman, M. A., I. D. Yalom, and M. D. Miles. *Encounter groups: First facts.* New York: Basic Books, 1973.

Lundin, W., and B. Aronow. The use of co-therapists in group psychotherapy. *Journal of Consulting Psychology,* 1952, *16,* 76–80.

Mackler, B. Black on white or white on black: Harlem and white professionals. *Professional Psychology,* 1971, *2,* 257–50.

MacLennan, B. The personalities of group leaders: Implications for selection and training. *International Journal of Group Psychotherapy,* 1975, *25,* 177–83.

Mahler, C. A. *Group counseling in the schools.* Boston: Houghton Mifflin, 1969.

May, O. P., and C. Thompson. Perceived levels of self-disclosure, mental health, and helpfulness of group leaders. *Journal of Counseling Psychology,* 1973, *20,* 349–52.

Moreno, J. L. *Psychodrama.* New York: Beacon, 1946.

Mullan, H., and M. Rosenbaum. *Group Psychotherapy.* New York: The Free Press, 1962.

Mullan, H., and I. Sangiuliano. *The therapist's contribution to the treatment process.* Springfield, IL: Charles C Thomas, 1964.

Ohlsen, M. M. *Group counseling.* New York: Holt, 1970.

Parker, R. Some personal qualities enhancing group therapist effectiveness. *The Journal of Clinical Issues in Psychology,* 1972, *4,* 26–28.

Parloff, M. Discussion of accelerated interaction: A time-limited approach based on the brief intensive group. *International Journal of Psychotherapy,* 1968, *28,* 329–44.

Roback, H. Experimental comparison of outcomes in insight and noninsight-oriented therapy groups. *Journal of Consulting and Clinical Psychology,* 1972, *38,* 411–17.

Rogers, C. The necessary and sufficient conditions of therapeutic personality change. *Journal of Consulting Psychology,* 1957, *21,* 95–103.

Rogers, C. Carl Rogers describes his ways of facilitating encounter groups. *American Journal of Nursing,* 1971, *71,* 275–79.

Rosenbaum L. L., and W. B. Rosenbaum. Morale and productivity consequences of group leadership style, stress, and type of task. *Journal of Applied Psychology,* 1971, *55,* 343–48.

Rothaus, P., D. L. Johnson, P. G. Hanson, and F. A. Lyle. Participation and sociometry in autonomous and suainer-led patient groups. *Journal of Counseling Psychology,* 1966, *13,* 68–76.

Seligman, M., and R. E. Desmond. Leaderless groups: A review. *The Counseling Psychologist,* 1973, *4,* 70–87.

Seligman, M., and R. Desmond. The leaderless group phenomenon: A historical perspective. *International Journal of Group Psychotherapy,* 1975, *25,* 277–90.

Shaw, M. E., and J. M. Blum. Effects of leadership style upon group performance as a function of task structure. *Journal of Personality and Social Psychology,* 1966, *3,* 238–41.

Simmons, J. J. A study of leadership styles in task-oriented committees. *Journal of Applied Behavioral Science,* 1972, *8,* 241–47.

Slavson, S. R. Personality qualifications of a group psychotherapist. *International Journal of Group Psychotherapy,* 1962, *12,* 411–20.

Smith, P. B. Correlations among some tests of T-group learning. *Journal of Applied Behavioral Science,* 1971, *7,* 508–11.

Stern, D. M., and M. Seligman. Further comparisons of verbal behavior in therapist-led, leaderless, and alternating group psychotherapy sessions. *Journal of Counseling Psychology,* 1971, *18,* 472–77.

Trotzer, James P. Using communication exercises in groups. *Personnel and Guidance Journal,* 1973, *51,* 373–77.

Truax, C. B., and R. R. Carkhuff. *Toward effective counseling and psychotherapy.* Chicago: Aldine, 1967.

Vondrachek, S., and F. Vondrachek. The manipulation and measurement of self-disclosure in pre-adolescence. *Merl-Palmer Quarterly,* 1971, *17,* 51–58.

Vontress, C. E. Racial differences: Impediments to rapport. *Journal of Counseling Psychology,* 1971, *18,* 7–13.

Warner, R. W., Jr., and J. C. Hansen. Verbal-reinforcement and model-reinforcement: Group counseling with alienated students. *Journal of Counseling Psychology,* 1970, *17,* 168–72.

Warner, R. W., Jr., J. D. Swisher, and J. J. Horan. Drug abuse prevention: A behavioral approach. *NASSP Bulletin,* 1973, *373,* 49–54.

Weigel, R. G., N. Dinges, R. Dyer, and A. Straumfjord. Perceived self-disclosure, mental health, and who is liked in group treatment. *Journal of Counseling Psychology,* 1972, *19,* 47–52.

Weinstein, I. Guidelines of a choice of a co-therapist. *Psychotherapy: Theory, Research, and Practice,* 1971, *8,* 301–03.

Wolf, A. The psychoanalysis of groups. In M. Rosenbaum and M. Berger (Eds.), *Group psychotherapy and group function.* New York: Basic Books, 1963, 273–327.

Wolf, A., and E. Schwartz. *Psychoanalysis in groups.* New York: Grune and Stratton, 1962.

Worthy, G. Self-disclosure as an exchange process. *Journal of Personality and Social Psychology,* 1969, *13,* 59–63.

Yalom, I. D. *The theory and practice of group psychotherapy.* New York: Basic Books, 1975.

Zimpfer, D. G. Multi-leader approaches to groups in counseling and therapy. In J. C. Hansen and S. H. Cramer (Eds.), *Group guidance and counseling in the schools: Selected readings.* New York: Appleton-Century-Crofts, 1971, 305–20.

13
Group Membership

The success of any group is a function of the abilities of the leader, the quality of the relationships among group members, and the interaction between the leader and the group. Perhaps the most overlooked aspect of the triad is the area of membership. The research on group counseling has tended to focus on the role of the leader of the process, but equally important is the role of the group members. Zaleznik and Moment (1964) described group member roles as the attributes that each member knows about each other. These roles become the guides that provide for a stable, predictable framework within the group on one hand, and provide a structure through which members behave consistent with other members' knowledge and expectation of them on the other hand. How this interaction actually takes place is discussed in Chapters 14 and 15. First, it is necessary to examine in some detail various aspects of and influence on group membership that a counselor must consider. The counselor needs to ask such questions as: What are the effects of previous experience on group members? What are the personality factors that are predictive of successful group membership? What factors contribute to a good relationship among members? How are the group norms and group roles established? What factors in group membership may hinder the process of counseling?

FACTORS AFFECTING ROLE PERFORMANCE IN GROUPS

The roles that individual members choose to fulfill within a group are not the product of a random choice process; rather, they are the product of four major influences: (1) the expectations of self and others; (2) personality factors; (3) the characteristics of the leader; and (4) the characteristics of the group. Factors emanating from these four areas interact to produce the actual behavior of any individual within the group. Hence, a discussion of member roles begins by examining these four areas.

Expectations of Self and Others: Effects on Role Performance

Each individual is a product, at least in part, of past experiences. Some of these experiences are determined by the particular physical and social environment of the individual. Some are determined by biological differences such as sex, age, race, and general physical capacity or incapacity. Regardless of the reason, individuals do come to the group with their own personal history, and this history will affect their performance in the group situation. When an individual enters a group and begins to interact, he or she is not interacting in isolation, but is interacting on the basis of past as well as present. Hence, any interaction is based on more than the actual situation.

Social Role   Every individual comes to the group representing some social role. Largely, this role is the product of the occupation of the individual and carries with it a certain social status ascribed to it by the larger society. Imagine a group composed of a physician, a bricklayer, a housewife, a custodian, an unemployed individual, a teacher, and an unskilled laborer. In such a group each individual has patterns of behavior that are associated with his or her position, and every other member has expectations of the other members' behaviors based on their ideas of how such people behave. In our hypothetical group we can expect the unemployed individual to be ascribed a low status, the physician to be treated with extreme respect, and the other members to fall somewhere in between. Thus, the interaction between the members in the group, at least initially, is a product of stereotyping rather than actual behavior. Beyond that, it is also true that each one of us, to some degree, attempts to behave in the fashion that we feel is appropriate to our social status. Social roles of students are apparent in schools. Hence, social roles affect both the individual's expectations of self and the expectations of others toward him or her.

Past Group Experiences   Related to ascribed social status is the fact that we all have had previous group experiences. The child is born into a group, the family, and from that moment on life is a process of joining, sustaining, and leaving groups. In each of these groups, individuals develop modes of behavior, attitudes, expectancies, and values which carry over to other groups. An individual who generally has been accorded high status in many group associations will most probably come to group counseling fully expecting to be given high status in the new group. Similarly, the individual whose group experiences have largely consisted of behaving as a follower will bring that behavior to the group. In short, the past group experiences of individuals will lead them to adopt certain behaviors in the group and, unless the counselor is aware of those past experiences, individuals will simply maintain old group behaviors rather than develop new ones. That being the case, there will be little opportunity for self-growth, which is the purpose of counseling. Hence the counselor, being aware of an individual's past experiences, must help the member integrate past with present so that the past acts as a guide but not a determiner of present behavior.

External Members' Influence   Counselors also need to be aware of influences on the group members from external individuals. The child in a group may well be influenced in his or her behavior by parents with whom the child shares the group experience. A wife whose husband is not an actual member of the group may still be influenced by his views, and vice versa. These external individuals, while not members of the actual group, are in a sense an extended membership of the group. They participate through the actual member, and the counselor must be attuned to these subtle influences on actual members. Individuals who allow non-group members to influence their behavior in the group will suffer the same difficulties as those members who permit past experiences to dominate their current behavior. In both cases, the opportunity for growth is severely curtailed.

Effects of Personality Factors on Role Performance

Just as past experiences affect a member's interaction in a group, so, too, do underlying personality traits. Such descriptive terms as aggressive, passive, dependent, independent, authoritarian, aloof, demanding, hostile, masculine, or feminine are used to define behavioral characteristics of individuals. Each of these terms implies some long-standing pattern of behavior on the part of the individual. Obviously, such patterns of behavior, which have been established outside the group, will have a carry-over to behavior in the group. It cannot be expected that an individual who is very aggressive outside the group will suddenly become a very passive member upon entering the group, or vice versa. Rather, we can expect that the dominant personality traits that the individual brings to the group process will have both overt and covert impacts on the individual's behavior within the group.

Effect on Role Performance   Stock and Thelen (1963) suggest the personality traits that lead an individual to behave differently in three important areas of group functioning. The first, and most basic of these, they believe, is the area of concern. "By area of concern we mean an affect-laden problem that, on some internal, possibly unconscious, level is felt to be significant by the individual and mobilizes his psychic energies (p. 75)." Thus, some individuals will come to the group concerned about their feelings of aggression; others, about their feelings of dependency; and yet others, about feelings of inadequacy. Often these feelings, although hidden by the individuals, will act to affect their particular mode of behavior in the group. The individual concerned about dependency may act to deny this by attempting to behave extremely independently in the group, while the individual who feels inadequate may strive to establish his or her adequacy.

A second area suggested by Stock and Thelen (1963) is culture preference, which refers to an individual's preference for certain work atmospheres. One individual may prefer a climate that is highly charged with emotion, while another may prefer a very intellectual climate where feelings are held to a minimum. Both will act to maintain the climate with which they feel comfortable.

The final area delineated by Stock and Thelen (1963) is affective approach. Here they refer to the manner in which an individual responds to the group culture.

One individual may fight if the culture is unpleasant, while another may retreat and withdraw from group participation.

Effect on Other Members   The ways that personality traits affect the individual's behavior in the group are extremely significant, but an equally important area is how these personality traits affect the behaviors of other members of the group.

A personality trait generally exists only in abstract form until it dictates a behavior toward another person. That is, when we describe an individual as aggressive, we usually mean the individual is aggressive toward other people. Hence, personality traits not only determine the individual's behavior, but they also act to stimulate behavior in the person toward whom the original behavior is directed. As pointed out by Zaleznik and Moment (1964), it is clear that while personality traits may be thought of as characteristics of individuals, for the most part they refer to the individual's interaction with other individuals.

Thus it becomes important to understand how the behavior of one individual affects the behavior of others. Each behavior of an individual will trigger a complementary behavior from a second individual. Leary (1957) defined this as an interpersonal reflex. It is a reflex in the sense that it is not consciously thought out and the response is complementary to the original act. If one group member says something to another which in effect challenges the competence of the second member, it can be expected that the second member will respond in a defensive fashion. Aggression from one will provoke aggression from some, but may generate submission in others. In either case, the response is one of habit, not thought (Zaleznik and Moment, 1964), and the behaviors of any individuals within the group are systematically related. The particular form of this relationship can be positive or negative depending on the climate within the group. If there exists a competitive, noncaring atmosphere, there is a high probability of negative exchanges. On the other hand, if there is a general feeling of cohesion and trust, these exchanges can be productive growth-producing exchanges. More will be said about complementary behavior and Leary's model in the section on communication between group members.

Personality factors do affect, often in unconscious ways, the performance of both actor and audience in the group. The group counselor must be attuned to the dynamics involved and help the individual become aware of his or her particular mode of behavior and its effects on others. Likewise, the counselor must help the other group members examine their interpersonal reflex behaviors in terms of whether they are productive or counterproductive. As with the effects of past experiences, the effects of personality patterns can hinder both self-growth and group functioning if left unattended by the group counselor. For example, the individual who behaves out of a defensive position may contribute to the group discussion, but "besides talking about the topic, he thinks about how to appear to others, how he may be seen more favorably, how he may win, dominate, impress, or escape punishment (Gibb, 1961, p. 141)." If such individuals are never forced to examine how this aspect of their personality is affecting their behavior in the group, and if the group never examines its reactions to this behavior, then both the group and the individuals will not move beyond this point.

Regarding the research findings on the correlates between personality characteristics and successful group memberships, Giedt (1961) reported that the best predictors of successful group membership were an individual's communication skills, degree of cooperative behavior, and overall adjustment. McFarland, Nelson, and Rossi (1962) reported that intelligence was positively related to successful membership. In one extensive review of the literature, Heslin (1964) suggested that there were fairly consistent findings that group member success was positively related to overall intellectual ability, overall adjustment, degree of extroversion, and ability to describe one's self. Jacobson and Smith (1972) concluded that individuals who preferred low rates of social interchange prior to an encounter group experience were more likely to change as a result of the experience.

Inclusion   Because the personalities of the members will have an effect on group performance, the counselor must be aware of each individual included in the group. It is imperative that members selected for the group are motivated for counseling in general and for group interaction in particular. Individuals who are reluctant to participate in the group should not be included. An individual's reluctant attitude regarding group counseling may be modified in the pre-counseling interview with the counselor; however, the counselor should not sell the idea of group counseling or need to convince the client to participate. Such efforts by the counselor will only lead to future problems in the group. Beyond the aspect of member motivation, it is difficult to establish the criteria for inclusion in the group. Not only is one considering the personality of the individual member but also how the members interact. However, Yalom (1975) identified two studies which note important variables predictive of success for individual clients. These variables include the members' attraction to the group and their general popularity in the group. It was also noted that such individuals had a high level of self-disclosure. Activity in the group and ability to introspect were variables which led to group popularity.

The encounter group study by Lieberman, Yalom, and Miles (1972) reported that members who profited most from the group experience valued and desired personal change, viewed themselves as deficient in understanding their own feelings and in their sensitivity to feelings of others, had a high expectation for the group, and anticipated that the experience would provide relevant opportunities for communication and help them correct their deficiencies. Data from these two studies indicate that members who are motivated to participate in the group, expect a positive outcome from the group, participate significantly in the group, and are liked by their group members are the members most likely to gain from the group experience.

The counselor must consider not only the personal variables of the individual member but must also examine the working relationship that may occur between the total group membership. Therefore, the counselor will select individuals that may play an important role for other individuals in the group. The circumplex communication model at the end of this chapter is one method to use in selecting a variety of members. For example, a group may profit from having an assertive individual as well as individuals who communicate in more passive styles. It may be helpful to have individuals with communication styles from each of the quadrants of negative and positive as well as assertive and passive.

Another important effect of the member's personality is the impact the member has on the counselor. If the counselor likes the individual, his or her interaction with and effect on the counselor will make the group a more positive experience. However, if the counselor experiences a dislike or disinterest in the individual, it may be more appropriate to refer the client to another group.

Members are satisfied with their groups when they view the group as meeting their personal needs, derive satisfaction from their relationships with other members, derive satisfaction from participation in the group task, and derive satisfaction from group membership vis-a-vis the outside world (Yalom, 1975).

Exclusion   Unfortunately, at this time more is known about whom to exclude from group counseling than whom to include. As Yalom (1975) suggests, it is easier to study failure criteria than it is to study the reasons for success. In general, the research indicates that individuals who are at the extremes of any behavioral or attitudinal continuum should be excluded from the group process. The individual who is extremely aggressive or hostile in interpersonal interactions will likely carry that behavior to the group and will act to keep the group from functioning. Similarly, an individual who is extremely withdrawn may find the the group situation such a threat that she or he may become even more withdrawn. Any individual who represents an extreme of behavior may consume so much of the group members' and leader's attention that the group process is dangerously inhibited. As a rule, these individuals are poor risks because of their inability to participate in the primary task of the group. They soon construct an interpersonal role which proves to be detrimental to themselves as well as the group (Yalom, 1975). While the preceding suggests a general guide for counselors that is best used in the initial screening process, there is a prevalent consensus that individuals who fall into any of the following behavioral categories should be excluded from groups: paranoid, narcissistic, hypochondriacal, suicidal, drug dependent, psychotic, and sociopathic (Yalom, 1975). Quite obviously, it is only through effective selection procedures that these individuals will be excluded. Nonetheless, some such individuals will still be selected for groups, often because the counselor is willing to take the risk, and the counselor must be prepared for the problem client who does enter the group.

Leader Characteristics and Member Role Performance

Just as the past experiences and personality characteristics of members influence the kinds of roles adopted in a group, so, too, do the past experiences and personality characteristics of the group leader. In addition, the leader brings along a theoretical position toward human development, maladjustment, and counseling, and this theoretical position will also act to influence the kinds of roles that exist within a group.

Past History of the Leader   Like the group members, the group leader does not come to the group from a vacuum but enters with an entire array of past experiences. The most important in terms of their impact on members are the leader's past group experiences. If in the past the leader operated non-directively and was not very successful, then he or she is likely to enter the group with some anxieties that will affect his or her behavior and in turn affect the roles of the members. If, on the other hand, the leader has experienced success by being somewhat directive, it is likely that he or she will continue this mode of operation. In either case, the past history of the leader is acting to restrict the range of member roles which will be seen as acceptable by the leader.

Personality Characteristics   The leader's personality traits act in two ways which affect members' role performance. First of all, the leader's personality will affect the kinds of leader behaviors that she or he can utilize. For example, it is difficult to conceive of a leader who can be described as domineering leading a group in a completely democratic fashion. The leader's personality traits will also cause the same type of interpersonal reflexes in members as do other members' personalities.

Theoretical Position of Leader   The theoretical position of the leader dictates the reasons for the group being constituted and may be a factor in the inclusion of certain individuals in the group. By including only certain types of individuals, the leader controls the range of roles. Theory also affects the type of role behaviors to which the leader will be attuned. The leader who holds that insight into past conflicts is a necessary step in counseling is going to encourage member roles that facilitate the explanations of past histories of members. Similarly, a counselor who adheres to more of a Gestalt position will encourage member roles that keep the group focused on the here-and-now situation. In either case, the theoretical position of the counselor has an effect on the kinds of roles that are acceptable and encouraged, and on the discouragement of other kinds of roles.

The characteristics of a leader's impact on member role performance described here are probably most profound early in the group process. Nevertheless, the leader must be aware of his or her impact on role behavior. This means that the leader must be aware of the kinds of roles encouraged or discouraged by his or her theory, past, and personality. In such an examination, the counselor may decide either to attempt certain modifications in order to facilitate different roles within the group, or to continue as is because the roles encouraged are the ones desired.

Characteristics of the Group Affecting Role Performance

Individual Status Within the Group   One of the chief factors affecting roles of group members is the individual member's concern with internal and external status or prestige. Internally, the individual must feel that she or he is a valued member of the group. This does not necessarily mean holding the top position, but it does mean that the individual cannot always feel that he or she is on the bottom rung of the status ladder. The counselor must be attuned to the problem of status within the group, for it acts to prescribe the kinds of roles people will be able to assume. As Hare (1962) indicates, if the counselor permits a power structure to form early in the group, those members who initially attain superior status and those who are accorded low status will remain in those positions and this will hinder the forming of a cohesive group. Harvey and Consalvi (1960) point out that in a group where high and low status situations are constant, those at the two extremes of status are not likely to be open to change within the group; hence, flexible role taking is limited.

External Evaluation of Group Status   Related to the problem of status within the group is the prestige assigned to the group by external forces. This is particularly true in schools and other institutions where individuals outside the group may either admire someone for being in a group or look down on anyone who is taking part in a group. If the counselor has not developed a feeling in the work setting that groups are a valuable experience, he or she can expect that external forces on the group will be of a negative nature. In this situation, there is a strong possibility that members will adopt role behaviors unconducive to group development, for they will feel no real commitment to the group or to the assumption of roles that are group-task oriented.

Group Composition and Role Performance   Another factor affecting role performance in the group is the actual composition of the group. This, of course, raises the question of homogeneity and heterogeneity. What is relatively clear from the research is that heterogeneous groups tend to permit and, indeed, encourage a wide range of group roles, while the homogeneous groups may act to restrict the kinds of roles used. The homogeneous groups tend to encourage the adoption of roles that are concerned with the social atmosphere of the group. The heterogeneous groups, on the other hand, will have a tendency to permit the adoption of social roles as well as group task roles, and it is a balance of roles that is needed for the most productive groups. Some members do need to be concerned about the social atmosphere, but the group also needs individuals who will push the group toward its goal through such behaviors as confrontation, initiation, and coordination.

Group Norms and Role Performance   If a collection of individuals are to form into a group that will have a therapeutic atmosphere, the individuals need to establish norms for behavior in the group. Group norms are a prescribed set of rules which define the types of acceptable behavior within the group and sometimes behavior outside the group (Bonney, 1972). A group will rapidly establish its own rules, procedures, and structure, and some of these will be explicit and some implicit. Most often these norms will facilitate interaction, but they can act to interfere with the therapeutic atmosphere of the group. As mentioned earlier, the norms of the group have a great deal to do with an individual's feelings of affiliation or attraction to a group. If norms are established that define rigid status lines and rigid role requirements, permit strong subgrouping, allow the discussion of only superficial material, and permit noncaring attacks on other members, it is likely that any individual's affiliation for the group will be rather weak. In such cases, it is to be expected that group cohesion will not occur.

If, on the other hand, norms are established that encourage dynamic interaction and help individuals sense a common goal or a shared purpose, then affiliation, attractiveness, and cohesion of the group is enhanced. As Mowrer (1972) suggests, norms that encourage individuals to operate on the basis of honesty, responsibility, and involvement will be the most therapeutic for group members.

While it is essential that norms be established and made as explicit as possible, members need to be willing to modify the norms as events within the group change. For example, early in the life of the group it is probably not appropriate for members to engage in a confrontive role, but such a role does become appropriate later in the group process.

It can be seen from the preceding discussion that one of the chief functions of group norms is the establishment of a counseling atmosphere that encourages members to feel part of and committed to the group. (In Chapter 14, which deals with the establishment of the group, more will be said on how that process takes place.) A second function of norms is the influence they have on the roles members play within the group. In this sense, norms act to maintain the group by encouraging member roles that facilitate the group process. Norms act as a force on the individual members, and they act to establish "the behavior expected from others to the self and by the self to others . . . , [and they can] in each case, extend from that which is required to that which is prohibited (Hare, 1962, pp. 103–4)." Norms can be established that protect status or that permit individual members a great deal of flexibility in their membership roles. The latter type of norm is essential for a productive group. Norms that act to reduce flexibility will act to channel communication in specific directions and inhibit individuals' attempts to try new behaviors. Group norms, then, have a great deal to do with the kinds of roles that individuals will take in the group. Conversely, it is also true that the initial roles that individuals bring to the group will affect the kinds of norms that are established.

Group Process and Role Performance   Membership roles are ways of defining the relationship between an individual and a group. In the group, individuals expect certain behaviors from other members and are themselves the focus of expected behaviors from others, and these expected behaviors are rather stable (Sherif and Sherif, 1964). A group role "describes the individual's interaction with other individuals, the psychological conditions within him as he interacts, and his effects on other group members (Zaleznik and Moment, 1964, p. 181)." Very early in the group process, these role expectations begin to take shape and act to establish the roles that individuals expect of themselves and that others expect of them. In a productive group, these roles do not remain static; rather, individuals move in and out of roles as the forces within the group act on them. As the group progresses through its normal developmental stages, different roles become necessary if the group is to progress, and a good group member has the flexibility to adopt roles that are appropriate for her or him and for the group. If a group has gone through a period of intense emotion in which there has been strife, confrontation, and competition among members, then those roles which act to bring harmony back to the group are appropriate and should be encouraged by the leader. Conversely, a group that is bogged down in social pleasantries needs members to take roles which will move them toward the accomplishment of their tasks. The point is that the actual life stage of the group should have an influence on the role performance of members.

Having considered four major influences on the role performance of members

—expectations of self and others, personality factors of members, leader characteristics, and group characteristics—it is now appropriate to turn to a more specific discussion of the roles to be expected from participants in group counseling.

MEMBERSHIP ROLES

Almost every writer in the field of group work has developed his or her own list of expected roles in group counseling. As might be expected, many of these lists describe the same set of behaviors but simply use different names to describe them. There has also been a tendency to describe either rather broad categories of roles (group task roles) or to use long lists of rather specific roles (resistor). The attempt here will be to synthesize the thinking in this area.

General Classification of Roles

Carter (1967), in a summary of the research on membership roles, suggested that the various statements of roles within a group could be classified into three broad areas: individual prominence, group goal facilitation, and group sociability. In a similar vein, Benne and Sheats (1948) used three classifications: individual roles, group task roles, and group building and maintenance roles. In both cases they appear to be describing similar behaviors, and their general grouping seems to be a useful way in which to classify and make more understandable more specific roles. Both see individual roles as that category of roles which individuals adopt that have little to do with the purposes of the group. They tend to be narcissistic in nature and often hinder the group process. Benne and Sheats' group building and maintenance roles and Carter's group sociability roles are roles which act to form the collection of individuals into a group and act to maintain group cohesiveness. Group goal facilitation and group task roles are those roles that facilitate the group's progress toward the accomplishment of its goals. It may be helpful to think of the building and maintenance roles as the base building or relationship phase of group counseling, and the group task roles as being the action phases of counseling, with the individual roles generally consisting of blocks or defenses against therapeutic progress.

Another useful system for the classification of member behaviors has been proposed by Bales (1951). Bales divides the types of roles in a group into two areas: (1) the instrumental or task acts, and (2) the social-emotional or expressive acts. He posits that groups move in a cyclical fashion between interest in the task and interest in the social-emotive atmosphere of the group. Work on the group task always creates at least some tension in the group, and when the tension mounts to a certain point it must be reduced. At this point, roles come into play that act to reduce the tension and restore a cohesive social-emotional balance within the group. It is Bales' contention that a group must go through these cycles to be productive. If a group persists in attending to the social-emotional atmosphere, no progress toward the accomplishment of the task will be made. On the other hand, if the group focuses exclusively on the task, then the amount of tension produced will be so high that the group will disintegrate. This is the reason that his system, as well as the Benne and Sheats system, calls for a notion of flexible role behaviors.

A close examination of Bales' system of classifying roles reveals that it is very compatible with the one developed by Benne and Sheats. While Bales uses only two major categories, he does subdivide the social-emotional roles into positive and negative behaviors, as illustrated in Table 2.

It is apparent that the task roles in the Bales system are similar to the Benne and Sheats task roles. Further, what Bales defines as positive social-emotional roles have a relationship to Benne and Sheats' group building and maintenance roles, and the negative social-emotional roles of Bales are comparable with the individual roles of Benne and Sheats. Both systems are based on the belief that changing conditions within the group call for individuals to adopt different roles.

When the group is in the task phase of its process, member roles that focus on the task are prominent. During those phases where the reaffirmation of group cohesion is needed, socially and emotionally expressive roles are necessary. Thus, a functional set of roles is achieved in a group when group members can act in ways that are appropriate to the particular phase of the group process. If this process does not take place, the structure of the group is weakened. Both of these systems, then, emphasize the necessity for flexible role taking. This means that most group members are capable of changing roles in relation to group needs, which enhances both individual and group growth.

Specific Membership Roles

To examine the specific roles, keeping in mind the overlap between the two systems of role analysis, the broad headings of Benne and Sheats (1942) are used here, with the subheadings in parentheses indicating the Bales (1951) system. The writings of several individuals will be incorporated within each specific role behavior, with heavy reliance on the lists developed by Benne and Sheats (1942), Bales (1951), Sherif and Sherif (1964), Ohlsen (1970), Yalom (1975), and Andrews (1972). It should also be noted that some of the specific roles can shift from one general category to another. It should also be kept in mind that a counselor will seldom experience a group in which all members represent a "pure" role. Rather, an individual most often will represent several roles. It is to be expected that these roles will share a common theme. Of course, it is to be hoped that as the group progresses, all members will find less need for the use of individual roles and will shift to the use of group-oriented roles.

Group Building and Maintenance Roles (Positive Social-Emotional Roles)

1. Facilitator or Encourager Individuals in this role act to encourage a feeling of friendship and security within the group. They sometimes do this because they view themselves as the counselor's helpers. They want to make sure everyone feels a part of the group. Counselors need to be aware that an individual may be encouraging others in order to keep the focus on others and away from himself or herself.

2. Gatekeeper or Expediter This role calls for an individual to keep the

Table 2   Classification of Roles Within a Group (after Bales, 1951)

Task Roles	Social-Emotional Roles	
	Positive	Negative
1. Provides orientation, information	7. Provides help, status	10. Shows passive resistance, disagrees
2. Gives opinions, evaluates and analyzes group data	8. Facilitates tension reduction	11. Creates tension, seeks help, withdraws
3. Directs and suggests	9. Shows under- standing and compliance	12. Acts aggressive, antagonistic
4. Seeks information		
5. Seeks direction or action		
6. Encourages evaluation and analysis of group data and experiences		

group operating within its norms. In many ways this individual is a kind of referee in the group and, as with the facilitator, may be acting as the counselor's assistant. The development of such a role within the group can free the leader from the sole responsibility of guiding the group, but once again the individual may be keeping the focus off herself or himself. Further, if the individual becomes too active a Gatekeeper, he or she may be the recipient of hostility from other group members.

   3.   Standard or Goal Setter   This role is highly related to the Gatekeeper. Here, however, the individual is pushing for the establishment of group norms and for a definition of what the final product should be. There is a tendency to push for high-sounding goals based on some outside standard. Individuals who take this role are often unsure of themselves but are concerned about being involved in a process which others will see as being worthwhile.

   4.   Harmonizer or Conciliator   This individual will strive to mediate any differences between group members. He or she acts to keep emotions level and to keep the group from polarizing, and will often attempt to bring subgroups together. In attempting to keep emotions under control, such individuals may hinder the productive nature of conflict. That is, they are so opposed to, or anxious about, conflict that they desire to flee from it and want the group to do the same.

   5.   Compromiser or Neutralizer   This role is highly related to the preceding role, but whereas the preceding role places emphasis on emotional balance, this role places emphasis on suggesting alternatives. As such, it is more cognitive in approach to the same problem. The internal dynamics of the individual in this role may be exactly the same as the Conciliator.

   6.   Group Observer   The Group Observer acts to provide feedback to the group. He or she may do this by summarizing either the content or the process of the group. Such individuals can be helpful, but they often feel above the group. Rather than really participating, they see themselves as being able to help others.

   7.   Follower or Neuter   This individual is there but does not really partici- pate. He or she swings with the group wherever they go. Such individuals express a lot of agreement with what is being said, but often are so unsure of themselves that they will never really offer any part of themselves to the group.

As noted earlier, the preceding roles generally focus on the social-emotional atmosphere of the group and act to facilitate the forming of a collection of individuals into a cohesive group. Also noted earlier were the dynamics within an individual which cause the individual to adopt a certain role. At times the role will be adopted in a true effort to facilitate group cohesion, but at other times the role may be adopted as a means of protecting the individual from true involvement.

Group Task Roles (Instrumental or Task Roles)

Once the social-emotional atmosphere of the group has been established, certain task roles become more prominent. Some of these roles, which will be apparent from the very beginning of the group, have the characteristic of moving the group toward the accomplishment of its tasks. The group task may be very specific (i.e., the development of a specific plan of action for the group as a whole) or it may have to do with more subjective, personal tasks of each member (i.e., the resolution of each member's specific personal difficulty). In either case, the task has been defined in the group formation stage, and more attention is given to developing solutions to the problem. In this state, the counselor can expect the development of the following roles.

1. Initiator-Energizer This is the individual who prods for action from the group. In doing so, the individual will often confront the group for its lack of action, or attempt to move the group by suggesting some new ideas or ways of looking at things. Such a role may be welcomed by a group that really desires to move forward, but it can also be the recipient of hassling from a group that feels threatened by any attempt to move beyond the warm, comfortable stage.

2. Information or Opinion Seeker This role, in fact, may often break into two roles. The Information Seeker is an individual who is concerned with cognitive areas and who seeks information in an attempt to clarify facts. The Opinion Seeker is concerned about the affective domain, and focuses on the clarification of values and attitudes. Despite the difference, both roles are attempts to seek more data for the group to act upon. While this is a necessary role, a danger here is that the individual fulfilling this role may push a group member either into a defensive position or into a self-disclosure that the individual is really not prepared to give. Obviously, such a development is counterproductive to task resolution.

3. Information or Opinion Giver A counter to the preceding role(s) is the individual who either seeks to provide information or advice (cognitive) or opinions (conative) to other members. Often this person acts from a position of assumed authority. That is, this person assumes she or he has the "correct" facts or the "proper" attitudes which the other members need to adopt. Despite this somewhat high-handed approach, often the facts or attitudes expressed by this individual can act as catalytic agents for the group.

4. Elaborator and/or Coordinator This role focuses on making sure that the group considers the relationship between ideas expressed by various members (Coordinator) and develops a full explanation of the workability of ideas expressed (Elaborator). In a real sense, this individual is the reality orientor in the group, making sure the group does not get lost in a dreamlike, unrealistic world. Often, the very logic of this individual may be such as to hinder any creative efforts by the group.

5. *Orientor-Evaluator* This individual acts as the group's judge both in terms of how close it is to a resolution of the task and in terms of the quality of the goals achieved. Such an individual can be very helpful in keeping the group focused on the task, but may also act to impose unrealistic goals on the group. The development of this role toward the end of the group sessions can be particularly troublesome to the group and the leader. At this point the individual may be acting to prevent the dissolution of the group.

6. *Procedural Technician* This role is very similar to the Gatekeeper role discussed under group building roles. It is one of keeping the group operating on acceptable norms. Generally, an individual filling this role is really somewhat of a follower but is concerned that the group achieve its goals. Such an individual is also likely to be overly concerned about the expression of emotion in the group.

As with the group building roles, the group task roles are seldom found in pure form. The focus of these roles is on movement or action; that is, moving the group toward a resolution of those things that brought it together. Hence, the roles will produce more conflict within the group, but it is conflict that is necessary for individual members' growth. It is a seeking, testing, confronting period in the group's life. If the group does not develop these roles, then it will not move beyond the stage of cohesion. As with the maintenance roles, the counselor must be aware when roles are being used for constructive purposes within the group and when they are being used as a defensive or protective cover by a particular individual. Generally, when one individual rigidly adheres to one particular role, he or she is doing so out of a defensive posture. In such cases, it is imperative that the group leader provide the individual the opportunity to examine his or her behavior.

Both the group building and the group task roles facilitate the progress of the group. As such they form an intricate part of the interaction process between leader behaviors and member behaviors which lead to positive counseling outcomes. The trained group leader is able to both recognize and utilize these member roles without letting them interfere with the process of the group. That is, the trained leader recognizes when the various role behaviors are actually facilitative and when they are defensive behaviors on the part of the group members. In the latter case, the counselor is able to focus the member's attention on the inappropriate way he or she is using the behavior.

Individual Roles (Negative Social-Emotional Roles)

The general nature of those individual roles which are counterproductive to positive counseling outcome is discussed here. Individual roles have the characteristics of being self-serving rather than group-oriented. Individuals who act as Blockers, Recognition Seekers, Self-confessors, Dominators, or Monopolists do so in an attempt to fulfill individual needs. They tend to be persons who can benefit a great deal from group work because their individual needs are such that they have a great deal of difficulty in their interpersonal relations. Thus, it is important that such people not be excluded from the group situation. Yet, their very presence makes the smooth operation of the group extremely difficult. The group leader must be sensitive to the personal needs of the individuals who engage in these antigroup behaviors and help them work through their needs. This is difficult for the leader because the leader's own feelings of frustration are likely to be brought forth by individuals who are actively interfering with the group process. This is where it is essential that the counselor have a good grip on himself or herself. In a cohesive group, other members will usually help the leader deal with individual role behavior by confronting the member using such behavior. But if they do not, the leader must help the member focus on the self-defeating behavior. This can often be accomplished by getting the other group members to react to the member's behavior. The leader may have to lead the way—saying something like: "John, it seems to be that every time some of us really get into something, you feel a need to distract us. How do the rest of you feel about this?" Plainly, the counselor must take care that John is ready to deal with such a statement, as well as being convinced that the rest of the group will react in a positive way by trying to help John deal with the behavior.

The belief of the current authors is that the group counselor should focus attention on all three broad categories of roles, as well as the more specific behaviors. The crucial question is: Does the individual member behavior seem appropriate for the developmental stage of the group? A group task role that is pushing the group toward the accomplishment of the group task before the members have really formed into a group is inappropriate, and the counselor needs to point out these discrepancies to the individual involved. In a similar vein, the counselor must not only be aware of that group of member behaviors classified as individual roles, or negative social-emotional roles, which interfere with the group but, as noted in the preceding section on member roles, he or she must also be aware of the use of normally productive roles for self-serving or self-productive reasons by individual members. Possessing the skill to accurately perceive the roles members are taking in the group will enable the group leader to maximize the potential of the group. That is, the leader will be able to use his or her leadership skills in a blend with the behaviors of group members. If, after the group has formed, the leader perceives a member acting as an Energizer or Initiator for the group, the leader can leave this task to the member. If, on the other hand, no one seems prepared to fill that role, the leader needs to assume it as part of the leadership task. In such a way, the therapeutic potential of the group, as well as the leader, can be fully released.

SPECIAL CONSIDERATIONS AND MEMBER ROLES

Some of the special considerations that act to affect actual role behavior discussed in this section are the problems created by role definition, group mentality, subgrouping, dropouts, and preparation for membership.

Role Definition

Earlier in this chapter, it was pointed out that members of a group do not operate in isolation from factors outside the group. They are influenced by external factors, and this can affect the roles they find themselves taking in the group. Of course, they are also affected by the dynamics of the group itself and this, too, affects the roles they take in the group. Often these external and internal factors cause some role definition problems for individuals, which in turn act to incapacitate them in the group. Hare (1962) has outlined four problems in this area which may cause individuals difficulty and thereby drain energy away from the therapeutic potential of the group. They are role collision, role incompatibility, role confusion, and role transition.

Role Collision   When an individual has one role in a real-world situation and is pressured by group norms to adopt another role in the group, role collision may occur. The administrator who is expected to make decisions for many people in a work role may find in a group that such behavior is not only not expected but is greeted with negative feelings from other members. In short, the administrator's natural mode of behavior collides head on with expected group behavior.

Role Incompatibility   When an individual feels pressured into an undesired role in a group, that person is suffering from role incompatibility. In some groups, an individual will be handed the leadership role by group members even though the individual has neither sought such a role nor wants it. Hence, the individual is caught between personal needs and the needs of the group.

Role Confusion   When an individual and/or the group is unsure of the expected roles, role confusion results. This often occurs in leaderless groups or in groups where the counselor has operated in an extremely nondirecting fashion. The members simply do not have enough guidelines with which to guide their behavior.

Role Transition   An individual may suffer some anxiety as the group moves from one stage of group development to the next. As has been pointed out, different roles are called for as the group progresses, and this can cause some difficulty to individuals who are forced to give up what has become a comfortable role for a new one.

All four of these problems act to keep individuals preoccupied with their position or role within the group, thereby distracting their attention from the true purposes of the group. Until the counselor or other group members can help the individual work through these role problems, the individual cannot become a productive member of the group. Part of this problem can be prevented by the counselor's guidance of the group toward the establishment of therapeutic group norms. The reader will recall that good group norms encourage flexibility in member roles and status. Thus, they encourage the working through of such difficulties. The counselor still must be alert to their development and, when they do occur, help the individual concerned process the difficulty he or she has been having.

Preparation of Members for the Group

As stated earlier in this chapter, there has been an emphasis on the training and preparation of group leaders, but the success of any group is also a function of the members. It would seem to follow, then, that potential members might also benefit from some training in group procedures. Part of this training should take place in the individual interviews preceding actual selection. It is also possible to use one of the interpersonal interaction scales discussed earlier in this chapter. Neither of these methods, however, gives a potential group member any actual experience in a group.

Goldstein, Heller, and Sechrest (1966) suggest using either trial or simulated groups for helping the counselor prepare individuals for the group process and also to aid in the selection process. In a trial group, potential members are placed in a temporary group for a short number of sessions, during which time their behavior is observed. Based on these observations, individuals who appear to demonstrate skills that will enable them to be group members are selected for inclusion in a regular group. If the counselor is composing several groups, he or she can also use these observations to place individuals in groups with the importance of balanced membership in mind. Schools or other institutions where there is a large number of potential members are most appropriate for this procedure. A group of juniors, for example, might be placed in a discussion group (the trial group) and on the basis of performance in the trial group be placed in a final group that is appropriate to their individual needs and behaviors.

A second procedure which is more feasible in situations lacking a large pool of potential members is the simulated group. Here the potential member listens to an audio tape or observes a video tape of a group session and is asked to respond as though she or he were a member of the group. As in the trial group, the individual's behavior is observed and the data used in the selection procedure. The simulated group also provides the potential member with an idea of the kinds of behaviors that are expected in the group process.

Both the trial group and the simulated group provide the counselor more data upon which to base a selection procedure and, very importantly, provide some pretraining to potential group members. This pretraining may remove some of the anxiety and uncertainty from early group meetings, thereby speeding up the process of individuals forming into a cohesive, working group.

Attendance

Attendance and punctuality issues usually arise in the early stages of the group. Members present a variety of excuses for their inability to attend a particular meeting or for being late. Lack of punctuality and irregular attendance typically indicate resistance to the group process and should be regarded in the same way a counselor handles resistance in individual counseling. If several members are late or absent, the counselor must examine the source of the group resistance. More frequently it is an individual resistance rather than the whole group. The counselor must help these members to recognize and work through the resistance if they are to be effective members in the group. Irregular attendance or even frequent tardiness is detrimental to cohesive development of the group. It becomes impossible to really work on an issue if important members are absent. In many groups, tardiness and irregular attendance become one of the issues which springs the conflict and confrontation stage among members. Tardiness and absence are examples of behavior which reflect the members' characteristic patterns of behaving to others. Yalom (1975) points out that the behavior is a part of the member's social microcosm, and, if handled properly, may be helpful in self-understanding. However, for both the individual and the group, the behavior must be corrected before it can be analyzed.

It is important that the counselor be convinced of the importance of group counseling and the necessity of regular attendance. The counselor will transmit these values by arriving punctually and beginning the group on time. The counselor begins by emphasizing attendance and punctuality in the preliminary meeting with individual members, and follows this up with a discussion during the first session.

Structure and Member Behavior

There has been considerable interest in the use of structure in initiating group work and its effect on facilitating group development and client outcome. Crews and Melnick (1976) conducted a study with three different levels of structured learning situations with groups of students meeting in interpersonal growth groups. They assessed the effects of the structure on member anxiety, cohesiveness, and the quality of interpersonal interaction at two different points in the stages of the groups. In the beginning meetings, members of the groups that received initial structure engaged in more self-disclosure than members in the other groups. However, in later sessions the differences disappeared as self-disclosure in other groups rose to the level of the initial structured groups. The level of interpersonal feedback, group confrontation, or cohesiveness was not effected by the type of structure.

Locus of Control   Earlier studies have suggested the utilization of the locus of control variable as a predictor of client counseling compatibility. The literature suggests that an unstructured counselor role would reinforce the internal-oriented person's need for personal control, while an external-oriented client would be more likely to benefit from a counselor's role that provided considerable structure and guidance. Kilmann (1974) predicted that externals would prefer a controlled leadership group while internals would prefer a shared leadership group. However, when he had students indicate their preference for the two types of groups prior to entering them, externals were found to significantly prefer the shared leadership group, while the internals showed no significant difference in preference for one group over the other. However, when actually experiencing the group, Kilmann et al. (1975) report that the locus of control did make a difference in outcome. The internal-oriented subjects in the unstructured group reflected a significantly higher increase on the inner-directedness scale of the Personal Orientation Inventory. Likewise, in the more structured groups the external subjects evidenced a greater shift than the internal subjects. It is important to notice that the changes in inner-directedness remained significant at the follow-up investigation. Internal subjects became more assertive, more avoiding, and less cooperative than internal subjects in the structured, traditional group. One might tentatively suggest that external-oriented subjects may achieve most significant benefits from a structured counselor within a specific space-time format, while internal-oriented members may profit more from a counselor with minimum control and structure.

Risk Taking   Melnick and Wicher (1977) designed a study to explore the characteristics of risk-taking propensity as a client variable in growth groups. Their finding indicates the importance of having high risk-takers as group members. They suggested high risk-takers are viewed by other group members as more self-disclosing, risk-taking, and verbally active than low risk-taking members. Although one cannot say risk-takers are more valuable in the group, Melnick and Wicher suggest there is ao aevantage to have some risk-taking members in the group to stimulate interaction.

Evensen (1976) and Lee (1975) found that high risk-takers function best in low-structured environments. In such an environment, high risk-taking clients were able to initiate self-disclosure, feedback, and group confrontation, all of which are important for group development. Low risk-takers perform best in a high-structured situation specifically designed to give them practice in self-disclosure, feedback, and confrontation.

Melnick and Wicher suggest that the alert counselor might use a highly structured environment in which a high-anxiety, low-risk client is invited to check out self-perceptions with feedback from others, and that this environment might reduce distortion, decrease anxiety, and minimize the potential for damage.

The Development of Group Mentality

At times when the emotional tone of the group is highly charged, there is a danger of a type of mass hysteria. In such a situation, the emotional tension of the group reaches such a point that the group will do almost anything to reduce the emotional level. The group in this situation submerges individual reactions and group responses begin to take over (Loeser, 1971). The group begins to act as one mind and in the process suspends the use of sound judgment. In short, these members will follow any lead to get themselves away from the anxiety-producing situation. If no member steps forward to point out to the other members what is happening, then the leader must intercede. While this development may not take place very often, it is crucial that it be stopped when it does occur. If left unchecked, the group may decide it is finished and will move toward premature termination.

Friendship in the Group

A tendency among group members is to let the friendships which develop in a group interfere with the group progress. In such circumstances, the group shifts away from a focus on the reason for the establishment of the group to a concern for maintaining a friendly atmosphere. This often precludes individuals from really interacting with one another in a meaningful way. It can be likened to an individual counselor or a group leader being so concerned that all clients like him or her that he or she never really helps the client(s). Part of this problem can be avoided by not selecting friends for inclusion in the same group. However, the problem still may develop, and the counselor must not allow the group to forego its tasks for the sake of friendship. A good way to deal with this is to talk about what real friendship means. Real friendship is more than smiling and agreeing; it also means being honest and open with one another.

Subgrouping

Subgrouping, which is the forming of an alliance among two or more members of a larger group, occurs because of the tendency of individual members to seek support from other members who have characteristics and ideals in common with them. The attractiveness of a group can be either increased or decreased by subgrouping. It may be positive in that it helps an individual establish contact with someone in the group with whom he or she can identify. In so doing, an individual's narcissistic behavior may be broken down, and the subgroup acts as mutual support for its members. Two individuals who are extremely unsure of themselves may form a subgroup as a defense against the rest of the group. If such a subgroup is used as an initial behavior in the group, or is used in a constructive supporting fashion, the subgrouping may be productive. This aspect of subgroups accounts for the effectiveness of various interpersonal exercises early in the group process. Many of these exercises utilize dyads or foursomes. As Asch (1967) suggests, a supporting partner can protect a participant from unwarranted pressure to give in to the feelings of the majority of the group.

Unfortunately, forming subgroups within a larger group often leads to hard lines being drawn between the various subgroups. In such cases, the lines of communication between group members are severely disrupted. Comments are weighed in terms of their impact on the subgroup rather than on their meaning for particular individuals. The disruptive effects can also be understood in terms of role conflict generated by subgroup membership. The subgroup member finds that he or she is caught between the norms and pressures of the subgroup and the norms stemming from identification with the overall group. In these cases the subgroup lines have been permitted to harden; the prospects of the total group developing the kind of cohesion all members must feel for the total group is minimal. In order to prevent this, the leader must be attuned to the early formation of subgroups.

The easiest way for the counselor to identify subgrouping is to observe the interaction patterns. The patterns of support or rejection of ideas among members must be observed. Individuals who constantly agree with one another whenever a group issue is raised are operating as a subgroup. The counselor has the responsibility for determining when such subgrouping is beneficial to members (usually only in the early meetings when members may need support), and when it becomes a resistance to group or individual progress. In the latter instance, the counselor should encourage a discussion and analysis of all the subgroups within the larger group. The counselor may need to take the lead in this by revealing his or her own emotional reactions to a subgroup; for example, how the subgroup may be acting to keep the leader at a distance, or to block progress. The ultimate aim of the leader must be to help those individuals involved in subgrouping realize how such behavior prevents the development of meaningful interactions with all members of the group, and how this behavior may be similar to behavior they exhibit in the outside world.

A counselor can also do much to prevent subgrouping as he or she goes through the selection procedures. The selection of two very close friends, husband and wife, siblings, or other such combinations for inclusion in a group almost guarantees the formation of a subgroup that may hinder the process of the group.

Self-disclosure

Self-disclosure is a process of making one's self known to other persons by revealing personal information (Jourard, 1958). Self-disclosure is considered a significant part of the member's therapeutic treatment. Members must disclose personal information if they are to become a cohesive group and the group counseling become a successful experience for members.

In most social situations, one person's self-disclosure will lead to another's self-disclosure. Usually the first person begins by offering a lower level of personal disclosure. The second person is likely to feel charged with some responsibility or obligation to the individual who has disclosed personal information, and responds to this disclosure with some appropriate comment and often some disclosure about herself or himself. Thus, both members have disclosed something about themselves and therefore feel somewhat vulnerable in what the other person knows about them. As the individuals make more open disclosures to each other, a deeper personal relationship is reached.

Self-disclosure is a necessary ingredient in the formation of a cohesive group interaction. After numerous disclosures, the group gradually increases the level of involvement with one another. Cohesiveness is certainly enhanced as members receive and reveal intimate information with each other. In addition to contributing to the cohesiveness of the group, it is also very beneficial for the individual member. There is a feeling of exhilaration when the member discloses material that has irked him or her for some time and feels understood and accepted by fellow group members. After an individual has been able to self-disclose in the group, he or she may also generalize this behavior to personal relationships outside the group.

Jourard (1971) suggested that the relationship between self-disclosure and mental health may be curvilinear; that is, too much or too little self-disclosure may indicate maladaptive or inappropriate interpersonal behaviors. If a member of the group does not reveal personal information, he or she is limited in the opportunity to test reality, and forfeits an opportunity to obtain feedback from the other members. In addition, such behavior prevents interpersonal relationships from developing since other members will discontinue further self-disclosure with that member. If several members offer too little self-disclosure, the group will stagnate. Members who do not self-disclose in the group are less likely to receive acceptance from the other members. They therefore have little chance of increasing their self-esteem or changing behaviors, which reduces the success of change due to group counseling. Self-disclosure does involve some personal risk, and members may feel that disclosing information is dangerous because it makes them vulnerable to other people in the group. When someone in the group has disclosed personal information that has been accepted and understood within the group, additional members may feel safe enough to self-disclose.

Some individuals self-disclose too much too early and then feel vulnerability and a need to withdraw. In addition, a great deal of self-disclosure may threaten other members of the group, causing them to withdraw rather than support the individual who self-disclosed.

The counselor must help individual members disclose an appropriate amount at the appropriate time. A lower level of self-disclosure is appropriate during the initial stage of the group, and every member should participate. As the group becomes more involved with each other, a deeper level of self-disclosure is important. After the group has become cohesive and individuals are working in a productive stage, a more personal self-disclosure is required.

Adding Members

In an open group, members will terminate at different times, thus leaving room for new members to be added. Even in some closed groups members may withdraw and the group census may fall to a level in which the counselor prefers to add new members. In a closed group, this is likely to happen during the early stages of the group prior to a real cohesiveness being established. In the open group, it will occur after the group has become cohesive and, through the productiveness of the group, some members are able to terminate.

Adding new members to an existing group is an important task for the leader and a significant event for the members in the group. One of the major variables in adding new members involves proper timing. A group which is in crisis or actively entering into a new phase of development is not in a favorable position for adding new members. A better time for adding new members is during a lull in the group interaction.

When new members are added to the group, older members often provide a rite of initiation. Group members may feel hostility toward the new member which is either verbally expressed or expressed by ignoring the individual. The group may spend considerable time discussing "the good old days" and describe members who have previously terminated from group or talk about past history which will leave new members out. New members may be discussed in terms of the resemblances they show to past members.

This type of transference is similar to that occurring between members in the initial phase of any group. Obviously, there are also feelings of welcome and support for new members. Older members may be facilitative and helpful to new members and assist them in overcoming their initial fear and defensiveness. Often members will provide a testimony to the effectiveness of the group and the assistance given to previous members, and they may provide a summary of the dynamics in the group.

Apparently, older members experience some ambivalence regarding the addition of new members. Some older members may prize the solidarity and cohesiveness of the group and feel a threat with the new members entering. Individuals who are concerned about control and dominance may be concerned regarding a threat to the present hierarchy of power. Others will be concerned that the new members will now receive undue attention and time from the leader. A common concern in the group is that new members will now slow the group, and therefore slow their progress in the group.

In an attempt to overcome the problems of adding new members to the group, the counselor must prepare both the new members and the old group. The counselor must prepare the individual for the types of stresses that are likely to occur for a member entering a group in process, and must help the individual be aware of the potential feelings of exclusion and bewilderment at the process. New members should be assured that they are allowed to participate at their own rate. In some groups, the counselor may want to discusss the process and events that are presently taking place in the group. Yalom (1975) suggests that counselors may want to introduce two new members at a time. This has the advantage for the group of conserving time by assimilating two individuals at once. Also, the new members may ally with each other and feel less alien in the situation.

Racial Differences

Groups often contain members of various racial groups and therefore the leader will also be of a different race from some of the members. Lanier and Robertiello (1977) concluded that there is usually a covert contract between racially different clients and counselors to use denial in relation to the issue of race. Both clients and counselors try to avoid confronting it, or at least attempt to play down its relevance or importance in the therapeutic process. They also concluded that it was not appropriate to expect a client to raise the issue. They note one of the most striking differences between black and white clients was the absolute and total denial of the white clients of any reaction whatsoever to the color of their therapist. Many members enter a group looking for help, and the race of the counselor or the other group members is not an issue. During the group process, however, the issue of race may get raised, and members begin to get in touch with racial feelings within themselves that they have not consciously been aware of.

Lanier and Robertiello report a discussion by counselors at a workshop focusing on the difficulty of patients and therapists of different races. A white client raised the issue of bringing up racial differences with the leader. There was concern about feeling guilty about being a racist, fearing retaliation for this, and being afraid of hurting the feelings of the counselor by raising the issue that the counselor might see as putting him or her at a disadvantage. The same feelings may be true in a black client's raising the issue with a white counselor. Race seems to be an important issue between people, although many clients deny it when entering the group. Black clients are generally more aware of color differences, and their degree of denial about racial concerns is not as great as white clients. It is the counselor's role to raise the issue and to do so early in the counseling process. If a client insists on not dealing with the issue at the time, the counselor should not force it; but at least the counselor has made an honest effort, not just a cursory one, to confront it.

Counselors from a minority group warned that there is a pitfall in overidentifying with a client because of a commonality of race. Being black does not mean being the same or having had common experiences in terms of racism. Lanier and

Robertiello (1977) suggest that many transferential and countertransferential sub-tleties indicate the need to examine the implications and ramifications of issues of race and racism in black situations.

Group members and counselors agree that the more important considerations in the interracial therapeutic relationship include the personality, skill, and psychic dovetailing between the clients and the counselor. These aspects transcend the racial differences without minimizing the fact and the importance of racial differences.

Interracial interactions in counseling tend to be very complex and very hidden. There tends to be a covert agreement on the part of clients and counselors to avoid the issue. For these reasons, counselors' self-awareness is extremely crucial in the process of resolving whatever problems arise.

Group Casualties

Group counseling may contribute negative outcomes as well as positive outcomes. Some members who participate in groups may have personal characteristics which are affected by the specific group situation which contribute to a negative outcome. An increasing awareness of the group casualty member has emerged since the preliminary report of encounter group casualties by Lieberman, Yalom, and Miles (1972). In their study of encounter group members, they found sixteen individuals, or 9.4 percent of the participants who completed the experience, showed evidence of durable negative outcome of more than a mild degree. They defined negative outcome or the group casualty as an individual who, as a result of encounter group experience, suffered some enduring psychological harm that was evident six to eight months after the end of the group. Their definition of a casualty was a member who had undergone some psychological decomposition and there was some evidence that the group experience was the responsible agent. A member was not considered a casualty who was shaken up or very distressed by the group but who, within a few days, had recovered equilibrium, nor did they define a casualty as a member who had experienced some difficulty that was not due to the group experience.

The most accurate predictor of the casualty was by peer judgment. Other members of the group were aware of the member who was hurt by the experience. One of the least accurate predictors was the leader's ratings; in fact, some leaders were completely unaware that there had been casualties in their groups. Group leaders who do not provide follow-up interviews with their group members do not have necessary information to make a statement about the hazards of their groups.

To identify the potential casualty, Lieberman, Yalom, and Miles (1972) developed a number of indicators: request for emergency psychiatric help, peer evaluation, dropping out of the group, steep decline in self-esteem, subject testimony, leader's negative rating of change, and taking psychotherapy. What contributes to a member's being hurt in a group experience? The data on the encounter group casualties showed rather clearly that a pre-existing personality disposition and expectations interacted with certain leadership styles and group climates.

Members who became casualties had some personal predisposition before they entered the group which contributed to their experience in the group. Individuals who became casualties were more psychologically vulnerable, e.g., showed lower self-esteem, less self-perceived mental health, and more sense of psychological distance from others. They also had very high hopes and expectations for the potential growth experience of the group. A second contributing variable was the leadership style. Some leaders appeared to create group conditions in which strong attack or rejection occurred. Far more casualties occur with a stressful leadership style characterized by intrusive, aggressive stimulation, high charisma, high challenging and confrontation of each of the members, and authoritarian control. Both attack and rejection are variables which may contribute to casualties in the group. A laissez-faire type leader may permit attack by group members which will hurt one of the members. It is also possible that rejection by the leader or the members may contribute detrimental impact on a member. Another contribution to a casualty experience may be input overload. Individuals may be so challenged or overstimulated that rather than assimilate new perspectives on themselves and their world, they may be sucked into a maelstrom of confusion and uncertainty. Still another form of injury may occur when a member observes other members quickly experiencing and expressing high-intensity affect. When they observe the apparent discrepancy between others' productions and their own, they may juege themselves as emotionally deficient and therefore identify themselves as hollow people.

It is apparent that group leaders have a responsibility to select individuals who can be helped through the group experience and to exclude those who should work in individual therapy rather than with a group. In addition, the leader has a responsibility to conduct a group in a manner which will be beneficial for the group members and to maintain contact with members to evaluate their progress.

It should be noted that many members of a group will experience upset, concern, and emotional disturbance during the process. The insight and changing of behavior is an anxiety-producing situation and a natural part of a counseling process. Confronting anxiety is essential for fully experiencing life and hence awareness and growth. Posthuma and Posthuma (1973) indicate that individuals who avoid this type of confrontation may be casualties in our society.

Dropouts

Given the proper preparation of potential members, good selection procedures, and an atmosphere in which membership in a group is seen as a potentially positive experience, the number of dropouts from a group will be minimized. This is extremely important in that the counselor can expect a dropout rate that may range from 25 to 57 percent (Yalom, 1975). Such early termination is not only a failure for the individual who drops out, but also has a debilitating effect on the remaining group members. In effect, when individuals leave the group, the group remaining is a new group, and it must go through a process of reforming. This process can be adversely affected by the remaining members dwelling on the reasons certain individuals left the group, and they may begin to question the efficacy of the group for themselves.

Yalom (1975) suggests the counselor needs to be aware of nine major reasons for individuals dropping out of a group:

1. **External Factors**   These are factors largely out of the control of the counselor. They may consist of the kind of external pressure from nongroup members discussed earlier, or they may simply be unavoidable circumstances.

2. **Group Deviance**   This is where an individual makes it through the selection procedure and turns out to be quite different from the other members. Hopefully, the counselor will be able to keep these to a minimum through good selection procedures.

3. **Inadequate Orientation to Therapy**   See the preceding section on preparation of members.

4. **Complications from Subgrouping**   See the section on the problems of subgrouping.

5. **Problems of Intimacy**   An individual member may feel pressured by group norms into self-disclosing behavior. In such cases, the member may disclose too much too early, and then feel compelled to withdraw; or, the pressure for disclosing is not something the individual is ready to face, and he or she withdraws to avoid it. To prevent such problems, the counselor must help the group establish norms that do not bring intolerable pressures on individual members.

6. **Fear of Emotional Contagion**   Here an individual member begins to fear that he or she is going to take on all the problems of the other group members. The member feels the "disease" is contagious, and drops out to avoid it. This is extremely difficult for the counselor. About all the counselor can do is in preparing the members, to point out that there will be individual differences in the group and that the process of the group will be therapeutic, not contaminating.

7. **Inability to Share Counselor**   The individual cannot deal with the situation in which the counselor gives equal attention to all members. The individual wants a one-to-one relationship with the counselor, who needs to try to break the dependency relationship by trying to get the group member to examine the nature of relationship and how it is acting as a negative focus in the growth process.

8. **Early Provocation**   Frequently one member is confronted by other members or the leader before the member is able to deal with such a confrontation. Here again, the counselor must lead the way in establishing group norms that will inhibit this behavior. It may also be necessary for the counselor to protect the member under attack if he or she perceives that the member is incapable of dealing with the problem at the time.

9. **Competition of Individual and Group Counseling**   At times, when an individual is being seen both individually and in a group, the two processes will cause inner conflict and the individual will drop out of the group. When the two processes are perceived in this fashion, termination of one of the processes is generally an advisable procedure.

In general, individuals drop out because they have received inadequate preparation for the group; the group norms are not conducive for growth; or, finally, they simply do not possess the necessary personal characteristics for group membership, They have less capacity for stress, and less desire for empathy from others and, conversely, they are less able to achieve emotional rapport with other group members (Yalom, 1975). In short, they seem to lack the element of "social hunger" referred to in the discussion of exclusion earlier in the chapter (Slavson, 1964). All of the special considerations noted here are ones for which the counselor can effectively plan. The key words are "plan" and "anticipate."

The focus to this point has been on the influences on roles; the ways in which roles may be classified; some specific role behaviors; and some special considerations affecting member roles. The important question yet to be explored is how these roles are communicated in the group qrocess. Or, how do the communication patterns, verbal and nonverbal, operate in groups?

COMMUNICATION IN GROUPS

In the earlier discussion of the effects of personality on role behavior, Leary's (1957) concept of interpersonal reflex was introduced. The interpersonal reflex is an unconscious, immediate response to a behavioral act of another individual. Taking this reflex into account is an important element in understanding the interpersonal meaning of behavior in a group.

Circumplex Model

To classify interpersonal behavior, Leary (1957) developed a two-dimensional schema called the Circumplex Model. On the vertical axis, behavior is classified across a continuum from dominance to submission, and on the horizontal axis, from hostility to affection.

Leary (1957) felt that all interpersonal behavior can be located somewhere around these axes. By using the two dimensions together (see Figure 13), one can understand the reciprocity of interpersonal behavior. For example, as shown in the position of four members in relation to the axes in the figure, member C may respond to member D's overly dependent behavior by providing help and taking active control. Member C becomes dominant and member D submissive. In this way, member C is demonstrating caring behavior and member D responds with similar feelings (Luft, 1970). Along the same dimensions, member A may respond to member B's passive aggression behavior by rejection. Once again, member A is dominant and the other member submissive, but in a far different manner from member C and member D. In both cases the members' responses are interpersonal reflexes. In Leary's scheme, the intersection of the two dimensions represents an emotionally neutral interaction. As one moves out from the center, the intensity of emotion increases.

The important concept for the group counselor in this schema is the recognition that a behavior by one individual will pull a complementary behavior from another individual. It is important to recognize that both the original behavior and the

Figure 13   Two-Dimensional Schema for Classifying Interpersonal Behavior (after Leary, 1957)

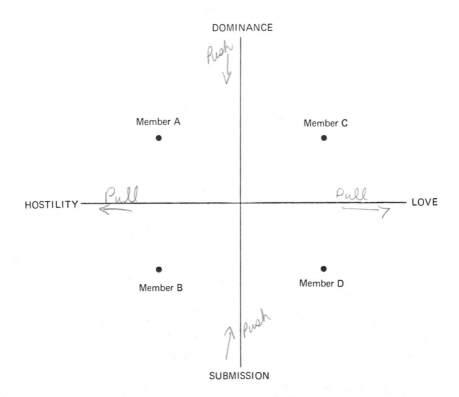

response may be activated even though neither party in the interaction meant to communicate what they actually did. An individual may be communicating a dominating behavior through the role of initiator without recognizing what he or she is communicating. This, in turn, may produce a submissive but hostile reaction on the part of other group members. In such cases, neither party may recognize the reasons for the behavior; this is where it is essential that the counselor possess the skill to help individuals recognize the nature of their behavior and the reactions it produces.

In using the model, it is important to recognize that the complementary act to an interpersonal act along the vertical axis will tend to evoke the opposite of that behavior from others (dominant-submissive). Behavioral acts along the horizontal axis, however, will tend to produce a similar response. Thus, a behavior that expresses affection will tend to produce a friendly response (Zaleznik and Moment, 1964).

The perception of the person acting will also influence the response. If the individual who is dominating the group is seen as someone who has proper authority, then the responses to that behavior will likely be submissive, but if the individual is not perceived as having the proper authority, the dominating behavior may produce similar, but competing, dominating behaviors from others.

In general, those individuals who are reasonably well-adjusted will demonstrate behaviors from all segments of the model when such behaviors are appropriate. A good indication of disturbance, however, is the individual whose behavior repeatedly comes from one quadrant of the schema regardless of the circumstances. In general, such people will try to change other individuals' behaviors rather than change their own, and the counselor must help them work through this process (Luft, 1970).

The model of interpersonal behavior developed by Leary provides the group counselor with an important tool for understanding the communication among members of the group. Using the model, the counselor can provide meaningful feedback to individuals in regard to both their originating behavior and their automatic reflexes, thus helping all members recognize the ways in which they communicate with one another at both the conscious and unconscious levels.

Johari Awareness Model

A second useful tool for examining the dynamics of communication in groups is the Johari Awareness Model. It not only provides a useful way of examining individual awareness but is also extremely useful in explaining the kinds of human interaction in groups.

The model, often referred to as the Johari Window, was developed by Joseph Luft and Harry Ingham in 1955. Since that time, it has received considerable attention from those concerned with group work. Much of the material here is based on Luft's book *Of Human Interaction* (1969). Readers who desire a more complete discussion of the model are urged to examine that text.

The Johari Awareness Model divides the total individual into four quadrants. Each of the quadrants represents an area of awareness or nonawareness of both uhe individual and those with whom he or she interacts. Awareness refers to knowledge of behavior, feelings, and motivation. In which quadrant the behavior, feeling, or motivation appears depends on who is aware of it. Figure 14 illustrates the model diagrammatically. The four areas are defined as:

Quadrant 1   The open quadrant consists of that material about self which is known to both the individual and to those with whom the individual interacts.

Quadrant 2   The blind quadrant consists of that material about self which is known to others but not to oneself.

Quadrant 3   The hidden quadrant consists of that material about self of which the individual is aware, but which is not known to those with whom the individual interacts.

Quadrant 4   The unknown quadrant consists of material about self that is out of awareness of both the individual and those with whom the individual interacts (Luft, 1969).

Each individual is composed of all four quadrants, although the relative size of each quadrant is dependent on the makeup of that individual. As a general rule,

Figure 14 Johari Awareness Model (after Luft, 1969)

	Known to Self	Not Known to Self
Known to Others	1 Open	2 Blind
Not Known to Others	3 Hidden	4 Unknown

the more material about self that is contained in the open quadrant, the better will be the functioning of the individual. It follows that those individuals experiencing some difficulty will most probably have a restricted open quadrant. Hence, one of the purposes of counseling is to help the individual move material from Quadrants 2, 3, and 4 into Quadrant 1. To do this, Luft describes eleven principles of change:

1. A change in any one quadrant will affect all other quadrants.
2. It takes energy to hide, deny, or be blind to behavior that is involved in interaction.
3. Threat tends to decrease awareness; mutual trust tends to increase awareness.
4. Forced awareness (exposure) is undesirable and usually ineffective.
5. Interpersonal learning means a change has occurred that makes Quadrant 1 larger, and one or more of the other quadrants smaller.
6. Working with others is facilitated by a large enough area of free activity so that more of the resources and skills of the persons involved can be applied to the task at hand.
7. The smaller the first quadrant, the poorer the communication.
8. There is a universal curiosity about the unknown area, but this is held in check by custom, social training, and diverse fears.
9. Sensitivity means appreciating the covert aspects of behavior in Quadrants 2, 3, and 4, and respecting the desire of others to keep them so.
10. Learning about group processes, as they are being experienced, helps to

increase awareness (enlarging Quadrant 1) for the group as a whole as well as for the individual members.

11.   The value system of a group and its membership may be noted in the way unknowns in the life of the group are confronted (1969, pp. 13–14).

Relative Openness of Quadrant 1   Each individual can be characterized by the relative size of his or her open quadrant. While, for differing persons and situations, the particular individual may have a larger or a smaller Quadrant 1, it is relatively stable across all individuals. People may enlarge their open area in interactions with their spouses, and restrict the open area with their bosses. The size of Quadrant 1 in any interaction, then, determines the degree to which two or more individuals can freely give and take, work together, and share experiences. The larger the open quadrant, the greater is the individual's contact with reality, and the more available are the individual's abilities and needs both to self and others.

The more an individual feels a need for self-protection, the smaller will be the amount of material in Quadrant 1. Having a need to protect oneself generally means that the amount of material placed in Quadrant 3 will be increased. Individuals who are unsure of themselves will try to hide more of their feelings and motivations in Quadrant 3. At the same time, the amount of material in Quadrant 2 is also increased. As the need for self-protection increases, the less apt the individual is to be aware of behavior which others see but he or she does not see. Quadrant 4 is also increased as this individual literally pushes events out of awareness. This area is similar to the Freudian concept of unconscious material of which neither the individual nor those around the individual are aware. Figure 15 diagrammatically illustrates this individual, while Figure 16 represents a fully functioning individual.

Note that even in a fully functioning individual, there are some feelings, attitudes, motivations, and behaviors that are located in Quadrants 2, 3, and 4. The key difference between the individuals represented in the two figures is the size of the open quadrant. The individual represented by Figure 16 is much more aware and self-confident, and is therefore much more able to interact in a meaningful way with others. In a very real sense, an overriding goal of counseling is to help individuals move from the situation represented in Figure 15 to the situation represented in Figure 16.

In a new group situation, most individuals will look like Figure 15. People tend to behave in a relatively polite and superficial manner as normal social rules prevail. Because the open area is relatively small for all members, the interaction in the group will be limited and guarded. If the group is to become a truly cohesive and working group, the individuals within the group must move toward the orientation represented by Figure 16. Here, interaction is at a meaningful level as the individual members are open to most of their feelings and behaviors and are willing to share them with others.

Relative Openness in Groups   Counselors should not expect that all groups

Figure 15   Constricted Individual (after Luft, 1969)

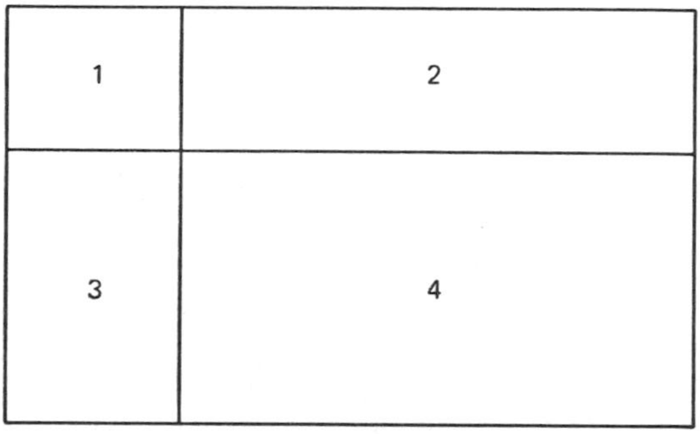

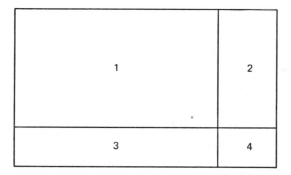

Figure 16   Fully Functioning Individual (after Luft, 1969)

are going to begin exactly like the group represented in Figure 17, nor will they all move to the state of awareness represented in Figure 18 (Luft, 1970). Rather, these two figures represent the average beginning point of a group and what a good working group might look like. In all stages of group development, differing individuals will have differing levels of openness. Even in very productive groups, one individual may still have a small open quadrant. In general, however, in groups in which there is a large area of free activity, individuals will feel less threat or fear, and there will be a higher probability that the skills and resources of each member can be utilized to work on the group task (Luft, 1970).

The implication of this model for the communication of roles is that initially members will communicate from the role position they feel most comfortable in sharing. Hence, a member may assume a submissive or compliant follower role because he or she feels that will be both an expected and an accepted role by the counselor, as well as by other members. Or, the member may engage in

Figure 17   Initial Group Session (after Luft, 1970)

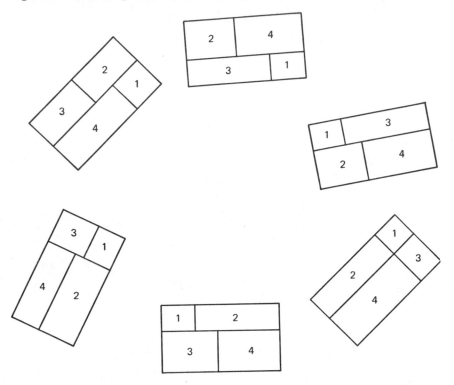

blocking behavior because he or she feels that is what other members expect. In either case, the member is operating with a restricted open area, and the behavior can be characterized as not being appropriate for the group process. The counselor can assume that members who operate only from one role position are operating with a small area and are expending a great amount of energy in keeping material hidden from the group and from themselves.

It is to be hoped that, as the group progresses, each individual enlarges the open quadrant, thus allowing for a greater flow of information, opinions, and ideas among the members. Since less energy is required to keep material hidden, more of the individuals' needs are free to be expressed, and there is an increased likelihood of satisfaction and involvement in the group (Luft, 1970). In this circumstance, members are freer to adopt flexible role behaviors—behaviors that both meet the individuals' needs and are productive to the group process.

The question then is: How do counselors and group members help individuals move from a restricted open quadrant qosition to an enlarged open quadrant? Members of a new group will begin to expand the small first quadrant by voluntary and involuntary shifts of private knowledge into the open (Luft, 1969). The voluntary shifts are initially from Quadrant 3 to Quadrant 1; the involuntary material

Figure 18   Adaptive Group Behavior (after Luft, 1970)

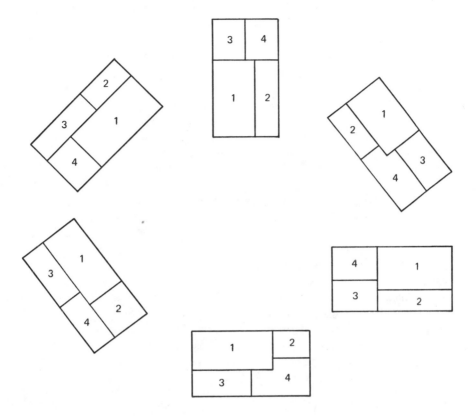

comes from Quadrant 2. The degree to which there is a feeling of mutual trust within the group will regulate how much data any one individual will knowingly move into the new quadrant.

As defined earlier, Quadrant 2, or the blind quadrant, contains material about the self which other group members can perceive but which is unavailable to the individual. Thus, other group members can confront the individual with personal material with which the individual is not ready to deal. If this happens, the amount of transfer from Quadrant 3 will also be restricted, as the individual feels a need for self-protection. "In the individual, the denial of the forced disclosure is probably the most common reaction," says Luft (1969,p. 36). Hence, it is extremely impor- tant that the counselor lead the way toward the establishment of group norms where mutual trust and reciprocity are supreme. If an inappropriate attack on an individual does occur, the counselor needs to use the incident to help the group examine its own dynamics. Luft points out that what often occurs is that other members may come to the defense of the member under attack by bringing into the open the motives of the individual doing the attacking; the counselor must help all members examine this process.

Given the establishment of mutual trust, members are more likely to engage in behaviors that will facilitate the exploration of self and others (Luft, 1969). Individuals come to see more of each other's blind areas. They feel less need to distort their own feelings and behaviors. Role behaviors become more open and flexible, and the members are then able to react more specifically and appropriately to each other, thereby going beyond superficial relationships. Members begin to voluntarily move material from Quadrant 3 to Quadrant 1 and, as they feel nonthreatened, they are also able to examine material from their own blind area. "Eventually, by restoring contact with self through exploration and sensing, one rediscovers more of one's selfness. In this way, one may restore part of the lost openness to the world, the world of inner life (Luft, 1969, p. 21)."

In such an atmosphere, it is also probable the material in Quadrant 4, the unknown, will move to Quadrant 3 and then perhaps to Quadrant 1. Direct movement from Quadrant 4 to Quadrant 1 may occur in an emotionally charged group session, but such disclosures are generally to be avoided if possible (Luft, 1969). The individual should have time to examine this material before moving it into the open area. If the material moves directly from the unknown to the open area without passing through the hidden area, this will not be possible.

In summary, the Johari Window is a useful tool for the counselor as she or he considers and tries to understand where each individual in the group is in the group process, why the individual is engaging in a particular role, and what the individual is communicating to the rest of the group. This can facilitate both the leader's understanding of the group process and also his or her ability to select the proper techniques for moving the group forward.

Nonverbal Communication

Much of the material presented on the Circumplex Model and the Johari Awareness Model has indicated the importance of nonverbal communication without actually mentioning it. In discussing how people communicate with one another, there is a tendency to forget that feelings and attitudes are communicated in nonverbal as well as verbal ways. One group member reaching out and touching another without saying a word may be communicating caring behavior on the one hand, or curtailing behavior on the other hand, depending on how the touching behavior is executed. Similarly, body posture, facial expressions, and eye contact can communicate quite effectively.

Nonverbal communication is particularly effective in imparting feelings and attitudes that members do not feel free to express verbally. Thus, an individual who is turned off by what another member is expressing may look out the window, fidget, or scowl; all of these acts communicate a lack of interest. A withdrawn individual may actually physically shrink from the group by moving a chair back or curling up in it. A dominating member may point, wave hands, pound a table, or pursue any number of other nonverbal behaviors that demonstrate an attempt to dominate the group. It may also be that this dominating behavior is really an attempt by the individual to keep the focus of attention away from his or her inner feelings. In short, nonverbal behavior is often the real key to what a group member is feeling. A member, in order to be accepted by the group, may verbally express very positive feelings about the group. At the same time, the member's nervous nonverbal behaviors may be a clue to real feelings of discomfort. It is particularly important that the group counselor have the ability to pick up these mixed messages. If the counselor simply responds to the overt verbal message and misses the real message being communicated nonverbally, he or she may never facilitate any positive growth in that group member. Obviously, the counselor must feed his or her perceptions on the nonverbal behavior back to the group member in a nonthreatening manner, or the individual may further retreat into a shell. In similar fashion, an entire group may be communicating feelings of discomfort, fear, or anger in nonverbal ways, and the counselor must be attuned to these expressions and feed them back to the entire group. If they are missed, the group will not move beyond superficial matters.

We will discuss two theoretical models to help counselors to understand the complexity of nonverbal communication. These conceptual models of nonverbal communication may help counselors bring order out of the confusion of the myriad of nonverbal behaviors.

Kagan's Model   Kagan and his colleagues (1967) observed clients in interviews and inferentially developed a framework of nonverbal behavior. They discovered that clients frequently used nonverbal behaviors as cues to important feelings or ideas at critical points in the interview. They established a framework of nonverbal behavior based upon three elements: the source of nonverbal behavior, the awareness of nonverbal behavior, and the duration of the nonverbal behavior.

The source of nonverbal behavior could be related either to the verbal content of the interview or to the affect of experience of the individual in the interview. While both content and affect occur simultaneously, nonverbal behaviors seem to be related only to one and seldom to both at once. The content of the interview refers to the topic of conversation at the time, while affect refers to the feelings being experienced by the individual regarding self, the situation, or the topic.

A client's nonverbal communication may occur at one of three levels of awareness: awareness, potential awareness, and lack of awareoess. The level of awareness involves both the client's knowing of behavior and an intention for it to occur. Potential awareness indicates that the individual could be aware of the behavior if his or her attention were drawn to it, but since the individual is involved in an interview, there is no direct awareoess. Lack of awareness means the client is entirely unaware of the behavior and if his or her attention were directed to it, there would be no awareness of it occurring.

The duration of time in the nonverbal behavior is the third element of the framework. Nonverbal behaviors can be arranged in regular fashion according to the amount of time each behavior lasts, from a quick motion of a fraction of a second to a motion which could continue for several minutes or occur continuously through an interview.

The interrelationship of the source and awareness of nonverbal behavior is described in six distinct categories of nonverbal behavior: emphasis, facilitation, portrayal, revelation—unaware, revelation—aware, and affect demonstration. Each category is named according to the major function of behavior in that category, implying that every nonverbal communication has meaning.

Emphasis The category of emphasis includes gestures used for emphasis which are generally brief, forceful, and accompany a particular verbal comment. The client is generally unaware of the gesture.

Facilitation This category includes gestures used to assist in increasing clarification. These include hand and arm gestures when the client is somewhat at a loss for words or is feeling that the communication is inadequate. The hands and arms typically move in a quick, upward, and outward motion as if to release words from within and speed them in communication. The individual is probably unaware of the facilitative gestures unless it is called to his or her attention. Thus, it is described as in a potentially aware category.

Portrayal Communication in this category occurs when a client wants to demonstrate what is meant and can only portray it by means of a gesture. These gestures give an example or picture of the topic being communicated, and are generally consciously used to specifically add to the verbal communication.

Affect Demonstration Nonverbal behaviors used deliberately to demonstrate feelings are in this category. These nonverbal behaviors are intentional and fully in the awareness of the client, such as facial expression to communicate feelings of distaste.

Revelation—Aware Gestures in this category include those of which the client is aware but attributes to habit and seldom recognizes the basic motivation for. Ring twisting, pencil tapping, or other nervous gestures may be explained by the client as a habit.

Revelation—Unaware Gestures in this category include the tension-motivated behavior of which the member is totally unaware. This is the most frequently critical nonverbal behavior in counseling. The member is more concerned with verbalizing content than with nonverbal behavior, and the tension that is present in a situation motivates the nonverbal behavior. These gestures may be continuous or repeated for an extended period of time.

Kagan et al. conducted additional research studies which contribute important information regarding nonverbal behavior. They focused on the level of intensity in the individual's feelings and also how congruent the nonverbal behavior was with the feeling the individual was verbalizing. They suggest the counselor should be aware of the high, middle, or low level of affective intensity of the nonverbal behavior being communicated. The congruency dimension represents whether a person's statement is congruent with the nature of the affect felt or whether it is at variance with it. If the verbal statement is at variance with the nonverbal statement, there seems to be two basic ways in which this occurs. The verbal statement might be similar to the affect perceived!but different in intensity, understating or overstating in words what is the perceived affect. A second way in which variances may occur is in terms of the lack of correspondence between the verbal statement and the perceived affect in which the verbal statement reflects a very different emotion from the nonverbal behavior.

Ekman's Model Another conceptualization of nonverbal behavior was proposed by Ekman (1973) from his research. There are some similarities and differences between Ekman's and Kagan's conceptualizations of nonverbal behavior; however, integrating the two greatly enhances the counselor's awareness of nonverbal behaviors.

Ekman presents circumstances to observe when nonverbal behavior occurs. When a member uses nonverbal communication, the counselor should be aware of conditions such as the environmental setting and the intangible circumstances such as the emotional tone of their interaction. Second, the counselor should be aware of the relationship of the nonverbal to the verbal behavior to see if it illustrates, repeats, or contradicts the accompanying speech. Third, the client's level of awareness that he or she is enacting or performing is closely related to the fourth circumstance, that of the client's intention to communicate through nonverbal means. Fifth, the counselor should be aware of the external feedback, or what the counselor or other members did with the information the client said. Sixth, the type of information conveyed that is distinguished between idiosyncratic and shared information needs to be determined.

Ekman offers a model and five categories that help to delineate nonverbal behaviors. The first category is emblems, those acts or positions that have a direct verbal translation into a word or two. Emblems are generally identified by their shared meaning and their intention to communicate to the other person, such as the "V" made with two fingers upheld. This would probably be categorized in Kagan's area of portrayal. A second category of behaviors is the illustrators which are direct accompaniments of speech and serve as pictographs to shape the referent visually. This is nearly the same description as Kagan's portrayal. Affect displays comprise a third category. The face is the location of most behaviors included in this category. Facial behaviors convey more information about an emotion than body movements. Although there are socially and culturally learned behaviors and rules of display, Ekman proposes that the actual facial displaying of primary emotions such as happiness, surprise, and anger are sufficiently alike to be recognizable across cultures. The affect display measures get a greater amount of attention than other nonverbal behaviors. The sender generally deliberately communicates, and often the receiver comments on receiving such information. The fourth category is termed regulators because the behaviors are seen as regulating the conversational flow between individuals. A head nod is an example of a widely used regulator. This conception suggests that particular regulators are related to ethnicity, social class, and culture, and that their misinterpretation is one of the more perplexing sources of misunderstanding that can occur between individuals. Adapters are the fifth category and cover nonverbal behaviors that are abbreviated versions of activities originally learned in childhood for purposes of coping with needs. Three sub-types of adapters are identified: self-adapters, alter-adapters, and object-adapters. The self-adapting act of a hand wiping the corner of an eye may have originally been used to rub away tears but later can be used to communicate when a person feels hurt or sad. Self-adapters generally involve the hand touching the face or head. Alter-adapters generally involve the hands moving in space rather than having contact with the person. Alter-adapters were learned in the course of managing previous interpersonal contacts, and include behaviors performed to protect oneself from attack or to withdraw. Object-adapters are behaviors learned to perform a task, such as smoking, using a typewriter, or shuffling cards. They are often used when some aspect of the interaction stimulates a reenactment.

The adapters are used in understanding nonverbal leakage and as clues to deceptive communication. Ekman examines deceptive interactions and tries to distinguish between self-deception and deceiving the other person. There are three characteristics of deceptive interaction that differentiate them from other types of social interaction. One is whether there is a conscious focus on deception by at least one of the individuals. The second characteristic is whether there is implicit or explicit agreement between the two to be collaborators or antagonists in the deception. The third involves the adoption of either a deceptor or detective role.

Counselors should note that actions of the face, hands, and legs differ in the amount of message they send and the amount of feedback they receive. A person's face is the best sender and receives the most attention. The legs and feet are the poorest communicators because their transmission time is slow and the repertoire is small. In understanding deception, the face is the best liar, the hands are the next, and the legs are the poorest. The legs would be a primary source of leakage of clues to deception because leg movement is rare and seldom employed deliberately. Among hand action users, Ekman suggests that it is the self-adapters who most often give away their deception such as chatting and smiling while they are making a fist. Object-adapters such as nervously playing with a pencil may also be giveaways. Ekman uses research to support this theory, illustrating that individuals viewing films of people telling the truth and lies could not differentiate by seeing their faces, while they could differentiate the two by watching bodies. There are many more self-adapters used by individuals not telling the truth. Self-adapters, that is, hands touching the face or head, tend to increase with anxiety or discomfort.

SUMMARY

The place of member roles in the group process has been the focus of this chapter. The ways in which people come to groups, how these factors as well as other external and internal factors affect the roles taken in a group, and two major systems of role classification have been discussed. Specific member roles in terms of their appropriateness or inappropriateness have also been examined. Finally, the concept of interpersonal communication of roles was introduced to illustrate some of the expected dynamics in a group.

This analysis was undertaken because of the authors' belief that the success of any group depends on the interaction between leader and members. The advantage of group counseling is the potential of added therapeutic benefits from the members, and in order to release this potential, a counselor must be aware of the dynamics of membership. The ways in which leader behaviors and member behaviors interact throughout the life of a group will be the concern of the next two chapters.

References

Addison, R. E. The racially different patient in individual and group psychotherapy. *Journal of Contemporary Psychotherapy,* 1977, *9,* 39–40.

Andrews, E. E. Therapeutic interaction in adult therapy groups. In R. C. Diedrich and H. A. Dye (Eds.), *Group procedures: Purposes, processes, and outcomes: Selected readings for the counselor.* Boston: Houghton Mifflin, 1972, 151–69.

Asch, S. E. Opinions and social pressure. In A. P. Hare, E. F. Borgatta, and R. F. Bales (Eds.), *Small groups: Studies in social interaction.* New York: Knopf, 1967, 318–24.

Bales, R. F. *Interaction process analysis.* Cambridge, MA: Addison-Wesley, 1951.

Benne, K. D., and P. Sheats. Functional roles of group members. *Journal of Social Issues,* 1948, 4, 2.

Bonney. W. C. Pressures toward conformity in group counseling. In R. C. Diedrich and H. A. Dye (Eds.), *Group procedures: Purposes, processes and outcomes: Selected readings for the counselor.* Boston: Houghton Mifflin, 1972, 144–50.

Carter, L. F. Recording and evaluating the performance of individuals as members of small groups. In A. P. Hare, E. F. Borgatta, and R. F. Bales (Eds.), *Small groups: Studies in social interaction.* New York: Knopf, 1967, 282–87.

Crews, C. Y., and J. Melnick. Use of initial and delayed structure in facilitating group development. *Journal of Counseling Psychology,* 1976, *23,* 92–98.

Ekman, P., and A. Gattozzi. Studies in communication through nonverbal behavior. In J. Segal (Ed.), *Mental health program reports,* 6. Washington, DC: U.S. Government Printing Office, 1973.

Evensen, P. *The effects of structure and risk taking disposition on early group development.* Unpublished doctoral dissertation. University of Kentucky, 1976.

Gazda, C. M. *Group counseling: A developmental approach.* Boston: Allyn and Bacon, 1971.

Gibb, J. R. Defensive communication. *Journal of Communication,* 1961, *11,* 141–48.

Giedt, F. H. Predicting suitability for group psychotherapy. *American Journal of Psychotherapy,* 1961, *15,* 582–91.

Goldstein, P., K. Heller, and L. Sechrest. *Psychotherapy and the psychology of behavior change.* New York: Wiley, 1966.

Hare, A. P. *Handbook of small group research.* Glencoe, IL: Free Press of Glencoe, 1962.

Harvey, O. J., and C. Consalvi. Status and conformity to pressure in informal groups. *Journal of Abnormal and Social Psychology,* 1960, *60,* 182–87.

Heslin, R. Predicting group task effectiveness from member characteristics. *Psychological Bulletin,* 1964, *62,* 248–56.

Jacobson, E. A., and S. J. Smith. Effect of weekend encounter group experiences upon interpersonal orientations. *Journal of Consulting and Clinical Psychology,* 1972, *38,* 403–10.

Jourard, S. *Personal adjustment: An approach through the study of healthy personality.* New York: Macmillan, 1958.

Jourard, S. *Self-disclosure: An experimental analysis of the transparent self.* New York: Wiley, 1971.

Kagan, N., et al. *Studies in human interaction, interpersonal process recall, stimulated by video-tape.* Final Report Project No. 5-0800, Washington, DC: U.S. Department of Health, Education, and Welfare, 1967.

Kilmann, P. Locus of control and preference for type of group counseling. *Journal of Clinical Psychology,* 1974, *30,* 226–27.

Kilmann, P., B. Albert, and W. Sotile. Relationship between locus of control, structure of therapy, and outcome. *Journal of Consulting and Clinical Psychology,* 1975, *43,* 588.

Lanier, E., and R. C. Robertiello. A small group of patients discuss their experiences and feelings about working with therapists of different races. *Journal of Contemporary Psychotherapy,* 1977, *9,* 42–44.

Leary, T. *Interpersonal diagnosis of personality.* New York: Ronald Press, 1957.

Lee, F. T. *The effects of sex, risk-taking, and structure on prescribed group behavior, cohesion, and evaluative attitudes in a simulated early training phase of group therapy.* Unpublished doctoral dissertation. University of Kentucky, 1975.

Lieberman, M. A., I. D. Yalom, and M. B. Miles. The impact of encounter groups on participants: Some preliminary findings. *Journal of Applied Behavioral Science,* 1972, *8,* 29–50.

Loeser, L. H. Some aspects of group dynamics. In J. C. Hansen and S. H. Cramer (Eds.), *Group guidance and counseling in the schools.* New York: Appleton-Century-Crofts, 1971, 207–17.

Luft, J. *Of human interaction.* Palo Alto, CA: National Press Books, 1969.

Luft, J. *Group processes: An introduction to group dynamics.* Palo Alto, CA: National Press Books, 1970. (2nd ed.)

McFarland, R. L., C. L. Nelson, and A. M. Rossi. Prediction of participation in group psychotherapy from measures of intelligence and verbal behavior. *Psychological Reports,* 1962, *11,* 291–98.

Melnick, J., and D. Wicher. Social risk taking propensity and anxiety as predictors of group performance. *Journal of Counseling Psychology,* 1977, *24,* 415–19.

Mowrer, H. Integrity groups: principles and procedures. *Counseling Psychologist,* 1972, *3,* 7–33.

Ohlsen, M. M. *Group counseling.* New York: Holt, 1970.

Posthuma, A. B., and B. W. Posthuma. Some observations on encounter group casualties. *Journal of Applied Behavioral Science,* 1973, *9,* 595–608.

Reddy, W. B. On affection, group composition, and self-actualization in sensitivity training. *Journal of Consulting and Clinical Psychology,* 1972, *38,* 211–214.

Sherif, M., and C. W. Sherif. *Reference groups.* New York: Harper & Row, 1964.

Slavson, S. *A textbook in analytic group psychotherapy.* New York: International Universities Press, 1964.

Stock, D., and H. A. Thelen. Emotional dynamics and group culture. In M. Rosenbaum and M. Berger (Eds.), *Group psychotherapy and group function.* New York: Basic Books, 1963, 71–91.

Thelen, H. *Dynamics of groups at work.* Chicago: U. of Chicago Press, 1954.

Yalom, I. D. A study of group therapy drop-outs. *Archives of General Psychiatry,* 1966, *14,* 393–414.

Yalom, I. D. *The theory and practice of group psychotherapy* (2nd ed.). New York: Basic Books, 1975.

Yalom, I. D., and M. A. Lieberman. A study of encounter group casualties. *Archives of General Psychiatry,* 1971, *25,* 17–30.

Zaleznik, A., and D. Moment. *The dynamics of interpersonal behavior.* New York: Wiley, 1964.

14

Establishing the Group

Groups are complex social systems in which many variables change simultaneously. For an individual entering a group and unaware of all the dynamics of the situation, this state of flux may be disconcerting. The individual may feel that the events are occurring in a confused, disordered, and unpredictable manner, and may need the help of an experienced counselor to discern order and patterns in the process.

LIFE STAGES OF A GROUP

A number of social scientists have described certain changes in the life of a group. Concepts of these phases, cycles, and developmental stages vary according to the type of group being studied, the goal of the group, and the professional interest of the theorist. Developmental stages have been identified in learning groups (Mills, 1964; Thelen and Dickerman, 1949; Runkel et al., 1971; Lacouriere, 1974); training groups (Miles, 1953; R. D. Mann, 1966, 1971; Dunphy, 1968); and counseling or therapy groups (Martin and Hill, 1957; Whitaker and Lieberman, 1964; J. Mann, 1953; Mahler, 1969; Shambaugh and Kanter, 1969; Heckel et al., 1971; Gazda, 1972; Bonnoy, 1074). Bearing in mind that the current concepts are based on the observation of only a few groups, and that some variation in life stages has been discovered in different types of groups, one can still assume a basic pattern of development within most groups. An understanding of these life stages can help the counselor place a single event in perspective and bring order out of confusion to the members of the group. To provide the most meaningful experience for participants in the groups they lead, counselors must understand how groups develop and how they evolve through a systematic process.

Chapters 14 and 15 explore the process of the development of a group and the maintaining and functioning of group behavior through the life stages. Five stages of group development will be examined: the initiation of the group, a conflict and confrontations stage, a stage of developing cohesiveness, a productive stage, and termination. Each stage is a composite of models presented in the literature as well as the process involved.

It seems reasonable for a group to begin with insecurity, apprehension, and unsureness about behavior and group structure, and to feel dependent upon the counselor for direction. At this stage the individual will start to engage in the counseling process by accepting influence from others in order to gain a favorable reaction. This is characteristic of the stage of initiation.

A second stage generally involves a period of conflict. The members' negative emotional response to the situation and to each other may pose a threat to further development.

If this feeling of stress is overcome, they develop sensitivity to one another and a spirit of working together. During this stage of cohesiveness, the members develop an identification with the leader and group, and have a feeling of commitment to the purposes of the group.

The group can then be functional and devote energy to realistic appraisal of individual and group goals and to achieving these goals. During the productive stage, individuals are able to internalize the insights from their interpersonal interactions and begin modifying their behaviors.

As they are able to generalize their behaviors outside the group, they approach a point of termination. When members have established personal bonds and reached some of their goals, they will have mixed feelings about separation.

Groups differ in the length of time spent in any one stage and the specifics of the problems faced in any stage. The developmental stages of a group are rarely clearly differentiated. A group does not necessarily move step by step through the life stages, but may move backward and forward as part of its general development.

It is important for the counselor to have a clear conception of the developmental stages of groups, for then he or she is better able to assist the group members in the formation of norms and to prevent the establishment of norms that hinder their personal and group development. It will also help the counselor diagnose group blockage and intervene in the process to help the group members proceed to a more productive stage. Moreover, the counselor's awareness of broad developmental stages will prevent personal feelings of confusion and anxiety, which would only compound similar feelings in the group members.

PREPARATION FOR THE GROUP

The counselor's decisions prior to initiation of the group are as important as behaviors in the group. Such issues as size of group, the process of selection, the open or closed character of the group, meeting times, and duration of the group must be decided. As noted in the preceding chapter, there should be some preparation of each member for the group process prior to actual initiation of the group.

The Setting

The counselor must locate an appropriate place for the group to meet and establish policy about the duration of the group, the duration of each session, admission of new members, and the size of the group.

Group sessions may be held in any setting that affords some degree of comfort as well as privacy, and is free from distractions. A table may be used as long as it permits all members to see each other. In the early stages of a group, the table will serve as a protection for the members, thus providing some psychological comfort. Individuals sometimes feel uncomfortable with nothing in the center, although the absence of a table permits the client's entire body to be visible so that nonverbal responses are more readily seen. Comfortable chairs and a carpeted floor permit the members to relax, move about, and change positions.

Another part of the setting may include the use of audio or visual recording equipment. Even if the equipment is not visible, it is a part of the setting. The group members should be made aware of its use. It may take them some time to work through such issues, but usually they forget about the recording very quickly.

Size

A consensus of the literature, although mostly not based on research, suggests that the ideal size for a group in counseling is seven to eight members, with a range from five to ten. The lower limit is determined by the fact that when the group is much smaller, it ceases to operate as a group, and the individuals find themselves involved in individual counseling within the group setting. In addition, opportunities for utilizing the dynamics within the group are reduced. Such pressure is put on each individual that he or she cannot choose to remain silent, and the comfort level is reduced. The upper limit is determined by the fact that less time is available for working through individual problems when there are additional members. As the group size increases, it is more difficult for the less forceful members to express their ideas. The competition for "air time" becomes critical.

An increase in the size of the group brings a corresponding tendency for disruptive subgroups to form (Hare, 1962). Castore (1962) investigated the relationship between the size of the group and the number of different member-to-member relationships that were initiated. The results indicated a marked reduction in interactions between members when the group size reached nine members, and a second marked reduction when it reached seventeen or more members.

A counselor might expect one or two members to drop out during the early stages. It is therefore advisable to start the group slightly larger than the desired size to anticipate this possibility.

Selection

A counselor can increase the chances of success within the group by careful selection of clients. Clients should be thoroughly screened so the counselor will understand as much as possible about them. The counselor may wish to review a history of the client's family background, childhood, adolescence, and other developmental areas. It may be helpful to be acquainted with the client's medical history.

Success is certainly increased by selecting clients who volunteer for a group after they know what is expected of them and what they can expect from the experience. Johnson (1963) and Rickard (1965) suggest that clients who volunteer and show a higher motivation for group membership are good prospects for group counseling. Individuals who seek counseling on their own are more open to help than individuals who are coerced by family and friends. Other variables, including capacity for insight, degree of flexibility, desire for growth, and some experiences with authority figures who possessed a measure of steadiness, helpfulness, direction, and maturity also contribute to more productive group membership (Stranham, Schwartzman, and Atkin, 1957). It is also important that the group members be interested in helping each other. The group experience will be more productive if the members are able to become emotionally involved in helping each other and receive satisfaction from seeing others solve their problems (Allport, 1960).

Boer and Lantz (1974) offer suggestions for selecting members in an adolescent group. Many of these suggestions are appropriate for other groups as well. They begin by suggesting that the age span of members should be as small as possible, probably no more than three years since there is a large variation in maturation levels of adolescents. The individual must, of course, be taken into mind. It is also advantageous to have roughly an equal number of males and females in the group. Sexuality is an important issue for adolescents as well as adults, and the information input and reality for this topic can be helpful for both.

When accepting referrals or accepting individuals in a group, it is important to realize that the group counseling should be the preferred mode of treatment. The group treatment is most appropriate when the members express difficulty in their relationships with others. Individuals with antisocial or asocial attitudes may need individual work prior to entering a group.

An important prerequisite for admission to a group is stated individual goals. A prerequisite for attending a group should be a verbalized contract regarding personal change. Individuals who know what they are interested in prior to beginning a group are more likely to participate.

All group members should have a relationship with the therapist prior to entering the group. This is important since there is always a great deal of anxiety associated with group membership in the early stages. This relationship will help members handle the anxiety until they begin relating with other group members.

Group Composition

Should a counseling group be homogeneous or heterogeneous? That is, should it comprise one sex, age, socioeconomic level, or problem area as opposed to varying these factors within the same group?

Homogeneous groups become cohesive more quickly, have better attendance and less conflict, offer more immediate support to each other, and provide more quick symptomatic relief. However, it is believed that the homogeneous group is more likely to remain at a superficial level and to be less effective in permanently altering behavior.

Whether or not to select homogeneous clients is an issue that the counselor must resolve. If the counselor does decide to select homogeneous members, which characteristics are important? Ohlsen (1970) suggest four areas to consider: age, intellectual ability, sex, and common problems. There is some advantage to, and in many cases a necessity of, working with children at or near the same age level. In many school settings, counselors work with children from the same grade. Actually it is a social maturity factor that is most important, rather than the chronological age. The age variable is probably most important in working with children and adolescents, although even with adults a wide age range may impede the discussions. A client who feels much older or younger than the other group members frequently feels left out and inappropriate.

It is possible that variations in a level of intelligence can create problems in the group. Less educated or intelligent members may be dominated by more verbally fluent members and may feel out of place. The counselor may wish to either observe the level of verbal fluency or obtain some actual measure of verbal capacity prior to selecting group members.

Some groups may be more productive when they are separated on the basis of sex. During certain stages of development, girls will be more mature than boys and be able to handle topics in the group discussion more effectively. Even so, the group experience is an excellent opportunity for boys to learn more adaptive skills. Most adolescents and adults need and want reactions from the opposite sex.

Clients generally feel a sense of belonging when they discover other members in the group have similar problems. Although they have the same general problem, they also become aware that each is unique and that there are different underlying causes in each case. In such a situation, the group members are more motivated and interested in helping each other. There is an atmosphere in which both their similarities and their differences are recognized, and the group members utilize their differing perceptions as they work to resolve a common concern.

Some counselors suggest that the group be as heterogeneous as possible to insure that maximum interaction occurs. In such a group, members would be selected from different behavioral patterns and problem areas, and from all races, social strata, and educational backgrounds, as well as varying ages and both sexes. In the heterogeneous group, each member receives greater stimulation and is forced to examine and understand what is different about the other group members. The heterogeneous group also provides greater opportunities for reality testing.

A heterogeneous group still involves careful selection rather than a haphazard composition. If the counselor has a sound understanding of the personality dynamics and patterns of the individuals, he or she can more effectively organize a group.

Due to the limited amount of research specifically relating group composition to group process and outcome, there are no firm guidelines available. There is considerable theoretical speculation regarding the impact of composition for certain types of interaction. One theoretical position may be called the social microcosm theory; it suggests that a group is a representation of society in miniature. Learning takes place as the group members are exposed to others who are different from themselves. An ideal composition would allow a member to find parents, siblings, and interact with other individuals who could be transferred meaningful people in their lives. Obviously it would be difficult to compose a group of eight to ten individuals who could fill the microcosm for each of those members. A dissent theory suggests that individuals would learn new behaviors when their customary ways of behaving do not achieve their aim and, therefore, a heterogeneous group would maximize the learning opportunities for the members. The cohesion theory recommends that groups be formed along homogeneous lines since members who are alike are expected to have more in common and be more comfortable with one another and more quickly establish a warm supportive atmosphere in which to work. Another theoretical position has been called the support plus confrontation position; this suggests moderate diversity in the group composition. This type of composition would provide an atmosphere which supports group members, confronts their behavior, and provides alternatives. Most of the research regarding the different theoretical concepts has been of a laboratory nature, with few of them related to group counseling or therapy (Melnick and Woods, 1976).

From their review of the theory and research regarding group composition, Melnick and Woods (1976) propose some guidelines regarding group composition. They suggest that when attempting to resolve the issue of homogeneity—heterogeneity, it is helpful to look at the range of "patient—normal" interpersonal skills and behaviors of the members. Since group maintenance is an important issue in a patient population, they suggest a more homogeneous composition to decrease the initial discomfort and anxiety of the group members. When group members are "more normal," they can tolerate greater degrees of discomfort and conflict with less risk of premature dropouts, which would suggest composition in the direction of greater heterogeneity.

To best insure group maintenance, they suggest utilizing the available selection criteria for individuals with less risk of becoming deviant or prematurely terminating. There is also a recommendation to exclude individuals with a high probability of being incompatible with the total group or extremely incompatible with one other member. It is recommended that pre-training be used to work with members that are composed into a group.

Melnick and Woods suggest using the conceptualization of compatibility rather than homogeneity. Compatibility would insure personal attraction, cooperation, and productive interactions among the members. They suggest looking for homogeneity in composition and relying on the group task to provide sufficient conflict. Heterogeneity of membership is beneficial to the extent that it does not cost in cohesiveness. This principle would suggest avoiding extreme demographic heterogeneity and selecting to insure that group resources are varied enough to generate a warm responsive interaction and yet create confrontations and dissent sufficient to provide alternative behavior models.

Bugen (1977) conducted a study concerning the level of homogeneous grouping most conducive to the development of cohesion. He reported that groups composed of members with a moderate need for inclusion developed into the most cohesive groups. He suggested that individuals with both a high need for belonging and a low need for belonging were marked by deflated cohesive scores, indicating that counselors should be aware of personality extremes in composing their groups.

Lawlis and Klein (1973) found that cohesive ratings have a significant relationship after group therapy. They concluded that group cohesion relates to the outcomes of an interpersonal behavior, and recommend that compatibility of group members would be an asset to the final outcome and that leaders use compatibility as a measure of selection.

Open or Closed Group

A decision must be made before beginning the group as to whether it is to be open or closed. In a closed group, no new members are admitted, and it may meet for a predetermined number of sessions or until the group decides to terminate. In an open group, members are replaced as they leave the group so that it continues to function without a predetermined conclusion. A closed group is effective in that it has a stable population and time limits within which to work. It does present certain difficulties, however, as members decide to drop out or move.

Pros and Cons Many groups conducted in outpatient clinics are open groups. This permits the counselor to bring new members into the group as someone terminates, thus allowing the group to continue indefinitely. One advantage to this type of group is that members have new individuals with whom to interact and from whom to receive feedback. New members entering the group have old members to use as models. A major weakness of the open group concept is that the new members are not aware of the content that has been discussed previously, nor of the functioning of the group. An open group would have members at different levels of commitment to the process, and the group members would not be at the same stages of development. Such weaknesses would lead the group to less effectively working through the life stages to help each other.

Differences Four characteristics can be considered in differentiating between an open and a closed group: the time perspective, equilibrium, frame of reference, and the changing membership (Ziller, 1965).

The members of a closed group are together for a given period of time, while those of an open group are more aware of the transitory nature of their relationships. The closed group provides a more stable environment in which to develop reciprocity and loyalty. In an open group, reciprocity must be assumed, but it probably becomes a function of the individual and the group as a group.

The concept of equilibrium is concerned with the adjustment that must take place within the group as membership changes. Instability is a basic shortcoming of an open group. It is assumed that a constant state of disequilibrium is nonfunctional. Members of an open group would need to develop some coping procedures to minimize the disruptive effects. It would be important for the counselor to maintain a flow of members in and out of the group that would retain enough members and provide an appropriate heterogeneity to insure a steady state.

Frame of reference refers to the ground against which the figure is perceived.

In an open group, members have a larger population as a frame of reference with which to compare themselves than in a selected closed group.

The most obvious distinction between open and closed groups is the changing of group membership. Changes may be made strategically or merely in response to the exigencies of group life. Ziller (1965) gives considerable attention to an individual's power over another member. Power is relatively permanent in a closed group. In an open group, either member may leave, thereby changing the balance of power. As new members enter a group, the subgroups will be concerned about their allegiance. Obviously, this will affect the equilibrium of the group. If the counselor conducts an open group she or he must develop a strategy to work through individual termination and its effect on the group as well as the assimilation of the new member into the group.

Duration

Most groups take considerable time to warm up to personal communication and to work through some of the major themes in the session. It is difficult for a group to become personally involved and productive in less than ninety minutes or more than two hours. Much of the folklore around the conduct of groups assumes that after a period of two hours, the members become less productive and a point of diminishing returns is reached.

There has been considerable experimentation with time. The most widely publicized variation has involved the marathon group, which may meet for twelve, twenty-four, or forty-eight hours. The participants remain together for the entire designated times, during which meals are served and rest breaks are scheduled. The impetus on the group is total self-disclosure with intensive affective involvement and interpersonal confrontation. Several advantages have been claimed for the extended use of time in the group. The development of the group is said to accelerate more quickly, members undergo a more intense emotional experience, and the entire course of counseling may be covered in one period of time. The fatigue resulting from the constant interaction and lack of sleep contributes to the members abandoning their usual facades. To date, research indicating that the extended time concept is more beneficial for group functioning or individual member growth has been inconclusive. For most counseling groups, the extended time concept is not necessary. Consequently, limited time duration sessions are usually the rule. This also permits members to take advantage of growth between sessions.

Another aspect of the duration of the group involves the number of times the group will meet. Although some intensive groups meet two to five times per week, the majority of groups meet once a week.

A further component of the duration of the group involves the number of meetings. In an open group, the number of meetings could vary for each member. In a closed group, however, it is possible to establish a specific number of meetings. The advantage of a specific number of meetings is that a time limit on the life of a group is provided, and members are forced to work within that time span. Such a requirement can reduce resistance and encourage the members to work quickly to achieve their goals. Obviously, it is possible for members to use the time limit to protect themselves and to avoid getting involved in working through specific areas. A weakness of the specified number of meetings could arise when a group has not sufficiently worked through the stages of interaction to such a point that it has productively met group and individual goals. Termination at such a specific point would then be highly frustrating to the group members, and it may be advisable to renegotiate at that time for another specified number of meetings.

Preparation Interview

The counselor should inform the members of the meeting place, the length of each meeting, and the number of group meetings per week. Most clients who enter group counseling appreciate an explanation of how the group will proceed. Even so, this explanation will generally not suffice in alerting the client to the actual counseling process.

Yalom (1975) states that the most effective use of the preparation interview is to help the clients recognize and work through misconceptions and unrealistic beliefs or expectations of group counseling. The counselor may help members to participate more effectively by offering a structure or outlining some concepts about the group's behavior. Misconceptions and expectations need to be explored in detail and given a sufficient discussion. A counselor can help the group in its development by offering a conceptual framework and clear guidelines to effective behavior. Each member's preparation is individualized according to expressed concerns and the amount of prior knowledge he or she may have about group counseling.

Each member should be given a brief explanation about the group process. The majority of problems that are experienced by people involve conflicts in relating with others. Consequently, a social situation can provide the best opportunity to learn new modes of behavior. The member is warned that working within the group will not be easy, but that open and honest responses to the other members will be beneficial to others as well as to the member. There are obvious risks to be taken in learning new behaviors, but the group setting provides a place for reality testing.

The clients are warned of some of the discouraging feelings that may occur in early meetings. Some of their expectations will not be met, and they may be frustrated with the functioning of the group. However, they are encouraged to remain with the group rather than withdraw.

Most counselors suggest that the members do not socialize outside the group meetings. The group is a situation for one to resolve social problems and not a place to meet new friends. Even so, when members do meet outside the group, it is important that they discuss the incident and the content of their meeting when they return to the group.

Yalom (1975) offers two practical observations about the preparation interview. First, the counselor should deliberately repeat and emphasize the important points of the preparation, because clients are frequently in a state of high anxiety and have a tendency toward selective attention, or they may misunderstand. Second, he suggests that the counselor would be wiser to conduct a group with smaller membership than to try to sell the group to a client.

Pre-Counseling Training   One of the major problems in effectively initiating group counseling is transforming a group of individuals into a productive counseling group. Bednar et al. (1974) reviewed the literature and gave guidelines regarding pre-counseling training. They concluded that the clarity with which clients understand the process of group developments, group goals, counselor and client roles, and the benefits that can be gained from group participation represent the general parameters of effective group treatment. Secondly, pre-counseling training, in which the counselor systematically prepares clients for group participation at both the cognitive and behavioral levels, seems to be an effective and responsible way of achieving the benefits that can result from clients understanding their role in group counseling.

Pre-counseling training is usually defined in terms of (1) clarifying client role expectations, (2) clarifying the counseling process, and (3) providing video or audio models of desirable client behavior. A review of the literature suggests that vicarious learning is particularly influential in pre-counseling training in effecting both process and outcome. Bednar et al. suggest that a full explanation and description of the value of the expected behavior should precede the vicarious learning situation. Cognitive learning should precede vicarious behavior learning with an audio or video tape presentation of a group counseling session.

Heitler (1974) conducted a study on the preparation of lower-class clients for group counseling. He reported that the group counselor tended to rate the prepared clients as more involved, as closer to the ideal model group counseling client, as demonstrating more dependable and self-initiated collaborative efforts in exploring personal difficulty, and as having more hopeful prognosis than controlled clients. The direct observational measure consistently indicated that they tended to have lower latencies for voluntary participation, to communicate more frequently, to spend more clock time communicating, to communicate more frequently on a self-initiated basis, and to engage in exploratory efforts more frequently.

Structure

The general goal of group counseling is to induce positive psychological change in the client. Most counselors emphasize client self-exploration, insight, and self-understanding leading to behavior change as a method of attaining client goals. Opinions differ regarding how the group should be structured to accomplish this process.

Those advocating an unstructured situation believe that such an atmosphere is more relevant to client needs, and is conducive to self-exploration and the acquisition of more effective behavior repertoires. The less structured the goals, tasks, and activities of the group, the more capable it becomes of gaining awareness of the psychological relationships among its members. The purpose of the counseling group is generally to uncover the work through the member's problem areas to an emotionally corrective experience. Analyzing the relationships among the group members serves as a major method for understanding inter- and intrapersonal conflicts. To the individual, it may seem that analyzing the members' relationships is irrelevant to solving his or her particular problem; the individual generally may not acknowledge that his or her feelings and behavior in the group situation are similar to those in outside life. There may be a resistance to discussing a problem with other individuals.

To escape the distress and anxiety inherent in unstructured situations, the members of any group devise their own structure through tasks, rules, status differential, activities, and goals. In addition, they resort to habitual ways of coping with anxiety by invoking their defense mechanisms. Structuring the group situation with more formal goal-directed procedures serves to inhibit a deeper experiencing of self.

Critics of the unstructured approach argue that the lack of structure in early sessions fails to facilitate group development and feeds client distortions and interpersonal fears (Bednar, Melnick, and Kaul, 1974). Since patterns of behavior established early in the group tend to persist, it is important to help the members develop productive behaviors.

It is suggested that structured interpersonal exercises can be used to enhance learning new behaviors that can facilitate group development and client improvement. Structured experiences may vary from encounter group exercises to merely modeling and describing appropriate behaviors.

Bednar, Melnick, and Kaul (1974) present a framework for early group structure which includes cognitive learning, vicarious learning, and behavioral practice. Group members can be exposed to the concepts of group counseling by the counselor's discussing the fact that most group members usually have some interpersonal difficulties, and although they may find it difficult at first, they need to explore their own feelings with the other members. The group members should also be warned that unrealistic expectations for quick change may lead to discouragement.

After discussing the process of interpersonal openness and sharing feelings, the group may be exposed to audio- or videotaped examples of appropriate behaviors. Through this experience, they can see or hear examples of self-exploration, interpersonal feedback, and group confrontation. It is important to discuss their feelings and attitudes about the examples.

After observing the process, members can engage in practicing some of the behaviors under low-threat conditions. They can share personal information with dyads or triads, and then with the whole group.

It is assumed that after a structured beginning the group will move quickly, express the specific content of their problems, and respond with more appropriate behaviors. Once the group begins, individual personalities will come into play, and it will take considerable time to work out consistent member roles.

The Bednar et al. (1974) model proposes that client exposure to levels of personal risk and responsibility most conducive to optimal group and individual development can be regulated by the use of group structure. It is suggested that structure tends to reduce the members' personal responsibility for behavior in early group sessions, thereby increasing the potential for high risking behaviors and the development of group cohesion in later group meetings. The risk of meaningful interpersonal exploration at high levels of personal responsibility is reduced by the successful development of cohesion at the appropriate levels. Group development is viewed as proceeding through sequential steps of initial ambiguity, increased structure, increased risk taking, development of group cohesion from shared group experiences, and increased personal responsibility.

Lee and Bednar (1977) conducted a study of the effects of group structure and risk-taking disposition on the members' behavior and attitudes. They found that both structure and risk-taking disposition were potent determinants of the degree to which members participated in behaviors which are presumed to be relevant to positive change. The high-structure condition dramatically increased the level of relevant, and presumably risky, communication of the low risk-taking members. In fact, the observed behavior of the low risk-taking members in the high-structure conditions was essentially identical to that of the high risk-taking members. It is interesting to note that the evaluative attitudes and group cohesion were the most negative in the treatment condition with the highest levels of meaningful interpersonal communication. Lee and Bednar argued that the high structure and high risk-taking disposition conditions did produce the highest frequency of personal and interpersonal communication and simultaneously could be the most meaningful and distressing. The assessment of the group experience and atmosphere made in close proximity to the peak periods of subjective distress could contribute to the negative feelings. Even so, the candid quality of the group interaction was sufficiently attractive to the members that, irrespective of the discomfort involved, seven out of twelve treatment groups continued meeting after the group workshop was completed.

Lee and Bednar pointed out that the concepts of group structure and risk-taking disposition are potent variables affecting early group behavior and attitudes. Both the helpful and harmful effects of these variables need further programmatic research.

Levin and Kurtz (1974) examined the effects of structured and nonstructured groups on human relations training, and stated that members in structured groups reported greater ego involvement, self-perceived personality changes, and group unity than did group members in nonstructured groups. The greater ego involvement and unity in structured groups may result from a greater opportunity for participation afforded by the use of structured exercises. Structured exercises not only permit but to some extent require all members to participate in the group interaction. Also, structured exercises often require members to behave in ways which are not ordinarily encouraged or sanctioned in their other interactions. In a nonstructured group, the nonverbal, shy, or apprehensive members can maintain an inactive role, and thereby experience little or no opportunity for personality change.

Crews and Melnick (1976) examined the facilitative effect of initial and delayed structure on group development. They found that initial structure was associated with increased levels of self-disclosure during early group meetings as well as higher levels of anxiety among group members. However, the effects of structure dissipated over time. The structure did not have an influence on the degree of group cohesion. It appears that structuring the group during the initial phases is an effective way to increase self-disclosure among members. Likewise, it appears that it will increase the anxiety of the members, and the leader must be prepared to deal with this.

There are some suggestions for using structure in the early stages of counseling. The structured exercises should be consistent with the expected outcomes of group participation. Another consideration guiding the choice of structured exercises should be the central role of feedback in group interaction. The exercises should provide opportunity for giving and receiving feedback; however, an atmosphere of psychological safety is a necessary condition for this to occur. Early exercises can be designed to foster the development of such an atmosphere, while later exercises may focus primarily on feedback and, still later, on confrontation. Structured exercises are presented in numerous group manuals.

The concepts discussed above underscore the amount of thought and preparation involved in the process of group development even before the initial session. The extent to which the counselor has worked out decisions in each of these areas will be reflected in the critical initiation phase of group development.

STAGE ONE: INITIATING THE GROUP

The first aspect of group development is the process of getting acquainted. During this period of time, the members generally reveal their "safer" or more public aspects. They describe themselves in terms of previous experience, but this seldom includes personally relevant material that has not been rehearsed or told before. Some members may adopt a protective withdrawal from even that process.

The behavior of members during the initial stage is relatively restricted. The usual social code for behavior with strangers or company is typically followed. Problems presented are usually discussed rationally, and members tend to be supportive and polite to each other. This social behavior permits members to learn who may respond favorably to them and whom they may fear or respect. From these interactions, they begin to formulate a concept of the role each expects to play in the group. The early stage of the group is thus characterized by a degree of caution and self-verification behavior.

The primary task for the members in a new group is to determine a method of achieving their individual goals. As a part of that primary task, they must resolve their social relationships in the group. Generally, they are wondering if they will be liked and respected or rejected by the other members. If they are unsure or think they may be rejected, they are prone to deprecate the group and feel that it is an artificial situation. Individuals frequently wonder what is expected, how much of themselves will have to be revealed, and what type of commitment must be made to these other people. The type of self-exploration that does occur in early meetings is not a spontaneous searching but more of a description of past experiences. People describe themselves to others as if they were objects. Only that which is safe to describe is revealed during this stage.

It is common for people who come together in a counseling group to initially interact almost entirely in terms of transference: they project their unconscious fantasy objects upon other members and then try to manipulate them accordingly. Each member will stay in the role assigned by another only if it happens to coincide with his or her own fantasies. Group members tend to approach a new group setting by merely repeating old patterns of behavior with new individuals. This behavior may be successful or unsuccessful, and frequently becomes the focus of the interaction process.

During the initial stage, an individual tends to perceive the group as an undifferentiated mass. He or she may pick one or two individuals for special attention, but this will probably be on the basis of a transference. At the same time, most other members in the group are perceiving the group in a similar way. So the first shared perception of the group members is that the group is an undifferentiated mass. This creates a rather tenuous state of affairs. If a member acts on his or her perception of a specific individual in the group, the distorted view of the latter will likely produce an abortive or confused interaction. If the member behaves according to the perception of the group as an undifferentiated mass, he or she may suddenly hear a rather overwhelming echo from the other group members.

For a while a culture evolves in the group that maximizes the opportunity for most members to play their private roles. However, as time goes by, more and more reality begins to intrude into their perceptions of one another. The most dramatic aspect is brought about by having a common object for fantasy projections. The presence of an ambiguous authority figure allows the members to share fantasy. It is through the process of developing this shared realtionship that a new reality is formed that permits the members to confront one another.

The sharing of fantasies about the leader tends to rescue the members from the situation; initially, it is the best group remedy. The leader is differentiated from the mass partly because it is easier to do so, but also to counterbalance this mass, to create a hero or heroine. But this differentiated leader does not necessarily produce clear differentiations among the members. There are many groups that do not progress far beyond this point. It may take an attack on the leader—a type of revolt—to bring forward the differences in the members' attitudes toward the leader. In other words, the group could not effectively revolt as long as it perceives itself as a mass.

This whole process may concern the individual because it blurs the boundary between self and the group as a whole. Slater (1966) suggests that the blurring of boundaries between the individual and the group tends to occur when the group members experience sudden reinforcement by the group of feelings, impulses, and fantasies of which they are not fully conscious. Bion's (1959) concept of flight and fight are both mechanisms for warding off this state when it arises. (See discussion in context of psychoanalytic theory, Chapter 2.) Both fight and flight serve to protect the boundaries that distinguish one individual from another. By fighting, the individual is saying "I am I, and I am different from you." By fleeing, the individual simply removes himself or herself from involvement.

Slater (1966) indicates that fight-flight pertains to a primitive level of boundary awareness and that it can be expected in the early sessions of a group. Groups frequently display a polite and civilized veneer while their acquaintanceships are still casual. There may be long and tense silences in which unconscious fears of group envelopment may be pressing, and there may be manic flights when no one listens to anyone else but only talks loudly to herself or himself. As the group continues, involvement increases, and more layers of the personality are engaged in the group situation. Cultural techniques of interpersonal facade generally fall away and deeper feelings surface. At the same time, self-awareness, awareness of group identity, and intragroup differentiation are all increasing, so that at the point where these most primitive fears about the group might become visible, they are already in a state of decay.

The Relationship

The first major concern of counselors is to provide a situation that reduces the threat to the members, thereby permitting them further self-exploration. If counselors are to be helpful to the group, a relationship must exist which is characterized by the counselors' genuineness, experiencing of positive regard for the members, and expression of empathic understanding.

Counselors must be genuine or congruent in the relationship. They must not display a facade or play a role but must behave exactly as they feel. They not only mean what they say, but also match what they feel to what they are expressing—behavior, feelings, and attitudes that exist within them. This is the only way the relationship can have reality for the group member.

Another facilitative condition in the relationship is the counselor's experiencing an empathic understanding of the member's world and being able to commuicate this to the member. The counselor senses the feelings and personal meaning that the individual is experiencing. When the counselor is able to perceive these as they seem to the group member and can successfully communicate some of this understanding this condition is fulfilled.

A good counseling relationship requires that the counselor experience a warm, positive attitude toward the client. This probably is the first element that the counselor must be able to communicate to the group member. It means that the counselor cares for the individual in a nonpossessive way as a person with potentiality. The counselor respects the client and gives him or her positive regard. The more the positive regard is unconditional, the more effective and safer the relationship will be. The fewer the conditions a counselor places on the client, the more unconditional his or her positive regard will be. This is an acceptance of and regard for the person's attributes at the moment, no matter how negative or positive they may be—there are no strings attached. Acceptance of the fluctuating feelings of the individual makes the client-counselor relationship warm and safe. It means the individual does not have to hide parts of himself or herself, behave in certain ways, or play a certain game for the counselor to pay attention and accept him or her as a person.

Nichols and Taylor (1975) conducted a study of the impact of counselor interventions on early sessions; they chose this focus because the group is probably more susceptible to influence during its initiation. They analyzed the three dimensions of facilitation, interpretation, and confrontation interventions that were made to individuals, total group, two or more persons, and the co-leader. Simple facilitation tends to produce higher mean focusing than all other types of interventions. Apparently, in early sessions the most productive interventions are those designed simply to encourage clients to talk and interact. Clarifications and interpretations may be more productive after group cohesiveness is developed.

Although we have presented the facilitative conditions a counselor offers, it becomes paramount that group members offer the same conditions to each other. Members must accept other members. The counselor will serve as a model for the group members in providing an atmosphere that is safe enough for self-exploration.

Goal Setting

Goal setting is a process of stating desired outcomes to be carried out in the group process. It is accomplished by defining group goals and subgoals that implement individual behavioral objectives. The more specific and operational the goals are, the more value they will be to the group. When nonoperational goals are established, there is a tendency toward greater apathy and intragroup conflict, as well as confusion.

Counseling goals can be process goals, general group goals, and individual goals. Process goals come out of self-exploration and interpersonal interaction of the members. Such process goals will lead to greater self-understanding in the areas of concern to the individuals. The self-understanding serves as a base for action in carrying out desired behavior. Group goals involve the process goals but may include generally accepted areas of concern. Individual goals are the subgoals of specific concern.

The desired outcomes that will take effect in the members as a result of the counseling process may suggest changes in the way members think or feel about themselves, or may involve behavioral changes. Generally, changes in the way a person thinks or feels also include establishing new behaviors. Broad goals can be expected to hold for all members in the group. In addition, individual members will establish subgoals and probably specific objectives for themselves.

Ryan (1973) focuses attention on the importance of operationalizing group counseling goals. Group goals are operationalized when broad statements of intent for the group are analyzed into cognitive, affective, and behavioral dimensions, which in turn can be described as behavioral objectives for individual members. Behavioral objectives include specific, pertinent, obtainable, measurable, and observable behavior that will result from planned intervention. Ryan suggests that operationalizing group goals has four advantages that increase the likelihood of counseling success: (1) operationalized goals produce more homogeneity in the group's shared interest; (2) operationalized goals contribute to more realistic expectations; (3) operationalized goals lead to more highly motivated members because they know what they are working for; and (4) operationalized goals make the group members more interdependent as they are able to see how goals for other members fit into their objectives as well.

There are certain problems in the process of goal setting for a group. The importance of a particular group goal for any person in the group may be influenced by individual needs. Obviously, goal setting is a part of the counseling process which must be accomplished jointly by the counselor and the group members. If a counselor establishes the goals for the group, he or she may not be aware of the members' individual goals underneath the umbrella of the general goal for the group. The extent to which group goals implement personal goals will vary from time to time throughout the group. Despite these difficulties involved in the goal-setting process, however, it is one of the most important avenues to success in group counseling.

Contracting   Contract negotiations help establish the therapeutic atmosphere in the group quickly. Contracts also acquaint the group with each other's difficulties and provide an opportunity for the counselor to clarify the fact that his or her sincere desire to help is circumscribed. This reduces vague promises that the group may somehow enrich life or provide instant happiness.

Meeks (1973) recommends the use of contracts rather than a list of rules. He believes that the treatment contract obviates the need for routine rules. He does mention the advisability of regular attendance, with notification if members are going to miss. He also mentions the advisability of announcing the planned duration of the group and discussing the need for confidentiality and commitment to confidential material. The counselor also begins the group with an emphasis that all group members commit themselves to the clear treatment contract. This contract represents an agreement between the counselor and each member concerning the member's goals. It is serious, concrete, and usually binding. That is, the member agrees to work as hard as possible and to achieve the goal. Every effort is made to have the contract specific and behaviorally concrete; however, general goals may be appropriate in this early stage, and they may be re-defined or made more specific when the group reaches a more productive stage.

Meeks (1973) talks about the idea of acceptable temporary contracts in counseling. This suggests that the group may begin with working toward temporary contracts, and indicates the need to re-define goals once the group reaches a more productive stage.

Structure   Structure is a multidimensional concept that can be useful for deliberately influencing group processes by focusing and controlling group attention and behavior. Recent literature suggests that the appropriate use of structure, particularly in the early stages of the group, represents a powerful force which does affect both group participant attitudes and behaviors. It has been proposed that client exposure to levels of risk and responsibility most conducive to group development can be regulated by the use of group structure (Bednar, Melnick, and Kaul, 1974). The conceptual model assumes that the structure tends to reduce group members' personal responsibility during early sessions, thereby increasing the potential for higher risk-taking behavior and the development of group cohesion from shared group experiences. In later group sessions, the risk of meaningful interpersonal exploration at higher levels of personal responsibility is reduced by the level of group cohesion appropriate to the group task. Although a great deal of focus is placed on pre-group structuring, there is a place for structuring again during the group process. Group development is viewed as beginning with the initial ambiguity, followed by increased structure from the leader, which can lead to increased risk taking and development of group cohesion, which can lead to increased personal responsibility.

Some approaches to group counseling minimize the conceptual importance and practical use of structure as a means of facilitating a group process, personal insight, and behavior change. Other approaches maximize the role of structure and goal-oriented group processes. Bednar and Battersby (1976) investigated the effects of three pre-group mediated messages on the early group development. The messages focused on group clarity, behavioral instructions, and persuasive explanations.

A consistent and relevant finding of the study was that specific behavior instructions were associated with desirable group development as measured by group cohesion, work-oriented interpersonal communication, and favorable attitudes toward groups. An interesting part of this study was the finding that goal clarity and expectations for improvement in interpersonal behavior have long been considered important variables. A possible explanation offered for their lack of influence was that brevity of the messages contravened the power and complexity of the concepts so that they could not activate client behavior. On the other hand, the behavioral descriptions were more concrete and provided tangible and immediate guides for behavior.

Group Identity

The effective development of any group requires that members share an image of the group. In the beginning, members bring individual images of the group. Each anticipates what the group will do, what its purposes are, and how it should function. These concepts are based primarily on past experience. Although each individual has a separate image for the group, there are usually enough shared ideas to find some common ground on which to build. To develop stability, order, and a pattern of interaction to meet their goals, a group is involved in the process of achieving a common identity in the minds of the group members. This identity is a definition of the situation held in common, which provides a source of continuing expectations of behavior of one's self and others (Zaleznik and Moment, 1964).

The definition of the situation involves the processes through which the members select and organize perceptions of reality as a basis for their action. In the early phases of group development, the members spend considerable time in developing a definition of the situation that can be held collectively. This permits a degree of routine in the interaction between the members, and their behavior becomes more predictable. The combination of routine and predictability reduces the ambiguity and anxiety, and it permits the members to focus their attention on achieving the group goals. When the situation is vague and members are not sure of what they are to do or of other members' behaviors, uncertainty and tension will be evoked. It should be noted that complete routine and predictability are neither beneficial nor possible. When unexpected behavior does occur, some members will be uncomfortable and the group will focus its attention on reducing the discomfort.

In any strange social situation, an individual assumes the most comfortable behavior in an attempt to deal with the ambiguity. After the individual has gathered the "lay of the land," he or she will have more flexibility in behavior or will work out an accommodation. A joking behavior between members who feel uncomfortable in a situation is one way of coping with the ambiguity. Some individuals isolate themselves from the group to minimize interaction and thus reduce anxiety. In other instances, some members may use one individual as a scapegoat. It is more socially acceptable to deal with disagreements by joking or withdrawing than to confront disjunctive ideas with other members in the group.

The definition of a situation involves the use of experience and learned behavior from the past with persons in the present. As the members' expectations are met, some sense of routine, predictability, and emotional balance will develop. Thus, in defining the situation, there is a consensus in the minds of the group members around a common set of images of the present group.

Not all definitions of the situation have positive effects. In fact, a shared acceptance of routine and predictability can serve as a dysfunction in the group. For example, the process of stereotyping consists of classifying new experiences and individuals by using symbols learned in the past. If the group members stereotype one of their group, there may be a consensus about that person, but it would be dysfunctional in the group as they would not get to know the person as an individual. The more the group can experiment in interpersonal relationships rather than relying on routine past interactions, the more the group members can learn. One of the chief characteristics of creative persons is their high capacity to tolerate ambiguity without becoming overanxious. Consequently, if the group develops a stable routine interaction, it may decrease their problem solving and creative work.

Overt and Covert Definitions   It is important to understand the two levels of group identity. One level is the overt and manifest identity, while the other is covert or hidden from the conscious awareness of the members. If there are conflicts between the overt and covert definitions, productive behavior may be blocked. This type of conflict is frequently considered as a hidden agenda, in which the announced goals of the group may be used to provide content for a covert goal. Although the stated goal of the group centers around a task to be accomplished, members may have a hidden agenda, such as competition or flirtation.

Dimensions of Group Identity   It is important to identify the elements that can contribute to the establishment of group identity. Zaleznik and Moment (1964) suggest four dimensions which provide cues in the development of group identity: (1) the location of the group in time and space; (2) the expectation conditioned by past exerience; (3) the symbols expressing the definition of the situation; and (4) the membership in the group, that is, the characteristics of the persons included and excluded from participation.

Time and Space   The place of the group in time and space is an important element in the development of group identity. Time places a group at some point in the cycle or rhythm of the day and the week, and individual responses are governed in large part by the routine of a day. There is also a time span expectancy of the group. Group members come to expect Wednesday afternoon as a time of the group. It is a time in the rhythm of life, not only of that day but of the total week. In the same sense, they may build a time span expectancy in which they know this will occur for ten weeks or six months or until they decide to terminate. The more transient a group is in the life of its members, the less it may command membership involvement. Even so, a short-term group with an important purpose may create a sense of urgency in the members and a high degree of emotional commitment.

The location of a group also helps in the development of an identity. The physical setting in which the group functions becomes important in its definition. Just as it is important that a family's space in the house presents boundaries separating it from others, each group needs a sense of privacy and boundaries to establish its separate identity. A group will usually develop some identification with the location of the room, and protect that privacy and the boundaries from infringement. Even after the group has terminated, the members will carry images of the room as well as people within the setting. Thus, a specific time and space helps individuals conceptualize themselves as a part of this particular group.

Expectations   Individuals who enter a group bring expectations conditioned by past experiences. The situation is anticipated in at least two senses: the taking of roles, and affective or emotional states. Role taking involves acting in accordance with a specific behavior pattern. The acts are usually tied to norms of how persons should behave in a specific situation. These should usually define a range of appropriate actions, and each individual plays the role as an integral part of his or her personality within this range. The roles that a person uses in the group will be affected by his or her own personality. Nonetheless, role taking will also be defined by the activities performed by other group members and by the style of interaction that is expected from them. The anticipation of taking certain roles is a form of fantasy in which the person imagines future events and fantasizes what people will do. The sources of these images are usually carry-overs from past experiences. Since everyone may not mesh in the roles that they take, or may not meet the expectations of other people, it may take time to develop an identity of who different members are, the roles they play, and eventually the establishment of some predictable way of interacting with each other. These elements are all part of the process that leads to a stronger group identity and eventual cohesiveness.

Without a set of emotions appropriate to the situation, role taking would be empty and would proceed without any involvement. Members learn to associate a particular range of emotional states with situational requirements. Situations also have the capacity to induce the appropriate state in the members. Some of this stems from sharing a mood once the group begins. The sharing is related to the contagion emotions, but much of the induction of emotion states that are appropriate to it become a part of identifying with the group.

Symbols and Group Identity   Symbols in a situation can play an important part in formulating group identity. The importance of the symbolic value of objects resides in their capacity to become invested with emotion and meaning. In certain types of groups—not related to counseling—there may be tangible objects which help members to identify with the group. Such objects as sweatshirts, insignia, or tools are all overt symbols of an identification with a particular group. In counseling groups, persons frequently give off cues or symbols that have to do with personal identification. In a newly formed group, the members will observe a series of cues given off by other members, either consciously or unconsciously. These cues will symbolize how the individuals want to be perceived and the kinds of positions or roles they expect to fulfill in the group. Some of these personal symbols will have to do with factors that the individual cannot control, such as age, sex, and race, and expectations of a person relating to age and sex may develop. Other attributes of the symbols of position and role are less obvious. Such attributes as education, ethnic and religious background, socioeconomic class, occupation, and marital status can be converted into cues in the course of interaction. The way the person dresses, stands, or sits, and the way the person talks communicate cues which other individuals recognize; the cues indicate how the person expects to relate to others. An individual will also verbally communicate some expectations, which may be symbols for personal identification; that is, the individual may communicate a wish for a dependency relationship, thereby symbolizing himself or herself as a weaker individual.

The individual symbols do not contribute to group identity and do not show a group identity. As noted above, a counseling group does not usually wear a sweatshirt symbolizing identification with the group, nor will it usually present other external symbols of the group identity.

Membership   Assigned membership to a group should not be confused with actual membership in the social-sociological sense. Who is accepted or rejected is an integral part of the identity of a group, and this process conditions behavior and attitudes of the members. Merely because a client is selected by the counselor to participate in the group is no sure sign that the client will accept the membership or that other members will accept the client. To accept membership, the individual must be willing to go along with the goals of the group. To be accepted by the other members, the individual needs to participate in the process.

Members usually search for and are delighted to find similarities among the other members. They are happy to find individuals who agree with their ideas and have had similar experiences. It is gratifying to find that one's problems are not unique. This process offers some relief and early support to members and suggests areas in which group cohesiveness can be found.

Determinants of Group Identity   What are some of the variables that determine the ease with which an individual can develop identity with the group? Zaleznik and Moment (1964) propose three main classes of determinants of group identity: (1) the culture, (2) the group purpose, and (3) identification with the leader.

The Culture   A culture is learned by an individual as a result of belonging to a particular group—constituting that part of learned behavior which is shared by others in that group. It is the individual's social legacy—the total way of life of a people. The term is an abstraction referring to the interrelated modes of behavior that an individual learns as a member in a particular society, and that the individual brings into new groups. It is a way of thinking, feeling, and believing. The culture is the group knowledge that is stored up for future use.

The experience of an individual in and through a culture will determine the individual's behavior in a group. Obviously, groups can create new forms of behavior that will result in cultural change over time.

Although all the elements of group identity are culturally derived, no two individuals experience a culture the same way. A pluralistic society contains regional, ethnic, and socioeconomic class differences that permit wide variations in styles of life and cultural values.

The counselor needs to be alert to the effect of varying values and perceptions of events that are based on cultural conditioning. Group relationships will be affected in terms of past cultural experiences of the individuals. The development of group identity will generally resemble the shared patterns taken from the cultural experiences of the group members. In groups with a great degree of heterogeneity, the process of developing a group identity becomes more difficult simply because the cultural backgrounds of the members vary. Until the members are able to develop a common definition of the situation, some feelings of conflict will exist, particularly where group members are motivated to remain in the group and overt withdrawal is not easy.

The Group Purpose　Another force in determining identity of a group stems from the goals of the group. If there is a clear purpose for the group's existence, members will be able to develop some identity with that purpose, since it meets a personal need. However, if the purpose of the group is vaguely defined, or if the individuals cannot personally identify with the purpose of the group, there will be a slower and more difficult process of defining the situation and developing a total group identity. Groups in which the participants are selected or placed rather than volunteering are more likely to experience difficulty in identifying with the purpose of the group. This is not to say that they will not develop this identification with the group purpose, but the process may take longer.

Identification with the Leader　The leader can serve as a source of cohesion among group members in their shared attachment to her or him. Their identification with the leader becomes a common element in the experience of the group members and helps bind them to each other. When group members identify with the leader, their loyalties serve to establish a definition of the situation. Many of the relationships are bound in the leader's activity, and the leader's values are accepted by the group members. In addition, the leader's behavior becomes a model for them.

Jeske (1973) found that clients feel a more positive change when they identify more frequently with group members. While the results do not demonstrate that improvement in therapy is caused by identification, they do suggest that members in group therapy who identify frequently receive a greater benefit than those who identify rarely. This suggests that identification in the group should be encouraged and opportunities for maximum identification between group members should be created. While homogeneous grouping of clients is one method of providing opportunities for identification, identification also took place with subjects whose problems were different from their own presenting problems.

Engagement in the Process

To enable the counseling process to move forward effectively, the client must become involved in the process. When people approach group counseling, they usually have some ambivalent feelings about it. They would like to improve—provided the experiences necessary to bring about their improvement are not too threatening. Any learning situation, however, does pose a threat to the individual's perception of self and to the perceptions others have of the individual. The questions that face each member are: How much a self-investment am I willing to make? How close do I want to be to the other group members? Each is concerned about acceptance by the group and about the ability to measure up to the expectations of others. Each member is uncertain as to what he or she can contribute, and defense mechanisms are high (Bradford, 1963). The counselor then must help the clients deal with these feelings of ambivalence. Each client has to learn how to "allow himself to experience certain feelings despite strong resistances to them and he must express these feelings; he must be trained to talk (Kelman, 1963, p. 403)."

Kelman (1963) viewed the role of the counselor in this part of the process as essentially that of a trainer. The counselor helps the clients learn appropriate behavior in the counseling sessions by responding to those statements of the clients that will lead to patterns of growth. The counselor directs the tone of the sessions by approving of some behaviors and disapproving of others. An active counselor will interpret statements and on occasion will confront a member. A more nondirective counselor will indicate a desired direction by responding to some statements and not to others. The group member becomes aware of these subtle cues and learns to respond in the expected manner. These responses to the cues of the counselor indicate some compliance on the part of the member. In essence the member is agreeing to play the game by the counselor's rules. The danger is that the member does just that—plays the game. The member learns all the right phrases and the right behavior, but without any emotional involvement. He or she is then at a superficial level, a level at which lasting behavior change will not occur. The issue at this point involves the ways the group can help the individual member engage in the counseling process. Corsini (1957) states that while the group leader may be of greatest value to the group process because of special training, the leader is far from the sole ingredient. To fail to consider the impact of the total group would be an error.

Hobbs (1951) suggests that the counselor's most challenging task in a new group situation is the need to release the therapeutic potential of the group itself. Kelman (1963) feels that "the group members can serve as additional sanctioning agents who can apply various kinds of pressure on the individual client to conform to the requirements of the situation and engage in therapeutic work (p. 410)." The group has many powerful techniques for influencing the behavior of its members. The most persuasive of these is the individual's desire to become an accepted member of the group. Because the individual is seeking this membership, peer efforts at influence may be more clearly heard than efforts made by the counselor. If the individual complies with the group's expectations and engages in the counseling process, he or she may be rewarded by the group through praise and encouragement. On the other hand, the group can be just as powerful in discouraging behavior that detracts from the counseling process. Hence the individual responds to demands of the group to the extent that the group acts as a source of acceptance and approval for that individual.

By virtue of its power to establish the norms for the counseling sessions, the group can help or hinder the counseling process. The norms of the group may be established in such a way that to engage in the counseling process reduces the individual's value in the eyes of fellow group members. The counselor must be aware of this possibility, and his or her influence must be used to encourage the group to develop norms that are conducive to the counseling process. In this stage of counseling, it is imperative that the counselor and the group cooperate to create a climate in which each individual will become engaged in a counseling process.

Self-Exploration   The process of counseling involves the group in providing a facilitative relationship in which each individual will feel safe enough to explore himself or herself. This self-exploration and interpersonal feedback from other members will lead to a greater degree of self-understanding as well as a better understanding of the environment. Ideally, this increased understanding would lead to the person's behavior changing to become more effective. When the person is able to behave more effectively, he or she will have an increase in self-regard. In many cases, however, the understanding does not lead directly to change in behavior, and the counselor must intervene to help the individual try some new behaviors.

Therefore, the counselor encourages self-exploration as a major goal in the initial stage, keeping in mind the different levels of self-exploration of each individual. Carkhuff (1967) has propsoed a five-point scale to examine self-exploration. At the first level, the client avoids any self-description or self-exploration that would reveal personal feelings to the group. At this level, clients probably do not trust their own feelings and may not like themselves well enough to offer their inner feelings. This lack of self-exploration is a common occurrence in beginning counseling. At the second level of self-exploration, the client will respond with discussion to the introduction of personally relevant material by the counselor or another member. Such responses, however, are mechanical in manner and do not demonstrate any real feeling. The client is answering personal questions but is not doing any self-exploration. At this level the group will be able to learn about the member's present self-concept. At the third level, the member voluntarily introduces discussions of personally relevant material but does so mechanically and without demonstrating much feeling. This frequently is a volunteering of material that has already been privately rehearsed or has possibly been discussed with other persons previously. There is no spontaneity and no inward probing for new feelings or experiences. At the fourth level, the client voluntarily introduces personally relevant material in a spontaneous manner. The client is dealing with his or her present feeling level. This behavior may lead to the fifth level, in which clients actively and spontaneously probe into newly discovered feelings and experiences about themselves and their situation.

When this concept is expanded to the whole group, it can be described in Berzon's (1964) six stages of personalization. These stages are:

1. No personally relevant material is discussed.

2. Facts about public aspects of oneself are presented in an aloof, superficial manner.

3. There is "inward reference" for material.

4. There is increased emotional involvement on the part of group members in their own contributions and own reactions.

5. There is tentative probing and effort toward self-exploration and an inward search for discovery of new feelings.

6. Members are actively exploring their feelings, values, perceptions of others, fears, and life choices with emotional proximity to the material.

What are some things the counselor can do to help the group members engage in self-exploration? As well as presenting the various levels to conceptualize self-exploration, Carkhuff (1971) has suggested a number of guidelines to assist the counselor in the exploratory stage of counseling. First, the counselor must establish self-exploration by the member as an immediate goal. Without this starting point, the individual will not gain new insights and new understanding, nor will the individual be able to incorporate new behaviors into his or her pattern. Second, the counselor needs initially to understand the individual at the level of self-exploration presented. Exploration of personal material is most likely to occur when there is an understanding and a withholding of judgment by the counselor and the group. The member will move increasingly to initiate exploration and spontaneity if the counselor and group are willing to accept the member at each level. Third, the counselor should initially offer minimal levels of the facilitative conditions. When the counselor offers minimal levels of empathy, respect, concreteness, and genuineness, he or she establishes a relationship in which individuals can both explore and experience themselves. The minimal facilitative conditions enable individuals to know that the counselor understands them on their own terms and also provide them with the feedback necessary for later reformulations. The group members will use the counselor as a model, trying to accept and understand the individual. Fourth, the counselor should employ the individual's self-sustaining level of self-exploration as a guide for moving to the next stage in the counseling process. Within a given problem or topic area, the criterion for movement to the next stage of counseling can be the person's ability to deal with self-explorations. Fifth, the counselor should recognize a repetition of the cycle of self-exploration both within and between different content areas. When the group member works through the process and is able to explore herself or himself in terms of a situation with parents, for example, the member may begin at the first level of self-exploration again when the topic turns to the relationship with employer or teacher.

When the individual is able to deal with self-exploration and the immediate feelings, the counselor can help draw together the fragmented insights and help the person develop self-understanding. The early phase of self-exploration and understanding may lead to some action, but usually the implementation and follow-through occur during later stages of the group.

When a member presents a problem to the group, the other members typically offer advice through some practical solution. Although the advice is seldom effective in resolving the problem, it does provide an avenue for members to express an interest toward each other. However, the fact that simple solutions are not appropriate to their problems also yields some frustration with the group process.

What If the Group Is Not Working?

If the group does not seem to be moving and is apparently unproductive, it is imperative for the leader to examine self, style, and techniques. As members struggle with their concerns about the relevance of the group activity to their personal goals and with their attempts to establish an identity within the group, they will look to the leader. The leader must determine whether or not he or she has been successful in creating a constructive therapeutic climate. Has the leader been genuine, communicating positive regard, listening and responding empathically? If not, that situation needs to be remedied first. If the leader has been successful in this aspect, he or she needs to look further to find ways to draw members into the process. The leader can use himself or herself as a model, or can reinforce other modeling behaviors that occur in the group. If it is an open group, the leader may seed the group with a model member from another group who then continues therapy in this group.

During this stage, the group needs structuring. The initial task of the leader is to help members determine goals and understand why they are there. The leader must encourage people in the process of the group, otherwise resistence will increase. The leader should encourage some self-disclosure as well as interaction among members. As a role model, the leader can reflect member statements and draw other members out by encouraging them to respond to each other. The failure to provide structure in early sessions not only fails to facilitate early group development but actually feeds clients' distortions, interpersonal fears, and subjective distress which interfere with group development. The earlier structure can be provided, the greater the likelihood of reducing anxiety.

There are a number of exercises or techniques to help move members into the interactional process of the group. Stopping to look at the process of the group at any given time is a helpful approach in this situation. Just getting members to verbalize about what is going on can draw reluctant individuals into the interaction.

If members are frightened of self-disclosures, Yalom (1975) suggests asking for metadisclosures, that is, a disclosure about the disclosure. Members can be asked to talk about how they feel about talking about themselves. It is often helpful after the first session or so to examine the process of the group and ask members how they feel about what is going on. This creates more involvement and responsibility from individuals within the group. It is incumbent upon the leader to know how to apply group dynamics and to be as emotionally honest as possible in order to help the members interact appropriately.

Moving Out of Stage One

The most important part of initiating the group is an agreement on its goals. Although each member will have individual goals, there must be enough consensus on the common goals and purposes of group behavior to permit the members to participate in the process. The leader and the group members will state their goals for the group. In counseling groups, the task is usually to help individuals develop self-insight and constructive behavior change. The members will seek some boundaries or guidelines by looking to the counselor or possibly another strong member in the group. Thus, the first problem of establishing group goals is solved in a dependent way. The members' dependency needs are frequently not met, for in most counseling groups the counselor defines his or her role quite differently. The members' expectations are derived from previous leaders, i.e., parents or teachers. When the counselor disappoints them by not fitting the familiar role, their anxiety may be aroused. They may consider the counselor external to them and perhaps resent his or her familiarity with groups.

Bion (1959) described a sequence of emotional modalities in groups. He suggests that at times in the group's development, there seems to be a covert consensus among the members around an emotional theme that is relevant to their sharing of problems. Early in the group, there is a response to a dependency-counterdependency theme. This centers around the leader. At first the group will feel very dependent upon the leader and want him or her to set up a structure and tell them how to behave. There also may be feelings of counterdependency toward the leader in a reaction to his or her control of the group. (When the group becomes more mature, attitudes of independence and interdependence can develop).

In this initial stage, there is not much cohesion or unity in the group. It is composed of individuals having little or no identification with the group—only their private conceptions. The members are socially isolated from each other, and the only justification for calling it a group is that it meets regularly with a counselor. The counselor is often the focal point to whom the individual members relate. A group structure, which helps individuals know what to expect or how to behave, has not yet been able to converge. Martin and Hill (1957) characterize this stage as having "no interpersonal, group-relevant structure, and the group is essentially a conjure of social isolates held in loose association by a vague awareness of the counselor and his role (p.24)."

Individual members may try to establish some group structure. They will assume some indigenous leadership in establishing group goals and norms of behavior. Frequently, members responding from their own conception of the group purpose will begin behaving in ways that they think are appropriate. One example involves a member expressing feelings in the form of a catharsis. Such a member's assumption is that to have self-understanding, one must be involved in self-disclosure. This self-disclosure may frighten other members of the group who do not have that level of readiness, or those who have other goals in mind for the group. This involves another theme modality involving fight or flight. Fight is a mood of aggression, while flight is psychologically moving away from an unknown danger by sharing in the fantasy.

At the conclusion of this stage, the group is frequently disillusioned and confused. The members' preconceived ideas of how a group functions and how members and the counselor should behave have been inadequate. They tend to withdraw from complex issues and suppress their personal feelings.

STAGE TWO: CONFLICT AND CONFRONTATION

In the second stage of group development, the members' dissatisfaction with the operation of the group is manifested. Following the initial acquaintance period, members are frequently frustrated in their attempts to evolve new patterns of behavior through which to work toward group goals. The discrepancy between individuals' real selves and their stereotyped images of the group may lead to conflict. Group members may challenge others' reactions to them and insist on their own rights. Some conflict may erupt when certain issues are discovered to be more complex than the group members originally perceived. The process of conflict and confrontation also occurs as group members begin to perceive and experience difficulty implementing changes in behavior.

Although the members' frustration is first provoked by the leader, it soon extends to their relations with each other. By becoming hostile with others, members seek to express their individuality and their resistance to the situation. There is conflict among members over entering the unknown of interpersonal relations. The anxiety felt by members comes from their fear of being judged by others, their need for more structure than can be provided at this time, and their uncertainty and frustration while goals, methods, and standards of desired behavior have not yet been established. The lack of unity is an outstanding characteristic during this stage.

Mills (1964) has termed this period boundary testing and role modeling because during this time, the members retest the limits of their preconceived ideas and try new behavioral roles in an attempt to become effective. It is a time when individuals must reexamine their concepts of groups and their own behavior patterns to determine which are appropriate and which need modification. Some members test their importance by being absent; others by giving only their best ideas and at other times remaining silent. Members test each other's commitment to the group by challenge or silent critique.

Individuals test the boundary of intimacy to see how much they can reveal to others and how much difference they can tolerate in others. Hence, the interaction is quite uneven. Infighting may occur between some members, while others regress to the security of dependence; detached observation as well as aggressive attacks are common kinds of behavior throughout this stage.

During this stage of group development, the group's preoccupation shifts to concern with dominance, control, and power. The conflict that is manifested is between the members or between the members and the leader. Individuals frequently will attempt to establish a role in the group, and gradually a power hierarchy is formed.

At this stage, advice giving and social conventions are abandoned, and members criticize others' behaviors or attitudes. Overt comments and criticism are more frequent between members.

It is a time in the life of the group when there is likely to be some suspension of the ordinary social mores and appropriate social behavior in the interest of fermenting ordinarily private and covert processes so that they become public and manifest for the sake of learning. This may include sanctioning responses that may lead to hurt feelings if they are taken personally rather than as manifestations of transference. As the group develops, the leader may point out the possibility that such personal comments may have more relevance to the inner world of the attacker than to the person under fire. Nevertheless, group members experience their anger toward each other in the present, and this can be uncomfortable. In cases where the leader is not very active, the degree of anxiety will increase, and there are times when the leader must pay sensitive attention to reducing the anxiety in the group to a manageable level.

Attack the Leader

At the beginning of this stage, the leader is seen as a frustrating figure because he or she refuses to fit the stereotype and tell members what to do. The leader may become the recipient of their hostility, which may be expressed openly. Some members try to force the leader into a more active role. If this proves unsuccessful, they may become hostile, rebellious, or silent. During this period, the conflict of dependency-counterdependency emerges with a challenge to the authority.

The occurrence of hostility toward the counselor is inevitable in this process. Considering the unrealistic attitude that many members feel toward the leader when the group begins, it is obvious that the counselor cannot fulfill all their concepts. The members' expectations are so grand that regardless of the counselor's competence, she or he will disappoint them. As they recognize the counselor's real personal and professional limitations, the process of disenchantment will begin. This is a slow process and frequently not intentional. Even when a group counselor attemps to avoid the traditional leading style by refusing to answer questions or offer solutions or redirect the members to explore their own resources, the group will project the leadership role onto the counselor. After several sessions, the group will come to realize that the counselor will frustrate their private expectations of his or her behavior.

Yalom (1975) suggests that one source of resentment derives from the recognition that each member will not be the one most favored by the leader. Through the precounseling interview, most members expect that the counselor is his or her own counselor. However, in the early meetings, each member begins to realize that the counselor is equally interested in the other members or may perceive a degree of unequal investment by the leader.

Seldom is there a unified group attack on the counselor. Generally, some individuals will defend the counselor. The individuals or subgroups who make up the attackers and defenders may serve as a guide for understanding attitudes and behaviors of each other. There is generally much information dealing with counter-dependency and independence arising from the conflict and confrontation stage.

Slater (1966) suggests three alternatives in the members' attitudes toward the leader after an attack: they behave as they did previously, they seem to view the leader in a far more realistic fashion, or they act with a more detached caring.

A first impression following an attack on a leader is that little has changed in the leader-members relationship, although patterns of behavior now seem to increase in independence among the members. The leader may then become aware that he or she no longer plays such a necessary part in the group. Frequently, the leader finds that his or her roles may be partially filled by other members in the group. The second impression the group leader receives is that of being viewed more realistically. Other members in the group can offer interpretations and adopt the leader's techniques and functions. The third impression a leader receives is that a worshipful attitude is still present, although it is detached from his or her person. It may be less in evidence than before, but it is quite visible. The attitude may attach itself to many other things, even something outside the group that usually both represents the group as a whole and also has some temporal or spatial association with the leader. Seldom will another group member be invested with the leader's attributes, because this will be met with sibling rivalry.

Prior to a revolt directed at the leader, three entities are bound together: the person of the group leader, the object of the members' worshipful attitude or dependency needs, and a set of abstract skills and qualities which are desired by the group members. After the revolt toward the leader, these three attitudes are separated. The qualities of wisdom, understanding, and interpretative skill are recognized as abstract principles no longer inherent in any particular person and hence capable of being shared by the group members. Before this time, there may have been a deep conviction, for example, that only the leader knew what was going on in the group. Although the leader may have assured the members that the same data are available to everyone and that it is simply a question of keeping one's eyes and ears open, they reply with earnest intensity that the leader has more knowledge and experience in these matters. The revolt reverses all three of these attitudes to a considerable extent. Although the leader may be a more skillful interpreter, the members are able to admit that they have the power to interpret even the behavior of the leader.

Although some conflict or confrontation between the members and the counselor is typical in groups, the magnitude differs from group to group. The needs of the members in the group will have some effect on it, but certainly the counselor's behavior will be a major contribution. This stage is difficult for most group counselors. Beginning counselors must recognize that they are essential for the group, and that they must differentiate between an attack on them personally and an attack on their role in the group. Confronting the counselor is an important process for the group, and inhibiting their conflicting feelings would be counterproductive. A counselor who is able to work through an attack without being destroyed or retaliating is able to provide a model for the members in handling aggression. If the counselor is able to understand and get to the sources and effects of the confrontation, the other members can learn that aggression need not be punitive or destructive—that it can be expressed and be a productive part of the group (Yalom, 1975).

Resistance

Resistance may be exhibited in attacks on subject matter, the group, or the leader. Other forms of resistance include misunderstanding the goals and the procedures, avoiding work, and attempting to get more structure from the leader. This is particularly true in a counseling group focusing on self-disclosure, self-understanding, and behavior change. At this point the members resist the demands that these tasks make upon them as individuals. There is frequently a discrepancy between the members' usual behavior and what is demanded of them by the group.

Aronson (1967) describes resistance as a decrease in the efficiency of the members' past behavior in the counseling session. It is manifested in the intensification of the members' characteristic transference distortions, defense mechanisms, and defensive maneuvers. The purpose of resistance behavior is to ward off anxiety stirred up by interpersonal stimuli that come closer to the awareness of the individual because of internal pressures or are triggered by the counselor or other members' comments. Aronson (1967) discusses both individual resistance in the group situation and a total group resistance.

Individual Resistance The group may be conceived as a task-oriented work group in which the participants and counselor engage in specific task behavior oriented toward a maximum flow of direct verbal communication. Such spontaneous interaction permits the counselor and group members to work through the conflicts of each member of the group. Members must not only talk about themselves and interact spontaneously with the counselor, but are also called upon to express their thoughts and feelings concerning the other members of the group. Each member is expected to act reciprocally with the other members in the group, to participate with them in their attempts to work through their problems, to maintain an ongoing relationship with each other despite temporary interpersonal differences. After all members have revealed their characteristic mode of behaving in the group, the counselor can detect resistance whenever he or she observes a decrease in the efficiency of a member's behavior. One of the behaviors that may be observed would be a persistent transference, whether positive or negative, toward any other member or subgroup or the entire group that prevents the members from engaging in open direct communication. In addition, any change or increase in the member's usual defense mechanisms is an indication of resistance.

This may include blockages or displacement in the flow of verbal communication; increases in the ratio of nonverbal to verbal communication; changes in the relative weight given to thoughts, feelings, and action; changes in the emphasis placed on current materials as compared to historical material; and increases in characteristic tension level. When members are not talking about themselves, it is quite difficult to detect changes in defenses without direct questioning in the group. The counselor may rely on observations of nonverbal behavior including gestures, posture, and facial expression. Another form of individual resistance may be seen in the use of defensive maneuvers. The most obvious maneuver is an attempt to terminate the group or the relationship to it. The member may state the difficulty of talking about himself or herself in the group as compared to talking with the counselor individually. Or, quite frequently, the member will see the counselor individually after the session to discuss things that should be done in the group.

A specific kind of resistance is shown in clients known as help-rejecting complainers, who characteristically ask for help but equally characteristically never accept it. They frustrate all who attempt to help them. The help-rejecting complainer is a particularly difficult client in group counseling. Peters and Grunebaum (1977) proposed an approach in which the counselor sides with the member's hopelessness and helplessness by making use of hyperbole and irony, and eschews reassurance and support.

The usual dilemma involves the client looking to the counselor for rescue but not willing to accept help. This leads to the client's feeling disappointed and seeing the counselor as a persecutor. At the same time, the counselor feels frustrated and begins to store up anger at the client which interferes with effective counseling.

The proposed strategy avoids the role of rescuer by consistently sidestepping the expression of optimism, encouragement, or advice. The counselor outdoes the client's negativity through hyperbole and irony. Because the counselor refuses to respond in the way the client is accustomed, the client is forced to adopt attitudes and views which can lead to a new range of choices. This attitude can help the client and counselor avoid the typical negative struggles, and allows for a more genuine contact.

Group Resistance Aronson (1967) believes one of the most difficult tasks confronting the counselor is the recognition and resolution of total group resistance; that is, the simultaneous resistance of most or all of the members of the group. Unless the counselor handles the resistance successfully, the group may remain at an impasse, become fragmented, or dissolve. The counselor cannot rely solely on experience in dealing with individual resistance when coping with the total group resistance. Special skills for detecting and working with it must be developed.

A group leader may encounter the small group that shows little substance, involvement, commitment, or prospect for change. Gustafson (1976) examined two types of intergroup tensions that may contribute to passivity in the group. The group may act as if it is involved in a shared magical thinking that limits their involvement, or the group may act as if it has made a negative judgment about the safety of the situation in the group.

The group that is passive because it is involved in a shared magical fantasy has been described by Bion (1961). Bion suggested that small groups of people tended to bring out in each person the same or similar unconscious attitude, and the group acts as if there were a shared magical assumption. Bion described the three principal assumptions. First, the group may act as if it had gathered to be completely taken care of and nurtured by a god-like figure and it need only wait for this god to revive them with what they need. This involves the basic assumption of dependency. Secondly, the group may act as if it need only fight or flee from the presupposed object; this basic assumption is called flight-fight. Thirdly, the group may act as if it only needed to wait for a creative pair of people to produce a messiah or messianic idea to save the group. This is the basic assumption of pairing. A group that becomes caught up in following or waiting for dependency, fight-flight, or pairing leadership may have little capacity to be involved in the work of the group. Bion suggested that the basic assumption of magical thinking continually occurs despite the best efforts to keep it under control.

This type of thought process and passivity in the group may be a type of resistance forerunner to the conflict and confrontation. When members find that their shared magical fantasy does not occur, they may respond with anger toward the leader, other members, or the group situation.

Another possibility for the passivity in the group may be the shared judgment that the situation is unsafe or uncertain for sharing thoughts and feelings openly. Members may silently observe the fate of others who take the risk of self-disclosing before the group, or they may observe the injury or slighting of contributions and wait to see if other offerings are made. Individual members may test the situation to judge the reception of minor risks before offering more.

For the leader to work further with the passive group, he or she must renegotiate a task that the members can join. Members may be encouraged to discuss the feelings about the safety of the group. The concern about the conditions of safety in the group may be questioning the dependency of the leader. The leader should bring up relevant issues regarding the group's passive attitudes and behaviors. In some cases, the counselor may confront individuals or the group with their behavior.

After the group moves through the initial stage of development, the extent to which the majority of members contribute to or detract from the group goals by maximizing the direct communication and spontaneous interaction may be used as a gauge by the counselor. Decreases in the operating efficiency of the group may be detected by observing the changes in transference distortion, defense mechanisms, and defensive maneuvering. It is important that the counselor, in estimating the degree of group resistance, rule out the possibility that his or her own countertransferences may be distorting this judgment. Saretsky (1972) suggests that resistance in the group may be a function of the counselor's countertransference expectations. He states that there is a tendency for counselors to avoid facing their own anxiety by labeling the client's behavior as resistance. If the individual or the group remains at a standstill or drops out, it is easier for the counselor to absolve himself or herself by saying that the group really wasn't working. This defense, however, may blind the counselor to his or her own fear failure, and may prevent the counselor from constantly dealing with the guilt and anxiety that are aroused when clients do not improve. Much of this can be done through self-awareness. However, continued supervision, even for the experienced counselor, is certainly beneficial. If the counselor clarifies how values affect procedures and the impact on the group, the counselor can integrate this insight with an understanding of the way in which the clients' evoked resistances relate to their preexisting transference potentials.

Group resistance should be differentiated from other problems that impair the efficiency of the group, problems that may resemble it on the manifest level but arise from other causes. Examples of these include groups that do not function efficiently because of an initially unworkable constellation, short-term blockages in the early stages of the group, or normal periods of consolidation in member behaviors. Aronson points out that the presence of a group resistance presupposes that the counselor has failed to adequately deal with individual resistances in the group. He suggests that the most serious errors occur in the preparatory phase, when the counselor selects someone for a group without a sufficient opportunity to really know the individual and his or her potential impact on the group. Another error in handling resistance may occur in the group itself. If the counselor unduly delays working through the developing resistances of individual members, this delay could set the stage for additional individual resistance, developing into a total group resistance. A crucial error is to fail to analyze and work through the reactions of the group members to some common stimulus configuration that impinges strongly on many or all of the members. In some situations, these may come from one or more group members or possibly some figure outside the group; most often, however, the attitudes and actions of the counselor constitute the most important focus of resistance. As in individual counseling, self-awareness may help the counselor understand his or her countertransferences. However, most counselors can profit from supervision from peers or more experienced counselors.

Confrontation

Confrontation may be defined as one person pointing out a discrepancy between his or her and another's way of viewing reality. The process involves intentional confrontation or a confrontation used as a specific skill. By pointing out a confrontation between their views, one person is causing the other to look at this situation. Confrontation is a counselor technique; however, a group member may use the technique with the counselor or another member.

Egan (1976) describes confrontation as an invitation. Confrontation as thus used is anything that the counselor does that invites a member to examine his or her behavior and its consequences more carefully. Discrepancies in the member's thinking and action appear most frequently in three areas: between the ideal and real self; between insight and action; and between reality and illusion. "The purpose of confrontation is to reduce the ambiguity and the incongruencies in the client's experiencing and communication. In effect, it is a challenge to the client to become integrated; that is, at one with own experience (Carkhuff and Berenson, 1967, p. 171)."

The term confrontation frequently conjures the idea of a hostile act; however, this need not be true. Confrontation is hostile to the unhealthy patterns of the client that have developed, but the challenge can be considered healthy rather than destructive.

Berenson and Mitchell (1974) describe five types of confrontation: experiential, didactic, strength, weakness, and encouragement to action. Experiential confrontation is the counselor's response to any discrepancy between what the client said about himself or herself and how the counselor experiences the client. A didactic confrontation is the counselor's response to a client's misinformation, lack of information, or need for information regarding a topic of discussion or the group process. A confrontation of weakness occurs when the counselor focuses on the client's liabilities or pathology while confrontation of strength focuses on constructive resources. Encouragement to action occurs when the counselor presses the client to act in life in some constructive manner, or discourages the client's passive stance.

Carkhuff and Berenson (1967) state that confrontation may range from a light challenge to a direct collision. It constitutes a challenge to the client to mobilize personal resources and take a step toward deeper self-recognition or constructive action. It may precipitate a crisis that disturbs, at least temporarily, the client's equilibrium. Carkhuff and Berenson view crisis as the very fabric of growth, invoking new responses and charting new developments. In fact, growth is viewed as a series of endless self-confrontations. A confrontation is a vehicle that ultimately translates the awareness of insights into action.

Effects of Confrontation   The client may feel powerless to do something and feels whatever happens is in someone else's control. The member particularly searches for someone who will do something, and waits for the magical moment when someone gives direction or meaning to life. The member often knows that his or her life is not satisfactory but feels there is nothing that can be done to change it. The member continues as a passive-reactive individual. By the use of confrontation, the counselor or other group members can force the individual to choose between that continuing life and becoming an active force in his or her own life.

Confrontation has a number of potential beneficial effects. It permits the counselor and other members to express real thought and feelings, and provides a model to help the client learn to accept and express thoughts and feelings and to test perceptions against other members' reality. The client learns that there are many ways of viewing a person or a situation, and that people may disagree without harboring hostile feelings for each other. Constructive confrontation gives members an honest and immediate experience: by becoming aware of the impact they have on the other person, they begin to realize their impact on themselves. Confrontation can also indicate to clients a measure of respect for their capacity and self-determination. The counselor is not handling them with kid gloves for fear of overwhelming or hurting them. By directly communicating his or her own position to clients, the counselor allows the clients to make their stand clear and to evaluate it by checking and comparing the views with other members. Clients learn to recognize and face the inter- and intrapersonal discrepancies that are an inevitable part of life (Anderson, 1968).

Egan (1976) is aware that confrontation can be beneficial or detrimental to the individual member, and that the manner of confrontation is as important as the type of confrontation. He offers some guidelines on how the confrontation should take place. His first suggestion is that confrontation be offered in a spirit of accurate empathy. The fact is that accurate empathy is in itself often challenging to the client. If confrontation does not come from an accurate understanding, it will almost inevitably be either ineffective or destructive. A second guideline emphasizes that confrontation should take place tentatively, especially in the early stages of a group. The tentativeness permits the receiving member an opportunity to hear and examine the other person's perspective without having it forced upon him or her. It does need to be mentioned that although good confrontations are not accusatory, they should not be so qualified and tentative as to lose their force. A third principle in confronting involves basic respect for the individual being confronted so that the confrontation is done with care. The confrontation is a way of getting involved with the individual and a way of communicating you care enough to mutually help the person. Confrontation should be proportioned to the relationship between the two individuals in the interaction. A caring confrontation presupposes some kind of intimacy between the confronter and the confronted. A fourth suggestion in using confrontation is using successive approximations. Confrontation may be more effective if it is gradual. The person has an opportunity to assimilate what is being said. It is not good to demand everything at once.

The counselor can model good confronting behavior, but during a period of time when conflict is existing in the group, the counselor can also help the process by giving practical hints concerning the matter of confrontation to group members. One of the best ways of confronting is to keep current. If one member's behavior is of concern, others should not keep the concern locked up by bottling the feelings or ignoring the person or engaging in other substitutes for the direct confrontation. If the members stay current to what is going on within the group, issues can be faced directly as they come up. This doesn't mean that members should become picky and challenge every point. However, it does keep members from carrying feelings around and bringing them up later when it is less appropriate. A second practical hint is that nonverbal behavior is insufficient. Nonverbal hints about what you are thinking or feeling in the group are not enough. If you are silent or look at someone or look away, you are certainly sending messages which may be challenging, but these messages should be supported by words which are more direct in helping the person understand his or her attitudes and behaviors. One of the most helpful ways of confronting is to use describing behavior. You describe what you see as counterproductive behavior to the person and describe the impact you think it has on that person, yourself, and others in the group. Commanding, judging, and accusing statements are not effective forms of confrontation. Describing behavior has more objectivity to it, and helps the person being confronted avoid a defensiveness that arises with confrontation'

The Right to Confront   Does everyone in the group have the right to confront fellow members? Egan suggests that it may not be appropriate. Members must earn the right to confront others, and in general they must live up to that type of relationship. Only active members really earn the right to confront. Berenson and Mitchell (1974) describe certain qualities that must characterize the member before he or she has the right to confront. One of the major qualities involves relationship building. If the member has not developed a relationship with the other person, he or she should not confront; mere acquaintance does not supply enough solid foundation for confrontation. Leave the confrontation to someone who has a more solid relationship. This indicates that members must get into the group and not just be peripheral members if they are really going to participate. Another quality involves understanding of the individual. Members should be encouraged not to confront until they have spent enough time understanding the other individual. Effective confrontation is built on understanding and should flow from it. Unless the other member feels the confronter understands her or him, the member will probably not listen to the confrontation anyway. A third aspect of confronting involves disclosing something of oneself. Do not confront others unless you are active in revealing yourself appropriately in the group. When you self-disclose, you also open yourself up to confrontation. The mutuality provides a better relationship. The person who confronts should be in touch with his or her own emotionality and should have a feeling for the strength of the relationship with the confronted member. In addition, it is important for the person to know why he or she is confronting. Members should be encouraged to confront only those with whom their relationship is growing. If they confront another person on a kind of interpersonal plateau, delay confrontation and find out why nothing is happening between them. Unless you have a sense of interpersonal movement with the other, the confrontation may be stale or ill-timed. Another suggestion is not to confront unless you are the kind of person who also challenges yourself. Finally, members should be encouraged to confront only when they have learned how to respond well to confrontations.

Responding to Confrontation   What constitutes an effective response to confrontation? When someone confronts, they are actually inviting the other person to do something or, in some cases, demanding that they do something. What are the implications of this invitation or demand?

First, the confronted member should strive to understand what the other person is saying. Often the confronting member finds it difficult to say what he or she feels should be said; out of caring respect, the confronting member may not say it straight. The receiving member may have to struggle with his or her own emotions in order to understand. The confrontation, even when it is reasonable, may feel like an attack, and an attack calls for a defense or possibly a counterattack. Therefore, it is imperative to make sure the individual gets the message straight and understands what is being said.

Second, since the member is in a group, he or she should use the resources of the group. If the member is confused or doesn't understand, deal with the confusion in the group. Throw the question open to the group, and receive additional information regarding the point that is being confronted and possible help in understanding that point.

Third, once you understand what is being said, respond to the confrontation. Whether you decide to change your ideas or behaviors at this point, examine your values, relate it to the issue, and respond in the group. It may take time for a particular confrontation to sink in and take effect. A good response to confrontation does not mean immediately leaping into action. Give the other member time, provided it is not just a way of resisting the issues.

What If the Group Is Not Working?

There are times when the group will not move from the initial orientation stage into a conflict stage. Individuals continue to respond to each other with stereotypical behaviors but are not confronted. The members look to the leader for leadership, and when it is not to their liking, they are passive.

What can the leader do to help individuals or the group as a whole to move into and through the conflict stage?

There are a number of ways the counselor could help to make this stage effective. The importance of careful preparation of members before they enter the group situation must be stressed. This preparation can include accurate information and discussion regarding the conflict that might be expected. It needs to be emphasized that working on their relationships directly with other group members may not be easy, but that is extremely important since the working through of interpersonal issues within the group will most likely lead to more satisfying relationships in other parts of their lives. Sometimes clients express a fear of being torn to pieces and are extremely reluctant to enter into a group situation. They need to be assured that certain ground rules will prevail, and they may be asked to listen to a tape of a group session in which the conflict was dealt with effectively.

After the group is functioning, a primary concern of the counselor must be that a consistent and positive relationship with group members exists. The basic atmosphere of the counselor must be one of acceptance, genuineness, and empathy. The creation of a constructive therapeutic relationship provides a foundation which permits effective conflict and confrontation to occur.

In order for the conflict to be productive, norms must be established that make it clear that people are there to understand themselves and not to punish or defeat others. It is up to the counselor to vigorously intervene when conflict gets dirty or out of hand, and to restate or model the fair-fighting norms of the group.

Furthermore, the counselor can make this stage more effective by serving as a model. The counselor can demonstrate both the giving and the receiving of confrontation behavior in a way that is constructive rather than destructive. The counselor needs to set a model which includes responsibility and appropriate restraints while maintaining a basic position of honesty. The counselor also needs to accept and admit his or her fallibility when accusations or anger directed toward him or her are true. For the counselor's own comfort as well as the effective handling of the situation, he or she needs to be prepared for an expected attack by the group or an individual member. Leaders must not present themselves as too frail so that members would consider an attack impossible. An attack on the leader presents an important model-setting opportunity. It is important for the leader to discriminate between a personal attack and an attack on the leadership role.

There are a number of sources of hostility in a group. Yalom (1975) discusses attacks on a leader which occur from recognition that each member will not be favored or that the leader is not able to fulfill their unrealistic expectations. Other sources of hostility include transference, rivalry, rejective identification, and differences on outlook based on different life experiences. Whatever the reason, the counselor needs to help the group in an exploration of the sources of the anger, keeping in mind the developmental stage of the group and their tolerance of conflict.

When individuals enter a group, they carry with them their personal beliefs, biases, and commitments. It is not feasible to expect individuals to abandon their feelings in favor of a total commitment to the group. The members will often make initial statements that sound biased or selfish which lead to situations of conflict. In such issues as power struggles, disillusionment, and anger between members or with the leader, it is necessary to help the members focus on the dynamics of the process and encourage them to deal with what is going on.

Moving Out of Stage Two

In many counseling groups, Stage Two may not emerge early or may be avoided completely unless there is enough commitment to the group so that the members will risk open confrontation. In fact, the conflict may not be expressed openly but through passive resistance. The members may remain silent rather than confront each other or the counselor. Open conflict and confrontation is not often seen in group counseling conducted in school settings or other short-term counseling situations in which the counselor is perceived as an authority figure.

Without working through this phase and establishing appropriate norms of behavior, only a superficial level of cohesiveness can develop. As the group members work through their differences of opinions about appropriate behavior for each other and the counselor, they are able to accept the real persons rather than the stereotyped images. This can lead to a great feeling of identity with the group. It is important to recall that even when the group moves into a cohesive stage, it may regress to periods of conflict and confrontation.

The necessity for working through the stage of conflict and confrontation cannot be emphasized too strongly. For groups to evolve from a superficial to a more truly effective level of functioning, this painful and difficult period must be experienced and dealt with successfully.

SUMMARY

This chapter has presented the concept of life stages in a group. The counselor's awareness of the broad developmental stages may help in understanding the process and interviewing effectively. This chapter examined the important variables in preparing for group counseling as well as the first two stages of development in establishing a group. Chapter 15 continues the examination of the life stages in group counseling through cohesiveness, production, and termination.

References

Allport, G. W. *Personality and social encounter.* Boston: Beacon Press, 1960. psychotherapy. *American Journal of Psychotherapy,* 1967, 94.

Anderson, S. Effects of confrontation by high- and low-functioning therapists. *Journal of Counseling Psychology,* 1968, *15,* 411–16.

Aronson, M. Resistance in individual and group psychotherapy. *American Journal of Psychotherapy,* 1967, *21,* 86–94.

Bach, G. R. *Intensive group psychotherapy.* New York: Ronald Press, 1954.

Bednar, R. L., and C. P. Battersby. The effects of specific structure on early group development. *Journal of Applied Behavioral Science,* 1976, *12,* 513–22.

Bednar, R., J. Melnick, and T. Kaul. Responsibility and structure: A conceptual framework for initiating group counseling and psychotherapy. *Journal of Counseling Psychology,* 1974, *21,* 31–38.

Bednar, R. L., C. Weet, P. Evensen, D. Lanier, and J. Melnick. Empirical guidelines for group therapy: Pre-training, cohesion, and modeling. *Journal of Applied Behavior Science,* 1974, *10,* 149–63.

Berenson, B., and K. Mitchell. *Confrontation: For better or worse.* Amherst, MA: Human Resource Development Press, 1974.

Berzon, B. The dimensions of interpersonal responsibility in therapeutic groups. (Mimeographed reports 1–3, The Intensive Group Experience.) San Diego: Western Behavioral Sciences Institute, 1964.

Bion, W. *Experiences in groups.* New York: Basic Books, 1959.

Boer, A. K., and J. E. Lantz. Adolescent group therapy member selection. *Clinical Social Work Journal,* 1974, *2,* 172–81.

Bonney, W. C. The maturation of groups. *Small Group Behavior,* 1974, *5,* 455–61.

Bradford, L. P,. J. R. Gibb, and K. D. Benne (Eds.). *T-group theory and laboratory method: Innovation in re-education.* New York: Wiley, 1964, 190–214.

Bugen, L. A. Composition and orientation effects on group cohesion. *Psychological Reports,* 1977, *40,* 175–81.

Carkhuff, R. Toward a comprehensive model of facilitative interpersonal functioning. *Journal of Counseling Psychology,* 1967, *14,* 67–73.

Carkhuff, R. *Helping and human relations, Vols. I and II.* New York: Holt, Rinehart and Winston, 1971.

Carkhuff, R., and B. Berenson. *Beyond counseling and therapy.* New York: Holt, Rinehart and Winston, 1967.

Castore, G. Number of verbal interrelationships as a determinant of group size. *Journal of Abnormal and Social Psychology,* 1962, *64,* 456–57.

Corsini, I. Methods of group psychotherapy. New York: McGraw-Hill, 1957.

Crews, C. Y., and J. Melnick. Use of initial and delayed structure in facilitating group development. *Journal of Counseling Psychology,* 1976, *23,* 92–98.

Dunphy, D. Phases, roles and myths in self-analytic groups. *Journal of Applied Behavioral Science,* 1968, *4*(2), 195–225.

Egan, G. Confrontation. *Group and Organizational studies,* 1976, *1,* 223–43.

Gazda, L. M. *Group counseling: A developmental approach.* Boston: Allyn & Bacon, 1972.

Gustafson, J. P. The passive small group: Working concepts. *Human Relations, 1976, 29,* 793–803.

Hare, A. *Handbook of small group research.* New York: Free Press of Glencoe, 1962.

Heckel, R. V., G. R. Holmes, and C. J. Rosecrans. A factor analytic study of process variables in group therapy. *Journal of Clinical Psychology,* 1971, *27*(1), 146–50.

Heitler, J. B. Preparation of lower class patients for expressive group psychotherapy. *Journal of Consulting and Clinical Psychology,* 1973, *41,* 251–60.

Heitler, J. B. Clinical impressions of an experimental attempt to prepare lower class patients for expressive group psychotherapy. *International Journal of Group Psychotherapy,* 1974, *24,* 308–22.

Hobbs, N. Group-centered psychotherapy. In C. (Ed.), Rogers *Client-centered therapy.* Boston: Houghton Mifflin, 1951.

Jeske, J. O. Identification and therapeutic effectiveness in group therapy. *Journal of Counseling Psychology,* 1973, *20,* 528–30.

Johnson, J. A. *Group therapy: A practical approach.* New York: McGraw-Hill, 1963.

Kelman, H. C. The role of the group in the induction of therapeutic change. *International Journal of Group Psychotherapy,* 1963, *13,* 399–432.

Kilmann, E. R., B. M. Albert, and W. M. Sotile. Relationship between locus of control, structure of therapy, and outcome. *Journal of Consulting and Clinical Psychology,* 1975, *43,* 588.

Lacoursiere, R. A group method to facilitate learning during the stages of a psychiatric affiliation. *International Journal of Group Psychotherapy,* 1974, 114–19.

Lawlis, G. F., and R. Klein. Interpersonal cohesion and feeling orientation: An application of matrix algebra. *Sociological Reports,* 1973, *32,* 807–12.

Lee, F., and R. L. Bednar. Effects of group structure and risk taking disposition on group behavior, attitudes, and atmosphere. *Journal of Counseling Psychology,* 1977, *24,* 191–99.

Levin, E. N., and R. R. Kurtz. Structured and non-structured human relations training. *Journal of Counseling Psychology,* 1974, *21,* 526–31.

Mahler, C. *Group counseling in the schools.* Boston: Houghton Mifflin, 1969.

Mann, J. Group therapy with adults. *American Journal of Orthopsychiatry,* 1953, *23,* 332–37.

Mann, R. D. The development of the member-trainer relationship in self-analytic groups. *Human Relations,* 1966, *19,* 85–116.

Mann, R. D. The development of the member-trainer relationship in self-analytic groups. In C. L. Cooper and I. L. Mangham (Eds.), *T-groups: A survey of research.* London: Wiley-Interscience, 1971.

Martin, E., and W. Hill. Toward a theory of group development: Six phases of therapy group development. *International Journal of Group Psychotherapy,* 1957, *7,* 20–30.

Meeks, J. E. Structuring the early phase of group psychotherapy with adolescents. *International Journal of Child Psychotherapy,* 1973, *2,* 391–405.

Melnick, J., and M. Woods. Analysis of group composition research and theory for psychotherapeutic and group-oriented groups. *Journal of Applied Behavioral Science,* 1976, *12,* 493–512.

Miles, M. Human relations training: How a group grows. *Teachers College Record,* 1953, *55,* 90–96.

Mills, T. *Group transformation.* Englewood Cliffs, N.J.: Prentice-Hall, 1964.

Nicholas, M. P., and T. Y. Taylor. Impact of therapist interventions on early sessions of group therapy. *Journal of Clinical Psychology,* 1975, *31,* 725–29.

Ohlsen, M. *Group counseling.* New York: Holt, Rinehart and Winston, 1970.

Peters, C. B., and H. Grunebaum. It could be worse: Affective group psychotherapy with the help-rejecting complainer. *International Journal of Group Psychotherapy,* 1977, *27,* 471–80.

Rickard, H. C. Tailored criteria of change in psychotherapy. *Journal of General Psychology,* 1965, *72,* 63–69. Runkel, P., et al. Stages of group development: An empirical test of Tuckman's hypothesis. *The Journal of Applied Behavioral Science,* 1971, *7.* 180–93.

Ryan, T. A. Goal setting in group counseling. *Educational Technology,* January 1973, 19–25.

Sadock, B., and H. Kaplan. Selection of patients in the dynamic and structural organization of the group. In H. Kaplan, and B. Sadock (Eds.), *The evolution of group psychotherapy.* New York: E. P. Dutton, 1972.

Saretsky, T. Resistance in a group as a function of the therapist counter-transference expectations. *Psychotherapy: Theory, Research and Practice,* 1972, *9,* 265–66.

Shambaugh, P., and S. Kanter. Spouses under stress: Group meetings with spouses of patients on hemodialysis. *American Journal of Psychiatry,* 1969, *125,* 928–36.

Slater, P. *Microcosm.* New York: Wiley, 1966.

Stranham, M., C. Schwartzman, and E. Atkin. Group treatment for emotionally disturbed and potentially delinquent boys and girls. *American Journal of Orthopsychiatry,* 1957, *27,* 58.

Thelen, H. and W. Dickerman. Stereotypes and the growth of groups. *Educational Leadership,* 1949, *6,* 309–16.

Whitaker, D., and M. Lieberman. *Psychotherapy through the group process.* New York: Atherton, 1964.

Yalom, I. *The theory and practice of group psychotherapy.* New York: Basic Books, 1970.

Zaleznik, A., and D. Moment. *The dynamics of interpersonal behavior.* New York: Wiley, 1964.

Ziller, R. C. Toward a theory of open and closed groups. *Psychological Bulletin,* 1965, *64,* 164–82.

15

Maintaining the Group

Whether a group progresses to a level of maturity and productivity depends in a large measure on the successful negotiation of the establishment stages. Beyond this, the group needs to learn behaviors that contribute to commitment to the working mores of the group. This may be accomplished during the cohesiveness stage as the members evolve increased acceptance and support for the leader and each other. When the group develops cohesiveness, it is ready to progress to the productive stage in which internalization of insights and rehersal of new behavior patterns may be manifest. Finally, as the goals of the members are achieved and generalizations to outside life situations are accomplished, the members are ready to consider separation from the group and the resultant termination of the experience. This chapter is concerned with the processes of these three stages: cohesiveness, productiveness, and termination.

STAGE THREE: COHESIVENESS

Following the stage of conflict and confrontation, the group gradually develops feelings of cohesiveness. During this stage there is an increase of mutual trust and group morale. The primary interest of the group is with its intimacy and closeness. In fact, after a period of conflict the group may want peace at all costs and may develop a false type of cohesiveness as a form of protection. The group may suppress all expression of negative affect—everybody seems to love everyone else. Only when all affects can be expressed and constructively worked through does the group become cohesive enough to be a mature, productive, functioning group (Yalom, 1975).

Cohesiveness generally refers to the amount of "groupness," which is a sense of solidarity or "we-ness." It can also refer to the attractiveness of the group for its members. There could, then, be a difference between total group cohesiveness and an individual member's perception of cohesiveness. The two are plainly interdependent since group cohesiveness would be the summing of individual members' attractiveness. However, it is important to realize that some individuals within a group will have a greater feeling of cohesiveness than others. Those with a greater sense of value in the group will be more likely to defend it against internal and external threats.

Cohesiveness is an important precondition for a productive stage in group counseling, but by itself it is not a curative factor. Many counselors feel that when the group reaches a stage of cohesiveness it is successful, and they permit the group process to stop.

Yalom (1975) quotes some research indicating tentative evidence supporting self-perceived positive outcome as being related to individual attraction to the group and to total group cohesiveness. Members of a group generally consider the level of cohesiveness a prime aspect of help in their experience. Individuals with a positive outcome generally report more mutually satisfying intermember relationships. The research focusing on the level of cohesiveness and individual outcome is rather meager. But numerous studies involving laboratory groups indicate that increased group cohesiveness is related to various positive outcome variables. For example, better attendance, greater participation, and greater responsiveness and openness of the members are some of the variables that might contribute to positive counseling outcomes.

Cohesiveness may be obtained on two major dimensions: interpersonal respect. The balance between the two determines the maturity of the group. Interpersonal respect could include respect for task-relevant skills, attention to expressions of individual ideas and feelings, and the right to individual and differing opinions. Bonney (1974) suggests that if interpersonal respect is sufficiently well developed, interpersonal attraction becomes relatively unimportant. However, some degrees of original attraction is probably prerequisite for the development of respect. If cohesiveness is based almost solely on interpersonal attraction, it will inhibit task-relevant activities and thereby restrict the movement toward the pre-established goals of the group.

How can the leader's behavior facilitate group cohesiveness? Krumboltz and Potter (1973) offer some behavioral techniques to help in developing trust and cohesiveness. They suggest that the counselor can observe those behaviors and words that indicate trust between people. When individuals do not trust each other, different behaviors will be observed. The counselor should be able to use behaviors indicative of trust and cohesiveness that serve as a model for the other group members.

A four-step approach for the counselor is suggested. First, the counselor must define operationally exactly which behaviors indicate the presence of trust and cohesiveness. These are the behaviors he or she wants to increase. The counselor would want to reinforce statements referring to "we" or the whole group, expressions of liking for the group, expressions of desire to continue the group, talk directed to other group members, talk relevant to other members' previous statements, and cooperative statements. Second, the counselor should diagnose the level of cohesiveness in the group. The counselor can observe a sample of the number of statements indicating cohesive feelings among the members by listening to a ten-minute segment from a group meeting. Third, the counselor may intervene by modeling cohesive behavior. He or she may also cue the situation by asking questions or making comments which lead others to make cohesive statements. Following such a statement, the counselor, of course, would reinforce both the statement and the person making it. The counselor would also try to extinguish either by ignoring or negatively reinforcing statements that detract from the cohesiveness of the group. Fourth, the counselor should assess the impact of his or her intervention. The same behaviors that were measured earlier should be counted again to see if there has been an increase in the level of cohesiveness in the discussions of the group members.

Liberman (1970) demonstrated that systematic social reinforcement will increase group cohesiveness. Groups that were socially reinforced for intermember cohesiveness behaviors also showed earlier systematic improvement and developed more independence from the counselor than did members of the comparison group.

Commitment to the Counseling Process

Besides complying with the norms established by the group and the counselor, the individual member must be personally committed to the counseling process in order for any real behavior change to occur. The member must be motivated to stay with the group and to work for positive change. The member must believe that the counseling process is personally beneficial and that any sacrifices made are worth the eventual benefits. To feel free to express and carry himself or herself before the group, a member must feel secure. The member must develop an attitude of trust toward both the counselor and the total group. If the group situation is not perceived as safe, the member's defense mechanisms will remain intact.

Identification   Kelman (1963) suggests that the member's commitment to counseling takes place through a process of identification. This process is twofold: the individual identifies with the counselor, and with the group. A successful group counseling experience depends largely on an association, however temporary, with those people involved. The more difficult and delicate the problem areas, the more carefully the association must be developed, and the more open, stable, and trusting it must become (Bradford et al., 1964).

The counselor's role in furthering the identification process is largely that of an accepting, permissive, expert listener. Most theories of counseling acknowledge the need for the establishment of a relationship between the counselor and the clients. Regardless of the theoretical orientation of the group counselor, self-exploration of the group members is an important part of the process. The individual first explores personal feelings, attitudes, values, and behaviors. Then, through the interaction with other members in the group, a better self-understanding can be gained. Increased self-understanding can eventually lead the individual to active changing of the behavior, either overtly or covertly. Cohesiveness will be increased as the level of facilitative conditions are increased. Truax (1961) studied forty-five hospitalized patients in three heterogeneous groups and found that patients in cohesive groups were significantly more inclined to engage in deep and extensive self-exploration.

Although group members' acceptance of one another is crucial, it is frequently slow to develop. For the counselor to offer higher levels of facilitative conditions is not enough; the member-to-member acceptance and understanding will be even more significant. When the members come to view each other as being more equal and alike, then the offering of the increase in facilitative conditions will be particularly meaningful to them. This relationship fosters in the member the belief that he or she is understood and accepted. Through this relationship with the counselor, the individual can develop self-esteem. The basis upon which the behavior change must be built is that the individual feels enough self-worth to motivate himself or herself for further changes.

Another way that the counselor fosters the group member's commitment to the counseling processes is by the apparent ability to help the person deal with problems. The member derives hope from a belief that the counselor places confidence in her or him, and this feeling of hope leads to an even greater commitment to counseling. Although essential, this strong attachment to the counselor can become an end in itself. That is, the individual becomes so attached to the counselor that the purpose of counseling becomes simply to meet with the counselor. While this process may help a person to develop some self-identity, and intrinsically may be of great value to the client, the danger is that any change in behavior is made only because of the relationship with the counselor. Changes made at this level are likely to persist only so long as the relationship exists and may never be internalized.

The individual's commitment to the process of counseling is also nurtured by membership in the group itself. Membership gives one the opportunity for growth through contributing out of one's own resources and through concern (Bradford et al., 1964). Through membership in the group, the individual discovers that he or she is not isolated, that there are similar people with similar problems. This awareness of similarity and a common fate increases the likelihood of identification with the group and of personal commitment.

Identification with the group is also encouraged through the building of meaningful relationships between group members. Individuals learn that they are accepted for what they are notwithstanding all obvious deficiencies. This acceptance by other members of the group may be more important to the person than being accepted by the counselor. The difference is that being accepted by the counselor encourages individual growth, but being accepted by the members of the group enhances growth potential. A group of peers has more sources of data, a wider range of reactions, and more possibilities for identification than can be afforded by the counselor. Finally, since behavioral change must be carried out by the individual in the outside world, learning through the influence of peers provides the opportunity to try out new behaviors with people who are representative of those in the outside world (Bradford et al., 1964). As the relationships within the group become stronger, the members discover there is much they can learn from each other. The group experience "provides the opportunity for each member to offer help to others, thus contributing directly to the definition of meaning in individual existence (Muro and Freeman, 1968, p. 10)." Another aspect of the group that encourages individual commitment is the provision of a comparison group that may have more meaning to the individual than do associated outside the counseling group. The group affords the opportunity to compare one's progress to those in the group with similar difficulties, rather than to those in one's daily life who are not faced with those problems. Further, seeing other members in the group progress toward solutions to their problems encourages the individual to feel that his or her difficulties also will be solved.

As in the case of a strong attachment to the counselor, there is a danger that the individual becomes more attached to the group; that membership in the group itself becomes the end. There is also a danger that the group will not accept the individual as is, thus forcing the individual to keep defense mechanisms intact. The counselor must be constantly aware of these tasks and must use his or her ability to protect the individual member from the dangers. The counselor must set the tone in the group so that each member is accepted, and should strive to move the individual members beyond the point of dependence upon the group.

Developing Group Patterns

After dropping certain preconceptions, attempting different kinds of behavior, and gaining some sense of direction, the group becomes concerned with establishing a set of norms for its behavior—deciding what should and should not be done. Such norms of behavior will grow out of members' values and preferences. Attempts are made to set the criteria for members' behavior, i.e., "the right of members to consume the time to make a personal point, the right of silent members to receive without giving, the right of absent members to return without paying a price (Mills, 1964, p. 36)."

Group patterns or structures represent the more observable part of group interaction. These refer to the properties of the group that result from the members' interaction and can be observed. A group structure is achieved through time and becomes a representable and recurrent pattern of relationships through which the group's activities are channeled. A pattern of stable relationships is thus established.

Behaviors among individuals do not result from random fluctuation and tend to recur in the course of new interaction. Even the changes that occur result from the existence of forces within the pattern. A basic element of group life is the fact that who participates with whom in a particular sequence is probably a process to be repeated in future interactions.

With an active leader and understandable goals, group members tend to identify with one another and internalize the group's goals. Some degree of identification with the group members and internalization of the group standards must take place if the member is to begin functioning effectively as a group member. The group must develop self-regulating internal mechanisms to function in the absence of constant policing. Internalization of the group's goals and standards demonstrates the transitional steps from an externally experienced group situation to an internally experienced and regulated dialogue between personal feelings and group pressures.

As a result of the interactions, sentiments associated with the stable relationships contribute to the group pattern. Such variables as members' influence on each other, liking or hostility toward each other, and the formation of subgroups within the total group influence the members to produce the behavior out of which a pattern emerges (Zaleznik and Moment, 1964).

Patterns of Influence   As a group develops identity and moves into a stage of commitment to the process, it becomes apparent that some individuals have been more influential in the movement of the group than others. The counselor will probably be one of the more influential individuals in the group, but there are many others who will exert varying degrees of authority. (This structure evolves out of the roles members assume or are given. See Chapter 13.) The structure of authority will be based on the degree to which members' actions influence other members to change their behavior or attitudes. Attempts by a member to influence are probably more frequent than is success in influencing. Authority exists only insofar as attempts to influence are successful. Hence, the structure of authority in a group represents the differences in influence among the members' actions. When a member is considered an authority figure, it is because she or he has been successful in influencing the other members, and the other members expect that that person's future actions will also be influential. Obviously, the amount of authority an individual has will vary directly with past successes that led to rewarding experience for the other members. This develops an expectancy of reward for following the influence of a particular member.

The maturity and emotional climate of the group is determined by the extent to which its members can influence one another. Members who are totally inaccessible to the influence of others are not actually members of the group in the psychological sense, while individuals who are so suggestible in the group that they virtually lack any personal initiative are not strong contributors. Most individuals in the group approach and withdraw from the boundaries that they erect and maintain against mutual influence. The boundaries may be subtly permeated by an appeal, or bypassed by diversion or evasion, or sometimes frontally assaulted by hostility and criticism. Even so, the boundaries may remain firmly entrenched. One method of penetrating the boundaries of isolation and distrust seems to be the expression of feelings or asking for help. The effectiveness of this approach is twofold; not only is the individual initiating the act willing to be influenced, but the other members who respond to the act are also influenced by their participation in it.

Patterns of Communication   This is the heart of the structural property of a group, fundamental to any description of group behavior. The pattern of communication is so significant that some researchers have based their entire conception of group counseling on it.

The quantitative aspect of communication is related to the fact that the group operates in time and members must share this time. Obviously, the use of time is not equal. Usually members who are high in influence will participate more than members who are low in influence. In fact, the high-influence figures are frequently encouraged to participate, while the low-influence figures may be discouraged. There are several ways for a counselor to observe the quantitative communication. One method of observation is the frequency of interaction—the number of times a member talks during the sessions. Another indication of the quantity of the communications involves the duration of interaction. The amount of participation is a more accurate indication of the time one member holds the attention of the group than is frequency. Obviously, the counselor will not be able to tally or time the interactions that take place during the group, but the observation of who is participating in the process is a major indicator of the group interaction.

Another aspect of the communication interaction is based on the selectivity in communication. This selectivity becomes a network that typifies who speaks to whom. The emergence of group patterns is influenced by which members initiate topics—presenting information or asking other people for the information. Also, the members who recieve more interactions become significant. As a rule, members who either initiate more or recieve more interaction will become more influential in the group. Probably the most important variable in a communication interaction is the number of members in the group with whom an individual interacts. Members will vary considerably in their tendency to develop relationships. While some restrict their interaction to a few persons, others will develop a relatively wide-spread communication pattern. Usually the wider the range of interaction, the more influential the member will become (Zaleznik and Moment, 1964).

The counselor will observe interaction patterns in the group to be aware of who communicates with whom. This communication pattern will give some indication of the subgroups that are formed as well as the roles that the individual members assume. The counselor could not maintain a system such as the Bales Interaction Matrix (1951), but an awareness of the variables involved in that system can be helpful in observing both the role-taking behavior and the communication pattern.

Patterns of Subgrouping   The discussion of subgroups in Chapter 13 pointed out that subgrouping is a structural dimension closely related to the interactions within a group. In fact, subgrouping is a structural dimension closely related to the interactions within a group. In fact, subgrouping usually results from a repeated interaction. Following a period of conflict, members have generally found other members they agreed with and felt protected by, as well as members they liked less, differed with, attacked, or felt attacked by. This alliance could be transient or could endure throughout the life of the group, frequently becoming a disruptive feature in the group.

Those members who are included into a subgroup frequently find they have a greater loyalty to the subgroup and the goals of the subgroup than to the total group. In some cases, this dual loyalty causes a conflict within the individual. The member who does not support the subgroup goals or behaviors risks exclusion and the imposition of a type of social sanction. Because subgroups are somewhat discouraged by group leaders, when two members do form a particularly close relationship or personal allegiance to each other, they hesitate to bring it out in the group. This frequently leads to their withholding interaction from each other within the total group. If members are revealing information in a subgroup that is not disclosed in the regular group meeting, they are holding back information that may be helpful for other individuals within the group. In addition, they may not be getting as much feedback from this process as they would otherwise.

The members who are excluded from a subgroup may feel less accepted and less desired in a social sense. Frequently these feelings have been involved before, and this type of situation only contributes to their difficulties rather than helping resolve them. If someone is able to bring this type of feeling about subgroups into the open, however, a productive discussion can ensue.

Subgrouping is not necessarily a negative force within the group. If the goals of the subgroup are consistent with the goals of the total group, the subgrouping may enhance the total cohesiveness. It is a common policy to have members report on the discussions of meetings held outside the group. When members find this difficult to do, the counselor may initiate such discussions. If the counselor openly discusses and analyzes the subgroup interactions, both inside and outside group meetings, it may free the members to discuss their reactions.

Generally, it is productive for the counselor to explain to potential group members before entering group counseling that all material discussed outside the group counseling that all material discussed outside the group should be brought back into the total group. Although subgrouping will occur, the counselor should not encourage it. The counselor may need to explain to the members that group counseling will help develop skills necessary to establish durable relationships, but its purpose is not to provide those relationships. Presumably members will generalize their learning from the group situation to other social relationships outside the group (Yalom, 1975).

Patterns of Role Taking

Group member role is such a significant aspect of group counseling that an entire chapter (Chapter 13) has been devoted to it. Here we only touch on that component as it relates to the structural picture of the group. Role taking is another way of examining the process of interaction as it is represented by the behavioral acts of the members. Role taking involves the performances of individuals that relate to a continuing process of the group.

The spirit of active emotional exchange is adopted, and there is interaction and sharing of interpersonal perceptions. The immediate task is to differentiate group members and give them individual identities. Differences among group members are acknowledged and tolerated, so long as each member contributes effort toward reaching the goal. Collaborating roles are important: supporting roles, conciliating roles, and integrative roles help bring members together. Many of the group member roles that build and maintain the group atmosphere are apparent at this point.

Following each personal confrontation, the group has a vast amount of new material to sift through and interpret. A great deal of information about each member comes out. Interaction, including the expression of anxiety, threat, and resistance, may be accomplished by the strengthening of personal bonds between members. Some of these relationships are symbolic, others hierarchical, and others complementary. This is a synthesizing process, in which seemingly random interactions are made more dynamic, orderly, and lawful because they are seen as a system of underlying relationships in the group. As the group develops cohesiveness, the roles assumed by members tend to take on some stability. The assumption or allocation of roles represents a division of function amoung the members. A workable role structure exists when members assume or are allocated roles that fulfill needed functions at the appropriate times. When this occurs, the roles will complement rather than compete with each other. Subgroup alignments develop with indigenous leadership, much of which has shifted to the hands of the group members.

Each member's personality and social behaviors can be conceptualized into various role categories. Although a counselor would not use a system such as Bales (1951) or Benne and Sheats (1948) to analyze a group in process, he or she must be aware of each individual's role taking as well as the general role areas in which the group is functioning.

Patterns of Interpersonal Sentiments   The structural aspects of groups can also be described in another way. While the pattern of interpersonal sentiments that develops among the members may not be observed directly because it exists in the feeling or attitudes that one member may have about another, these sentiments will underlie the behavior and can be inferred from what a person does and says. Making inferences about sentiments, however, will play a very important part in the group process. Whether members like or dislike each other influences the roles that they take with each other, the communication pattern, and the subgroups that will be formed (Zaleznik and Moment, 1964).

Although cohesiveness within the group is demonstrated by acceptance and understanding, it also permits a greater expression of hostility and conflict. One aspect of congruence involves effective communication of what one is feeling. Hence, masking one's anger or hostile feelings would hamper interpersonal learning. Unexpressed conflict cannot lead to a resolution; the individual would break off communication and lessen any opportunity for attitudinal change. A high degree of cohesiveness permits individuals to express their conflicts and hostility toward each other in an attempt to resolve them. The members of the group must mean enough to each other to be willing to bear the discomfort of working through a conflict. When the conflict can be constructively worked through in the group, communication becomes more authentic. It can be a good learning experience for members to have others angry with them, differ with them, and still care for them. Conversely, ti is an important learning experience for the others that they can be angry, can express it, and not be rejected.

Acceptance by others and self-acceptance are frequently interdependent. Self-acceptance is to a large degree dependent upon acceptance by others. Obviously, the degree to which a group can influence an individual's self-esteem is a function of its cohesiveness. The more the group means to the member, the more that individual respects the judgment of other members and the more he or she will try to behave so as to gain their esteem. In some cases, there may be a discrepancy between the individual's self-esteem and the esteem in which she or he is held by the group. When the group evaluates the individual less than the individual does, she or he may deny or distort the group's evaluation. If this is a pattern of behavior and the group is effective, it will eventually break through and confront the individual with the reality. The individual may rationalize the discrepancy by devaluing the group. If the individual needs to use this method to deal with the discrepancy, it may well lead to termination from the group. A more productive way of resolving discrepancy is to attempt to raise the esteem in which he or she is held by changing those attributes that have been criticized by the group. This behavior is more likely when the individual is highly attracted to the group and the discrepancy is not too great.

More frequently, the group evalates the individual more highly than the individual does. When this occurs, the individual may be cautious in self-disclosure, causing guilt feelings to develop. However, as the group comes to mean more, the individual will risk revealing inadequacies. Some individuals attempt to lower the group's esteem by revealing inadequacies, but this behavior generally has the opposite effect. As the individual receives higher levels of facilitation, he or she can self-explore more deeply and with greater understanding raise the level of self-esteem.

Generally, group members are better accepted and liked when they participate actively and are involved in self-exploration and self-disclosure. Yalom (1975) points out that most counseling groups value acceptance of the client role, self-disclosure, honesty about oneself and other members, nondefensiveness, interest and acceptance of others, support of the group, and personal improvement. These behaviors, which build cohesiveness, are also a part of the productive stage of group counseling. The individual is participating in the group and being reinforced for adaptive social skills.

Cohesiveness and Collaboration

Dailey (1977) offered an important theoretical model of the effects of cohesiveness and collaboration on the group. He believes that both cohesiveness and collaboration are co-determinants of group productivity and effective responses of group members. Cohesiveness is often viewed by all social scientists as a structural characteristic of groups and thus a determinative of group performance and processes. It is conceptualized as an indicator of the group members' desire to remain and work in the group. Collaboration has been a group process of considerable importance in collective problem solving but has received only limited attention in the therapy literature. Aram and Morgan (1976) define collaboration in work settings as the presence of mutual influences between persons, open and direct communication, conflict resolution, and support for innovation and experimentation. In the majority of studies conducted in laboratory situated small groups, cooperative and collaborative group processes consistently yield superior performance when compared with competitive processes. Collaboration is composed of three factors: (1) problem solving through support and integration; (2) open authentic communication; and (3) knowledge-based risk taking.

Although the literature emphasizes the fact that both cohesiveness and collaboration are related to a variety of important group and individual outcomes, little attention has been directed to the interactive impact of these two variables on the group members. Cohesiveness and collaboration are each positively related to productivity. Dailey proposes a model that predicts cohesiveness to be positively associated with collaboration and to function as an antecedent of collaboration. Cohesiveness provides a basis for the emergence of collaborative group processes. In other wores, cohesiveness is seen as a necessary but not a sufficient condition for maintenance of group productivity.

Dailey describes four possible situations that could arise in the group. One possibility would be a group that exhibited low cohesion and collaboration. Such a group would demonstrate a weak sense of mutual attraction, low inter-member respect, and low-level trust. Furthermore, the group would be non-collaborative in the sense of problem solving and working toward resolution. The counselor in such a group would need to work to increase the cohesion and collaboration by providing a great deal of supporative and structural behavior. A second possibility involves groups that are highly cohesive but low on collaboration. Such a group would occur if members were strongly attracted to other group members and used the group for social interaction rather than collaborative work toward problem resolution. A third possible group is one that poseses low cohesion and high collaboration. This type of group would probably seldom occur in a counseling situation, where it would suggest a group that was recently formed but willing to collaborate on information and problem solving. This may be a more common phenomenon in task-oriented groups. The last possibility is a group that exhibits high cohesion and high collaboration at the same time. In such a group, a strong sense of mutual attraction would exist, and they would confront problems and conflicts in an open and trusting manner. It is assumed that such groups would be most productive. It should be noted, however, that high collaboration and cohesion are not necessarily enduring properties of the group. It seems possible that as a group moves through various stages, it may experience different possible combinations of cohesiveness and collaboration.

What If the Group Is Not Working?

There are times when a group moves through the beginning orientation and social behavior and into a period of oonflict. Through the conflict period, hidden behaviors may become more obvious, and the stereotypes established in the early sessions are disconfirmed. Members express opposing points of view on some issues, and this may create both mistrust and new alliances. Instead of an argument being understood in terms of facts, it may be a testing ground for personal influence and prestige. Hopefully, the group moves through this period by facing its own destructive tendencies, comes to understand the confrontation, and works to get people together into a movement of cohesiveness. After a period of conflict, a group typically moves into a period of cohesiveness; at least, the counselor expects this to occur. When the group or subgroups or individuals do not feel cohesive, the group will not come together and not be able to move on to more productive behavior.

What can the counselor do to facilitate this movement and feeling of cohesiveness? It may be necessary for the group to explore further some of the areas of disagreement, either between individuals or subgroups, or possibly with the leader. The leader needs to review and attempt to correct the possible snags that could interfere with the development of cohesiveness. Has the group worked out norms of behavior and are they governing each other in their conduct? Has the counselor been successful in creating a therapeutic climate? Are the members interacting with each other rather than with just the leader? Is there an open expression of emotion, both positive and negative? Has the leader demonstrated the successful handling of an attack? Are members safe when they are self- disclosing? The counselor may want to present the problems of lack of cohesiveness within the group and invite their input. If members are willing to process what is going on in the group and their feelings about it, they may be able to pinpoint the snags that are interfering with their cohesiveness. In most cases, this will stimulate additional conflict between members or subgroups, or between members and the leader. It will take a period of time to work through the issues before the group develops a more genuine feeling of cohesiveness.

Moving Out of Stage Three

During Stage Three, members respond more readily to subtle cues. They indicate agreement or disagreement tentatively, rather than with flat acceptance or rejection. Members accept the group and each other's idiosyncrasies. The group becomes an entity by virtue of the members' mutual acceptance, their desire to maintain the group and to establish new group norms to ensure its existence. As the group evaluates, selects, and decides, it becomes a unique social system with its own values, norms, and internal arrangements. A nucleus of members is committed to the normative system, and conflicts are avoided. Harmony is of maximum importance. In fact, Miles (1957) states that a "false acceptance" may appear, in which disagreements are carefully submerged into an anxiety-avoiding search for consensus. Glossing over differences in order to keep harmony may present a problem. The real test for the group is whether it can skillfully move out of this stage to become an instrument geared for action, directed toward improvement. The group must break out of its complacency, because too prolonged a complacence period is an obstacle to further growth. Security is not a sufficient goal in itself.

Many counseling groups never progress beyond this stage. The counselor may be satisfied when the clients give emotional feedback and show increasing awareness of their effect on others. Group members find it difficult to move beyond the stage in which they love each other but do not really accomplish anything.

In groups where interpersonal bonds are genuine and strong, a remarkable amount of cohesiveness develops, and members give mutual evaluative support, which is a prime requisite for successful behavior change. Having discovered that some members are insightful and productive, the group attempts to follow their lead.

STAGE FOUR: PRODUCTIVENESS

The behavior of the group during the stage of productiveness is not clear-cut. The group has met for some time, worked through some of its conflicts, and worked to a realistic level of cohesiveness in which members accept each other with their problems and try to help resolve them. Although all of these procedures involve a certain amount of productive behavior change, it is not until a high level of cohesiveness is established that the members feel they are giving and receiving higher levels of facilitative conditions and thereby feel safer to explore themselves at deeper levels.

When a group achieves some degree of stability in its pattern of behaving, a long working process begins. Because members are more deeply committed to the group, they may reveal more of themselves and their problems in living.

The established group now directs itself toward individual as well as group goals, attempting to produce something of a general and lasting value. In a counseling group, the task may be to develop insight into personal and interpersonal processes and to affect constructive personality change.

There is awareness that the group is a group. At first, a group is dependent upon the leader for concepts and models, but now the members have developed some leadership skills. The group has developed a pattern of distributive leadership in which realistic individual roles are maintained. These roles are assigned on the basis of relative abilities and are accepted accordingly. The counselor serves as one source of internal standard, but not the only one.

In this stage, group structure tends to be functional. Norms of behavior are useful and not maintained simply for their own sake. A sort of casual, constant attention is given to the work process. Locating goals, developing procedure, summarizing, and operating systematically are some of the activities needed to balance the interpersonal emotional aspects of the group. It is helpful for the counselor as well as the members to be aware of structural patterns of behavior that have developed to a higher level of stability. No one can offer procedural guidelines for the productive period. In general, the counselor can maximize the development of the group through the application of the basic principles in the counselor's role. (These roles and techniques were discussed more specifically in Chapter 12.)

Because interpersonal bonds are strong, evaluation, criticism, discussion, and reevaluation can be undertaken. The group directs itself to members as objects since subjective relations have been established. Members view individual behavior in the group with greater objectivity. They show greater ease in making decisions, and more flexibility in controlling group processes. Because they have learned to relate to others as social entities, role structure is not an issue. Members can adopt and play roles that will enhance the effectiveness of the group.

Despite this encouraging picture, a group frequently regresses from the constructive behavior. It may exhaust the process in dynamics, and it may revert to a lower level of operation in order to regenerate.

Corrective Emotional Experiences

Productiveness as an outcome of counseling must be measured in terms of changes made by the group members. The changes may be view in terms of their behavior within the group situation, as well as changes in the behavior outside. The counselor and group members have to exert influence on the individual member's behavior within the group setting in order to be certain that the member will engage in the counseling process and open up to the potential of the situation. Kelman (1963) suggests a group situation in which the client is both freed and forced to overcome resistances and to think and talk about things ordinarily avoided. The greater freedom allows the client to experience certain feelings within the group and to express these feelings as they are experienced.

For lasting changes to take place, the client must undergo what Kelman (1963) calls "corrective emotional experiences." These are based on the manifestations in the group setting of distorted, self-defeating, and troubling attitudes that the individual brings to real- life relationships. A corrective experience is possible if the feelings the member experiences when expressing these attitudes in the group situation are as real and intense as they are under usual circumstances. The difference between the group setting and real-life situations is that in the group, the individual is encouraged to examine these feelings as they occur. With the help of the counselor and group members, the individual can see his or her attitudes in their true light, recognize their distorted and self-defeating aspects, and gain some understanding of their origins.

The significance of corrective emotional experiences is that the individual's examination of attitudes and behavior patterns occurs simultaneously with their actual manifestation at a real-life level of emotional intensity. The individual is still experiencing the relevant feelings, making it more than an intellectual exercise. This type of experience can be the basis for internalized changes in the individual's self-concept and concept of interpersonal behaviors. The individual gains new insight, new understandings of the attitudes and behaviors that he or she characteristically uses in interpersonal relationships, the result of those behaviors, and the exceptations of others' reactions that generally guide him or her. From the new insights, a more realistic attitude and expectation can be developed.

The individual's compliance and identification are usually necessary before such an experience can occur. The three processes—compliance, identification, and corrective emotional experiences—represent sequential steps in the process. The individual begins by complying, that is, following the basic rule and engaging in the counseling process. Identification occurs as the individual gets some satisfaction from the relationship with the counselor and possibly the group. As the member continues to engage in the counseling process, the corrective emotional experiences can occur and internal changes can be built on them.

The emphasis in the group is on demonstrating to the individual how certain motives, of which the individual is partially unaware, influence behavior. The communication involves awakening some latent emotional resistance and defenses against the intellectual material, thus making them explicit and permitting resolution of the resistance. In contrast to most learning situations, the long-range goal in a group requires an interference with the members' initial hope that things would remain on a comfortable and intellectual level.

For this process to occur, the counselor and group members must influence the individual to overcome resistances, to allow himself or herself to experience some threatening feelings, to express these feelings at the same time they are being felt, and to examine them. That is to say, the counselor and group members influence the individual member within the counseling situation to increasingly meet the requirements of a therapeutic self-exploration process.

The counselor contributes to this process by confronting a group member with the distorted and self-defeating aspects of the member's attitudes and behaviors, as well as by other methods of encouraging self-examination. The group makes a special contribution to this process by providing many ways of stimulating the individual's habitual interpersonal reactions, which can then be examined and form the basis for a corrective experience. The group members present a wide range of interaction possibilities for the individual, thus increasing the chances that the attitudes and patterns which trouble the individual in real life can be evoked during the counseling situation. When the individual manifests some troublesome interpersonal attitude or behavior, the individual can be confronted not only with the character of the behavior but also with the reactions it elicits in others. The consensual validation by group members in describing their reactions to the individual's behavior would be more dramatic than would just a counselor's response.

One study (Mainord, Burk, and Collins, 1965) compared counselor behaviors in group therapy where counselors were either confronting or diverting in their responses. The confronting approach was direct, maximally affective, immediate, and concrete. In the diverting treatment, the counselor attempted to direct the group away from discussion of the personal to impersonal and more generalized topics. Many of the group members showed signs of discomfort during the confronting approach; it was reported, however, that such discomfort was transient and considered necessary for the positive effects. Obviously, the diverting approach resulted in less discomfort during the group. The study found that the confronting approach was clearly superior in changing behaviors leading to more successful terminations. As indicated, although the group members may experience discomfort during a stage of confrontation, their attention may focus on specific emotional thoughts or behaviors which eventually would be more productive in meeting their personal objectives.

Kaye (1973) argued that change, in the sense of the occurrence of interpersonal learning in attitude modification among group members, depends on the development with the group of a member-centered and emotionally involving mode of action. He conducted a study using the Hill interaction matrix to examine the effect of group interaction on interpersonal learning. He found that increased leader time and interaction provoked an interpersonal focus. When the leader structured activities and took more time in parti cipation, the group moved more quickly into involvement in relational issues. Kaye concluded that short-term changes in behavior and in personal and interpersonal construct are related to the content and style of interaction in the groups. He also suggests that for long-term change to occur, a more confrontive mode of behavior is required over a time period which permits the development of tolerance for such confrontation to avoid defensiveness.

McMurrian and Gazda (1974) researched the level of facilitative communication that occurred during the developmental stages of a group. They found that facilitative functioning was highest in the central portion of the group interaction, and was lower for the beginning and terminal phases. During the productive stage, or what Gazda calls the action stage, there was a qualitatively different style of interaction. An increase in the level of functioning shows a systematic process characteristic in those interviews. During this stage productive, growth-oriented interchanges were appropriately confrontive, showed immediacy, and incorporated facilitative action dimensions of genuiness, concreteness, and appropriate self-disclosure. There was a slight regression seen during this stage of interaction which was considered to be a result of confrontation that went beyond the facilitative level of the group.

Self-Understanding   This period should not be interpreted as a hostile one. The confrontation by the counselor and group is a feedback process involving high levels of the facilitative conditions. The focus is on the individual's stated problem areas—it is not a probing process. Should there be too much threat, the counselor would defend the individual.

When the group member is able to deal with immediate feelings and self-exploration, the counselor can help draw together the fragmented insights and help the person develop self-understanding. The counselor can concentrate on constructing or reconstructing the member's communication process. More effective communication—intrapersonal as well as interpersonal—is a primary goal leading to constructive action. To begin, the counselor may focus on the more competent areas of the individual's functioning, since the probability of the client's understanding and acting upon the situation is greatest in the areas in which the individual is functioning at the highest levels. Success in these experiences will increase the probability of understanding and action in other areas. The counselor may offer minimal levels of facilitative conditions as he or she establishes the relationship. Then, with greater exploration and an improvement in self-understanding, the counselor can increase the level of facilitative conditions. When the member is safe enough to explore and is gaining new insight, he or she is able to handle additive responses within the given content areas. As the individual gains in self-understanding and is able to sustain the level of affective understanding, the counselor can shift attention to the next stage of counseling—action. The counselor needs to recognize a repetition in the cycle of self-exploration to understanding to action. The early phase of self-exploration and understanding may lead to some action. This action will then provide feedback that can modify the original concepts and elicit further explorations leading to a deeper level of understanding, culminating in new action (Carkhuff, 1971).

Modifying Behaviors

Insights derived from a corrective emotional experience are not sufficient. To be productive, counseling must produce changes in the individual's behavior with people in daily life, outside of the group setting. The counseling situation helps develop insight and plans for behaviors to bring about new attitudes, experiences, and behaviors. But the real payoff is derived from generalizing these to life outside. Changing the behaviors outside the group will be even more difficult than working through the situation inside the group. It will be necessary for the group to exert influence on the individual's behavior so that he or she can apply new insights into those situations in which previous behavior has not been satisfactory. The counselor and group members encourage the person to test new patterns by providing a frame of reference for analyzing his or her own behavior and by reviewing with the person some of his or her attempts to apply the learning to outside interactions. During the later part of the productiveness stage, the group will be involved with directly influencing the individual's behavior outside the group situation while counseling is still in process.

Action   The immediate goal should be to help the individual toward constructive action. The ultimate goal of counseling is constructive action toward behavior change for the client. There is an interrelatedness between the client's self-understanding and action, with each serving to sharpen the other. As noted in the preceding section, the counselor emphasizes action in the area in which the client functions best. Areas of greatest self-understanding offer the highest probability of successful action. As the client increases understanding in other spheres and approaches action, the counselor can then increase the level of action orientation. Carkhuff (1971) suggests that the counselor begin to initiate more activities based on experience in the situation, thus serving as both a model and agent for the client to do likewise. While the emphasis for the member is on acting according to one's experience, the counselor attempts to ensure generalization of learning and acting in relationships outside the counseling situation.

Generalization to life outside can be done more effectively when a full description of the goals of counseling can be expressed. When the counselor and client are able to describe the dimensions desired, a plan can be put into operation to meet those goals. Vaguely delineated goals are not helpful in developing procedures for attainment. When operational goals have been established, step-by-step procedures for their accomplishment can be developed. Each step represents a systematic progression toward the goal. The more fully the goals have been described, the more fully the steps can be described and implemented. Once the individual is able to employ constructive action in one area, the counselor can repeat the cycle in another problem area; that is to say, once the person has been able to put into action some new behaviors, this will have a positive effect on self-concept, and the person will have more confidence in attempting new action.

Experimentation   Changes that are produced within the counseling situation should have an important effect on the individual's behavior outside. Generalization of the learning to the outside situations requires that the person experiment with new behaviors. As the person tries to change actions and interpersonal situations, he or she will become even more aware of the unrealistic nature of earlier attitudes and gain additional confidence to reorient behavior. Although the experimenting with new behaviors will continue after termination of counseling, it is important that it occur while counseling is still in progress. The member can experiment on ideas that are still fresh in the mind, can bring back the experiences from outside to discuss in the group, and can carry out experimentation with the support of the counselor and group, who give reassurance when difficulties arise.

The counselor's contribution to this process involves offering a relationship that will enhance the self-concept and feelings of hope. The importance of the facilitative conditions, for instance, is very evident during this period of time. Equally significant are the apparent expertness and personal characteristics of the counselor, which inspire belief in the counselor's ability to help the individual. If the individual has faith that the counselor and other group members can help, feelings of possible success will be enhanced, and feelings of helplessness will be diminished. Identification with the counselor will increase the commitment of the member to the group situation and his or her role requirements within it. The counselor must remember, however, that this is only a part of the process and not an end in itself.

Kelman (1963) refers to the counselor as "an imaginary interlocutor." When the individual is in a real-life situation that was discussed in the group, the counselor tends to be represented as a third party with whom the individual engages in imaginary conversation. Knowing that he or she will report the behavior in the next session increases the likelihood that the individual will live up to the counselor's expectation and his or her own commitment to try out new behaviors. Thus, the individual may try a new behavior expecting the counselor to approve it, or may refrain from a behavior assuming it will be disapproved by the counselor. Group members play a similar part in this process by reinforcing the counselor's position. They are an "anticipated audience" before whom the individual must report on behavior outside of the group.

The ultimate goal of counseling is achieved when the individual generalizes the insights gained to specific situations in life outside. The individual is able to examine situations in which former behavior has been inefficient or inappropriate, and to analyze the attitudes and expectations brought to such situations, and the kind of interaction pattern which typically evolves. In such an examination, the individual applies the insights learned from the group situation to the real-life situation.

When the individual talks about trying a new behavior in light of new insights, the group can help to anticipate the reactions that such behavior is likely to elicit from others. Group members are representatives of society and can remind the individual of the social expectations that circumscribe behavior. They can point out the unrealistic aspects of his or her expectations, and whether the individual is underestimating or overestimating the effects of the planned behavior on others. The practice session within the group allows the individual to reality test the new behavior under conditions that are realistic but also protective.

When the individual comes back to the group and reports experimentation, he or she can gain benefit from the group's reaction. The group members can indicate directly how they would have reacted if they had been participants in the situation, and the individual can gain a fuller understanding of the adequacy of his or her expectations of the social effect of the new behavior.

The effect of the counselor and group on the individual's changes in behavior outside of counseling will be limited to the time the individual remains in the group. It is anticipated, however, that success with the new behaviors will provide sufficient reinforcement to continue on one's own.

What If the Group Is Not Working?

The productive stage in group counseling occurs when the members are at a point where they can work out specific problems within the group. It is important at this stage for the leader to review what the individual members are working toward. Often their original goals have changed as members have progressed through the different stages. The leader must be sensitive to any shift in goals and to understand that, as members interact with each other over a number of weeks or months, their initial goals may change. This is particularly important in an open group. They have experienced initial feelings of anxiety as they oriented themselves to the group, undergone conflict when it arose, become closer and more cohesive as members, until they are finally ready to trust themselves in the group enough to work toward specific goals. There are times, however, when individuals or the group as a whole may reach this point and then not be able to work toward specific goals. Although the group has become cohesive, it does not work and become productive.

What can a leader do when the individual or entire group has difficulty moving toward productivity? In making the productive stage effective, the leader must continue to encourage self-exploration. The members must be encouraged to explore more deeply than in earlier meetings, and this can only be accomplished if there is an atmosphere of trust. Through self-disclosure and the responses of the group members, each individual can gain insight to personal behavior and begin changing it.

The first task for the counselor at this point is to establish the goals which are perceived as achievable and meaningful for each member in order for them to arrive at personal satisfaction and change as a result of the experience. This reevaluation of goals should usually occur as members move from the cohesive stage to production. This renewed focus can help the individuals in the group to explore themselves and the situations they want to work on.

When members are not moving into the productive stage, the leader may want to examine the amount of cohesiveness present. In addition, the leader may want to examine the relationship between the cohesiveness and the collaborativeness of the individuals in the group. Perhaps the group has been cohesive as a whole but a particular member still does not feel free to share a deeper level. The leader can help the member examine his or her feelings toward others in the group, especially feelings of trust.

The leader can involve the group in an evaluation of the level of cohesiveness and examine the process that is going on within the group. As the group processes its own behavior, it may help them clarify what they are doing or not doing, and the self-exploration of some individuals in that process may help move them and the remainder of the group into a productive stage.

The leader must also remain a model of confrontive behavior. By this stage in the group, the members should be able to confront each other and work through the confrontation. At this point, cohesiveness is an obvious prerequisite.

Another possibility for the leader when a member is not moving into this stage is to make a contract. It can even be a written contract. The contract would state the goals, and the member would be encouraged to move toward them. A firm verbal commitment or promise to work on new behavior may also be appropriate.

Leading an open group causes additional complications for the leader. With the continual entry of new members into the group, the stages have a tendency to overlap and even be repeated for some older members. One of the results of this situation is that production is an ongoing phase, but it usually takes place more readily between several older members. Many times, older members form a nucleus of the group, with newer members moving into that nucleus as they become more identified with the group. The effect of this on newer members is usually a positive one, in that it enables them to become aware of the process of working on specific goals. As they observe older members who are acting more directly with each other and dealing with confrontation, they are often encouraged to become active members within their group. As they watch older members model facilitative behavior and deal with confrontation, they feel safer about opening up and exploring themselves. The element of trust is enhanced as they also begin to reveal more of themselves in a more than superficial manner. The leader must be aware of the individual's goals so that each member can be encouraged and move into his or her personal productive stage.

Moving Out of Stage Four

While an individual's first engagement in the counseling process and later commitment to that process are important stages, the productiveness stage in the model is most crucial. To sum up, it is during this stage that the individual internalizes such new values and new patterns of behavior as have been acquired. In earlier stages, any changes in the individual are likely to be the result of playing the game, and later changes are usually dependent upon the relationship with the counselor or the group. In either case the changes while perhaps helpful to the individual, do not become a part of internalized structure. Only when the new, more realistic behavior patterns become part of the individual's personality has the counseling attained its goal.

In order for lasting changes to take place, the client must undergo corrective emotional experiences. These are brought about in the counseling situation through the individual's objective evaluations of past behavior. The individual is led to examine his or her feelings and behavior and to recognize their distorted and often self-defeating aspects. As a result of these new insights, the client may develop more realistic attitudes and behavior patterns. The counselor can help the client see the nature of the self-defeating behavior by confronting the client with these behavior patterns, by offering interpretations of them, or by encouraging self-examination in other ways.

The group members also offer opportunities for corrective emotional experiences. In individual counseling, the only interaction possible is between the counselor and the client; in the group setting, there are many individuals with whom to interact. The wide range of personal and social characteristics represented by the various members of the group provide greater stimulation for the person's feelings and attitudes. "As a group member engages in his own inquiry process, sharing it through discussion with his peers, he will receive immediately the feedback which reinforces or extinguishes the tentative idea, meaning, or value he is exploring (Muro and Freeman, 1968, p. 10)." In effect, the group becomes a miniature society in which the individual has the opportunity to examine attitudes and values and ways of behaving.

The group can also produce behavior-modifying experiences through its reaction to the individual's behavior. When a group member exhibits a troublesome attitude or kind of behavior, she or he can be confronted not only with the self-defeating nature of the behavior but also with the reaction that the behavior elicits in other group members. The member is able to obtain a clearer picture of the meaning of such behavior, and is led to a deeper understanding of how it causes difficulty with other individuals in the outside world. The individual may be able to build upon this experience in the group situation and apply this new learning to other situations in daily life.

The group situation can also help the member learn how to operate in other social situations outside of counseling. This can be an extremely important contribution, because most behaviors occur in group situations. In group counseling, as in all other groups, there is competition for the leader's attention, struggles for power status within the group, attempts at impressing other members, and other forms of group competition. Being forced to deal with the interpersonal situation caused by these struggles in the counseling group, the individual can learn to handle everyday situations outside the counseling group in ways that are self-enhancing, rather than self-defeating.

STAGE FIVE: TERMINATION

Termination is one of the most significant aspects of the group process. If handled inappropriately, it may not only conclude this experience without effective change for the member or members, but also so adversely affect individuals that they may not seek further help when necessary. If handled adequately, the process of termination in itself can be an important force in helping individuals develop new behaviors.

During the process of termination, it is important that the members put their new learning into practice. The transition from the group to the members' daily lives is made easier if the counselor has emphasized the importance of taking action and making changes in attitudes and behavior. During the productiveness stage, opportunities should have been provided for members to initiate action in establishing new behavior patterns. The group experience will give the members a good start and an incentive to continue the learning process after the group ends. During the termination stage, the group members may focus on ways of working on things that they have learned in the group when they no longer have the group situation to use.

A review of the literature indicates very little written on the topic. However, the literature does suggest that termination is often not handled well. This is less surprising considering that the affects most commonly associated with termination seem to vary from sad to downright morbid. McGee et al. (1972) described termination as one of the most difficult and emotionally involving processes for the members during group therapy because it arouses feelings of separation, loss, dissolution, impotence, dependency, death, and abandonment. Pleasant or not, termination is built into the group process from its very beginning because the intention of the members is to eventually leave the group. In an open group, termination is a more constant part of the group process. Changes in membership and sometimes in counselors keep the issue of termination constantly alive. Whenever anyone leaves the group, it has a profound impact on that individual and often a direct impact on the other members. Each time termination occurs as an issue, it can serve to accelerate the group and deepen the individual gain for each member. However, when termination is poorly handled, the threat that arises is difficult for the entire group.

Considerations in Termination

The appropriateness and effectiveness of a termination may be related to the institutional ethos, the group culture, or the counselor's attitudes and actions in relation to the process (McGee, Schuman, and Racusen, 1972). Within an institution with a limited commitment to group counseling, there may be less concern with the process of working through a termination. In some institutions, such as an inpatient hospital unit, the pressure from the group may not be a part of the group process but a decision made by physician that the member is ready for a discharge from the hospital. The lack of continuity of care in such a situation does not permit the group to be an effective method of achieving insight and behavior change.

The group culture is made up of the members and the counselor. In an open group, the assimilation of new members and the dropping out of others may damage the group culture. If cohesiveness is low, the counselor and group must face the situation openly. They may raise issues about termination as new members enter the group, and focus on any other issues that arise. Excessive absence or premature departure of a member, for example, are signs of weakness in cohesiveness and should be explored. If members assume that they can drift along and drop out when they so desire, without an obligation to the rest of the group, the atmosphere will be detrimental to the counseling process.

Sisson et al. (1973), in their examination of client verbal interaction in group counseling, found that the last quarter of counseling showed a decrease in the amount of interaction among the members. It should be noted that while there was some decreasing in the amount of interaction, they did maintain a high degree of therapeutic interaction with an increase in some topic-centered pre-worked categories. McMurrian and Gazda (1974) studied the level of facilitative function throughout the stages of the group. They found a dispersion of data during the last three or four sessions of that thirty-two session group. At that point, there was a strong identity with the group, and there were conflicting feelings of cohesiveness and closeness on one hand and recognition that the group was about to end on the other. More interaction would be inappropriate, and the group was preparing to disband. It seems that as individuals are preparing to terminate, they become less facilitative, have less therapeutic interaction, and start to pull back.

The meaning of termination as a continuing process within the therapeutic experience has rarely been systematically examined. Kauff (1977) states that termination is most often treated as an isolated event. She believes that although there are differences in the kinds of termination, an interesting set of shared fantasies and feelings appear regularly in therapists and clients regardless of the exact termination circumstances. She proposes that termination issues are involved with the transference of members or the countertransference of the counselor.

One transference response that occurs for a group as a whole may occur when the therapist is going to leave the group and a new therapist will take over. There may be a fantasy about the terminating therapist that he or she is too good to lose. Or there may be a fantasy that the incoming therapist is a dangerous intruder, is going to be a bad parent, or needs to go through a time of trial.

There are some situations in which the counselor may have a countertransference which interferes with the termination process. A counselor who has a need to cling and has not fully resolved his or her own dependency issues will have difficulty trusting the growth of clients. It is not uncommon for a client to regress to remain with such a counselor. In a situation where a counselor feels there are not enough members in the group, a client may feel a necessary member. Thus the counselor's unconscious intervention could interfere when the client is considering termination.

In contrast to the clinging type of counselor is the leader who rejects a client whose tentative shift toward the environment is experienced as a loss. A counselor who is vulnerable to such feelings when the client approaches termination may neglect or reject the member rather than productively work through the termination process.

Another transference issue may occur when the client first considers termination and the counselor appears to agree. Even though the client has initiated the idea of termination, the counselor's agreement may be felt as a rejection.

Transference in the group is not only to the leader but may be to the group as a whole. As a closed group approaches termination, an individual or the entire group may feel the group become more important because of the threatened loss.

There are times when termination of members is a threat to the remainder of the group. The group may respond with an undue holding on. Some members will have fears of being trapped by the group or by the counselor. The individuals who remain may have feelings of abandonment as though the other person is moving away from them. This may stimulate anger at the individual who is terminating, and possibly at the group situation.

Kauff (1977) suggests that the counselor examine closely the member who exhibits no visible reaction to his or her own termination or that of another member of the group or the counselor. Often, anger underlies such a defensive posture when an individual repeatedly manifests this type of nonresponse.

It is unusual for a group to examine feelings about termination without being encouraged by the counselor. The counselor must help the members to differentiate between appropriate termination and other forms of departure from the group.

Premature termination can be dealt with openly in the group. The member considering departure can be confronted with its implications, both for herself or himself and for the group.

Yalom (1975) outlines three common forms of termination from a group:the termination of the unsucessful client, the termination of a successful client, and the termination of the entire group.

The Unsuccessful Client

Usually, a considerable amount of stress in the group underlies the reasons for a member's terminating early. Some early dropouts have developed inappropriate interpersonal patterns to handle the demands for candor and intimacy that are involved in the group. They may be confused about the procedure and suspect that the group interaction has little relevance to their problems. Finally, throughout this period of stress, too little support emerges for them to sustain their hope that something positive will come from the experience.

Rosenzweig and Folman (1974) review some of the variables affecting premature termination in group therapy. They examined some client, counselor, and treatment variables that may affect members and premature termination. A review of the literature indicated that the difference between individuals who stay in counseling and drop out is that the stayers tend to be more anxious, more self-dissatisfied, more verbal, and more self-aware than the leavers. The early terminators also have less education than the remainers. Group therapy terminators tended to be more socially effective than continuers.

Rosenzweig and Folman found that therapists' impressions were highly predictive of the clients remaining in counseling. They found a highly significant relationship between the counselor's responses on an attitude questionnaire and therapy dropout. However, of all the psychological tests and demographic variables on the clients, only the level of education was significantly related to therapy outcome, with the remaining members more highly educated than the leavers. It has been suggested that the individuals remaining demonstrated a greater goal-directed persistence. Another interpretation is that the counselor's bias may have been present in favor of the more educated and more highly verbal individuals.

The findings from the therapists' attitude questionnaire indicate that the counselor is probably the most reliable judge of members he or she can help. The counselor's feeling toward the client and toward how long he or she expects the client to remain may be a self-fulfilling prophesy or may indicate a useful intuitive-based diagnostic skill.

Members terminating from an open-ended group can be divided into at least four different classes (McGee, Schuman, and Racusen, 1972), three of which involved premature termination. The comparison of the four classes is made according to the completeness of the experience and the degree to which the terminating member, the group, and the counselor are able to deal with the feelings about separation.

In the first level separation, there is complete avoidance of dealing with the importance of the loss. The member may handle this by denying or repressing at this level through the use of a letter or phone call to the counselor, or by repeated absences from the group meeting. Typical separations at this level occur during the early stages when the group is immature or when there has been an error in the member-selection process. Individuals who terminate in such a manner are generally called dropouts.

The second level of termination may be referred to as "a flight into health." A member may have been involved in some self-exploration with some self-understanding, and may possibly have made some experimental behavior changes. At this point, the member acknowledges the gains that have been made and feels no need to continue in the group. This is a difficult procedure to handle because in come cases, the member may be ready to leave the group. When, however, the member has not successfully made the generalization to the outside situations, but is just "feeling good" about some success without working through the self-exploration and understanding, the termination is premature.

At the third level of termination, the individual may be satisfied with the successful insight and change in behavior and be unwilling to proceed further. This is a step beyond the second level because the individual has worked through with some degree of success the area focused on and, although recognizing a need for further involvement, decides not to proceed further. Often after this level of success, the departing member may feel that the group support is not needed any longer. The member is determined to handle life on his or her own.

The fourth level is actually an appropriate procedure. At this level of termination, the individual announces in advance that he or she is considering termination, establishes an approximate date, and works toward the date by discussing personal feelings and interacting with other members around the issue of leaving. The group helps the member analyze behavior and the process of leaving, and supports the decision. At this level the terminating member, the other members, and the counselor all participate in working through the leaving process.

There may be many reasons for an individual to leave the group without reaching the fourth level of termination. Changing work, moving, becoming ill, or being discharged from a hospital are all reasons for discontinuing without an appropriate level of termination.

An inexperienced counselor may feel threatened by a client who announces an intention to drop out. During a stage with a lot of conflict, several clients may consider terminating, and at this point the counselor may feel considerable discomfort. It is important for the counselor to learn that dropouts in the early stages are an inevitable part of the group and probably do not reflect a personal failure. If a counselor puts pressure on a client to continue, the counselor may be asking the client to do something for the counselor rather than for himself or herself.

One method of reducing dropouts is to provide an understanding of the process to the members during the precounseling interview. If each member has an idea about the process, it may reduce the initial anxiety that stems from uncertainty and confusion. The counselor may also anticipate some of the group concerns during the early stages of the process, and can comment that it is typical in group interactions for some members to feel they need to withdraw.

Despite preparation and discussion of the process, some members will consider dropping out. It is typical for members to discuss this with the counselor individually before announcing it to the group. A counselor generally approaches this problem, as most other problems, by suggesting the member return to the group and discuss it with the other group members. It is assumed that the group members will help the individual work through the concerns, and that group pressure will keep the individual from terminating. This process, however, may not be successful.

When the individual member decides to drop out, the counselor may suggest a few individual sessions to discuss the group process and the member's plan for future behavior. If these meetings are productive, the individual may seek another counseling experience. This whole process suggests that the counselor must work to make each termination a constructive experience for the client. All too often, both the member and the counselor have feelings of failure and are more prone to avoid each other than to work through the process to understand what has happened and to make productive future plans.

Termination of the Successful Client

In an open group, individuals will terminate at various times although the group continues to function. In such a group, the process of life stages that have been described earlier will obviously vary more than in a closed group. Each client enters, participates, and terminates in a highly individualized manner.

The timing for termination is very important, although inexact. Individuals in the group usually become aware that they are handling their life in a more appropriate manner and are able to devote more attention in the group to helping others. In the open group, clients are able to see new members enter the group and others terminate. They are able to observe the counselor beginning the process with the new members, and watch individuals work through their termination. The member contemplating termination should be encouraged to present this intention to the group. Instead of being an open announcement, however, it usually comes with cues that are picked up and presented by members of a subgroup. Although the interest in termination is usually initiated by the group members, the counselor must play an active role in the process. Occasionally the counselor may have to take an active role when a member has become too dependent on the group situation.

Members may delay termination because of a belief that the group needs them and that they have assumed a helping role for other members. Others may postpone termination because the group has become a social life for them rather than the place to learn new skills. However, group members are usually helpful in working with each other to decide about termination. As with the unsuccessful client, the counselor must be aware of his or her own feelings during termination with a successful member. The counselor must be careful neither to encourage termination too early for members with whom he or she is less close, nor to attempt to hold individuals whom he or she particularly enjoys.

The announcement of intention to terminate should be made far enough in advance to permit group discussion. It is too difficult to examine the feelings regarding termination if it is announced during the same session at which the member intends to leave.

Termination from a group is an extended and comprehensive process. McGee, Schuman, and Racusen (1972) suggest a process of continuous phases that are usually manifest during the group:

1. Feelings about termination usually arise in the individual's preparation interview and as other members leave the group.

2. A member will usually make some indication of a wish or intent to terminate from the group.

3. There will be some discussion of the member's plan to terminate and the implication of termination for both the individual and the other group members.

4. After some discussion regarding the termination during the group sessions, the terminating member will confirm the decision.

5. The member attends his or her last meeting, and the separation occurs.

6. The group discusses the member's termination and its implications during the next few sessions.

7. A new member will enter the group.

An effective termination involves the departing member in openly acknowledging what the group has meant and how he or she will function without it. The group will also acknowledge what the departing member has meant to them and how they feel about functioning without him or her. Termination from the group is considered irrevocable; when everyone accepts the finality of the termination, they can be relatively certain that a departing member is ready for this action. Through the discussion of the finality, unresolved feelings about the group can be examined. The aspect of finality will force the terminating member and the other group members to examine the concept of loss.

Termination of the Group

Many closed groups have specific time limits that are established at the beginning. However, an entire group may be terminated due to other circumstances. A few closed groups begin on an open-ended time schedule and then work out a decision for a time of termination.

A group frequently tries to avoid the difficult process of working through a termination, and the counselor must help them focus on the task. The conclusion of the group is a significant loss. Although members may continue to see each other, it is a fragmentation of the group and that atmosphere will be gone forever. As the group moves toward termination, the counselor will need to help the members overcome the avoidance of the issue. With a group that has worked through the various stages and become productive, the members can be reminded that it is their group and they must decide how they are going to terminate. Frequently, new problems occur during this stage—problems of separation and loneliness—that will generate new concerns for the members. Other members may have difficulty with any separation and try to withdraw by increasing absence, denial of the situation, or not wanting to discuss it until the final meeting. Because it is an important part of group development, the counselor must help the group members talk about their feelings of separation and the death of the group.

While the counselor and group members are terminating a joint experience, they are doing so with varying degrees of readiness. Although the group may go through the general life stages together, individuals within the group may not have reached a point of generalizing insights into behaviors for outside situations. It is important that the group members and counselor examine their feelings regarding the upcoming termination and prepare themselves for the process. In a closed group, in which the entire group terminates, the members do not have to examine the issue of how the group will function without them, nor do they deal with feelings about leaving a vital process that continues after they are gone. Both of these areas are important in the process of termination from an open, ongoing group.

Group members may discuss fear and pain regarding the loss of the group, which often leads to sharing past experiences. Members may discuss the more exciting group events, remind each other of the way they were, and give personal testimonials about how much they have been helped. The counselor must also deal with feelings about separation. He or she is as vulnerable as the other group members and may facilitate the process of the group by disclosing personal feelings.

Summary of Termination

In a group that runs on a schedule, the last meeting is fixed in advance. In other groups, the approaching termination becomes apparent. Its approach raises a complex set of issues and demands. Near the end of the time, members anticipate the loss and feel the need for closure. They make various attempts to deny the full impact of their separation.

As members approach the last meetings, they spend some effort generating new interpretations of the problems. While noting successful events, they dwell on some of the group's failures. They reflect with chagrin that the hopes of realizing come soals are dwindling. It is not uncommon for one such goal to be an intimate relationship with the counselor. There is a pressure for the counselor to affirm the extraordinary quality of the group and to give it his or her blessings.

Some stifled frustation, insecurity, and anger may emerge before termination. It may be that these feelings were unexpressed or unheeded throughout the group's sessions. The resurgence of anxiety and hostility also serves as a distancing device preparatory to separation. Members often withdraw by first expressing their negative feelings about others, then their positive feelings.

They frequently insist that the group will never end, because each person will carry the group away with them. Although they did not accomplish as much as they had hoped, they feel that knowing each other was significant, and they reflect on their roles and what they gave and received. They seek confirmation that their choice to join the group was a good one. They express positive feelings about the experience and thank one another for their contributions. They feel the results will be evident after the group is over and they are on their own.

Evaluation of Group Stages Concept

A number of observers who have studied group development have found some basic patterns that occur within most groups. Groups tend to differ in length of time spent in any one stage, and the stages are usually not clearly separated. In fact, they are likely to go forward and backward to some degree as part of the general progression through the stages. However, most groups, and individuals that compose them, probably go through the stages. It seems resonable to assume that engagement in the process, a part of the initial stage, is a necessary condition of effectiveness. Members need to get past a superficial, polite behavior that is more appropriate at social situations and begin to engage in self-disclosing and self-exploration behaviors. Both individual and group goals must be established so that members can have clear conceptions of what they are working toward. Groups do need to work out individual roles and behaviors, handle stereotypical behavior, and establish guidelines.

However, the type of conflict that exists in confrontation would certainly be different in different groups. Many groups would not experience the stage with the connotation of fighting and retaliation. However, in order for a group to progress, differences must be resolved or accepted so that defensiveness can be diminished. The consensus suggests that cohesiveness is crucial so that group power can help people change. This sense of working together is considered to be one of the curative factors in group counseling. Just as it would be hard to imagine positive outcomes with a poor relationship in individual counseling, it is difficult to conceive of positive outcomes without cohesiveness in a group. Certainly the productive stage is necessary if one is considering effectiveness of the group, particularly if productiveness is equated with changes in behavior by the individual members. In some groups, however, cohesiveness is a measure of group effectiveness when it is generally only a necessary prerequisite for production.

Tuckman (1965) reviewed fifty-five articles dealing with stages of small group development, and generated a model of changes involving four stages: forming, storming, norming, and performing. In 1977 he reviewed the literature again to see if the research was consistent with the stages. Not all of the twenty-two studies agreed; however, there was a general pattern. This second review found considerably more evidence of a termination stage, so Tuckerman added adjourning to his previous stages.

Is It Necessary?   Although groups do seem to go through stages, there is a serious question regarding the necessity of a group or all individuals in the group to experience the stages. Does the group have to go through the stages to be effective? What if an individual does not feel consistent with the group stage?

"Each group, like each individual, is unique, can be understood in terms of exceptions, and in terms of when, how and why changes and development occur (Napier and Gershenfeld, p. 248, 1973)." One variable that may affect the group's conduct through the stages is whether it is an open or closed group. In an open group, the stages may be met for some members, even reoccuring as new members enter and not occuring at all for some members. Some new members in an open group experience conflict and cohesiveness, but do not yet feel safe enough within the confines of the group to express their feelings. They have entered the group as it is in process, and in spite of the initial screening and orientation of the leader they may feel uneasy about becoming active participants. Therefore, they withdraw and observe the group process. Such individuals would be described as still in the initial stage of group orientation while the majority of the group is experiencing a conflict stage. Such members can feel isolated from the other members and have difficulty gaining a feeling of cohesiveness.

Often a group member does not quite fit in. This is a difficult and uncomfortable situation for that individual and possibly other members of the group. Even with careful selection, consistent development through the stages cannot be assured. Most people develop at different rates in other areas of life, and it is unlikely that group development would be any different. The leader need not force members to speak to the process or to hold others back. The development is a natural process, and individuals should be allowed to go through the stages at their own pace. The leader does need to be aware of the differences in the stages for individual members, and assist individuals in their process and progress in the group.

A number of things could happen to the individual who is not in line with the stages of group development. Other members may use this individual as a scapegoat. The scapegoat may be the victim of jokes or teasing, or may be confronted with probing questions. The individual could be isolated by other members and not taken seriously or even ignored. If the person is strong enough but continues to not feel a part of the group, he or she may drop from the group. The individual may become the target of hostility, anger, or ridicule by the majority of the group, either because he or she is inhibiting the progress of the group, or because he or she is more eager to move ahead than the majority.

A member may be out of stage with the other group members for several reasons. A member may not feel safe with the material being discussed by the group. This would indicate a lack of trust toward the other group members. The member would be too anxious to self-disclose, and would discuss material at the intellectual rather than the personal level. Another reason for inconsistent behavior would be the member's feeling deviant from the remainder of the group. This could occur if the group is selected from a self-contained population such as alcoholics or acting-out adolescents attending a program. Although general populations seem to share characteristics, a great deal of variability does exist in each member. A deviant member becomes isolated, while most of the members form an alliance. The leader should attempt to draw this member closer to the mainstream of the group.

If a member is not consistent, can he or she still profit from the group experience? The goals of individual members may be satisfied before all stages have occurred. That is, some members may feel satisfied at the cohesive stage if their goals were related to human closeness. True behavior change within a time-limited group may be an unrealistic expectation for some people. Although the stated purposes of the group are not fully realized, there are secondary gains that are not to be dismissed. Participants may acquire an increased sense of responsibility by seeing how their behavior affects others. It could be the first time a member has felt a sense of belongingness or has identified with a group of people. The educational aspect of group counseling is also important. In most groups, participants learn how to interact on a deeper level. Stereotypes that they may have held in earlier sessions begin to fall away as members discover numerous aspects about one another. The feedback one receives in the group is an invaluable lesson in human interaction that one can relate to the outside world. Individuals can learn more about themselves from reflecting upon the roles they assume in groups and comparing them to their life situations. Even if a member leaves the group before regular termination, he or she may learn that group counseling may not be an appropriate mode of therapy for them.

The person who is not consistent with the stage of the rest of the group would probably be somewhat of an isolate and considered deviant by the other members. It is likely that such a person will drop out early. Not only does this represent a potential loss to the individual, but it can also have a demoralizing effect on the other group members The counselor needs to do something to help individuals stay somewhat consistent with the stage at which the group is working. The counselor begins by careful selection of members, screening out individuals who are poor risks for group counseling situations and who may not be compatible with other members selected for the group. Once the person is part of the group and is not behaving in the ways which are consistent in the particular stage, the counselor needs to look at himself or herself to determine whether he or she has been successfully created a constructive therapeutic climate. There are a number of exercises or techniques to help members into the interactional process of the group. Attempting to look at the process of the group at any given time is a helpful approach to the situation. Just getting a person to verbalize about what is going on draws the person into the process. If the member is frightened of self-disclosure, the leader can ask for metadisclosures, or even a disclosure about the concern of disclosing. Asking for positive disclosures can be effective if a member is frightened of expressing negative or angry feelings. To help members who are having trouble being cohesive with the rest of the group, the leader can work at creating an interaction network in which the member interacts with certain members rather than directing comments at or through the leader.

If a member moves successfully through the early stages but gets bogged down in a productive phase by not making any modifications in behavior, the counselor must help the group help the individual toward constructive action. The counselor can encourage the members to test out new behavior patterns with the group, and the group members can provide feedback. Members are then encouraged to experiment outside the group to enhance generalization to others.

The leader must be cautious not to force the sequence of stages to occur. Yalom (1975) comments that the determination of the natural history of the group is made even more complex when leaders may anticipate a certain developmental stage and unknowingly guide the group through the predicted stages.

Given that production and accomplishment of group goals is a desired outcome of the group, building blocks of a good foundation need to be set before the working through can occur. It would be difficult for members to accept constructive criticism if feelings of trust, respect, intimacy, and commitment were not there. By going through the stages, members learn about themselves and their relationship to the group, individual roles, behaviors, and patterns of communication. Without these events occurring, members lose a chance to learn about themselves in various important situations. It seems logical that a group must first deal with why they have come together and how they are going to run their organization, then with differences of opinion regarding their roles and behavior. Later, shared experiences increase with issues of intimacy and closeness.

In summary, it appears that groups go through developmental stages. However, individuals and groups will have various time patterns in their development. A counselor's awareness of the stages can help him or her place a single event in perspective and provide appropriate leadership for the group. Although it is group counseling, the counselor has a responsibility to each individual.

References

Aram, J. D., and C. P. Morgan. The role of project team collaboration in research and development performance. *Management Science,* 1976, *22,* 1127–37.

Bales, R. R. *Interaction process analysis.* Cambridge, MA.: Addison-Wesley, 1951.

Benne, K. D., and P. Sheats. Functional roles of group members. *Journal of Social Issues,* Spring 1948, *4,* 2.

Bonney, W. The maturation of groups. *Small Group Behavior,* 1974, *5,* 445–61.

Bradford, L. P., J. R. Gibb, and K. E. Benne (Eds.). *T-group theory and laboratory method: Innovation in re-education.* New York: Wiley, 1964, 190–214.

Carkhuff, R. *Helping and human relations Vols. 1 and 2.* New York: Holt, Rinehart and Winston, 1971.

Dailey, R. C. The effects of cohesiveness and collaboration on work groups: A theoretical model. *Group and Organizational Studies,* 1977, *2,* 461–69.

Kauff, P. F. The termination process: Its relationship to separation—individuation phase of development. *International Journal of Group Psychotherapy,* 1977, *27,* 3–18.

Kaye, J. D. Group interaction and interpersonal learning. *Small Group Behavior,* 1973, *4,* 424–48.

Kelman, H. C. The role of the group in the induction of therapeutic change. *International Journal of Group Psychotherapy,* 1963, *13,* 399–432.

Krumboltz, J., and B. Potter. Behavioral techniques for developing trust, cohesiveness and goal accomplishment. *Educational Technology,* January 1973, 26–30.

Liberman, R. A behavioral approach to group dynamics: 1. Reinforcement and prompting cohesiveness in group therapy. *Behavior Therapy,* 1970, *1,* 141–175.

Mainord, W., H. Burk, and G. Collins. Confrontation Versus Diversion in group therapy with chronic schizophenia as measured by a "Positive incident" criterion. *Journal of Clinical Psychology,* 1965, *21,* 222–25.

McGee, T., B. Schuman, and F. Racusen. Termination in group psychotherapy. *American Journal of Psychotherapy,* 1972.

McMurrian, T. T., and G. M. Gazda. Extended group interaction interpersonal functioning as a developmental process variable. *Small Group Behavior,* 1974, *5,* 393–403.

Miles, M. B. Human relations training: How a group grows. *Teachers College Record,* 1957, *55,* 90–96

Mills, T. *Group transformation.* Englewood Cliffs, NJ: Prentice-Hall, 1964.

Muro, J.M., and S. L. Freeman (Eds.). *Reading in group counseling.* Scranton, PA: Intext Educational Publishers, 1968, 5–12.

Napier, R., and M. Gershenfeld. *Groups: Theory and experience.* Boston: Houghton Mifflin, 1973.

Rosenzweig, S. P., and R. Folman. Patient and therapist variables affecting premature termination in group psychotherapy. *Psychotherapy: Theory, Research and Practice,* 1974, *11,* 76–79.

Sisson, P., C. Sisson,and G. Gazda. Extended group counseling with psychiatric residents. *Small Group Behavior,* 1973, *4,* 466–75.

Truax, C. The process of group therapy; Relationship between hypothesized therapeutic conditions and intrapersonal exploration. *Psychological Monograph,* 1961, *75,* No. 5111.

Tuckman, B. W. Developmental sequence in small groups. *Psychological Bulletin,* 1965, *63,* 384–99.

Tuckman, B. W., and M. A. Jensen. Stages of small group development revisited. *Group and Organizational Studies,* 1977, *2,* 419–27.

Yalom, I. *The theory and practice of group psychotherapy* (2nd ed.). New York: Basic Books, 1975.

Zaleznik, A., and D. Moment. *The dynamics of interpersonal behavior.* New York: Wiley, 1964.

16

Issues and Guidelines in Ethics and Training

Robert Rossberg

Organized group activities under the most widely imaginable labels have become a major social, therapeutic, and organizational procedure in our society. Experiences in groups are virtually everywhere and have appeared in almost every conceivable social setting. In addition to the traditional varieties of group therapy conducted in clinics, hospitals, educational settings and in private practice, it is possible to catalogue group activities in churches, businesses, and social clubs. One astonishing phenomenon is the elevation of the organized group activity, therapeutic or otherwise, to the status of "feature attraction" in many resort settings. The guests that flock to these vacation and recreation centers seem perfectly happy to substitute the "weekend encounter" or the "self-help group" for their favorite rock group or comedian.

One may conjecture about the reason for this amazing popularity of the group experience and offer explanations ranging all the way from the simplistic notion of a passing social fad to more subtle concerns about the breakdown of the American family and concomitant search for substitute primary groups. Whatever the most thoughtful explanation is found to be, the explosion of activities in this arena over the past several years must give rise to thoughts about the implications of these activities for the well-being of the participant.

One team of writers suggests that "with man's experiencing alienation and seeking more intimacy with his fellow man, the small group appeared to offer the ideal medium through which he could achieve this closeness (Gazda et al., 1971, p. 637)." This widespread attempt to find increased intimacy and to alleviate loneliness in an environment perceived as increasingly hostile and depersonalized, is undoubtedly one explanation for the increasing popularity of the variety of group experiences offered to a receptive public.

These newly available experiences evolved at a time when the marketplace particularly welcomed such opportunities. A public wary of formal approaches to treatment responded with eager enthusiasm to the new product. In the first place, the new labels under which the experiences were offered were much more acceptable than more traditional approaches to treatment under the labels of the various psychotherapies sponsored by traditionally educated psychiatrists, psychoanalysts, and social workers. In addition, the latter treatments were frequently offered through agencies and institutions whose credibility and social acceptability were suspect. Now churches, businesses, educational institutions, and recreational settings provided the opportunity for "growth" experiences, along with a reduction of the potential negative stigma associated with some traditional forms and loci of treatment. Attending the new varieties of group growth experiences became a shared social experience with friends and family, an admirable personal asset rather than a potential social liability. The "Tuesday Night Group" became a focus for social conversation in peer groups. "My leader" or "my trainer" became a badge of honor worn proudly by housewives and businessmen alike. Couples' groups developed new significance to marital communication. In short, changed labels, altered sponsorship, increased accessibility, and the reduction of stigma brought many new adherents to group experiences.

However, as one writer notes,

> there are dangers in all group encounters—groups are crucibles of intense emotional and intellectual reaction and one can never say exactly what will happen. It can be said generally, however, that well-trained people are equipped to recognize and deal with problems (and successes) before, while, and after they happen, and that ill-trained or untrained people often are not (Shostrom, 1972, p. 475).

The question of training, control, and the development of guidelines for providing help through groups will be explored in this chapter—defining the issues, examining the origins and scope of the problems implied, and developing a set of guidelines that may be potentially useful to prospective group leaders.

FUNCTION OF ETHICAL GUIDELINES

It is certainly not possible to regulate and codify behavior dealing with the entire group movement. Some of it occurs outside the role of psychology and counseling. Some of the activities are so close to the edge of the professional practice of the professions of psychology and counseling that practitioners at the fringe could easily disclaim adherence to any code of professional behavior. Nevertheless, professional practitioners bearing some allegiance to the helping professions might well be aided by attempts to provide guidelines for practice in this area. As Whiteley (1970) notes, "specific ethical standards for those portions relevant to psychology and counseling . . . are essential—to guide the practicing professional, to inform the general public and potential clientele, and to indicate what aspects of the group movement are to be considered within the purview of the practicing psychologist (p. 62)."

Ethical guidelines are particularly useful to practitioners in helping to resolve conflict situations that arise out of practice. They provide an outline for the implementation of the counselor's responsibility to his or her clients, and they inform the latter of what legitimately may be expected from the professional offering service. They may help place specific practices within the framework of the general objectives and goals of the profession, and perhaps limit activities that are contrary to these goals. Ethical guidelines may also suggest approaches to practice that are consistent with social expectations and general codes of moral behavior. Finally, they may offer some protection for the professional by clearly stating the limits of professional practice in particular areas (Whiteley, 1970).

Sources of Ethical Guidelines

It should be made clear at the outset that guidelines, principles, and ethics derive from moral codes and social values. In our system of thought, the relativity of these moral codes and values is painfully apparent. Along with Nagel (1960), the current authors reject the assumption "that there are absolute moral standards immune to revision, no matter what scientific study reveals, and binding upon all men at all times and in all cultures (p. 666)."

Nagel's notion implies that there are no unchanging ethics, values, and moral codes that need permanently restrict behavior, limit options, or circumscribe the possibilities for change in beliefs and behavior. We can certainly subscribe to the ultimate implications of these concepts. Nevertheless, the issues of behavior confront us with the reality that men and women are continuously searching for the origins of principles of "what ought to be," and attempting to understand and harness forces "that promote the good in human affairs, simply in individual human desires or ideals, or in social decision (Faust, 1960, p. 66)."

Absolute or Relative Standards   Men and women continuously search for guiding principles to reach ultimate ideals of the common good and the general welfare. In the course of this search they evolve principles, values, and moral codes, which, however temporary, guide their behavior. These, in turn, become codified into laws, folkways, and mores or institutional procedures (Golightly, 1971). "A particular behavior is good or right if it is consistent with the accepted norm (p. 290)." The danger in this process is that the temporary nature of the codes of behavior is frequently forgotten, and the notions of "good" and "right" are promoted to the status of absolutes which resist change until beliefs are changed by practice or, heaven forbid, by social or political revolution.

Despite this tendency of human beings to solve ethical dilemmas "once and for all," and an inclination to move toward absolute standards, the answer does not lie in the rejection of codes of behavior. Rather, it lies in a recognition of the temporary status and the fragile and relativistic base from which such codes are derived and perhaps, most importantly, in a recognition of our uncertainty in these areas. "All of our terms of ultimate reference—'the public good' with respect to society, for example, and 'maturity' or 'adjustment' to society with respect to the individual—have the same unsatisfactory ultimate point of reference (Faust, 1960, p. 669)."

The search for guiding principles, for satisfactory ultimate points of reference, for commonly accepted propositions and values regarding the relationship of human beings to their world and universe has occupied theologians and philosophers for centuries. It is certainly beyond the scope and competence of this brief discussion. We do not profess to be able to provide answers, guidelines, and resolutions to issues of this level of profundity. Indeed, the philosophical dilemma arising from a position of relativism is evident, as are the arguments of the critics of the relativistic position who posit that it may "engender a moral vacuum," and that relativism itself may be elevated to the status of a religion (Peterson, 1970, p. 173). Nevertheless, we are more comfortable with this position, given the alternative of arguing the validity of universal and permanent values.

Within the context of this position of relativism, however, "an ethical system or code of ethics is a guideline for action based upon commonly held values (Peterson, 1970, p. 120)." Furthermore, these codes of ethics are generally reflective of values commonly held by the society, and represent an attempt to codify the specific efforts of a given profession to implement its own values within that framework. Professional codes of ethics are generally a response to perceived social mandates from the society to specially qualified groups to implement particular elements of commonly held values. As Peterson (1970) notes, "Before a group can state an ethical code, it must first seek out commonly agreed-upon underlying values and responsibilities (p. 120)." Virtually every attempt to codify professional behavior in general, and within the psychological helping professions in particular, reflects this process.

Conflicting Individual and Social Needs   On the surface, this might appear to be rather simple. Certainly, on first examination, statements of first principles which deal with such issues as the unlimited potentiality of the individual, the right to maximum opportunities for freedom of choice, and the imperative of self-determination for each individual seem hardly arguable and perhaps even benign in their implications. However, these value commitments to maximizing human potentiality are not free of implicit conflict, because the enthusiastic implementation of such values may sometimes conflict with issues of broader social needs and social imperatives. Implicit in this dilemma are the conflicting tendencies in men and women to be completely free to search for self-actualization, self-determination, and pleasure and, at the same time, to seek security, shelter, and comfort by establishing social institutions for protection from oneself and others. In our society, in particular, the conflict in the need and desire for collective responsibility and the need and desire for unfettered human freedom—both emanating from innate sources of motivation—lead to value conflict between individuals and groups, and individuals and institutions. In commenting on this tangled web of conflicting motives, Peterson (1970) offers the following observation pertaining to ethical practice:

> This makes ethical matters problematic in counseling as long as one approaches them in a dualistic manner. There exist conflicting loyalties on the part of the counselor to the client, society, employing institution, the profession, and to himself. The subjectivism of the individual clashes with the objectivism of societal standards. Such conflicts

can be resolved only by recourse to a framework of values. Although an ethical code may serve as a guideline, the final judgment rests upon the individual counselor, his values, and his perceptions of the axiological dilemma. To make such decisions requires great moral courage and integrity on the part of the counselor (p. 121).

Indeed, one might also observe that despite the presence of ethical codes of behavior, which frequently result from strenuous public efforts to provide guidelines to the professionally perplexed, the most important ethical decisions are present ones. These decisions are frequently made in lonely contemplation, weighing the public and private costs and the agonizing comparison of equally attractive or unattractive alternatives. Values are only important when conflicts arise between one's individual needs and one's social responsibilities. Ethical guidlines, at best, can only serve as parameters of those value conflicts. The ultimate decision to stand in one place or another, or on one ethical principle or another, is a highly personal matter.

We are convinced that this ethical subjectivism "instead of being a danger, is more likely to be an advantage to morality. Could it be brought home to people that there is no absolute standard in morality, they would perhaps be on the one hand more tolerant and on the other hand more critical in their judgments (Westermarck, 1932, p. 59)."

General Attempts at Evolving Ethical Guidelines

Most professions ultimately evolve codes of ethics that provide guidelines for practice. At best, these codes attempt to provide broad standards for practitioners and have as one of their major functions the prevention of obvious errors in practice.

The American Personnel and Guidance Association Code of Ethics (APGA Ethical Standards, *Personnel and Guidance Journal,* 1971) describes the general characteristics deemed desirable for its membership and provides principles for practice in six general areas of concern: counseling, testing, research and publication, consulting and private practice, personnel administration, and preparation for professional practice. In addition, the code offers some general principles to the professional to aid each person in defining the obligations and responsibilities that membership in that profession implies.

Specifically, the code attempts to delineate the professional counselor's responsibility to the profession, to clients, to the institutions he or she serves, and to the general public.

The American Psychological Association has also established a code of practice for its membership (*American Psychologist,* 1968, 23, 5, 357–64). In many ways similar to the code promulgated by the American Personnel and Guidance Association, it too deals with broad responsibilities of the psychologist to the profession, to clients, to organizations and institutions that employ his or her services, and to the general public. This code provides specific principles dealing with behavior of professionals relating to service to clients, testing, research and publication, representation to the public, and general competence, among others.

Both codes begin with a general statement of values that have considerable areas of agreement. For example, the preamble to the Code of the American Personnel and Guidance Association includes the general statement that the organization is "dedicated to service to society (and that) this service is committed to profound faith in the worth, dignity, and great potentiality of the individual human being (APGA Ethical Standards, 1971)." Similarly, the American Psychological Association's Code of Ethical Standards states in part in its preamble that "the psychologist believes in the dignity and worth of the individual human being. He is committed to increasing man's understanding of himself and others (Ethical Standards of Psychologists, 1968)."

Following these general statements of values, the specific principles enunciated in both codes attempt to implement the general statements in the specific areas of practice covered. They provide guidelines to those who provide counseling services, and may be useful starting points for consideration for practitioners who offer these services to groups of clients. Unfortunately, neither set of ethical standards deals specifically with the practice of group work. Both sets of standards were developed and disseminated before the group movement grew to its current state of popularity, and specific mention of practice in groups is simply not covered. While it is possible to extrapolate guidelines and principles that may be applicable to group activities from these ethical codes, the fact remains that specific guidelines are lacking, and providing such guidelines constitutes a present important necessity for the fields of counseling and psychology.

THE NEED FOR A CODE OF ETHICS FOR GROUP LEADERS

A number of writers in the field have noted the proliferation of group practices that have become available to the general public in the past decade (Whiteley, 1970; Zimpfer, 1971; Gazda, 1971). Yalom (1975) notes that group practices in his own region of the country include "a bewildering array of approaches: psychoanalytic groups, psychodrama groups, crisis groups, Synanon, Recovery, Inc., Alcoholics Anonymous, marital couples' groups, marathon encounter groups, family therapy groups, traditional T-groups, personal growth T-groups, nude therapy groups, multimedia groups, nonverbal sensory awareness groups, and gestalt therapy groups (p. 6)."

As is the case with any strong therapy, group experiences have the potential to help or to harm. In the wake of the popularity of the group movement, reports of both useful and harmful experiences have begun to filter back to practitioners in the field. Some of the literature has even begun to characterize reports of negative experiences with the group movement as a backlash (Gazda et al., 1971).

In one survey of practice in which there were 164 respondents to a questionaire, Gazda noted that while there were "only 20 reported violations of ethical practice on behavior," he was less concerned with the relatively small number of apparent violations than he was with their nature and with the potential "harm done to the participants as well as the damage done to the helping professions as a result of the 'bad press' (Gazda et al., 1971, p. 639)."

Among the violations reported by Gazda were the following:

1. "Encounter groups" conducted by a professor of counseling which students were "required to attend."

2. The use of drugs by group participants encouraged by a group leader.

3. "Nude encounter groups with sexual experimentations" for new teachers in a school system.

4. The onset of a psychotic episode in a participant in a group marathon during which the leader permitted abuse to be inflicted on the victim.

5. No provision for follow-up in a sensitivity training group.

6. A professional untrained in group work doing family group therapy as well as hypnosis as part of the experience.

Parenthetically, it might be noted that the first of Gazda's reported violations gave the current authors a few uncomfortable moments. As part of the program for the education of counselors, students are encouraged to participate in an activity—groups that actually foster growth. While students are informed of the existence of the experience at the time of their admission interview, and while tacit agreement to participate in such activities is obtained, there does exist some concern as to whether the beginning students are fully aware of the implications of the activity and whether every precaution is always taken to prevent potential psychological injury to the participant in the activity. Many graduate training programs in counseling and psychology provide similar experiences for prospective counselors and clinicians. They are either explicitly or implicitly required. At the heart of this problem is the question of whether every effort is being exerted to make sure that they are ethically and professionally conducted. We are then led to ask: What are the ethical guidelines to be followed? Furthermore, if there is a degree of looseness within the university vis-a-vis these activities, what might be the nature of practice in less controlled environments and in settings where professional peer pressure and support is less readily available?

In this vein, Lakin (1969) reports:

> It has come to my attention that there are inadequately prepared trainers who lead student groups on college campuses without supervision. Several eyewitness accounts of these groups suggest that highest value is placed upon intensity of emotionality and on dramatic confrontations. Screening of participants is virtually unknown and follow-up investigation of the effect of these groups is unheard of. Their leaders are usually individuals who have participated in only one or two experiences themselves. Most disturbing of all, there is no sign that these leaders are aware of or concerned about their professional limitations (p. 924).

The standards and codes of the American Psychological Association and the American Personnel and Guidance Association are fairly explicit on the subject of counselor responsibility in the one-to-one counseling situation for maintaining conditions that protect the client's privacy and well-being. The special dynamic nature of the group situation alters the balance of responsibility considerably. Zimpfer (1971) points out:

In forming a group, a counselor yields some measure of his authority and control simply because he is outnumbered. If in addition he desires to distribute equitably the time for talking, his influence is straitened considerably further. If he also chooses to encourage the members to exchange feelings, offer feedback, and confront each other, he reduces his power even more (p. 283).

The potential for negative effects on members in a group situation is much greater than in a one-to-one counseling situation precisely because of the complex relationships within groups and the encouragement of participants to act as "quasi-counselors" for each other (Zimpfer, 1971).

The nature of the group situation raises other dynamic issues that may have ethical implications For example, how much protection of the group and the individual members should the leader maintain with respect to topics to be discussed, protection of silent members, or group pressures to conform to particular procedures and ideologies within the group (Zimpfer, 1971)?

The issue of confidentiality in groups is assuredly more complicated than it is in individual counseling situations. The potential for violation of confidentiality is certainly multiplied by the number of participants in the group. Other issues in group practice that ultimately lead to the need for developing ethical guidelines include experimenting with new methods, the need for follow-up of group members, implications of training and education of leaders, and the need to be explicit with respect to the ground rules of the particular group experience (Zimpfer, 1971).

The proliferation of group experiences and the variety of individuals who offer them pose issues of public protection that need to be dealt with explicitly in terms of ethical codes of practice. As Shostrom (1972) points out,

The demand for group experience—whether in the form of actualization groups, as I call them, or T-groups, synanonlike attack-ins, sensitivity training groups, or marathons, nude and otherwise—has grown so tremendously that there are not now enough trained psychologists, psychiatrists, or social workers to meet it directly. As a result, groups organized by lay leaders have proliferated. While some of these lay groups have honestly and efficiently fulfilled their almost miraculous promises, others have been useless, stupid, dangerous, corrupt, and even fatal. I shall make it clear that I am not arguing against lay leadership, but rather for lay leadership that has been trained in such a way that the public will be protected (p. 474).

The point of Shostrom's warning about the implicit danger in the proliferation of groups with respect to ethical standards of practice is not that such standards per se will eliminate potentially dangerous psychological hazards. The reality is that certain group activities conducted outside the role of organized professional activities are subject neither to legal control nor to the mores of ethical professional practice. Rather, the implication of Shostrom's observation is that both the curious public and the concerned professional have no baseline or standards from which to operate in dealing with the questions posed above.

The professional psychologist or counselor, faced with a query from a member of the public who asks for "advice" concerning participation in a particular group experience, is left strictly on his or her own in rendering judgments and in responding to such requests. There must necessarily be a degree of uncertainty in the responses one is able to make to the public in the absence of guidelines or standards of practice.

Mykel in her investigation of the application of general professional ethical codes to practitioners of group psychotherapy discovered there were differential applications of published ethical standards to group practice by professional practitioners (Mykel, 1971). She makes the point that the application of the general codes of ethical behavior "may reflect varied interpretations of the [published standards] (Mykel, 1971, p. 254)." Her conclusion is that specific ethical guidelines designed to aid practitioners engaged in group practice are very much needed. She specifically notes that unique conflict areas include issues of confidentiality and invasion of privacy, applications of community standards within the group, limits of client relations, and matters of client welfare.

Mykel also deals with the issue of conflict of interest of the therapist. "Psychotherapists doing family and group therapy are especially open to charges of conflict of interest (Mykel, p. 253)." This is particularly true when therapists are seeing clients in selective individual treatment.

One of Mykel's respondents wrote, "I had one group member in individual therapy with me. The intense relationship that developed created problems in the group; it was seen as favoritism, etc. While this could have been dealt with (and was), I was unclear in my own mind whether, in fact, the special relationship did result in a reduction of my effectiveness as a therapist in the group (Mykel, p. 253)."

Several writers have called for the creation of joint professional commissions to deal with the special issues of group practice. Lakin is especially concerned that this be done with regard to the issue of sensitivity training. He suggests the "immediate creation of a commission by our professional organization to investigate training practices, standards of training preparation, and to recommend a code of ethics for accredited trainees (Lakin, 1969, p. 928)."

Lakin also points out that the time has arrived "to distinguish between good and bad theory, good and marginal practice. It is time to demand better standards of trainer development and preparation. It is indeed time for a thorough self-assessment on the part of the training movement. The 'state of the art' and consumer welfare require it (Lakin, 1970, p. 70)."

Zimpfer (1971) points out that the APGA standards as currently constituted do not address themselves to issues pertinent to group practice. He does indicate that "The National Training Laboratories, after more than twenty years of operation, have recently published their *Standards for Use of the Laboratory Method*. Although prominent use of similar procedures in counseling and guidance is more recent, APGA cannot afford to wait so long (p. 282)."

Whiteley makes a similar point in noting that while the ethical standards and codes of ethical practice of both the American Psychological Association and the American Personnel and Guidance Association provide useful guidelines for practice, "they were not intended to provide, nor do they provide, specific standards relating to various aspects of groups (Whiteley, 1970, p. 63)." He proposes the establishment of study commissions within the organizations cited to establish "at a basic minimum" the areas of proper concern for these professions and standards of practice within that framework.

Gazda's proposal is much more ambitious than those cited above. He states:

> It would be ideal if such associations as APA, APGA, the NTE Institute, the American Group Psychotherapy Association, the American Society of Group Psychotherapy and Psychodrama, and the American Psychiatric Association could send representatives to a national conference for the purpose of reaching some consensus on definitions of group practices, on subsequent setting of goals, training or competencies required, and clientele to be served by each one, and on similar criteria which would lead to some mutual understandings among professionals of related disciplines and would provide some guidelines for practitioners (Gazda et al., 1971, p. 641).

It seems reasonably clear that the unique and idiosyncratic substantive characteristics of the group work movement have created special problems in the area of ethical practice. Current codes of ethical practice and standards, with the possible exception of the specific recommendations of the National Training Laboratory, do not deal with these issues. Hence, there is a need for the evolution of standards of practice in this area of professional activity.

Issues of Concern in Group Work

The major areas of concern and ethical issues of group work (Whiteley, 1970; Zimpfer, 1971; Gazda et al., 1971; Olsen, 1971) are identified with fairly broad agreement in the literature. Perhaps the most comprehensive listing is provided by Whiteley, who suggests several critical areas that need to be studied and for which guidelines need to be developed. These are the matters of leadership, responsibility toward participants, safeguards against injury, questions of process, confidentiality, informed consent, freedom of choice, and research considerations. Each of the areas will be examined in turn, the questions and issues involved in them will be considered, and an attempt will be made to formulate a set of tentative principles of practice to provide preliminary guidelines for practitioners.

The Question of Leadership The issue of leadership must be considered primary in the hierarchy of concerns about ethical practices in groups. Groups deal with many issues in their lives, but none is as widespread and significant as the nature of the leadership of a professionally led group. Styles of leadership vary, and philosophical and dynamic assumptions concerning leadership differ from individual to individual. However, one statement can be made without equivocation, namely, that groups are *about* the leadership and leaders more than they are about anything else. The leader is central to the process, irrespective of his or her personal view of leadership. The primary and ultimate responsibility for what occurs in groups is centered on the leader, however eagerly or reluctantly he or she accepts this mantle. The fact of the leader's presence, the act of offering service, places the leader in the position of valuing the activity proffered and bearing the major responsibility for what occurs in the group. The leader is the indispensable presence, the source of coveted approval, support, security, safety, love restrictions, limits, prohibitions, and punishments. The leader may relinquish this responsibility to the group as a whole or to individuals in the group to a greater or lesser degree. He or she may be challenged, resisted, seduced, attacked, and even rejected over issues of leadership. However, the leader is the focus of all these dynamics, and learning occurs through mediation of his or her presence. More than anything else, groups are about leaders.

These observations naturally lead to questions concerning the characteristics, training, and responsibilities of group leaders. Are there specific personal characteristics of group leaders that can and ought to be identified? What kind of education and training is necessary and desirable for specific kinds of group experiences? It is possible to legislate and codify the ethical responsibilities of group leaders?

The state of the art of group practice probably precludes general and universally applicable answers to these questions. Nevertheless, there are several principles pertaining to those questions to which the authors subscribe, as well as a number of notions that warrant explanation.

Leaders need to be educated about the particular service they are offering through the medium of groups. This education involves formal and experiential elements to prepare the potential leader to be minimally competent in his or her activity. (More about formal training appears later in the chapter.) We agree wholeheartedly with Rosenbaum (1972), who observes that "enthusiasm is no substitute for thought (p. 511)." Prospective leaders need to be informed about group modalities through some formal process, and need to have had the opportunity to evolve a theoretical rationale for practice. "It is only when psychotherapists (counselors) are informed about their goals and the issues involved that group therapy (counseling) can be carried out effectively and honestly. No amount of technique gimmickry and quick appeals to the immediate experience will serve as a substitute for a theoretic rationale (Rosenbaum, 1972, p. 512)."

Principle 1:   Group leaders have a responsibility to develop a theoretical rationale for group practice which will enable them to identify the goals of their activity.

This is consistent with Zimpfer's position which maintains that the group leader "should have articulated a philosophical base and rationale regarding interpersonal relationships that permit peer and group activity to be an important part of the growth/change process (Zimpfer, 1971, p. 280)." Endorsement of "the maintenance of high standards of professional competence" by Olsen (1971) also concurs with this principle. The position of the American Psychological Association with respect to conducting growth groups (APA, 1973) and the standards of the National Training Laboratory (NTL, 1972) run parallel to this principle.

In effect, the principle endorses the notion that there are both cognitive and experiential aspects to group work practice. It makes it an ethical imperative that professional practitioners know "why" they are functioning in specific ways with specific goals, in addition to knowing "how" to provide the experience. The principle is consistent with the idea, the source of which has long since disappeared from view, that "feeling good is not enough." This position is exemplified by the statement that only through the cognitive integration occurring through dialogue can learning occur. "Both the experiential and the cognitive integration are necessary for effective learning (Dreyfus and Kremenliev, 1972, p. 503)." This is certainly true for group experiences and makes it necessary for the group leader to be capable of providing that integration.

Principle 2:   Group leaders have a responsibility to limit their group practice to developed levels of competence and skills, and to reveal these limits to clients.

Implicit in this principle is the imperative that all who offer services through groups need specific education and training in the techniques of those proffered services, and that only those competencies specifically held by the leader are to be implemented in this individual's practice. A further obligation is also implied: to disclose the nature of that competence to the participants in this particular group experience and, in addition, to stay within the limits of that competence in practice.

Principle 3:   Group leaders have the responsibility to be familiar with the standards and codes of ethical behavior of their parent professional organization and to apply them, where appropriate, to group practice.

While published codes, as indicated earlier, do not deal specifically with issues pertaining to group practice, the general principles in them do apply to general professional practice and have specific application in a variety of situations.

Principle 4:   Group leaders should be relatively congruent and stable individuals, free from gross pathology and with developed insight into their own unique characteristics and needs.

The nature of the group situation places more complex and subtle personal demands on the group leader than does the traditional one-to-one counseling situation. The assaults on the leader's ego may be more frequent, persistent and, by virtue of the number of group members, probably more potent than in traditional one-to-one situations. Consequently, the group leader must have demonstrated by prior participation in similar experiences and by carefully scrutinized behavior in training, that he or she has the personal stability and strength to cope with the special stress that devolves upon the leader in the group situation.

In short, the position taken is that the group leader who offers service in a field that comes under the rubric of the professional practice of counseling and/or psychology, should present levels of education commensurate with the services offered. He or she should have developed a rationale for that practice based on appropriate cognitive and experiential training. He or she should be able to articulate the goals and limits of that practice and, in general, be obliged to function within the framework of the ethical codes and standards of the parent profession. Finally, it is our conviction that the group leader must demonstrate the personal strength and stability to function consistently and effectively in implementing the stated goals of the proffered services.

Participants   It is conceivable that there are appropriate groups for every potential participant. The literature is replete with references to groups conducted in institutions whose residents are among the most seriously psychologically ill in our society, as well as to short-term groups of relatively normal, intact individuals. Hence, it seems inappropriate to proscribe group experiences for any participant.

What does seem appropriate, however, is that some concern should be demonstrated over whether the particular group experience is suitable to the potential

participants. The following principle needs to be implemented to ensure the latter:
Principle 5: Potential group members should be screened to ensure that they are capable of benefiting from the particular experience offered.

The APA *Guidelines for Psychologists Conducting Growth Groups* (1973) suggests that "a screening interview should be conducted by the group leader prior to the acceptance of any participant. It is the responsibility of the leader to screen out those individuals for whom he or she judges the group experience to be inappropriate (p. 933)." Other writers also recommend a screening procedure to ensure that there is congruence between the potential experience and the participants (Olsen, 1971; Zimpfer, 1971; Gazda, 1971).

The National Training Laboratory, which specifically defines the goal and objectives of group experiences offered under its sponsorship, precisely delineates both the circumstances and the characteristics of individuals that would preclude participation. This list includes individuals who are required to attend based on someone else's demand, those whose goal is to alleviate emotional illness, or those who are particularly susceptible to stress situations. In the published standards of the NTL is the specific statement that "to the limited extent that personal difficulties are predictable and screening procedures make it possible, prospective participants should be screened for these conditions (NTL, 1972, p. 523)."

Another issue with respect to the participants deals with the particular nature of the grouping. Gazda makes the point that "special consideration must be given to methods of grouping individuals for training and treatment. For example, the degree of risk involved in working with close associates such as superiors and subordinates may preclude the potential benefits of such a group if adequate safeguards are not established (Gazda et al., 1971, p. 642)."

Principle 6: If participants include individuals whose normal relationships involve extragroup contact, such as employment, educational, and even personal relationships, safeguards should be taken to minimize the risks of "spill over" from the group experiences.

One of the safeguards implicit in Principle Six deals with the experience of the participant after separation from the group or following the termination of the group process. This may involve what Olsen refers to as "necessary follow-up and assistance to protect member welfare (Olsen, 1971, p. 288)." It implies that responsibility to the participant is not limited to the actual meeting time of the group, but rather that the welfare of individual members may, on occasion, call for assistance outside the group through consultation andor referral. In addition, it also implies that the leader must be available to evaluate the impact of the experience on individual members outside the group and after the group is terminated.

Principle 7: The welfare of participants should be protected by assuring adequate follow-up efforts, which include making available relevant consulting and referral sources. Responsibility for participant welfare does not necessarily end at the point of termination of the group.

The relevant ethical issues with respect to participants deal primarily with client welfare. To ensure the latter, ethical guidelines concerned with screening, issues of grouping, and follow-up need to be implemented.

Limits of Permissible Behavior in the Group Process   A great variety of activities are currently conducted under the rubric of group behaviors. Many of them are of debatable value, although each is offered under the guise of a rationale leading to personal growth. Some of these include within the process a degree of verbal and physical abuse. Others encourage physical contact, including sexual exploratory behavior, under the rationale of individual growth and "finding oneself." Perhaps some of the allowable techniques actually do produce the desired outcome. Nevertheless, the current authors believe that professionally conducted group activities do impose certain limits on what is permissible in the process. Gazda takes the position that "some direction must be given to protect the group participants from some potentially harmful, nonverbal methods and physical contacts (Gazda et al., 1971, p. 642)." Olsen (1971) makes the point in his suggested code of ethics that it is the leader's responsibility to show a "sensible regard for the social codes, moral expectations, and laws that set limits on the behavior of one individual toward another (p. 288)."

Principle 8:   In general, professionally conducted groups should limit the process to those verbal and nonverbal techniques that do not have the potential to harm participants. Physical assaults, sexual behavior between participants, and excessive verbal abuse are unacceptable.

The authors have little difficulty in agreeing that physical assaults and sexual behavior between participants in the group cannot be condoned. While we recognize that some practitioners consider these activities part of general growth behavior among individuals, to us they are beyond the pale of acceptability. In addition, defining "excessive" verbal abuse presents another difficulty. Certainly, conflict and hostility between members are to be expected as part of the process of group interactions. Nevertheless, condoning verbal assaults as cathartic for the participants, or even as a means of illuminating reality, seems to be at the fringes of acceptable ethical practice. In general, the leader must make a judgment of what is "excessive" verbal abuse in the context of its occurrence. The main guiding principle would seem to be whether the behavior does harm to a participant in a group situation without a reasonable expectation that it will aid in his or her growth process.

Confidentiality   In the traditional one-to-one counseling situation, the issue of confidentiality pertains primarily to the counselor's behavior in maintaining the privacy of the consulting room. The content is the property of the client, and his or her expectation is that the counselor will treat the shared knowledge with respect and discretion. Existing ethical codes prescribe limitations on confidential behavior for the counselor, and even carry with them potential sanctions for violators through the actions of appropriate ethical practices committees. While these sanctions are admittedly weak and rarely enforced, the situation with regard to confidentiality in the one-to-one situation seems incredibly simple as compared to the same issue with regard to group approaches. Olsen (1971) notes that "while the leader can vouch only for his respect for confidentiality in the group, he must inform the members of their responsibility for confidentiality, and also make them aware that he cannot speak for anyone other than himself (p. 288)."

The problem is undoubtedly a difficult one to resolve and implement. As Whiteley (1970) notes, "Sanctions on group participants through the profession don't exist as they do on the counselor (p. 63)." Nevertheless, attempts should be made at appropriate times during the group process to deal with the issue of confidentiality and to discuss frankly all of the ramifications and issues involved in responsible maintenance of confidentiality, as well as the potential violations of the privacy of individual members that may result from their participation in the group process. inciple 9: Every effort should be made to ensure the maximum privacy of participants in the group process by appropriate discussion of the principles, needs, and implications of the concept of confidentiality. Leaders should frankly confront the fact that they are able to guarantee only their own commitment to the privacy of group discussions.

The Issue of Informed Consent Virtually all participation in group experiences is "voluntary." That is, the participant generally appears of his or her own volition and agrees to participate in the activity. For many practitioners, the fact that no coercion was used to obtain participants absolves the leader of responsibility for further explanation of the implications of that involvement to the participants. Much more needs to be done to ensure that the prospective participants fully understand the nature of their commitment. The very fact that the service is offered places this special responsibility on the practitioner and the institution he or she represents. At the very least, the full implications and nature of the potential experiences must be explored during the screening and orientation process. The leader must be convinced that the potential group member truly understands all that may be involved in the process and that the leader has provided as much information as possible about the conditions of treatment before any assumption regarding informed consent may be made.

Principle 10: In general, group practice should be limited to volunteer participants who have had ample opportunity to obtain information concerning the process and to evaluate the implications of their own participation, and are thereby able to make a commitment from as fully informed a vantage point as possible.

There is a corollary issue to the above principle. Some groups, organized particularly for the purpose of education and training are not, strictly speaking, voluntary. This aspect of the education program for prospective psychologists, counselors, social workers, and other helpers is undoubtedly discussed as part of the process of admission to such programs of education. As mentioned earlier, acceptance of admission to such programs generally is taken as meeting the requirements for voluntary participation. The corollary issue derives from Principle Ten and deals with the matter of informed consent. Certainly, prospective professionals who are required to participate in groups as part of their professional development must be offered the same right to informed consent as any other potential participant in a group.

Some professional educators point to another side of this issue. Their position is that the educator bears an ethical responsibility to ensure that those individuals he or she is training as professional helpers are exposed to both cognitive and experiential opportunities for growth. If this includes a "required" experience in a group, so be it. As long as the group is formed along the lines of sound ethical practice, and the prospective helper is provided all the safeguards of informed consent, no ethical issue really is involved.

There are unresolved issues regarding the structure of such required groups. Gazda notes that what he finds "especially questionable is the practice of placing students or trainees with classmates in a group led by the instructor for that course (Gazda et al., 1971, p. 642)." In the absence of specific guidelines from the profession, however, each educational institution will of necessity have to resolve its own stand on this issue—hopefully, with full cognizance of those limited guidelines currently available.

Freedom of Choice   When is an individual free to withdraw from a group experience? Obviously, in some absolute sense, one could answer the question by glibly stating that a person is free to withdraw whenever he or she so chooses, just as one is free not to participate in the first place. We already have indicated an important limitation on the freedom *not* to participate in the case of so-called required or compulsory groups. In one instance, that of education or training, a rationale for the restriction of freedom has been stated. There are other settings, such as employment situations, mental hospitals, prisons, even in society at large, where the perceived pressure to join in such activities is powerful and difficult for individuals to resist. Certainly, during the screening process, the leader has an obligation to determine if the potential client is truly exercising freedom of choice in the matter, and the leader-screener has an obligation to aid the client in making the decision. Actually, Principle Five, which deals with screening procedures, covers by implication the issue of freedom of choice at the point of entering the group process. Principle Ten, which deals with the matter of informed consent, is even more explicit on this issue of freedom.

There does remain, however, the issue of separation from the group and the actual freedom of choice provided the group member to exercise such freedom. Closed groups obviously will exert pressure on members to remain in the setting. Subtle pressures may emanate from both group members and the leader to block the flight of a member. One writer believes that each client has the "right to withdraw from any given activity or from the group itself without being exposed to pressure from the group members or leadership." In addition, to fully implement this right to free choice, the individual must not be subjected or "threatened by humiliation, reprisal, rejection or ridicule (Whitely, 1970, p. 64)." In general, the current authors endorse this position.

Principle 11:   Each participant should have the right to exercise complete freedom of choice with respect to participation in particular group activities or to separation from the group. This right of the individual participant shall be exercised free of undue pressure from the group leader or other group members.

A clarifying comment is probably in order with respect to what constitutes "undue pressure." Certainly, we are aware that resistance, situational stress, and traumatic occurrences may lead a client to express a desire to withdraw from the group. If the leader determines that the latter is the case and reasonable efforts have been extended to have the individual continue, the leader is obligated to aid the client to separate from the group with the least possible damage to that client. Of course, if the leader feels that it is in the best interests of the client to withdraw from the group, there is no issue for the leader. Even in this situation, however, he or she may need to act to protect the client's right to freedom of choice and to freedom from continuing pressure outside the group from the other members or from the community in which the activity is being conducted. In the final analysis, whatever the leader judges to be the therapeutic impact of the act of withdrawal on the client, the client's ultimate right to freedom of choice must be implemented.

Accountability, Effectiveness, and Research   Group practice is an evolving activity that ought to be subject to refinement and restructuring. Also, some evaluation of the effectiveness of the activity is an ethical concern of institutions and practitioners supporting such activities.

Principle 12:   Individuals and institutions that offer and support group activities have the obligation to evaluate those activities periodically. Furthermore, those professionals and institutions have an obligation to participate in research activities designed to reform and refine practice and to determine the effectiveness of variations in practice.

This principle is largely self-explanatory. It follows from the assumptions stated above.

Summing up the Guidelines

The guidelines enunciated here provide very broad parameters for the ethical and professio nal conduct of groups. They have been presented in the context of existing issues and standards of professional practice in this area, and the relativistic and tentative nature of such guidelines have been indicated.

Despite the latter, some guiding principles are necessary, and those presented here are deemed to be minimally essential for ethically sound professional practice in this area.

Issues in the Education and Training of the Group Leader

Historically, most training programs for mental health workers evolved from the individual counseling and therapy model. Education in the application of group counseling and therapy skills was either elective in such programs or even nonexistent. Yalom notes that "it is not unusual for students to be given excellent intensive individual therapy supervision and then, early in their program, to be asked to lead therapy groups with no specialized guidance whatsoever. The program directors apparently expect that the student will be able, somehow, to translate his individual therapy training into group therapy skills (Yalom, 1975, p. 503)."

Probably the diversity of the population of practitioners in this area accounted for the historical laxity in training in group process and tereapy. As one survey revealed, practitioners came from such disciplines as medicine, psychology, social work, counseling, and the ministry (Kadis et al., 1974, p. 159).

There are a variety of models that are possible to employ in the education of competently trained group leaders. A number of writers have described alternative models (Kadis, 1974; Berman, 1975; Yalom, 1975; and Gazda, 1978). What follows is an approach which may be applied in both traditional academic settings as well as those that are more experientially oriented. It is an attempt to provide guidelines to those aspects of training that are minimally necessary to ensure competent professional performance.

There is a clear, interactive relationship between ethical practice and competent performance, in our view. The first three principles developed earlier in the chapter with respect to ethical guidelines governing group practice are directly concerned with the education and training of the leader. In a very real sense, this is the foundation of ethical group practice. Certainly the matter of competence relates quite specifically to professionally sound group leadership, and insight into the personal limitations of that competence can only derive from familiarity with the skills necessary to function as a successful group leader.

In addition, the same study pointed out that the primary source of training for those practitioners included traditional academic settings, specialized institutions devoted to post-graduate therapeutic training, inservice activities as part of a residency or internship program in hospital or clinical settings, and others (Kadis, 1974).

Even though the practice of treatment in a group context has a history of many decades, it is clear that the availability of formal training has been desultory and even unorganized to a certain extent. Despite the long history, we are still dealing with an area in the practice of mental health intervention that remains at the frontier of professional practice. It has been observed that "these pioneers began working in the area long before the availability of formal instruction. They trained others via preceptorships and other relatively informal procedures. It is not surprising, therefore, that there is a considerable proportion of group psychotherapists without much formal training (Kadis et al., 1974, p. 162)."

To ensure minimally competent professional group leadership, the following framework for the education and training of group leaders is proposed.

The Foundations The position of the current authors is that a firm foundation in individual approaches to counseling is a necessary underpinning of successful group practice. While many practitioners of group techniques approach the modality from a variety of viewpoints, including the position that group practice is quite different in orientation and objectives from individual counseling and psychotherapy, our stand on this issue is much more traditional.

A thorough grounding in personality dynamics, human development, psychopathology, and the process of human socialization, which undergirds individual practice in this area, is also necessary background for successful group practice. In addition, thorough understanding of and experience in individual approaches to counseling and psychotherapy are a necessary prerequisite to most successful training in group approaches to human intervention. Certainly, as indicated earlier in the text, the dynamics of group counseling and psychotherapy are different and more complex than those of individual approaches. It is precisely for that reason that we take the position we do with regard to this foundation of training.

Issues of selection and retention, understanding of individual behavior, and unique needs of individuals in groups are predicated on an understanding of the individual group members. Special personal problems, as they arise, are similarly dependent on the understanding of personality dynamics and even psychopathology. Consequently, didactic and experiential training in group counseling and psychotherapy must be superimposed on a firm professional grounding in individual approaches to counseling and psychotherapy.

Didactic Training   Keeping in mind that most, if not all, practitioners in this field are continually adding to their repertory of skills by obtaining additional training in the area of group practice, a minimum didactic education for human intervention specialists in the area of group practice can be outlined.

First, practitioners should be familiar with the basic literature in the field of group dynamics. This would include rather extensive coverage of the areas of group formation, the process of group development, leadership, group membership, and the material generally covered under the rubric of dynamics, styles, and impact of permanent and temporary groups in contemporary society.

Much of this material is specifically unrelated to group counseling and psychotherapy, and much more generally concerned with the impact of primary and secondary groups on the lives of people in general. However, since group counseling and psychotherapy are viewed as a uniquely designed intervention process which utilizes the force of group processes already in existence in society, some basic understanding of general group dynamics is necessary for practioners in this field.

A second major focus of didactic training in this area deals with the theoretical issues inherent in the application of theory and techniques to the actual process of group counseling and psychotherapy. For example, an orientation to the varieties of group approaches to treatment is certainly indicated, including reasonably thorough grounding in the various theoretical options available to prospective practitioners.

This does not mean that a group counselor or psychotherapist may not opt for a specific theoretical orientation; quite the contrary. If it is consistent and congruent with the practitioner's basic philosophy and assumptions about human behavior, this is a desirable ultimate outcome. However, an orientation to the wide variety of theoretical possibilities that exist in this field should be included in the didactic experience.

Following the generic orientation to group dynamics and the theoretical orientation to practice in the field, didactic training should then deal with the specific issues and problems of practice that face the prospective counselor or therapist. Discussions concerning the techniques and problems of selecting members for the group, starting and maintaining a group, problems of leadership, issues dealing with subgroup dynamics, nonverbal communications, silence in the group, acting-out behavior by members of the group, transference and countertransference phenomena, and termination of group sessions need to be taken up in the training period. In addition, special settings bring forth other didactic issues, including open or closed groups, attendance, goals of the group experience, and the like. These topics may be dealt with in terms of both the theoretical implications of the issues and the specific techniques to be employed by the practitioners.

Finally, didactic training should include some approaches to the evaluation of the group process. Some background and understanding of the effectiveness of local experiences should be provided. Also, the training should attempt to relate these approaches to the rather extensive literature dealing with the research in the field of group counseling and psychotherapy.

In short, didactic training in this field of practice must encompass an orientation to understanding group dynamics in its broadest social and psychological context; knowledge of the varieties of theoretical approaches to group counseling and psychotherapy; an awareness of the issues and techniques of conducting groups; and some familiarity with the approaches to evaluation of the effectiveness of group practice in their broadest and most specific applications in research.

Supervised Practice   The applied aspects of the didactic training presented above are equally important to the acquisition of knowledge in this field. Supervised practice is an integral part of professional development, and the relationship between didactic knowledge and supervised practice is reciprocal and developmental.

Ideally, supervised practice and didactic experience should proceed concurrently. Although other models of experience are certainly reasonable, a concurrent model would maximize the reciprocal nature of that relationship. Furthermore, supervised practice may proceed through a series of developmental plateaus concurrent with didactic learning. For example, the prospective group leader might progress developmentally from group member, to observer, to coleader, and finally to full leader status.

At each step, opportunities for integrating content and experience should be provided through the supervision process, although the process may take somewhat different forms at various stages of practical experience. As an example, integration at the group member stage may be accomplished by having the student relate theoretical learning to personal experiences through a series of academic exercises. Integration at the observer or coleader stage may be accomplished under the supervision of the group leader. Finally, integration during the instance of first full responsibility for the leadership of a group may be accomplished by intensive one-to-one supervision by a preceptor designated for this purpose.

To sum up, supervised practice is certainly necessary in the development of group counseling and psychotherapy skills. More important, it should be integrated with didactic training through a series of planned experiences which ensure the developmental and reciprocal nature of that process.

Personal Participation in a Group Experience   Obviously, one need not participate personally in every possible human experience to be expert in any given area. One can point to the obstetrician who has never given birth, or the neurosurgeon who has never had a tumor removed, to say nothing of the observation by the unknown wag that chickens know considerably less about omelettes than do human beings. Nonetheless, where possible and logical, experiencing that process for which one is later responsible may have a salutary educational impact on the practitioner. The viewpoint taken here is that participation in a group counseling or therapy group, or even in a development group, has the positive effect of providing the prospective group leader with a view of the process from the "other side of the desk." There is also the added benefit of increased self-knowledge and insight that such an experience may engender. Finally, this experience is a first developmental step in the supervisory process as outlined above. For these reasons, personal participation in a group experience is strongly recommended as a necessary part of training for prospective group leaders.

Continuous Learning and Growth   It goes without saying that even after completing a sequence of education and experience as outlined above, there is a need for continued attention to refinement of skills and updating of knowledge in this field.

Attendance at workshops for this purpose, membership in appropriate professional organizations, and a periodic return to the supervisory process may help ensure continued development of professional competence in group counseling and psychotherapy.

SUMMARY

This chapter has outlined the imperatives to ethical practice for those who practice group counseling and psychotherapy. While there are general ethical standards governing professional practice in counseling and psychology, the special nature of this area of practice makes it necessary to explore ancillary ethical principles of practice. These have been presented as a series of ethical principles of practice for group practitioners.

The point has been made that part of the ethical imperatives involves the matter of professional competence. It is hoped that the paradigm of education and training developed here will ensure minimum professional competence and, hence, compliance with the principles enunciated.

References

American Personnel and Guidance Association. Ethical standards. *Personnel and Guidance Journal,* 1971, *50,* 327–30.

American Psychological Association. Ethical standards of psychologists. *American Psychologist,* 1968, *23,* 357–64.

American Psychological Association. Guidelines for psychologists conducting growth groups. *American Psychologist,* 1973, *28,* 933.

Berman, A. L. Group psychotherapy training, issues and models. *Small Group Behavior,* August 1975, 325–44.

Dreyfus, E. A, and E. Kremenliev. Innovative group techniques: Handle with care. In R. C. Diedrich and H. A. Dye (Eds.), *Group procedures: Purposes, processes and outcomes.* Boston: Houghton Mifflin, 1972, 502–8.

Faust, C. The search for answers. In Lyman Bryson (Ed.), *An outline of man's knowledge of the modern world.* Garden City, NY: Doubleday, 1960, 667–77.

Gazda, G. M. *Group counseling: A developmental approach.* Boston: Allyn and Bacon, 1978, 425.

Gazda, G. M., J. A. Duncan, and P. J. Sisson. Professional issues in group work. *Personnel and Guidance Journal,* 1971, *49,* 637–43.

Golightly, C. A. A philosopher's view of values and ethics. *Personnel and Guidance Journal,* 1971, *50,* 289–94.

Kadis, A. L., J. D. Krasner, M. F. Weiner, C. Winick, and S. N. Foulkes. *Practicum of group psychotherapy* (2nd ed.). Hagerstown, MD: Harper & Row, 1974, 171.

Lakin, M. Some ethical issues in sensitivity training. *American Psychologist,* 1969, *24,* 923–28.

Group sensitivity training and encounter: Uses and abuses of a method. *The Counseling Psychologist,* 1970, *2,* 66–70.

Mykel, N. The application of ethical standards to group psychotherapy in a community. *International Journal of Group Psychotherapy,* 1971, *21,* 248–54.

Nagel, E. The mission of philosophy. In Lyman Bryson (Ed.), *An outline of man's knowledge of the modern world.* Garden City, NY: Doubleday, 1960, 543–666.

National Training Laboratory Institute for Applied Behavioral Science. Standards for the use of laboratory method. In R. C. Diedrich and H. A. Dye (Eds.), *Group procedures: Purposes, processes and outcomes.* Boston: Houghton Mifflin, 1972, 520–28.

Olsen, L. C. Ethical standards for group leaders. *Personnel and Guidance Journal,* 1971, *50,* 288.

Peterson, J. A. *Counseling and values.* Scranton, PA: Intext Educational Publishers, 1970.

Rosenbaum, M. The responsibility of the group psychotherapy practitioner for a therapeutic rationale. In R. C. Diedrich and H. A. Dye (Eds.), *Group procedures· Purposes, processes and outcomes.* Boston: Houghton Mifflin, 1972, 509–19.

Shostrom, E. Group therapy: Let the buyer beware. In R. C. Diedrich and H. A. Dye (Eds.), *Group procedures: Purposes, processes and outcomes.* Bostom :Houghton Mifflin, 1972, 471–77.

Westermarck, E. *Ethical reality.* London: Routledge and Kegan Paul, Ltd., 1932.

Whiteley, J. M. Editorial. *The Counseling Psychologist,* 1970, *2,* 62–65.

Yalom, I. D. *The theory and practice of group psychotherapy* (2nd ed.). New York: Basic Books, 1975.

Zimpfer, D. Needed: Professional ethics for working with groups. *Personnel and Guidance Journal,* 1971 *50,* 280–87.

Credits

Chapter 8   Three figures adapted from Eric Berne's *Games People Play*. Reprinted by permission of Random House, Inc. Copyright © 1964 by Eric Berne. One figure adapted from Eric Berne's *Principles of Group Treatment*. New York: Oxford University Press, 1966.
Two figures adapted from *Transactional Analysis After Eric Berne: Teachings and Practices of Three TA Schools*, edited by Graham Barnes. Copyright © 1977 by Graham Barnes. Reprinted with permission of Harper's College Press.

Chapter 10   A figure adapted from D. H. Frey, "Conceptualizing Counseling Theories: A Content Analysis of Process and Goal Statements." *Counselor Education and Supervision*, 1972, *11,* 4, 243–250. Copyright © 1972 American Personnel and Guidance Association. Reprinted with permission.

Chapter 13   A figure adapted from Timothy Leary, *Interpersonal Diagnosis of Personality—A Functional Theory and Methodology for Personality Evaluation.* Copyright © 1957, The Ronald Press Company, New York.
Three figures adapted from *Of Human Interaction* by Joseph Luft by permission of Mayfield Publishing Company. Copyright © 1969 by The National Press.
Two figures adapted from *Group Processes: An Introduction to Group Dynamics* by Joseph Luft by permission of Mayfield Publishing Company. Copyright © 1963, 1970 by Joseph Luft.

Name Index

Subject Index